EDUCATION
94/95

Twenty-First Edition

Editor

Fred Schultz
University of Akron

Fred Schultz, professor of education at the University of Akron, attended Indiana University to earn a B.S. in social science education in 1962, an M.S. in the history and philosophy of education in 1966, and a Ph.D. in the history and philosophy of education and American studies in 1969. His B.A. in Spanish was conferred from the University of Akron in May 1985. He is actively involved in researching the development and history of American education with a primary focus on the history of ideas and social philosophy of education. He also likes to study languages.

SCHOOL OF EDUCATION
CURRICULUM LABORATORY
UM-DEARBORN

Cover illustration by Mike Eagle

Annual Editions
A Library of Information from the Public Press

The Dushkin Publishing Group, Inc.
Sluice Dock, Guilford, Connecticut 06437

The Annual Editions Series

Annual Editions is a series of over 60 volumes designed to provide the reader with convenient, low-cost access to a wide range of current, carefully selected articles from some of the most important magazines, newspapers, and journals published today. Annual Editions are updated on an annual basis through a continuous monitoring of over 300 periodical sources. All Annual Editions have a number of features designed to make them particularly useful, including topic guides, annotated tables of contents, unit overviews, and indexes. For the teacher using Annual Editions in the classroom, an Instructor's Resource Guide with test questions is available for each volume.

VOLUMES AVAILABLE

Africa
Aging
American Foreign Policy
American Government
American History, Pre-Civil War
American History, Post-Civil War
Anthropology
Biology
Business Ethics
Canadian Politics
Child Growth and Development
China
Comparative Politics
Computers in Education
Computers in Business
Computers in Society
Criminal Justice
Drugs, Society, and Behavior
Dying, Death, and Bereavement
Early Childhood Education
Economics
Educating Exceptional Children
Education
Educational Psychology
Environment
Geography
Global Issues
Health
Human Development
Human Resources
Human Sexuality
India and South Asia
International Business
Japan and the Pacific Rim

Latin America
Life Management
Macroeconomics
Management
Marketing
Marriage and Family
Mass Media
Microeconomics
Middle East and the Islamic World
Money and Banking
Multicultural Education
Nutrition
Personal Growth and Behavior
Physical Anthropology
Psychology
Public Administration
Race and Ethnic Relations
Russia, Eurasia, and Central/Eastern Europe
Social Problems
Sociology
State and Local Government
Third World
Urban Society
Violence and Terrorism
Western Civilization, Pre-Reformation
Western Civilization, Post-Reformation
Western Europe
World History, Pre-Modern
World History, Modern
World Politics

Library of Congress Cataloging in Publication Data
Main entry under title: Annual editions: Education. 1994/95.
    1. Education—Periodicals. I. Schultz, Fred, comp. II. Title: Education.
370'.5   73-78580   ISBN: 1-56134-272-6
LB41.A673

© 1994 by The Dushkin Publishing Group, Inc., Guilford, CT 06437

Twenty-First Edition

Manufactured in the United States of America

Editors/ Advisory Board

EDITOR

Fred Schultz
University of Akron

ADVISORY BOARD

Members of the Advisory Board are instrumental in the final selection of articles for each edition of Annual Editions. Their review of articles for content, level, currentness, and appropriateness provides critical direction to the editor and staff. We think you'll find their careful consideration well reflected in this volume.

STAFF

To the Reader

In publishing ANNUAL EDITIONS we recognize the enormous role played by the magazines, newspapers, and journals of the *public press* in providing current, first-rate educational information in a broad spectrum of interest areas. Within the articles, the best scientists, practitioners, researchers, and commentators draw issues into new perspective as accepted theories and viewpoints are called into account by new events, recent discoveries change old facts, and fresh debate breaks out over important controversies.

Many of the articles resulting from this enormous editorial effort are appropriate for students, researchers, and professionals seeking accurate, current material to help bridge the gap between principles and theories and the real world. These articles, however, become more useful for study when those of lasting value are carefully *collected, organized, indexed,* and *reproduced* in a *low-cost format,* which provides easy and permanent access when the material is needed. That is the role played by *Annual Editions.* Under the direction of each volume's *Editor,* who is an expert in the subject area, and with the guidance of an *Advisory Board,* we seek each year to provide in each ANNUAL EDITION a current, well-balanced, carefully selected collection of the best of the public press for your study and enjoyment. We think you'll find this volume useful, and we hope you'll take a moment to let us know what you think.

Discourse over the purposes of schooling is intense, as always. Debate over the relative strengths and weaknesses of North American educational systems continues. There is intense competition for the loyalty of our respective "publics" among those who champion alternative and differing educational destinies for our youth. The journal literature reflects intensive differences among those who champion the public tax-supported schools and those who favor either some form of "voucher" plan or efforts to "privatize" sectors of our educational systems. The American Federation of Teachers has adopted a policy statement calling for improvements in traditional models of public schooling as well as for the development of new types of learning institutions for our youth. The National Education Association is vigorously defending the efforts of the public schools. The debate continues over standardization of the national curriculum for elementary and secondary schools. There are several equity (social justice) issues yet unresolved that are receiving intensive analysis in the journal and monographic literatures in educational studies.

There is critical discourse over the nature and the quality of various alternative forms of schooling, both within the public school sector and in the private school sector. This critical discourse occurs when major demographic changes occur in the social and economic conditions affecting our youth. More than 23 percent of children in the United States live in households that are classified as at or below the poverty level. In 1993 the cultural composition of the United States indicated that 30 percent of all American school children were from cultural minority groups. Minority student populations are growing at a much faster rate than traditional Caucasian populations. Many scholars argue that the distinction between majority and minority school populations is being steadily eroded and will become relatively meaningless by the year 2030. If demographic trends continue, Caucasian (white) students may be the minority by 2030. The dramatic shifts in cultural composition gives greater urgency to the need to deal affirmatively and decisively with the remaining social justice issues to guarantee students' educational rights and to create a just set of social and educational opportunity structures.

With each passing year, the government, as well as leaders in the private sector of the economy, want to prepare our youth for a rapidly changing economic future. This has led to the advancement of several alternative educational agendas for the future of North American educational systems.

Dialogue and compromise continue to be the order of the day. The various interest groups within the educational field reflect a broad spectrum of perspectives from various behaviorist and cognitive development perspectives to various humanistic ones. The interests of students, parents, state or provincial governments, and the corporate world continue to reflect many differing views on how people should learn.

In assembling this volume, we make every effort to stay in touch with movements in educational studies and with the social forces at work in the schools. Members of the advisory board contribute valuable insights, and the production and editorial staff at The Dushkin Publishing Group coordinates our efforts. Through this process we collect a wide range of articles on a variety of topics relevant to education in North America.

The following readings explore the social and academic goals of education, the current condition of North American educational systems, the teaching profession, and the future of American education. In addition, these selections address the issues of change and the moral and ethical foundations of schooling.

As always, we would like you to help us improve this volume. Please rate the material in this edition on the form at the back of the book and send it to us. We care about what you think. Give us the public feedback that we need.

Fred Schultz

Fred Schultz
Editor

Contents

Unit 1

How Others See Us and How We See Ourselves

Five articles examine today's most significant educational issues: the debate over privatization, the quality of schools, and the current public opinion about U.S. schools.

The concepts in bold italics are developed in the article. For further expansion please refer to the Topic Guide and the Index.

Unit 2

Change and Rethinking of the Educative Effort

Four articles discuss the tension between ideals and socioeconomic reality at work in today's educational system.

Unit 3

Striving for Excellence: The Drive for Quality

Five selections examine the debate over achieving excellence in education by addressing issues relating to questions of how best to teach and how best to test.

The concepts in bold italics are developed in the article. For further expansion please refer to the Topic Guide and the Index.

Unit 4

Morality and Values in Education

Three articles examine the role of American schools in teaching morality and social values.

Unit 5

Managing Life in Classrooms

Five selections consider the importance of building effective teacher-student and student-student relationships in the classrooms.

The concepts in bold italics are developed in the article. For further expansion please refer to the Topic Guide and the Index.

Unit 6

Equality of Educational Opportunity

Five articles discuss issues relating to fairness and
justice for students from all cultural backgrounds, and
how curricula should respond to culturally pluralistic
student populations.

Unit 7

Serving Special Needs and Concerns

Seven articles examine some of the important aspects of special educational needs and building cooperative learning communities in the classroom setting.

The concepts in bold italics are developed in the article. For further expansion please refer to the Topic Guide and the Index.

Unit 8

The Profession of Teaching Today

Eight articles assess the current state of teaching in
American schools and how well today's teachers
approach subject matter learning.

Unit 9

A Look to the Future

Four articles look at new forms of schooling that break
from traditional conceptions of education
in America.

The concepts in bold italics are developed in the article. For further expansion please refer to the Topic Guide and the Index.

Topic Guide

This topic guide suggests how the selections in this book relate to topics of traditional concern to students and professional educators involved with the study of education. It is useful for locating articles that relate to each other for reading and research. The guide is arranged alphabetically according to topic. Articles may, of course, treat topics that do not appear in the topic guide. In turn, entries in the topic guide do not necessarily constitute a comprehensive listing of all the contents of each selection.

TOPIC AREA	TREATED IN:	TOPIC AREA	TREATED IN:
Accountability	10. Launching a Revolution in Standards and Assessments 11. How the National Board Builds Professionalism 12. Magnet Schools and Issues of Education Quality 35. What Makes a Good Teacher? 37. Exploring the Thinking of Thoughtful Teachers 40. Five Standards of Authentic Instruction	Culture and Schools (cont'd)	24. Teachers and Cultural Styles in a Pluralistic Society 25. Crisis in Education 26. Investing in Our Children 27. Concerns About Teaching Culturally Diverse Students
		Defense of Public Schools	1. Preserving the American Dream 7. Changing Schools From Within 13. Myth of Public School Failure
Alternative Schools	4. Little Schools That Could 8. World of Choice in Education 9. Question of Choice 14. Should We Push the Button?	Demographic Change	2. Strengths and Weaknesses of American Education 3. American Education: The Good, the Bad, and the Task 43. Where We Go From Here 44. Education 2000 A.D.: A Peek Into the Future
Change and Schooling	6. U.S. Education: The Task Before Us 7. Changing Schools From Within 8. World of Choice in Education 9. Question of Choice		
Child Care	29. Child Care: What Do Families Really Want?	Discipline	18. Discipline With Dignity in the Classroom 19. Constructivist Approach to Conflict Resolution 20. Practical Peacemaking Techniques for Educators 21. From Individual Differences to Learning Communities 22. Resolving Teacher-Student Conflict
"Choice" and Schooling	4. Little Schools That Could 8. World of Choice in Education 9. Question of Choice 14. Should We Push the Button?		
Classroom Management	18. Discipline With Dignity in the Classroom 19. Constructivist Approach to Conflict Resolution 20. Practical Peacemaking Techniques for Educators 21. From Individual Differences to Learning Communities 22. Resolving Teacher-Student Conflict	Equity and Schooling	23. Canon Debate, Knowledge Construction, and Multicultural Education 24. Teachers and Cultural Styles in a Pluralistic Society 25. Crisis in Education 26. Investing in Our Children 27. Concerns About Teaching Culturally Diverse Students 28. Blowing Up the Tracks
Communities and Schools	1. Preserving the American Dream 3. American Education: The Good, the Bad, and the Task 4. Little Schools That Could 5. 25th Annual Phi Delta Kappa/Gallup Poll 6. U.S. Education: The Task Before Us 8. World of Choice in Education	Ethics and Teaching	15. Right and Wrong 16. Why Johnny Can't Tell Right From Wrong 17. Ethical Communication in the Classroom
Conflict Resolution in Schools	19. Constructivist Approach to Conflict Resolution 20. Practical Peacemaking Techniques for Educators 22. Resolving Teacher-Student Conflict	Eurocentric versus Multicultural Curriculum	23. Canon Debate, Knowledge Construction, and Multicultural Education
Creativity and Teaching	35. What Makes a Good Teacher? 38. Better Way to Learn	Excellence and Schooling	10. Launching a Revolution in Standards and Assessments 11. How the National Board Builds Professionalism 12. Magnet Schools and Issues of Education Quality 13. Myth of Public School Failure 14. Should We Push the Button?
Culture and Schools	23. Canon Debate, Knowledge Construction, and Multicultural Education		

How Others See Us and How We See Ourselves

There is serious dialogue going on regarding the use of public tax funds to enhance parental "choice" plans to permit greater "privatization" of schooling. Advocates of the public schools are fiercely defending the importance of retaining the "common school" tradition of tax support for public institutions only. The defenders of private corporate intervention into education argue that greater privatization of education at the K–12 levels will give parents and children more real choices among schooling alternatives. Defenders of the public schools argue that the development of a two-tired national educational system, one public and one private, would undermine the basic democratic traditions of tax-supported education by creating even greater levels of segregation among socioeconomic groups. Private sector schools will have students from higher socioeconomic backgrounds, while students remaining in the public schools with be the "have nots" and the learning disabled. (The readings in unit 2 go into this debate in great depth.) Yet, even in this first unit of essays the public perceptions of the "choice" issue in schooling are raised from both within and without the education profession.

Concerns regarding the quality of public schooling need to be seen in the social context of the dramatic demographic changes currently taking place in North America and especially in the United States, which is experiencing the second largest wave of immigration in its history. Cuts in federal government funding of such important early educational programs as Head Start over the past 12 years have created a situation in some areas of the nation (such as West Virginia) where only about one in three eligible children from poverty-level homes can have a place in Head Start programs. In addition, school dropout rates, adult and youth illiteracy, the increasing rate of teenage pregnancy, and several interrelated health and security issues in schools cause continued public concern.

The public's perception of the costs and effectiveness of new school programs is vague at best because we are uncertain about the long-term success of certain models of innovation. For instance, some state departments of education are imposing 9th and 12th grade exit standards that are academically demanding, as well as "tiered diplomas" (qualitatively different exit credentials) for high school graduates. We are not sure what the overall public reactions to such innovations will be even though the competency testing has been going on in several states and provinces for some time.

There is public uncertainty, as well, whether or not state and provincial legislators will accept a greater state government role in funding needed changes in the schools. There continues to be intense controversy among citizens about the quality and adequacy of schools. Meanwhile the plight of many of the continent's children is getting worse, not better. Some have estimated a child is molested or neglected in the United States every 47 seconds; a student drops out of school every 8 seconds. More than a third of the children in the United States have no health insurance coverage. The litany of tragedy for the children and teenagers could be extended; however, the message is clear. There is grave, serious business yet to be attended to by the social service and educational agencies that try to serve North American youth. People are impatient to see some fundamental efforts to meet the basic needs of young people in the mid-1990s. The problems are the greatest in major cities and in more isolated rural areas. Public perceptions of the schools are affected by high levels of economic deprivation among large minority sectors of the population and the economic pressures that our interdependent world economy produces as a result of international competition for the world's markets.

Studies conducted in the past few years, particularly the Carnegie Corporation's study of adolescents in America, document the plight of millions of young persons in North America. Some authors point out that although there was much talk about educational change in the 1990s, those changes were marginal and cosmetic at best. States responded by demanding more course work and tougher exit standards from school. However, the underlying courses of poor academic achievement received insufficient attention. With still more than 25 percent of school children in the United States living at or below the poverty level and almost a third of them in more economically and socially vulnerable nontraditional family settings, the overall social situation for young persons in North America continues to be difficult. The public wants more effective governmental responses to public needs.

Alternative approaches to attracting new and talented teachers have received sympathetic support among many sectors of the public, but these alternative teacher certification approaches have met with stiff opposition from large segments of the incumbents of North American education systems. Many states are exploring and experimenting with such programs at the urging of government and business leaders. Yet many of these alternative programs are too superficial and fail to teach the candidates

in these programs the new knowledge base on teaching and learning that has been developed in recent years.

So, in the face of major demographic shifts and the persistence of many long-term social problems, the public watches closely how schools respond to new as well as old challenges. In recent years, these challenges have aggravated rather than allayed the public's concerns about the efficacy of public schooling as conducted in most places. Alternative educational agendas continue to be articulated by various political, cultural, corporate, and philanthropic interests. At the same time, the "incumbents" of the educational system respond with their own educational agendas reflecting their views of the system from the inside. The well-being and academic progress of students are the motivating forces behind the recommendations of all well-meaning interest groups in this dialogue. New national strategic goals for future educational development may come from this dialogue.

Looking Ahead: Challenge Questions

What educational issues are of greatest concern to citizens today?

What ought to be the policy directions of national and state governments regarding educational reform?

What are the most important problems blocking efforts to improve educational standards?

What technological changes in the world economy influence the directions of educational change?

What economic factors affect educational development?

How can we best build a national public consensus regarding the structure and purposes of schooling?

What social factors encourage at-risk students to leave school early?

What are the differences between the myth and the reality of North American schooling? Have the schools done anything right?

What are the best ways to accurately assess public perceptions of the educational system?

What is the functional effect of public opinion on national public policy regarding educational development?

What generalizations can one draw concerning public schools in the United States from the Phi Delta Kappa/ Gallup poll data?

How can existing public concerns regarding schooling be addressed more effectively by state or provincial legislatures?

Preserving the American Dream

toward a recommitment to Public Education in America

Privatization advocates would abandon America's commitment to educational equity. Pluralism, educational excellence, and democratic governance are at stake.

Don Cameron

DON CAMERON is Executive Director of the National Education Association.

Envision the following scenario of American K–12 education in the year 2010: All children are provided government vouchers which their parents sign over to the school their children attend.

There are two distinct kinds of school systems. The first is public and is financed through public funds derived from tax dollars. It is staffed by employees who work for the public. These schools are automatically open to all children without exception. They are obliged to admit and retain every child. Parents pay no additional enrollment costs beyond their tax dollars. These public schools are directly accountable to state and local authorities and must comply with all federal and state statutes, such as those on desegregation and education of the handicapped.

The second school system is private and is financed through a combination of private funds and public tax dollars in the form of vouchers. It is staffed by employees who work for the school's owner. Many of these schools are created and run by private, profit-making corporations; others are owned and run by religious groups. They are able to accept

From *Educational Horizons*, Vol. 71, No. 1, Fall 1992, pp. 31-36. Reprinted with permission from *Educational HORIZONS*, quarterly journal of Pi Lamda Theta, International Honor and Professional Association in Education, 4101 E. Third Street, Bloomington, IN 47407-6626.

This scenario of a two-tier education system in the year 2010—one tier for the haves and another for the have-nots—is ugly.

or reject students based upon virtually any criteria they wish, and they charge parents tuition over and above the amount of the government voucher. These private schools are accountable only to their owners and need not comply with most of the state and federal laws applicable to the public schools.

Since the private schools' viability and profitability depend on producing a quality product, they accept only the most promising students. They refuse to accept children with physical or mental disabilities or children whose learning abilities are marred by poverty, neglect, or dysfunctional families. They even shy away from children for whom English is not the language spoken at home.

Tuition, when added to the public's tax dollars, allows private schools to enjoy smaller classes, employ teacher assistants, and purchase more computers and other learning materials. The tuition not covered by the government voucher likely will range between $2,000 and $7,000 a year by 2010—more than a poor family (or even some middle-class families with more than one child) can afford.

Accordingly, in the 2010 scenario, private school students tend to emanate from wealthier families and those families that can afford to place a high priority on education. Students, by and large, come to the private schools ready to learn.

And what about public schools in this 2010 scenario? They are simply responsible for all children who don't attend a private school, including the poor, the disadvantaged, the disabled, and those whose families are not particularly education oriented.

The education of such children is more expensive, yet public schools have less money with which to operate than their private counterparts. They enroll and retain students who are harder to educate and require more individual attention. They have larger classes, fewer computers, and less equipment.

This scenario of a two-tier education system in the year 2010—one tier for the haves and another for the have-nots—is ugly. It's a scenario that would further stratify our already stratified society. It would further undermine America's ability to produce an educated citizenry capable of meeting the challenges of the twenty-first century. Such a scenario, if it becomes a reality, is wrong for education. And it's wrong for America.

Unfortunately, there is a distinct possibility that such a scenario could, indeed, become reality. Since the advent of the Reagan Administration in 1981, there has been a continuing drumbeat to privatize American public education by providing public tax dollars for private and parochial schools. This privatization juggernaut is often masked by employing the feel-good word "choice."

Private school choice is the heart of the Bush Administration's education strategy.[1] Last year the Administration proposed to take $530 million from the public treasury for the use of private and parochial schools, to allow the $6.2 billion in Chapter 1 funds to be used as vouchers at private schools, and to use $225 million in education block grants to encourage choice programs.[2] Privatization zealots have been active at the state level as well. During the 1991–92 school year, twenty five states considered legislation that would create a voucher program allowing public funds to be used for private education, placed a privatization initiative on the ballot, or had a voucher experiment in place.[3]

American business has more than signalled its readiness to become involved in profit-making schools in a big way. Best known is Christopher Whittle's Edison Project. Whittle plans to spend $2.5 to $3 billion to develop a blueprint for a new kind of private, profit-making school, and he plans to open two hundred such schools by 1995. By the year 2010, he plans to operate one thousand schools serving two million students.

Jefferson, Horace Mann, John Dewey, and others recognized the critical role of education in forming and maintaining a democratic society and the imperative of making schooling a public, governmental function . . .

Another private, for-profit company, the Minneapolis-based Education Alternatives, Inc., is already running a newly built public school, South Pointe Elementary in Miami Beach, Florida. Education Alternatives also has a five-year contract to run nine schools in Baltimore, Maryland starting in the 1992–93 school year. K–12 education potentially is big business: 46 million students, expenditures of $200 billion a year.

Indispensable to Democracy

But public education in the United States is profoundly more than an untapped new market for private entrepreneurs. Public education is the bedrock of American democracy. Further, America's public schools have given meaning to our nation's commitment to equal opportunity and cultural diversity. They are the ties that bind America's diverse and pluralistic society into a nation—teaching children to get along with those who are different from themselves, helping all citizens learn to balance individual interests with the common good.

Thomas Jefferson called education "the anvil upon which democracy is forged." Jefferson, Horace Mann, John Dewey, and others recognized the critical role of education in forming and maintaining a democratic society and the imperative of making schooling a public, governmental function—universally accessible and accountable to the people. The founders and definers of America's public schools understood that "public education stands at the critical intersection of government and civil society."[4]

America's public schools—directly accountable to the communities they serve—are indispensable to democracy. They provide a critical venue for balancing the interests of parents and other taxpayers, for setting priorities, for providing a well-educated citizenry. When a community debates the school budget, considers passing a school bond issue, or considers the costs versus the benefits of a full-day kindergar-

ten program, it is weighing its responsibility to the children of that community against competing demands.

Education is not simply the concern of parents of school-age children, and by no means is it a local phenomenon. Our system of public education is premised on the idea that the education of America's children is not only a family responsibility but also a national investment. That investment is in the very fabric of America's dream—its social and economic well-being.

Public schooling has its problems. But the solution is not to give up on public schools and on democracy. That is precisely what the advocates of privatization would have us do. They would turn over the decisions about the education of America's children, now made in the public arena, to the marketplace. Schools would no longer be community-based institutions, run by the public for the public. They would become private institutions, run by their owners for their students and their parents.

The Market Model

Privatization advocates want to remove schools from democratic governance. In *Politics, Markets and American Schools*, the neo-manifesto of privatization, John Chubb and Terry Moe state, "The problem of poor [school] performance is just as much a normal, enduring part of the political landscape as school boards and superintendents are. It is one of the prices Americans pay for choosing to exercise direct democratic control over their schools."[5]

Is competition in the marketplace better suited to educating America's future generations than democratic governance? Privatization proponents argue that competition will force ineffective and inefficient schools to close, eventually leaving America with a world class network of private and public schools. Hogwash!

Public schools, already strapped for funds and facing even deeper

The motivation is profit, not efficiency; the goal is private and religious control, not improving the quality of the public schools. You don't have to be a mystic to see that beneath the sheep's clothing of "competition," the profiteering wolf hides.

cuts because of the exodus of public tax dollars to private schools, could not possibly compete with tax-bank-rolled private institutions awash in both private and public funding. The motivation is profit, not efficiency; the goal is private and religious control, not improving the quality of the public schools. You don't have to be a mystic to see that beneath the sheep's clothing of "competition," the profiteering wolf hides. Public schools have their problems, but the solution is not to dismember them, not to relegate them and their young occupants to the lower rungs of the socio-educational ladder.

Under the privatization scenario, we know what will happen to "ineffective" and "inefficient" students—those unfortunate enough to have impediments of one kind or another that make it difficult for them to learn. They will suffer even more. And when they do, so does this nation. Under the privatization scenario, we know what will happen to "inefficient" communities—those that are impoverished or overrun by drugs, violence, and social dislocation. They will atrophy even further. In a two-tier education system, millions of children and thousands of communities will be condemned to the schools of last resort—the public schools.

If you want a practical example, look at health care, a service of public importance firmly controlled by the private sector. Doctors, hospitals, and other medical services are in short supply in many communities, especially in communities where there is a disproportionate number of poor people who cannot afford quality medical care. Under-staffed and underfunded public hospitals and clinics struggle desperately to meet the health needs of America's have-nots, and they do so with fewer and fewer human and financial resources. In a two-tier educational structure, America's public schools will be left struggling to educate the children of the have-nots; and with fewer and fewer resources.

There's no question that the market works. The question that must be asked is whether the invisible economic hand, the free-for-all of the marketplace, is best suited to meet America's educational needs. Will the harsh realities of the market assure that every child in the United States will reach his or her potential? I don't believe so. In any event, we should not gamble: the stakes are too high.

Educational Starvation

Privatizing America's schools won't begin to address this country's fundamental educational problem—inequity. The real issue in American public education isn't that parents don't have the option to choose a good school for their children. The real issue is that all schools aren't good schools. Privatization of education won't assure good schools for everyone any more than privatized health care, housing, and transportation have provided good medical care, homes, and means of travel for everyone.

Our public schools need systemic, radical reform. They need restructuring. They need a bottom-up overhaul. They are burdened by cumbersome, top-down bureaucracies that were designed to accommodate the long-outmoded industrial model of the early twentieth century. The schools must be revamped and recharged if they are to meet the twenty first century head-on. To do so will cost money and time—commodities that are difficult to come by, especially in poor communities.

In *Savage Inequalities*, Jonathan Kozol documents the gross and damaging inequities among America's public schools.[6] The book takes readers on a tour through inner-city and suburban schools, describing in devastating detail the differences in facilities, equipment, learning materials, and teacher-student ratios, as well as the environments in which children are growing up. Kozol cites per-pupil

There's a certain irony to this educational starvation, this call for emasculation of the public schools.

spending figures for the wealthy suburban school districts that are three, four, and five times higher than per-pupil spending in impoverished inner cities.

America, as well as education, is living with the unwholesome political legacy of the 1980s. We're feeling the effect of three administrations committed to removing government from as many public venues as possible, with little regard for the public good. Look at our national parks. Look at the airlines. The effect of the political philosophy of the past twelve years, coupled with the current recession, has been to stretch the financial capabilities of state and local governments to the breaking point. Squeezed between federal funding cuts and reduced local revenues, state and local governments—which provide 94 percent of the funding for public education—can't even afford to continue funding schools at the current inadequate levels.

There's a certain irony to this educational starvation, this call for emasculation of the public schools. Here we are in the last decade of the twentieth century, knowing full well that a good education for every youngster is essential to coping successfully with an increasingly complex world. America's population is aging, which means that there are fewer and fewer workers to support each retiree, thereby placing a burgeoning strain on the Social Security system. In 1950 there were eighteen workers supporting each retiree; in 2035 there will be just two.[7] The children in our schools today are the children we will depend on tomorrow. Not some of them—all of them. Yet, increasing numbers of children are at risk—in danger of failing in school. Poverty is the most prevalent indicator of school problems, and the poverty rate among children is increasing rapidly. Today in the United States one of every four children under the age of six lives in poverty.[8] Of the people in U.S. prisons, 82 percent are high school dropouts.[9]

In "The Milwaukee Parental Choice Program," Herbert Grover, Wisconsin superintendent of public instruction, and Julie K. Underwood, an associate professor at the University of Wisconsin-Madison, ask how privatization addresses the real problems confronting America's children and schools:

What impact will choice have on improving the conditions that surround the children? Will such a program improve the United States' nineteenth-place ranking among the nations of the world in infant mortality rates and twenty-ninth in low birth weight babies? Will it address the reality that . . . this country ranks eighth among industrialized nations in childhood poverty? . . . How does it resolve the Milwaukee condition in which 60 percent of the pupils come from low-income families; 28 percent within the minority community are unemployed; 7,700 child abuse cases are reported; 2,500 children are homeless; the teen pregnancy rate is twice the national average; and 35 percent of the pupils change schools each year because of family housing or employment situations?

How can children learn when their lives are in such turmoil? It takes hard work, dedication, prudent investment, and the ability to resist glitzy, quick fixes. How is it that, between 1982 and 1989, 2.1 million children fell into poverty while the number of American billionaires quintupled? How was this nation able to invest $1.9 trillion in national defense while cutting $10 billion from programs to defend poor children and families? And why does this society spend $27,000 a year to keep a juvenile in custody but only $2,500 a year to support a child in Head Start?[10]

The United States is experiencing the second largest wave of immigration in our nation's history. This is a time of rapidly growing ethnic and racial diversity, a time when it is more important than ever for America to educate all its children well. It is projected that by the year 2010, 38 percent of America's youth population will be members of minority groups. By that year, the "minority" youth population of six states (Hawaii, Texas, California, Florida, New York, and Louisiana) will in fact be the majority.[11]

Renewing the Commitment

It is no exaggeration to suggest that now, more than at any time in our nation's history, America must renew its commitment to pluralism, equality of opportunity, and educational excellence. To do so effectively, we need public institutions, including public education, that unite the diverse American constituency. We need to work out new models for living and working together that respect diversity while holding fast to the notion of "one nation, indivisible."

This is scarcely the time to withdraw support from yet another public institution—especially one as essential to democracy as the schools. It's exactly the wrong time to trade democratic governance for the bottom lines of profiteers. It's exactly the wrong time to abandon America's commitment to educational equity. It's exactly the wrong time to privatize American public education.

Real education reform and restructuring are happening in public schools all across the United States. Teachers, administrators, education associations, colleges of education, and communities are working together to fundamentally change their schools, to provide meaningful choices within the public schools, and to build stronger links between schools and their communities. In schools associated with Ted Sizer's Coalition of Essential Schools, John Goodlad's National Network for Educational Improvement, James Comer's School Development Program, and the National Education Association's National Center for Innovation, educators are struggling with the hard questions of school improvement, student learning, and teacher preparation. These are not showy, one-shot, publicity-seeking efforts. They are long-term restructuring efforts that address the fundamental problems facing America's children and schools.

This bottom-up approach to school renewal is not to be confused with the plethora of quick-fix school "reforms" enacted in the last decade. Most legislated prescriptions for school change called for more of the same—more graduation requirements, more regulations, more standardized tests, more time in school. That kind of school reform no more addresses the real, urgent issues of equity and excellence than do private school vouchers. Simplistic state mandates, such as the Bush Administration's America 2000 with its call for parental choice and the development of 535 New American Schools, only tinker around the edges of our nation's education problem.

The kind of educational improvement that's needed—and the kind that's already underway in hundreds of public schools—fundamentally questions all the traditional assumptions of schooling, from how schools and students are organized to how teachers teach and students learn. This is the kind of change that needs to be supported within institutions that are universally accessible and publicly accountable—within the democratically run public schools.

Far from moving to the private-sector, competitive market model, America needs to recommit itself to creating universally excellent public schools. Markets create winners and losers. America cannot afford any more educational losers.

1. *America 2000: An Education Strategy* (Washington, D.C.: U.S. Department of Education, 1991).
2. "Report on Privatization Initiatives" (NEA Government Relations, April 1992), 15.
3. "Privatization Initiatives," 2–9.
4. Ann Bastian, "Keeping the Public in Public Education," in *Why We Still Need Public Schools*, ed. Art Must, Jr. (Buffalo, N.Y.: Prometheus Books, 1992), 297.
5. John E. Chubb and Terry M. Moe, *Politics, Markets, and America's Schools* (Washington, D.C.: The Brookings Institution, 1990), 2.
6. Jonathan Kozol, *Savage Inequalities* (New York: Crown Publishers, 1991).
7. Harold L. Hodgkinson, *A Demographic Look at Tomorrow*, (Washington, D.C.: Institute for Educational Leadership, 1992), 12.
8. Reports on U.S. Census Bureau poverty figures. *The New York Times* and *The Washington Post*, 4 September 1992.
9. Ibid., 3.
10. Herbert Grover and Julie K. Underwood, "The Milwaukee Parental Choice Program," in *Why We Still Need Public Schools*, 242.
11. Ibid., 6–7.

Strengths and Weaknesses of American Education

Taking the time to examine the strengths of the U.S. education system helps to put our problems in perspective, Mr. Kirst suggests. There is no evidence that abandoning our public schools will improve the situation.

MICHAEL W. KIRST

MICHAEL W. KIRST (Stanford University Chapter) is co-director of Policy Analysis for California Education and a professor in the Department of Administration and Policy Analysis, School of Education, Stanford University, Stanford, Calif.

(United Nations photo)

THE PUBLIC education system in the U.S. has served this nation well. Today and in the future, it must meet unprecedented challenges. However, arguments about whether the performance of our students has declined over time miss the point. The 1990 Oldsmobile was better than any Olds made before. But was it good enough to meet worldwide competition in 1990? A similar question faces U.S. education: Are we good enough to stand up to worldwide competition?

The time is right to assess the strengths and weaknesses of the U.S. public education system. We need to build on its strengths and shore up its weaknesses.

We know more than ever about how to do this, but serious questions remain about the resources we are willing to de-

 From *Phi Delta Kappan*, April 1993, pp. 613-616, 618. Reprinted with permission of *Phi Delta Kappan* and the author.

vote to the task and about our political will to get the job done.

WHAT IS RIGHT

Inclusiveness. The U.S. K-12 education system as we know it today was created in the mid-20th century to serve all pupils for 12 years and not weed them out at an earlier age. Until very recently, this policy provided high retention

> *Is there a better technical university in Japan or Germany than MIT, Cal Tech, or Stanford?*

rates compared to those of other nations. Since 1970, however, other industrialized nations (e.g., Great Britain, Australia, and Japan) have increased their retention rates dramatically. The inclusiveness of our system through high school is no longer the competitive edge it once was, although 88% of our young people have earned high school diplomas or the equivalent by age 25.

Nevertheless, we should strengthen our efforts at dropout prevention and expand the second-chance opportunities we offer to dropouts who wish to resume their schooling. The GED (General Education Development) program, broad access to community colleges, and high school adult education programs are parts of the U.S. system that are frequently overlooked. Moreover, their curricular standards are a concern and need to be reviewed, but the role they play in the U.S. education system should not be underestimated.

Postsecondary education. The most commonly cited indicators of the health of education in the U.S. — international assessments, the National Assessment of Educational Progress (NAEP), scores on college entrance exams, scores on standardized achievement tests, and the results of state assessment programs — all ignore the value added by the postsecondary education system. However, in the international arena, the U.S. system of postsecondary education — including community colleges, trade schools, and universities — is one of our chief strengths.

For example, in 1988 the U.S. spent a higher percentage of its gross national product on public and private higher education than any other country in the world. Moreover, U.S. spending on higher education as a percentage of all education spending was 39.4%, compared to 20.8% for West Germany and 21.4% for Japan.[1] The principal reason for the high level of U.S. spending on higher education is that the proportion of the population participating in higher education is greater here than in any other large nation.[2] But the U.S. per-student expenditure on public and private higher education is also high. For example, in 1988 the U.S. spent about $9,844 per pupil for higher education while Japan spent $6,105 and France, $4,362.[3]

We should also be pleased with the *total* years or days of schooling that young people in the U.S. accumulate through age 25. Much is made in the press about our 180-day school year, compared to a school year of 240 days in Japan. But it is rarely mentioned that in the U.S. the highest percentage of 24-year-olds in the world graduate from a four-year college or university. Our particular advantage is in the percentage of females who graduate from colleges and universities. The U.S. graduates 24% of its 24-year-old females; Japan, 12.4%; West Germany, 10%.

Many studies have emphasized that U.S. students complete little homework and do not work hard on academic subjects in high school.[4] But U.S. students are often confronted with a demanding academic regimen in college. The adjustment to the academic pressures of the university in freshman year can be difficult for many U.S. students, but they do make up for the ground lost in high school.

The difficulty of the postsecondary experience in the U.S. contrasts sharply with the situation in Japan, where the university years are viewed as a time to take it easy between the intense academic pressure of high school and the demands of Japanese business. Japanese universities are not as challenging as those in the U.S., especially for the many Japanese women, who often take a less-rigorous academic curriculum that prepares them for homemaking.[5] A 1988 study of teacher education students in the U.S. and Japan concluded:

> Although American students seem to know less about global issues than Japanese students at the beginning of college, by graduation they are performing as well. This is attributable to a considerable positive difference between U.S. freshmen and seniors, and a small difference between Japanese freshmen and seniors. This finding corroborates recent statements by Japanese scholars expressing concern about the quality of higher education.[6]

The preeminence of U.S. graduate schools is widely recognized. The U.S. attracts a large number of foreign students, and our most prestigious research universities are certainly competitive by world standards — many consider them to be the best in the world. Is there a better technical university in Japan or Germany than MIT, Cal Tech, or Stanford? Given the overall quality of all U.S. research universities, it is likely that some of the international academic gap is closed at this final stage, at least for our most outstanding science and math students.

Content standards and assessment. A recent international study concluded that U.S. 9- and 14-year-olds compared quite favorably with their counterparts in other industrialized nations in reading.[7] While basic reading looks relatively good, we still have a long way to go before the majority of U.S. students can comprehend complex passages and grasp the tone and mood of the author. Moreover, math and science appear very weak in international comparisons. The U.S. math and science curricula do not expose the mass of students to very much problem solving, statistical inference, chemistry, or physics.[8]

Some help appears to be on the way. For example, by the end of the 1990s, the U.S. will probably have national curriculum standards and subject-matter frameworks, though not a detailed national curriculum. Currently, de facto national "policies" are all around us — set by the school accreditation agencies, such as the North Central Association of Schools and Colleges; the College Entrance Examination Board; and the National Collegiate Athletic Association.

The movement toward national content standards in various curricular areas is justified by several concerns.

• Current state and local standards for pupil achievement and teacher performance are lacking in rigor and do not provide uniform data on outcomes — data crucial for interstate or local comparisons.

• Commonly used multiple-choice tests are excessively oriented to low-level basic skills that inappropriately emphasize single right answers. Moreover, local education agencies tend to choose commercial tests that do not adequately emphasize analysis, statistical inference, mathematical problem solving, experimental science, synthesis, expository writing, and complex reading. Many widely available standardized tests — such as the Comprehensive Tests of Basic Skills, the Stanford Achievement Tests, and the Metropolitan Achievement Tests — are not geared to the high curricular standards of our economic competitors in Europe and Asia. Since the U.S. is involved in worldwide economic competition, complete local control of tests and curricula is a luxury we can no longer afford.

• Since the commonly used standardized multiple-choice tests are pitched at such low levels, parents and the general public receive a "phony story" that exaggerates what U.S. pupils know and can do today — compared to prior decades or to students in other nations. The "Lake Wobegon" effect, in which all the students are above average, then becomes the reality.

• U.S. tests and exams often do not have "high stakes" for the pupils who take them. Few employers look at the transcripts of high school graduates, and state assessments are not used for college entrance. The Scholastic Aptitude Test is not aligned with the high school curriculum and purports to measure "aptitude" rather than achievement.

A coalition of policy leaders has concluded that national subject-matter curricular standards that meet world-class benchmarks are needed.[9] This coalition contends that a nationwide system of exams should be developed and aligned to these world-class standards in five core

subjects — English, mathematics, science, social studies, and foreign languages. Moreover, the results should be reported for individual students, and "high-stakes" decisions should be based largely on student performance. Specifically, the coalition contends that employers should use the results of national exams when hiring high school graduates and that universities should consider scores on national exams as well as high school grades. Furthermore, these initiatives for national standards need to be part of any state-level strategy for systemic reform, especially in the areas of staff development and teacher training.

Local flexibility. Despite the likely evolution of national standards, the locally based education system in the U.S. is flexible and can innovate without feeling the heavy hand of national control. The 15,000 school districts provide the U.S. with the ability to adapt to diverse local contexts. While many districts are stuck in political gridlock, others are increasingly on the move. Citizens with the resources to relocate can find many educational choices to suit their tastes. Despite growing state control, there is still a large range of options in local education. Districts differ in their mix of secondary school curricula and in their stress on extracurricular activities. They also differ in their local tax burdens.

Socialization and the common school. The U.S. system of public education has been a crucial element in unifying a nation of immigrants, producing the *unum* from the *pluribus*. More immigrants entered the U.S. in the two decades between 1970 and 1990 than in any previous 20-year period. Consequently, the need to teach community values and concepts is just as urgent as it was during the rise of common schools at the turn of the century. If the public schools do not include the vast majority of our children, the only other common transmitter of our culture will be television. And so far television does not seem to have had a positive influence on American youth.

We have lost much of the national cohesiveness that the common school crusaders helped to create. Today, powerful and well-organized interest groups — whether labor, business, or agriculture — have no inclination to unite with other segments of the community to explore differences and work toward the common good. Although the leaders of these interest groups are not irresponsible, they

have developed attitudes that make collaboration with others almost impossible. Since each group feels that it is not getting what it deserves, the leaders are in no mood to work with others to shape a constructive future.

PROBLEMS WITH U.S. SCHOOLS

The bottom half. The U.S. is particularly weak in providing higher-order skills to those students — roughly half — who do not go on to postsecondary education.

> *The U.S. has no national strategy for staff development that provides depth and breadth for its teachers.*

In part, this failure is caused by the declining conditions of children and the relative lack of support here for children, compared to other nations in the industrialized world.

Today, more than 20% of children in the U.S. live in poverty, up from 14% in 1969.[10] The median income of families in the bottom income quintile (lowest 20%) has eroded over time, and the gap between the incomes of the poorest and wealthiest families has grown.[11] The decline in real income for those in the lowest quintile has been accompanied by gains for those in the top 40% of the income distribution. Race and ethnicity, gender, and family structure are strongly associated with the likelihood of living in poverty. In 1992, half of families headed by single women lived in poverty, compared to only 11.4% of two-parent families.[12]

While many children fare well in low-income households, studies have shown that children in such circumstances are more likely to die in infancy and early childhood, suffer serious illnesses, become pregnant during their teen years, or drop out of school. They are also less likely to continue education beyond high school.[13] Despite the statistical association of these outcomes with poverty, the direction of causality is less clear. The diminished life chances of the poor may be linked to the lack of access to adequate health care and nutrition, the often lower quality of schooling in low-income neighborhoods, the stress of poverty on family relationships, or a variety of other elements.

Family structure. Traditionally, most institutions that serve children and youths make the implicit assumption that children live with two biological parents, one working in the home and the other working in the formal labor market. This traditional family type now accounts for less than one-third of all families. Forty-six percent of children live in homes in which both parents (or the only parent) work outside the home.[14] Because of an increase in divorce and in the number of births to single mothers, about 60% of all children and youths will live in a single-parent family for some period of their lives.[15]

Teachers. While the U.S. is developing challenging and better-conceived curricula and exams, there is no commensurate effort under way to improve the training or the working conditions of teachers. Teachers still work in a structure that inhibits collaboration and professional growth. Staff development programs are typically one-shot affairs with scant follow-up and coaching. The U.S. has no national strategy for staff development that provides depth and breadth for its 2.2 million teachers. The U.S. also lacks levers to improve teacher preparation, which is largely controlled by independent universities and driven by state requirements. The probable result will be minimal classroom implementation of the high-level national content standards.

Fragmentation and gridlock. In the 1950s and 1960s, the politics of education was a "closed system" that was unresponsive to communities and political constituencies. Now the situation is quite different. Numerous actors and constituencies have created a sense of fragmentation and have led to complaints that no one is in charge of U.S. education policy.

This fragmentation of interests inhibits coherent reform. For example, it is very difficult to align categorical programs with the standards developed by the National Council of Teachers of Mathematics. Moreover, it is difficult to sustain education reform over a long period of time because newly elected politicians do not generally want to continue reforms that they did not originate.

Most of the social movements of the 1990s differ from those of the 19th century that led to the creation of such social institutions as the public schools. Today, social movements are interested in challenging public institutions and trying to make them more responsive to forces outside the local administrative structure. Some would even assert that these movements help fragment decision making so that schools cannot function effectively. This conclusion is reinforced by the almost unremitting litany of the media suggesting that violence, vandalism, and declining test scores are the predominant conditions of public education.

In California, for example, this situation has become so serious that the schools increasingly suffer from shock and overload characterized by poor morale and too few resources to operate all the programs that the society expects schools to offer. The issue then becomes how much change and agitation a public institution can take and still continue to function effectively. Californians have confronted numerous initiatives, such as Proposition 13, vouchers, and spending limits. Citizens in California and elsewhere go to their local school boards and superintendents expecting redress of their problems only to find that the decision-making power rests with the state. The impression grows that *no one* is in charge of public education.

All of this does not mean that local school authorities are helpless. Rather, it means that they cannot control their agendas or shape outcomes as much as they could in the past. Superintendents must deal with shifting and ephemeral coalitions that might yield some temporary local advantages, but many important policy items on the local agenda arise from external forces, such as state and federal governments or the pressures of interest groups, including teachers.

There is a feeling abroad in the land that the education system *cannot* be restructured on a massive scale. According to this view, the most that we can expect is incremental improvement, along with a few showcase anomalies of structural change. More "projects" do not seem to be the answer. But national exams on their own are not a sufficient policy either. Perhaps our biggest weakness is our uncertainty about what to do next in pursuit of comprehensive and systemic change.

THE WEAKNESSES of U.S. education are most evident in big cities, and the strengths are clearest in suburbs with high incomes and high levels of education. NAEP results, however, highlight significant weaknesses even in the upper ranges of achievement in terms of problem solving, synthesis, analysis, statistical inference, and comprehension of complex passages of prose.

Despite a century of education reforms, nothing much has changed at the classroom level. Reforms that have lasted have usually been structural additions that are easily monitored and create a long-term influential constituency. Some examples are vocational education and the use of Carnegie units. But overcoming the weaknesses discussed above will require reform at the lowest unit — teachers and teaching — in addition to systemic restructuring. It will also require the political will to stick with a coherent strategy directed toward improving student outcomes in all parts of the education system. Our democracy leads us to make frequent changes in leadership, and new policy makers must overcome the tendency to throw out their predecessors' approaches automatically.

Analyses on a national scale mask urgent problems that specific U.S. regions confront. In the Southwest, for example, students with limited facility in English are a large and growing portion of the population. One of every eight schoolchildren in the nation lives in California, but more than 20% have limited proficiency in English, and by the year 2000 half of California children will be Hispanic or Asian. The educational problems of these children never make the top of national lists, which suggests that a nationwide analysis may not always lead to the right approach in specific regions.

It is probable that the Clinton Administration will focus on job creation through policies that emphasize the transition between high school and the workplace.

However, it is doubtful that apprenticeships will provide a complete answer to the problems of the bottom half outlined above. It seems more likely that apprenticeship initiatives will have but scattered and limited impact. Other strategies to meet this challenge may be even less effective. Some proponents of national exams contend that, if employers ask for national exam scores, students will be motivated to work harder in school. This theory has never been tested in the U.S. and will require large-scale mobilization of employers.

Taking the time to examine the strengths of the U.S. education system helps to put our myriad problems in perspective. There is no evidence that abandoning our public education system will improve the situation. A great deal of rhetoric and numerous theories surround the alleged panacea of choice. But the strengths of the U.S. education system are embedded in our culture and history, and we should not discard them easily or without better data about what choice would actually accomplish. The U.S. education system is gigantic, with roughly $250 billion spent annually, 2.6 million employees, and 44 million pupils. Untested schemes, such as vouchers, are dangerous and represent a plunge into unknown waters. We already know quite a bit about systemic education reform and school improvement.

1. Arthur Hauptman, Eileen O'Brien, and Lauren Supena, *Higher Education Expenditures and Participation: An International Comparison* (Washington, D.C.: American Council for Educational Research, 1991).

2. *Education at a Glance* (Paris: Organisation for Economic Cooperation and Development, 1992), p. 77.

3. Ibid., p. 57.

4. Joseph Murphy, *The Education Reform Movement of the 1980s* (Berkeley, Calif.: McCutchan, 1990), pp. 10-19.

5. Michael W. Kirst, "Japanese Education: Its Implications for Economic Competition in the 1980s," *Phi Delta Kappan*, June 1981, pp. 707-8. For a critique of U.S. higher education, see Ray Marshall and Marc Tucker, *Thinking for a Living* (New York: Basic Books, 1992).

6. John Cogan, Judith Torney-Purta, and Douglas Anderson, "Knowledge and Attitudes Toward Global Issues: Students in Japan and the U.S.," *Comparative Education Review*, vol. 32, 1988, pp. 282-97.

7. Warwick B. Elley, *How in the World Do Students Read?* (New York: International Association for the Evaluation of Educational Achievement, July 1992).

8. For direct comparisons of achievement in the U.S. with that in other nations, see *Education at a Glance*.

9. See *Raising Standards for American Education* (Washington, D.C.: National Council on Education Standards and Testing, 1992).

10. See Harold Hodgkinson, *A Demographic Look at Tomorrow* (Washington, D.C.: Institute for Educational Leadership, 1992), p. 4.

11. Ibid., pp. 7-10.

12. Ibid., pp. 4, 7, 8.

13. Ibid.

14. Ibid., p. 4.

15. Ibid; see also Marshall and Tucker, op. cit.

American Education: The Good, the Bad, And the Task

Photo by Kathy Sloane

Mr. Hodgkinson discerns a clear message amid the data on shifting populations, on test scores, and on students' socio-economic status. The figures are telling us that we must turn our attention to the students who are at the highest risk of school failure.

HAROLD HODGKINSON

HAROLD HODGKINSON is director of the Center for Demographic Policy, Institute for Educational Leadership, Washington, D.C.

MY AIMS IN this brief article are to describe the unique diversity of the American student body and the magnitude of the demographic changes that are to come, to consider our accomplishments with this student body by looking at test data, to point out the failures of the system in working effectively with certain students, and to indicate what needs to be done to make the system work more effectively for *all* young Americans.

DIVERSITY

While the national population grew 9.8% during the 1980s, certain groups grew very rapidly, and others posted only small increases. The number of non-Hispanic whites grew by 6%; of African-Americans, by 13.2%; of Native Americans, by 37.9%; of Asian-Pacific Island-

From *Phi Delta Kappan*, April 1993, pp. 619-623. Reprinted with permission of *Phi Delta Kappan* and the author.

ers, by 107.8%; of Hispanics of all races, by 53%.

While about 22% of the total population can be described as minority, 30% of school-age children are minority, a number that will reach 36% shortly after the year 2000. A look at immigration rates can give us a clue as to why this is so. Between 1820 and 1945, the nations that sent us the largest numbers of immigrants were (in rank order): Germany, Italy, Ireland, the United Kingdom, the Soviet Union, Canada, and Sweden. The nations that send us the most immigrants now and that are projected to do so through the year 2000 are (in rank order): Mexico, the Philippines, Korea, China/ Taiwan, India, Cuba, the Dominican Republic, Jamaica, Canada, Vietnam, the United Kingdom, and Iran.

It is clear from the former list that we have not really been a "nation of nations," as both Carl Sandburg and Walt Whitman proclaimed; rather we have been a nation of Europeans. There was a common European culture that the schools could use in socializing millions of immigrant children. The latter list indicates that we face a brand-new challenge: the population of American schools today truly represents the world. Children come to school today with different diets, different religions (there were more Moslems than Episcopalians in the U.S. in 1991), different individual and group loyalties, different music, different languages. The most diverse segment of our society is our children. While these children bring new energy and talents to our nation, they also represent new challenges for instruction.

In the 1990 Census, for the first time in history, only three states accounted for more than half of the nation's growth in a decade. These states were California, Florida, and Texas. They also picked up a total of 14 seats in the U.S. House of Representatives, while New York, Pennsylvania, Ohio, Indiana, and Illinois lost an equivalent number of seats. California will have to prepare for a 41% increase in high school graduates by 1995, with 52% of them being "minority," a term that loses its meaning in such a situation. By the year 2010, the number of minority young people in the U.S. will increase by 4.4 million, while the number of non-Hispanic white young people will decline by 3.8 million.

The states that are growing fastest have high percentages of "minority" youth. If the large minority population of New York is added to the large and fast-growing minority populations of California, Texas, and Florida, these four states will have more than one-third of the nation's young people in 2010, and the youth population of each state will be over 52% "minority." In 2010 about 12 states will have "majority minority" youth populations, while Maine's youth population will be 3% minority. It makes little sense to focus solely on the national changes when the states are becoming much more diverse in terms of ethnicity, age of population, job production, population density, family types, and youth poverty.[1]

CHILDREN AT RISK AND SCHOOLS

In 1993 more than 23% of America's children were living below the poverty line and thus were at risk of failing to fulfill their physical and mental promise. This is one of the highest youth poverty rates in the "developed" world and has shown little inclination to decline. Most of these children live in our nation's inner cities and rural areas, in about equal numbers. (The issue of youth poverty in rural America has not been addressed seriously by the nation's leaders.) Because these children bring the risks with them on the first day of kindergarten, it becomes a vital job of the schools to overcome these risks. Schools should be assessed on how well they and other agencies responsible for youth development meet the challenges posed by these children.

Since the publication of *A Nation at Risk* in 1983, there has been a general impression that American students have slumped from a previous position of world leadership to near the bottom in terms of academic achievement. (Of course, we have had similar waves of criticism of public school standards in previous decades; Arthur Bestor's *Educational Wastelands*, James Bryant Conant's reform movement, and the many responses to Sputnik I — suggesting that American students were hopelessly behind those of the Soviet Union — spring immediately to mind, along with a long list of books suggesting that American education is "falling behind.")

Behind what? That question is seldom voiced, though its implied answer is clear to readers of the literature of decline: schools are falling behind some previous Golden Age during which American public school students were the world's best in every aspect of the curriculum. In reality, if you look at the data from 30 years of international achievement testing, you will find *no* period during which American students led the world in school achievement.

Anyone who questions the methodology of the international comparisons on which much of the literature of decline is based will usually be accused of advocating "complacency." Those who ask such questions are thus shown to be enemies of excellence. However, a variety of data suggest that the picture is not as universally bleak as it is sometimes painted.

A report from the Sandia National Laboratories, carefully assessing a wide variety of data sources, concluded that American education has done well in most areas of performance. That report has never formally seen the light of day. The largest-ever international study of reading, directed by a distinguished U.S. researcher, tested thousands of students in more than 30 countries. It found that U.S. students were among the best in the world in reading, surpassed only by Finland. Only *USA Today* covered the story, and the U.S. Department of Education immediately discredited the results by saying that higher levels of difficulty were not assessed, and therefore the U.S. was not interested in the findings. Actually, the data were politically unacceptable rather than cripplingly flawed.

The fact is that all the international studies of educational achievement have a number of built-in flaws. First, translation is an art, not a science, and an item in one language can seldom be translated into another language with the identical set of culturally derived meanings. All items have a cultural "spin" based on the values behind the words. If a student can correctly identify a harpsichord as a musical instrument, we learn little about that student's intelligence but a lot about his or her family and social class. Moreover, there is no way to control for the differing motivation of the students who take the tests. (For details on this and other flaws in international comparisons, see the article by David Berliner, "Mythology and the American System of Education," *Phi Delta Kappan,* April 1993.)

In addition, international comparisons are not diagnostic: they don't help students (or nations) understand their mistakes in order to improve performance. They don't help policy makers figure out what is wrong with an education system in order to improve it. Outside of a major preoccupation with finding out who's "number one" in some vague terms, it is hard to see how any education system in any nation has been helped by these tests. It's hard to tell from these test scores what specifically needs to be fixed in American education. One can wonder what the return has been on this considerable investment.

TEST DATA IN THE U.S.

Let's look at test data from our own country and see what we can make out of them, starting with the performance of younger children and ending with that of graduate students. For this purpose I'll rely on an excellent compendium titled *Performance at the Top*, recently issued by the Educational Testing Service (ETS).[2]

With regard to reading, the data show that one 9-year-old in six can search for specific information, relate ideas, and make generalizations — the same fraction as in 1971. But we also learn that whites do much better and that Hispanics actually do a little better than blacks, despite the complications associated with English as a second language for many Hispanic children. Most important, there are spectacular differences in reading that are associated with parents' level of education: 22% of children whose parents have had some college can read at this higher level of comprehension, but only 6% of the children of high school dropouts can. Indeed, parents' level of education is one of the very best predictors of students' educational achievement.

The implications of the importance of parents' education for our education reform efforts are huge, and they have been largely neglected by the reform initiatives that issued from the Bush White House under the banner of the America 2000 strategy. Poverty would seem to be the root cause of educational deficiency (college graduates being unusually low on poverty measures), yet the reforms suggested as part of America 2000 seldom mention poverty or disadvantage.

If a child who was poor and a member of a minority group is allowed to enter the middle class — as happens if the parents become college graduates and move to the suburbs — then that child will tend to perform in school like other children whose parents are college graduates living in suburbs. This means that we should not let go of the American Dream just yet; if given the chance, it still works.

In math, slightly more 9-year-olds (20%) can perform at intermediate levels. Again, there has been no change over

the years, although the first data are from 1978. But whites still do far better, and the scores of blacks are slightly lower than those of Hispanics. Geographically speaking, the Southeast and the West don't do as well as the Northeast and the Central U.S. But again, differences in parents' level of education reveal much: 29% of the children of college graduates perform at the intermediate level, while only 6% of the children of high school dropouts do so.

In science, about one-fourth of 9-year-olds can apply basic scientific information, a figure unchanged since 1977. Here, racial and ethnic differences are somewhat smaller, and blacks do a little better than Hispanics. Regional differences are also smaller. But once again, the differences between the children of college graduates and the children of high school dropouts are the greatest: 36% of the former do well in science versus only 9% of the latter. (Oddly enough, children whose parents had some additional education past high school do better than the children of college graduates, but only by 3%.)

The data on the performance of 13-year-olds in reading reveal patterns similar to those of 9-year-olds. Again, whites do better than minorities, but the differences have narrowed among the 13-year-olds, and the scores of blacks are slighter higher than those of Hispanics. Regional differences are also smaller. However, differences associated with parents' level of education remain quite large: 15% of 13-year-old children of college graduates read at the "figuring out" level, but only 6% of the children of high school dropouts can. (Other subjects use different comparisons and are therefore not included. Among 17-year-olds, the data for comparing regions and parents' education are not comparable, although there is no evidence of systematic declines in subject areas.)

As we look past high school, some fascinating numbers are present. The Advanced Placement (AP) testing program has grown rapidly since its inception — jumping by more than 500% in the last two decades. The numbers of minority test-takers have also shown large increases, reaching about one-fifth of all test-takers in 1990, though Asian-Americans make up about half of all the minority students tested. The program has become very popular in a variety of schools, ranging from the inner cities to the wealthy suburbs; the number of test-

takers grew from about 100,000 in 1978 to 320,000 in 1990.

In most testing situations, expanding the pool of test-takers lowers the average scores. The AP program proves to be the exception, as the scores have remained virtually stable for the past two decades. One interpretation in the ETS report suggests that the limits of the pool have not been reached and that many more students could successfully complete college work in high school through AP-type programs. (This is particularly exciting for low-income and minority youths, as I have contended that inner-city students will often rise to a challenge, no matter how depressed their background may be.) The data certainly suggest that the consistency of AP scores cannot be explained by the conventional wisdom that all schools are terrible and getting worse.

When we finally get to scores on the Scholastic Aptitude Test (SAT), we find that the declines of the 1970s were largely recouped during the 1980s in terms of the percentage of students scoring 600 or above on either the verbal or the math sections. (The percentage of students achieving high scores in math has been about twice as large as the percentage achieving high verbal scores, which could have some useful implications for high schools.) Even more interesting with regard to the "high end" scores are those for the College Board's Achievement Tests, which are designed to test what is actually taught in high school courses. About 8% of high school seniors take these tests. Their average SAT verbal and math scores have steadily increased since 1977, and their average scores on the Achievement Tests have increased since 1979. It seems clear that the performance of our top students is, in some senses, improving over time.

If we look at issues of equity with regard to college attendance and graduation, we find that about 23% of all white high school graduates in the classes of 1972 and 1980 received a bachelor's degree, while the corresponding figure for black high school graduates actually declined from 17.5% for the class of 1972 to 13.9% for the class of 1980. The rate at which Hispanics earned college degrees actually improved a little, from 10.7% in 1972 to 11.2% for the 1980 class, even though Hispanics' percentages of college completion were consistently below those of blacks. The 1992 *Almanac* of the *Chronicle of Higher Education*, however, shows an increase in college enrollment for all minorities during the 1980s, although degree data are not given.

Coordinating services in the best interests of young people would make a fine agenda for the next decade.

It seems that during the 1980s, when minority scores were improving on many K-12 measures, *access* to higher education was slipping for many minority groups. Whether this was a result of shifts in financial aid policies (converting grant programs to loans) or of other factors is not clear. However, half of our graduating seniors enter college, and about one-fourth of them receive bachelor's degrees. Two percent then enter graduate school, and 3% enter professional schools. While minorities were steadily increasing their numbers through high school graduation, their participation in the higher education pipeline showed some disturbing trends. In 1992 minorities represented about 30% of public school students, 20% of college students, and 14% of recipients of bachelor's degrees. (Note that an increase in the number of high school diplomas earned by minorities will take five or more years to show up as an increase in bachelor's degrees.)

Even more striking is a look at the ETS data on high-ability students. While half did earn a bachelor's degree, 10% of high-ability seniors did not attend *any* higher education program after high school, and 40% of those who did so attended a community college, from which some transferred later to four-year programs. Given our stereotype that community colleges have virtually none of the high-ability students, it appears that they

actually enroll about two-fifths of them, which may explain why students who transfer to four-year programs do quite well.

When we come to the question of entrance to graduate school and consider scores on the Graduate Record Examination, we find even more interesting issues. From 1981 to 1990, the number of test-takers increased 16%, from 135,000 to 157,000, while the mean verbal score rose 16 points, the mean quantitative score rose 36 points, and the mean analytical score rose 30 points. The average score on the Graduate Management Admissions Test has gone from 481 in 1982 to 503 in 1990, while the number of test-takers surged from 114,000 in 1984 to 160,000 in 1990. Scores on the Medical School Admissions Test and on the Law School Admissions Test have also shown great stability (and some score increases), even with a more diverse group of test-takers. From these data it appears that both the diversity and the quality of our future scientists, researchers, and professional workers have increased simultaneously.

AN EXPLANATION

We now need to try to find some way of explaining all the data we have examined. Below, I offer a brief summary, and then I propose one explanation that fits all the data.

First, the top 20% of our high school graduates are world class — and getting better. However, talented minority youths do not get as far in the educational pipeline as they should. (The production of black Ph.D.s declined by more than one-third during the 1980s, a factor that cannot be explained in terms of declining test scores for blacks or declining numbers of blacks in the pool.)

As Iris Rotberg and others have pointed out, 40% of all research articles in the world are published by U.S. scholars; no other nation produces more than 7%.[3] There seems to be little doubt that the American intellectual elite, particularly in math and the sciences, is retaining its dominant position. The problem is that, if all public schools are doing such a miserable job, how do colleges make up for that loss and produce the world's best graduate students? (Note that the vast majority of U.S. graduate students are U.S. citizens, not Asian citizens; only at the doctoral level in the areas of engineering and computer science are U.S. stu-

dents not holding their own.) The data on the AP tests and graduate school admissions tests certainly suggest that our best are already world class, have been improving, and probably will continue to improve, despite more diversity in the examinees.

Second, the 40% right behind the top 20% are mostly capable of completing a college education, although some will need remediation in writing and science. A large number of minorities are probably now in this group, the first generation in their families to get a crack at a college education. Many students from low-income backgrounds are also in this group. We have colleges that serve a wide range of student abilities in the U.S., which explains the large American middle class. Having a wide range of undergraduate institutions that specialize in different kinds of students from different backgrounds is vital to success in a highly diverse nation.

Third, the lowest 40% of students are in very bad educational shape, a situation caused mostly by problems they brought with them to the kindergarten door, particularly poverty, physical and emotional handicaps, lack of health care, difficult family conditions, and violent neighborhoods. (Using indicators of these conditions, it is very easy to predict in the early grades which children will be at risk of school failure.) Because many of these children stay in our schools until age 18, while in most other countries they would be on the streets, our test scores reflect our commitment to try to keep them in school. These are the children who are tracked into the "general" curriculum in high school, which prepares them neither for college nor for a job. We know exactly where most of these very difficult students reside — in our inner cities and in our rural areas.

If we can locate the young people who need help the most, why do we not target our resources and focus our concern on improving the entire system by working on the students who are at the highest risk of school failure? Most of our top students are going to do well with very little effort from the school system. But the students in the bottom 40% have few resources they can bring to the school: their parents are often high school dropouts, and they know very few people who have benefited from education. Without assistance and concern from the school, they are destined for failure. If half of the students in the bottom third of U.S.

schools were stimulated to do well, developed some intellectual and job skills, and moved into the middle class, everyone in the nation would benefit.

The best way to deal with this problem is to provide a "seamless web" of services, combining education, health care, housing, transportation, and social welfare. Such efforts represent an attempt to reduce the vulnerability to school failure of the lower 40% of students. Head Start and follow-up programs can give very young children a sense of their own accomplishment and potential and can help in building a supportive and enthusiastic home environment. Chapter 1 can continue the battle in the early grades, while TRIO, Upward Bound, and Project Talent can keep the achievement level up through the high school years and on into college, where other programs are available to improve graduation rates.

On the health-care front, one of the best ways to improve education would be to make sure that every pregnant woman in America received at least one physical exam during the first trimester of her pregnancy (which would reduce births of handicapped infants by around 10%); a second way would be to make sure that every child is immunized against polio, diphtheria, and measles before entering school. All the components of the "seamless web" of services are in place, but it's not clear that we know how to coordinate these services in the best interests of young people. That would make a fine agenda for the next decade.

It is also clear that American students have regained any ground lost during the 1970s and that students are doing approximately as well as when the National Assessment of Educational Progress began more than two decades ago. Some might say that that level of achievement is not high enough for today's world, and that's a reasonable position. But then one must specify what level is needed and why. The idea of making America "number one in math and science" is meaningless unless we understand what skills and habits of mind we wish to develop and *why*. Certainly becoming numero uno on the existing international tests would not necessarily increase the number of graduate students in science and math, would not increase the scholarly output of our universities, and would not increase the number of patents or inventions (indeed we might see a reduction in creativity, since these tests do not reward innovative or divergent thinking). Broadening the educational pipeline to include more disadvantaged students with an interest in science might work, but no one has proposed that.

So where should the U.S. bend its energies and talents in education? It seems very clear to me: we should focus on the students who are at greatest risk of school failure, numbering close to one-third of the children born in 1992. These children will become the college freshmen of 2010. We know where these children are; we know that they are smart and energetic, even when doing illegal things; we know what they need in order to become successful students; and, generally, we have the resources they need (although local, state, and federal programs are largely uncoordinated). What we lack is the will to make this a national direction. Yet if we were told that an unfriendly foreign power had disabled one-third of our youth, rendering them incapable of reasonable performance in school, we would view it as an act of war. We don't need to imagine a foreign enemy; by systematically neglecting the needs and potential of disadvantaged children, we have done the damage to ourselves.

1. For a complete discussion of diversity, see Harold Hodgkinson, *A Demographic Look at Tomorrow* (Washington, D.C.: Center for Demographic Policy, Institute for Educational Leadership, 1992); and Harold Hodgkinson, Janice Hamilton Duttz, and Anita Obarakpor, *The Nation and the States* (Washington, D.C.: Center for Demographic Policy, Institute for Educational Leadership, 1992).
2. Paul E. Barton and Richard J. Coley, *Performance at the Top: From Elementary Through Graduate School* (Princeton, N.J.: Educational Testing Service, 1991).
3. Iris Rotberg, "Measuring Up to the Competition: A Few Hard Questions," *Technos*, Winter 1992, pp. 12-15.

UP AGAINST THE SYSTEM

THE LITTLE SCHOOLS THAT COULD

Deborah W. Meier

Deborah W. Meier is principal of Central Park East Secondary School in New York City.

"Too Good for Its Own Good? Bronx School Backs Quality" ran the front-page August 10 headline of *The New York Times*. The story was about the threatened closure of the Bronx New School, a small, highly innovative elementary school in New York City, on the eve of moving to its larger site. The new District Superintendent, John Reehill, was quoted as saying that the school was too autonomous, that its effort to maintain a racial balance and its insistence on being different made it "elitist," too much like a "private school." He said he intended to dismiss its teacher-director and merge it with another, more traditional school.

All over the country efforts similar to the Bronx New School face or have met similar fates. The question is, Why? What's puzzling is not that such schools make enemies but that their enemies are so successful in today's presumably pro-reform educational climate. Brave groups of parents and teachers stick their necks out, but their work rarely gets off the ground, or if it does get off the ground the schools they invent rarely survive the founding fathers and mothers. They get subtly or not so subtly transformed by bringing in new leadership more "compatible" with the system and less "abrasive," more beholden to the authorities above, not to the school's own constituents. And where they succeed in avoiding all these pitfalls, they know enough to keep a low profile.

Rather than contributing to the reform movement, such schools have quietly gone underground, praying just to sneak through another year. The innovators shun the news media. Fame they don't need. Instead of helping to revitalize public education, their short-lived success stories help breed cynicism about public institutions. The movement to privatize American education, which has gathered considerable momentum in the past decade, thrives on their stories [see Meier, "Choice Can *Save* Public Education," *The Nation*, March 4, 1991].

The Bronx New School's record of achievement is not in dispute. It served a largely "at risk" population but also attracted some middle-class families. Begun three years ago by a group of Bronx parents dissatisfied with the local public schools, it operated out of the small cramped basement of a local church while it awaited and helped redesign a larger space that would enable it to expand from under a hundred students to several hundred. It always intended to stay small, at least in comparison with the huge size of the average New York City public school, and envisioned gradually adding a middle or secondary school. But it didn't intend to change its style, roughly modeled after the successful Central Park East schools in East Harlem, to which some parents had earlier bused their children at considerable inconvenience.

The Bronx New School operated on the basis of a close collaboration between school and family, under a teacher-director who had many years of experience as director of a nursery co-op. It was characterized by inter-age grouping and it didn't separate children by academic ability, two currently much-approved reforms. Children learned at their own pace in a classroom community in which depth rather than superficial coverage of material was emphasized, and children were encouraged to work both collectively and individually, depending on the task and their preferences. The curriculum was built around the interests of young people, and the school's small rooms were alive with activity—hands-on use of scientific and mathematical materials and lots of creative writing and art work, which covered the walls. The parents and staff built their own library by collecting used books and buying new ones with private funds—a practice that Superintendent Reehill criticized, charging them with creating a "private" library. They painted their drab space and built or scrounged for "extras." A parent coordinator to help maintain the high level of family participation, a part-time curriculum specialist and additional library materials were the result of the school's skill at seeking private-sector grants. The additional "riches" that offended the Superintendent were thus not taken away from

From *The Nation*, September 23, 1991, pp. 321, 338–340. Copyright © 1991 by The Nation Company, Inc. Reprinted by permission.

other district schools. The district's per-pupil expenditure on the Bronx New School was approximately the same as it spent on any other school. The school struggled over the appropriate division of labor between parents and professional staff but didn't give up its belief in the importance of each having a say in the school.

The school's parent body was predominantly low-income; two-thirds were either Latino or African-American. By design, a third were white or "other." Families applied for admission and were selected by lottery; many more than there was space for applied. Both parents and their children loved it. Few students left and none were kicked out. Attendance was nearly perfect. While technically an annex of an existing traditional neighborhood elementary school, in fact its teacher-director reported to the former superintendent and the school had considerable autonomy.

But, as Evelyn Nieves of the *Times* reported, "such success . . . may be the school's downfall." The current plan is to eliminate its leadership, merge it with classes from the nearby neighborhood school and place it under the direct control of that school's principal. That will be the end, parents and staff agree.

The most interesting part of the story is that few school reformers get exercised over such events. The people who kill such schools count on this. The death of the Bronx New School seems a small matter in the larger scheme of things. The reformers find such small-scale, homemade changes of little importance—after all, the Bronx New School affects only a few hundred kids. New York, they say, has a million pupils. What is needed, they claim, are macro reform measures that affect all schools equally and reach desperate millions, rather than highly personalized inventions of a small group of practitioners, parents and kids. Some reformers even agree with Superintendent Reehill that such schools are inherently unfair because they provide for a lucky few a quality education that remains inaccessible to the vast majority. But that's like attacking a low-income housing project because it hasn't solved the housing problems of *all* low-income people.

It's precisely this mindset, not the authoritarianism of a particular superintendent or the political ambitions of a particular school board member, that is killing the Bronx New School, and by extension hundreds of others like it. What Reehill found most offensive may have been the Bronx New School's independent style: hiring a director who hadn't come up through the system, creating the alleged "private library," developing a different form of decision making. "They have to realize that in New York City they have rules and regulations. . . . It is a public school, not a private school," he told the *Times*. That bureaucrats should resent schools that thrive on acting with unauthorized autonomy is understandable. That bureaucrats can get away with dismantling these schools at a time when educational reform is such a popular cause is less understandable. Why so little protest from those education policy-makers busy attending conferences and joining task forces? They are not likely to be sympathetic to Reehill's distaste for autonomy. But when he charges the Bronx New School with being "unfair," he hits a responsive chord.

How else to explain the indifference of educators over the past fifteen years to the kind of reforms that occurred in the now-famous East Harlem District 4, and the mere trickle of efforts to replicate the success of the Central Park East schools, with which I have been intimately involved over the past eighteen years? The lessons of hundreds of successful alternative schools are always dismissed in the same way: "It's really very nice; in fact it's really even remarkable; it's clearly a success story and deserving of praise, but . . ."

What's the but? They aren't reproducible models that can be imposed on unwilling participants. They won't change those who don't want to change. Such schools offer no detailed blueprint for success; they depend too much on idiosyncratic individuals, the right mix of parents and staff, dedicated teachers, unusual families.

What these critics seem to be looking for is a model that mediocre people can carry out, that's standardized and factory-made, that anyone can duplicate by implementing the new curriculum, the latest tests or a new form of governance. "We want reforms that will produce schools like yours," they insist, "but we want ones that are replicable by people who aren't like you."

They're both right and wrong. They're right in saying that the Bronx New Schools of this world are by nature replica-proof. That's the secret of their success. They're wrong, because a good school is by definition unique. The Bronx New School may have been inspired by East Harlem's Central Park East schools, but what people created in the Bronx was not another C.P.E. school but a school that fit their own needs. What the "system" can do is create the structural conditions that encourage people to want to change and give them sufficient autonomy to do so, and that provide support and encouragement even when they blunder in the course of creating their interpretation of the "good school." But in the end the change must be home-grown.

Such a reform agenda won't unleash a massive movement to remake schools overnight. Until we have a sufficiently large number of such different and successful schools we can't and shouldn't win over the skeptics. You can make temporary improvements by decree . . . perhaps. But without substantially increased resources even this is dubious. None of the reforms being touted today in pedagogy, curriculum or governance will in themselves create schools for the future. The essential ingredient for schools that produce intelligent adults is the presence of a community of people exercising their intelligence on a daily basis, coming up with ideas for change and then having the freedom to act on the conclusions they reach. Nothing less than that will work (although more than that is also needed). That's what's so special about the Bronx New School. The people who founded it argued over ideas—the design of a new curriculum, the place of rote learning, noncompetitive ways of evaluating student performance, homework that doesn't baffle parents, the difficulties that can arise between parents and teachers when both want more power.

The only way to produce schools like the Bronx New School

is to encourage that sense of "specialness," not attack it. It's a specialness that grows out of the fact that the school is the hard-won and carefully crafted creation of a particular group of people: an act of willed intelligence. A good school is always particular.

But there are potential macro strategies that encourage such innovations. In New York City, Chancellor Joseph Fernandez's "school-based management/shared decision making" concept is not an end in itself, as critics who have followed its history as a national reform agenda have been quick to point out. But it is intended as a strategy, not a solution. The Chicago plan, which turns schools over to a council of parents and teachers with considerable freedom of action, is another macro strategy that can provide a framework for innovation. What is needed is a legislative strategy designed to nurture such particularity, that offers parents and teachers an incentive to break the mold, and some protection once they get under way. To have national impact the new schools must be open to criticism from without—careful and thoughtful responses to their pedagogy and curriculum, and close attention to how well their students are learning.

A good school is always "experimental," always learning from its own experiences. It's a place in which the "having of wonderful ideas," as educator Eleanor Duckworth noted in a book by that title, becomes the essence of education. Not only does such an environment encourage wonderful ideas by its staff, it creates a community powerful enough to convince young people that having wonderful ideas is at the heart of a good life.

The impact upon young people of such an education is long-range and powerful. This is not conjecture; it has been proved time and again. The latest study of the graduates of the Central Park East elementary schools showed that almost every one of them finished high school and most went on to college. In interviews the students described how much it had meant to them to study in a climate in which their ideas were taken seriously. The success of the C.P.E. secondary school in transforming the lives and hopes of its overwhelmingly low-income African-American and Latino students is equally indisputable. What the C.P.E. schools, like the Bronx New School, are about is the creation of powerful communities of people who know one another well and take one another seriously (which involves quarreling).

Above all, what such communities produce is lots of face-to-face exchanges about the meaning of their institutions, and the power and autonomy to change them. They reproduce a powerful public discourse on what it means to be a well-educated person. Weekly staff meetings generate lively discussions over everything from the appropriate dress code to improved ways to report students' performance to their parents. What, if any, common set of facts all students should know is the kind of topic that in the context of a real school setting, focusing on real young people, engenders thoughtful discussion that enriches not only teachers but parents and students. A school community that together looks at samples of student work and argues over its merits, as well as ways to respond, is engaged in the most effective form of staff development. The debate over multiculturalism and Eurocentrism takes place publicly in such schools and can't be sidestepped with generalities. In designing a one-year curriculum around the "peopling of the Americas," the Central Park East school system spent considerable time thinking through the differences between voluntary and forced migrations, ways to tell the Columbus story and so on. It worked out ways to focus on essential "habits of mind" that made it possible to use a wide variety of texts, even many traditional Eurocentric ones, as stimulants to deeper thought on the part of the C.P.E. faculty and students. Such schools are living examples to their students of the power of ideas and the value of education.

For those of us who believe that public education is feasible and essential to democracy, the capacity of public institutions to allow for autonomy is critical. There is no reason that public schools can't be as imaginative and exciting as independent schools. Public doesn't have to mean drab and uniform, standardized and bureaucratic. Let's give reform a chance by letting parents, students and teachers invent their own schools. When critics say "not fair," let's respond by offering them the same deal, rather than taking it away from those who are using it so well.

The 25th Annual Phi Delta Kappa/ GALLUP POLL
Of the Public's Attitudes Toward the Public Schools

Stanley M. Elam,
Lowell C. Rose, and
Alec M. Gallup

AMERICANS ARE well aware of the "savage inequalities" that characterize the funding of U.S. public schools. The public agrees with professionals that differences in funding from state to state and from district to district are largely responsible for the uneven quality of public education in America, and a 2-1 majority states a willingness to pay more taxes to bring schools in poorer states and communities up to standard.

These are among the major findings of the 25th annual Phi Delta Kappa/Gallup Poll of the Public's Attitudes Toward the Public Schools. Other significant poll results:

• For the first time since 1971, "inadequate funding" is clearly number one among the "biggest problems" people perceive in their local public schools.

• Asked to grade the local public schools as teachers grade students, almost half (47%) of the poll's respondents awarded A's or B's, a gain of 7 percentage points since last year and the highest percentage since the 48% recorded when the question was first asked in 1974.

• Previous Phi Delta Kappa/Gallup surveys have shown that substantial majorities of Americans would welcome more attention to values and character education in the public schools. The 1993 poll shows that about seven in 10 respondents also believe that it is possible to achieve local consensus on a set of basic values to be taught in the public schools. However, as responses to a sample set of values show, the trick will be to find an acceptable set.

• The public disagrees by a 3-1 margin with last year's U.S. Supreme Court ruling that declared government-sanctioned prayer at public school commencement ceremonies unconstitutional.

• The public is enthusiastic about the Clinton Administration proposal to give young people an opportunity to earn up to $10,000 in credit toward a college education through a year or two of public service; 81% approve, 14% disapprove.

• President Clinton edges former President Bush by 38% to 33% as likely to do a better job of school improvement, while 16% of respondents see no difference. Clinton's lead of 5 percentage points matches his margin of victory in the Presidential election.

• Two out of three Americans (67%) would like to see their children take up teaching as a career — up from 51% in 1990 and the highest percentage recorded in 20 years. The percentage rises to 80% among blacks.

• Americans believe lack of money for a college education is keeping minorities out of the teaching profession, while the minority student population is exploding and the percentage of minority teachers is no larger than a decade ago.

• About two out of three Americans (65%) support choice in the public schools, virtually the same proportion as reported support for public school choice in previous years — but 74% oppose allowing parents to send their children to private schools at public expense.

The report that follows provides details about these and other findings of this 25th annual Phi Delta Kappa/Gallup poll.

Grading the Public Schools

This year's Phi Delta Kappa/Gallup poll registered the largest one-year improvement in the grades given by the public to their local public schools since the question was first asked in 1974. The percentage of respondents awarding A's or B's jumped from 40% in 1992 to 47% in 1993, after nearly a decade of relative stability. College graduates in particular gave high ratings (54% A or B).

The question:

Students are often given the grades A, B, C, D, and FAIL to denote the quality of their work. Suppose the *public* schools themselves, in this community, were graded in the same way. What grade would you give the public schools here — A, B, C, D, or FAIL?

Ratings Given the Local Public Schools

	National Totals %	No Children In School %	Public School Parents %	Nonpublic School Parents %
A & B	47	44	56	37
A	10	10	12	5
B	37	34	44	32
C	31	32	28	41
D	11	10	12	9
FAIL	4	4	4	11
Don't know	7	10	*	2

*Less than one-half of 1%.

From *Phi Delta Kappan,* October 1993, pp. 138-152. Copyright © 1993 by Phi Delta Kappan, Inc. Reprinted by permission.

1. HOW OTHERS SEE US AND HOW WE SEE OURSELVES

Ratings Given the Local Public Schools

	1993 %	1992 %	1991 %	1990 %	1989 %	1988 %	1987 %	1986 %	1985 %	1984 %	1983 %
A & B	47	40	42	41	43	40	43	41	43	42	31
A	10	9	10	8	8	9	12	11	9	10	6
B	37	31	32	33	35	31	31	30	34	32	25
C	31	33	33	34	33	34	31	28	30	32	32
D	11	12	10	12	11	10	9	11	10	11	13
FAIL	4	5	5	5	4	4	4	5	4	4	7
Don't know	7	10	10	8	9	12	14	15	13	8	17

Poll respondents were also asked to grade the *nation's* public schools. As has been true in all past years, the "nation's schools" came off a poor second to "local schools" in the current poll. Whereas 47% of the public thought their own schools merit either an A or a B, only 19% awarded these grades to schools of the nation as a whole.

The second question:

How about the public schools in the nation as a whole? What grade would you give the public schools nationally — A, B, C, D, or FAIL?

Ratings Given the Nation's Public Schools

	National Totals %	No Children In School %	Public School Parents %	Nonpublic School Parents %
A & B	19	20	19	15
A	2	1	3	6
B	17	19	16	9
C	48	47	49	48
D	17	16	17	15
FAIL	4	4	4	12
Don't know	12	13	11	10

Finally, public school parents were again asked to rate the public school attended by their oldest child. Seventy-two percent of these parents gave the school their oldest child attends an A or a B, and among parents whose oldest child is doing above-average academic work the figure rises to 83%. The differences between these grades and the national rankings suggest that the better people know the public schools, the higher their opinion of school quality.

The third question:

Using the A, B, C, D, FAIL scale again, what grade would you give the school your oldest child attends?

	1993 %	1992 %	1991 %	1990 %	1989 %	1988 %	1987 %	1986 %
A & B	72	64	73	72	71	70	69	65
A	27	22	29	27	25	22	28	28
B	45	42	44	45	46	48	41	37
C	18	24	21	19	19	22	20	26
D	5	6	2	5	5	3	5	4
FAIL	2	4	4	2	1	2	2	2
Don't know	3	2	*	2	4	3	4	3

*Less than one-half of 1%.

Biggest Problems Facing Local Public Schools

In the 25-year history of the Phi Delta Kappa/Gallup education poll, three school problems uppermost in the minds of respondents have been discipline, drugs, and finances. Between 1969 and 1985, discipline was the most frequently mentioned problem each year except 1971, when finances were identified as a major problem by 23% of the public. Drug abuse by students then became the most frequently mentioned problem for six years, 1986 through 1991. In 1992 drugs and lack of proper financial support were each mentioned by 22% of the respondents.

In 1993 lack of proper financial support has clearly emerged as the number one public school problem. Twenty-one percent of poll respondents named it, while 16% cited drug abuse and 15% mentioned lack of discipline. Significantly, the respondents who most clearly recognized the inadequacy of school financing were college graduates, upper-income and professional and business groups, and public school parents.

Concern about the problem of financial support was considerably greater in the West (30%) and the Midwest (29%) than in the South (13%) and East (15%). In the South and East, concern about drug abuse was mentioned more often (by 18% and 19% respectively) than was lack of financial support.

The question:

What do you think are the biggest problems with which the public schools of this community must deal?

	National Totals %	No Children In School %	Public School Parents %	Nonpublic School Parents %
Lack of proper financial support	21	19	24	13
Drug abuse	16	17	14	9
Lack of discipline	15	15	15	19
Fighting/violence/gangs	13	12	14	17
Standards/quality of education	9	9	8	18
Overcrowded schools	8	6	11	10
Difficulty in getting good teachers	5	4	7	3
Parents' lack of support/interest	4	5	4	3
Integration/segregation, racial discrimination	4	4	4	4
Pupils' lack of interest, poor attitudes, truancy	4	3	4	4
Low pay for teachers	3	4	3	2
Moral standards, dress code, sex/pregnancy	3	3	3	9
There are no problems	1	1	3	2
Miscellaneous**	3	3	2	*
Don't know	14	17	10	16

*Less than one-half of 1%.

**A total of 36 different kinds of problems were mentioned by 2% or fewer respondents.

(Figures add to more than 100% because of multiple answers.)

The table below shows how public perceptions of the three public school problems most often mentioned have fluctuated over the past decade.

Percentages Mentioning Each Major Problem

	1993 %	1992 %	1991 %	1990 %	1989 %	1988 %	1987 %	1986 %	1985 %	1984 %
Lack of proper financial support	21	22	18	13	13	12	14	11	9*	14**
Drug abuse	16	22	22	38	34	32	30	28	18	18
Lack of discipline	15	17	20	19	19	19	22	24	25	27

*Ranked fifth among problems
**Ranked fourth among problems

Will Clinton Improve Schools More Than Bush Did?

In recent years thousands of officials at all levels of government have publicly committed themselves to school improvement. Last year's Phi Delta Kappa/Gallup poll asked respondents to grade these officials on their success to date. Dissatisfaction was rampant. These figures are illustrative: President Bush, 15% A or B, 46% D or Fail; members of the U.S. Congress, 7% A or B, 52% D or Fail; state governors, 19% A or B, 41% D or Fail; and state legislators, 14% A or B, 40% D or Fail.

In the current poll, we asked only whether people believe President Clinton will do a better or worse job of school improvement than President Bush did. The poll was taken when Clinton's approval ratings were particularly low for a recently inaugurated President, yet Clinton edged Bush by 5 percentage points (38% to 33%) on potential to bring about school improvement — his exact margin of victory in the November election. The region most strongly for Clinton in November — the East — was also his best in terms of the public's response to this question. In the East, 46% said they believe that Clinton will do better than Bush did, while 28% said they believe that he will do worse.

Further evidence of how political this question is comes from breakdowns of responses by respondents' political affiliation. By a wide margin, Democrats said that Clinton will do a better job than Bush; Republicans supported Bush by almost as wide a margin.

The question:

Do you believe that President Clinton will do a better job of school improvement than President Bush or a worse job?

	National Totals %	No Children In School %	Public School Parents %	Nonpublic School Parents %
Clinton better job	38	39	38	34
Clinton worse job	33	32	34	42
No difference (volunteered)	16	17	15	16
Don't know	13	12	13	8

5. 25th Annual Phi Delta Kappa/Gallup Poll

	National Totals %	Political Affiliation Rep. %	Dem. %	Ind. %
Clinton better job	38	17	68	29
Clinton worse job	33	59	9	33
No difference (volunteered)	16	16	10	23
Don't know	13	8	13	15

Prioritizing the Six National Goals

Since the six national goals for education (to be reached by the year 2000) were announced early in 1990 by President Bush and the 50 state governors, these polls have tracked opinion about various aspects of the goals, including levels of public awareness and approval of the goals, the priority that should be given to achieving each of them, levels of public confidence that the goals can be reached in this decade, and public perceptions of progress toward meeting the goals. Public approval of all six goals has always been high, and people have assigned a high priority to reaching each of them. For example, in 1990 every goal but one was given either a "very high" or "high" priority by more than 80% of the respondents. Even the goal that "American students will be first in the world in mathematics and science achievement" gained 76% of the "very high/high" vote.

However, people were very skeptical about the possibility of realizing the goals by the year 2000, and public awareness of the goals was still low as recently as last year. Only about a quarter of respondents said they had heard of each of the goals. And, in 1992, majorities said they believed that little progress had been made toward realizing the goals. But — as might be expected — many answered "don't know" to that question.

This year we again asked the public to assign priorities to each of the goals. The priorities assigned this year are, generally, even higher than they were in 1990. For example, 71% assigned a "very high" priority to the goal that "every school in America will be free of drugs and violence and will offer a disciplined environment conducive to learning." The comparable figure for 1990 was 55%.

The question:

Now, some questions about the national education goals that have been recommended for attainment by the year 2000. How high a priority do you think each goal should have for the remainder of the decade — very high, high, low, or very low?

1. HOW OTHERS SEE US AND HOW WE SEE OURSELVES

	Very High %	High %	Low %	Very Low %	Don't Know %	1993 %	1990 %
	Priority Assigned					**National Totals**	
						Very High	
By the year 2000, all children in America will start school ready to learn.	41	48	8	1	2	41	44
By the year 2000, the high school graduation rate will increase to at least 90%.	54	38	6	1	1	54	45
By the year 2000, American students will leave grades 4, 8, and 12 having demonstrated competency in challenging subject matter, including English, mathematics, science, history, and geography. In addition, every school will insure that all students will learn to use their minds well so that they may be prepared for responsible citizenship, further learning, and productive employment in a modern economy.	59	33	6	1	1	59	46
By the year 2000, American students will be first in the world in science and mathematics achievement.	45	43	9	2	1	45	34
By the year 2000, every adult American will be literate and will possess the knowledge and skills necessary to compete in a global economy and to exercise the rights and responsibilities of citizenship.	54	37	7	1	1	54	45
By the year 2000, every school in America will be free of drugs and violence and will offer a disciplined environment conducive to learning.	71	19	7	2	1	71	55

Exploring Equal Funding

In at least 26 states, the long-standing American tradition of spending tax money on schools in the community where the money is raised has collided violently in recent years with a principle of fairness that is also traditional. This principle of fairness is not usually stated explicitly, but it might read as follows: All children deserve an equal opportunity, through education, to reach their full potential; to achieve this end, greater equality in school funding is essential.

In most cases, the fairness principle is winning. The issue was settled long ago in California. Four years ago the Kentucky Supreme Court ruled the entire school system of the Bluegrass State unconstitutional, and the legislature built a new system, with equal funding for every school. A Kansas judge has ruled that property taxes must be spent equally across that state, regardless of where they are collected. And last spring an Alabama court declared that state's entire school system unconstitutional, and state officials are re-inventing the system.

In Texas, after voters rejected a court-ordered redistribution plan last spring, the legislature sought to reduce funding disparities by effectively transferring property wealth from rich to poor school districts. The law will be in effect in the 1993-94 school year, though an appeal is likely and the law itself may be changed.

In a series of seven questions, this poll explores public opinion on several of the issues involved in the debate over equal funding. The responses should hearten educators who have fought for the fairness principle. People appear to understand the problems, and they support fairness in funding. They are even willing to pay higher taxes in order to achieve fairness — or so they tell pollsters.

Specifically, people are aware that the quality of public schools varies greatly from district to district and that in most states the amount of money spent on schools differs considerably from district to district. A sizable majority (68%) believes that the quality of schooling depends a great deal or quite a lot on the amount of money spent, and an overwhelming majority (90% yes, 8% no) believes more should be done to improve the quality of public schools in the poorer states and poorer communities. People also believe, by a large majority, that the amount of money allocated to public education from all sources should be the same for all students, whether they live in wealthy or poor districts.

The first question:

Just your impression, how much would you say the quality of the education provided by the public schools in your state differs from school district to school district — a great deal, quite a lot, not too much, or not at all?

	National Totals %	No Children In School %	Public School Parents %	Nonpublic School Parents %
A great deal	33	31	35	44
Quite a lot	29	30	27	28
Not too much	30	30	33	22
Not at all	1	1	1	1
Don't know	7	8	4	5

The second question:

Again, just your impression, how much would you say the amount of money spent on the public schools in your state differs from school district to school district — a great deal, quite a lot, not too much, or not at all?

	National Totals %	No Children In School %	Public School Parents %	Nonpublic School Parents %
A great deal	28	28	26	31
Quite a lot	26	24	32	32
Not too much	33	34	32	29
Not at all	3	3	3	5
Don't know	10	11	7	3

The third question:

In your opinion, how much does the amount of money spent on a public school student's education affect the quality of his or her education — a great deal, quite a lot, not too much, or not at all?

	National Totals %	No Children In School %	Public School Parents %	Nonpublic School Parents %
A great deal	38	37	40	33
Quite a lot	30	30	30	31
Not too much	25	25	25	30
Not at all	5	6	2	5
Don't know	2	2	3	1

The fourth question in this series gave respondents the generally accepted view of educators: that differences in money spent on schools make a real and measurable difference in the quality of education. It then asked about correcting inequities. Because the same question was asked in 1989, it is possible to check for change over time.

The fourth question:

The quality of the public schools varies greatly from community to community and from state to state because of differences in the amount of taxes taken in to support the schools. Do you think more should be done to improve the quality of the public schools in the poorer states and in the poorer communities or not?

	National Totals %		No Children In School %		Public School Parents %		Nonpublic School Parents %	
	'93	'89	'93	'89	'93	'89	'93	'89
Yes	90	83	89	82	93	86	86	85
No	8	9	10	9	5	8	12	7
Don't know	2	8	1	9	2	6	2	8

The responses to this question show that the public is almost unanimous in believing that more should be done to improve the quality of public schools in the poorer states and communities. Respondents seem to agree with the premise that inequality is largely a result of uneven funding. Even parents of students in nonpublic schools were overwhelmingly in favor of doing more for the poorer public schools. Interestingly, 100% of blacks answered yes to this question. Ninety-five percent of Democrats and 85% of Republicans answered yes.

The fifth question (asked of those who answered yes):

Would you be willing or not willing to pay more taxes to improve the quality of the public schools in the poorer states and poorer communities?

	National Totals %	No Children In School %	Public School Parents %	Nonpublic School Parents %
Willing	68	66	71	60
Not willing	30	31	27	35
Don't know	2	3	2	5

About six out of 10 Americans (61%) think that more should be done to improve the quality of the public schools in poorer states and communities *and* are willing to pay more taxes to improve these schools — an increase of 10 percentage points over the 51% who felt that way in 1989.

Support for higher taxes to improve poor schools is fairly consistent among all demographic groups. Nonwhites are es-

pecially supportive; they favor the idea of paying more taxes to improve quality in poorer schools by a 73% to 25% margin. People in the West and South are most likely to approve additional taxes to improve schools in poor states and communities.

Answers to the final two questions in this series on funding show clearly that an overwhelming majority of people believe that the amount of money allocated to public education should be the same for all students, regardless of whether they live in wealthy or poor districts. Moreover, Americans feel just as strongly that money allocated for public education should be the same for all students even if that means taking money from wealthy districts and giving it to poor districts. Interestingly, responses to both these questions were consistent across income levels.

The sixth question:

Do you think that the amount of money allocated to public education in your state, from all sources, should or should not be the same for all students, regardless of whether they live in wealthy or poor school districts?

	National Totals %	No Children In School %	Public School Parents %	Nonpublic School Parents %
Should	88	87	89	88
Should not	10	11	10	10
Don't know	2	2	1	2

The seventh question:

Do you think that the amount of money allocated to education in your state should or should not be the same for all students, even if it means taking funding from some wealthy school districts and giving it to poor districts?

	National Totals %	No Children In School %	Public School Parents %	Nonpublic School Parents %
Should	85	85	86	79
Should not	12	12	12	14
Don't know	3	3	2	7

Support for Improving Inner-City Schools

Alarm about the condition of America's inner-city schools has been growing rapidly in recent years, as many of these schools continue to deteriorate. The concerns of educators who are familiar with the problem have been graphically described in Jonathan Kozol's most recent book, *Savage In-*

equalities. The poll shows that this concern is widely shared by the lay public. A large majority (81%) views it as very important to improve inner-city schools, and another 15% regard it as fairly important. Only 3% of respondents say it is not very important or not important at all to improve these schools. This represents an increase in concern since the question was first asked in the 1989 Phi Delta Kappa/Gallup poll, when 74% said the problem was very important.

More significantly, 1993 respondents also expressed a willingness to pay more federal taxes to improve the quality of the nation's inner-city schools. The margin here was 60% to 38%. This willingness is evident among virtually every demographic and geographic group.

The first question:

How important do you think it is to improve the nation's inner-city schools — very important, fairly important, not very important, or not important at all?

	National Totals %	No Children In School %	Public School Parents %	Nonpublic School Parents %
Very important	81	80	81	79
Fairly important	15	15	16	13
Not very important	2	2	2	3
Not important at all	1	1	*	4
Don't know	1	2	1	1

*Less than one-half of 1%.

	National Totals	
	1993 %	1989 %
Very important	81	74
Fairly important	15	19
Not very important	2	2
Not important at all	1	*
Don't know	1	5

*Less than one-half of 1%.

The second question:

Would you be willing or not willing to pay more federal taxes to improve the quality of the nation's inner-city schools?

	National Totals %	No Children In School %	Public School Parents %	Nonpublic School Parents %
Yes, willing	60	59	62	52
No, not willing	38	38	37	47
Don't know	2	3	1	1

Preschool Programs: Value and Means of Financing

As the general public increasingly recognizes how important a good start in school is for future success, preschool programs have become more and more popular. At least part of this popularity is no doubt associated with the growing percentage of mothers of young children who work outside the home.

Head Start, established by Congress under the Economic Opportunity Act of 1964, was initially aimed at poor children and helped to prepare them for elementary school. Later, it was extended to children above the poverty level, whose parents then paid for it according to income. Although some recent research suggests that the advantages gained by Head Start children tend to disappear in later grades, other research shows that the better programs are enormously cost-effective. The usual figure quoted is a $3 return for every dollar spent on Head Start.

In the 1992 poll, the public affirmed that early care and education are valuable. Thirty-nine percent said they believed that preschool programs would help low-income youngsters perform a great deal better in their teenage years, and 35% said they would help such youngsters perform quite a lot better. Moreover, a plurality (49% yes, 42% no) said they would be willing to pay more taxes to fund free preschool programs for children from low-income and poverty-level households.

The current poll asked two questions about early child care which show that public support for these programs continues — and, in fact, suggests that it may be increasing slowly. In response to a trend question asked previously in 1976, 1981, and 1985, taxpayers for the first time this year, by a comfortable margin of 59% to 38%, state that they would be willing to pay for child-care centers within the public school system for all preschool children.

The second question asks whether the public would approve of the idea of using tax money for preschool programs *only* when parents are unable to pay for them. This question elicited marginally more support, 61% to 36%, than the previous one, although somewhat less support than might have been expected given the implied lower cost to taxpayers.

The first question:

A proposal has been made to make child-care centers available for all preschool children as part of the public school system. This program would be supported by taxes. Would you favor or oppose such a program in your school district?

	National Totals %	No Children In School %	Public School Parents %	Nonpublic School Parents %
Favor	59	56	67	47
Oppose	38	40	32	52
Don't know	3	4	1	1

	National Totals			
	1993 %	1985 %	1981 %	1976 %
Favor	59	43	46	46
Oppose	38	45	47	49
Don't know	3	12	7	5

The second question:

Let's assume that preschool programs are to be paid for only by those parents whose children use the programs. Would you be willing, or not willing, to pay more taxes for funding free preschool programs for those children whose parents are unable to pay for them?

	National Totals %	No Children In School %	Public School Parents %	Nonpublic School Parents %
Willing to pay	61	62	62	46
Not willing to pay	36	35	34	51
Don't know	3	3	4	3

Health and Social Services as Part Of the Public School Program

The 1992 Phi Delta Kappa/Gallup poll showed considerable public support (77% in favor, 16% opposed) for using public school buildings and facilities for the delivery of health and social services to students. That question specified, however, that these services at school sites would be administered and coordinated by various other governmental agencies. This year poll respondents were asked to indicate approval or disapproval of six specific services that might be offered by the public schools in their communities. In some schools several of these services are already being provided at taxpayer expense, but consensus has not been reached on most of them. No reference was made to administration or coordination by other governmental agencies.

In almost every case, the public strongly favored the provision of these services by their local public schools, as the table below shows. Only dental exams did not get overwhelming support. In most cases, there was very little variation in support among different demographic groups. It may be worth noting, however, that Republicans were generally less supportive than Democrats. Also, 87% of nonwhites, but only 57% of whites, favored after-school care for children of working parents.

The question:

I am going to read a list of health and social services that the public schools in your community might provide to students. As I read off each service, one at a time, please indicate whether you think the local schools should provide this service to students, or not.

Should Provide	National Totals %	No Children In School %	Public School Parents %	Nonpublic School Parents %
Examinations to detect sight and hearing defects	92	91	94	83
Free or low-cost luncheons	87	84	93	86
Inoculations against communicable diseases	84	85	83	77
Free or low-cost breakfasts	74	70	80	73
After-school care for children of working parents	62	59	69	55
Examinations to detect dental needs	58	57	61	50

The Curriculum: Broad and Shallow, Or Narrow and Deep?

Although it waxes and wanes over the years, there appears to be a perennial "back to the basics" movement in American education; it coexists with constant pressures for a wide range of new subject matter, from computer use to AIDS prevention. Today, "less is more" is the rallying cry for a powerful set of school reformers, and many secondary schools have reduced the scope of their curricula in order to concentrate on what the third national goal calls "challenging subject matter" in English, mathematics, science, history, and geography. Believers say it is better for all children to learn a few essential subjects thoroughly than to elect from a broad but sometimes trivialized curriculum. To get some sense of the public's views on this issue, the current poll revived a question first asked in 1979.

The question:

Public high schools can offer students a wide variety of courses, or they can concentrate on fewer, basic courses, such as English, mathematics, history, and science. Which of these two policies do you think the local high schools should follow in planning their curricula — a wide variety of courses or fewer but more basic courses?

	National Totals %	No Children In School %	Public School Parents %	Nonpublic School Parents %
Wide variety of courses	48	44	55	54
Basic courses	51	54	44	43
Don't know	1	2	1	3

	National Totals 1993 %	1979 %
Wide variety of courses	48	44
Basic courses	51	49
Don't know	1	7

Values Education: Time for Greater Emphasis?

Since 1975 the Phi Delta Kappa/Gallup polls have been sampling public attitudes toward values or ethics/morals education as a function of the public schools. In 1975, 79% of the public favored instruction in the public schools that would deal with morals and moral behavior. In the 1976 poll, 67% of the respondents said that the public schools should "take on a share of parents' responsibilities for the moral behavior of their children." The same poll rated "high moral standards" among the top four qualities to be developed in children. Respondents to the 1984 poll identified "to develop standards of right and wrong" as second only to "developing the ability to speak and write correctly" as the most important goal for the public schools.

1. HOW OTHERS SEE US AND HOW WE SEE OURSELVES

After Secretary of Education William Bennett made character education one of his prime emphases in 1986, the 1987 poll asked respondents whether they thought courses aimed at helping students develop personal values and ethical behavior should be taught in the public schools or left to the students' parents and the churches. Forty-three percent said the schools should teach such courses, but 36% thought the task should be left to parents and churches. However, another 13% volunteered that both (schools *and* churches/parents) should teach values and ethical behavior. In the same 1987 poll, 62% of respondents thought it would be possible "to develop subject matter for a character education course that would be acceptable to most people in the community," while 23% disagreed and 15% said that they did not know.

Why haven't the public schools responded more positively to the evident public desire for character education? Kevin Ryan of Boston University's Center for the Advancement of Ethics and Character points to many problems and changes that keep schoolpeople from pursuing more vigorously what was once a tradition of teaching core values. There is increasing diversity and lack of consensus in the larger society, and character education has become a gray area in the curriculum, Ryan says.

The current poll asked two questions about values in the public schools, the first a repeat of the 1987 question on whether local communities could agree on a set of basic values to be taught in the public schools. Again, as in 1987, a solid majority (69%) said yes. The second question, which sought opinion on a sample set of 12 specific values, showed considerable agreement on a number of them but demonstrated the potential for conflict in this area.

The first question:

Do you think it would be possible, or not possible, to get people in your community to agree on a set of basic values, such as honesty and patriotism, that would be taught in the local public schools?

	National Totals %	No Children In School %	Public School Parents %	Nonpublic School Parents %
Yes, possible	69	67	73	73
No, not possible	27	28	25	26
Don't know	4	5	2	1

The second question:

I am going to read a list of different values that might be taught in the public schools. For each one, please tell me whether you think it should be taught, or should not be taught, to all students in the public schools of your community.

Should Be Taught	National Totals %	No Children In School %	Public School Parents %	Nonpublic School Parents %
Honesty	97	97	97	95
Democracy	93	92	93	98
Acceptance of people of different races and ethnic backgrounds	93	92	96	92
Patriotism, love of country	91	91	93	89
Caring for friends and family members	91	90	93	90
Moral courage	91	91	94	83
The golden rule	90	90	89	88
Acceptance of people who hold different religious beliefs	87	87	87	86
Acceptance of people who hold unpopular or controversial political or social views	73	73	75	70
Sexual abstinence outside of marriage	66	66	67	69
Acceptance of the right of a woman to choose abortion	56	56	57	38
Acceptance of people with different sexual orientations: that is, homosexuals or bisexuals	51	52	50	43

The respondents strongly approved (at least 87% in favor) the teaching of eight values in the public schools. Indeed, the level of endorsement for the teaching of honesty reached 97% — an almost unanimous vote of approval.

However, on four values that are more controversial there was significant disagreement by category of respondent. For example, younger people (ages 18-29) were much more likely than persons 50 and older (61% yes to 46% yes) to favor teaching acceptance of persons with different sexual orientations. Similar differences appear between whites (48% yes, 49% no) and nonwhites (63% yes, 36% no). Southerners were much less likely to approve of teaching this value than people in other regions: South 40%, East 63%, West 54%, and Midwest 49% yes. Public school parents are also divided: 50% for, 47% against. Only 46% of men would teach acceptance of homosexuals and bisexuals, compared with 55% of women who would do so.

Sexual abstinence outside of marriage was favored as a topic for public school instruction by a 2-1 margin (66% to 32%). Acceptance of the right of women to choose abortion was approved as a topic for instruction by rather small margins in most demographic groups. Oddly, 61% of men but only 52% of women approved it. Democrats approved (62% to 35%), while Republicans were slightly opposed (45% yes, 54% no).

Required Community Service

When a question on offering high school credit for community service was first asked in these polls in 1978, it was framed to imply that community service would be an option, not a requirement. As a result, public approval was very high (87% for, 8% against). In 1984 the same question brought a slightly lower approval rating (79% for, 16% against).

In 1989, the public was asked if community service should be made a *requirement* for high school graduation. Although there was less support for the requirement than for the elective, a majority of respondents still approved (61% in favor, 30% opposed).

In the current poll, approval of community service as a requirement showed some gain (70% in favor, 29% opposed). There was little variation in support among demographic categories.

The question:

Would you favor or oppose a requirement that all students in the local public schools perform some kind of community service in order to graduate?

	National Totals %		No Children In School %		Public School Parents %		Nonpublic School Parents %	
	'93	'89	'93	'89	'93	'89	'93	'89
Favor	70	61	70	60	69	63	70	69
Oppose	29	30	28	30	30	32	29	25
Don't know	1	9	2	10	1	5	1	6

National Service to Pay for College

One of the more popular education policies advocated by candidate Bill Clinton was that young people who might not otherwise be able to afford a college education be offered the opportunity to earn up to $10,000 in credit toward college by public service over a period of one or two years. Although President Clinton appears to have been forced by budget considerations to reduce the scope of his proposal, the idea remains very popular. Respondents nationwide approved of the idea by an 81% to 14% margin. Almost all demographic groups favored it overwhelmingly, even Republicans.

The question:

President Clinton has proposed a national service program to help young people pay for college. Under this program, anyone over age 17 could work in a public service position for one or two years and earn up to $10,000 credit toward the cost of a college education. Do you favor or oppose such a program?

	National Totals %	No Children In School %	Public School Parents %	Nonpublic School Parents %
Favor	81	81	83	71
Oppose	14	15	12	23
Don't know	5	4	5	6

Bilingual Education

Public school people have long debated the best ways of dealing with students from homes where English is not spoken, or not spoken well. Debate over the problem heated up this year as Congress considered reauthorizing the Bilingual Education Act first passed 25 years ago.

In recent years, with new waves of immigration from many countries, but particularly from Spanish-speaking nations and Asia, bilingual education has become more perplexing and expensive than ever. For example, how many teachers can teach in Tagalog, a language spoken by nearly one million U.S. residents over age 5? In all, one in seven U.S. residents speaks a language other than English at home, according to the Census Bureau. That's 31.8 million people, up from 23.1 million a decade ago.

The 1968 bilingual education program authorized by Congress embodies the theory that students with limited English-speaking skills lose ground in traditional academic subjects unless they are taught in their native tongue. Some educators have challenged the federally mandated bilingual education program as "fraudulent, designed to keep kids trapped in the program."

The 1980 poll in this series found that 82% of the lay public at that time thought children who cannot speak English should be required to learn English in special classes before they are enrolled in public schools. (The question did not specify whether these special classes would be a part of the tax-supported public school system.) In the current poll we have asked respondents to choose one of three options in handling students with limited ability in English. The results suggest that the public supports the advocates of English instruction first.

The question:

Many families who come from other countries have school-age children who cannot speak English. Which one of the following three approaches do you think is the best way for the public schools to deal with non-English-speaking students?

	National Totals %	No Children In School %	Public School Parents %	Nonpublic School Parents %
Require children to learn English in special classes at their parents' expense before they are enrolled in the public schools	25	27	23	20
Provide public school instruction in all subjects in the students' native languages while they learn English	27	26	30	29
Require students to learn English in public schools before they receive instruction in any other subjects	46	45	45	47
Don't know	2	2	2	4

National Testing and Its Purposes

The public has repeatedly endorsed the use of standardized national tests to measure the academic achievement of U.S. students. As early as 1976, 65% of poll respondents thought all high school students should be required to pass a standard examination in order to get a high school diploma; 31% were opposed. The same question produced similar results in 1984 (65% yes, 29% no), but by 1988 the level of support had risen to 73% for, 22% against. The public also has a long history of support for national tests that would allow comparisons of the educational achievement of students in different communities. The following table displays responses from previous years to the question, Would you like to see students in the local schools given national tests so that their educational achievement could be compared with students in other communities?

| | National Totals | | | | |
	1988 %	1986 %	1983 %	1971 %	1970 %
Yes	81	77	75	70	75
No	14	16	17	21	16
Don't know	5	7	8	9	9

The reform movement of recent years has brought pressure for establishing higher national standards of student achievement. A series of questions asked in the 1989 Phi Delta Kappa/Gallup poll found that the public not only understands that there is no single set of national achievement standards and goals for all public schools, but that people also favor, by a 70% to 19% margin, requiring the public schools to conform to national achievement goals and standards. In that same year people approved, 77% to 14%, requiring U.S. public schools to use standardized national tests to measure the academic achievement of students.

In 1992 the poll repeated the 1989 question about requiring local schools to use standardized national tests to measure student achievement, but it also asked how else the results of those tests should be used. The latter question was asked again this year. In both years, the public placed highest value on identifying areas in which students need extra help and on identifying areas in which teachers need to improve their teaching skills. Respondents placed less value on ranking schools in terms of student achievement, determining if a student advances to the next grade, determining how much teachers should be paid, and determining the level of funding for each local school.

The question:

In addition to measuring the academic achievement of students, do you think standardized national tests should be used or should not be used in the public schools in this community for the following purposes?

Should Be Used	National Totals %	No Children In School %	Public School Parents %	Nonpublic School Parents %
To identify areas in which students need extra help	91	91	92	92
To identify areas in which teachers need to improve their teaching skills	87	88	87	82
To rank the local public schools in terms of student achievement	72	74	68	69
To determine if a student advances to the next grade level of schooling	70	72	66	64
To determine the level of funding each local school should receive	49	52	45	44
To determine how much teachers should be paid	46	48	43	34

Longer School Day and Year

Over a 25-year period, these polls have shown that the U.S. public usually favors a change or innovation in the public schools if the change promises improvement.* But it has taken the public nearly a decade to recognize that the traditional nine-month school year may no longer suffice in a post-industrial, knowledge-driven, and increasingly global society.

Beginning in 1982, the following question was periodically asked in the Phi Delta Kappa/Gallup polls: In some nations, students attend school as many as 240 days a year as compared to about 180 in the U.S. How do you feel about extending the public school year in this community by 30 days, making the school year about 210 days or 10 months long? Do you favor or oppose this idea?

The proposal finally gained majority approval in 1991, as the table below shows:

| | Extend School Year 30 Days | | | | |
	1992 %	1991 %	1984 %	1983 %	1982 %
Favor	55	51	44	40	37
Oppose	35	42	50	49	53
Don't know	10	7	6	11	10

In the current poll, the question was put differently.

*See Stanley Elam, ed., *The Gallup/Phi Delta Kappa Polls of Attitudes Toward the Public Schools, 1969-88* (Bloomington, Ind.: Phi Delta Kappa, 1989), pp. 7-8, in which the approval/disapproval ratings of 53 suggested changes are summarized. Forty of the 53 won public approval by sizable margins.

The question:

Some public schools in the nation have increased the amount of time students spend in school by extending the school year or the school day. Do you favor or oppose increasing the amount of time students spend in the public schools in your community?

	National Totals %	No Children In School %	Public School Parents %	Nonpublic School Parents %
Favor	52	53	50	54
Oppose	47	45	49	43
Don't know	1	2	1	3

The current poll asked respondents which way they would prefer to increase the amount of time children spend in school: increasing the number of days in the school year, increasing the number of hours in the school day, or holding Saturday morning classes. A plurality (47%) favored more days in the year, but 33% favored increasing the number of hours in the school day. Saturday classes ran a poor third, gaining a favorable vote from only 5% of the respondents.

The question:

Which one of these plans for increasing the amount of time students spend in school would you prefer — increasing the number of days in the school year, increasing the number of hours in the school day, or having classes on Saturday morning?

	National Totals %	No Children In School %	Public School Parents %	Nonpublic School Parents %
Increasing number of days in school year	47	46	50	45
Increasing number of hours in school day	33	34	33	31
Saturday morning classes	5	5	6	1
A combination of these (volunteered)	2	2	1	5
None of these (volunteered)	12	12	10	18
Don't know	1	1	*	*

*Less than one-half of 1%.

Attractiveness of Teaching as a Career

For the past quarter century, these polls have tracked the attractiveness to parents of teaching as a career for their children. The popularity of teaching as a profession has apparently rebounded from its doldrums during the 1970s and 1980s. In the current survey, two out of three Americans say they would like a child of theirs to take up teaching in the public schools, an increase of 16 percentage points since the question was last asked in 1990. At that time only about half of the respondents (51%) wanted a child of theirs to enter the teaching profession.

Public perceptions of the desirability of teaching as a career have been measured eight times since the initial reading taken in the first poll in the Phi Delta Kappa/Gallup series in 1969. During the ensuing quarter century, the attractiveness of the profession to the public has fluctuated greatly (by 30 percentage points) depending on impressions at the time regarding teacher salaries and the state of the public schools. The high was recorded in 1969, when 75% of the respondents said that they would like a child of theirs to become a teacher; the low came in 1983, when the figure was only 45%.

The question:

Would you like to have a child of yours take up teaching in the public schools as a career?

	National Totals							
	1993 %	1990 %	1988 %	1983 %	1981 %	1980 %	1972 %	1969 %
Yes	67	51	58	45	46	48	67	75
No	29	38	31	33	43	40	22	15
Don't know	4	11	11	22	11	12	11	10

Minorities and the Teaching Profession

Approximately 70% of students in U.S. public schools today are white non-Hispanics. Minorities account for roughly the following percentages of the student population: blacks, 16%; Hispanics, 12%; Asians and Pacific Islanders, 3%; and American Indians, 1%.* At the same time, the Education Information Branch of the U.S. Department of Education reports that 86.8% of the public school teaching force is white, 8% black, and 5.3% other.

The disproportion between the percentage of minorities in the student population and the percentage of minorities in the teaching force is likely to grow rapidly in the future, because the number of minority students is increasing very rapidly, and the minority component of the teaching force is not. These disparities are troublesome because of the need for teachers to be conscious of and sympathetic to the cultural backgrounds that minority students bring to school. Critics argue that even well-prepared white teachers often fail to understand these differences. Why does the disproportion exist? In a question asked in this year's poll, the public was invited to choose among five plausible explanations. Respondents felt that "not being able to afford the college preparation required for teachers" was the most important factor. Seventy-three percent identified this factor as "very important" (46%) or "quite important" (27%). Minorities themselves confirmed this impression: 80% of nonwhites judged inability to pay for college "very important" or "quite important."

The question:

As you may know, a relatively small percentage of people from minority groups enter the teaching profession. As I read off possible reasons for this, one at a time, please tell me how important you think that reason is in keeping minorities out of teaching. Do you think it is very important, quite important, not too important, or not at all important?

*Conversation with Vance Grant, National Center for Education Statistics.

	Very Important %	Quite Important %	Not Too Important %	Not at All Important %	Don't Know %
Unable to afford college preparation	46	27	13	11	3
Low salaries	37	23	22	16	2
Little chance for advancement	31	25	23	19	2
Believe they will face discrimination in the profession	27	21	27	22	3
Low prestige or status of teaching	26	19	29	21	5

Those Responding "Very Important"

	National %	Whites %	Nonwhites %	Hispanics %	Blacks %
Unable to afford college preparation	46	44	59	58	67
Low salaries	37	33	55	56	65
Little chance for advancement	31	27	54	38	60
Believe they will face discrimination in the profession	27	23	56	48	61
Low prestige or status of teaching	26	24	34	43	34

Parent Involvement

Teachers are quick to point out that children are far more likely to do well in school if their parents are actively engaged in the children's education. A recent National PTA survey found that parents themselves also understand this very well. Ninety-five percent of parents surveyed by the PTA said they favor written plans for parent involvement because they believe such involvement is crucial to school success. They want guidance in how they can help.

The current poll reveals almost total unanimity in every demographic group on the importance of encouraging parent involvement. Ninety-six percent of the public said parent involvement is very important.

The question:

How important do you think it is to encourage parents to take a more active part in educating their children — very important, fairly important, not too important, or not at all important?

	National Totals %	No Children In School %	Public School Parents %	Nonpublic School Parents %
Very important	96	97	95	95
Fairly important	3	2	5	5
Not too important	1	1	*	*
Not at all important	*	*	*	*
Don't know	*	*	*	*

*Less than one-half of 1%.

Prayers at Public School Graduation Ceremonies

Last June the U.S. Supreme Court let stand a Fifth Circuit Court of Appeals ruling in Texas that approved student-initiated and student-led invocations and benedictions at graduation ceremonies. The circuit court held that a senior class could vote on whether to include prayers at graduation, so long as the prayers were delivered by student volunteers and were "nonsectarian and nonproselytizing in nature." The court said a majority of students can do what the state cannot do, referring to the Supreme Court's 5-4 decision last year in *Lee* v. *Weisman*. That decision ruled unconstitutional a Providence, Rhode Island, school district policy of inviting local clergy to deliver graduation prayers.

But the long battle over prayer at graduations has probably not been settled. For one thing, the Fifth Circuit ruling is legally binding only in Texas, Louisiana, and Mississippi. Prayer advocates say the Supreme Court "affirmed" the student-initiated approach. Meanwhile, Gwendolyn Gregory, deputy counsel for the National School Boards Association, which asked the Court to review the Fifth Circuit's ruling, said, "We needed some help and we didn't get it." The American Civil Liberties Union, the American Jewish Congress, and Americans United for Separation of Church and State have also maintained that the appeals court ruling was wrong.

The American Center for Law and Justice, a public interest law firm associated with religious broadcaster Pat Robertson, has sent letters to 15,000 U.S. school administrators urging them to allow student-led prayers at graduation ceremonies. Rev. Robertson said the Supreme Court's action in the Texas case and the Court's recent unanimous decision giving religious groups after-hours access to school facilities on the same basis as other community groups have "opened a wide and effective door for Christian people of this country to proclaim their faith." (See Larry Barber, "Prayer at Public School Graduation: A Survey," *Phi Delta Kappan,* October 1993 for information about a Phi Delta Kappa study of school districts' responses to the Court's decision in *Lee* v. *Weismann*.)

The current Phi Delta Kappa/Gallup poll was conducted before the Supreme Court decided to let stand the Fifth Circuit ruling that approved student-led prayers. But a question referring to the *Lee* v. *Weisman* decision outlawing officially sponsored prayers was asked. The response shows how generally public sentiment favors prayer at graduation ceremonies. The margin is approximately 3-1 in favor. People in the South were particularly positive. Other interesting differences by respondent category are shown in the second table below.

The question:

The U.S. Supreme Court has ruled that conducting religious prayers at any public school graduation ceremony is unconstitutional because it violates the First Amendment, which concerns the separation between church and state. Do you, yourself, believe that prayers should or should not be part of public school graduation ceremonies?

	National Totals %	No Children In School %	Public School Parents %	Nonpublic School Parents %
Should be allowed	74	71	79	82
Should not be allowed	23	26	19	17
Don't know	3	3	2	1

	National Totals %	Age 18-29 %	Age 30-49 %	Age 50 & Older %	Religion Protestant %	Religion Roman Catholic %	Jews/ Others %
Should be allowed	74	61	73	83	82	72	58
Should not be allowed	23	36	24	14	16	27	35
Don't know	3	3	3	3	2	1	7

School Choice

President Bush made school choice the centerpiece of his education reform strategy, campaigning for tuition tax credits and other voucher-like plans that would give at least some parents public money to use for private schools. Thirteen states and many more school districts have adopted some kind of choice plan involving public schools but not private schools in the past five years. However, the public has not generally accepted the voucher idea. Three populous states — Pennsylvania, California, and Colorado — have turned thumbs down on voucher plans since December 1991 — Colorado by a 67% majority in the November 1992 election.

Last spring the Carnegie Foundation for the Advancement of Teaching released a 118-page report, *School Choice*, based on a yearlong study. It questions claims about the benefits of school choice, saying "they greatly outdistance the evidence, thus far." The report praises some districtwide choice programs but argues that statewide plans have failed to demonstrate any educational impact and could increase disparities among districts. Moreover, according to Foundation President Ernest Boyer, most public school parents have little desire for such a system. In states where choice has been adopted, the report states that fewer than 2% of eligible parents participate. Moreover, parents who transfer their children to other schools do so mostly for nonacademic reasons.

The Carnegie report has had its critics. Joe Nathan, director of the Center for School Change at the University of Minnesota, claims he found "64 significant misstatements of fact or distortions in one chapter." But Richard Rothstein of the Economic Policy Institute in Washington, D.C., says the report "confirms what most people who have studied the issue have observed. And that is that there's no reason to believe that choice in itself will be a force for inspiring schools."

The Phi Delta Kappa/Gallup polls have dealt extensively with the choice issue.* This year four questions on choice were asked. All four have been asked before in the series. Few changes in opinions have occurred.

The first question:

Do you favor or oppose allowing students and their parents to choose which public schools in this community the students attend, regardless of where they live?

	National Totals %	No Children In School %	Public School Parents %	Nonpublic School Parents %
Favor	65	65	68	61
Oppose	33	33	31	38
Don't know	2	2	1	1

*For details, see the poll reports in the September issues for 1987, 1989, 1990, and 1991, *Phi Delta Kappan*.

National Totals

	1993 %	1991 %	1990 %	1989 %
Favor	65	62	62	60
Oppose	33	33	31	31
Don't know	2	5	7	9

The second question:

Do you favor or oppose allowing students and parents to choose a private school to attend at public expense?

	National Totals %	No Children In School %	Public School Parents %	Nonpublic School Parents %
Favor	24	21	27	45
Oppose	74	76	72	55
Don't know	2	3	1	*

*Less than one-half of 1%.

National Totals

	1993 %	1991 %
Favor	24	26
Oppose	74	68
Don't know	2	6

The third question:

Do you think private schools that accept government tuition payments for these students should be accountable to public school authorities or not?

Acknowledgments

A 12-member panel of distinguished educators and others interested in education helped frame the questions for the 1993 Phi Delta Kappa/Gallup Poll of the Public's Attitudes Toward the Public Schools. After editing and compilation, these questions were rated for appropriateness by the same panel. The authors of this report chose the final set of questions from the panel-approved list.

Panelists: Gregory R. Anrig, president, Educational Testing Service, Princeton, N.J.; Gerald W. Bracey, education writer and consultant, Alexandria, Va.; Edward A. Brainard, former president, CFK Ltd. (originator of the Gallup education poll), now retired from the assistant superintendency, Aurora (Colo.) Public Schools; Anne Campbell, former commissioner of education, Nebraska; David L. Clark, professor of education, University of North Carolina, Chapel Hill; Luvern Cunningham, partner, Leadership Development Associates, Columbus, Ohio, and Fawcett Professor of Educational Administration (emeritus), Ohio State University; Joseph Cronin, president, Bentley College, Waltham, Mass.; Lowell C. Rose, executive director, Phi Delta Kappa, Bloomington, Ind.; Sam Sava, executive director, National Association of Elementary School Principals, Alexandria, Va.; M. Donald Thomas, partner, School Management Study Group, Salt Lake City, Utah; Ray Tobiason, director of programs, Washington State Association of School Administrators, Fox Island, Wash.; and Carolyn Warner, president, Carolyn Warner and Associates, Phoenix, Ariz. — SME

	National Totals %	No Children In School %	Public School Parents %	Nonpublic School Parents %
Yes, should	63	62	67	40
No, shouldn't	34	35	31	57
Don't know	3	3	2	3

Of the 24% who said they favored allowing students and parents to choose a private school to attend at public expense, 54% said that these private schools should be accountable to public school authorities — a drop of 9 percentage points since 1991.

The fourth question:

What effect do you think allowing students and their parents to choose the students' schools would have on the public schools of this community? Do you think it would improve all schools, hurt all schools, or would it improve some and hurt others?

	National Totals %	No Children In School %	Public School Parents %	Nonpublic School Parents %
Improve all schools	21	20	24	27
Hurt all schools	6	6	4	4
Improve some, hurt others	69	69	70	66
Don't know	4	5	2	3

	National Totals	
	1993 %	1989 %
Improve all schools	21	21
Hurt all schools	6	14
Improve some, hurt others	69	51
Don't know	4	14

Distribution of Condoms by Schools

The 1992 Phi Delta Kappa/Gallup poll asked two questions about the distribution of condoms by public schools. On a question that was *not* repeated this year, the 1992 poll found that 40% of poll respondents believed condom distribution would increase sexual promiscuity among students, while 13% said it would decrease promiscuity, and 42% volunteered the response that it would make no difference. But by large majorities, 1992 respondents thought these programs would decrease pregnancies among students and decrease the likelihood of students' contracting AIDS or other sexually transmitted diseases. The following question was repeated in 1993.

The question:

Which one of the following plans regarding condoms would you prefer in the public schools in this community? Provide condoms for all students who want them, provide condoms only to those students who have the consent of their parents, or don't provide condoms to any student?

	National Totals % '93 '92		No Children In School % '93 '92		Public School Parents % '93 '92		Nonpublic School Parents % '93 '92	
Provide condoms for all students who want them	41	43	41	44	42	41	36	38
Require consent of parents	19	25	17	24	23	27	17	24
Don't provide	38	25	39	23	34	27	45	29
Don't know	2	7	3	9	1	5	2	9

It appears that support for the idea of condom distribution by public schools declined slightly over the past year. Nevertheless, 60% of respondents still approve of condom distribution (though 19% of them would require parental consent), compared with 38% who disapprove.

Research Procedure

The Sample. The sample used in this survey embraced a total of 1,306 adults (18 years of age and older). A description of the sample and methodology can be found elsewhere in this report.

Time of Interviewing. The fieldwork for this study was carried out during the period of 21 May to 9 June 1993.

The Report. In the tables used in this report, "Nonpublic School Parents" includes parents of students who attend parochial schools and parents of students who attend private or independent schools.

Due allowance must be made for statistical variation, especially in the case of findings for groups consisting of relatively few respondents, e.g., nonpublic school parents.

The findings of this report apply only to the U.S. as a whole and not to individual communities. Local surveys, using the same questions, can be conducted to determine how local areas compare with the national norm.

For tables showing recommended allowances for sampling error of a percentage and for sampling error of the difference between two percentages, see the September 1992 *Phi Delta Kappan*, page 53.

Design of the Sample

For the 1993 survey the Gallup Organization used its standard national telephone sample, i.e., an unclustered, directory-assisted, random-digit telephone sample, based on a proportionate stratified sampling design.

The random-digit aspect of the sample was used to avoid "listing" bias. Numerous studies have shown that households with unlisted telephone numbers are different in important ways from listed households. "Unlistedness" is due to household mobility or to customer requests to prevent publication of the telephone number.

To avoid this source of bias, a random-digit procedure designed to provide representation of both listed and unlisted (including not-yet-listed) numbers was used.

Telephone numbers for the continental United States were stratified into four regions of the country and, within each region, further stratified into three size-of-community strata.

Only working banks of telephone numbers were selected. Eliminating nonworking banks from the sample increased the likelihood that any sampled telephone number would be associated with a residence.

The sample of telephone numbers produced by the described method is representative of all telephone households within the continental United States.

Within each contacted household, an interview was sought with the youngest man 18 years of age or older who was at home. If no man was home, an interview was sought with the oldest woman at home. This method of respondent selection within households produced an age distribution by sex that closely approximates the age distribution by sex of the total population.

Up to three calls were made to each selected telephone number to complete an interview. The time of day and the day of the week for callbacks were varied so as to maximize the chances of finding a respondent at home. All interviews were conducted on weekends or weekday evenings in order to contact potential respondents among the working population.

The final sample was weighted so that the distribution of the sample matched current estimates derived from the U.S. Census Bureau's Current Population Survey (CPS) for the adult population living in telephone households in the continental U.S.

As has been the case in recent years in the Phi Delta Kappa/Gallup poll series, parents of public school children were oversampled in the 1993 poll. This procedure produced a large enough sample to ensure that findings reported for "public school parents" are statistically significant.

Composition of the Sample

Adults	%
No children in school	64
Public school parents	33*
Nonpublic school parents	5*

*Total exceeds 36% because some parents have children attending more than one kind of school.

Sex	%
Men	46
Women	54

Race	%
White	85
Nonwhite	11
Undesignated	4

Age	%
18-29 years	23
30-49 years	42
50 and over	34
Undesignated	1

Occupation	%
(Chief Wage Earner)	
Business and professional	34
Clerical and sales	9
Manual labor	32
Nonlabor force	2

Farm	1
Undesignated	22

Income	%
$40,000 and over	36
$30,000-$39,999	14
$20,000-$29,999	17
$10,000-$19,999	16
Under $10,000	9
Undesignated	8

Region	%
East	24
Midwest	25
South	31
West	20

Community Size	%
Urban	37
Suburban	34
Rural	29

Education	%
Total College	44
College graduate	22
College incomplete	22
Total high school	55
High school graduate	40
High school incomplete	15
Undesignated	1

Conducting Your Own Poll

The Phi Delta Kappa Center for Dissemination of Innovative Programs makes available PACE (Polling Attitudes of the Community on Education) materials to enable nonspecialists to conduct scientific polls of attitude and opinion on education. The PACE manual provides detailed information on constructing questionnaires, sampling, interviewing, and analyzing data. It also includes updated census figures and new material on conducting a telephone survey.

For information about using PACE materials, write or phone Neville Robertson at Phi Delta Kappa, P.O. Box 789, Bloomington, IN 47402-0789. Ph. 800/766-1156.

How to Order the Poll

The minimum order for reprints of the published version of the Phi Delta Kappa/Gallup education poll is 25 copies for $10. Additional copies are 25 cents each. This price includes postage for delivery (at the library rate). Where possible, enclose a check or money order. Address your order to Phi Delta Kappa, P.O. Box 789, Bloomington, IN 47402. Ph. 800/766-1156.

If faster delivery is desired, do not include a remittance with your order. You will be billed at the above rates plus any additional cost involved in the method of delivery.

Persons who wish to order the 382-page document that is the basis for this report should write to the Gallup Organization (47 Hulfish St., Princeton, NJ 08542) or phone 609/924-9600. The price is $95 per copy, postage included.

Change and Rethinking of the Educative Effort

There is intensive and complex dialogue around the continent regarding how the forms and content of schooling should change. A rich literature on change in schooling has developed to reflect this dialogue. In the midst of this dialogue is the fierce debate over parental and student "choice" of where students attend schools. Defenders of the public schools who oppose extending parental "choice" options, which would allow them to send their children to other public school districts or to private schools, argue that parental choice in education will undermine the public schools. Defenders of school choice proposals argue, among other things, that parental choice will motivate less effective public schools to try harder to do well. The argument gets far more complex than this. The debate to rethink and change the educational system is focusing on ways the alternative curricula can be developed in existing public schools. The question

of developing alternative forms of learning environments for children and teenagers is also debated. What will these new models of learning environments look like? Will they be public or private? Probably both public and private alternative models for schooling will be developed. The current debate over reform and change in public education has been going on for well over 10 years, and one thing learned from this debate is that there are no easy, painless "one-shot fixes" for qualitative improvement of a public school system.

We have to consider the social and ideological differences among those representing opposing school reform agendas for change. The differences over how and in what directions change is to occur in our educational systems rest on which educational values are to prevail. These values form the bases for differing conceptions of the purposes of schooling. Thus, the differing agendas for change in American education have to be situated (positioned) within the context of the different ideological value systems that underpin each alternative agenda for change.

There are several currently contending (and frequently conceptually conflicting) strategies for restructuring life in schools as well as the options open to parents in choosing the schools their children may attend. On the one hand, we have to find ways to empower students and teachers to improve the quality of academic life in classrooms. On the other hand, there appear to be powerful forces contending over whether control over educational services should be even more centralized or decentralized (site-based). Those who favor greater parental and teacher control of schools support greater decentralized site management and community control conceptions of school governance. Yet the ratio of teachers to nonteaching personnel (administrators, counselors, school psychologists, and others) continues to decline as public school system bureaucracies get more and more "top heavy."

In this unit, the efforts to reconceive, redefine, and deconstruct existing patterns of curriculum and instruction at the elementary and secondary levels of schooling are considered and related to the efforts to reconceive existing conflicting patterns of teacher education. There is a broad spectrum of dialogue developing in North America, the British Commonwealth, Russia, Central Eurasia, and other areas of the world regarding the redirecting of the learning opportunities of citizens.

Prospective teachers are encouraged to question their own educational experiences as a part of the process of becoming more reflective professional persons. Cultural institutions and values affect our ideas about curriculum content and the purpose of educating others. This is perceived as vitally important in the developing dialogue over liberating students' capacities to function as independent inquirers. The dramatic economic and demographic changes in North American society necessitate fundamental reconceptualization of how schools ought to respond to the social contexts in which they are located.

Fundamental rethinking is underway regarding the process of curriculum development in elementary and secondary schools and in teacher education. This has developed as an intellectual movement with participants in the dialogue coming from the entire range of ideological, political, and cultural perspectives reflected in public debate regarding the social purposes of educational systems and the quality of teaching and learning. The current efforts to restructure and to redefine professional purposes are closely related to the efforts to achieve meaningful qualitative improvement in what and how students learn in schools. The varied and pluralistic perspectives that shape the lives of students in their formal educational experiences in schools have been under critical review. This process is leading to fascinating reconception of what is possible in our efforts to educate others.

The effort to reassess and reconceive the education of others is a part of broader reform efforts in society as well as a dynamic dialectic in its own right. How can schools, for instance, better reflect the varied communities of interest that they serve? How can they be better perceived as more just, fairer places in which young people seek to achieve learning and self-fulfillment?

This is not the first period in which North Americans have searched their minds and souls to redirect, construct, and, if necessary, deconstruct their understandings regarding formal educational systems. The debate over what ought to be the conceptual and structural underpinnings of national educational opportunity structures has continued since the first mass educational system was formed in the nineteenth century.

When we think of continuity and change, we think of the conceptual balance between cherished traditions and innovations that may facilitate learning without compromising cherished core values or standards. When one thinks of change in education, one is reminded of such great educational experiments of earlier times as (1) John Dewey's Laboratory School at the University of Chicago, (2) Maria Montessori's Casi di Bambini (children's

houses), and (3) A. S. Neil's controversial Summerhill School in England, as well as many other earlier and later innovative experiments in learning theories. Our own time has seen similarly dramatic experimentation.

What constitutes desirable change is directly related to one's own core values regarding the purposes and content of educational experiences. When considering a proposed change in an educational system or a particular classroom, some questions to ask include: What is the purpose of the proposed change? What are the human and social benefits and costs of the proposed change (in teachers' work, in students' learning tasks, etc.)? What defensible alternatives are possible? What are our best ideas? How does the proposed change affect traditional practice? The past thirty or more years of research on teaching and learning have led us to be concerned over the need to improve the quality of learning while also broadening educational opportunity structures for young people.

Each of the essays in this unit relates directly, in some relevant way, to the conceptual tension involved in reconceiving how educational development should proceed in response to dramatic social and economic changes in society.

Looking Ahead: Challenge Questions

What are the most important problems to be considered when we talk about restructuring schools?

What concepts in our thoughts about education need reconceptualization?

What are the social forces that affect human responses to change?

What can teachers do to improve critical reasoning skills in themselves and their students?

To what extent can schooling be reconstructed to most effectively emphasize academic achievement as well as intangible but important factors such as character or initiative or freedom of thought?

Are there more political and economic pressures on educators than they can reasonably be expected to manage? Is this pressure avoidable? Why or why not?

What knowledge bases (disciplines or interdisciplines) ought senior high school students to study?

If it is true there should be a common curriculum at the primary and middle grade levels, should there also be a common curriculum at the secondary level?

What values ought to be at the basis of any effort to reconceptualize the social purposes of schools?

U.S. EDUCATION: THE TASK BEFORE US

Improving the Traditional Model, Creating the New Model

After nearly ten years of sustained effort—some of it fruitful, some of it not—on behalf of education reform, it is possible to distill two primary strategic principles to guide future action. First, we must continue the work to create a different kind of learning institution to replace the traditional school. This effort represents our greatest hope for making a major educational breakthrough. Second, while those efforts continue, we must move ahead with changes that we know will greatly improve our existing traditional schools. In that regard, we have much to learn from the world's other industrialized democracies, whose schools, while quite traditional, continue to dramatically outpace ours on a broad range of educational measures.

The sweeping policy discussion that follows sets forth the rationale for these strategies and describes how we can proceed on both fronts. It was adopted by AFT delegates meeting in convention this past summer. For a copy in brochure form, write the AFT Order Department, 555 New Jersey Ave., N.W., Washington, DC 20001 and ask for item #23.

As the crisis in American education continues, it is becoming a national crisis—one that affects our democratic system, our values, and our way of life. As it persists, the gap between what we stand for as a nation and what we really are is widening. A generation is growing up unprepared for citizenship, work, and family life.

We have problems throughout the system—at all levels, with all students. At one end of the spectrum, a huge number of students leave school, either as dropouts or graduates, with such low levels of achievement that their employment prospects are very poor. Many have never overcome the overwhelming social problems they brought with them to school. At the other end of the spectrum our schools produce among the smallest percentage of high achieving graduates in the industrialized countries. Our average achieving students compare poorly with their counterparts abroad. No policies, whether federal, state, or local, have yet successfully addressed the problem of substantially improving the educational attainment of all of our children.

This is not, as has been suggested, the result of "decline" from some Golden Age, since if a Golden Age ever existed it existed only for the few. Yet, those who have written recently to say that all is well with American education are not right either. It is true that our schools are performing, in most respects, better than they ever performed before. They are educating more students and more difficult students to levels attained in earlier times by only a small and favored group. But success is not assured merely by doing better than we did in the past.

The real issue is that our schools are not doing as well as they need to do to prepare the citizens of a democratic society and the productive workers of a world-competitive economy. We are simply not doing well in comparison to other industrialized countries.

To be sure, comparisons with other countries are difficult to make. They are imperfect. Some unfairly compare a large (and broadly representative) group of U.S. students who are still in school with a smaller, more select group elsewhere. Nevertheless, the many careful comparisons that have been made show other countries doing much better with all groups of students—those in the top, middle, and lowest achievement groups.

There are five tasks before us:

■ We must continue the efforts to create a different kind of learning institution to replace the traditional school.

■ We must improve our traditional schools so that they are at least as effective as the traditional schools in other industrialized countries.

■ We should strive to place both these new and traditional schools in a clear system-wide framework where high national (not federal) standards shape curriculum, where the curriculum to be taught is known to all stakeholders, and where outcomes are set and measured to determine successes and failures. This framework should define policies at the federal, state, and local levels.

■ We must convince the American people that the differences in the support for education and children in other countries—the higher percentage of GNP they spend on education, family, and health supports—are part of the reason for their success.

■ We must continue to fight against public monies being used to support private schools over which taxpayers have no control.

To pursue these goals, we must do the following:

Create a Different Kind of School

AFT locals throughout the country continue to support major restructuring efforts. These must continue. They represent our greatest hope for making a major educational breakthrough. Schools that require children to sit most of the day, learn mainly by listening, and learn at the same rate and in the same way rarely succeed with a majority of students. This model of schooling has remained relatively unchanged for over a century. A new model must be developed.

Our experience has been that school-based management and shared decision making are necessary, but not sufficient, conditions for school change. By themselves, these innovations don't necessarily lead to school improvement. We have strong evidence that these arrangements and other components of restructuring will not succeed unless we first agree on what all students must know and be able to do. (School-based management and shared decision making are essential in deciding how best to meet academic standards that have been adopted.) Only then will we know what faculty must know and be able to teach.

Having agreed upon what students should learn, we must develop school

structures and teaching techniques that take into account the many obstacles that now impede student learning. In transforming our schools, we should learn from the practices of school systems abroad and we should incorporate into our reforms the kinds of supports we know students and teachers need, including:

■ Agreement by management and union to grant a school that is undergoing serious restructuring efforts freedom from many regulations over a long period of time.

■ Substantial time for staff planning, training, and cooperation.

■ Professionalization of teachers so that they are capable of using all the alternatives to whole-class teaching, including team teaching, cooperative learning, peer tutoring, and discussion seminars.

■ Staff training in the educational use of technology—not just computers, but also audiotapes, video, and Fax.

■ Pre-service preparation and staff development that will lead to higher levels of subject teaching skill mastery than have been required up to now.

■ An opportunity for school staff to explore alternative school models that combine all or some of these elements, such as the German Köln-Holweide model, Montessori schools, the Key School, some schools featured by the Coalition of Essential Schools, and the one-room schoolhouse.

Improve Traditional Schools: Use Lessons from the Systems of Other Industrialized Countries

Most of the schools in other countries are performing better than ours. They may have some features we identify with restructuring, but generally they are traditional. This demonstrates that those not engaged in developing new types of schools can work to cre-

ate successful traditional schools. In fact, getting Americans to adopt the key elements of these traditional schools is no less a revolutionary task than school restructuring. We need to work on both—substantially improving the schools we have while at the same time working to create a new model.

What General Motors and the United Auto Workers are doing with cars is very similar. In developing the new Saturn model, UAW and GM are mounting a great effort to create a car that can successfully compete using a new manufacturing process—one that does not resemble the old factory system. While this effort has been going on and is successful, GM has not stopped making its other cars. Many buyers still wanted the traditional models. So GM continued to improve them, too. The changeover from our current schools to those of the future will be evolutionary in the same way.

In improving our traditional schools, we should learn from our school system and those of other industrialized countries.

■ Schools in other countries are run by professionals, with relatively little regular interference by laypeople or school boards.

■ Schools in other countries generally have a national curriculum. Consequently, teacher training, textbooks, and assessments are

> The many careful comparisons that have been made show other countries doing much better with all groups of students.

much more effective than ours because they can be geared to a specific curriculum. Moreover, students know that as they go from teacher to teacher or school to school, there will be continuity.

- Assessments, at least for the college bound, are curriculum-based and challenging. As a result, "teaching to the test" is a constructive way to spend class time.

- Because other countries produce many more students who reach the highest levels of achievement, there is an adequate supply of highly educated people to staff positions in business, government, the military, and educational institutions. These nations can guarantee that all classrooms are staffed by highly knowledgeable, skilled teachers.

- A number of other countries group students by achievement level. In the U.S., student grouping has usually had negative effects on students because students in the "slow" groups are not given challenging work. In other countries, student grouping has positive effects because all students are given challenging work. Also, U.S. student grouping often starts in the first grade with reading groups. Other countries avoid any grouping until much later. Germany starts grouping earlier than most—in the fifth grade. All others do so in later grades, and all group students in high school. Also, in the U.S. there is a danger that grouping of students could be used not for educational purposes but to increase racial separation.

- Good systems in other countries have clearly visible consequences for student performance. There are high college entry standards and clear employment standards. Since success is rewarded in all tracks, all students are expected to work hard—and their teachers and parents push them.

- Schools are relatively safe and free of many of the disruptions of U.S. schools because the legal system supports school regulations needed to maintain a proper educational atmosphere.

- School systems in other countries have much smaller school bureaucracies. In many cases, principals and other supervisors continue to teach.

If traditional U.S. schools are to reach the attainment levels of our industrial competitors, we must try to incorporate these practices, or reasonable equivalents, into our schools. With respect to the above points, these are possible U.S. responses.

1. Experiment with different forms of school governance that free schools from micromanagement by school boards and superintendents. Some of these are discussed in the recent report of the 20th Century Fund. There should be experimentation with various systems of management recommended in the report.

2. States and districts should adopt the best curricula and curriculum frameworks available and require everyone in the system to work faithfully within them. The National Council of Teachers of Mathematics developed such a curriculum. California has developed outstanding curriculum frameworks in history and language arts. Instead of trying to develop separate curricula in each school, district, or state, we should use the best of what is available. At the same time we should support national and state efforts to produce new and better curricula and develop common national standards.

3. We should use the best kinds of assessments available. As one example, California has developed assessments based on its curriculum frameworks. Advanced Placement exams, the International Baccalaureate, and the older New York State Regents examinations should be used as models while new ones are developed that relate to new, improved curriculum frameworks. AFT should support the commitment of federal, state, and private funds for the development of a national system of assessments—one that also includes assessments for vocational and other non-academic track students.

4. Since teacher standards are always related to student standards, we necessarily will need to raise the knowledge and skill levels of many teachers when we raise student standards. While a smaller percentage of U.S. teachers are now adequate to the tasks ahead than in many other countries, we do have a great deal of exceptional talent, and, even when shortcomings are evident, there aren't any replacements with the needed skills, knowledge, and talents available. So, we should encourage some of the same strategies used in the private sector when faced with similar problems.

One answer is teaming and sharing skills—with two, three, four, or five teachers working together in such a way that all students have access to at least one teacher who is top-notch in each area. In some cases technology can help. We should also support "pay for knowledge." This means that, in the future, salary differentials might be based on acquiring the knowledge and skills to teach in an area of shortage. Or, they might be granted to those receiving certification by the National Board for Professional Teaching Standards, which would indicate that a teacher had reached the highest levels of competence in a given field.

5. We need to move away from the ideological debate about student grouping. In fact, there are successful examples of both heterogeneous and homogeneous systems. The basic issue

> When assessments are curriculum based and challenging, "teaching to the test" is a constructive way to spend class time.

is to determine what practices are needed to make the system work for all students. Heterogeneous grouping can work if there is relatively little teacher talk and if the school is organized around individual student work or by subgroups within the class, much like the one-room schoolhouse or the workings of a Boy Scout troop.

Or, as Harold Stevenson and James Stigler have shown in their book, *The Learning Gap,* whole class direct instruction can also be effective with heterogeneous groups—when very carefully team-prepared lessons are adhered to by all teachers who, instead of trying to cover a great deal, work with the class to carefully review how each student solved a single problem, the different ways of reaching successful answers, and the common pitfalls that led to mistakes. However, if teachers are going to talk a great deal and cover much ground, classes must be grouped homogeneously so that students can follow together.

Where there is grouping, we should follow the practices of other countries. Students are grouped on the basis of achievement—a combination of effort, ability, and level of development and not on the basis of presumed innate ability. Students are not grouped any earlier than the fifth grade, and, for the most part, not at all in elementary school. At the elementary level students are given the same work and are pressed and are helped to do it. At the point where students are grouped, all students in all groups are given challenging work that is designed to have all learn to the maximum of their abilities. Students who do exceptionally well are moved to more challenging groups and, in the best situations, student grouping may be different in each subject to reflect different subject strengths and weaknesses.

6. AFT should support incentive systems to increase the motivation of students to work hard and achieve in school. We should favor the development of world-class college entry standards over a given period of time. The college graduation rates of other countries lead us to believe that we would not reduce the number of college graduates if we maintained high standards. There should be provisions for ongoing education for those students who do not meet college requirements, and it must be possible for those who do not reach college entry standards by the time they are 18 to meet them at a later time. We also favor the establishment of school-to-work links and legislation that would involve all businesses in providing on-the-job apprenticeships and training programs for all employees.

Extrinsic incentives are needed, but intrinsic incentives are most important. Anticipated college and employment standards are not likely to motivate elementary and middle school students. For them, among the strongest incentives is recognition within a group small enough so that all know each other—something that is further made possible when teachers and students remain with each other for a number of years to develop close relationships.

7. AFT should engage in ongoing meetings with school, parent, civil rights, and other groups in an effort to modify current laws and/or practices that make U.S. schools the least safe and most disorderly in the industrialized world.

Implement Public Policies that Support Schools

Educational results do not depend only on what teachers and schools do. Much of the success of other countries is due to the social and economic context within which education takes place.

- In other industrialized countries, the amount spent on the education of children is about the same throughout the country. In other industrialized countries, the amount spent on a child's education does not depend on local real estate values or the wealth of a local community. Most other countries have national systems in which the same is spent on all children, with the exception of additional funds that are provided for children with special needs. Even where there are some differences,

they are very small by American standards. Jonathan Kozol has dramatically portrayed the shameful conditions in thousands of our worst schools. Even if it's not possible in our system to reach equality in spending, at the very least we need a set of high minimum standards that includes special compensation for the most deprived, so that no child is denied an education.

- Other countries spend more on elementary and secondary education than we do. We need to spend comparable amounts.

- The income gap between the top 10 percent and the bottom 10 percent is greater in the U.S. than elsewhere. This translates into different educational chances for students.

- National health care systems in other countries and child and family leave policies provide a system of support that improves school chances.

We do not propose to relieve our schools or our profession of the responsibility for doing better; but we recognize that even if we in education were to do everything as well as others do, without these other external impacts our results are likely to remain worse than those of our competitors.

> Other countries spend more on elementary and secondary education than we do. We need to spend comparable amounts.

Monitor the Changes

The National Assessment of Educational Progress (NAEP) should be adequately funded to be able to continue its valuable sample assessments. They are an important and vital indicator of our nation's educational performance. Increased funding for NAEP would permit more essay, performance, and open-ended questions as well as more regular assessments in those areas now rarely tested.

Improve We Must

We face a fight for the very existence of public education. In order to defeat privatization and voucher schemes, we need to do the following:

■ Educate our members and the general public as to the potential dangers to our society if schools in the future were to be organized on the basis of race, ethnicity, religion, and class.

■ Disseminate information that shows that private and parochial schools: a) have students from higher socioeconomic groups; b) reject students who are difficult; and c) still don't produce results that are much better than the public schools.

■ Analyze and take seriously the reasons why parents remove students from public schools so that we can address their concerns with aggressive retention efforts.

■ In order to reduce the pressure for private school choice, we should increase choice in public schools.

Since voucher or private school choice plans are under consideration, we must demand freedom from all but essential laws and regulations covering civil rights, health, safety, and quality standards. And we must demand that whatever regulations are deemed necessary and in the public interest must also be required of any non-public schools whose students are publicly funded. The theory of school competition will certainly not work if public schools are saddled with unnecessary, unpopular rules while private schools are not.

We should strive to incorporate into public schools three of the elements of private and parochial school education that are most attractive: the ability to separate out students who are consistently so troublesome as to prevent others from learning, smaller class size, and often the requirement that students take more academic courses.

We need to return to the idea of the common school: the idea that children of all races, religions, classes, and national backgrounds should get a common education and set of values so that they can learn to live together in a diverse democratic society. This means an emphasis on history, civics, democracy, and commonly shared and held values. It means learning about the contributions of all peoples to our multicultural society. It means teaching history accurately, with pride in our national achievement, but also awareness of our past sins and present shortcomings. But it means opposition to those social studies programs that pit groups against each other and stress differences and conflict.

We must also vastly increase our political efforts in opposition to vouchers as well as our cooperative school improvement efforts with business and other groups. Still, we must face the possibility—even the probability—that soon, somewhere, in some state, one of these schemes will pass. AFT should prepare materials on how public schools can effectively compete should such a system be instituted.

A strong public school system is essential for our democracy. To support our public education system we will dedicate ourselves to oppose politically all efforts to use public monies for private schools and to engage in strong and ongoing efforts to create new type of schools and vastly improve existing ones.

QUESTIONS & ANSWERS

Why is it important to make our education system world-class?

■ *To Remain Economically Competitive*
It's no secret that our economy is in bad shape. Our trade deficit is growing, productivity is waning, and the job market is shrinking. Increasingly, we find ourselves being outperformed by such countries as Japan and Germany. Rather than leading, we seem to be struggling just to keep up.

The past two decades have seen a 12 percent decrease in the real average weekly earnings of Americans. These falling wages have primarily hurt low- and middle-income citizens, while those at the top of the income scale have continued to prosper.

Two years ago, the Commission on the Skills of the American Workforce issued a sobering report (*America's Choice: High Skills or Low Wages!*) characterizing the nature of our economic problems. The key to maintaining—and improving—our standard of living, the commission argued, is to increase productivity and our competitive standing in the global marketplace.

As computer and communications technology development make for what is being termed the third industrial revolution, businesses worldwide are recognizing a need to turn to new forms of work organization. In Japan and Germany, for example, companies are cutting middle management and giving front-line workers more responsibility. Such an approach places far greater demands on the skills of employees and, in turn, on the education systems that prepare them. In the United States, by contrast, highly skilled workers are in short supply, so companies opt for low productivity and archaic, labor-intensive work patterns.

If we hope to remain economically competitive and provide a decent standard of living for a larger number of our citizens, we must follow the lead of our competitors. The problem is that we are not presently equipped to do this. Too many students leave our secondary schools—both dropping out and graduating—without a firm grounding in core subjects and lacking the communication and analytical skills necessary for them to become productive employees in any occupation.

■ *To Strengthen Our Democratic Way of Life*
As vital as improving the education of our children is to our economic health, it is also indispensable to our democratic way of life. Democratic government relies on an informed, well-educated citizenry for its strength and substance, and schools are an essential civic resource.

An improved education system is also important in our fight against crime, poverty, drug abuse, and other social ills. To be sure, these problems cannot and should not be left for our schools to solve by themselves, but schools play a significant role in the quest to teach our youth a greater sense of discipline and values.

Are our students really doing worse than their counterparts in other countries?

Whether students go to college or not, they must be equipped with the necessary knowledge and skills to become productive members of the work force and responsible, law-abiding citizens of our democracy. Unfortunately, the evidence indicates that our elementary and secondary schools are falling short.

Ever since "A Nation at Risk" disclosed the poor performance of American students 10 years ago, a multitude of reports have emphasized the same point. While in some cases the data may be flawed, the sheer number of studies (a leading testing company estimates the total at more than 150) published—all with similar findings—certainly drives the message home. Consider:

■ National Assessment of Educational Progress data from 1990 show that students in the fourth, eighth, and 12th grades couldn't handle

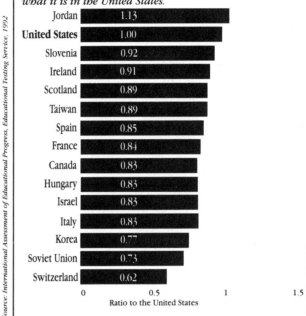

The Achievement Gap

Not only do American 13-year-olds rank near the bottom on international comparisons, but the disparities between the performance of our top and bottom students are also among the largest in the world. As this chart shows, only Jordan has greater disparities among its students in math achievement. Achievement disparity is computed as the range between the performance of the bottom 10th and the top 10th of students, divided by the average for that country. In Switzerland, for example, the gap between the highest and the lowest performing students is almost half what it is in the United States.

Country	Ratio to the United States
Jordan	1.13
United States	1.00
Slovenia	0.92
Ireland	0.91
Scotland	0.89
Taiwan	0.89
Spain	0.85
France	0.84
Canada	0.83
Hungary	0.83
Israel	0.83
Italy	0.83
Korea	0.77
Soviet Union	0.73
Switzerland	0.62

Ratio to the United States

Source: International Assessment of Educational Progress, Educational Testing Service, 1992

challenging subject matter in science or math (*The 1990 Science Report Card* and *The State of Mathematics Achievement*).

■ In science, for example, the NAEP results showed that fewer than half the 12th graders demonstrated the ability to apply knowledge to interpret graphs and tables, evaluate and design experiments, or show detailed knowledge of scientific information. In math, fewer than half the 12th graders demonstrated a consistent grasp of decimals, percents, fractions, and simple algebra. Just 5 percent of the seniors showed skills in advanced algebra and geometry necessary for college-level work or high-technology jobs.

■ Results from the 1992 International Assessment for Educational Progress (*Learning Science* and *Learning Mathematics*) placed U.S. 13-year-olds 14th out of 15 countries in math (ahead of only Jordan) and 13th out of 15 in science (Jordan and Ireland scored lower).

■ A 1988 report from the International Association for the Evaluation of Educational Achievement (*Science Achievement in 17 Countries*), which showed a similar pattern of poor American performance in science, includes a revealing comparison. It takes the lowest-scoring school in the highest-scoring country and compares the results from that school to the performance of all schools in the other countries. The results: for 10-year-olds, 38 percent of American schools scored below the lowest-scoring school in Japan; for 14-year-olds, 30 percent of American schools scored below the lowest-scoring school in Hungary. The numbers are even more striking for American 12th graders: In biology, 98 percent of the schools scored below the lowest-scoring school in Singapore; in chemistry, 48 percent scored below the lowest-scoring schools in Hong Kong, Singapore, and England; and in physics, 89 percent scored below the lowest-scoring school in Hong Kong. Only Italy scored worse across the board.

■ Nor do top American students match up very well against countries such as Japan. A 1989 report from the National Research Council (*Everybody Counts*) showed that the performance of the top 5 percent of U.S. students in math is matched by the top 50 percent of Japanese students. And it found that the top 1 percent of American students scored the lowest of the top 1 percent in all participating countries.

How is the reform agenda outlined in "The Task Before Us" consistent with our existing efforts to restructure schools?

We have one agenda: to create schools that produce students who are among the best educated in the world. Whether they are restructuring or not, all our schools could benefit from examining the traditional schools in other industrialized countries. Much of the success of schools abroad is due to clear educational policies that outline rigorous national standards for all students, define curriculum based on those standards, and assess students' results in reaching those standards.

■ Shared decision making, the centerpiece of most restructuring until now, can't succeed until teachers know what they're supposed to do. Once standards are set, shared decision making can focus on establishing policies that help all students reach the standards.

■ Other practices we associate with restructured schools would likewise benefit if we establish clear standards and expectations. We could better define the purposes of staff development and explain why teachers need time to improve

their subject-matter expertise and related instructional methods. We could shape experiments in cooperative learning, team teaching, peer tutoring, and discussion seminars around a common substantive agenda growing from national standards.

What impact would rigorous national standards—translated into curriculum frameworks and a national system of assessments—have on the mission of our schools to generate equal opportunity? Will some populations—the poor and the disadvantaged minorities, for example—face added hurdles in their struggles to make good on the American dream?

On the contrary, if everyone knew the meaning of success in hard, substantive terms, we could eradicate the double standards that give so many of our high school graduates a false sense of accomplishment. We could no longer delude ourselves into believing that "improvement" equals success because the national standards would make the gap between expectations and true performance glaringly apparent. These tough tools would give us a more realistic diagnosis of the extent of our problems and a better basis for focusing remedial help where it's needed.

■ Urban schools that serve the poor have been the least successful in fostering equal educational opportunity. The depiction of their performance gap will be more dramatic once high national standards are in place, making more compelling our arguments that low-income students deserve a level playing field when it comes to resources. It's better to know fully the disastrous predicament of our educationally disadvantaged populations so we can face the consequences head on.

■ The basic-skills thrust of the late 1970s and resulting state movements to implement minimum-competency tests are as close as we've come to setting a national learning agenda. As inadequate as these minimum standards were—they were set at low levels and ignored higher-order thinking skills—they contributed to tremendous achievement gains by minorities and the disadvantaged across the country. For example, the gap in reading achievement between African-American and white students has closed by 50 percent in the last 20 years. High standards and curriculum guidelines that incorporate problem solving and thinking skills should have an even more profound effect.

■ Nonetheless, the attachment of serious consequences to student performance on the assessments should be phased in over time, simultaneous to channeling more resources and assistance to schools whose students need the most help to perform well and which are often funded inadequately.

Don't other countries track students in ways that perpetuate inequality? In shaping our system, shouldn't we hold on to our belief that all students deserve a good education and none should be relegated to dead-end tracks?

None of our major competitors track or group children by level of achievement until at least the fifth grade. Many wait until later. In the United States, we give loud lip service to the idea that such grouping is bad, even as we group students as early as first grade.

When other systems begin grouping in the secondary years, many also offer extra instruction, enabling all students to keep up and meet the standards appropriate to their grade level and academic program. And when grouping becomes a matter of practical aspiration in the late secondary years, with vocational and higher education tracks, clear standards ensure that all students, regardless of track, will be exposed to core academic content. Moreover, these standards show students in those countries what they're expected to know and be able to do, and—unlike our general-track students—they know all the tracks will lead to opportunities after they graduate.

■ Even in American elementary schools, we have different expectations for different students, and those expectations translate into watered-down curriculum for students in the slow tracks. The disparities in content become more striking in junior high and high school. A NAEP report on math, for example, pointed out the differences in eighth-grade math curricula. High-performing groups tended to study algebra and functions and learn to use calculators, while low-performing classes were still covering arithmetic and completing work sheets. Most math classes, but especially those with low-performing students, continued to rely on textbooks, work sheets, and frequent tests.

■ Achievement grouping is defensible only if all groups are taught in ways that maximize their potential. Practices that relegate low achievers

to a dumping ground of low standards and expectations can't be tolerated. Students should be constantly re-evaluated so that they are always placed in a group that challenges them to do their best.

Doesn't the idea of national standards run counter to the traditional American idea of local control?

■ In reality, we've already ceded local control of the curriculum—and in effect, standards—to commercial textbook publishers and test developers. Unfortunately, they give us little more than basic skills. Our best chance to displace this minimalist material is by creating an excellent, prestigious curriculum based on world-class standards.

■ Even in countries with a national curriculum, local areas and individual teachers retain some discretion over what to teach. And teachers are still free to use whatever methods they think are best for teaching the curriculum. In this country, even with national standards, a large part of the curriculum would continue to be developed locally.

Wouldn't national standards serve to homogenize our unique and vibrant diversity and impede progress toward a more multicultural curriculum?

■ National standards in the humanities subjects will ensure that all students, of all backgrounds, receive some instruction in common. In the humanities, much of that instruction will relate to our common history and literature. But, as AFT's resolution on multicultural education says, this nation is "one of the world's most diverse multicultural societies." Properly understood, America's common culture is itself extremely multicultural. While there will certainly be difficult and hard-fought debates about the content that should be included in national standards and related curriculum frameworks, we believe that the result would reflect the reality of America's multicultural inheritance.

Why is it necessary to tie college admission and employment to student performance?

■ One of the greatest trials of teaching is motivating students who feel they have little stake in learning the material. This is a greater challenge for American teachers than for their overseas counterparts because we are one of the few countries in which students' school performance has so little impact on their future success. In most European and Asian systems, students' ability to get admitted to college or to a good apprenticeship program depends on how well they do in school. As a result, students in these other countries have a strong impetus to work hard in their classes.

■ Under our educational system, in contrast, the onus for getting a child to learn is on the teacher, not the student. Most students face no great consequences if they don't do well in school. For those who are college bound, average grades will get them into all but the nation's best colleges. And the work-bound know their potential employers will have little interest in their high school performance. A recent poll by Louis Harris and Associates confirms that belief: Only 24 percent of employers said they "pay a great deal of attention" to the high school records of the average applicant.

Why should teachers be "paid for knowledge"?

■ Good teaching requires both pedagogical knowledge and deep understanding of the content area one teaches. If the difficulty of the content is greatly increased, it follows that teachers will need to greatly strengthen their own content understanding. In California, for example, where demanding new curriculum frameworks are now in place, researchers are finding that to successfully teach the new curriculum, many teachers need a stronger grasp of their content area.

■ If we substantially raise national standards for students, we will need to create a variety of opportunities and incentives for teachers to strengthen their content knowledge. One way to do this would be to modify current salary schedules so that salary differentials would be awarded only for course work in a teacher's content field, not for methodology courses.

■ Once the National Board for Professional Teaching Standards begins issuing credentials, salary differentials could be provided for teachers who meet new advanced certification standards. The AFT has opposed merit pay because it has traditionally been awarded in arbitrary ways. But the National Board offers a vehicle for rewarding excellent teaching performance in a fair, objective way.

Changing Schools from Within

Robert E. Rubinstein

Robert E. Rubinstein is a public school teacher, children's author, and professional storyteller from Eugene, Oregon.

So many little parts of our educational system "need to be changed"—discipline, test scores, sex education—that we often fail to see that the whole system needs massive restructuring.

It is difficult for the public—as well as teachers and administrators—to see that we need to move our schools and students to meet the demands of the next century. Teachers must move out of the isolated classrooms and, for the sake of our children, make schools viable places of practical, enthusiastic, lifelong learning.

Together we must dramatically change the use of school funds within a district, organization of curriculum and class time, teaching methods, school structure, assessment of students and grades, administration, teacher education, and who decides what will be taught.

FUNDING

We know that the most important part of a building is its foundation. Without a good foundation, sooner or later the building will collapse. Such is happen-ing to the public school system in America.

Usually, money, services, and special staff go first to the high schools, and last to the elementary schools. Studies have shown that classes with more than 15 students per teacher do not allow the teacher to keep in personal touch with students. Students' progress, success, and enjoyment of learning diminish as class size increases. Many school districts today have 30 or more students per class in elementary school, and then school officials and the public wonder why many children cannot read or write at "class levels," have behavior problems, and do not like school.

In most school districts, high schools get first claim on funds, vehicle use, updated equipment, special teacher training, and specialized programs. However, a large percentage of students arriving at high school are ready to drop out because they are frustrated, aren't succeeding, don't feel supported, and can't see how school will benefit them. "High school dropout" is really a misnomer; most decided to drop out in middle school.

If, instead, the funds and resources were focused on the early years of school to build a solid foundation, many of these students might feel they can learn and succeed, and see the benefits of education in their futures. The pattern for contin-ued success would then have been established.

ORGANIZATION AND TIME

I wonder how many of the experts on national committees are actually active classroom teachers. They do not seem to realize that merely adding time to the school day is an exercise in futility.

By 2:00 P.M., in most schools, the students have had their fill of school and, often, the teachers have had their fill of dealing with students. To extend the school day until four or five o'clock then would only heighten the tension and teacher burnout.

Indeed, educational systems elsewhere in the world do have longer school days, but from 12–2 P.M. the students have free time to have lunch, relax, or socialize. This provides them with a psychological break, and they return with a more open and positive attitude and are more productive until even five or six.

Where, besides the traditional American school, do students run from one 40- or 50-minute period to another, with just four-minute passing times, and try to digest six to eight unrelated curriculums? Could we adults do that? I couldn't. Yet, we ask 10 to 18 year olds, with all their personal concerns and distractions, hormones, and body changes to successfully manage this schedule. That does not make sense.

Some schools have developed block periods where students only meet four classes a day in 70-minute or two-hour periods every other day. In this way, science labs can be conducted in more depth; extended class activities can happen—all in a more relaxed atmosphere where students can ask questions and learn more effectively.

Socialization, an important part of a student's life, should also happen in school. Again, many schools in other countries allow students 15–30 minutes between classes. This permits them to relax, eat or drink, use the restroom, maybe shoot a hoop or two, and meet with friends. Most significantly, this span between classes allows students to digest what they've heard in the previous class before they turn their attention to a completely new subject. They need time to make that mind-switch.

With all that natural energy artificially suppressed by classroom rules, students through ninth grade need at least a morning and an afternoon time to participate in some activity. Can we adults sit in a class for two hours without getting restless?

Our summer school breaks also have become unrealistic, a holdover from the time when children had to work on the farms. Our economic focus has changed, but schools have not adjusted. Today, with the problems of the American family, lack of parental supervision, and children wandering the streets, the extended summer offers great opportunities for gangs to recruit members and for teen crime. The long break also makes students forget what they've learned, so more time must be spent in review during the fall.

In Europe and in other parts of the world, students may have a two- or three-week break

■

Without a good foundation, sooner or later the building will collapse. Such is happening to the public school system in America.

■

between terms and maybe a full month or six weeks off from school in the summer. Frequently, as in Japan, students have minimal work to complete during these vacations. The students keep abreast, and the teacher does not have to review material in the fall.

HOW AND WHAT TEACHERS TEACH

Most teachers, especially in high school and more so in classes for college-bound students, stand in front of the room and lecture. They emit huge mounds of information that they expect students to memorize and then feed back to them on a comprehensive exam. Studies have shown that within two days after the exam, students forget 80 to 90 percent of that information. So, what is the sense in teaching this way?

Ironically, as we enter what has been termed the "Information Age," what teachers should *not* be emphasizing is information. Known information doubles about every 18 months. No one can be an expert anymore. There's just too much to learn. As Einstein stated: "Don't commit to

memory what you can look up."

Teachers must teach how to know what information is available, how to find that information, and then how to use it effectively in what you want to do. Teachers have to be concerned with how students perceive the curriculum: How do they understand it? How is it relevant to their world? The learning approach, as such, must focus on active student participation and interaction with the teacher, not lectures. A Chinese proverb states:

What I hear I forget.
What I see I remember.
What I do I understand.

We must not be so consumed with getting from point A to point B in our curriculum that we lose students along the way.

Teachers also need to teach for the future. Stephen Glenn, the noted educator, has stated that it takes 2 years for a new idea to be incorporated into the business community and 16 years to be accepted into the education community. How can we prepare students for the future if it is already passed? There is no going "back to basics," just as there is no going back from plane travel to horse and wagon.

In conjunction with this active approach to learning, schools need to teach socialization skills. Almost 80 percent of young people 16–25 years of age who lose jobs do so not because they lack knowledge or skills, but because they cannot cooperate with fellow workers, have little sense of responsibility, and will not or cannot follow directions. When there were two-parent families and stable homes, many might have learned those skills at home, but not so today. The only place these young people can learn life-skills is in school.

CONTINUITY

As noted earlier, U.S. education is a backwards system that works from the top down. So-called national experts state how every school should educate children. Superintendents and "downtown" administrators with little knowledge of what goes on in the classroom determine policy and prescribe what teachers should teach and how.

Very often high school social studies teachers, for example, instruct middle or junior high social studies teachers what they should teach and how, and what materials they can or cannot use. Some become irate if a middle school teacher should transgress on their social studies territory. Then, middle schools sometimes tell elementary teachers what they should teach.

Often, little or no communication occurs among a district's primary and secondary schools. The student, as such, is passed through a 12-year continuum with only a vague awareness of what he or she has learned as opposed to what should have been learned. In a profession whose main ingredient must be positive, successful communication, there is often little.

If schools are truly concerned with educating, this process should be reversed. The kindergarten teacher would tell the first-grade teacher what has been taught and what the students need to learn to succeed. This communication then would continue up through high school, with the student, not the teacher or curriculum, as the focus. High-school programs should be flexible enough to adapt to students' needs and interests, providing links and experiences in the real world to prepare students for adulthood.

But then there are the all-powerful colleges that dictate, through the Standard Achieve-

■ *Follow the leader:* **School reform should start with the bottom line, which is children and their classroom teachers.**

ment Test, what ought to be taught. Isn't it amazing that a student goes through 12 years of school and takes one test to account for all that he or she has accomplished? Where do we do this in real life? And this is an information-parroting test, not even a test of skills and understanding. If a student has a bad day, has test anxiety (as many do), then what? Maybe we need to communicate to the colleges that basing admission on these exams is not acceptable.

Also, what happens to those who do not want to go on to col-

lege? In most cases—little. There's little interest in these students, little counseling, less quality teachers, and fewer noncollege-bound classes offered. In essence, we throw these students away—and wonder why they do not like school, feel negative about learning, turn to crime, and cannot function in society.

COMPETITION

We too often promote competition in our schools in personally destructive ways. Our society states that to progress and succeed, we must tear down the old to build the new.

In school we do the same, only we use tests, grades, awards, and curves. These all point out students who have "succeeded" and others who have "failed," or are less valued. Harold Gardner, the Harvard professor of education, noted that of the seven different ways of learning that people have, schools use only two: logical and linear learning. He also stated that only 20 percent of the students utilize these two intelligences. As such, we often label the other 80 percent as "failures" because their ways of learning are different from those the teachers use.

This does not make sense in terms of personal development or in terms of education and learning. We should learn from the Japanese business practices that focus more on cooperation than competition. They honor instead of tearing down the "old," and then collectively decide to improve and move on to further develop their product or service. Employees at all levels, with a wide variety of perceptions, are invited to contribute their ideas to the process. They feel valued and usually work more effectively.

Schools likewise need to engage in cooperative learning, developing skills of sharing, responsibility, and helping each other succeed. If all students are valued and part of the learning process, everybody benefits.

We know that there are 2.5 million reported cases of child abuse each year, that 95,000 children commit suicide annually, and that a 12-year-old had a better chance of reaching the age of 25 in good health in 1935 than he or she does today.

Each child, starting from the third grade on, regardless of socioeconomic background, should take part in a survival class in school. Taught by coun-

■

Each child, starting from the third grade on, regardless of socioeconomic background, should take part in a survival class in school.

■

selors, nurses, and guests from other community agencies, this class should focus on identifying nutritious food, cooking a basic meal, sewing to repair clothing, dealing with conflict, knowing how to handle money, living with dysfunctional families, and knowing which agencies to contact for help.

For people to feel part of the community, they must be able to contribute to it and to be valued by it. Kids aren't. If we want to reduce vandalism and crime, we must encourage our young people to consistently take part in and invest themselves in their communities.

From kindergarten on through high school, some form of weekly community service should be part of the curriculum. This might range from growing a communal garden to caring for the homes and yards of the elderly and disabled, painting houses or murals, visiting retirement or nursing homes, visiting hospitals, helping younger children, and so forth. Young people need that sense of worth that the present school curriculum does not accord them. If they do feel they are valued, that school is relevant to the outside world in positive ways, then the natural inclination is to want to be valued more. The school is the ideal place to learn

skills that enhance their own self-image and importance.

ADMINISTRATION

The school administration—or "downtown" as it is often called—consists of the superintendent, the school board, assistant superintendents, curriculum coordinators, special services, personnel, business offices, purchasing, and maintenance. Here again the problem usually is a lack of communication. Although these "downtown" people determine policy for the school and the teacher, they rarely know what's happening inside the classroom.

Teachers need communication. The administrative people should come out to the school at least twice a year to find out what they need to do for students, teachers, and schools. Their job should be to provide support to teachers and students rather than to simply dictate policy.

EVALUATIONS

In most districts, teachers receive some sort of formal yearly evaluation. This is often a stressful and an artificial experience for the teacher, who prepares for that one visit. Evaluating teacher performance should, of course, be a continual, informal process. The principal, vice principal, counselor, and other teachers should feel free to drop in on any teacher's class to enjoy what's happening there. The teacher should feel relaxed enough to welcome or even invite guests without feeling threatened. These guests could give that teacher some informal feedback about what they enjoyed and what could be improved.

Why don't teachers have the opportunity to evaluate department heads, administrators, downtown people, and the superintendent? Since they are the ones who supposedly support teachers it seems logical that teachers evaluate their performance.

COLLEGES OF EDUCATION

In 22 years of teaching, I have rarely met teachers who had anything positive to say about the college education classes they took to prepare for the job. This must change.

There are some fine college teachers who are actively involved in public schools, who provide insightful, relevant training and positive modeling for students in the teacher-training programs. These people, however, are few and far between. Most of those teaching our future teachers fall into one of the following categories: those who have left the public schools because they did not want to teach there anymore; those who have been asked to leave the public schools; and those who have never taught in the public schools (little or no contact with schoolchildren).

Perhaps there should be some part-time arrangement for

■

Students arriving at high school are ready to drop out because they are frustrated, aren't succeeding, don't feel supported, and can't see how school will benefit them.

■

classroom teachers to teach future public school teachers. Any college instructor teaching teachers should spend part of one term teaching or working with schoolchildren every three years. This would give them a reality check.

Just as teachers receive evaluations, education teachers should also be evaluated. Teaching well and effectively must come before doing research papers and working on grants.

Future teachers might work as volunteers, tutors, or classroom aides to gain experience and discover early in their college careers if they want to be teachers.

Many states now require teacher certification examinations, but the ones I have seen were created by college professors and had little relevance to a person's ability to teach. Any such test should be prepared by classroom teachers.

The above mentioned reforms will require changing the traditional paradigms. These dramatic changes need to be made now—and they must have the understanding and active support of parents, the public, school administrators, teachers, and the students. There is no going back or standing still. There is only the future. Teachers and schools must prepare our children for that future as well as they can.

A WORLD OF CHOICE IN EDUCATION

Clifford F. Thies

Clifford F. Thies is the Durell Professor of Money, Banking, and Finance at Shenandoah University, Winchester, Virginia, and is an adjunct scholar at the Heritage Foundation.

In many places in the United States, parents can choose among public, Catholic, evangelical Christian, Jewish, Islamic, and secular private schools for their children. This right has been affirmed by no less an authority than the U.S. Supreme Court, which, in 1925, in overturning an attempt by the state of Oregon to prohibit private and religious schools, declared that the child "is not the mere creature of the state."

And so it is in just about every other democratic country. Except that there is a difference. In most other democratic countries, parents who choose to send their children to religious or private schools do not have to fully pay a second time in tuition for what they have already paid in taxes. Parental choice in education is not biased by the funding of some, but not other, schools. Parents of modest means are not forced to weigh the sacrifices in family budget and educational quality against the value they place in sending their children to schools that affirm the faith and morals taught at home.

Explicit protection of parental choice in education is incorporated into many state and national constitutions. Article 42 of the constitution of the Republic of Ireland, for example, declares the family to be the "natural educator" of the child and "guarantees to respect the inalienable right and duty of parents to educate their children." Article 23 of the Dutch constitution guarantees government spending on an equal basis for all schools chosen by parents meeting regulatory standards.

The Alberta Act of 1905, whereby that province joined the Canadian confederation, establishes a right to Catholic or Protestant schools with funding equal to that provided to public schools. Article 27 of the Spanish constitution guarantees the freedom of parents to choose the religious and moral education of their children.

The United States is just about the only democracy today that does not support parental choice in education. The United States, the most diverse and religious country in the world, has the most uniform system of education and the fewest children receiving religious instruction. And, not coincidentally, the United States, which spends the most money on education per public school student, scores the lowest in internationally administered tests of knowledge and reasoning ability.

In Scotland, the first public schools were founded in 1872 and were administered by the established (Presbyterian) church. Forty-six years later, Catholics obtained full government support for their schools. In England, fully supported nondenominational public schools were founded in 1870. Thirty-two years later, the government allowed about 90 percent of the operating costs of church-related "voluntary schools" to be paid by local educational authorities.

In France, public schools separate from the schools run by the Catholic Church were officially begun in 1850. Before the Third Republic, the emperor had supported the reestablishment of the Catholic Church through governmental support of its schools. During the Third Republic, the public schools were secularized, and aid was denied to independent schools; the Third Republic was anticlerical, viewing the church, and its schools, as an enemy of the state. By 1904, the government had gone so far as to prohibit members of religious orders from teaching. But, with the increasing secularization of public schools, the private sector grew in popularity; and, with the approach of World War I, the authorities turned a blind eye toward religious schools. Finally, in 1918, independent schools began to be aided, primarily with grants to support teacher salaries.

In Belgium, a state school system was formed in 1842. Initial cooperation between the ruling Liberal Party and the church was soon replaced by anticlerical sentiment. In 1879, the government decided that all schools receiving public support would be under its exclusive jurisdiction and sought to replace religious teaching with secularized moral instruction.

Within months, 30 percent of students and 20 percent of teachers withdrew from the public school system and formed "free" Catholic schools. And, five years later, after having defeated the Liberal Party at the polls, the Catholic Party returned control of schooling to local governments.

In the election of 1958, which largely revolved on the issue of education, the Christian People's Party (successor to the Catholic Party) did surprisingly well. Following the election, it, the Liberal, and the Socialist parties joined into the "Pacte Scolaire," cementing aid to independent schools on the same basis as that given to public schools. Only the Communist Party held out. Today, over half of Belgian children attend independent schools.

The school struggle, or *schoolstrijl*, is perhaps best illustrated in the Netherlands. A secular state school system was established early during the nineteenth century. In 1848, a constitutional amendment secured the right to independent schools for the Dutch Catholic minority. At about the same time, a revival of Calvinism split the Protestant majority into liberal and Calvinist camps. Liberal Protestants preferred a universal *secular* public school system, and the Calvinists preferred a universal *Protestant* public school system. It was clear that no single group—the Catholics, the liberals, or the Calvinist Protestants—constituted a majority.

In 1889, a Catholic-Calvinist-Protestant coalition came to power and gained limited financial aid for independent schools. Over the next twenty-four years, support of independent schools gradually increased but remained less than the support given public schools. Following the election of 1913, agreement in principle to equal funding of independent schools was obtained. This principle was incorporated into the constitution of 1917 and was enacted into legislation in 1920. Today, over 70 percent of Dutch children at-

The town of Vienna, Virginia, attempted to close the Fairfax Christian School for zoning reasons.

tend independent schools, roughly half of which are Catholic and half Protestant.

THE SCHOOL STRUGGLE TODAY

All over the world, the school struggle continues to this day. In the last generation, important victories have been won in Australia, Canada, Japan, and elsewhere. Several of the newly democratic countries of eastern Europe and the former Soviet Union are implementing plans for parental choice in education. In the Hispanic world, Chile, Mexico, the Philippines, and Spain have relaxed restrictions against religious instruction, decentralized control of public schools, and extended financial support to independent schools. Also significant, defeat has been averted in a number of countries, most notably France and Greece, in which left-socialist parties attacked parental choice.

In the eastern provinces of Canada, parental choice in education evolved some time ago. The province of Ontario, for example, supports denominational schools—most of them Catholic, a few of them Protestant—that are organized as "separate" schools within the public sector. During the 1970s, parental choice was provided in the west, as the provinces of British Columbia, Manitoba, and Saskatchewan began to provide financial support to independent schools on the basis of per capita grants.

In Australia, modest grants to independent schools, most of which were Catholic, were first approved during the 1960s. Opposition to this aid then emerged from government teachers' unions, parent groups, secularists, and Protestants. By the 1980s, because of the increasing secularization of the government school system, the funding of independent schools was no longer a Catholic versus non-Catholic issue. Instead, it became a religious versus secular issue. This shift enabled the coalition supporting parental choice in education to win a commitment for substantial support. Grants to independent schools were put onto a per capita basis and increased to about half the funding level of government schools.

Following World War II, independent high schools in Japan expanded rapidly. Several reasons can be cited for this expansion, including: demand for education in excess of the number of seats available in government schools and the encouragement of bank loans to finance the construction of independent schools. During the 1970s, many of these independent schools encountered financial difficulties due to rising labor costs and their debt burdens. The government thereupon increased its assistance to them, providing up to 50 percent of their expenses.

In Norway, since the 1970s, increasing disenchantment with government schools, as well as with the welfare state in general, has led to several education reforms upon the ascendancy of a center-right government, including decentralization and greater accountability in the public sector and a significant increase in state aid to independent schools.

PRÉCIS

In the United States, parents are free to send their children to any school they choose—public, religious, or secular private—but they must still pay taxes to support public schools, receiving no financial help from the government to support the tuition of the alternative school. The United States is about the only democracy that does not fund parental choice in education.

Most other democratic countries—including Ireland, Canada, the United Kingdom, France, Belgium, the Netherlands, Japan, Australia, Chile, Mexico, the Philippines, Spain, Greece, and others—are different. There, parents who choose religious or private schools do not have to pay fully a second time in tuition for what they have already paid in taxes.

In most of those, choice in education is not biased by funding only some schools, and low-income parents are not forced to weigh sacrificing family budget and educational quality against sending their children to schools that affirm the home's faith and morals.

Educational choice can be achieved here as was every civil right—despite the intransigent U.S. educational establishment and its interest in the status quo—through years of persevering struggle, consolidation of small victories, and appealing on the basis of justice.

EDUCATION IN THE UNITED KINGDOM

Some 20 percent of students in the United Kingdom attend *grant-maintained* independent schools, treated as part of the government sector. Another 6 percent attend *private schools*, treated as separate from the government sector. In addition to the financial support given to the grant-maintained schools, the government gives scholarships to bright children of parents of modest means so they can attend private schools.

Parental choice in education evolved in the United Kingdom in a way that naturally accommodates religious diversity. At first, this meant allowing Catholics, Methodists, and Jews to have their own schools, just as had the established Church of England. More recently, and in spite of some initial resistance, it has meant also allowing Muslims and Hindus to have their own schools. This religious diversity has not proven to be divisive. Instead, other concerns have received attention, for example, elitist private schools, vocational versus comprehensive high schools, and restriction of choice to schools within geographic districts.

During the election of 1979, the Conservative Party promised to reinvigorate parental choice. Margaret Thatcher characterized the public school bureaucracy as an unresponsive monopoly. After winning the election, the new Conservative government required Local Education Authorities to relax geographic restrictions on choosing schools.

In 1988, several additional steps were taken to bypass the public school bureaucracy. A number of vocational high schools were formed in metropolitan areas outside of the control of Local Education Authorities. In addition, public schools were allowed to "opt out" of the government school system to become grant-maintained independent schools and private schools were allowed to "opt in."

Within a year, 25 public schools opted out and another 120 expressed an interest in doing so. In addition, a few of the growing number of (mostly small) Muslim and evangelical Christian private schools applied to opt in.

These Muslim and evangelical Christian schools often started as little more than Koran and Bible schools, basically supplementing the education received in the public schools during evening or weekend meetings. But, due to the increasingly materialistic philosophy taught in the public schools, as well as their discrimination in matters such as dress, diet, and prayer opportunities, these Koran and Bible schools tended to evolve into full-fledged elementary and secondary schools.

In order to keep costs—and tuition—to a minimum, these schools often utilize church buildings, rely on parent volunteer labor, and make do with few certified teachers. The Oak Hill School, run by the Bristol Christian Fellowship, for example, is housed in a church building and uses the Accelerated Christian Education (ACE) method of instruction, which relies heavily on student workbooks. The Islamic College, a high school in London,

Parental Choice in Education: A Selective Survey

Australia	Per capita grants.
Belgium	Funding of independent schools, mostly Catholic, on a basis equal to the funding of government schools.
Canada	Varies by province: in the east includes support of "separate" schools, mostly denominational, within public sector; and, in the west, per capita grants.
France	Ranges from support of teachers' salaries to funding on an equal basis, with concomitant variation in state regulation.
Germany	Varies by state. Includes per capita grants and support of teachers' salaries.
Japan	Per capita grants to independent senior high schools.
The Netherlands	100 percent voucher system.
Norway	Per capita grants to folk schools.
United Kingdom	Support of "voluntary" schools within the public sector, and scholarships to private schools for children of poor parents.

teaches mathematics and science—for which Muslims have the highest regard—with a minimum of computer and laboratory facilities.

In a perfect example of catch-22 reasoning, the applications for grant-maintained status by thirteen of these evangelical Christian schools were rejected by Local Educational Authorities because they could not afford the kind of resources expected of grant-maintained schools. Thus, because they needed assistance, they were denied assistance. Concluded the report of the inspector of one of these schools:

"The school undoubtedly has the best interests of its pupils at heart and wishes to provide for them as well as possible within the framework of its strongly held religious convictions, but the present pro-

vision is still far from achieving acceptable standards."

The application of Islamia Primary School, in London's Brent district, was denied by a party-line vote of its Local Educational Authority, with Tory members supporting and Labor members opposing the application. The stated reason for the rejection was unused capacity in the public schools. Another catch-22: Because many parents found the public schools to be so unacceptable that they withdrew their children from them, leaving these public schools with empty seats, the private schools could not be funded.

In France, upon the election of François Mitterrand in 1981, the socialist left attempted to restrict that country's plan of parental choice in education. The new government proposed to gain the power to appoint teachers and administrators in independent schools, to gain exclusive power to conduct teacher training, and to restrict parental choice—both private as well as public—to schools within geographic boundaries.

These proposals were seen by private schools to be a threat to their independence. Public opinion polls showed that an overwhelming majority of the French—including many who described themselves as socialists or as communists—supported parental choice in education. In June 1984, more than a million people participated in a massive demonstration in Paris to oppose the proposals. The center-right parties rose to the defense of parental choice and, in part because of this, won control of the National Assembly in the elections of 1986. His lesson learned, when Mitterrand ran for reelection two years later, he abstained from attacking independent schools.

HOW IS PARENTAL CHOICE IMPLEMENTED?

There are many ways in which parental choice in education is implemented. In some countries, such as Italy, government funding of primary and secondary schools has evolved in such a way that no clear distinction can be made between government-financed private and public schools. Just about all Italian schools can be said to be both quasi-private as well as quasi-public.

Other countries allow parents to opt out of the government school system, which is either secular or reflects the dominant religion, in respect of religious diversity. In Belgium and France, the government's school systems are, or at one time were, more than simply secular but anti-clerical. Choice in education in these countries originated from the desire of Catholic parents to send their children to religious schools.

The Canadian province of Quebec, where Catholic schools dominate the public school system, gives Protestant parents alternative schools. In other provinces of Canada, as well as in Australia, England, and Scotland, the government's school systems have shifted over the years from Protestant to secular. Choice gives Catholic and, more recently, Protestant parents an alternative.

Sweden allows parents to opt out of the government's schools, which are run by the Church of Sweden (the established church), and send their children to other Christian schools or secular schools such as Montessori and Waldorf schools. Moderate Arab countries, including Egypt and Saudi Arabia, give Christians an alternative to the government's Islamic schools.

Parental choice in education can help ethnic as well as religious minorities finance their own schools. The Chinese schools of Southeast Asia—in Indonesia until they were shut down by the government and in Singapore—are an example. In England, a number of schools have been organized along ethnic lines, including Afro-Caribbean, Asian, and Irish schools. The Marcus Garvey School in Midlands, for example, offers parents an

alternative to the racism implicit in the low expectations of teachers in public schools for minority children. Without these schools, more minority children would be sent "home," for example, to the Caribbean, to live with relatives and attend school there.

Allowing for parental choice in education can also help finance other dimensions of diversity. In Scandinavian countries and northern German states, choice in education enables parents to enroll their children in the *folk schools* that are traditional to these countries. These folk schools are small, rural-based boarding schools in which elements of the standard high school curriculum are incorporated into a program that emphasizes experience-based learning and the dynamics of living, working, and studying together.

There are many different folk schools; some are church sponsored and all display a wide variety in structure and discipline, curricula, and facilities. An example is the Kolding Hojskole in Denmark. Set in a medium-sized provincial town, this folk school features a kib-

butzlike organization of work and studies, along with a non-Marxist, left-wing criticism of capitalism and materialism.

In Japan, choice in education has almost a purely economic rationale. In that country, public financing of independent schools enables those who do not gain a seat in the government's high schools to nevertheless continue their education. Thus, the government schools are the high-quality schools, available only to a few (i.e., those who do best in competitive examinations). The independent schools are, more or less, the schools for the masses.

In certain places, the language of instruction is a vital decision in the education of children. In Quebec, increasing numbers of parents were choosing English-language schools for their children because they believed that this would enhance their children's future prospects in a predominantly English-speaking North American and world economy. For a similar reason, in Belgium, the French language spread into the schools of the traditionally Dutch-speaking province of Flanders. In both cases, parental choice in language was preempted by the government in order to preserve the provincial language. Children of French-speaking parents in Quebec or of Dutch-speaking parents in Flanders are not allowed to attend English- or French-language schools, respectively, even though parental choice is otherwise respected.

THE CATHOLIC CHURCH AND EDUCATIONAL CHOICE

No discussion of parental choice in education would be complete without some reference to the Catholic Church. In almost every part of the world, and for almost two hundred years, Catholics have been resisting state encroachment on the right of parents to choose the kind

The United States is just about the only democracy today that does not support parental choice in education.

of education given their children. The Catholic position was stated by Pope Paul VI in his 1965 encyclical on religious freedom, *Dignitatis Humanae*, "Government, in consequence, must acknowledge the right of parents to make a genuinely free choice of schools and other means of education, and the use of this freedom of choice is not to be made a reason for imposing unjust burdens on parents, whether directly or indirectly."

In Great Britain, during the nineteenth-century debates on education, Irish members of Parliament were most eloquent in their defense of parental choice in education. At the time, Irish members held the balance of power in Parliament, neither the conservative nor liberal factions consistently constituting a majority. Liberals desired to extend education to all children, and the more radical liberals desired to secularize schools. Conservatives desired to continue support of church schools, meaning primarily the schools of the established Anglican Church. What eventually resulted had something for each faction of Parliament: a commitment to universal access to education, with secular government schools to be established where church schools were inadequate, and support of Catholic as well as Anglican schools.

In our generation, a reinvigoration of the Catholic faith has revived support for explicitly Catholic schools. During the attack on private schooling in France, Cardinal Jean-Marie Lustiger, archbishop of Paris, defended church schools, arguing: "The child does not belong to anyone, and certainly not to the state. He is given by God to parents who are not his owners but are responsible for him as a gift entrusted to them. In order for this child to become what he is—free, in the image of a free God—it is necessary that his parents, those primarily responsible, initiate him into freedom!" And Pope John Paul II has intervened in France, as well as in Spain, to defend the right to operate church schools as a matter of religious liberty.

Jewish experience in the matter of independent schooling is in many ways similar to, and intertwined with, Catholic experience. In the Third Republic of France, the attack on church schools was an attack on Jewish as well as Catholic schools. Liberals in France opposed the observance of Shabbot and Jewish dietary law by schools, and the speaking of Yiddish in schools, whether these were religious or secular Jewish day schools, or public schools serving Jewish children.

Even though Jewish schools were, at the time, facilitating the assimilation of Jewish immigrants from eastern Europe, liberals sought to close these schools and to force the integration of Jewish immigrant children into French schools. Although Jews were a small minority in France and no real threat to the regime, liberals—some of whom were themselves Jewish—saw in the toleration of Jewish schools an excuse for Catholics to demand the restoration of their own schools.

A 1982 survey of Jewish schooling in the diaspora (outside Israel) found a remarkable difference in enrollments. In the United States, where there is no financial support of parental choice in education, only 12 percent of Jewish children were found to attend Jewish day schools. But, in other industrial democracies, in which there is support, 34 percent were found to attend Jewish day schools. In Australia, 48 percent of Jewish children attend Jewish day schools, and in South Africa, 53 percent.

IDEOLOGY AND THE 'COMMON SCHOOL'

Americans are rightfully proud of the common heritage of their public schools. In fact, American public schools were never truly common schools—in the north, the Protestant orientation of public schools alienated Catholic immigrants and, in the south, blacks were segregated from whites by forced busing. Nevertheless, American public schools by and large served to develop a sense of community, locally, and to forge a unique national identity.

It is important to realize that this had less to do with these schools being *public* than with these schools being subject to *local democratic control*. Today, as control of U.S. public schools shifts from parents to bureaucrats, their common heritage is at risk of being replaced by an ideological orientation.

The distinction between ideological schools and common schools is best illustrated in the schools of totalitarian countries. In Cuba, in 1961, and in Angola, in 1976, schools were "nationalized," specifically to transform them from culture-preserving institutions serving parents' interests into radical institutions serving the interests of the state.

In nontotalitarian countries, the role of ideology imposed by the government is more subtle. Ever since its revolution, there has been an ongoing struggle over control of France's schools. There has been little pretense of "neutral" education, and secularists have openly coveted the power of the state to use schools to subvert the values of parents and to replace belief in transcendent values with materialism and secular humanism.

In Germany, Otto von Bismarck's Kulturkampf was an attempt to subject his country's Protestant and Catholic schools to the state. In 1872, all schools were put under direct control of the state in Prussia, and members of religious orders were barred from teaching. Resistance by Catholics, especially, preserved a certain degree of autonomy for church schools. Nevertheless, all schools came to be expected to serve the state.

A half-century later, Adolf Hitler was more effective. As a candidate for office, he promised to respect the autonomy of Christian schools and to close only Jewish schools. But upon consolidation of power, Hitler imposed a "Germanized" religion on all schools. "This Reich," he declared, "will hand over its youth to no one."

After Germany's defeat, the occupying powers in the West debated restoring denominational schooling versus establishing U.S.-style secular public schools. Because the church was Germany's only social institution to survive the Nazi era with any honor, the occupying powers allowed denominational schools to be formed, where supported by popular vote. As a result, in some states, Catholic, Protestant, and nondenominational Christian schools are organized within the public sector; in other states, church schools are classified as private schools, but they are supported with public funds by a variety of formulas.

When Ferdinand Marcos declared martial law in the Philippines in 1972, he tightened central control of schools and attempted to use them to advance his nationalistic policies. This included using public schools to promote the Filipino language, even though parents wanted their children to learn English (or Arabic in the southern islands) in order to be more successful in the global economy. Following her country's transition back to democracy, President Corazon Aquino restored parental choice in education by returning control of schools to local governments and supporting private schools.

During the regime of Salvador Allende in Chile, schools were subjected to radical politicalization. In 1973, after Gen. Augusto Pinochet overthrew Allende, he moved to eliminate Marxist influence from schools and to return them to local governmental and parental control; schools were to honor the preferential rights of parents to oversee the education of children. In addition to preparing young people to be productive, schools were to inculcate love for family and country, and respect for the dignity and rights of mankind. When democracy was finally restored to Chile in 1990, the new president, Patricio Aylwin, promised to maintain the commitment to local and parental control of schools.

In Poland, when the communists were overthrown, not only was the curriculum de-Sovietized, but vouchers for private and religious schools equal in value to half the per-pupil cost of public education were instituted. Within a year, two hundred private schools with over ten thousand students were formed.

PARENTAL CHOICE AND SECTARIANISM

In England, commitment to parental choice in education long ago overcame the potential divisiveness of sectarianism. This was in part due to the fact that people with distinct religious views have not been worried that the next turn of politics would undermine their control of their children's education. Also, the strong tendency for denominational education to teach toleration of others in addition to their own distinctive beliefs has helped to create unity.

For Americans, who have little experience with parental choice in education, the received wisdom is to forbid the teaching of religion for fear of offending anyone. But, in a pluralistic society, unity comes from explicitly acknowledging religious beliefs rather than from suppressing the differences.

Soon after its founding, the United States faced the issue of the establishment of religion. While the Constitution prohibited the U.S. Congress from establishing religion, states were not so enjoined until the ratification of the Fourteenth Amendment. Proponents of religious liberty, including Thomas Jefferson of Virginia and Horace Mann of Massachusetts, argued that sectarianism should be excluded from the public schools of their states and that only the most basic, shared beliefs, common to all religions, should be taught.

But whereas Jefferson argued that there should be a "wall of separation" between the state and religion, the Supreme Court in this century has erected, in Justice Hugo Black's words, a "high

---

Today, as control of U.S. public schools shifts from parents to bureaucrats, their common heritage is at risk of being replaced by an ideological orientation.

---

and impregnable" wall of separation. No religious doctrine would be allowed in public schools because—taking Jefferson's and Mann's argument to its illogical conclusion—there are no religious beliefs common to the American public, being as it is Protestant and Catholic, Christian and Jew, Muslim and Hindu, religious, atheist, and agnostic.

Not only is the complete absence of religion in school unsatisfactory to many parents, but a variety of beliefs objectionable to many parents have made their way into public schools, such as sex education that seems to endorse promiscuity. Given the fact that public schools are today prohibited from teaching civil religion, one can only guess what Jefferson or Mann would think about our present predicament. Struggle over the content of public school instruction has been inevitable.

Some historical exceptions to local control of public schools illustrate this struggle. During the nineteenth century, a number of state legislatures in the north, which were dominated by Protestants, intervened in local control of public schools to suppress the Catholic influence in the schools of the large cities that would result from the growing number of Catholic immigrants concentrated there. In certain southern states, racial integration was prohibited even in church-affiliated schools.

In 1890, German-language Lutheran schools became part of the school debate in Illinois. Republicans, supported by Baptists, Congregationists, and Methodists, sought to use the regulatory power of the state to prohibit the teaching of religion and culture through the medium of the German language. Democrats, joined by Catholics, Jews, and Quakers, rose to the defense of Lutheran schools, declaring in their state platform that "the parental right to direct and control the education of the child shall remain forever inviolate." Ultimately, the view of the Democrats prevailed.

In Oregon, in 1922, a citizens' initiative completely outlawing private schools was placed on the ballot by the Ku Klux Klan because they wanted the white Protestant majority to control the schools. By a vote of 115,506 to 103,685, it was approved on election day. By the time the U.S. Supreme Court overturned this law, the *Chicago Tribune* and most other major papers that had supported state interventions into parental and local control of education, as in prohibiting the use of the German language, changed their positions. John Dewey commented that the Oregon law seemed "to strike at the root of American toleration."

In most other democracies, parental choice in education is today part of the core of the common school experience. Constitutional-level protection of equal treatment of all schools chosen by parents commit these countries to true diversity. In America, "diversity" is superficial, referring only to the most obvious differences among people—for example, race and gender. With choice, "diversity" goes to the very soul.

PARENTAL CHOICE AND THE RIGHTS OF PARENTS

Parental choice in education is often predicated on recognition of the rights of parents to raise their children in their own culture and religion. While this sentiment is idealistic and commendable, the reality has been that parental choice has usually been achieved for much more base reasons—it provides a trucelike solution to internecine battles for control of government schools, keeping independent schools afloat is less costly than expanding the public school system, and it increases the quality of education by introducing an element of competition. But, once the commitment to choice in education is made, its idealistic justification becomes undeniable.

That the U.S. Constitution has no explicit reference to the responsible freedom of parents to direct the education of their children reflects the innocence of our nation at its founding. We had not yet eaten of the tree of the knowledge of state education. Until recently, our public schools were locally controlled and financed, and they reflected the values of the community. But, today, they are heavily bureaucratic, the would-be instruments of competing social engineers.

Other democratic countries have constitutional-level protection of the family *because* they went through the essentially religious war we have only recently been dragged into, which is a struggle to determine to whom God has entrusted children: to their parents or to the state. Those who worship the state—whether from the left or from the right—have always envied the authority of parents over their children.

Today, we in the United States are in the midst of the second great campaign to gain parental choice in education. The first great campaign occurred during the 1960s and early '70s, when limited support of parental choice was achieved in several states. New York, Pennsylvania, and Rhode Island passed legislation providing financial support for private schooling, including per capita grants and tax relief.

That first great campaign to gain parental choice was defeated by a series of U.S. Supreme Court decisions that were designed to establish a "high and impregnable" wall of separation between church and state. While the Supreme Court today remains resolutely hostile to teaching religion in public schools, there is some evidence that it may allow public funding of private schools that teach religion, as long as certain safeguards are provided.

The ability of the educational establishment to protect its interest in the status quo should not be understated. Nevertheless, if history is a guide, parental choice in education will be achieved in this country the way it has been achieved elsewhere in the world, which is the same way every civil right has been won: through years, even generations, of struggle, through perseverance in the face of frustration, through consolidation of initially small victories, and ultimately through appealing to people on the basis of justice.

A Question of Choice

Call it "the permanent crisis."

Ever since the launching of the Russian satellite Sputnik in 1957, the American education system has been in a state of permanent revolution. Over the course of two generations, nearly every would-be remedy for the nation's education crisis, from the "new math" to "back to basics," has been tried – most, many times over.

The bad news is that it hasn't worked.

By now, anyone who cares about the future of education is familiar with the falling test scores, high dropout rates, and verbal and mathematical illiteracy that have become the scarlet letters of America's classrooms. Liberals and conservatives alike agree: our schools are failing.

In the course of two generations, nearly every would-be remedy for the nation's education crisis has been tried.

And it isn't for lack of trying. Across the country, governors have raised both taxes and state education budgets, sometimes at the cost of their own jobs. By the end of the 1980s, education spending, adjusted for inflation, was one-third higher than it had been at the beginning, and this after its having climbed by some 40 percent the decade before. In Milwaukee's troubled public schools, to cite just one example, state education funding soared from $129 million in 1980-81 to $310 million in 1991-92 – all to little effect.

What went wrong?

Brookings Institution social scientists John Chubb and Terry Moe, among the most prominent school-reform critics, contend that this patchwork of conventional school reforms simply "does not get to the root of the problem." Their review of 500 schools and 22,000 students, carried out as part of their controversial 1990 study *Politics, Markets, and America's Schools*, suggests that the blame for poor academic performance lies not with teachers and classrooms as much as it does with the calcified institutions – school boards, teachers' unions, and administrative superstructures – that govern them.

THE FAILURE OF SCHOOL REFORM

Education journalist Tom Toch offers a disturbing glimpse into this institutional inertia in his 1991 book *In the Name of Excellence*. Over the 1980s, he points out, 46 states raised their graduation standards for science and mathematics in an effort to boost student learning. Yet in his tour of schools around the country, Mr. Toch found that "tremendous numbers of students are being permitted to satisfy new graduation requirements with a host of insipid courses that are appearing where requirements have been raised."

In Florida, for instance, high school students could fulfill their 4-year science mandate without having to take a single course in biology, chemistry, or physics; in the high school general math sequence, young people studied nothing but arithmetic for 4 years. Mr. Toch observed similar patterns in Bill Clinton's Arkansas, where course-taking requirements are nominally among the nation's most stringent.

Disconcerting as these watered-down curricula might be, other observers contend that miserliness rather than miseducation remains the real problem. "We need to substantially increase our funding for education," insists the Milwaukee-based advocacy group Rethinking Schools. "The bottom line is our schools need more resources." Jonathan Kozol, the fiery education critic and author of last year's *Savage Inequalities*, says that nothing less than a "massive" infusion of money into urban schools, to bring them up to the level of their suburban counterparts will do the job.

If so, inner-city students may be shortchanged for a long time to come. After a spending boom in the 1980s that bought few lasting gains, state officials are increasingly wary of pouring scarce dollars into education. And many states simply can't afford it. As for sizeable increases in Federal funding, the political forecast is simple: forget it.

ENTER SCHOOL CHOICE

It's into this environment of failed reforms and falling resources that the white horse of educational reform – school choice – has come charging. From a virtual footnote in Republican party platforms of the pre-Reagan era, school choice has become the "most prevalent reform idea of the 1990s," in the words of University of Wisconsin political scientist John F. Witt.

The data bear him out. Already, 13 states and scores of local systems boast school choice arrangements of one form or another, with fully 37 states having considered choice legislation in 1992 alone. And the numbers keep on growing:

■ Minnesota, Massachusetts, and Milwaukee – all of which adopted high-profile choice plans in the 1980s – continue to expand coverage under those plans. More recently, statewide choice initiatives have become the centerpiece of school-reform efforts in such bellwether states as California, Colorado, Florida, and Pennsylvania.

■ Following on the widely reported success with public-school choice in East Harlem, New York City Schools Chancellor Joseph A. Fernandez announced in September that, beginning next year, his office would allow parents throughout the New York area to send their children to any public school in the city's five boroughs—in one stroke producing the largest urban choice plan in the country. School superintendents in cities ranging from San Francisco to Washington, D.C., and from Austin, Tex., to East Orange, N.J., have proposed comparable plans for their own schools.

For a generation of young people already struggling with their educational futures, the debate over choice is a great deal more than a passing fad or a political fancy.

■ Not content with current educational offerings, communications entrepreneur Christopher Whittle last year launched his $3.1 billion Edison Project, designed to create from scratch 1,000 "break-the-mold" choice schools by early in the next century. In a separate move, the state of California this September joined Minnesota in authorizing "charter schools" – learning centers formed by parents and teachers independently of the public school system.

Not all the news is good news for the advocates of school choice, of course. Two years ago, voters in Oregon soundly defeated a proposal to grant state tax credits for private and home schooling. This year, Colorado voters rejected a similar plan, while opponents of choice managed to block a statewide choice initiative from even reaching the ballot in California. Nationally, Congress has repeatedly turned back attempts to experiment with choice arrangements involving private schools.

Still, with the tidal wave of activity in the states, it's hard to fault the enthusiasm of Marquette University political scientist Quentin Quade, director of the university's new Center of Parental Freedom in Education, "There's no question that there is a tremendous momentum around the country behind [the choice] movement," he says. "It's just a question of time before the dam breaks."

TURNING SCHOOLS UPSIDE DOWN

To some, this prospect is as unwelcome as the collapse of the Hoover Dam might be to residents of Las Vegas – especially when private schools are involved. Allowing kids to opt out of their neighborhood public school, asserts Chicago School Supt. Ted D. Kimbrough, is "anti-American. It is anti-democratic. It is anti-everything we stand for . . ." It is, in Jonathan Kozol's words, "a triage of the worst kind."

Indeed, about all that contenders in the choice debate can agree upon is the magnitude of change implied by school choice—a change that would literally turn the infrastructure of public education upside down. They acknowledge that, with rare exceptions, the traditional neighborhood-based school system inextricably ties families to their local public school—unless the family pays extra for the privilege of sending their children elsewhere. Choice plans, to a greater or lesser degree, would break this iron link between home and classroom, and thereby set free the "captive audience" that the local public schools have long held.

The resulting competition for students, say proponents of choice, would bring to the education system the diversity and quality that free economic markets have recently brought to computers, communications equipment, and cable television. Opponents charge that school choice would do just that – producing academic C-SPANs for the rich and the educational equivalent of "Wheel of Fortune" reruns for everyone else.

For a generation of young people already struggling with their educational futures, the debate over choice is a great deal more than a passing fad or a political fancy. It is, instead, a roll of some very large dice. School choice might prove to be these youths' first step toward intellectual salvation – or it might plunge the most vulnerable among them even further into ignorance, perhaps beyond rescue. It's hard to imagine a *political* choice more fundamental – or consequential – than that.

Striving for Excellence: The Drive for Quality

There are many things happening in the numerous efforts to improve the quality of schooling in North America. These efforts offer great promise both for the improvement of students' academic achievement levels and for the improvement of the quality of teacher education and licensure. We have defensible reason to believe that this decade will see some major qualitative breakthroughs on both fronts. The Carnegie Corporation National Board for Professional Teaching Standards offers great hope and promise for motivating the nation's teaching force to strive for high levels of professional competence. National Certification of teachers is an option that will give many competent teachers renewed hope for greater professional recognition and status.

We see some fascinating alternatives that could open to us if we have the will to make them happen. In the decade of the 1980s, those reforms that were to lead us to a higher level of qualitative growth in the conduct of schooling tended to be what education historian David Tyack referred to in *The One Best System* (Harvard University Press, 1974) as "structural" reforms. Structural reforms consisted of demands for standardized testing of students and teaching, reorganization of teacher education programs, legalized actions to provide alternative routes into the teaching profession, efforts to recruit more talented people into teaching, and laws to enable greater parental choice as to where their children may attend school. However, these structural reforms cannot, as Tyack noted as early as 1974, in and of themselves, produce higher levels of student achievement. We need to explore a broad range of possible and deeply important aims of schooling requiring a broadly conceived conception of what it means to be a literate person. Also, we need to reconsider what is implied in speaking of the "quality" of the effects of our children having been schooled.

The cognitive goals of schooling cannot be de-emphasized; we cannot "deskill" (Apple, *Education and Power*, 1982) students by denying them the opportunity to learn how to be skilled inquirers, persons able to reason well on their own. When we speak of quality and excellence as aims of education, we must remember that these terms encompass aesthetic and affective as well as cognitive processes. Young people cannot achieve that full range of intellectual capacity to solve problems on their own simply by being obedient and memorizing factual data. How students encounter their teachers in classrooms and how teachers interact with their students are concerns that encompass aesthetic as well as cognitive dimensions. We see reflected in the current literature on this topic critical

reactions to standardized testing as well as vigorous defenses of it. Perhaps, and this is probably the case, there is a need to enforce intellectual (cognitive) standards and to make schools creative places in which to learn, places where students learn to explore and to imagine and to hope.

European nations give more qualitative forms of examinations in the sciences and mathematics and written essay examinations in the humanities and social sciences, as well as oral exit examinations from secondary school by committees of teachers. "Top down" solutions have been traditional to educational problems in the United States, Canada, and the rest of the world. Perhaps this is not avoidable due to the logical necessity of governmental financing of public, tax-supported school systems. However, the top-down pattern of national-state (provincial) policy development for schooling needs to be tempered by even more "bottom-up," grass-roots efforts at improving the quality of schools such as is now under way in many school systems across the North American continent. Imaginative inquiry and assessment strategies need to be developed by teachers working in their classrooms with the support of professional colleagues and parents.

Excellence is the goal: the means to achieve it is what is in dispute. There is a new dimension to the debate over the assessment of the academic achievement of elementary and secondary school students. In addition, there is a continuing struggle of conflicting academic (as well as political) interests over improving the quality of preparation of future teachers.

Few conscientious educators would oppose the idea of excellence in education; as with motherhood and one's nation, some things are held in deep and generalized reverence. The problem in gaining consensus over excellence in education is that excellence is always defined against some standard. Since there are fundamentally opposing standards for determining what constitutes excellent student and teacher performances, it is debatable which standards of assessment should prevail. The current debate over excellence in teacher education clearly demonstrates how conflicting academic values can clash and lead to conflicting programmatic recommendations for educational reform.

The 1980s brought North American educators many important individual and commission reports on bringing qualitative improvement to the educational system at all levels. Some of the reports addressed higher education concerns (particularly relating to general studies requirements and teacher education), but most of them focused on the academic performance problems of elementary and secondary school students. There were literally dozens of such reports. There have been some common themes in these reports. However, there are professional teaching organizations that take exception to what they believe to be too heavily laden hidden business and political agendas underlying some of the public rhetoric on school reform. Educators in teacher education are not in agreement either.

The following are types of questions to be considered when developing policy alternatives for improvement of student achievement. Should schools with different missions be established at the secondary level as they are in Europe? If specialization is considered desirable or necessary at the secondary level, what specific types of specialized secondary schools should be established? Or should there be a common secondary school curriculum for all secondary school students? If existing American and Canadian elementary and secondary schools are not producing desired levels of academic competency, what specific course changes in school curricula are required?

What forms of teacher education and inservice reeducation of teachers are needed? Who pays for any of these programmatic options? Where and how are funds raised or redirected from other budgetary priorities to do these things? Will the "streaming" and "tracking" models of secondary school student placement that exists in Europe be adopted? How can we best assess (evaluate) academic performance? Will North Americans accept structural realignments in the educational system? How will handicapped learners be scheduled in schools? Is there a national commitment to heterogeneous grouping of students and to mainstreaming handicapped students in the United States? Many individual, private, and governmental reform efforts did not address and resolve the reform agenda issues that these questions raise.

Other industrialized nations have championed the need for alternative secondary schools to prepare young people for varied life goals and civic missions. The American dream of the common school translated into a comprehensive high school in the twentieth century. It was to be a high school for all the people with alternative diploma options and its students "tracked" into different programs. What is the next step? What can to be done? To succeed in improving the quality of student achievement, concepts related to our educational goals must be clarified, and political motivation must be separated from the demonstrable realities of student performance. We must clarify our goals. When we do this we get a clearer picture of "what knowledge is of most worth?" Which educational values and priorities are to prevail?

Looking Ahead: Challenge Questions

Identify some of the different points of view on achieving excellence in education. What value conflicts can be defined?

Do teachers see educational reform in the same light as governmental, philanthropic, or corporate-based school reform groups? On what matters would they agree? On what matters might they disagree?

What can we learn from other nations regarding "excellence" in education?

What are the minimum academic standards that all high school graduates should meet?

How will the National Board for Professional Teaching Standards improve the quality of the teaching force in the United States?

What can we learn from the experience of other nations in improving the academic achievement levels of students?

Launching a Revolution in Standards and Assessments

In the absence of national standards, we have evolved a haphazard, accidental, disconnected national curriculum based on mass-market textbooks and standardized, multiple-choice tests, Ms. Ravitch maintains.

DIANE RAVITCH

DIANE RAVITCH is a visiting fellow at the Brookings Institution, Washington, D.C.

Illustration by Mario Noche

DURING the brief period that Lamar Alexander was U.S. secretary of education, his department began several initiatives that altered the federal role in education. Before Alexander, the Department of Education was essentially a dispenser of formula grant monies, and the secretary was the nation's scold. During Alexander's tenure, the department became an advocate for educational *perestroika*, providing a platform for reformers, teachers, principals, community leaders, and anyone else who was willing to try new ways to improve schools and communities.

Lamar Alexander holds a rather paradoxical view of the federal role in education. On the one hand, he is an activist and a strategic planner, and when he was secretary he lent his influence to a wide

 From *Phi Delta Kappan*, June 1993, pp. 767-772. Reprinted with permission of *Phi Delta Kappan* and the author.

spectrum of efforts to shake up lethargic bureaucracies and to demonstrate that all children could reach high levels of learning. But on the other hand, he strongly believes that the federal government ought not to tell everyone else what to do; he is instinctively skeptical of those who want to use the federal government to impose their ideas on others.

I first met Lamar Alexander and David Kearns early in 1991 when they invited me to join them at the department. At first, I was not interested; I had never wanted to work in government, and I was in the middle of writing a book. But I changed my mind when Alexander said that I would have the lead in developing new national standards and assessments. The offer was one I could not refuse, knowing as I did that any federal activity in these areas would be historic and would have to be managed with extreme sensitivity to the principles of federalism.

Alexander explained to me that the purpose of everything he intended to do was to support the national education goals. The goals, forged in a bipartisan pact between the President and the nation's 50 governors, provided a unique sense of direction for American education. They also supplied the rationale for the America 2000 plan that Alexander and Kearns designed. America 2000 was not a federal program but a strategy to help the nation reach the national education goals.

The America 2000 plan had three fundamental objectives: 1) to encourage every community to adopt the national goals, develop its own local strategy, and prepare an annual community report card on its progress toward the goals; 2) to stimulate the creation of thousands of "break-the-mold schools" that would approach education in totally new ways to meet the needs of today's children and families; and 3) to develop voluntary "world-class" standards and American Achievement Tests.

Standards and assessments were critical because they would allow teachers, students, parents, and communities to determine whether they were aiming high enough and whether they were making progress. Without standards and assessments, the "new American schools" and the community-based reformers would not know whether their innovative efforts were making a difference.

It was clear to us that the nation could not make progress toward the goals unless there were high national standards and valid, reliable individual student assessments. Goals 3 and 4 specifically required new standards and assessments. As a nation, we were not likely to be "first in the world in math and science" unless we set standards that were at least as high as those in other leading industrialized nations and unless we had the means to find out whether our students measured up to those standards. Nor would we know whether students could "demonstrate mastery of challenging subject matter" in core subjects unless we were able to agree on standards for those subjects and on assessments that measured mastery.

We also knew from numerous surveys on education that most Americans, and especially parents, were misinformed and self-satisfied. They thought that there was a problem in the nation's schools, but they believed that their own schools were fine. Perhaps their own schools *were* fine, but they had no objective measures by which to reach that judgment. As Harold Stevenson has found in his studies of American and Asian parents, the complacency of American parents acts as an obstacle to education reform.

AT THE outset it was not clear whether there was an appropriate federal role in setting standards or developing national examinations. But it was very clear that these are subjects on which there is a great deal of disagreement among educators.

In 1991, shortly after taking office, Alexander persuaded Congress to establish the National Council on Educational Standards and Testing (NCEST), a 32-member bipartisan body, to consider whether and how to develop new standards and tests. Co-chaired by the leaders of the National Education Goals Panel, Gov. Carroll Campbell of South Carolina and Gov. Roy Romer of Colorado, NCEST was broadly representative of teachers, administrators, civic leaders, political leaders, policy makers, and people in higher education.

NCEST issued its report early in 1992, recommending the establishment of voluntary national standards in key subject areas and a national system of achievement tests. The panel opposed the development of a single national examination, suggesting instead that new assessments could be developed by individual states or groups of states working together. However these new assessments were created, they were to be based on common national standards.

Throughout the hearings held by NCEST, the work of the National Council of Teachers of Mathematics (NCTM) served as a model of the power of national standards to drive education reform in a coherent manner, while involving a broad array of participants. Several years earlier, the nation's math teachers had surveyed their field and decided that it was in dire need of change after the failure of the New Math and the ascendancy of the back-to-basics movement. Eager to raise students' expectations and achievement and to promote problem-solving activities as the core of teaching and learning mathematics, the NCTM sponsored the development of national standards. The process of reaching consensus eventually involved thousands of math teachers, who collaborated to determine what students should know and be able to do in mathematics.

Published in 1989, the NCTM standards quickly became a dynamic force in changing staff development, instructional practices, teacher education, textbooks, technology, and assessment. Every new commercial mathematics textbook or instructional program that entered the market since 1989 has claimed to incorporate the NCTM standards. According to the NCTM, 30% to 40% of the nation's mathematics teachers were using the new standards by 1992. Even the federally sponsored National Assessment of Educational Progress (NAEP) began to change in response to the NCTM standards.

The powerful advance of the NCTM standards demonstrated that standards could serve as both the starting point and the goal of education reform. Suddenly it seemed crystal clear that the reform of education begins with a consensus about what children should learn, and every other part of the system should work in concert to support that result. Textbooks should be based on a solid consensus about what children should learn — not on checklists prepared by textbook-adoption states. Staff development should help teachers understand and teach the new standards. Teacher education should prepare new teachers to teach what children should learn. Tests should measure what is worth learning, not just what is easy to measure. And the very process of developing standards is a valuable exercise that builds consensus within a given field by promoting discussion about what is most worth learning.

But what was to be the federal role in the growing movement for standards? This was not yet determined. As a historian of education, I knew that there had long been antagonism toward federal involvement in education because of widespread fear that a federal Department of Education might be too powerful and might try to usurp local control. I knew that any federal role in the creation of standards and assessments had to be shaped very thoughtfully, with great respect for the legitimate concerns of states and localities.

The principle of *federalism* does not mean the supremacy of the federal government, but rather a careful balancing of the interests of the different levels of government. In this case it meant steering a course between two extremes: the familiar pattern of complete local control — in which there are no standards or wildly different standards from district to district — and the imposition of a federal one-size-fits-all program. These are the Scylla and Charybdis of standards, both to be avoided.

I must confess that at the outset we knew what we wanted to accomplish but did not know how we would get there. We wanted to begin the process of setting national standards, but we did not want the federal government to have the power to impose standards on unwilling states and localities; we wanted to encourage the development of a national testing system, but we knew that the U.S. Department of Education did not have the authority to do this on its own. We quickly realized that the department must play a leadership role in helping the public understand the importance of a strong national system of standards and assessments.

As we were trying to figure out our strategy, a chance conversation in the summer of 1991 between Lamar Alexander and Frank Press of the National Academy of Sciences opened a new vista. They talked about how standards should be developed and who should do it. Shortly afterward, with the secretary's encouragement, the academy submitted a proposal to develop national standards in the sciences. It was generally recognized that the National Academy of Sciences was uniquely situated to convene the full complement of science organizations and to develop a consensus around what children should know and be able to do in the sciences. In September 1991 the department made a grant to the academy and launched the first of the federally funded standard-setting projects.

The science standards project defined the procedures and roles for subsequent efforts. The federal government would give funds to applicants who agreed to create a broad and inclusive process of arriving at consensus. The organizations involved in this process should be led by and include teachers, scholars, and other members of the public. The project would agree to examine the standards used in other nations and in leading states. The standards produced by these projects would be voluntary, not mandatory.

From the beginning, the department stressed the importance of both excellence and equity as outcomes for the standards projects. The object was not to create higher hurdles for students, but to demystify what was to be learned and to help all students reach higher levels of learning.

The National Center for History in the Schools submitted a proposal to develop national standards in history and won an award from the Department of Education in December 1991. The director of the center, Charlotte Crabtree, had gained the endorsement of every organization that was involved in the fields of history and social studies. In addition, the National Endowment for the Humanities agreed to join in providing financial support for the project.

As I have already noted, NCEST published its report, titled *Raising Standards in American Education*, in January 1992. The release of the report put the issues of standards and assessments in the public spotlight. NCEST recommended the development of high standards that were national, not federal (i.e., not controlled by the federal government); voluntary, not mandatory; and dynamic, not static. The standards should be developed through a participatory process, and they should be used to provide focus and direction, not to create a national curriculum. NCEST also recommended a national testing system that was fair and equitable, in which different tests would be linked to common standards.

I N THE YEAR following the release of the NCEST report, the Department of Education moved forward in a deliberate fashion to implement the council's recommendations. In a 12-month period, the department launched national standards projects in the arts, civics, geography, English, and foreign languages. (Each of these projects also received funding from the National Endowment for the Humanities.)

Five years before, even two years before, almost no one had spoken seriously about the possibility of national standards or a national testing system for individual students. Now both prospects were part of the national debate.

But while it was crucial to establish national standards, we saw that as only the first step in a process that would depend on the active participation of the states. We concluded that the best way to preserve the principle of federalism was to encourage states to develop their own K-12 curriculum frameworks *at the same time that the national standards were under development*. Some people thought that this was an odd approach and wondered why we did not insist on a linear progression: first national standards, then state curriculum frameworks based on the national standards.

The reason we rejected the linear approach was that we felt there were as many smart people in the states as there were at the national level (indeed, they were often the very same people). We wanted to encourage a synergy between the national projects and the creation of state curriculum frameworks, and this synergy was likeliest to occur if both were going on at the same time. Indeed, the "state systemic reform" awards from the National Science Foundation to nearly two dozen states meant that many of those states were already working on their curriculum frameworks in mathematics and science.

What is a state curriculum framework? It is a declaration of the state's standards for its children — a description of what it expects children to know and be able to do. State frameworks are usually more detailed than statements of national standards, and they usually serve as the basis for textbook adoptions or state assessments. A state curriculum framework should also be a strategic plan for education, starting with what children should know and using that as the basis for reforming teacher education, teacher certification, staff development, textbooks, assessments, and so on. (California, under Bill Honig's leadership, was the first state to develop this strategy of starting with the curriculum framework as a master plan for systemic reform.)

So, even as we were making awards to support national consensus projects, we launched competitions to fund the development of state curriculum frameworks in the same subject areas as those for which national standards were being established. To qualify for funding, the states had to demonstrate how they intended to use their own curriculum frameworks as the basis for reforming teacher education, teacher certification, staff development, and assessment.

Our strategy, you see, was not to put the federal government in the driver's seat, but to use federal funds to encourage the states to set their *own* standards and to use them to reform the other key parts of their own education systems. I never tired of reminding state officials that *they* controlled the marketplace in education. They had the power to shape teacher education by saying that they would not hire people who didn't know what the children were supposed to learn. They could shape teacher certification by saying that new teachers would be certified *only* if they knew what they were expected to teach. They could use staff development to help teachers learn what they needed to know to meet the state's own goals, and they could reform assessment by basing it on their own determination of what children needed to know and be able to do.

We also believed that the national standards would be widely accepted only if they were truly representative of the best thinking in the field and only if they were developed in a process that was open and broadly inclusive. If they succeeded in providing a vision for what should happen in the best of circumstances, then they could be incorporated as part of federal programs, such as Chapter 1 or the Dwight D. Eisenhower Mathematics and Science Programs.

After science and history, the next area funded was the arts. The arts were not mentioned in the national education goals — a source of considerable annoyance to arts educators. Because he believes that the arts should be part of everyone's education, Alexander decided that the subjects that are specifically named in the national goals (mathematics, science, history, geography, and English) are given as examples and are not meant to exclude other subjects. In June 1992 the Department of Education funded a standards proposal by the Music Educators National Conference, which joined in collaboration with the American Alliance for Theatre and Education, the National Art Education Association, and the National Dance Association.

On 1 July 1992 a press conference was held at the Supreme Court to announce the department's award to the Center for Civic Education to develop national standards in civics — another area not specifically mentioned in the goals. The center, headed by Charles Quigley, had contacts in every state and had assembled a broad umbrella coalition of organizations committed to civic education.

Three weeks later, at the National Geographic Society's headquarters, the department announced an award for a national standards project in geography. The award went to the National Council of Geographic Education, which represented a consortium of the Association of American Geographers, the National Geographic Society, and the American Geographical Society.

Then in September 1992 the department made an award to the Center for the Study of Reading (University of Illinois at Champaign), together with the National Council of Teachers of English and the International Reading Association, to create English standards.

Finally, in January 1993 an award was made to develop national standards in the teaching of foreign languages. The award went to the American Council of Teachers of Foreign Languages, in conjunction with organizations of teachers of German, Portuguese, and Spanish.

The law establishing the Department of Education states that the department shall not supervise, control, or direct the curriculum of the schools (this prohibition reflects the decades-old fear of a federal "takeover" of the schools). In funding the standards projects, the department made clear that its role was to provide the money and then to get out of the way. Although a member of the department's staff monitors the progress of each project, the department does not attempt to supervise, control, direct, or influence the deliberations of the projects in any way.

Each of the projects received funding to set high national standards and to lead a broadly inclusive participatory process. The department also provided a list of negatives — a description of what the projects are *not* to be. The projects are *not* to create standards for the elite, but to create them for *all* children. The projects are *not* to create a national curriculum, but to describe what children should know and be able to do in a particular field. Also, the projects are *not* to end the pedagogical disputes within each field; rather, the standards should leave to the wit and ingenuity of teachers decisions about *how* to teach (although there will probably be some emphases that blend the *what* and the *how*, such as problem-solving activities).

The standard-setting projects are well under way, and most expect to have a finished draft of national standards available by 1994-95. In addition, the work of creating state curriculum frameworks is moving steadily forward. My office sought funding from Congress to sponsor large competitions for state curriculum frameworks, but the money was not forthcoming. We were able to go forward on a limited basis through the Eisenhower National Program, which has made money available in math and science. Shortly before leaving office, I approved a competition for state frameworks in the other subject areas, to be supported by discretionary funds (which are quite limited).

My own view is that, in a time of fiscal stringency at all levels, it is a federal responsibility to help states reform their own standards in order to preserve federalism and promote both excellence and equity.

THE ISSUE of assessment has been far more complex than that of national standards. Until this time, the only meaningful federal role in assessment has been the department's sponsorship of the National Assessment of Educational Progress, which tests large national samples, not individual students. NCEST recommended tests for individual students, leaving the matter largely to the states or groups of states to manage.

This recommendation comes at a time of massive rethinking about testing. During the past several years, there has been much discussion about how to deemphasize the current reliance on tests that are standardized, machine scorable, and multiple choice. Many states, local districts, and individual schools are experimenting with ways to gauge student "performance" by "authentic assessment." At the leading edge of this reform have been the work and advocacy of Lauren Resnick and Marc Tucker of the New Standards Project, which is affiliated with a number of states and school districts.

Although the Alexander team had come

into office calling for American Achievement Tests (and the Phi Delta Kappa/Gallup Poll shows that a majority of the American public favors a national examination), there was no way to make such tests happen. There was no money in the department's budget to fund a national testing system, and Congress repeatedly made plain its strong hostility to any federal involvement in testing. The only visible exception was Sen. Claiborne Pell (D-R.I.), who has long been an advocate of a national academic achievement test. The House Committee on Education and Labor passed a flat prohibition against the department's support for assessment development (as well as a prohibition against national standards and even against new research on assessment).

There was, we thought, a perfectly reasonable and appropriate way for the department to support the improvement of assessment, and that was to offer funds competitively to states that were building new student assessments based on higher standards. We asked Congress for money to help states that were taking the lead in assessment reform, and again we were turned down.

We also thought that it was an appropriate federal role to support new research and development efforts related to assessment. Despite the fact that the department maintains a research center on assessment at the University of California at Los Angeles, we believed that there was a need for much more investment in research and development on this complex issue. More research was needed to understand how to administer and score performance assessments. Certainly new research was needed to figure out how to equate, link, and calibrate different assessments — one of NCEST's key recommendations. And more research was needed to understand issues of test fairness.

Unfortunately, though we asked for "only" $5 million for new research on assessment (one senator told me not to waste his time with such small requests), Congress denied those funds also.

Obviously, we were not able to produce American Achievement Tests during our brief tenure in office; given the lack of consensus among educators as well as the outright opposition in Congress, that is not surprising. Nonetheless, I would say that we managed to change the national discussion and to put onto the table questions that no one was raising before we got there. Whenever possible, we lent moral support (and, when funds were available, financial backing) to those who were trying to develop new kinds of assessment. We gave full support to the introduction of performance items on the NAEP.

The point is that standards will be meaningless if students continue to be tested without regard to them. Unless current tests change, the standards will wither and die. Teachers know that they will be judged by test results, and they will continue to teach to the tests by which they are judged. That is why we as an Administration sided with such people as Lauren Resnick and the leaders of the NCTM, who contend that the tests must test knowledge and skills that are meaningful to students. The tests should be based on what children learn in class, and what they learn in class should be worth knowing and doing and using.

STANDARDS ARE the starting point of education reform. You can't design an assessment unless you have agreement about what children should learn. In the absence of national standards, we have evolved a haphazard, accidental, disconnected national curriculum based on mass-market textbooks and standardized, multiple-choice tests.

Education reform must begin with broad agreement on what children should learn. Learning, after all, is the heart and soul of education. When there is no agreement regarding what students should learn, then each part of the education system pursues different, sometimes contradictory, goals. As a result, our education system is riddled with inequity, incoherence, and inefficiency.

In the summer of 1991 the department sponsored a meeting with education ministers from 15 Asian Pacific countries.

The subject of the meeting was standards for the 21st century. The United States was one of the few participants that had not established national standards. When we asked the various ministers why their society had set national standards, they all gave the same dual answer: to promote equality of opportunity and to promote high achievement. As they explained it, without explicit standards some schools would set high standards and others would not (and without assessments, no one would know the difference). Moreover, explicit standards enabled students to judge their performance against clear goals, thus raising everyone's expectations.

One of the joys of the federal position that I held for 18 months was that I was able to visit many school districts. Occasionally, I saw truly exciting programs in which schools were teaching all children to reach for very high standards. For example, at the Mission High School in San Francisco I witnessed the Interactive Mathematics Project, which engages inner-city youngsters in high-level problem solving that requires them to use algebra and geometry. At Portland Middle School in Portland, Michigan, I saw a mathematics program transformed by the hard work of the staff, and I saw children who understood what they were doing in math class and why.

I know full well that standards are not a panacea. I understand that there are children who are growing up in terrible situations, and no academic program alone will rescue them. I realize that there are school districts that have sustained devastating budget cuts. For dysfunctional families, social programs are needed. For financially strapped districts, more resources are needed. But if we are to attend to the learning that goes on in schools and if we are to take that responsibility seriously, then we must work to make national standards a reality. We must work together so that every state establishes curriculum frameworks that reflect the best thinking in the field, and we must continue to explore ways to improve student assessments.

I will always be grateful for the opportunity to have been part of these historic changes in American education.

How the National Board Builds Professionalism

Great teaching must be recognized not by putting one teacher on a pedestal but by creating a platform for thousands, says the National Board for Professional Teaching Standards.

Mary-Dean Barringer

Mary-Dean Barringer is Director Emeritus of the National Board for Professional Teaching Standards, 300 River Place, Suite 3600, Detroit, MI 48207.

When Rita Duarte Herrera, a middle school teacher from San Jose, California, was asked what National Board Certification might offer the professional teacher, she told how she had asked an accountant, an environmental lawyer, a minister, and several teachers the question, "What does it mean to be a professional?" The first three individuals had strikingly similar responses. The accountant, lawyer, and minister spoke of possessing special knowledge to perform their work, of holding themselves accountable to a particular standard of practice, of responsibility to their "clients."

Only when Herrera queried her fellow educators did the responses vary: "Don't talk to me about professionalism," the teachers said. "Professional? I don't even have a telephone or a computer at work. Professional? I can't get textbooks for my students."[1]

Herrera dramatically revealed to her audience of teachers and other education leaders what the National Board for Professional Teaching Standards (NBPTS) has

heard repeatedly across the country in similar state forums: the language of professionalism is still unfamiliar to many teachers. While no less devoted to their clients' welfare or to delivering their best services in the classroom, teachers more often speak of professionalism in terms of environmental conditions than of standards and dispositions.

Since 1987, the National Board has worked to create policies, processes, and products that teachers can use to build their profession. The initial policies that the 63-member board of directors (a majority of whom are practicing teachers) established have shaped the framework of certificates, the standards-setting process, the development of assessment exercises, and the proposed certification process.[2] As thousands of teachers across the country have joined the National Board in its developmental work, the conversation about professional teaching in faculty rooms is changing.[3]

Defining Standards of Excellence

In 1989, in a bold departure from current licensing language, the National Board devised a certification process that recognizes teachers for the expertise that *they* say matters: a developmental perspective on the range of students they teach and

the knowledge they impart to those particular students. The National Board will not award a professional distinction for "9th grade" or "resource room" knowledge, but will honor teachers who demonstrate what they know about students in "early childhood" or "adolescence through young adulthood."

Professional certification will also indicate a teacher's knowledge specialty, such as mathematics, art, or vocational education. Recognizing that many teachers call upon multiple subjects to organize instruction, the National Board is also developing a "generalist" certificate. Because the hallmark of *all* accomplished teaching is the professional judgment teachers use on behalf of children, the certificate framework acknowledges the kinds of expertise teachers draw upon to make those sound decisions.

The heartbeat of the National Board is a vision of excellence in teaching shaped by five core propositions (see fig. 1). "What Teachers Should Know and Be Able to Do" combines the wisdom of practice of outstanding teachers with consensus among the broader education community.[4] While holding to the premise that all excellent teaching encompasses certain generic qualities, the National Board recognizes that the age of students, the subject(s), and the context of teaching require that standards for the certificates reflect this specialization.

For each certificate area, a teacher-majority committee is working to set standards of teaching excellence that:

■ highlight critical aspects of teacher practice while emphasizing the holistic nature of teaching;

■ describe how the standard comes to life in different settings;

■ identify the knowledge, skills, and dispositions that support a teacher's performance on the standard at a high level;

■ show how a teacher's professional judgment is reflected in observable actions;

■ reflect the NBPTS policy on "What Teachers Should Know and Be Able to Do."

To date, committees have been working to set the standards for "what teachers should know and be able to do" in 16 certificate areas. The initial set of documents for three fields will be available this spring. By 1995, NBPTS expects to have standards committees at work in approximately 30 certificate areas.

Measuring Teaching Excellence

The policies and standards established by the National Board have introduced a new way for teachers to talk about what they love most about their work: teaching. Teachers have shifted the discourse from minimal teaching competencies, which have dominated both faculty and policy talk, to shape the public perception of teaching as a profession of complexity. The certification standards establish teaching as both intellectual and technical work, as both art and science. Most important, they illuminate highly accomplished teaching.

If the National Board has been passionate about removing the mystery of what constitutes great teaching, it has been equally persistent in creating a process where any teacher in America can seek recognition for achievement. Many of the teachers who serve on the NBPTS board of directors hold the distinction of having been a "teacher of the year," in some capacity. They are most persuasive in arguing that identifying great teachers must not result in a pedestal for one but a platform for thousands. The selection process must be perceived by the profession and the public as fair, credible, and capable of identifying aspects of teaching most worth honoring. In other words, the process must have great fidelity to what teachers actually do with students as they learn together.

Assessment Development Laboratory contractors have completed the prototype exercises for two certificates. In doing so, they were guided by the National Board's "Golden Apple" rule of assessment development, which states that methods must be administratively feasible, professionally credible, publicly acceptable, legally defensible, and economically affordable. The University of Pittsburgh, with the Connecticut Department of Education, developed the exercises for the Early Adolescence/English Language Arts (EA/ELA) certificate. The University of Georgia produced the assessments for the Early Adolescence/Generalist (EA/Generalist) certificate. Both assessment packages have undergone initial field-testing with teachers across the country. Each package has two modules: the school site and the assessment center. (See fig. 2 for EA/ELA Draft Standards Statements.)

The School Site Module

The work that a teacher completes for National Board Certification at the local site is organized into a portfolio. The exact exercises in each package (EA/ELA and EA/Generalist) vary but are organized around three elements in the portfolio: documentation, student work, and instruction.

The documentation segment allows

> The nature of the National Board's certification process does not lend itself to cramming or studying course guidebooks.

teachers to demonstrate how they analyze, evaluate, and modify their practice and act as advisor and advocate for students. Teachers also submit physical evidence of collaboration with colleagues, families, and other community members on instructional and school activities that benefit their students. Artifacts have included letters, transcripts of interviews, logs and diaries, minutes of meetings, newspaper articles, memos, student

---

Figure 1

What Teachers Should Know and Be Able to Do

1. Teachers are committed to students and their learning.

2. Teachers know the subjects they teach and how to teach those subjects to students.

3. Teachers are responsible for managing and monitoring student learning.

4. Teachers think systematically about their practice and learn from experience.

5. Teachers are members of learning communities.

Source: Core propositions from *Toward High and Rigorous Standards for the Teaching Profession: Initial Policies and Perspectives of the National Board for Professional Teaching Standards*, 2nd ed.

projects, instructional units, photographs, and products of working committees.[5]

Student work has a prominent place in the school site module. Teachers field-testing the EA/ELA assessment pilot were asked to assemble writing samples from two students—representative of the diversity in their classroom, over a three- to four-month period—with reflective commentaries about the samples. The student work for the EA/Generalist portfolio spanned six weeks and was a sampling of the products generated from the unit of instruction profiled on the teacher's videotaped classroom instruction.

Actual teaching was documented through videotape in both portfolios. For the EA/Generalist portfolio, the teacher had to submit an instructional unit supplemented by video clips and a commentary of the planned unit enacted in practice. The student work included must correspond to activities in the instructional unit. For the EA/ELA portfolio, candidates prepared two clips. One was a commentary and video from a three- to six-week unit of instruction of the teacher's choice. The other was a video of the teacher conducting a "post-reading interpretative discussion exercise." This second clip measured the teacher's skill at engaging students in language learning, reading, and fostering discourse.

Based on the early field-testing, the National Board projects that teachers will work on the school site portfolio over a period of six months during the school year. Preliminary estimates indicate that they spent approximately 50 hours compiling the materials for this part of the assessment process. Between the time they receive the instructions and the deadline for submitting the portfolios to the National Board for review, teachers have flexibility to choose when to complete the work.

The Assessment Center Exercises

Because teaching is performance-based and multifaceted, assessing excellence requires a series of exercises that capture the richness and complexity of the work. The second element of the assessment package for National Board Certification, which occurs away from the classroom, consists of pedagogical content knowledge examinations and various simulations.

Candidates seeking EA/ELA certification demonstrated their content knowledge in a variety of exercises during the field test. They were asked to write essays in response to prompts focusing on four broad domains in English language arts: composition, response to literature, language and language development, and issues that surround the teaching of English language arts to early adolescents. Candidates were also asked to read and write about professional articles that presented different sides of an issue or texts that they might encounter in their classrooms.

The participants in the EA/Generalist field test demonstrated their knowledge by creating an interdisciplinary unit of instruction that drew on content across the curriculum domains (mathematics, science, social studies/history, and English language arts). They were also asked to respond to pedagogical issues evident in student work samples they received at the assessment center.

Various simulations used during the field test mirrored the work that teachers perform in their classrooms. Candidates demonstrated how they met the National Board's standards by designing instructional units or individual lessons, evaluating samples of student work, and critiquing videos of another teacher's practice. Teachers particularly enjoyed exercises that involved collegial activity. Before arriving at the assessment center, the EA/ELA candidates were required to read eight novels. At the center, they met in small groups to discuss a particular curricular issue related to the assigned readings.

The EA/Generalist candidates praised the parent-teacher conference simulation in which a trained teacher assessor played the scripted part of "Heather's" parent. As one teacher later remarked, "I knew Heather when I read the report. I've taught Heather, and, boy, was I expecting Heather's mother!"[6] Role-playing allowed candidates to display their understanding of early adolescent intellectual, physical, social, and emotional development, as well as their ability to work as a member of a learning community.

Unlike many tests that teachers have come to either dread or dismiss, the certification exercises are "user-friendly." For each exercise, teachers receive a question-and-answer guide that explains the task, highlights the standards being measured, stipulates what the teacher assessors will look for in their performance, and suggests how to prepare for the exercise.

The nature of the National Board's certification process does not lend itself to cramming or studying course guidebooks. It does lend itself to coaching and collegial support. Some teachers involved in the field-testing formed study groups or "video clubs" to evaluate the videotapes of teaching against the draft standards. Portfolio work was also done together, and at the assessment center simulations involved collegial interaction.

Teachers who participated in field-testing the assessment packages all felt that the exercises captured what they do as teachers. Calling the experience a profound professional development activity, they also commented on the amount of work and effort the assessment process required and the demanding nature of the exercises. Since the National Board's vision of teaching excellence attempts to mirror professional teaching, it should not surprise anyone that the process is rigorous and demanding.

New Norms of Teaching Practice

The National Board for Professional Teaching Standards has set in motion a national conversation about teaching focused on advanced knowledge, skills, and habits of the mind.[7] As the plan unfolds, the tools of professional practice—standards of excellence and voluntary accountability to those standards—will be laid before America's teachers. Many teachers will welcome these tools as a means to build their profession, but their foundational work will require the support of the broader community if the full promise of National Board Certification is to be realized.

What will it mean to be a professional teacher? With the launch of the first certificate areas in 1994-95, teachers will begin to think about what becoming a National Board-certified teacher means for them. At the 1992 NBPTS National Forum, Rae Ellen McKee (1991 National Teacher of the Year) gave a heartfelt answer to this question:

> It will throw out a lifeline of incentives to teachers across America. It will save the many among them who know in their hearts what it means to be a professional educator—but who have lost the faith to try. It will bring deserved recognition to those who have plowed on in the name of excellence, knowing that what they do is the most important job in society. It will define teaching as the epitome of society's concept of a professional: one who deals with the most human problems. Most important, it will set into motion the cogs of more effective instruction— and that's the only school reform that will truly matter.[8]

Teachers who embrace National Board Certification will help institutionalize a vision of teaching excellence that currently goes unrecognized in our nation's schools. If the maxim is true that we assess what we value, then new norms of teaching practice will come forward. We will support collegiality among teachers because we will see that broadening teacher expertise enriches instruction for students. We will value giving teachers greater responsibility for the induction of novices because we will see how the wisdom of expert practitioners strengthens the work of beginning teachers. And we will make time for teacher reflection because we will see how learning benefits when teachers have time to make reflective commentaries and narrative assessments on students' work.

These instances of practice, artfully captured in the assessment process,

---

Figure 2

A Draft of the Standards for Language Arts Teachers (Early Adolescence)

1. Knowledge of Students—Teachers systematically acquire a sense of their students as individual language learners.

2. Curricular Choices—Teachers set attainable and worthwhile learning goals for students while extending to students an increasing measure of control over how those goals are pushed.

3. Engagement—Teachers elicit a concerted effort in language learning from each of their students.

4. Classroom Environment—Teachers create a caring, inclusive, and challenging classroom environment in which students actively learn.

5. Instructional Resources—Teachers select, adapt, and create curricular resources that support active student exploration of literature and language processes.

6. Reading—Teachers engage their students in reading, responding, interpretation, and thinking deeply about literature and other texts.

7. Discourse—Teachers foster thoughtful classroom discourse that provides opportunities for students to listen and speak in many ways and for many purposes.

8. Language Study—Teachers strengthen student sensitivity to a proficiency in the appropriate uses of language.

9. Integrated Instruction—Teachers integrate reading, writing, speaking, and listening opportunities in the creation and interpretation of meaningful texts.

10. Assessment—Teachers use a range of formal and informal assessment methods to monitor student progress, encourage student self-assessment, plan instruction, and report to various audiences.

11. Self-Reflection—Teachers constantly analyze and strengthen the effectiveness and quality of their teaching.

12. Professional Community—Teachers contribute to the improvement of instructional programs, advancement of knowledge, and practice of colleagues in the field.

13. Parent Outreach—Teachers work with families to serve the best interests of their children.

---

will become the norms. Most important, we will realize the relation between teaching excellence and lifelong learning, and we will begin to create professional development based on standards of excellence.

---

[1]Comments made by Rita Duarte Herrera, October 9, 1992, at the NBPTS California Regional Forum in San Diego.

[2]Policies are elaborated in the document *Toward High and Rigorous Standards: Initial Policies of the National Board for Professional Teaching Standards*, (1991), 3rd ed.

[3]Teachers are involved in the development of the NBPTS certification system as chairs and members of standards committees; members of advisory boards and merit review panels; assessment development laboratory contractors; participants in field-testing; and reviewers of draft standards.

[4]This statement can be found in Chapter 2 of *Toward High and Rigorous Standards*.

[5]These examples are from the materials presented by the University of Georgia Performance Assessment Laboratory to the NBPTS Assessment Methods and Processes Working Group on June 19, 1992.

[6]Videodocumentation on the evaluation of the assessment center exercises for the University of Georgia was conducted in August 1992 at the University of Southern Florida.

[7]Complementing its core functions regarding certification and assessment, the National Board plans to act on three reform issues related to the improvement of teaching and student learning: creating a more effective environment for teaching and learning in schools, increasing the supply of high-quality entrants into the profession (with a special emphasis on minorities), and strengthening teacher education and continuing professional development.

[8]Remarks made by Rae Ellen McKee, June 21, 1992, at the NBPTS National Forum in Las Vegas, Nevada.

Magnet Schools and Issues of Education Quality

ROLF K. BLANK and DOUGLAS A. ARCHBALD

Rolf K. Blank is director of indicators programs, State Education Assessment Center, Council of Chief State School Officers, Washington, D.C. Douglas A. Archbald is an assistant professor in the Department of Educational Development, University of Delaware, Newark.

Over the last fifteen years, magnet schools have become a primary method of innovation and reorganization in urban education. Education decision-makers at the local, state, and national levels have recognized that magnet schools, which are organized to enroll students through voluntary selection of a distinctive theme or specialty, have potential for addressing difficult policy issues of school desegregation, education quality, and choice.

Magnet schools grew out of changes in desegregation policy in the 1970s. Magnet schools could offer an alternative to mandatory assignment, and they provided incentives aimed at decreasing "white flight." Growth of magnet schools has been rapid. In the early 1970s there were programs in a handful of districts, in 1982 about one-third of large urban districts had magnet schools, and today, by the best estimates, almost all urban districts and many suburban districts have magnet schools. In the 1980s, federal funds for urban district programs spurred the development and expansion of magnet schools. Currently, federal funding to magnet schools is $110 million per year for sixty-four school districts.

Even considering the creation of magnet schools as a desegregation strategy, and the growth through federal support, the development of magnet schools in American education must also be attributed to the concerns of education decision-makers with improving the quality of education in our schools. Magnet schools have been shown to generate renewed motivation for education among students, parents, and teachers and, in some magnet schools, to improve the academic performance of students.

In the 1980s and 1990s, as broader approaches to choice in education are advocated, it is important to assess what is known from recent experience with magnet schools. Research on magnet schools can shed light on questions about the effects of school choice on equal opportunity, improved student outcomes, costs, and impacts on school systems.

We will outline here some of the major policy questions that are being analyzed in a national study of magnet schools to be completed in 1993. The study results will be examined closely by policymakers, educators, and researchers who want to determine the outcomes of the magnet school movement and to anticipate what can be expected from efforts to broaden programs of school choice.[1] The study is being conducted by the American Institutes for Research for the U.S. Department of Education. The authors of this article are members of the study team.[2]

How Many Magnet Schools Are There?

There are no current national figures on the number of magnet schools, the number of districts with magnet schools, or the number of students enrolled in magnet schools. The new Department of Education study includes a survey of a nationally representative sample of school districts to obtain accurate counts.

Currently, only rough estimates are available. In the first national study of magnet schools in 1981–83, one-third (138) of the largest school districts had magnet schools, and the total was over 1,000 magnet schools at the elementary and secondary levels (Blank et al. 1983). In 1988, the National Education Longitudinal Study classified 9 percent of all public schools with eighth-grade students as "schools of choice" (i.e., schools employing application or admission procedures) (Sosniak and Ethington 1992). The National School Boards Association conducted a survey of urban districts in 1990 and found that thirty-four of fifty-two responding districts had magnet schools (NSBA 1990). In 1989, the average large urban district with magnet schools enrolled 50 percent more students in magnet schools than in 1983, and about 20 percent of students in large urban districts were in magnet schools (Blank 1989). A 1992

From *The Clearing House*, Vol. 66, No. 2, November/December 1992, pp. 81–86. Reprinted with permission of the Helen Dwight Reid Educational Foundation. Published by Heldref Publications, 1319 Eighteenth St., NW, Washington, DC 20036-1802.

study of magnet schools in New York City reported that only 37 percent of high school students are in a non-magnet, comprehensive high school (Crain et al., 1992).

These studies may use somewhat different definitions of magnet schools and different methods of counting schools and students. How magnet schools are defined greatly affects final enrollment figures. For example, many districts have a variety of special schools and programs that enroll students from throughout the district: vocational schools, gifted and talented programs, GED programs, juvenile offender programs, schools for pregnant girls or young mothers, specialized professional schools, and others. These are generally not magnet schools because they serve no formally established racial integration purpose. However, sometimes they are labelled as magnet schools.

For the purposes of the current Department of Education national study, a magnet school is defined as a public school with any grades K through 12 that offers "whole-school" or "program-within-school" programs that have the following characteristics:[3]

- A specialized curricular theme or method of instruction intended to attract students district-wide
- At least some students who *volunteered* for admission and entered voluntarily (enrollment is not limited to neighborhood attendance zones)
- Racial/ethnic enrollment goals or controls of some type

This definition of magnet school will be used throughout the national study, and the discussions in this article will address this concept of a magnet school.

What Is Distinctive about Magnet Schools?

The first magnet schools were based on models from specialty schools in public education, such as the Bronx School of Science, Boston Latin school, and Chicago's Lane Tech, which have offered advanced programs to selected students for many years. Such specialty schools admit students by examination or other measures of performance or ability and tend to serve highly gifted students. The idea of a magnet school, however, was to attract and enroll students based on their *interest*, not ability level, in either a particular subject or career (such as science, art, or business) or to attract students because of a different instructional approach (such as an open school or a multicultural school).

By attracting students with common education interests but diverse abilities and socioeconomic backgrounds, a magnet school can enroll a racially heterogenous student body and provide a unique educational experience through a curriculum organized around a specific theme or instructional approach. A magnet school principal tries to attract and hire a faculty according to their specific interests in the magnet theme and thereby offer a working environment with greater cohesiveness and cooperation among the faculty. Dis-

trict policies or union regulations, however, often require selecting teachers based on seniority as the main criterion. At the district level, the goals of a magnet school program are typically to maintain or advance educational equity and to improve quality of education through diversity.

Generally, magnet schools can be classified according to (*a*) their instructional methods (how they teach) or (*b*) their content (what they teach). The range of alternatives in the "instructional methods" category is usually greatest in elementary magnet schools and tends to diminish at the secondary level. At the high school level, magnet schools are more likely to have a theme that focuses on specific subject areas.

Rossell's study of magnet schools in twenty urban districts identified the types of magnet school programs by school level. Table 1 provides an illustration of the types of programs found among a total of 342 magnet schools.

The national study for the Department of Education will provide national statistics on the types of magnet schools at different levels. The study will also provide

TABLE 1
Types of Magnet School Programs in Twenty Urban Districts

Magnet Program Type	N	%
Elementary/middle schools		
Basic skills/individualized	32	12
Foreign languages	31	11
Science/math/computers	31	11
Gifted and talented	27	10
Visual/performing/creative arts	26	10
Fundamental/traditional	22	8
College prep	20	7
Early childhood/Montessori	18	7
Multicultural/international	13	5
Extended day	11	4
Other	39	15
Elementary/middle total	270	100
High schools		
Science/engineering	14	19
Vocational/career preparation	10	14
Business/marketing	8	11
Creative and performing arts	7	10
College prep	5	7
Medical careers	5	7
International/multicultural	4	6
Communications/mass media	4	6
Law and criminal justice	3	4
Other	12	16
High school total	72	100

Source: Rossell, C. H. 1990. *The carrot or the stick for school desegregation policy: Magnet schools or forced busing?* Philadelphia, Pa.: Temple University Press.

statistics on the number of "whole-school" magnets vs. "program-within-school" magnets. The study will be able to analyze which types of magnet schools are offered according to district characteristics, suh as size and region, and school characteristics, such as racial/ethnic composition and student-teacher ratio.

Whether magnet schools offer a truly distinctive or unique educational experience consistent with their formal title or specialty can be difficult to assess. Educators, students, and parents want to know if the school actually offers a different kind or intensity of curriculum in a subject, or if teachers actually use teaching methods that are not found in a typical non-magnet school. That is, do students find something different and educationally valuable as a result of their choice. Or, is a magnet school unique only in the name and the fact that students choose to enroll.

The first national study of magnet schools (Blank et al. 1983) addressed the question of program distinctiveness. Comparative case studies were conducted with magnet schools in fifteen districts. The curriculum, staff, materials, teaching methods, student and teacher interaction, and student outcomes were analyzed in relation to a series of hypotheses about school effectiveness. The analyses showed that one-third of the magnet schools could be characterized as having "high education quality." About one-fifth of the schools demonstrated no unique or distinctive elements of school effectiveness. The remaining schools showed some aspects of distinctive "education quality." The study concluded that local planning and implementation of magnet schools varied widely from district to district and that magnet schools could provide distinctive education opportunities through careful, diligent efforts at the district and school levels, although not all magnet schools were distinctive.

The current national study for the Department of Education will further analyze the question of distinctive qualities of magnet schools, and these variables will be related to measures of student outcomes.

Do Magnet Schools Provide Equal Opportunities for Students to Enroll?

Several issues need to be examined concerning equality of opportunity: (a) whether students and parents have sufficient information about magnet schools; (b) the degree of selectivity in methods of enrolling magnet students; and (c) the rate of acceptance of magnet school applicants.

Access to Information

A major factor in equal opportunity is for students and parents to know about the magnet schools available and to have sufficient information to make a choice. Limited access to and understanding of information may be the key barrier to access for low-income parents,

who in big-city districts are most often black or Hispanic. A study of school choice in an open enrollment system found that parent educational attainment was associated with the probability that a parent was aware of having a choice; among those aware that they could choose, educational attainment was associated with the probability of investigating school options before enrolling (Nault and Uchitelle 1982). A study of school choices by inner-city black parents showed that the schools that received the most magnet applications had more parents with college degrees (Archbald 1988). A survey of randomly selected parents in seven schools in the Milwaukee system found that 93 percent of the non-low-income and 74 percent of the low-income respondents had heard about Milwaukee's magnets (MMPSSC 1986).

But social class differences are by no means predeterminate. In all systems with magnets, while the proportions may differ, parents from all strata and sociocultural groups enroll their children in magnet programs. This has been demonstrated most dramatically in the East Harlem school district, which serves a largely low-income clientele yet boasts of one of the most successful school choice programs in the country (Fiske 1988; Bensman 1987).

In school districts where all parents do not know about magnet schools, or districts where not all magnet applicants are accepted, the issue of "skimming" has often arisen. Critics claim magnets "skim" the brightest and/or most advantaged students from (non-magnet) neighborhood schools (Moore and Davenport 1989). Implicit here is the claim that magnet schools do not get their "fair share" of poor or low-achieving students (however this fair share should be determined).

Sustaining the "skimming" thesis are studies showing that magnet schools usually have fewer low-income students than non-magnet schools (Archbald and Witte 1985; Moore and Davenport 1989). However, a detailed analysis of inner-city enrollment patterns of black children in Milwaukee (Duax 1988) shows only a very small difference in the percentage of low-income black children in elementary magnets (without academically selective admissions policies) as compared with elementary non-magnets (82 percent vs. 85 percent). Duax argues that most comparisons of magnet and non-magnet schools indiscriminately lump academically selective magnets with nonselective magnets. However, selective schools and programs almost always have lower concentrations of low-income students, regardless of whether or not they are magnets.

Selectivity

Across the nation, magnet schools have very different methods of selection of students, varying from "highly selective" schools requiring high test scores and good grades to "moderately selective" schools requiring a C average and a recommendation to "non-selective" schools where selection is by lottery or order of application. Blank (1989) analyzed methods of student selection in seventy-two magnet schools in eight urban districts and found that fourteen of the seventy-two used moderate to highly selective methods.

Regardless of the formal method of student selection, all magnet schools have voluntary choice, or "self-selection," which in many communities results in magnets attracting students and parents with more information and higher interest in magnet schools. Often, these students are already doing better in school. For example, a study of eight magnet high schools in Dallas showed that the entering test scores of magnet students were significantly higher than the district average (Dallas ISD 1988). At the same time, Dallas has nonselective magnet enrollment and a high percentage of applicants to magnets are enrolled. Half of the magnet high schools are more racially integrated than the district average.

Rate of Applicants and Acceptance

The debate about skimming and selectivity of magnet schools is difficult to resolve at the national level, partly because detailed information is needed about individual district programs. The rate of acceptance, the total number of magnet schools, and the total number of magnet school "slots" at each grade level all affect the extent of equal opportunity. For example, skimming is a much larger issue in districts with only one or two magnet schools and in districts that have not expanded the number of slots after initial programs become well known. The rate of acceptance of applications to magnet schools varies widely. A follow-up survey with fifteen urban districts in the 1983 national magnet school study showed that the proportions of applying students that were accepted in magnet schools varied from 25 percent in Buffalo and Pittsburgh to 40 percent in Cincinnati to 90 percent in Houston, Lubbock, and St. Paul (Bland 1989). High application and acceptance ratios were also reported with the Cambridge "controlled choice" plan (Alves and Willie 1987).

The New York City magnet schools use a lottery system for selection, but acceptances are apportioned to represent the distribution of students by previous school achievement (Crain et al. 1992). Eighty-two percent of students entering high school in New York apply for a magnet school, and 50 percent receive their first choice. One-half of the enrollment in each magnet is selected by the school, and one-half is randomly selected from among applicants. One-sixth of those accepted in each magnet school are from the top one-sixth in the district on reading and math test scores, and one-sixth of those accepted are from the bottom one-sixth on test scores.

Although in many local districts self-selection produces more academically capable students in magnet schools, the strongest criticisms of "skimming" prob-

ably overstate differences in student composition between magnets and non-magnets and underestimate the accessibility of magnet schools to most urban families. Key issues being addressed by the national study are the methods of selection used with magnet schools and the characteristics of magnet school students, with the application of standard definitions across a national sample of districts.

Do Magnet Schools Improve Student Learning?

Magnet schools are popular methods of education reform in urban school systems. Many of the schools provide an innovative, distinctive approach to education. But the question that many educators and parents want answered is whether the quality of education is any better. Do students learn more in magnet schools than in non-magnet schools? Most district reports show that magnet schools have higher achievement test scores (Blank et al. 1983; Blank 1989). Critics contend that magnets schools' successes are the result of getting better students and more central office support. Undoubtedly, for some magnet schools this is the explanation. But there is evidence that this explanation is incomplete: studies comparing magnets to non-magnets with similar student characteristics show that student outcomes are higher in magnet schools, and other studies find organizational characteristics of magnet schools such as work relationships, innovation, and "team spirit" that are not logically traceable to student or resource characteristics.

Student Outcomes

First, there is strong evidence that some magnet schools do improve student learning. The East Harlem school district in the city of New York converted entirely to magnet schools over a decade ago. East Harlem, one of the poorest communities in the city, ranked thirty-second among the thirty-two community districts in the city on achievement scores when it initiated its school choice program. As of 1988 it ranked sixteenth. Student reading scores have risen steadily and are now above national averages; attendance has improved. School officials believe school choice was the major reason for the improvement (Fiske 1988; Bensman 1987). A new study of magnet career high schools in New York City demonstrates that eighth grade students who are randomly assigned to magnet schools have higher test scores than similar students who were not accepted in magnets (Crain et al. 1992).

A similar story occurred in the Montclair, New Jersey, school district, which turned all its schools into magnet schools in the early 1980s and subsequently experienced significant improvement in test scores (Clewell and Joy 1990). In Buffalo, New York, aggregate student test scores rose substantially on the state's Pupil Evaluation Program test over ten years (1976–86) after the district implemented its magnet school–based desegregation plan. Gains of 23 percent in reading and 37 percent in math occurred at the sixth grade level, and 8 and 14 percent, respectively, at third grade. Also, the pattern of declining scores at older grades—a common phenomenon in urban schooling—disappeared over the ten years (Rossell 1987).

A review of magnet school research and evaluation studies from twelve large urban districts shows the same pattern of findings (Blank 1989). Although most of the studies reviewed do not control adequately for student background characteristics and thus there are confounding effects from selection processes, the several using controls still show greater achievement gains in magnets. Studies in Montgomery County, Maryland (1988, 1990), Austin (1988), Dallas (1988), and San Diego (1988) employ statistical controls and analyze individual-level performance over time. Each found superior performance over time. Each found superior performance of students in magnet schools in such areas as reading, math, science, and writing. A larger study of effective schools in a major urban district found a statistically significant increment in test scores among students in magnet schools, after controlling for several student composition and organizational independent variables (Witte and Walsh 1990).

Thus, some studies demonstrate positive relationships between magnet schooling and student outcomes. It is difficult to control statistically for all differences between magnet and non-magnet schools. However, examination of studies that found rising *districtwide* scores after the development of magnet schools would be another approach to determining positive educational effects.

Magnet School Organization and Quality

Other studies have looked at the organizational characteristics of magnets. Rather than focusing on magnet/non-magnet differences in student outcomes, these studies examined if and why magnet schools differ on variables of organizational structure and internal social relations.

In 1983, Blank et al. analyzed magnet organization and process variables in forty-five magnet schools in fifteen urban districts, and the research showed that three variables were significantly related to education quality: principal leadership; coherence between the magnet theme and the curriculum and staffing; and district commitment and support.

Metz' (1986) ethnographic study of magnet school implementation in one district shows that top-down implementation can be detrimental to a positive school climate and that "faculty culture" is important in producing an innovative, effective magnet school. McNeil (1987) studied the impact of magnet schools on teachers in one urban district and found positive effects on teachers who participated in magnet school planning

and development and positive changes in teacher morale and career goals.

Archbald's (1988) study compared magnets to non-magnets on organizational quality ratings, using statistical controls for student composition. Magnet teachers reported higher levels of professional autonomy and parent involvement and higher ratings on a number of "effective schools" items. Analyses of the magnet school subsample found that magnets attended by students from neighborhoods with higher levels of parent education did not necessarily have more positive ratings than magnets attended by students from neighborhoods with lower levels of parent education. This lends support to the hypothesis that student composition differences do not fully account for more positive organizational ratings in magnets.

There is no research examining in any detail the educational effects of magnet schools. Typically, test scores are the one outcome examined, but many magnet school programs are not specifically aimed at building the skills reflected on standardized tests. Also, few studies have examined the features of magnet school organization, curriculum, staffing, and instruction that may produce higher achievement among magnet students. The second phase of the new national study will analyze questions concerning educational effects with a selected sub-sample of districts with magnet schools.

Summary

Magnet schools have become a major part of American public education, especially in urban school systems. In fact, magnet schools have been one of the key vehicles of innovation in urban schooling over the last several decades. Research and evaluation studies have shown that magnet schools are having positive educational effects, but these have mainly been studies of individual districts or schools. There are few carefully designed, comparative studies of magnet schools as educational innovations. The new national study being conducted for the Department of Education will help to address some of the major questions about magnet schools and will provide an extensive database for further research on the characteristics and effects of magnet schools.

There are several reasons why little is known about the effects of magnet schools on the quality of education in our schools. First, educators and researchers tend to view magnet schools as a strategy for desegregation in big-city systems, not as a strategy for educational reform. Second, magnet schools have been implemented at various points in time through local adoption and adaptation of a variety of models for reform, such as effective schools, alternative schools, career education, and site-based management. The focus on individual school innovations has drawn attention away from magnet schools collectively as a model for change.

3. STRIVING FOR EXCELLENCE: THE DRIVE FOR QUALITY

Third, recent analysis of the issue of school choice has subsumed the question of magnet schools, and choice has become a controversial political issue. As a result, some of the basic questions about magnet schools have not been systematically examined.

Within a year, results from the new national study will start to be released, and our collective knowledge of magnet schools and choice will be strengthened. This study should help resolve some of the debates involving magnet schools and should spur work by educators and researchers to analyze further the educational effects of magnet schools and their prospects for the future.

NOTES

1. This article discusses policy issues related to magnet schools and education quality. The national study is also examining the effects of magnet schools on desegregation and evaluating the effects of the federal program providing funding for magnet schools.

2. This article is partly based on a literature review written for the magnet schools study by Douglas Archbald, entitled "Magnet Schools and Issues of Public School Desegregation, Quality, and Choice" (March 1991).

3. Source: Draft National Survey Interview Protocol, Magnet Schools and Issues of Public School Desegregation, Quality, and Choice, American Institutes for Research, Palo Alto, California, 1990.

REFERENCES

Alves, M., and C. Willie. 1987. Controlled choice assignments: A new and more effective approach to school desegregation. *Urban Review* 19(2): 67–88.

Archbald, D. A. 1988. *Magnet schools, voluntary desegregation and public choice theory: Limits and possibilities in a big city school system.* Unpublished Ph.D. dissertation, University of Wisconsin-Madison.

_____. 1991. *Magnet schools and issues of public school desegregation, quality, and choice.* Palo Alto: American Institutes for Research.

Archbald, D. A., and J. Witte. 1985. *Metropolitan Milwaukee specialty schools and programs.* Milwaukee, Wis.: Report prepared for the Milwaukee Metropolitan Public Schools Study Commission.

Austin Independent School District. 1988. *Looking at magnet programs in AISD, 1987–88.* Austin: Austin Independent School District, Department of Management Information, Office of Research and Evaluation.

Bensman, D. 1987. The story of the Central Park East School. In *Quality education in the inner city,* edited by D. Bensman. New Brunswick: Rutgers University Press.

Blank, R. K. 1989. *Educational effects of magnet high schools.* Madison, Wis.: National Center on Effective Secondary Schools, University of Wisconsin-Madison.

Blank, R. K., R. A. Dentler, D. C. Baltzell, and K. Chabotar. 1983. *Survey of magnet schools: Analyzing a model for quality integated education.* Final report of a national study for the U.S. Department of Education. Washington, D.C.: James H. Lowry and Associates.

Clewell, B. C., and M. F. Joy. 1990. *Choice in Montclair, New Jersey: A policy information paper.* Princeton, N.J.: ETS Policy Information Center, Education Testing Service.

Crain, R. L., A. L. Heebner, and Y. P. Si. 1992. *The effectiveness of New York City's career magnet schools: An evaluation of ninth grade performance using an experimental design.* Berkeley: National Center for Research in Vocational Education.

Dallas Independent School District. 1988. *Evaluation of 1987–88 Vanguard, Academy, and Magnet high school programs.* Dallas: Dallas Independent School District, Department of Research, Evaluation and Information Systems.

Duax, T. 1988. *The impact of nonselective magnet schools on a predominantly black community.* Unpublished Ph.D. dissertation, University of Wisconsin-Milwaukee.

Fiske, E. 1988. Parental choice in public school gains. *New York Times* (July 11): 1.

McNeil, L. M. 1987. *Structuring excellence and barriers to excellence.* Washington, D.C.: Office of Educational Research and Improvement.

Metz, M. H. 1986. *Different by design: The context and character of three magnet schools.* New York: Routledge and Kegan.

Milwaukee Metropolitan Public Schools Study Commission (MMP-SSC). *Parents and schools.* Final report to the Milwaukee Metropolitan Public Schools Study Commission, Milwaukee, Wis.

Montgomery County Public Schools. 1988. *A microscope on magnet schools, 1983 to 1986. Volume 2: Pupil and parent outcomes.* Rockville, Md.: Montgomery County Public Schools, Department of Educational Accountability.

_____. 1990. *A microscope on magnet schools: Secondary school magnet programs.* Rockville, Md.: Montgomery County Public Schools, Department of Educational Accountability.

Moore, D. R. and S. Davenport. 1989. *The new improved sorting machine.* Madison, Wis.: National Center on Effective Secondary Schools.

National School Boards Association (NSBA). 1990. *A survey of public education in the nation's urban school districts.* Alexandria, Va.: National School Boards Association.

Nault, R., and S. Uchitelle. 1982. School choice in the public sector: A case study of parental decision making. In *Family choice in schooling,* edited by M. E. Manley-Casimir, 85–90. Lexington, Mass.: Lexington Books.

Rossell, C. H. 1987. The Buffalo controlled choice plan. *Urban Education* 22(3): 328–54.

_____. 1990. *The carrot or the stick for school desegregation policy: Magnet schools or forced busing?* Philadelphia, Pa.: Temple University Press.

San Diego City Schools. 1988. *San Diego High School, International Baccalaureate/Writing Academy Magnet Program, second year evaluation.* San Diego: San Diego City Schools, Planning, Research and Evaluation Division.

Sosniak, L. A., and C. A. Ethington. 1992. When public school choice is not academic: Findings from the National Education Longitudinal Study of 1988. *Education Evaluation and Policy Analysis* 14(1): 35–52.

Witte, J. F., and D. J. Walsh. 1990. A systematic test of the effective schools model. *Educational Evaluation and Policy Analysis* 12(2): 188–213.

The Myth of
Public School Failure

Richard Rothstein

Richard Rothstein is a research associate of the Economic Policy Institute and a columnist for the L.A. Weekly.

There's a conventional wisdom about public schools: Graduates don't have the skills needed for a technologically advanced economy. We've doubled funds for public education since the mid-1960s, but more money hasn't improved schools. Academic achievement is stagnant or declining. Public schools can't improve because teachers are smothered by bureaucracy. To address this system failure, structural reforms such as school-based decision making or parental choice of schools are imperative.

Liberals and conservatives share much of this view, parting only when the left proposes radical decentralization of public schools while the right calls for privatization with vouchers. Yet despite the broad consensus, each assertion in the conventional story is incorrect or misguided.

The truth is:

■ Public schools now produce most academic skills currently demanded by employers and, most likely, even the skills needed if industry adopted more flexible production methods.

■ While public education funding has more than doubled since 1965, little new money has gone to improve academic outcomes; instead, the funds have mostly pursued social goals like education of the handicapped, nutrition programs, and busing for integration. Teacher salary increases and class-size reductions have been insufficient to produce educational effects.

■ Despite relatively modest increases in regular education funding, real progress is reflected in reduced dropout rates, higher test scores for white and especially minority students, improved mi-

nority college attendance, and more students going into science and engineering.

■ Bureaucracy does stifle creativity, but school administration consumes few dollars, mostly to prevent discrimination, favoritism, or fraud, or to maintain minimum academic standards.

■ Consequently, systemic reforms like decentralization and school choice mostly address the wrong problems. Choice programs will increase race and class segregation and depress academic achievement for disadvantaged students. Radical decentralization could waste teacher time with routine administrative tasks.

■ Schools need incremental reforms like improved evaluation and training of teachers and principals and more curricular emphasis on conceptual and verbal skills. But the most important reform remains more money. Results are most likely from education of preschoolers, drastic class-size reductions for disadvantaged students, investments in health care for pregnant mothers, improved teacher pay, and workplace training for the non-college bound.

Public education advocates miscalculate when they attempt to mobilize support by attacking school outcomes. The strategy likely to enhance support for public schools is to highlight schools' accomplishments, suggesting that even greater gains are likely with additional resources.

The "Jobs-Skills Mismatch"

At President Clinton's December "Economic Summit" in Little Rock, Apple Computer Chairman John Sculley claimed that "[w]e're still trapped in a K–12 public education system which is preparing our young people for jobs that just don't exist anymore." After Sculley was seconded by Princeton economist Alan Blinder, Clinton challenged them:

"Only about 15 percent of the employers of this country report difficulty finding workers with appropriate occupational skills. Does that mean the employers don't know what they're talking about, or that we're wrong?"

Blinder evaded Clinton's probe, claiming there is no skills shortage only because of the recession—when hiring picks up, "Skills are going to be in short supply." But Blinder was mistaken. The employer-survey to which Clinton alluded was conducted by "The Commission on the Skills of the American Workforce" in *pre-recession* 1989. It found that over 80 percent of American employers were satisfied with new hires' education. Only 5 percent expected future increases in skill requirements. Nonetheless, illustrating the power of ideology over experience, employers who find little fault with their own workers' preparation frequently complain that the schools are failing, just as the public consistently tells pollsters that schools fail while the schools that their own children attend are doing just fine.

Academics, politicians, journalists, and business leaders seem to agree that schools' failure is confirmed by growing "returns to education"—each additional year of school boosts an individual's earnings by about 6 percent. In 1979, college graduates earned 38 percent more than high school grads. Today it's 57 percent more.

If employers pay more for college degrees, it seems reasonable to conclude that degrees are in short supply and to demand an increase in the number of graduates, focusing on shortcomings of public schools that produce too few students qualified for college. But while college grads do earn increasingly more than high school grads, many college graduates take jobs that don't require degrees. In 1990, 20 percent of college graduates had jobs that don't require higher education, or they couldn't find work at all, up from 18 percent in 1979 and 11 percent in 1968. There are now 644,000 college grads working as retail salespersons, 83,000 who are maids or janitors, and 166,000 driving trucks or buses. Blue-collar workers include 1.3 million college grads, twice as many as 15 years ago. Even before the current recession, 400,000 grads were unemployed—despite their credentials.

Not all graduates, of course, want professional or technical careers, but it's unlikely that voluntary blue-collar work explains much of this data, because technologically sophisticated occupations are not increasing rapidly. The oft-cited conclusion of the Department of Labor's *Workforce 2000* report that future jobs will require more education failed to weight data on increased educational requirements by the number of new jobs in each occupation, failed to offset increases in educational requirements for some jobs with decreases in requirements for others, and neglected to consider the growth of low-skill industries as well as those needing higher skill.

The Bureau of Labor Statistics, for example, expects "paralegals" to be the nation's fastest growing occupation, with employment increasing from 1988 to 2000 by 75 percent. But this growth means just 62,000 new jobs. Meanwhile, with only 19 percent growth, janitors and maids will gain 556,000 new jobs. In their re-analysis of *Workforce 2000*'s projections, the Economic Policy Institute's Lawrence Mishel and Ruy Texeira concluded that probable industrial shifts and occupational shifts within industries will require only that students entering the work force in the year 2000 will need one-fourth of a grade level more schooling than those who entered in 1955.

With a surplus of college grads, their higher relative earnings stem not from premiums paid for more education but rather from penalties exacted from those with less. The oversupply of college graduates is confirmed by a 10 percent drop in wages of college-educated workers since 1973. But high school graduates' earnings have dropped even more, by 16 percent. Greater returns to education suggest not a need to increase schooling but rather trade and labor market policies to reverse the earning declines of industrial and service workers.

A conclusion that schools now adequately prepare youth for expected job openings seems counterintuitive, especially in light of frequent anecdotes about ill-schooled youth. In one typical case, Pacific Telesis Chairman Sam Ginn complained to

From the movie *Stand and Deliver*

a 1991 press conference that his company gave a seventh-grade-level reading test to 6,400 "operator" job applicants, and more than half failed, proof of the need for improved education to provide "workers with skills that will allow us to be competitive into the next century."

But Ginn failed to mention that for the 2,700 who passed the test, there were only 700 openings, paying wages of less than $7 an hour. A more telling conclusion would have been that schools provided PacTel with nearly four times the number of qualified operator-candidates it needed, even at low wages. If the company offered wages above the poverty line, even more successful test takers might have applied.

Some critics, like Ray Marshall and Marc Tucker in their recent book, *Thinking for a Living*, acknowledge that schools prepare youth for today's jobs and even for the more sophisticated jobs expected to evolve. But this is no cause for complacency, they argue, since skills are now adequate only because we maintain outmoded assembly lines where workers follow detailed instructions to perform repetitive unskilled tasks. We will never accelerate productivity with these assembly lines, Marshall and Tucker claim. High-productivity organizations of the future already common in Japan and Germany require flexible workers who can perform many tasks, work together, and diagnose production problems. Were American companies to adopt high-productivity structures, skills would be insufficient.

But this argument may overestimate the schooling required even for high-performance work organizations. Ten years ago, Harley Shaiken began to study Ford Motor Company's new engine plant in Chihuahua, Mexico. Initially, he believed that Ford's gamble to save on labor costs in Mexico (where 6 years of school is the norm) would fail. Manufacturing engines is a sophisticated operation, with machine tolerances of one ten-thousandth of an inch. Coordination between production workers and technicians is essential. Yet while Ford required only 9 years of education for new hires in its Chihuahua facility, it has become the world's most productive engine plant and is now Ford's sole North American engine source.

Ford enrolled Mexican school dropouts in a 4-to-12-week technology institute program covering gasoline engines, mechanical drawing, and mathematics. New hires learned to tear down and reassemble an engine. Once on the job, they were rotated every 3 to 6 months to new tasks, so skills would be broadened further.

As the Chihuahua plant matured, Ford hired workers with less schooling and relied even more on its own training. As skilled technicians left, Ford replaced them with production workers promoted and trained from within, as required by Ford's Mexican union contract.

It's not evident that our schools fail to produce workers qualified to staff such a system. Even if American school standards are less than other nations', we have a plethora of underemployed grads whose skills are at least equal to those of Mexican dropouts. When General Motors implemented a high-performance work system at its Tennessee Saturn plant, American schooling was no impediment. But unlike other GM plants, Saturn gave 10 weeks of formal training to new hires and required ongoing classroom work for permanent employees. Most American corporations, however, make few training investments, so their claim that public schools can't provide qualified workers rings hollow.

School Funding Growth Since 1965

Irving Kristol recently attacked Clinton's social spending plans by asserting: "Look at the spending on public schools. It goes up and up, and the results go down and down and down."

When Benno Schmidt resigned Yale's presidency in 1992, he denounced public education to justify a new national for-profit private school chain:

> We have roughly doubled per-pupil spending (after inflation) in public schools since 1965....Yet dropout rates remain distressingly high...overall, high school students today are posting lower SAT scores than a generation ago. The nation's investment in educational improvement has produced very little return.

In 1990, the U.S. spent $5,521 per pupil on public schools, more than double the $2,611 (in 1990 dollars) spent 25 years earlier. More money for schools won't do any good, critics assert; it's just pouring good money after bad.

But spending more hasn't failed. It hasn't been tried. The truth is that little new money has been invested in regular educational improvements since 1965. How has the money been used?

Special Education. Nearly 30 percent of new education money has gone for "special education" of children with disabilities. Since 1975, federal law has required public schools to provide "a free appropriate education" to each child, no matter how seriously handicapped. By 1990, nearly 12 percent of all schoolchildren were in special education. Schools must design an "individualized education program" for each child with a learning, emotional, or physical disability. Publicly financed medical diagnoses, special transportation arrangements, personalized instruction, tiny class sizes, specially trained teachers, and the purchase of special equipment may be required to place a child in the "least restrictive environment." Parents dissatisfied with an individualized program are entitled to a hearing. The Supreme Court has ruled that cost cannot be an excuse for failing to design an appropriate program. If a handicap is too severe for a public setting, schools must pay the child's private tuition.

Education of the handicapped is worthwhile, but it is dishonest to suggest that special education funds should produce academic gains for regular students and, when they do not, claim proof that money spent on public schools is wasted.

Nutrition Programs. School breakfast and lunch programs have absorbed nearly 10 percent of increased costs. In 1965, nutrition programs were mostly self-supporting, selling milk and ice cream their main function. Today 35 percent of all students get free or reduced price meals, costing over $6 billion a year. Providing meals to needy children should also improve academic achievement, since nutrition is necessary for learning. However, such an expectation assumes that children are better nourished as a result. If, on the other hand, school food subsidies only offset deterioration in children's health since 1965, expecting academic gains from this program would be unrealistic.

Fourteen percent of Americans lived in poverty in 1992, the highest rate since 1964. Growth of overall poverty masks more drastic growth in child poverty. In 1990, nearly 25 percent of American children under age six were poor, an increase from 18 percent in 1979. With a probable deterioration in the nutritional condition of children when they come to school, it is questionable whether educational improvement can be expected from today's breakfast and lunch programs. Nor is it appropriate to suggest that maintenance of such expenditures would, from an educational point of view, be throwing good money after bad.

Smaller Classes. Nearly one-third of new school money has gone for smaller classes. Pupil-teacher ratios have declined by about 30 percent since 1965 and average class size is now about 24, requiring more teachers and extra classrooms. It seems reasonable that this investment should produce academic gains. Yet while reducing class size to 24 creates better teacher working conditions and may be needed for discipline—as education becomes more universal and society's authority norms weaken—it's not enough to improve academic outcomes as much as we'd like. Unless class sizes get small enough (around 15) so that the method of teaching can change to individualized instruction, smaller classes have no measurable academic effect.

Salary Increases. Teacher salaries have grown 21 percent—less than 1 percent a year—from an average of $27,221 in 1965 (1990 dollars) to $32,977 in 1990. This increase is responsible for another 8 percent of increased education costs. This added expenditure should result in improved student achievement if higher salaries attract more highly qualified graduates to teaching. But if other professional salaries grew more, higher teacher pay would not enable school districts to maintain teacher quality in the face of greater competition from other professions.

Since 1975, starting teacher pay increases have lagged behind pay increases of other beginning professionals with bachelors' degrees. Starting teacher salaries have grown by 149 percent since 1975, less than the rate of inflation. For beginning engineers, the increase was 153 percent; for marketing reps, 169 percent; for business administration grads, 171 percent; for mathematicians and statisticians, 163 percent; for economists and finance personnel, 161 percent; for liberal arts graduates, 183 percent. Teachers did better than chemists (144 percent) and accountants (130 percent).

Teacher salaries increased faster from 1965 to 1975 than after. But over 25 years the overall increase in real teacher pay at best maintained schools' ability to attract candidates. If anything, the increase has been inadequate to maintain teaching's competitive standing, since more professions have welcomed women since 1975. Highly qualified female college graduates are no longer captives of the teaching profession, so the same relative teachers' pay now attracts less qualified teachers than before. All told, we can't expect teachers' pay gains since 1965 to produce higher student achievement; for this result, we would need bigger pay boosts to attract higher quality college graduates to teaching.

Transportation. Transportation has consumed 5 percent of increased costs. In 1965, 40 percent of public school students were bused at an average cost of $214 (1990 dollars). By 1989, 59 percent were bused, and the cost jumped to $390.

Fewer Dropouts. About 3 percent of new spending stems from keeping more students in school. The oft-repeated worry that more students are dropping out has no factual basis. Since a student dropping out of one school may move to a new community and enroll there, the most accurate measurement of dropouts is not schools' own records but census information on young adults who have completed 12 years of school.

In 1970, 75 percent of youths between ages 25 and 29 had completed high school. By 1990, 86 percent had done so. Minority dropout rates have steadily declined—in 1940, only 12 percent of 25-to-29-year-old blacks had completed high school. In 1950, the black completion rate rose to 24 percent; in 1960, to 39 percent; in 1970, to 58 percent; in 1980, to 77 percent. The rate continued to rise in the 1980s, to 83 percent in 1990.

Hispanic dropout rates are less accessible because the 1980 decennial census was the first with separate data on Hispanics, and because many so-called Hispanic dropouts (young adults who have not completed high school) are immigrants, some of whom came to the U.S. too old to enroll in school. They shouldn't be considered "dropouts"—many never "dropped in." In 1990, only 58 percent of Hispanic 25-to-29-year-olds had completed high school. But for Hispanics in their forties (who were in their twenties in 1970), the rate was less—52 percent. And for those in their sixties (in their twenties in 1950), the rate was only 38 percent. Thus, it seems, Hispanic dropout rates are declining as well.

If the typical dropout completes 10.5 years of school, then the higher completion rate has increased per pupil costs by 1.3 percent since 1965. This added spending does not improve graduates' average

academic achievement. While preventing dropouts is important, lower dropout rates will also reduce average test scores, since a broader base is now tested, including those less academically motivated than earlier groups that did not include potential dropouts. Fewer dropouts will also generate more anecdotes about high school graduates who don't read or compute well. So, paradoxically, expenditures for more schooling can seem to reduce academic achievement while contributing to an improved education level for society.

In sum, special education, smaller classes, school lunches, better teacher pay, more buses, and fewer dropouts account for over 80 percent of new education money since 1965. That these produced few academic gains is no surprise. It is to the credit of the public schools and the teaching profession that real gains have occurred at all.

Improved School Outcomes Since 1965

Yet there have been real gains, partly due to higher academic standards and curricular reforms implemented in the last 15 years. In many classrooms, for example, conceptual math has embellished arithmetic, and literature has replaced basic readers. The 1983 report, *A Nation at Risk*, accelerated a curricular reform movement that was already gathering steam. Heightened consciousness of the ways in which low teacher expectations for working class and minority students become self-fulfilling have also helped boost student academic progress. New spending related to these curricular reforms, though modest in scope, has made a difference. Some new money has gone for education of the disadvantaged, in Chapter I and bilingual programs. Computers have been added to classrooms: 54 percent of public elementary students (including 43 percent of those in the lowest family income quartile) now use computers at school.

Thus with limited new investment, academic performance has improved, especially for minority students. This is one reason why schools' skills production has outpaced industry's ability to absorb educated workers.

It does seem that academic performance declined in the late 1960s and 1970s but rebounded dramatically in the last decade. School achievement, certainly for minority youth and most likely for whites as well, today exceeds not only 1970s standards but those of 25 years ago.

True, average Scholastic Aptitude Test

(SAT) scores have declined to 899 (math and verbal combined) in 1992 from 937 in 1972. Yet this favorite fact of headline writers tells a very partial story. Last year, 29 percent of SAT takers (students planning to go to college) were minority students, more than double the 13 percent 20 years earlier. In 1992, 43 percent of test takers ranked in the top fifth of their high school classes. In 1972, 48 percent were in the top fifth, a more elite group. In California, for example, where over half the test takers were minority students in 1992, only 66 percent came from homes where only English was spoken, and 20 percent spoke English as a second language, up from 13 percent just six years earlier. These shifts unsurprisingly produce lower average scores. Declines in average SAT scores stem mostly from expansion in the test takers' base, adding more disadvantaged students to a pool that earlier included mostly privileged students.

While average scores have gone down, minority scores have gone up. From 1976 (when the College Board began tracking group scores) to 1992, black student scores went from 686 to 737; Mexican-origin scores went from 781 to 797; and Puerto Rican scores went from 765 to 772. White scores declined, but this is due, at least in part, to the broadened social class base of white test takers. In 1976, the number of white test takers was equal to only 19 percent of the 17-year-old white population. In 1992, it was 25 percent, a less elite group.

The best way to improve average SAT scores would be to encourage only the best middle-class students to take the test. We used to do just this, which is why average scores were higher. Today we prepare more minority and lower-middle-class students to take college entrance exams. It's a sign of accomplishment, not failure.

A more accurate evaluation of SAT trends comes from examining not average scores but the percentage of all youths in the 17-year-old cohort (both test takers and non-takers) who perform well on the test. In 1992, test takers equal in number to 2.2 percent of all 17-year-olds had verbal scores of at least 600 (good enough to get into top-ranked universities), better than the 1.9 percent with such scores in 1976. In math, test takers equal in number to 5.4 percent of all 17-year-olds got at least 600 in 1992, up from only 3.8 percent who scored that well in 1976. The number of students who scored over 500, good enough for admission to academically respectable four-year colleges, grew as well. These data suggest improved grade and high school performance.

Reports of the National Assessment of Educational Progress, a federal attempt to test student achievement, mostly confirm this conclusion. White student reading levels have been stagnant, for example, but growth in minority scores has closed much of the gap in the last 20 years. The same is true for math and, to a lesser extent, science. Absolute scores still leave great room for improvement. The average 13-year-old, for example, reads adequately to "search for specific information, interrelate ideas, and make generalizations"; but only 11 percent of 13-year-olds can "find, understand, summarize and explain relatively complicated information."

SAT tests measure the ability of seniors who think about attending college. Actual enrollment data provides more evidence of improvement. White student college enrollment has jumped from 27 percent of all 18-to-24-year-olds in 1970 to 34 percent in 1991. In 1970, 16 percent of black 18-to-24-year-olds were enrolled in college. In 1991, 24 percent were enrolled. In 1972 (the earliest year for Hispanic census data), 13 percent of Hispanic 18-to-24-year-olds were enrolled in college, and by 1991, 18 percent were enrolled. While immigration confounds this statistic, if we consider only those who graduated from high school, the number of Hispanic youths enrolled in college jumped from 26 percent in 1972 to 34 percent in 1991.

From 1980 to 1991, the number of black students enrolled in four-year colleges jumped by 20 percent, despite the fact that black 18- to-24-year-olds in the population declined by 6 percent. Hispanic enrollment in four-year colleges increased by 76 percent, outpacing a population gain (including immigrants) for this age group of 41 percent. These data are no cause for complacency; minority participation rates in higher education still fall below white rates. And enrollment gains do not necessarily translate into college completion, which is affected as much by economics as academics. But these enrollment data are also no basis for condemning the preparation for college in public schools. On the contrary, we should look at what schools do right, so we can do more of it.

Contrary to a cherished myth, American science and engineering performance surpasses our competitors. Of every 10,000 Americans, 7.4 have bachelor's degrees in physical science

or engineering. Japan has 7.3 per 10,000 and West Germany, 6.7. American performance continues to improve: in 1987, 7 percent of 22-year-olds had a science or engineering degree, up from less than 5 percent in 1970. Only 6.5 percent of 22-year-olds in Japan and 4 percent of 22-year-olds in Germany had science or engineering degrees in 1987. Our advantage stems from greater commitment to educate women. In America, 35 percent of new scientists are women, compared with Japan's 10 percent.

During the cold war, Sandia National Laboratories in Albuquerque produced nuclear weapons components. With demand for warheads declining, and a belief that production of scientists was declining as well, the Bush administration asked Sandia to plan how "to pick up our society by its bootstraps and find a new mechanism to obtain science and math literacy."

Sandia gave the assignment to three systems analysts with experience in nuclear weapons, a subject too dangerous to approach with preconceptions. They took pride in their ability to examine facts dispassionately. In early 1991, the Sandia team prepared a report, asserting that "evidence of decline used to justify system-wide reform is based on misinterpretations or misrepresentations of the data."

The Sandia researchers have been muzzled. The Department of Education complained that the report was biased because "data shown are consistently supportive of a picture of U.S. education in a positive light." The report, Secretary of Energy James Watkins charged, "is a call for complacency at a time when just the opposite is required. The Department of Energy will not permit publication of the study as presently drafted." It has still not been released.

School Bureaucracy

Conventional wisdom has an all-purpose explanation for supposedly deteriorating education: public schools spend inordinate resources on administration, teacher creativity is stifled by centralized control, and funds for educational improvement are diverted to bureaucracy.

The claim, however, does not withstand scrutiny. In Los Angeles, typical of other California districts, schools spend 65 percent of their own resources (excluding state and federal programs) on "instruction," including salaries, benefits, and training of teachers and paraprofessional aides, textbooks, classroom equipment, and supplies. Counselors, psychologists, and nurses take

4 percent. Security and maintenance consume 11 percent. School administrators (principals, deans, attendance officers, and school clerical personnel) take 7 percent. Busing gets 6 percent. Miscellaneous expenses (such as library staff, library books, and educational television) take another 3 percent. This leaves central administration (the "bureaucracy"), including superintendents, accounting, payroll and purchasing, property and liability insurance, with only 5 percent of the annual budget. Its peak in the last decade was 6.6 percent. Although category definitions may vary, national data also show schools spending 61 percent of their budgets on instruction and 5 percent on administration.

Yet even these relatively modest bureaucratic expenditures are often characterized as wasteful, lending support to calls for decentralization, "school-site autonomy," or "school-based management."

In 1970, New York gave parent- and teacher-dominated community boards finance and hiring power. The relaxation of controls spawned scandals like loans of school funds to employees; theft of school property; hiring politicians' relatives as teacher aides; solicitation of bribes; ethnic-based hiring; and extorting political contributions from teachers. Despite his commitment to school-site decision making, New York School Superintendent Joseph Fernandez expanded the central bureaucracy's role in monitoring finances and appointments.

Schools' bureaucratic rules (such as centralized textbook selection, detailed curriculum requirements including the number of minutes spent on specified subjects, demands for attendance accounting and ethnic surveys, and restricted telephone or copying machine use) inhibit teacher creativity and should be reformed. But behind classroom doors, teachers are still the most autonomous and unsupervised of all professionals. Rarely acknowledged in school debates is that bureaucracy results from compromises made between spontaneity and creativity on the one hand, and eliminating discrimination, corruption, and incompetence on the other.

Decentralization can't stimulate creativity without also risking corruption. Schools with flexibility to buy classroom computers without cumbersome bidding also have opportunities to solicit bribes. A principal who can select unconventionally qualified candidates, ignoring credentials and test scores, can also discriminate in hiring teachers or custodians.

Centralized school systems restrict flexibility, yet districts have mostly been freed of corruption. Bureaucratic mazes have roots in earlier reforms to curb graft. After employees are caught in a kickback scheme, multiple signatures for purchases become required. Years ago, hiring relatives was routine in school employment. To avoid this abuse, school hiring is now governed by cumbersome civil service rules. Perhaps the most egregious exception is New York City's system of school building custodians who function more like entrepreneurs than employees. Reform will require more bureaucracy, not less. If decentralization of school bureaucracies proceeds, there will be calls for recentralization when scandals inevitably follow.

The trade-off between autonomy and accountability is most stark when academic standards at issue. Bilingual teaching for non-English speaking students is now national policy. School administrators train faculty and inspect schools to ensure that students get native language instruction while gaining English fluency. Data clerks track student progress to assure that appropriate tests for transition to English are administered. Without central monitoring, some schools might ignore language minority students. Indeed, many did, prior to 1978 when courts ordered bilingual teaching.

Special education requires tests to identify handicapped children and specialists who investigate whether special education is provided. Without watchful bureaucrats, some schools might ignore these expensive requirements. Before courts mandated these programs in 1974, many schools did so. Demands for less bureaucracy imply willingness to risk their doing so again.

Bureaucrats also review applications to determine which students get free lunch, which are eligible for subsidy, and which must pay full cost. It would of course be simpler and more expensive to provide meals to all. But few business or political leaders are prepared, despite anti-bureaucratic rhetoric, to commit additional tax funds to such administrative streamlining.

Simultaneous calls for greater school autonomy and higher national standards put the two basic "reform" drives in direct conflict. One wants higher standards, the other less administration. Yet bureaucracy must enforce mandates unless we allow each school to decide whether to teach math, science, or American history. Higher standards demand more bureaucracy, not

less. Many leaders say they want school-based decision making, but what they really seek is a chimera: all schools spontaneously deciding to do the "right" thing, without administrative enforcement.

Bureaucracy stifles, and school reform should reduce bureaucratic structures performing redundant or useless tasks. But lacking the willingness to abandon common standards and tolerate more corruption, calls for radical dismantling of school administration are mostly demagogic.

It's no surprise that school-based management experiments have mostly floundered. Good school principals have always involved teachers in school planning. But when, in contemporary reforms, teachers get formal powers to run schools, they often balk at time demands of administrative tasks. Good teachers, reformers have been discomfited to find, want to teach. They don't want to spend time in committee meetings, entertain textbook publishers, solicit low bids for supplies, or calculate race and ability distribution for classroom assignments.

The Fantasy of School Choice

Belief in schools' failure has also encouraged the notion that competition could force improvement by requiring that schools compete for clients. "Choice" supporters argue that if education producers (school staffs) tied their security to consumer (parents) satisfaction, quality would improve and high-performing schools would multiply, while unselected schools would lose enrollment.

But the customer-driven management analogy may not work for public education, where the "consumer" of school outcomes is the nation's economic, social, and moral standing, not merely the family whose child is taught.

Choice advocates assume that parental "purchasing power" will include knowledge of competing schools' academic strengths. Choice advocates assert without evidence that parents will not favor schools where academic mediocrity is offset by good athletic programs, a whiter student body, or a recent paint job. Illiterate immigrant and college-educated parents, they assume, will have equal information about alternatives. Unfortunately, however, parents with the least purchasing power (knowledge about educational alternatives) in a market model are the very parents whose communities most need school improvement.

Parent choice already plays a limited role

in public education. Specialized theme "magnet" schools in many urban districts give ambitious minority students a chance for integrated education and entice whites to stay in the city system. These are worthy goals but have little to do with the fantasy that the whip of competition will force schools to improve. In fact, "choice" schools like magnets may make neighborhood schools worse. Despite careful admissions restrictions, magnet programs attract the most highly motivated students, draining neighborhood schools of students and parents who could spur higher achievement levels. Controls cannot be subtle enough, for example, to prevent counselors from giving greater encouragement to middle-class magnet applicants than to poor students. While magnets have better academic records than neighborhood schools, this is because the motivated students they attract do well in any setting. Magnets provide no evidence for the free market idea that a need to be selected forces schools to improve. Analysis of student outcomes shows that magnet students generally do no better than neighborhood school students who applied to magnets but, because of space limitations, could not get in.

The greatest danger of choice, public or private, is that race and class segregation will grow if parents choose schools attended by children like their own. This likely effect of choice is suggested by other nations' experience. Since 1978, for example, Canada's British Columbia has subsidized private schools; wealthier and better educated parents took these subsidies, leaving public school students in a less advantaged milieu.

Since 1959, the French government has paid salaries of all teachers, public and private. Though France attempts to limit inequality by requiring comparable public and private class sizes, rich students are disproportionately enrolled in subsidized private schools, leaving immigrant students concentrated in the public system.

Israel recently established alternative schools with differing philosophies and curricula. They are academically superior to neighborhood schools; parents who choose them are wealthier and more educated. Choice schools are islands of excellence for the rich while Israel struggles to assimilate immigrants from North Africa and Russia.

Holland's choice system is 85 years old. The government pays for buildings and teacher salaries for any school that parents establish; two-thirds of all schools are privately run. School choice in Holland has enabled "white flight" from Turkish and Moroccan neighborhood schools. Recent Dutch studies show that Muslim students in segregated classrooms do worse than those who are in integrated classrooms, while most Dutch parents choose schools based on the socioeconomic status of students already enrolled, not on the school's academic performance.

Scotland got school choice in 1982; parents can send children to private or public schools outside their local district. According to a recent study by professors Doug Willms and Frank Echols, 27 percent of children whose parents were professionals chose to escape neighborhood schools, but less than .5 percent of children whose parents were semi-skilled blue-collar workers did so. Twenty-four percent of college-educated parents' children, but less than 1 percent of children whose parents had no college, escaped.

There is little doubt that wealthier parents believe their children gain advantage by attending schools with other privileged children. But the consequence of honoring this choice is diminished opportunity for less advantaged children. Historically, we have honored such choices. White, middle-class parents once moved to homogeneous suburbs to seek "better" schools. Today this method of exercising school choice is less available. Urban areas and their impoverished minority populations are now too large to permit easy escape within commuting distance of central cities. The incorporation of professionals into upper-income strata has expanded elite private school options previously reserved for the hereditary or corporate elite. As a result, desire for restorating the segregation that this class once knew has been transformed into demand for school choice. Cloaked in a faulty assessment of schools' academic decline, choice is presented as a necessity for broad school reform to benefit all children.

Reforms That Could Work

If the foregoing is true--that increasing returns to education are deceptive and we have a shortage of demanding jobs rather than of educated workers; that expanded educational resources since 1965 have not mostly been dedicated to academic improvement; that, nonetheless, public schools' academic achievement has risen; that bureaucracy is not stifling American

education; and that the most popular contemporary reforms, decentralization and choice, address the wrong problems and could do great damage—then it is hard to avoid an iconoclastic conclusion: the public school system is mostly on the right track and the best way to improve its results, especially for minority children, is to pour more money into it.

More resources are not the only improvement needed. Implementation of the curricular reforms of the last 15 years is essential. Better systems for hiring and evaluating principals and improved teacher training—for undergraduates as well as teachers already on the job—could contribute to better academic achievement. So too could a satisfactory method of removing poor teachers from the profession. But design of this reform is difficult because results produced by individual teachers are hard to measure statistically, so sustaining the removal of poor teachers through civil service or union procedures is improbable, unless child abuse or other criminal behavior is present.

Most teachers are competent, as the performance of our schools indicate. We could not claim improved outcomes without a teaching force that, on the whole, is dedicated, prepared, and increasingly creative. This is why, while weeding out uninspired teachers would be worthwhile, the most useful reform of public education remains more money. Here is how more resources could most productively be spent:

- **Equalized school funding.** In states which have not equalized funding between rich and poor districts, students continue to attend dilapidated schools without adequately paid teachers or necessary equipment. As Jonathan Kozol has pointed out, if money made no difference in education, wealthy districts would not be so determined to hoard it.

- **Reduced class size.** Educational research shows that class-size reduction has little effect if classes remain so large that teaching is mostly to large groups. Reducing class size to 15 or less, on the other hand, can have academic results. This is the most expensive school reform imaginable (reducing class size from 24 to 15 doubles the marginal costs of education), and it should perhaps be restricted to schools with the most disadvantaged students. But if we

want to close the gap between minority and white students more quickly, lowering class size could be effective.

- **Full funding of Head Start**. Preschool children exposed to books, manipulative toys, and literate adults are better prepared to succeed than those who are not. Quality school experiences cannot fully compensate for deprivation in preschool years. Yet Head Start funding is sufficient to enroll only 30 percent of eligible low-income children. While Head Start children's test scores surpass those of nonenrolled children in first to third grades, the advantage seems to be lost by fourth grade. Further investigation is needed to understand this loss, other evidence supports full funding. Head Start graduates are less frequently retained in grade, have better school attendance, lower dropout rates, higher employment rates, fewer criminal arrests, and less welfare dependency than youth from similar backgrounds but without the benefit of a preschool program.

- **A national prenatal health program.** It is a shibboleth of the education establishment, overcompensating for generations of contempt for poor and minority children, that all children can succeed if only their teachers communicate high expectations. This has an element of truth, but also an element of denial. Low-birthweight babies, or fetal drug-, nicotine-, or alcohol-addicted babies cannot mature into successful students to the extent healthy babies can. Giving all babies a healthy start in life would contribute to improved academic outcomes.

- **Improved apprenticeship and workplace training.** Schools presently send students with adequate numeric and literary skills into the work force. Work habits may not be adequate, and curricular reforms should emphasize team building and cooperative skills. But schools cannot be expected to provide the kind of practical technical training like Ford offers to Mexican dropouts in Chihuahua. The Clinton administration may propose requiring business to fund worker training, with the further mandate that training funds be expended on frontline as well as supervisory workers. Ongoing workplace training is needed to preserve the fruits of improved schooling.

- **Improved teacher salaries.** The highest achieving college students don't always make the best teachers, but teachers are too often recruited from college graduates whose grades or ambitions are not high enough to win places in more remunerative professions. Higher teacher salaries will improve the competitive position of education vis-à-vis law, accounting, engineering, medicine, and nursing. To attract good teachers, salaries need not be higher than in other professions, but improving relative teacher pay will improve schools' ability to attract more highly qualified graduates.

Especially because of the need to win more public funds for teacher salary increases, the role of some teacher-union leaders in education debates has been curious. Each Sunday, a paid *New York Times* advertisement by Albert Shanker, president of the American Federation of Teachers, analyzes American education, often denouncing school performance and contrasting the illiteracy of American youth with academic achievements of other nations' children.

If a teachers union goal is to mobilize support for public education and its employees, denunciation of school performance is a questionable strategy. The public is more likely to increase tax support for systems that perform well than for those that fail. Campaigns to highlight teachers' extraordinary accomplishment—the advance of universal education in a social system hostile to economic equality—could do more to mobilize opinion on teachers' behalf. Nonetheless, teachers unions around the country follow Shanker's lead, mounting attacks on their own school systems in the vain hope that the public will blame only administrators and not teachers for schools' purported failures.

The School Failure Myth in Perspective

The prevailing consensus that schools need radical systemic reform is at odds with economic and academic data. But it derives support from a political culture surviving the Reagan era—the suspicion of all public institutions and conviction that if public bureaucracy is responsible, performance must be deficient. The school failure myth also derives support from the nation's corporate leadership, anxious to find a scapegoat for high unemployment, racial division, and income inequality. Blaming the schools avoids confronting business deindustrialization strategies, failure to invest in high-wage jobs, and shortsighted trade policies. Faulting public education also excuses the business community's desire to reduce tax support of schools.

The myth of school failure derives support from liberals and minority group activists who too easily assume that youth unemployment must stem from lack of preparation, not lack of decent jobs. And the myth derives support from the right's privatization agenda; it is easier to mobilize support for private school subsidies if belief in public school failure gains currency—

> *If a teachers union goal is to mobilize support for public education and its employees, denunciation of school performance is a questionable strategy.*

thus the suppression of Sandia Labs' school performance report because it sent a message of "complacency."

Finally, the school failure myth is reinforced by experiences of many in the professional middle class who have their own anecdotes about ill-prepared (usually minority group) high school graduates. In some cases, the stories suffer from an idealized memory of how much better prepared graduates once were—discounting realities that not only did fewer students graduate in past decades, but many graduates had "general" or "vocational" diplomas in which carpentry or metal shop, not algebra, dominated the curriculum. Today nearly all graduates are in academic programs, both because our expectations of universal education have expanded and because jobs no longer exist for which vocational programs once trained.

There are still too many dropouts and too many high school graduates who can't read or compute at appropriate levels. Almost invariably, however, these are students without a consistent school experience, who have frequently moved, have no stable home support, or come from violence, drug or alcohol dominated environments. School reforms, no matter how creative, cannot substitute for a full employment program with jobs at good wages in minority communities.

Schools have done less well in developing disciplinary habits in students from social strata which, in earlier generations, dropped out. As the Commission on the Skills of the American Workforce put it, while few businesses find a lack of academic skills in entry-level workers, "the primary concern of more than 80 percent of employers was finding workers with a good work ethic and appropriate social behavior: 'reliable,' 'a good attitude,' 'a pleasant appearance,' 'a good personality.'" Conventional critiques of school performance, however, have little to say about this problem, and popular systemic solutions to education's alleged academic failures do not address it either.

We have no reason to be complacent about schools' performance. No democratic society should tolerate adults who cannot interpret bus schedules or newspaper articles. When job applicants can't pass a seventh-grade-level employment exam, we have a problem, even if the promise of jobs for those who pass is a false one. That school output may be adequate for industrial needs does not suggest that a more literate and mathematically sophisticated work force would not be even more productive. Industry should invest more in workplace training, and training can be more effective if workers bring greater literacy and numeric skills to their jobs.

But when schools are doing better than ever before, the best way to encourage continued improvement is not a concerted attack on school governance and organization. A more effective approach would be praise for accomplishment, provision of additional resources to programs whose results justify support, and reforms on the margin to correct programs and curricula shown to be ineffective. Unfortunately, school reform is now a crusade that eclipses attention from the true causes of youth unemployment and declining wages for those who graduate from high school but do not go to college. Reform of industrial, trade, and labor market policies hold more promise for income growth than does school reform.

SHOULD WE PUSH THE BUTTON?

B. Paul Komisar

B. PAUL KOMISAR retired from Temple University and is now an adjunct professor at Rowan College.

Once upon a time, there was a kid who used to draw a small circle on paper and blacken it in with a pencil. This was now "the button." Then he picked out whatever he wanted to happen—pass the test, get rid of George the bully, abolish spinach, or whatever—and pushed the button!

The button technique was amazingly reliable. George the bully, for example, just vanished, and to my knowledge he never returned. Gradually, knowledge of the button spread. There was even talk that military types planned to get some kids to use the button on the enemy. But no big contracts were involved, and nothing came of it. The military turned to Star Wars instead, and the button technique died out.

Or so it seemed. Then just yesterday some people put pencil to paper, made a button, and marked it "school vouchers." The technique seemed to retain all its old magic. Suddenly, just by poising a finger above the button, we had magnet schools, theme schools, industry schools for unwed mothers, state-run specialized high schools, and the city schools leased to a corporation. There was even talk of decentralizing the system (yet again) under the tricky title of "school-based management" with the goal of "empowering" teachers. It was enough to leave you breathless.

Still, there was one most curious omission: no voucher system. How could the voucher idea have inspired so much change when no one had actually pushed the button?

A Benevolent System

The present school system has been from its inception a benevolent, paternal one. Schools had some very good things to do for both society and individuals. Indeed, even before public schools got under way, the idea of knowledge as necessary for citizens in the new republic was pushed. Much later the mission was to fit the young into the melting pot, to Americanize them. More recently the idea was to give everyone a sort of equal shot at life's chances and help the young toward self-realization or something. Today we want to make the nation more competitive in world markets. Such ploys have justified the use of public funds to support an institution, ultimately a big bureaucratic institution. So perhaps we shy from actually pushing the voucher button because it would replace a benevolent system with what would seem to be a less-inspiring entrepreneurial one.

But not everyone in a paternal institution works from missionary zeal. It's easy to celebrate those who act in service of educational ideals, but bureaucrats in a benevolent institution can still gain power, position, status, even celebrity. These usual trappings of personal ambition represent for many a good return on one's investment. That doesn't appear to differ much from the entrepreneurial exchange of service for payment. So let's think of the public school system and those working in it as hybrid, combining a benevolent framework with a tradelike mentality.

So much is the system a hybrid that when society shifts toward an extreme individualism, the hybrid realizes that educational variety will now be looked on with favor and moves to provide it. And as in any competitive market, when another arrangement promises still more variety, the hybrid moves to it. If we just want more choice in schooling, then the hybrid system may do the job and make a voucher plan unnecessary. Why make revolutionary shifts when finally, a little more jostling of the present system will do?

Desperate Problems

But isn't there another basis for pushing the voucher button? Yes, there is. For a couple of decades we have been engaged in school reform, and the voucher idea is at least that old. So we can ask: what is impelling this idea *now*? Desperation, I think.

The consensus is that reforms have not solved the major school problems—problems of poor performance by U.S. students in comparison with their foreign counterparts in math and science, poor work or basic education skills in our work force, a decline in student achievement since the 1960s as shown in Scholastic Aptitude Test scores, and the prevalence of dysfunctional behavior in students, including violence, gun toting, drug use, and widespread dropouts.

Let's begin with the problem of poor performance of U.S. students in international competition, because it reveals best the unrecognized underlying situation. The comparison is suspect from the beginning. In the U.S. we have adopted a system of schooling stretched out twelve to fourteen years before the student does any serious majoring. We tie this to a democratic impulse to keep as many children as possible in school for as long as possible. To compare test scores of *these* students with foreign students from restricted early-specialization schools is like pitting amateurs against professionals. Naturally the scores reveal a difference in average levels of achievement. When the critic responds that the average scores of even the top groups differ, the only response is to declare that of course they do, given the differences in focus, expectation, and seriousness in the schools at the time the tests are given.

Timing is the key. If you want to

From *Educational Horizons*, Vol. 71, No. 1, Fall 1992, pp. 18-22. Reprinted with permission from *Educational HORIZONS*, quarterly journal of Pi Lamda Theta, International Honor and Professional Association in Education, 4101 E. Third Street, Bloomington, IN 47407-6626.

91

compare U.S. and foreign student achievement in specialized fields, the place to do it is further downstream, where there is a comparable degree of concentration on studies. Or better yet, why use tests at all? Why not compare the real thing? How do U.S. and foreign mathematicians and scientists perform on the Job? None of these people would stand still for anything as silly as achievement tests, but can't we use other measures, such as the number of Nobel prizes, patent rates, institutional rankings used in hiring, and a little of our version of industrial spying?

I don't contend that earlier tests are worthless. At the least they tell us the price we pay for our kind of school system. But levity aside, the point to keep in mind is that we are evaluating systems, not students. Perhaps we in the United States have adopted a bad system. Perhaps what we have done is to assume there is a buffer learning zone to work with so that students who don't major at age sixteen, can do so at ages twenty or twenty four or even later and make up in a reasonably short time what was not learned in the years spent in general studies or other majors. That is, we take a certain range as learning and assume it's never too late to focus, to get serious. Is this a mistake? It seems to be the case that our later majors are a match for those who focus earlier in foreign school systems, and plenty of students do one major, then start another (Sir Francis Crick, the codiscoverer of DNA, for one). And I recall reading of an Oxbridge debate following World War I over whether veterans planning to major in history could make up for the loss of crucial years of absorbing history. Things seem to have worked out nonetheless

With delay, some students get restive. We have to let some of them go, or rather get out of their way (computer hackers, for instance). Can't we carry delay to a point of absurdity, even danger, for those in fields where productive work comes

early? To put the matter concretely, is twelve to fourteen years of school and two more of general education in college simply too long? And what do we do with students during the delay? Must it be general education, core curriculum, or that hollow joke, distribution requirements?

One good move now fairly screams to us: put more variation, more choice points, in schooling. Here is where the voucher idea shines. The system, any system, even when oriented to choice has to maintain some uniformity simply because it is a system and can't abide chaos. But a voucher arrangement goes as far as human ingenuity will take you, and that can be pretty far.

Poor Work Skills

With regard to the problem of poor work or basic education skills in our work force, we can quickly dispense with the idea that poor education keeps our workers from high productivity and lowers our competitive advantage over Germany and Japan. Surely industrial leaders, not schoolteachers, bear most of the responsibility for our competitive decline and our slow pace in adapting to methods of lean production developed by Japanese auto makers. (Honda's success in making Accords in the United States and then exporting many of them to Japan tells us what well-led U.S. workers can do.)

There is nothing new in this attempt to blame schools for goofs made in high places. The early Soviet lead in space enterprises was blamed on poor science education in high schools, though it was never made clear (it couldn't be) how school science would advance space travel. But let's not knock it. A lot of good came from that foolishness. We got new textbooks, involvement of scientists and mathematicians in schools (too short-lived, sadly), and summer seminars for high school teachers. Most school people will play scapegoat anytime for those advantages.

Maybe it will work out that way again. Demands for improved na-

tional productivity through school reform just might get teachers some of what they need. But if adjustments in industry are finally under way, then let industry itself give workers the kind of training said to be needed. Industrialists seem to be maneuvering to get schools to do it. Of course, if it is just a better basic education they are after, they are right to ask schools for it. But they (someone) will have to be clearer on the kinds of basic skills needed. After all, it's *their* production line. The public rhetoric is useless when it comes to details, and that's where this debate is placed.

So if specialized work skills are needed, it is clearly industry's task. It would be too expensive and too inefficient to tool up vocational schools to prepare workers for industries already tooled up. But there is no reason why a school voucher can't be used by families to get classes in industries or in industry-run schools. With vouchers, the principle of putting the solution exactly where the problem is now has support.

Sometimes we tend to forget we are a pragmatic country. But it's easy to be cynical about this issue of school versus industry as the site for worker education. Our predicament is that our economy cannot create jobs as easily as it can start programs to train for them. There is no use trying to tell students that job training and job getting are separate, even if we teach about the economy along the way. It's impossible to break the perception that making the effort to learn job skills guarantees the job when the effort is done. Bad stories of this sort abound. It's a cynical point, but the voucher shifts blame to the family when the chosen training course turns out to be uncashable.

SAT Score Decline

We arrive now at the very real decline in SAT scores since the 1960s which is taken as indicating a reduction in school learning. Serious business. I'm not ready to take test scores as evidence of very much, but I do concede that they are an indirect measure of such things as drug abuse, intimidation, hostility to authority, and so forth. But given our kind of attenuated twelve to fourteen year system, these symptoms of negativism are no surprise. In fact, encouraging potential dropouts to stay in school just to get the credential when there are no new substantive experiences to offer them disenchants everyone. In this case the system is simply breeding its own degradation. Surely we must have something more hopeful to offer when the system reaches deadness.

One quick step is to slap the label "school program" on as many community practices as we can get away with and get students to enter them. Here the voucher works beautifully, for it is also a way to get money to a museum, a library, a child care center, an art gallery, clubs for adolescents, theaters, and so on. We get an infusion of human and financial life into the community, and have a certificate for completion. This is the route for many students and a voucher plan will get them there.

Thinking about Schooling

But my main concern here is not in working out school reforms. It's obvious what we should do, and it's even more obvious why we won't do it. The chief matter is how we conceive of schooling to begin with. In school you run into two worlds. Among the hybrid bureaucrats, drug use, assaults on teachers and students, intimidation in class, and dropouts are problems, often social problems. They have to be confronted, discussed, researched, made the content of reports and targets of recommendations. Problems are what's wrong; they are alien to the institution. It's a model of confronting and overcoming intrusions in the system.

Teachers tend to live in a different world. The problems of the system are the conditions of work. They are factors to be accommodated day by day in order to make the classroom as viable for effort and learning as

one can make it. If students won't listen or attend, you have to find ways to sneak the message through or set them more on their own. If they won't let themselves get excited about classroom matters (I've seen this phenomenon many times, and it always surprises me), then you need to treat the matter as humdrum so that it is acceptable to be bored about it. If students have little to offer, find something, anything they will do.

Teaching here, at this level, is making concrete moves bit by bit: a new idea here, a device there, even trying a different attitude or outlook. The thing that strikes you is that the slogans of the system (learning to learn, kids at risk, whole language approach) just vanish. In the classroom, that is just political rhetoric that counts for nothing in doing real work.

The key to classroom teaching is the precise move, what you do in a particular situation. Precise moves are what teaching competence amounts to, and its main working feature is absorbing conditions of the moment into the ongoing task. There need be no confrontation, no removal, even no solution in a way. The bored remain so, the obnoxious become no better tempered. *But the class is made to work.* We are not "problems" but are working within them. The "problems" are not alien. There are always troublesome conditions to work with; if not these, then others: student denseness (teaching, like sculpting, can be working with stone) or aloofness and later hostility when the teacher fails to acknowledge the student's invented superiority. Teaching is *always* one damned thing or another. To imagine otherwise is fantasy.

I don't mean to idealize classroom competence, just to characterize it. I don't suggest it can regularly turn class situations into great teaching. Most of us muddle through; there are not always happy moments. Conditions may require routine and you may have to lose the spontaneity and openness you prefer. Don't

you recall those "classroom treaties" reported in research wherein the teacher asked for little effort in exchange for no trouble from the students? At least the teachers could pull that off; the class didn't disintegrate.

Summary

We end up with a split decision in a double sense. The voucher splits public education on the line between credentialing and learning. If you are bent on a credential, a special one from a science high school or a school for international studies, then you can get it in the choice system we have now. The hybrid bureaucrat can broker such programs and other policies for us. Vouchers are not needed.

Of course, the hybrid can't guarantee you'll learn good science; you need to control the classroom to do that. The hybrid official can only wield the rhetoric of program slogans. These have a place in discourse, but they are not part of actual teaching; if you want learning, you'll have to choose schools, even classrooms, and do your own brokering. Then it's a voucher system that strips away layers of officialdom to tap in to teaching competence.

I've also called attention to another advantage of the use of vouchers. At a time when finances are very tight, vouchers are a way to use the big money tied up in school systems to support industrial education programs, museum and library activities, and a host of apprentice programs. By refiguring the use of public school funds, we get a voucher dividend.

Maybe that's what school people object to. When parents choose more glamorous schools and exotic programs, they leave the public schools with a mixture of the troubled and the uninterested. But isn't that what they should have competence to deal with? They've been in the game long enough. And anyway, where is it written that we must sacrifice the welfare of those who want to learn in favor of those who don't?

Morality and Values in Education

The family and socioeconomic contexts in which many children and teenagers live have become more multi-problematic over the years. Many children and teenagers live in crisis. Some teachers complain that many students no longer cherish or abide by basic traditional values such as honesty, honor, or respect for other persons. Educators believe that children and teenagers need instruction in how to make ethical decisions regarding what they should or should not do when problems arise in their lives. Frequently, many students are not being enculturated in many traditional civic values. A number of people argue that this is the responsibility of the family and religious organizations. Quite often teachers feel that they cannot do everything, but many of them also feel that they must do something. Teachers need to be good examples of responsible, ethical behavior for their students.

Many values regarding what we perceive to be worthwhile ideas or defensible behavior inform our reflections on professional practice as teachers. We are conscious of some of the values that inform our behavior, but we may not be conscious of all of those values that inform our preferences as to what we ought to do as teachers.

Values that we hold without being conscious of them are referred to as "tacit" values—values that we need to derive from reasoned reflection on our thought about teaching and learning. Much of our knowledge about teaching is "tacit" knowledge—knowledge that we need to bring into our conscious cognitive repertoire through reflection and conscious analysis of the concepts which "drive" our practice. We need to acknowledge how our values inform, or influence, our thoughts about teaching.

What part ought the schooling experience play in the formation of such things as character, informed compassion, conscience, honor, and respect for self and others? From Socrates forward (and before him) we have wrestled with these concerns. We address these things as educators in every human generation have had to address them. Aristotle noted in his *Politics* that there was no consensus as to what the purposes of education should be in Athens, that people disputed what Athenian youth ought to be taught by their teachers, and that youth did not always address their elders with respect. Apparently, we do not have a new problem on our hands here. It is one, however, of great importance that every generation of citizens in every nation addresses in one manner or another. Certainly the issue of public morality and the question of how to educate best for individually and collectively responsible social behavior is a matter of great significance in North America today.

Teachers need to help students develop within themselves a sense of critical social consciousness and a genuine concern for social justice. The debate on this issue continues in professional literature. Insight into the nature of moral decision-making should be taught in the context of real current and past social problems and lead students to develop their own skills in social analysis relating to the ethical dilemmas of human beings.

There is a need for teachers to develop principles of professional practice that will enable them to respond reasonably to the many ethical dilemmas they face. The knowledge base on how teachers derive their knowledge of professional ethics is developing. The study of how teachers come to be aware of their basic values and of how these values shape their professional practice is very important. Educational systems at all levels are based on the desirability to teach certain fundamental beliefs and the disciplines of knowledge (however they may be organized in different cultures). School curricula are based on certain moral assumptions (secular or religious) as to the worth of knowledge, and the belief that some forms of knowledge are more worthy than others. Schooling is not only to transmit national and cultural heritage, including the intellectual heritage, of a people; it is also a fundamentally moral enterprise. "Moral bases of education" is the evaluation of choices and the making of decisions on the knowledge and academic skills that ought to be taught. How persons answer the questions implied by the above remarks reflects their own ideological biases.

We see, therefore, that when we speak of morality and education there are process issues as to the most basic knowledge-seeking, epistemological foundations of learning. Hence, the controversy over morality in education deals with more than just the tensions between secular and religious interests in society, although to know about such tensions is a valuable, important matter. Moral education is also more than a debate over the merits of methods used to teach students to make morally sound, ethical choices in their lives—although this also is critically important and ought to be done. Thus, we argue that the construction of educational processes and the decisions about the substantive content of school curricula are also moral issues as well as epistemological ones having to do with how we discover, verify, and transmit knowledge.

One of the most compelling responsibilities of Canadian and American schools is the responsibility of preparing young persons for their moral duties as free citizens of free nations. The Canadian and American governments

communicable diseases, etc.? Or should they deny these requests? For whom do the schools exist? Is a teacher's primary responsibility to his or her client, the student, or to the student's parents? Do secondary school students have the right to study and to inquire into subjects not in officially sanctioned curricula? What are the moral issues surrounding censorship of student reading material? What ethical questions are raised by arbitrarily withholding information regarding alternative viewpoints on controversial topics?

Teachers cannot hide all of their moral preferences. However, they can learn to conduct just, open discussions of moral topics without succumbing to the temptation to indoctrinate students with their own views.

Teaching students to respect all people, to revere the sanctity of life, to uphold the right to dissent on the part of any citizen, to believe in the equality of all people before the law, to cherish the freedom to learn, and to respect the right of all people to their own convictions—these are principles of democracy and ideals worthy of being cherished. An understanding of the processes of ethical decision-making is needed by the citizens of any free nation; thus, this process should be taught in a free nation's schools.

The essays in this unit constitute a comprehensive overview of moral education with considerable historical and textual interpretation. Topics covered include public pressures on schools and the social responsibilities of schools. The unit can be used in courses dealing with the historical or philosophical foundations of education.

Looking Ahead: Challenge Questions

What is moral education? Why do so many people wish to see a form of moral education in schools?

Are there certain values about which most North Americans can agree? Should they be taught in schools?

Should local communities have total control of the content of moral instruction in local schools, as they did in the nineteenth century? Defend your answer.

Should schools be involved in teaching people to reason about moral questions? Why or why not? If not, who should do it? Why?

What is the difference between indoctrination and instruction?

Is there a national consensus concerning the form that moral education should take in schools? Is such a consensus likely if it does not now exist?

What attitudes and skills are most important to a responsible approach to moral decision-making?

have always wanted the schools to teach the principles of civic morality based on their respective constitutional traditions. Indeed, when the public school movement began in the United States in the 1830s and 1840s, the concept of universal public schooling as a mechanism for instilling a sense of national identity and civic morality was supported. In every nation, school curricula have certain value preferences imbedded in them.

Significant constitutional issues are at stake in the forms and directions moral education should take in the schools. Both theistic and nontheistic conceptions of what constitutes moral behavior compete for the loyalties of teachers and students. Extremist forces representing the ideological left and right, both religious and secular, wish to see their moral agendas incorporated into school curricula.

Do teachers have a responsibility to respond to student requests for information on sexuality, sexual morality,

RIGHT AND WRONG

*Teaching values makes a comeback, as schools
see a need to fill a moral vacuum*

Sonia L. Nazario

Ms. Nazario is a staff reporter in THE WALL STREET
JOURNAL's *Los Angeles Bureau.*

*To educate a person in mind and not in morals is to
educate a menace to society.*
—THEODORE ROOSEVELT

Clovis, Calif.—Music teacher Carolyn Barrett is determined that her fourth-graders don't grow up to imperil mankind.

So, in a classroom at Lincoln Elementary School here, she raises her baton and puts the tots through the usual paces. They sing about equality, racial tolerance and reliability. "Most of all, you can count on me! me! me!" the less-than-harmonious voices belt out, as 40 children point at their little chests. For the grand finale, the children interlock hands, sway in unison and sing, "We are the future. We stand for love."

"This class will stand for the right things," Ms. Barrett tells the children between songs. She coaxes the children to share what they think are the "right" values. A boy's hand shoots up. "Not doing drugs," he says proudly. "Caring for other people," says a girl. Ms. Barrett beams.

Values aren't always taught in the home. Or even in church. But at Clovis Unified Schools, there is an unrelenting drive to create people who know the difference between right and wrong. "I want every song to push a value," says Ms. Barrett, who speaks fearfully of increasing crime in Fresno, Clovis's southern neighbor.

Adds Clovis Associate Superintendent for support services Dale Stringer: "Values are the underpinning of everything we do."

A FAR CRY

It wasn't that long ago that such talk would have brought forth howls of protest from parents and educators, worried that children were being forced to swallow somebody else's values. Schools still have to be careful: They typically stick to teaching "safe" values, such as honesty, perseverance, respect and responsibility. But even groups as diverse as the liberal American Jewish Committee and Phyllis Schlafly's conservative Eagle Forum now tend to support values education, recognizing that schools must fill a growing moral vacuum.

The evidence of that moral vacuum is overwhelming. Two-thirds of high-school students say they would lie to achieve a business objective, one survey found. U.S. teen pregnancy, drug abuse and juvenile crime rates are among the highest in the industrialized world.

Often, both parents now work and don't live near an extended family or other support system. In Maryland, a Baltimore County public-school survey showed that parents spend only 15 minutes each week in "meaningful dialogue" with their children, who glean values mainly from peers and television. Parents "are tired when they get home," says Mabel Franks, a teacher in Clovis. "They worry less about values than how to pay the bills." Another blow to values has been the dwindling role of the church as the U.S. becomes an increasingly secular society.

The upshot: Children are prodded to make complex moral decisions—about sex, for example—at an increasingly tender age, often before they are developmentally able to, and with little adult guidance.

"Teachers have recognized that they have to do something, or not live through their classes," says Gary Edwards, president of the nonprofit Ethics Resource Center in Washington, D.C. Pluralistic societies need common values or "tribalism takes over," he warns.

FEWER PROBLEMS

Advocates of values education point to several studies to bolster their case. Major disciplinary problems dropped 25% in some Los Angeles schools, for instance, after one year of using the Jefferson Center for Character Education's 10-minute daily values lessons. Another study, by Jacques S. Benninga, an education professor at California State University, Fresno, tracked the effects of Clovis's efforts over four elementary school years; children registered significant improvements in helpfulness and cooperation, and ranked higher in these areas than control groups.

"If you present an environment where certain values are consistently recognized and nurtured, some of them will be internalized," says Richard Sparks, who heads Clovis's Curriculum Committee for Character Education.

According to gurus in the field of "values education," Clovis is a model for providing just such an environment.

Clovis, a bustling middle-class community, certainly has its share of problems. Last year, says Clovis resource teacher Sylvia Gamble, 47 of the 300 seventh-graders in her school were termed "at risk." Some were neglected, while others had alcohol or drug-abuse problems. One Clovis high-school student on PCP went into a convenience store in search of beer and stabbed the manager 21 times.

Lincoln fourth-grader Ziad Amro recalls his parents hitting the moral highlights when he was four years old: Don't do drugs, don't hitchhike, don't use cocaine, don't get in cars with strangers. That was it. Instead, the nine-year-old says, he has gotten moral lessons about life's seamier side by tuning in each day to TV's "A Current Affair"—and even "Wall Street Week."

Affluent students are no less at risk. Clovis teachers say. One sixth-grade girl in Gayle Peck's class sharpened her pencils, and left the shavings where they fell around her feet. When Ms. Peck told her to pick them up, the girl refused, saying it was the janitor's job. After a talk with the girl, Ms. Peck learned that she was used to having her maid pick up after her.

CHANGE IN THE '60S

Schools share some of the blame for the moral malaise. As the rigid cultural norms of the 1950s gave way to the free-style individualism of the 1960s, teachers were told that all values were relative and personal. Many texts with blatant moral messages of right and wrong—throwbacks to the McGuffey's Readers of the 1800s—were supplanted by values-neutered texts. One commonly used textbook described the Pilgrims not as seekers of religious freedom but as "people who take long trips."

"Schools didn't want to indoctrinate children," says University of Illinois values education expert Edward A. Wynne.

Instead, schools turned to "values clarification"—often exercises that tried to get children to figure out and embrace their own values, no matter what they were.

Typical were exercises where children were told that World War III was beginning, and only six of 10 individuals, whose personality traits were described, could enter the fallout shelter. If the child said the ax murderer should live and the nun should die, that was fine. Some teachers, notes Mr. Edwards of the Ethics Resource Center, began questioning, "What would we say to the little Charlie Manson who clarified his values?"

In contrast, at many schools today, there *are* values that are seen as right and wrong. Clovis's success, for instance, rests on zealously imparting values throughout its schools—from English classes to the football field. "We don't say, 'Oh! its time to learn your values,'" says Ms. Gamble, pointing to her watch. "We stick values in all over the place."

The cornerstone of Clovis's efforts is the district's much-coveted "Sparthenian" award—named after the physical and mental disciplines of Sparta and Athens in ancient Greece. Contenders each semester earn points for activities that develop their mind, body and spirit.

Clovis believes good values go beyond knowledge; they are ingrained habits embraced through experience. To earn points in the "spirit" category, students can choose from a host of offerings. For community service, they can train guide dogs for a local group. Or they can apply for an on-campus job, which includes lawn care or library monitor.

The activities often seek to foster cooperation. For points in the "super classroom" category, everyone in the class must avoid playground infractions and overdue library materials, and pitch in for a favorable janitor's rating each day for housekeeping. At Clovis's Valley Oak Elementary, winners get a certificate, which children proudly hang on the classroom wall, and a round of sugarless candy. Receiving the award in 10 of 18 weeks ensures an end-of-the-semester swim party at Clovis High School.

LITTLE IDLE TIME

Teachers prod each student to work toward Sparthenian goals; at Valley Oak, about 90% participate, keeping the school humming with activity long after hours and leaving children little idle time to gravitate toward less-desirable values. "I'm relentless," says Ms. Gamble. "Day after day, I ask them, 'What do you want to do after school?' I call it my hit list."

"I felt real proud to get [the award]," says 10-year-old Batia Epelbaum, as she works on a dry-ice experiment. "It's really hard to get it. A lot of kids don't."

In the classroom, Clovis promotes seven values—honesty, responsibility, respect, dedication, perseverance, self-respect and concern for others. Second-grade teacher Becky Maldonado selects a value-of-the-month and a famous person who exemplifies it. Typ-

A CRISIS OF VALUES

Moral Dilemmas

A 1989 survey of 5,000 students, conducted by Louis Harris & Associates for the Girl Scouts, found:

- **47%** of students would cheat on an important exam – **12%** by copying answers directly and **35%** by glancing for ideas.
- **5%** would take money from their parents without asking, if given the opportunity.
- **36%** would lie to protect a friend who has vandalized school property; **24%** would tell the truth.

In the same poll, students were asked: *If you were unsure of what was right or wrong in a situation, how would you decide what to do?*

Their responses:

Do what is best for everyone	**23%**
Follow advice of an authority	**21%**
Do what makes you happy	**18%**
Do what God or the Scriptures said	**16%**
Do what would improve your situation or get you ahead	**10%**
Follow conscience	**3%**
Don't know	**9%**

Condoning Rape

In 1988, the Rhode Island Rape Crisis Center asked this question of 1,700 students in the sixth to ninth grades: *Under which of the following situations does a male on a date have the right to a kiss/sexual intercourse against a woman's consent?*

	Kiss	Inter-course
He spent a lot of money on her	**51%**	**20%**
He is so turned on he can't stop	**41%**	**29%**
She has had sexual intercourse with other men	**32%**	**31%**
She is drunk	**36%**	**28%**
She let him touch her above the waist	**67%**	**47%**
She let him do it before	**74%**	**61%**
They have been dating a long time	**77%**	**59%**
She led him on	**74%**	**58%**
She gets him sexually excited	**58%**	**53%**
They are planning to get married	**85%**	**70%**
They are married	**89%**	**80%**

The Parents' View

When parents were asked to rank the relative importance of 25 educational goals, their top 10 were:

To develop the ability to speak and write correctly	**66%**
To develop standards of what is "right" and "wrong"	**64%**
To develop an understanding about different kinds of jobs and careers, including their requirements and rewards	**56%**
To develop skills needed to get jobs for those not planning to go to college	**54%**
To develop the ability to use mathematics in everyday problems	**54%**
To encourage respect for law and order	**52%**
To help students make realistic plans for what they will do after high-school graduation	**52%**
To develop the ability to live in a complex and changing world	**51%**
To develop the desire to excel	**51%**
To develop the ability to think – creatively, objectively, analytically	**51%**

Source: Gallup Poll done for Phi Delta Kappa

---

ically, one boy and one girl are picked who exhibit the traits of that value, and they are honored at monthly school assemblies. One of her students got the award after he displayed friendship by showing a new boy where the restroom and lunch lines were and inviting him home to play after school.

Values are infused into the academic curriculum, too. In junior-high English classes, for example, teens read "Charley Skedaddle," the tale of a Civil War drummer boy with lessons about honesty. Other classroom activities help students learn together and to get to know each other, with an emphasis on respect and a sense of community and cooperation.

Instructors are also expected to model the values they teach. Fifth-grade teacher David Piercy prods students to exhibit self-control and politeness. He has given up cursing at umpires at sporting events or at errant drivers. He doesn't buy beer anymore. "How can I let one of them see me with a six-pack at the grocery store?" he asks.

Sixth-grade teacher Gary Cohagan says that when he exhibits caring, by regularly attending his students' sporting games or calling them on weekends to see what they are up to, they respond with trust – and few disciplinary problems. Joe Garcia, one student who couldn't read, learned perseverance when Mr. Cohagan repeatedly stayed after school to read the sports pages with him. By the end of the year, Joe was one of the class's best readers.

Rules and values – also championed in posters around the school – are consistent and strict. The dress code stipulates that boys can't wear earrings or hair below the collar line; neither sex can wear shorts, except in the hottest months of the year. Intramural sports rules state that students can't quit after the first week until the semester ends. To help students pass on the good values they've learned, high-school students help elementary youngsters in dramatizations geared to instructing them how to deal with peer pressure in real-life situations.

FULL CIRCLE?

How U.S. schools teach values and morals has changed sharply through the century. Here are examples of exercises children have used—in the early part of the century, between the 1960s and the late 1980s, and now.

Early in the Century

Until the 1960s, U.S. schools often taught strong moral messages. The most strident can be found in McGuffey's Readers texts, which in the early 1900s trailed only the Bible in circulation.

Here are two examples from McGuffey's Readers.

THE HONEST BOY AND THE THIEF

Charles was an honest boy, but his neighbor, Jack Pilfer, was a thief. Charles would never take anything for his own which did not belong to him; but Jack would take whatever he could get.

Early one summer's morning, as Charles was going to school, he met a man opposite the public house, who had oranges to sell. The man wished to stop and get his breakfast, and asked Charles if he would hold his horse while he went into the house.

But first he inquired of the landlord if he knew Charles to be an honest boy, as he would not like to trust his oranges with him, if he was not. Yes, said the landlord, I have known Charles all his life, and have never known him to lie or steal.

The orange man then put the bridle into Charles's hand and went into the house to eat his breakfast. Very soon Jack Pilfer came along the road, and seeing Charles holding the horse, he asked him whose horse he had there, and what was in the baskets on the horse. Charles told him that the owner of the horse was in the house, and that there were oranges in the baskets.

As soon as Jack found there were oranges in the baskets, he determined to have one, and going up to the basket, he slipped in his hand and took out one of the largest, and was making off with it.

But Charles said, Jack, you shall not steal these oranges while I have the care of them, and so you may just put that one back in the basket.

Not I, said Jack, as I am the largest, I shall do as I please; but Charles was not afraid of him, and taking the orange out of his hand, he threw it back into the basket.

Jack then attempted to go around to the other side and take one from the other basket; but as he stepped too near the horse's heels, he received a violent kick, which sent him sprawling to the ground.

His cries soon brought out the people from the house, and when they learned what had happened, they said that Jack was rightly served; and the orange man, taking Charles's hat, filled it with oranges, as he said he had been so faithful in guarding them, he should have all these for his honesty.

After the story, students were asked:
1. *What is this story about?*
2. *Which was the honest boy?*
3. *What kind of a boy was Jack Pilfer?*
4. *What kind of a character did the landlord say that Charles had?*
5. *How can boys earn a good reputation?*
6. *What advantage is there in possessing a good character?*

Here's a poem, called "Lazy Ned," from McGuffey's Readers.

" 'Tis royal fun," cried Lazy Ned,
"To coast upon my fine, new sled,
And beat the other boys;
But then, I can not bear to climb
The tiresome hill, for every time
It more and more annoys."
So, while his schoolmates glided by,
And gladly tugged uphill, to try
Another merry race,
Too indolent to share their plays,
Ned was compelled to stand and gaze,
While shivering in his place.
Thus, he would never take the pains
To seek the prize that labor gains,
Until the time had passed;
For, all his life, he dreaded still
The silly bugbear of *uphill,*
And died a dunce at last.

Sources: "Educating for Character" by Thomas Lickona, published by Bantam Books; and "Moral, Character, and Civic Education in the Elementary School," edited by Jacques S. Benninga, published by Teachers College Press of Columbia University.

1960s

In the 1960s, many educators decided that teaching clear moral lessons was wrong. Values, they said, were relative and personal. Instead of being taught right from wrong, children should go through "values clarification" exercises that helped them understand their values, no matter what they were. Aspiring to be either a saint or an ax murderer was all right, as long as you knew what your values were.

Here is one such "values clarification" exercise.

FALLOUT SHELTER EXERCISE

Suppose you are a government decision maker in Washington, D.C., when World War III breaks out.

A fallout shelter under your administration in a remote Montana highland contains only enough space, air, food and water for six people for three months, but 10 people wish to be admitted.

The 10 have agreed by radio contact that for the survival of the human race you must decide which six of them shall be saved. You have exactly 30 minutes to make up your mind before Washington goes up in smoke. These are your choices.

1. *A 16-year-old girl of questionable IQ, a high-school dropout, pregnant.*
2. *A policeman with a gun (which cannot be taken from him), thrown off the force recently for brutality.*
3. *A clergyman, 75.*
4. *A woman physician, 36, known to be a confirmed racist.*
5. *A male violinist, 46, who served seven years for pushing narcotics.*
6. *A 20-year-old black militant, no special skills.*
7. *A former prostitute, female, 39.*
8. *An architect, a male homosexual.*
9. *A 26-year-old law student.*
10. *The law student's 25-year-old wife who spent the last nine months in a mental hospital, still heavily sedated. They refuse to be separated.*

Source: "Values in the Classroom" by C. B. Volkmor, A. L. Pasanella, & L. E. Raths, taken from "Moral, Character, and Civic Education in the Elementary School," edited by Jacques S. Benninga.

1980s

In the 1980s, some schools began to reject values clarification and returned to teaching some clear moral messages and the importance of abiding by certain core values—among them honesty, respect and responsibility.

Here is a typical exercise now in use.

Marta, Pedro, and Stella were walking home from school one day when they saw a small puppy playing in the street. It looked lost. They were late getting home, and they knew their parents would be worried if they were much later. They talked about the problem. Finally, they decided to pick up the puppy and to ask several people in the neighborhood if they knew whose puppy it was. Soon they found the owner. She was very happy and thanked the children again and again.

****

Mrs. Newman was an older woman and could no longer take care of her yard by herself. She paid two students to mow her lawn and help her around the house once a week. One of the students worked very well, but the other only did about half the work he was supposed to do even though both were paid the same amount.

Students are told that "when we talk about responsibility, we mean that a person has a duty to do something or not to do something." They are then asked:

1. *Who has responsibilities in each story?*
2. *What are the responsibilities?*
3. *To whom is each responsibility owed?*
4. *What rewards might the person receive for carrying out the responsibility?*
5. *What penalties might the person receive for not carrying out the responsibility?*
6. *Why might it be important to carry out the responsibility?*

Source: "Responsibility: Law in a Free Society Student Book," published by the Center for Civic Education, part of the State Bar of California.

4. MORALITY AND VALUES IN EDUCATION
INJURED ANIMALS

In their classrooms, teachers are given the freedom to impart values in very individual ways. To teach responsibility, Ms. Peck uses injured animals she finds as part of her work with a wildlife group. One is a screech owl called Larry. "If you are good, you can take him home. Everyone wants to take Larry home," says 11-year-old Laura Wagnon as Larry buzzes overhead. She instructed her parents about Larry's eating habits. "My parents were really impressed," she says, giggling. Students also get a sense of accomplishment returning nursed animals to the wild.

One boy with severe disciplinary problems, who had been cited for making racist remarks in school, was rewarded for improved behavior by being able to feed three owls and show them off in demonstration to other classes. "We set goals for him," Ms. Peck says. "His parents think it turned him around."

For children who learn the lessons well, there are rewards, and lots of them. Sylvia Gamble, the Lincoln Elementary summer principal, gives Tootsie Roll candy to students displaying the value of the month on the playground. Others get a "good-deed ticket," which they deposit in a bowl for a weekly prize drawing. At Valley Oak Elementary, the "Lion of the Month" award goes to two students in each classroom who best exhibit that month's value. September's value: honesty.

TEACHING PARENTS

Clovis's efforts extend to parents, who in a voluntary, six-week Family Wellness Survival Course learn parenting skills and values through coaching and role-playing. "You can work with these kids and change their values. But then they go home to a destructive environment," says Valerie Hill, who runs the program.

The cumulative effect of this values onslaught is noticeable: Vandalism and stealing, teachers report, are very low. Kids pick trash up off the school grounds without being asked. Etiquette prevails in lunchrooms, where food is eaten, not thrown. Even on the last day of summer school, children line up in five neat rows in front of buses outside Lincoln Elementary, and wait for Ms. Gamble's signal to board. As Dale Stringer drives down Clovis streets, he often sees students with the sign "student painter." They are doing community service painting the homes of the elderly in Clovis for a senior citizens' center.

Even at the Gateway school, where "problem students" are sent, Ms. Hill has never had anything stolen from her classroom. Students from troubled homes, whom Ms. Franks has to instruct to sit down when asked, now are paragons of politeness. They open doors for her. "They say thank you all the time," she marvels.

Early in the last school year, students in her class teased a boy with cerebral palsy. She took the students aside and explained his condition. The next week, they voted him class president. "Maybe this is the only time he'll have anything really special," one boy in the class explained.

Which is not to say that focusing on morality hasn't provided some delicate moments at Clovis schools. When Ms. Barrett, the music teacher, asked one day for a list of "right morals," one boy answered: "Going to church and worshiping God." She gets flustered remembering that moment. "Glad to hear it," she said. "Boy, I just passed right over that one."

Many teachers in other districts, surveys show, play hooky when they are assigned to teach about values. They wonder about the source of values being taught, fear conflicts and even lawsuits from parents, and worry that character-education programs will take away from the core mission of schools.

Teachers at Clovis also struggle with the inevitable questions students ask when school-taught values run counter to those in their homes.

Nine-year-old Joanne Condley says she has asked teachers why they are taught that alcohol and tobacco are bad, but her father smokes and drinks beer after work. Mr. Stringer recalls when one pony-tailed parent burst into his office fuming, complaining that his son had been suspended for wearing his hair below the shoulder. "Are you telling me I'm a bad person" for having long hair" he demanded of Mr. Stringer. When teachers are asked about thornier values, such as those relating to abortion or the death penalty, they are instructed to tell students that they must ask their parents about them.

'I WANT TO BE NICE'

But the net effect on little Joanne Condley is seemingly positive. "I want to be honest and not get in gangs or do drugs," she says, brushing the stringy blond hair from her face. "When I grow up, I don't want to be a killer or rob banks. I want to be a real nice person."

So does 10-year-old Dominique Avila. "You can't be rude to people," explains the fifth-grader. "You have to be cooperative." She won her class's "Falcon-of-the-Month" award, which rewards good values, when her teacher noticed how Dominique would pick up books after class and helped another girl with a division problem. "She started understanding," Dominique says of her struggling classmate. "It made me feel good."

She's also become a Sparthenian. "You do good things and you get it," she explains. "It makes me feel good to be a Sparthenian. I know I've tried my hardest." She recounts many exercises that helped her focus on self-control, honesty and being herself. "I will remember these lessons," she vows.

Why Johnny Can't Tell Right from Wrong

The most important lesson our schools don't teach

Kathleen Kennedy Townsend

Kathleen Kennedy Townsend is director of the Maryland Student Service Alliance of the Maryland Department of Education.

"What would you like to be when you graduate?" asked a grade school teacher of her students in a Baltimore County classroom I visited recently. A young man raised his hand: "A pimp. You can make good money." The teacher then turned to a female student and asked, "Would you work for him?" "I guess so," the young woman replied lethargically.

In my five years in the Maryland Department of Education, I've heard hundreds of similar stories—rueful teachers' lounge chronicles of abject moral collapse by children barely old enough to make grilled cheese sandwiches by themselves. But these days you don't need to work in education to hear such mind-numbing tales. Turn on the TV news and there you have it: Our schools are hotbeds of violence, vandalism, and unethical behavior. Recently we've heard of a student-run LSD ring in one Virginia school and the bartering of stolen college entrance exams in one of New York City's most selective high schools. Sixty-one percent of high school students say they cheated on an exam during the past year. Nationwide, assaults on teachers are up 700 percent since 1978. Each month 282,000 students are attacked. And for the first time ever, the risk of violence to teenagers is greater in school than on the streets.

Obviously, we've got a problem here—a problem not just of violence, but of values. Plain and simple, many of our kids don't seem to have any, or at least any of a socially constructive kind. But what to do about 12-year-old aspiring pimps and cheaters? You might think the solution lies with that "family values" constituency, the Republicans. Yet a year of podium-thumping in favor of "values" by the Bush administration was not backed by a single concrete plan of action. In his four years as president, George Bush offered nothing more substantial than a PR stunt—his Thousand Points of Light Foundation. Still, at least the Republicans have been willing to *talk* about values. For all of Bill Clinton's 12-point plans, he has yet to come up with a specific agenda for restoring values.

To explain away that omission, Democrats argue that the ultimate responsibility for inspiring values lies not with the government, but with the family. A day in one of the nation's public schools might well convince the average citizen that those Democrats need a reality check. Face it: In some homes, parents simply aren't paragons of civic or ethical virtue. If we rely on the family alone to instill values, we will fail. As one 21-year-old ex-con said, "Kids grow up with a father or an uncle who is robbing stores. They figure, 'If my father can do it, so can I.'" In other homes, parents simply aren't around. In a series of recent workshops sponsored by the Maryland state government, high school students suggested a number of solutions they thought would help them better withstand the antisocial pressures that buffet them. While much of what they said was expected—more information about drugs, greater student participation in school and county decisions-one was a real eye-opener: They asked that their parents have dinner with them more often.

A survey of 176 schools that have adopted a values curriculum found that 77 percent reported a decrease in discipline problems, 68 percent boasted an increase in attendance, and 64 percent showed a decrease in vandalism.

Ultimately, the goal should be to help parents raise kind and law-abiding children. But how do we get there? Why not turn to the one institution that sees the problem more closely than any, and that touches children on a regular and sustained basis: the public school. Why not teach values in school?

Before you dismiss this suggestion as a William Bennettesque ploy to end calls for more school resources, additional jobs programs, or parental-leave legislation—all worthy goals—hear me out. Teaching values does *not* mean using the classroom to push a particular point of view on any political issue—say, abortion or the death penalty—that has worked its way to the core of the values debate. We're not even talking about school prayer or requiring the Pledge of Allegiance. It's much simpler than that: Teaching values means quietly helping kids to learn honesty, responsibility, respect for others, the importance of serving one's community and nation—ideals which have sufficiently universal appeal to serve as the founding and guiding principles of this country. In the schools, values education means lessons about friendship and anger, stealing and responsibility, simply being polite, respecting others, serving the needs of those who may be less fortunate—all lessons sadly absent from today's curriculum.

Teaching these sorts of values does more than yield heart-warming anecdotes of students helping old ladies across the street. It brings results—tangible improvement to the lives of children and their families. A survey of 176 schools that have adopted a values curriculum found that 77 percent reported a decrease in discipline problems, 68 percent boasted an increase in attendance, and 64 percent showed a decrease in vandalism. Three years after the Jackie Robinson Middle School in New Haven, Connecticut, initiated a values curriculum, the number of student pregnancies went from 16 to zero. After the Merwin Elementary School in Irwindale, California, instituted a character education program, damage due to vandalism was reduced from $25,000 to $500; disciplinary action decreased by 80 percent; and—could it be?—academic test scores went up.

Teaching values is clearly worth the trouble. So why is "values education" still one of education's neglected stepchildren? Why is it that schools that now teach values are rare—most often independent efforts by one or two inspired educators? Because, despite the family values chitchat, there's been no political or popular consensus that values should be as much a part of the curriculum as reading and writing. We need a more organized approach. If we are ready to instill a sense of values in America's youth, it will take a concerted effort by both political leaders and educators to make it happen.

SELECTIVE SERVICE

So where to begin? How about with a notion relegated to the back burner in the get-it-while-you-can eighties: community service. Serving others is held in such low regard among our youth that 60 percent of high school students said in a recent survey they simply would not be willing to "volunteer to serve their community for a year." That's a remarkable figure not only because so many aren't willing to serve, but because so many of those who responded negatively have never served to begin with. The students' distaste for service could largely be a distaste for the unknown. But when students are exposed to this unknown—through activities such as tutoring, visiting the elderly, rehabilitating homeless shelters, lobbying for new laws—their reaction is appreciably different.

Alethea Kalandros, as a ninth-grade student in Baltimore County, missed more than 70 days of school and was tempted to drop out. The next year she missed two days of school. What

happened? She enrolled in a program that allows her to volunteer at the Maryland School for the Blind. "It gives me a reason to come to school," she says. Alethea is part of Maryland's pioneering effort in promoting community service. While the program is now voluntarily offered by only a couple of schools, Maryland, after years of heated debate, recently became the first state to require all high school students to perform community service in order to graduate. Starting next year, all students entering the ninth grade must complete 75 hours of service or classes which incorporate service into the lesson, such as stream testing in an environmental course or writing about visits to the elderly in an English class. As part of the program, students are required to "prepare and reflect." This means, for instance, complementing working in a soup kitchen with learning about the most common causes of homelessness.

Any of a wide variety of activities fulfill the requirement, from repairing a local playground to tutoring fellow students. The impact, however, goes beyond helping the needy. Community service, as the limited experience in schools has shown, teaches students values and citizenship. For instance, while fourth, fifth, and sixth graders at Jackson Elementary School in Salt Lake City, Utah, were studying ground water pollution, they discovered that barrels of toxic waste were buried just four blocks from their school. They waged a vigorous public relations and fundraising campaign to clean up the site, eventually winning the support of the city's mayor. When this effort was stymied—Utah state law does not allow for private donations to clean up such sites—they lobbied the legislature and changed the statute. And while service programs can help students make a difference outside the school, they also have an impact inside the classroom: They make learning more interesting by simply helping students to understand how to apply textbook lessons in the real world.

Despite successes in experimental programs, stubborn resistance to community service from educators is still the norm, even in Maryland where the Superintendents Association, the PTA, and the local boards of education all fought against the new service requirement. One of the most common knee-jerk reactions is cost. But ask educators in Atlanta, Georgia, who have been operating a regional service program for eight years, and they'll tell you it doesn't cost a dime. Of course, that doesn't mean all service programs can be run as efficiently, but it does show that costs can be kept low.

Beyond that, the arguments against service become more strained. The president of the Maryland Teachers Association, for example, called the proposal "enforced servitude" and claimed that it violated the Thirteenth Amendment. What's really bothering the educators? Probably the fact that they would be required to change their teaching methods. As Pat McCarthy, vice-president of the Thomas Jefferson Center, a non-profit foundation specializing in values education, says, "The biggest impediment to values education is teacher education." You can't teach community service out of a textbook; it takes time and thought, which, of course, takes effort. And that, for some educators, is a tough concept to accept.

While community service teaches values through hands-on experience, that's but one piece of the puzzle. If we want to instill values, why not take an even more straightforward approach: Teach them directly. It may sound radical, especially when we are talking about methods like memorizing passages from the Bible, "bribing" kids with discounts at the school store to behave decently, permitting students in class discussions to describe problems they face at home, and allowing teachers to make it clear that they might not approve of some parents' values. But while students are sometimes taught that what happens at home is not always a good thing, teaching values does not mean separating the parents from the lessons. Quite the contrary, a smart values program includes parents, too. Before a values program at Gauger's Junior High in Newmark, Delaware, was implemented, 100 people—parents, teachers, students and community representatives—attended a two-day conference in which they learned about the purpose and goals of the program and the ways they could help implement it. Parents provided input and teachers knew they had community support. And in the end, nobody had to worry that little Petey would bounce home from values class clutching the collected works of Lyndon LaRouche.

Is it really possible to teach values that we all agree upon? Of course. In fact, schools in an indirect way already present students with a set of values that is universally respected: What are our efforts to integrate our schools and prohibitions against stealing or drinking in school if not an education in values? It's not difficult to take this type of thinking one step further, creating a curriculum that teaches other values that are universally accepted but are almost never actually taught directly to our youth. In districts such as Sweet Home, New York, and in Howard and Baltimore counties, Maryland, superintendents formed representative groups of community leaders that included people as ideologically diverse as fundamentalist ministers and ACLU attorneys. They held public forums and listened to community opinion and after months of extensive discussion, the groups produced a list of values with which everyone was comfortable. Now, when people in these communities ask, "Whose values?" they can proudly say "Ours.

At places like Hebbville Elementary in a low-income section of Baltimore County, the results are impressive. There, teachers hold out the promise of tutoring the mentally retarded as a reward for children who have finished their assignments, done well on a test, shown improvement, or been helpful in class. The students actually vie for the privilege. Tiesha was picked to help out in a class of 15 seven- and eight-year-olds whose IQs are in the 30–45 range. "I like being a helper," she says. "I tried to teach my cousin that 100 percent and 100 percent equal 200 percent. When I saw her write two, I was so happy."

At the Waverly Elementary school in Baltimore City, values lessons are taught through discussions about peer pressure. The teacher chooses 15 students, divides them into four groups, and asks them to perform skits about peer pressure. One skit involves Daniel, whose three hip classmates mock him because he wears non-brand-name tennis shoes. Daniel persuades his parents to buy Nikes and when he returns to school, the gang accepts him. In reflecting upon the skit, Daniel says, "All the friends were making the decision rather than me making my own decision." Another student said, "Daniel could have decided to be different." It is significant that the students made up this fact pattern. In the kids-and-sneakers stories you usually hear, children are assaulting each other for Air Jordans. Here, they are girding themselves to accept an alternative.

That's well and good, but we're still missing one crucial element: accountability. For values education to succeed and prosper, schools need to show that it's paying off in tangible ways. That means, for instance, keeping track of indicators such as rates of crime and vandalism in schools or the number of students involved in community service where values are being taught.

CLASS WAR

Many may resent this call for values as a way for parents to shirk their own responsibility onto someone else, or may see it as another passing fad. As for parents, they may cling to concerns about which values their children should learn. But our collective trepidations pale next to the alternative: another generation of children growing up without a moral compass.

Changing will take courage, but we can take heart from one fifth-grade class I watched where the topic was "the right to be an individual." The purpose was to help the children decide when their own actions are inappropriate and to develop strategies for improving their classmates' behavior. The discussion began with a very simple story about a boy named Bobby who never washed himself and had no friends. Eventually he realized that he'd have to take a bath if he wanted his classmates to ask him to play. The immediate lesson was about cleanliness—about as innocuous a value as you can find. But the moral had pertinence even for frequent bathers: Sometimes change is not only good, but necessary. That's a lesson that should resonate, not just with fifth-graders, but with the next administration. Clearly, the old ways of inculcating values in our kids are no longer working. We grownups have got to change our thinking, too.

Ethical Communication in the Classroom

Michelle Dabel

Michelle Dabel teaches high-school English and coordinates curriculum in Fremont County Schools in Lander, Wyoming. She is completing her dissertation for a doctorate in Education and Rhetoric at New Mexico State University. Ms. Dabel has been a secondary and postsecondary teacher since 1975.

Most teachers would probably contend that they are good, effective communicators. After all, what is education if not the practice of effective communication? All that is positive or negative ultimately depends on communication and the use of language. But is there good ethical communication in the classroom—communication that exhibits equity of dialogue, mutual respect, and values the audience over the message?

The film about Nazi Germany ends. The fluorescent lights flicker back on. The teacher walks to the front of the room before the silence is broken. "If any of you think that the Nazis were right, then you are warped. Go ahead, open your texts to the questions, and get started."

The teacher finishes reading the fairy tale about the princess choosing a husband as her prince. The teacher closes the book and says, "Well, guys, I guess you just have to accept that women like rich men. Okay, it's break time. You have five minutes to go to the restroom. If you come back late, you won't get another break for the rest of the week."

The teacher begins a social studies activity. "I know that you have all heard something about the Clarence Thomas hearings. Do you know that the reason he was so controversial is that his would be a decisive, tie-breaking vote on the Supreme Court? Now, I know that you might have opinions on his stance on certain issues. We can't really discuss them, but think about them."

Interchanges of this type are fairly common every day in some American classrooms. Observation by educators and researchers indicates that teacher-talk, instruction giving, seatwork, and passive learning dominate the classroom (Apple 1985; Cazden 1988; Goodlad 1984; Shor 1986). In his monumental research of 1,000 American public schools, Goodlad (1984, 194) found strong similarities of how teachers teach. He generally describes classrooms as emotionally flat. Even when teachers start out with sound pedagogy and strong communication skills, the demands after a few years make them turn "to routines that make the least physical and emotional demands." Yet he found that successful schools "are more different, it seems, in the somewhat elusive qualities making up their ambience—the ways students and teachers relate to one another . . . ." Could this ambience be the levels of ethical communication? In some schools this type of communication does not seem to flourish. Why?

One-Way Communication

Instead of two-way communication, many teachers use one-way communication. This practice may arise because of a teacher's need to control, feelings of fear, or simply the belief that school is supposed to be that way. One main concern of teachers is control. As Elbow (1986) put it, "much teaching behavior really stems from an unwarranted fear of things falling apart." Elbow realized after studying and teaching for many years that a great deal of fear drove his teaching practices, a fear that "some unspecifiable chaos or confusion would ensue." He came to feel that this fear was unwarranted and found that in his own teaching, even when all did not go as planned, the students recovered—or found a new idea—and went on having learned something from the experience. How much extra control or power do teachers hoard that is driven by this underlying fear? Perhaps this fear changes classroom communication to the point of disempowering students. Perhaps it is this fear that creates unethical communication.

Cazden's (1988, 168) research on classroom discourse revealed teachers' perceptions of their own authority and social distance. Comparing distance on a continuum from close family members to fearful strangers, many teachers place themselves rather far from their students. "Many classroom observers have commented on the social distance that teachers either feel or wish to maintain between themselves and their students." She asks, "Even if teachers start most school years feeling like strangers to their students, why do these features of distance persist? Is it possible without expressions of humor and affection to achieve a shared sense of community?" This is also a call for good communication, effective classroom discourse—ethical communication.

This distancing sounds like the old cliché told to new teachers, "Don't smile until Christmas unless you want them walking all over you." Can there be a balance between control and unalienating communication? If a teacher chooses to be an ethical communicator, certainly he or she does not have to give up leadership control. Can students handle the dialogic, two-way give-and-take of ethical communication? Surely teachers can. If a teacher avoids two-way communication to maintain control, is the alienation of students a certain outcome? It often looks like the issue of control is juxtaposed with ethical communication.

Booth (1963) identifies the pedantic stance as one of three "unbalanced stances," the other two being the entertainer and the advertiser. He claims that the pedant ignores or undervalues the audience and focuses on the subject. The speaker's attitude toward the audience is a take-it-or-leave-it stance of neutrality and indifference. This unbalanced pedantic stance seems present in the illustration given above of a teacher's comments about the Nazis. He does not value the students' (audience's) opinion, focuses on the subject, and delivers a take-it-or-leave-it comment before moving on to material he has predetermined, perhaps to distract them from formulating any kind of response. Would not the teacher's stance—making a personal value judgment about student beliefs and trying to control their thinking—alienate them, no matter what their beliefs about Hitler were? What about the other teacher who believes that students cannot discuss politics? Is this a fear of losing control or a feeling of indifference to student opinions? Do the teachers reflect a caring attitude? Scorn?

These interactions have raised the idea of communication as dialogue rather than monologue. After all, true communication is not a one-way but a two-way transaction. Equity in communication cannot exist where there is no chance for one of the parties involved to respond. Unethical communication exists when there is little or no chance for an exchange of ideas (Johannesen 1990).

Buber (1958) examined two basic models of human relationships: I-Thou and I-It. He believed that the stance taken in a relationship directly affects communication. The I-Thou stance is characterized by openness, respect, and mutuality. The I-It stance, on the other hand, is characterized as perfunctory, unequal, and exploitative. In the I-It stance, people become "things," and the emphasis is on the communicator's message, not on the audience. Consequences are exaggerated, and choice is remote. The communicator's purpose is to coerce and command the listener. Is not this unethical communication? Is not this descriptive of a teacher's stance common in the classroom? Is it possible to resolve this dilemma?

Equal Communication

Habermas (1982) sets forth the "ideal speech situation," which he further discusses in terms of a discourse ethic. The four criteria call for *equal* opportunities to those involved to (1) initiate and continue communication, (2) express feelings, (3) forbid or permit communication, and (4) air all significant opinions. What does this mean in terms of the teacher who did not think that her students had significant opinions about the princess's choice? Students did not have an equal opportunity to initiate communication or express feelings. If the teacher was not willing to deal with student response to the fairy tale, why did she read it? What about student reaction to the comment about "how women are"? If the speaker (teacher) diminishes the worth or opinions of the audience

(students)—no matter what age, what number, or what subject matter—a skewed communication will result. What price control?

Looking again from the perspective of classroom discourse, how does this control manifest itself in schools? There may be communication rules for students—no talking, no whispering, no laughing, no turning to look at classmates, no passing notes, etc.—yet teachers can interrupt anybody anytime. On one level, students come to accept this as a well-established pattern in school, but on another level—especially as they develop opinions and independence—students become resentful and alienated and begin to resist authority. As Cazden (1988) points out, this lopsided communication also means that often the ones who need to communicate the most receive the least. Students who are shy, linguistically different, or otherwise insecure about communicating need reinforcement, practice, and a chance to "read" cues about language usage.

Spoken language creates social identity. In order to learn and grow, students need to use language in a school or social setting to begin to understand differences in how and when one says certain things. "While other institutions such as hospitals serve their clients in nonlinguistic ways, the basic purpose of school is achieved through communication" (Cazden 1988, 2). Classroom discourse affects the thought processes of students. What do students learn from unethical communication? Probably they do not learn humane and democratic values.

Elbow (1986, 69) states that teaching behaviors will be right "so long as they rest upon a symmetrical premise: an equal affirmation of the student's experience, his right to ground his behaviors in his experience . . . to embark on his own voyage of change. . . ." He feels that many poor teaching behaviors result from "some kind of pathology . . . the hunger to tell people things they did not ask you to tell them . . . unsolicited telling" that detracts from student growth and understanding. Elbow humorously states that we should "set up other arenas where teachers can work off this appetite."

Perhaps some classroom teachers may find this whole argument naive. Perhaps they would claim that teachers cannot practice ethical communication in the classroom. Some of the arguments or comments they may make follow. "The students are an unequal element of the communication seesaw. The students are not "heavy" enough to hold the weight. If the teacher permitted students to freely choose options, initiate dialogue, or air significant ideas, they would go wild and spiral completely out of control, running roughshod over the teacher. The class would never get anything done. Students must know their boundaries. They have little to offer because they are inexperienced, lacking knowledge and worthwhile opinions. Teachers have far too many students to let them all give voice to their opinions. They only reflect their parents' ideas and have not developed real opinions yet. Teachers are not therapists. They do not have time to help every student work out an opinion. The teacher's purpose is to dispense content knowledge and assess the students' progress. Teachers have a job to do! Let people engage in ethical communication elsewhere! It simply isn't practical or feasible in schools!"

Ethical Communication Strategies

So, where does this leave the argument? Teachers at this point have three choices: (1) The teacher can accept that he is not an ethical communicator because of any number of other priorities and sign off. (2) The teacher can say he or she already is an ethical communicator, practicing all of the criteria listed above. (3) Or the teacher can say that he or she would like to move toward becoming a

more ethical communicator by working out effective methods to manage the classroom and/or large numbers of students.

From my work at the secondary and postsecondary levels, I have observed and practiced strategies that assist in my becoming a more ethical communicator. For example, a teacher needs to be careful who is reinforced with feedback. Rather than take the first articulated answer, usually by an outspoken and successful student, the teacher can encourage others to build on an initial response or challenge the first student to carry the thought further, to think more deeply or in a different way. The teacher must ask himself why he judges particular discourse meaningful or even profound. On what criteria does a teacher use to base a decision? Just asking a question creates meaning. Carlsen (1991), examining questioning from a sociolinguistic perspective, states that "classroom questions are not simply teacher behaviors but mutual constructions of teachers and students." Teachers need to encourage students to formulate questions and answers for themselves. After all, asking a good question is often the first step in acquiring knowledge.

Another strategy, using analogy and metaphor to present ideas and concepts, can often help students see old thoughts in a new light. This is part of ethical communication because, rather than pushing ideas and biases on students, the teacher can structure an opportunity for them to examine attitudes freely. The teacher could use the analogy of a leaky roof, for example, to describe to teacher education students how the

> What do students learn from unethical communication? Probably they do not learn humane and democratic values.

goal of multicultural education is a challenge to the schools. If the roof is not leaking, everything is fine. If the roof is obviously dripping into the room, measures will be taken to fix it, but again everything will be fine. But if the roof is leaking into the structure of the building, hidden from sight, measures will not be taken to fix it, and eventually, the roof will fall in, harming the students and staff. Using such an analogy may externalize or objectify an idea in a way that will allow students to think more abstractly. The teacher can use a premise or begin questions with "What if . . .?" statements.

The teacher can try to be thoughtful, if not guarded, about expressing "expert" views. Teachers can monitor teacher talk, which can be very intimidating to a free exchange of ideas or may encourage students to manipulate opinions to garnish favor. Teachers can create and nurture an environment for student voices. They can strive to create a place of respect and safety where silent voices can be heard. Encouraging reluctant students, especially minority students, to participate and communicate reduces their feelings of marginality and gives other students a chance to hear about alternate social realities (Bigelow 1990). The students can examine their historical and biographical identity development. This should give them a clearer sense of why they think as they do.

When striving for ethical communication, basic attention to interpersonal skills is helpful. As Cazden (1988) points out, "classrooms are among the most crowded human environments." As a result, communication becomes abrupt, perfunctory, and routine. Common courtesy , which would be practiced elsewhere, is often dropped, especially when dealing with difficult students. The teacher should know students' names and establish eye contact whenever possible.

Ethical communication has to contain a sense that the speaker values the listener. An ethical communicator must exhibit involvement and a desire to understand the audience. Taking time to listen indicates to the student that he or she is worth the extra time. Saying "thank you" and "you are welcome" can be quite uplifting to a student. These are the common social graces that are often abandoned in the classroom. The students need to believe that the teacher is genuine and wishes them to reach their potential. How often can a teacher be heard to say "If you flunk, it is your own problem," or "If you don't turn in the assignment, it is just one less paper for me to grade"?

This is not to turn ethical communication into a superficial exercise in polite conversation. True, teachers have heavy workloads, which lead to frustration and fatigue. However, knowing that teachers have reasons for being abrupt or indifferent probably will not help students on a day-to-day basis nor will this fact make an unethical communication an ethical one. Also, ethical communication does not rule out confrontation and debate. Teachers can usually find a way to help students articulate and vent their frustrations. Working in small groups or writing about the topic can release much tension. Talking to students individually to promote mutual understanding can help a teacher see students' concerns more clearly. If the group is not too large, individual conferences can work miracles.

Teachers who want to be recognized as professionals have a mandate to practice ethical communication, regardless of the circumstances. If our school settings work against such a mandate, then we must change the circumstances under which we labor. Ours and our students' futures teeter in the balance.

The film about Nazi Germany ends. The fluorescent lights flicker back on. The teacher remains near the switch as students begin to talk. "That was a disturbing film, wasn't it? Let's take some time to discuss your reactions. We might consider that there are students of Jewish or German heritage among us who have mixed feelings about what happened. Let's hear some of your opinions."

The class finishes an oral reading of a fairy tale about a princess choosing a husband. The teacher says, "Wow, things have really changed in the way people choose spouses. Let's take some time to discuss our ideas about this tale. First, clarify your thoughts in a five-minute writing. What does this story say about men and women? How do you feel about the princess's choice? What would you have done if you were one of the characters? Okay, start writing, and in five minutes we will take our break. When we come back, we will begin talking about it."

The teacher opens the class. "How many of you heard about or watched the Clarence Thomas hearings? This will be the basis for discussion today. Remember the format we established: taking turns, no shouting or name-calling, respecting others' opinions. We all need to learn how to develop our opinions with others in society. That is how democracy works. Okay now, who wants to start?"

References

Apple, M. W. 1985. *Education and power.* Boston: Ark Paperbacks.

Bigelow, W. 1990. Inside the classroom: Social vision and critical pedagogy. *Teachers College Record* 91:437–48.

Booth, W. C. 1963. The rhetorical stance. *College Composition and Communication* 14:139–45.

Buber, M. 1958. *I and thou.* New York: Scribners.

Carlsen, W. S. 1991. Questioning in classrooms: A sociolinguistic perspective. *Review of Educational Research* 61:157–78.

Cazden, C. B. 1988. *Classroom discourse.* Portsmouth, N.H.: Heinemann Educational Books.

Elbow, P. 1986. *Embracing contraries: Explorations in learning and teaching.* New York: Oxford.

Goodlad, J. I. 1984. *A place called school.* New York: McGraw-Hill.

Habermas, J. 1982. A reply to my critics. In *Habermas: Critical debates*, ed. J. B. Thompson and D. Held. Cambridge: MIT Press.

Johannesen, R. L. 1990. *Ethics in human communication.* 3rd ed. Prospect Heights, Ill.: Waveland.

Shor, I. 1986. Equality is excellence: Transforming teacher education and the learning process. *Harvard Educational Review* 56:406–26.

Managing Life in Classrooms

We have witnessed in recent years the massive development of a knowledge base on life in the classroom, on teacher-student interaction in the teaching-learning process. Much of this knowledge has come from field-based research by teachers, psychologists, anthropologists, and others who have sought to explore "life" in classroom settings. We speak of managing life in classrooms because we now know that there are many factors that go into building effective teacher-student and student-student relationships. The traditional term "discipline" is too narrow and refers only to teachers' reactions to undesired student behavior. We better understand methods of managing student behavior when we look at the totality of what goes on in classrooms with teacher responses to student behavior as a part of that totality. Teachers have tremendous responsibility for the emotional climate that is set in a classroom. Whether students feel secure and safe and whether they want to learn depends to an enormous extent on the psychological frame of mind of the teacher. Teachers must be able to manage their own selves in order to manage effectively the development of a humane and caring classroom environment.

Teachers bear moral and ethical responsibilities for being witnesses to and examples of responsible social behavior in the classroom. There are many models of observing life in classrooms. When one speaks of life in classrooms, arranging the total physical environment of the room is a very important part of the teacher's planning for learning activities. Teachers need to expect the best work and behavior from students that they are capable of achieving. Respect and caring are attitudes a teacher must communicate to receive them in return. Reasonable expectations, emphasis on doing the best work one can, and communicating faith in the capacity of one's students to do their best work do wonders in developing positive classroom morale. Open lines of communication between teacher and students create the possibility for congenial, fair, dialogical resolution of problems as they occur.

Developing a high level of task orientation among students and encouraging cooperative learning and shared task achievement will foster camaraderie and self-confidence among students. Shared decision-making will build an *esprit de corps*, a sense of pride and confidence, which will feed on itself and blossom into high quality performance. Good class morale, well managed, never hurts academic achievement. The importance of emphasizing quality, helping students to achieve levels of performance they can feel proud of having attained, and

encouraging positive dialogue among them leads them to take ownership in the educative effort. When that happens, they literally empower themselves to do their best.

When talking with teachers and prospective teachers regarding what concerns them about their roles (or prospective roles) in the classroom, it is usual that "discipline," the management of student behavior, will rank near or at the top of their list. A teacher needs a clear understanding of what kind of learning environment is most appropriate for the subject matter and age of the students. Any person who wants to teach must also want his or her students to learn well, to learn basic values of respect for others, and to become more effective citizens. Humane and caring ways to do this are most valuable and effective.

There is considerable debate among educators regarding certain approaches used in schools to achieve a form of order in classrooms that also develops respect for self and others. The dialogue about this point is spirited and informative. The bottom line for any effective and humane approach to discipline in the classroom and the necessary starting point is the teacher's emotional balance and capacity for self-control. This precondition creates a further one—that the teacher wants to be in the classroom with his or her students. Unmotivated teachers have great difficulty motivating students.

Helping young people learn the skills of self-control and self-motivation to become productive, contributing, and knowledgeable adult participants in society is one of the most important tasks that good teachers undertake. These are teachable and learnable skills; they do not relate to heredity or social condition. They can be learned by any human being who wants to learn them and who is cognitively (intellectually) able to learn them. We further know that these skills are learnable by virtually all but the most severely cognitively disabled persons. There is a large knowledge base on how teachers can help students to learn self-control. All that is required is the willingness of teachers to learn these skills themselves and teach them to their students. No topic is more fundamentally related to any thorough examination of the social and cultural foundations of education.

There are many sound techniques that new teachers can use to achieve success in managing students' classroom behavior. They should not be afraid to ask colleagues questions and to develop peer support groups. These peer support groups should be composed of those colleagues with whom they work with confidence and trust. Educators at all levels encounter some behavioral problems with some students. Even educators of adults sometimes have behavioral management problems in training activities or educational programs. New teachers in the elementary and secondary schools are always concerned about how they will manage disruptive, disorderly, or disobedient students.

Teachers' core ethical principles come into play when deciding what constitutes defensible and desirable standards of student conduct. As in medicine, realistic preventive techniques combined with humane but clear principles of procedure seem to be effective. Teachers need to realize that, before they can control behavior, they must identify what student behaviors are desired in their classrooms. They need to reflect, as well, on the emotional tone and ethical principles implied by their own behaviors. To optimize their chances of achieving the classroom atmosphere they wish, teachers must strive for emotional balance within themselves; they must learn to be accurate observers; and they must develop just, fair strategies of intervention to aid students in learning self-control and good behavior. A good teacher is a good model of courtesy, respect, tact, and discretion. Children learn by observing how other persons behave and not just by being told how they are to behave.

Confidence in one's own innate worth and in one's ability to teach effectively goes a long way toward reducing or eliminating discipline problems in educational settings. Teachers often function as role models for their students without even being aware of it. Later in life, they might be told by former students what an impact they had; these revelations are precious to them. From the first day of the first year of teaching, good teachers maintain firm but caring control over their classes by continuing observation of and reflection on classroom activities. There is no substitute for positive, assertive teacher interaction with students in class.

This unit addresses many of the topics covered in basic foundations courses. The selections shed light on classroom management issues, teacher leadership skills, the legal foundations of education, and the rights and responsibilities of teachers and students. In addition, the articles can be discussed in foundations courses involving curriculum and instruction. This unit falls between the units on moral education and equal opportunity because it can be directly related to either or both of them.

Looking Ahead: Challenge Questions

What are good general rules, subject to amendment, which can guide a first-year teacher's initial efforts to manage student behavior?

What are some of the best techniques for helping someone to learn self-control?

What ethical issues may be raised in the management of student behavior in school settings?

What reliable information is available on the extent and severity of school discipline problems in North America? What sources contain such information?

What civil rights do students have? Do public schools have fewer rights than private schools in controlling student behavior problems? Why or why not? What are the rights of a teacher in managing student behavior?

Do any coercive approaches to behavioral management in schools work better than noncoercive ones?

Why is teacher self-control a major factor in just and effective classroom management strategies?

What are the moral responsibilities of teachers in managing student behavior?

What are some ways a teacher can help students take pride in their own work and in that of their classmates?

Discipline with Dignity in the Classroom: Seven Principles

Allen N. Mendler

Allen N. Mendler is a consultant, psychologist, educator, and author of What Do I Do When . . . ? How to Achieve Discipline with Dignity in the Classroom, *available for $18.95 from National Educational Service, 1610 W. 3rd St., P. O. Box 8, Bloomington, IN 47402 (800-733-6786). This article is condensed from Chapter 2, "Principles of Effective Discipline," pp. 25-42.*

HAVING worked with thousands of children and adults, I consider it fruitless to expect any discipline technique to work with all people with the same symptom. The competent teacher needs to get at the reasons or functions of a given maladaptive behavior to formulate a strategy likely to work. Educators must have a sound set of principles and guidelines from which they can use existing strategies or develop new ones:

1. Long-term behavior changes vs. short-term quick fixes. People take time! Dealing with discipline takes time. When children misbehave, they tell us they need help learning a better way. They are telling us there are basic needs not being met which are motivating the behavior. If all we do is focus on

what to do after the behavior, then there are simply better and worse solutions. The best time to deal with behavior is before there are problems. Focusing on and addressing basic needs is time well spent. Preventing discipline problems is far preferable to dealing with them after the fact.

If you believe that dealing with discipline is part of the job, you will give yourself enough time to plan for and deal with disruptive classroom situations in the most effective way for both the long and short term. You must bring the same professionalism, energy, and enthusiasm to discipline as to the content you teach.

For some students, discipline is the content of their school lives. Effective discipline means teaching kids how to become responsible. Within that framework, discipline problems are an opportunity to teach responsibility. Far too many children and adolescents have little idea of what it means to be responsible. They need to learn that they have choices and that they need to plan their behavior. They need someone who cares enough to engage them beyond tossing them out of the room, scolding them, or criticizing when they behave in irresponsible, perhaps outrageous ways.

Discipline is a job for everyone in the school when it is viewed as teaching kids how to be responsible. Long after kids forget facts, they will remember the people who most influ-

enced them. Dealing with discipline gives us many opportunities to really affect a child's life: 25 years ago and 25 years from now, it will still be important for those seeking successful employment to know how to get along with others.

2. Stop doing ineffective things. With regard to discipline, some kids simply do not respond to "common sense" or "empirically sound" strategies. Some children get worse when "positively reinforced." Some can be taught "social skills" and yet continue to misbehave. We need to let go of our common-sense notions when we encounter people who do not respond in "prescribed" fashion. Some suggestions, solutions, and interventions can best be termed "unconventional."

Accepting people as they are enables them to risk change. Consider a student who is chronically late to class and has not changed despite conventional interventions. Sally's teacher can decide to affirm her. She must suspend her belief in the primary importance of coming to class on time for Sally and seek behavior(s) she can genuinely affirm.

The next time Sally is late, she says: "Sally, as you know, I've been really angry with your lateness. Although I'd prefer you come to class on time, you participate very well when you are here and often have

Reprinted from *The Education Digest*, March 1993, pp. 4-15. Condensed from chapter 2 "Principles of Effective Discipline," pp. 25-42 from WHAT DO I DO WHEN. . . .? How to Achieve Discipline with Dignity in the Classroom, by Allen N. Mendler. Available from National Educational Service.

lots to share. Thanks for coming and contributing." She has moved the discussion beyond time to class and has found or rediscovered the primary importance of helping Sally realize that her value is more than whether she is punctual. Sally is much more likely to come to class on time.

The beliefs we hold about our capabilities influence our behavior. Changing behavior is a way of influencing those beliefs. We are most likely to facilitate change when we respect someone's current views and behaviors, while providing sufficient safety and support as he explores other possibilities.

3. I will be fair, and I won't always treat everyone the same.

Some who read the preceding scenario will be concerned about the disciplinary message to other kids. You may think it's great to treat all kids as individuals, but the consequence may be that kids accuse you of being unfair: "You made me stay after school, and you don't make Sally."

Teaching children how to be responsible means tailoring the consequences to the child. Children must be shown and taught the difference between being fair and treating everyone exactly the same. Being fair means giving each person what she needs, not treating everyone exactly the same. Equality means all people are born of equal value, but, since no two people are identical, it is absurd to think everyone should be treated exactly the same.

Being fair but not treating everyone the same allows you to have a foundation of rules based upon sound values for everyone. Specific consequences are implemented on an individual basis so each child can learn a better way based on his actions, beliefs, and needs. Have clear, specific rules, each having several possible consequences from which you, the teacher, can choose those most likely to best teach the child.

One way to teach students the difference between fair and equal is to ask them to imagine 10 patients waiting to see the doctor. One has a cold, one has a broken arm, one has poison ivy, one has diarrhea, and so on. The doctor comes out and an-nounces that today is aspirin day: All patients will be treated equally and given aspirin to solve their ailments. A lively discussion can ensue analyzing if the doctor is being fair although he is clearly being equal.

Keep being fair and not equal. Be preventive with this practice by sharing your discipline program with parents verbally and in writing. Let them know you seek consequences which teach each child a better, more responsible way.

4. Rules must make sense.

Rules viewed as stupid are least likely to be followed. Rules in schools should be the guidelines needed for success to happen.

In many instances, students are made servants of the rules rather than the rules being there to serve students. Students need to see how a rule benefits them. They need and deserve an explanation for why things are the way they are. Telling students your rules exist because "That's the way it's always been," "Rank has its privileges," "Someday you'll understand," or "Because I said so" deprives them of an opportunity to learn that education trains people to think. You become the enemy who extorts compliance through fear and will be targeted for either direct or "terrorist" attack.

5. Model what you expect.

Let students see you living by the same code of behavior you expect. If you assign homework, be sure to promptly do your own homework by getting their work back to them as quickly as possible. If assignments are not returned, students lose interest in doing them. When they are returned late (more than three days after they are turned in), the only students who benefit are those who care about their grades, because learning from mistakes rarely occurs following that interval.

Be visible in the halls between classes as a message of safety and security to your kids. Speak to them in a way you want them to speak to you. When conflict occurs, let them see you implement solutions that are respectful, nonviolent, and verbally non-aggressive. If you want to pro-mote friendliness among them, have a smile on your face as you greet them into the room. Teach the real, healing value of apologizing by saying you are sorry to a student when you lose your temper or otherwise blow it. Let them see you as a model of how you want them to be.

6. Responsibility is more important than obedience.

Obedience means "Do not question and certainly do not be different." The seeds of retaliation and rebellion are sown when people feel robbed of their personal freedom to make choices. The major tools of obedience models of discipline are rewards and punishments.

Responsibility means: Make the best decision you possibly can with the information you have available. In a responsibility model of discipline, children must accumulate information, see the options available, learn to anticipate consequences, and then choose the path they feel is in the best interest of themselves and others. Because learning to be responsible is an ongoing, dynamic process, bad decisions are viewed as opportunities by which children can learn to make better ones. The processes by which children increase their competence in learning responsibility are increased awareness, choosing, planning, and predicting.

"Obedience" is not always bad. Some elements of the "do-as-you-are-told" philosophy are *essential* for a civilized society to survive, such as when danger is an issue. In my work with "behaviorally disordered" and "juvenile delinquent" youth, a combination of obedience and responsibility methods is needed for growth and change to occur. Conventional behavioral methods which are obedience-oriented ("Do as I say and you will be rewarded or punished") are often required in the early stages for such youth to feel a sense of safety and security (someone else will put controls to the impulses which I cannot).

Unfortunately, most programs never proceed beyond this. Many children who have not been taught to behave responsibly may learn to behave well when monitored. But without the authority figure present, they often return to old, familiar behaviors. As they get older, they have more and more trouble responding to situations in which they are on their own. They become dependent on what the voice of authority demands. "Obedient" children listen to the authority that has the loudest, most persuasive voice. In far too many instances, that "voice" is the television, stereo, Nintendo game, peers, or even the neighborhood drug dealer.

We must develop discipline techniques that move beyond obedience. We must ask ourselves questions larger than, "Does it work?" We must consider: What happens later? What happens to motivation for learning? How does the discipline method affect self-esteem? What happens to an individual's dignity? How would we (the instructor) be affected if on the receiving end of the method?

Most students do not need any kind of systematic discipline method to behave. About 80 percent of all kids will behave well and respond with improved behavior to either good or bad methods of discipline. About 5 percent of all students chronically misbehave and generally respond very poorly to most conventional forms of discipline.

About 15 percent fence-sit, breaking rules on a somewhat regular basis. They do not blindly accept the classroom principles, and they fight the restrictions. Their motivation and achievement ranges from completely on to completely off, from high to low, and is affected by influences such as what happened at home that morning, how they perceive the classroom activity, the teacher's behavior toward them, their current status needs from others, etc. These students need a clear set of expectations and consequences. If they are not given enough structure, they can disrupt learning for all.

The goal of a good discipline plan is to provide structure and control for the 15 percent without alienating or overly regulating the 80 percent or backing the 5 percent into a corner.

Programs that are too heavily obedience-oriented give the illusion of success because they may provide short-term control of the 15 percent. In such classrooms, however, seeds are sown for them and the out-of-control student to explode in rebellion and for many among the 80 percent to lose interest in learning.

7. Always treat students with dignity. This is perhaps the most important of all the principles, because without dignity, students learn to hate school and learning. When we attack their dignity, we might get them to follow rules, but we lose them to anger and resentment. Discipline techniques must be compatible with helping students maintain or enhance their self-esteem. Some methods that attack dignity include put-downs, sarcasm, criticism, scolds, and threats delivered publicly.

It is easier to treat "good" kids with dignity, although all too often even they feel discounted, ignored, and put down by important adults. Listening to what a student thinks, being open to feedback from students, using I-messages to communicate your feelings to them, explaining why you want something done a certain way and how that will likely be of benefit to the student, and giving students some say in classroom affairs are ways of communicating dignity to them. The message is: You are important.

It is difficult to be dignified with students who tell you where to go and how to get there! Because we are human, when our buttons are pressed, we react from the gut. Yet it is precisely during these moments that displays of dignity become all the more necessary.

The student who attacks needs to learn non-attacking ways of dealing with stress. You can truly be a teacher in the purest sense by modeling alter-

natives during your own stressful moments with the student. Further, if you attack back, escalation results, and the power struggle gets worse. It is important that other students see you as capable and strong without being brutal when your or their well-being is disrupted. They need to realize there are alternatives to full-scale warfare even after the first bomb is dropped.

Discipline with dignity encourages teachers and other caregivers to be aware of how they communicate their expectations that students correct their behavior. Dignity in discipline can often be accomplished by using privacy, eye contact, and proximity (PEP) when you need to deliver a corrective message to a student. Make your comments quietly so only you and the student can hear, with eye contact (being sensitive to possible cultural or emotional issues regarding eye contact), and in close physical proximity. Many potentially explosive situations have been prevented with PEP.

For a discipline method to be effective for the short and long term, it must meet the following criteria:

● It must work to stop disruptive behavior and/or build constructive, prosocial behavior.

● You (the teacher) would find the method acceptable if you were on the receiving end. Use yourself and your feelings as a guide to the relative emotional benefits or liabilities of all methods.

● The method(s) are geared toward teaching responsibility (better decision-making) even when obedience is necessary (i.e., safety).

● You are willing to model the method, not merely preach it.

● You can identify and explain how following a rule or procedure can provide both immediate and long-term benefits.

● The method is compatible with the seven principles of effective discipline just described.

A Constructivist Approach to Conflict Resolution

Nancy Carlsson-Paige and Diane E. Levin

Nancy Carlsson-Paige (at Lesley College, Cambridge, Massachusetts) and Diane E. Levin (at Wheelock College, Boston), co-direct the Lesley-Wheelock Peace Center for Children, Families, and Schools. Condensed from Young Children, 48 *(November 1992), 4–13.*

Teachers can do a great deal to challenge the violence in children's social lives by intervening early and teaching specific skills to help them learn a broader repertoire for resolving conflicts. An approach for resolving conflicts that grows out of social psychology and is used with adults has also been taught in school conflict resolution and mediation programs primarily with children in late-elementary through high school.

This approach teaches elements of constructive conflict resolution: defining the problem, brainstorming solutions, using negotiation skills, and choosing solutions that satisfy both sides. Such skills require cognitive abilities typical of older children and adults.

We have been studying K–3 children to learn how their ideas about conflicts develop over time and how the skills they use to resolve conflict develop. The bulk of our data was collected in three classrooms (kindergarten, second grade, and third grade) in an urban school with a diverse ethnic, racial, and economic population. Insights from this research have helped us develop guidelines teachers can use in working with conflict resolution in classrooms. How can key elements of constructive conflict resolution used more commonly with older children and adults be adapted for young children, and how can we nurture these skills in developmentally appropriate ways?

How participants in a dispute define their problem has a lot to do with how they resolve it. Until the problem is seen as shared, working on a positive solution is hard.

Common Progression

Children go through a progression in learning to define a problem. Kindergartners tend to see problems in the immediate moment and in physical terms, from their own point of view. Only with age and experience do they learn to see problems in a larger context, in more abstract terms, and from more than their own point of view. Until then, the teacher needs to help.

Younger children have many conflicts over actions or visible things. If they argue during play, it is often over roles they will have (who does what) or actions or concrete aspects of things they make together. Children aged 7 or 8 often have conflicts involving words, feelings, and intentions.

Teachers can help children understand the problems that cause their conflicts in terms that make sense to them. For young children, this will mean helping them define problems in terms of physical objects and concrete actions. With lots of experience doing this with the teacher, children begin to be able to use concrete terms to talk about their problems on their own.

To understand a problem fully, the players need to be able to take the views of all players into account. There is a lot of progress from seeing one point of view to being able to coordinate two perspectives. In between, children begin to realize there are two points of view and that both need to agree, but they still assume the other player agrees with what they want. Teachers can help children see that their problems have two sides, showing them the two viewpoints in the immediate context of the problem they are having.

Understanding a conflict fully involves realizing what led up to it and how each action taken affects the other person (e.g., how any individual action escalated or de-escalated a conflict). Young children, however, see conflicts in the very moment they occur, often not knowing what caused them or how their own actions might have contributed.

Cause and Effect

As children develop, they become better able to link cause and effect and to predict the results of their actions. The five-year-olds in our study almost never spontaneously mentioned causes of conflict or where actions might lead, but eight-year-olds showed consistent and enthusiastic interest in these ideas.

Teachers can help children see the whole problem and how their behavior contributed to it. After a conflict occurs they can help children look at specific actions that led to the problem and what the effects of the children's actions were. Teachers can also try to enter into the heat of a conflict to help children think of what will happen if they do what they are headed toward.

Basic to constructive conflict resolution is learning to find a solution everyone can agree to—being able to think of potential solutions and then to think through negative and positive consequences of each, while taking into account points of view of both sides. Working on this with young children is challenging.

At all ages, some children offered a special type of winning solution—a novel one incorporating both people together.

Yet, we found that many children as young as five spontaneously thought of winning solutions to conflict stories. Children often seemed to love coming up with positive solutions. At the same time, their solutions reflected five-year-old thinking: Many offered global statements such as "they shared" or "they took turns" as endings for their conflict stories, without indicating how the solution might work in practice or how it took into account two different points of view. Still, the fact that young children invent positive solutions to conflict gives teachers something very important to work with.

Teachers can help children think of winning solutions when they have a hard time coming up with them. Teachers can also offer several winning solutions by suggesting various ways children can share or positive solutions that worked for them in the past.

Once children have tried out a winning solution, teachers can help them evaluate how it worked. A teacher can ask them to report how their solution worked and to describe it at a class meeting. Teachers can provide children an opportunity to reflect on their actions, acknowledge their success, and give others ideas about how they might solve their problems.

In all age groups studied, some children suggested a very special type of winning solution—a novel solution that incorporated both people together. Teachers can suggest winning solutions that recast the situation in some creative way to include children's joint participation. While some children did invent inclusive solutions, the solutions teachers suggested were often more "justice oriented," such as taking turns. Helping children find inclusive solutions can lead to more joint participation and cooperation than using only traditional win/win solutions, such as taking turns for equal time.

The most common solutions were losing ones. A majority of children of all ages ended their conflict stories with miserable outcomes. These seemed easier for young children to think of, and there are developmental factors that help explain this.

But developmental theory also predicts that with age, as children's thinking becomes more logical and flexible, they will become better able to think of win/win solutions. We did not find this, even when we saw general advances in cognitive levels. We wondered to what extent cultural factors influenced responses, and if the prevalence of violence in the United States and lack of exposure to models of positive solutions to conflict prevented children from developing an increasingly mutual orientation to conflict.

Children should have many opportunities to explore what happens in conflicts in which one or both participants lose. While most conflict-resolution training programs focus on win/win solutions, younger children are still working on understanding what happens as conflicts worsen and where hitting, fighting, and name calling can lead. It is often outside actual conflicts that teachers can help children see how bad leads to worse in a conflict and then help children use what they have learned when they have conflicts.

Negotiation—working out how to get from a problem to a solution—is critical to conflict resolution. It involves communication and give-and-take, a beginning understanding of two points of view, and the ability to see how different aspects of a conflict relate to each other. In their conflict stories, the five-year-olds almost never mentioned negotiation. They described conflicts and solutions but left out what might go on in between. When asked, they frequently had no idea.

Five-year-olds described conflicts and solutions but left out the in-between. If asked, they often had no idea about negotiation.

Younger children have a hard time moving from one state in a conflict to another or seeing how it might be done. They often seem totally immersed in the conflict, unable to see a way out. Only when children's thinking becomes more flexible and interconnected do they begin to see how to get from a state of conflict to a solution.

Teachers can help young children see what they need to do to put their positive solutions into practice. This often requires direct intervention in children's conflicts, helping them move from the conflict to a solution. Throughout negotiation, teachers can check to see if the children agree with each other's ideas, showing them that negotiation is a mutual process.

When we help children develop conflict-resolving skills, we help them feel they are capable of solving problems in the social realm. In the social arena, children need to feel, *I am a problem solver.* Many children we talked with expressed powerlessness about being able to do anything to work out their conflicts. They insisted there was nothing they could do to improve the difficult conflicts they described.

It's often easier for children to work on conflict-solving skills when they are not caught up in the heat of their own conflicts.

From an early age, no matter what developmental skills children have, one of the most important things we can do is to instill a sense of empowerment that they can do things to create more positive social relationships. The more children try out their skills and experience success in their own conflicts, the more they see themselves as successful and empowered and the more their skills evolve.

Conflict resolution skills must be practiced in a wide range of contexts to be meaningfully learned. The non-violent values underlying any program must be deeply connected to the overall curriculum and social climate in the classroom. Ideally, children would be immersed in a cooperative environment with opportunities for social encounters that foster cooperation and sharing rather than individualism and competition. In such a classroom, teachers would ask for and use children's ideas and involve children in various aspects of the decision-making process.

In the Class Curriculum

Many conflict-resolution activities and techniques can be incorporated into the class curriculum. It is often easier for children to work on conflict-solving skills when not caught up in the heat of their own conflicts. Then, when they are involved in conflicts, the teacher can bring in ideas discussed at these other times.

Children need lots of opportunities to experiment with their developing skills. A child mastering social skills needs to try them out in many different situations—to approximate, practice, test, and revise.

Children's social relationships are as important for discussion at group meetings as literacy skills, and new learnings should be "displayed" alongside accomplishments in other areas. There should be time and encouragement for children to share with others the approaches they tried in getting along together, what they think worked, and why. Lists of successful techniques can be made and referred to. As trust builds, children can talk about conflicts they are having, and classmates can help with problem solving.

Teachers can read books with conflict themes and elicit children's ideas about resolutions. Curriculum activities can spring from these discussions.

Teachers can show pictures of conflict situations to children, asking questions to encourage discussion: "What do you think is the problem here?" "How might they solve it so they're both happy?" What could they say to each other?" In such discussions, children benefit greatly from hearing each other's ideas and those of the teacher, and ideas the children can try in conflicts among themselves will accumulate.

Problem Puppets

Teachers can also use "problem puppets," simple sock puppets that role-play conflicts. The puppets can have disputes like those of children, and children can volunteer ideas about how the puppets might solve their problem, after which teachers can suggest new things. The range of conflict-resolution skills—defining the problem, negotiating, finding win/win solutions, and acting them out—can be worked on in an interactive and participatory way. Later, teachers can suggest a technique the puppets used to children having a conflict. Also, teachers can put the puppets in a special classroom area where children can role-play with them on their own.

Attitudes and skills for nonviolent conflict resolution that we help children construct in the early years provide the foundation they will need for making peace as adults in the twenty-first century. We must be able to see problems from more than a single point of view and have skills for negotiation that go beyond stating ultimatums and bottom lines. We must be able to find solutions that can work in the end for everyone—not solutions with winners and losers.

Especially in the 1990s, when children's lives are filled with violence and popular culture teaches them it is the common, acceptable way of resolving conflicts, we need to take this issue seriously. By introducing children to conflict-resolution skills in ways they understand and enjoy, teachers can begin to help this generation learn how to grapple creatively with conflict and make the kind of peace that can benefit everyone.

Practical Peacemaking Techniques for Educators

Peter Martin Commanday

Peter Martin Commanday is Director, Commanday Peacemaking Institute Corporation, Congers, New York. Condensed from School Safety, *Fall 1992, 15-17*

MOST school personnel are not taught practical trouble-handling techniques that would increase their chances for everyday survival. The Commanday Peacemaking Institute trains professionals to stay safer—in schools, on the streets, and at home. Offered here are concepts and techniques taught in Institute workshops in schools nationwide.

Emotions of individuals in trouble often cloud their judgment and their ability to effectively communicate. For instance, sometimes a disruptor's infuriating verbal abuse in your face feels like a personal attack, but in the disruptor's reality, it has nothing to do with you—you just happen to be there. To a disruptor, saving face will always be more important than adhering to any school rule. We answer what disruptors say instead of learning what they really mean. Too many of us believe a disruptor should "stop" just because we say so. The following mental self-defense techniques will help a person stay safe:

Never take it personally.

At the beginning of the day, students were coming into the building in reasonable order. A female teacher started up the stairs to her third-floor classroom and saw Jason sitting on the steps: "Hi, Jason." Silence. "Jason, it's time to go to your homeroom." Jason jumped to his feet, glared at her, and screamed, "Get the - - - - out of my face. Who do you think you are, bitch? Don't tell me what to do; you're not my mother!"

The great temptation is to respond with an angry lecture or sarcasm, but squelch that response. The remark is rarely related to you, even though the venom is directed at your face. No matter how personal the remark seems, whatever is said must not be taken personally. When you face this kind of verbal abuse,

If you don't respond in kind when you're cursed at, you disarm the disruptor of a potential weapon. Don't give disruptors ammunition.

detach yourself emotionally. Instead of an emotional response to "get back," use a peacemaking approach.

For example, you can respond with absolute silence, a very effective tool.

Most disruptive students cannot handle it. They become uncomfortable and break the silence either with a tirade of loud abuse or a demand to be left alone. Either way, the disruptor is now focused on you as the visual target. This gives you the opportunity to change the disruptor's behavior.

Another approach is to ignore the personal attack and respond with a neutral remark, such as "Jason, what's up?" This is not as casual as it might appear. You are offering the disruptor the opportunity to choose the topic for discussion. Sometimes, this elicits another personal attack, but more often, it stimulates the disruptor to say something related to the situation. After the first few words, the disruptor frequently reveals the real sources of frustration or fear, making it clear that the disruption is not concerned with you—you are just the recipient of the outburst.

A third type of response is a non sequitur. Say something totally unrelated to anything that has happened up to this point: "Jason, who let out the white rabbits?" The question has no value in itself but it may get the disruptor to stop, look up quizzically, and say, "Lady, you're crazy." Once again, you are the visual target—the focus of the disruptor's attention. This attention allows you to continue with your silence or casual remark—all in hopes of getting Jason to tell you what is upsetting him.

We have all been cursed at. Some-

 Reprinted from *The Education Digest*, March 1993, pp. 21-26. Condensed from *School Safety*, Fall 1992, pp. 15-17.

times we ignore it, sometimes we respond mildly, and other times we get verbally aggressive. When you choose not to respond in kind, you disarm the disruptor of a potential weapon. Do not give the disruptor ammunition—never take it personally.

Everybody saves face. Saving face has become a common term in school settings. When kids are "dissed" (insulted) in school, they are hurt and react very strongly to regain their status in school and on the streets. Kids can lose face in various types of situations:

The student is alone. Jason is sitting on the steps before class, with serious thoughts about his mom. She's in the hospital, and he isn't too sure what's wrong with her. He loves his mom and in their daily struggle to survive emotionally in the absence of a father in the house, they have formed a strong bond. He doesn't see or hear the teacher come up to him.

"Jason, what are you doing here? You belong in class. Please leave right now." In this setting, the student is alone—he has no audience. But he still loses face, as he feels the teacher should have read his mind and not bothered him with this stupidity. He loses face within himself with what seems to him an insensitive, disrespectful invasion of privacy. So, he

---

A peacemaker uses a personal tone of voice, rather than the cold, official tone we all know too well how to assume.

---

lashes out at the person who invaded his space—the teacher.

Even in a private setting with a disruptor, it is best not to give lectures or orders. Instead, take a more personal approach: "Jason, how's it going?" or "Jason, what's up?" If you don't know the student's name, leave it off. On a one-to-one basis, a peacemaker stays personal and avoids questions that come from his organizational identity as teacher, dean, or counselor.

Above all, a peacemaker uses a personal tone of voice, rather than the cold, official tone we all know too well how to assume. Convey to the student that you care about him, and you will more likely end up with a conversation rather than a disruptive incident.

The student has an audience. A student who loses face with peers watching will suffer many future indignities and has the curious goal, not of winning a conflict, but of prolonging it, to be seen by his peers as a "brave knight," defying the odds against the system no matter what the cost.

The goal of the peacemaker remains the same in this setting. Find a way to make yourself the visual target. Attract the disruptor's attention and, at the same time, offer the hope that if he will cease prolonging the conflict and allow intervention, there will be a positive outcome.

If the peacemaker has safely passed through the crowd and into the area of conflict of one or more disruptors, what do you do to make yourself the visual target? If you know both their names, try using humor, a great tool: "Sara, Janet—how much did you charge for tickets to this fight?"

If you do not know all names, use none. You do not want to attract the attention of only the person whose name you call. He or she may turn and become vulnerable to being hit. You also do not want to seem more favorably inclined toward the student whose name you know.

Another way to get the disruptors' attention is to use sound. Bang hard with your hand on something or slam down anything to make a loud noise. Or, you can whisper something startling to the disruptors that the crowd can't hear. When I am with boys, I sometimes whisper, "Your fly is open." To girls, I whisper, "He isn't worth it."

If the conflict is really heated—a screaming match about to erupt into an actual fight—you can use extreme measures. If there is a nearby chair or table, climb up on it. You can act crazy, say crazy things, start singing. (I once shouted a hodgepodge of nonsense syllables and said I was speaking a foreign language.)

Whether you play to the audience or to the combatants, remember that your immediate goal is to get the attention of the combatants in a way that allows each to save face. If you cause one or more of the volatile combatants to lose face, you will escalate the situation.

Once you have their attention, you want to move them away from the war zone. The further away they are from the crowd or the place of the conflict, the greater the possibility of keeping their attention.

A group of students has gathered. A group of students is assembling when they should be elsewhere. Let's assume the students are standing in a group in the hall just before class, but after the bell has rung.

When you approach a group of students, it is best not to address one or several of them by name. Instead, if you choose to speak, address the whole group. When students are in a group and doing something wrong (and they always know),

---

Whether playing to the audience or combatants, your immediate goal is to get the attention of the combatants in a way that allows each to save face.

---

calling their names will incense those who were singled out. You are likely to get the response, "Hey, man, why me? I'm not the only one here."

One very effective method of attracting and keeping the attention of groups is to use hand signals rather than voice command. Everyone saves face when you motion what to do rather than order what to do. As you attempt to move the disruptors from the combat zone to another room, motion with two hands, palms up, fingers together, and swing your hands in the direction you wish them to move. Do not single out any individual. This is usually successful. If it's not, try verbal requests, taking care always to keep your tone personal and calm.

Whether you are alone with a student, or with two kids with a surrounding crowd, or dealing with a group of kids which needs to move on, remember to allow all those involved to save face. If you show respect first, you increase the probability that the disruptors will respect your efforts.

No surprises. After the volatile behavior has been controlled and the peacemaker is making progress in defusing the incident, the disruptors do not want surprises. A disruptor will frequently re-escalate the situation if an unexpected factor is introduced into the equation.

How can a peacemaker prepare a disruptor for what happens next? This specific situation demonstrates the technique: You are in the hallway alone with John, who pulls a knife and waves it threateningly in the air, shouting to no one in particular how he plans to use it. You defuse the situation. John now asks, "What's going to happen next? Am I going to get suspended?"

Most people will think these two questions are connected. I think not. The first question is not related to being suspended or any other delayed consequence of his behavior. What is not being asked is a very different question: "In the next 90 seconds or so, what is going to happen to me?"

The unasked question can be answered, "John, we are going to go down this hallway to stairway six, down to the second floor, and across to room 223, as I want to see if the substitute teacher has showed up. Then we will go to stairway 1, down to the first floor to room 104. We'll go in, I'll close the door, and then you can tell me everything. I'm going to listen and not interrupt."

What you will probably see next is fascinating—a sigh of relief. The individual's body will actually show acceptance of your description of the next 90 seconds. The disruptor sees it as a time not to be frightened, a time of reasonable safety.

"No surprises" is a method of discussing before the fact what is about to immediately happen. Students live in a world of unexpected events. Surprises from parents, teachers, and the rest of the world are always happening to them and they are, for

---

You lessen tension and offer comfort and respect by verbalizing quietly, personally, matter-of-factly the immediate future.

---

the most part, not ready for the onslaught.

You lessen tension and offer comfort as well as respect by verbalizing quietly and personally, in a matter-of-fact manner, the details of the immediate future. The last part of your description should center around hope. By saying, "I will listen to everything you have to say, and will not interrupt," you offer the disruptor the hope of expressing what is on his mind to someone who wants to listen.

Win small, sequential victories. How often have you heard a teacher tell a student, "Stop that." In minor situations, that can work. In a conflict, when dealing with a disruptor, do not to try to stop everything all at once.

A moment ago, we mentioned John, who pulled his knife in the hallway. Let's look at what to say and not say in this situation. Some might say, "John, give me the knife"—and he may indeed do just that—"give it to you." Do not make such a dangerous suggestion. Very few combatants in this position will immediately weaken themselves by conceding to such a demand.

Instead, suggest very small, almost inconsequential moves: "John, please move that knife just a bit to the left. It

makes me nervous. See, I won't move—just a bit to the left. Thanks." Once this is done, follow with, "What's up?" Each time you talk about the knife, ask for a small movement. Win small sequential victories—these are easier for the disruptor to accept.

If you are in a room, the last step might be to get John to place the weapon on a table or chair. Once this is done, while you are talking, casually move in front of the item to put it out of John's sight. Then, when appropriate, place it in your back pocket. If in the hallway, you might not have such an easy series of moves. I have had the disruptor slowly lower the weapon until I finally suggested that he put it back in his pocket. Once we were in a room, away from the crowd, I then again attempted to get the weapon placed on a table.

It is important not to give an order to a person displaying a weapon in a threatening manner. Instead,

---

Don't give orders to a person displaying a weapon threateningly. Instead, try to win small, sequential victories.

---

try to win small, sequential victories.

In a dangerous world where people behave unpredictably, violence may often erupt immediately and suddenly. School personnel need practical techniques to reduce the probability that anyone will be hurt. Hopefully, these suggestions will be helpful.

[Commanday Peacemaking Institute offers a series of workshops on how to manage a crisis with "mental self-defense" techniques. Contact Peter Martin Commanday, 7 Greenfield Terrace, Congers, NY 10920, or phone (914) 268-4420.]

From Individual Differences to Learning Communities — Our Changing Focus

The emerging picture of teaching and learning raises a host of new questions, among them: How do we create a community of inquiry in the admittedly artificial environment of the classroom?

RICHARD S. PRAWAT

Richard S. Prawat is Professor and Chair, Michigan State University, College of Education, Department of Counseling, Educational Psychology and Special Education, East Lansing, MI 48824-1034.

Current conversations about the nature of teaching and learning differ dramatically from those 20 or 30 years ago — both in *what* is being discussed and in *who* is doing the discussing. Many researchers now include teachers as equal participants. They argue that involving practitioners in conversations about teaching and learning significantly improves the dialogue, leading to more useful and creative change. This practice coincides with the notion of "teacher empowerment," a key aspect of educational restructuring efforts under way in many parts of the country (Prawat in press).

These changes exemplify the role of educational theory and research. Ideas from educational theory and research influence how we think about teachers, students, and subject matter; they also enlarge our field of vision. Educational theory functions more as a "conversation starter," however, than as a final answer. It provokes better questions about important issues, but sometimes constrains our responses or hinders our evaluations (Prawat in press).

These observations about the past, present, and future of educational research offer a perspective on the impact of these "conversations" and could lead to additional, productive discussions.

Focus on Individual Students

Prior to the 17th century, Western philosophers equated education with inward, solitary searches for truth. Even gifted educators like Socrates were thought to play a relatively passive role in what was primarily viewed as a process of individual self-discovery. This focus on the individual continues to exert a powerful influence on today's education and educational research.

In 1914 Thorndike argued that researchers should focus their energies on describing the individual student. In response, his colleagues developed measures, such as intelligence tests, to assess the traits deemed relevant to individual performance in school. Before long, "individual difference" measures were used to sort students into ability groups, tracks, and special education programs.

Our preoccupation with individual differences contrasts sharply with other countries. Particularly in Asia, teachers downplay traits such as intelligence and emphasize instead "doing one's duty" to meet social expectations or group norms.

Until recently, researchers did little to challenge the individual differences approach. Instead, they devised ways to work around certain traits, especially ability or "rate of learning." One solution in the 1950s and 1960s was mastery learning. Elements of mastery learning, such as breaking the task into smaller pieces and providing immediate feedback at each segment of the learning sequence, figured prominently in successful training programs developed during World War II. It was hoped that applying these principles to individual learning would minimize the importance of the most pervasive individual difference: ability. The argument went something like this: If instructional materials are designed so that students work at their own pace through a carefully planned sequence of tasks, then ability will cease to be an important factor in student performance.

The concept of mastery learning — to design a curriculum so powerful that it overcomes deficiencies in learners and teachers alike — represented the first version of what came to be known as a "teacher-proof" curriculum. This notion was embraced by subject matter specialists during the 1960s. Although the curriculums developed by subject matter specialists — for example, "new math" — differed dramatically from those developed by educational researchers and often focused more on general inquiry or problem-solving skills — the concept was the same. The goal was to create a compelling stimulus environment to

By Richard S. Prawat, "From Individual Differences to Learning Communities—Our Changing Focus," *Educational Leadership,* Vol. 49, No. 7, April 1992, pp. 9-13.

carry students regardless of what they or the teacher bring to the learning task. The popularity of mastery learning and other similar curriculums grew logically from the focus on individuals. This perspective, in turn, was shaped in large part by the theoretical biases then evident in the research community.

Understandably, the notion of teacher-proof curriculums turned out to be a dead-end. Mastery learning, and other such curriculums, downplayed the role of teachers too much, making them little more than managers of instructional material. Rightfully so, teachers would not allow their classrooms to be "proofed." Subsequent research demonstrated that teachers play a vital role in the educational process, although honest differences of opinion continue as to how to characterize their role. Engelmann presents one perspective (1991, p. 218):

> Teachers should have a special kind of knowledge about teaching. That knowledge derives from the ability to execute the details of effective instruction. The teacher should know how to present tasks to students and should demonstrate appropriate pacing, appropriate inflections and stress, appropriate responses to students who perform well, and appropriate responses to students who make mistakes.

Engelmann adds some skills to this description, concluding that "the teacher, in summary, should be a technician." This view gained dominance in the 1970s.

Teachers as Technicians

During the late 1960s and early 1970s, it became apparent that not all teachers were up to the educational challenges that became more visible at that time. Thus was born the body of research that came to be known as "teacher effectiveness" research. Using various teacher observation instruments and traditional measures of student achievement as the index of effectiveness, researchers tried to determine what technical skills were possessed by more effective teachers. In an

approach elegant in its simplicity, researchers sat at the back of a classroom and noted the specifics of how teachers managed and instructed a class. For example, they studied how the teacher organized the group, introduced lessons, asked questions, or gave feedback to students. These "process" skills could then be correlated with student achievement (the "product") to assess effectiveness.

Across several teacher effectiveness studies, consistent relationships emerged: Teachers who were more effective in producing gains in student achievement were well organized, minimized student disruptions by monitoring behavior, and enforced rules in a consistent manner. Effective teachers programmed their instruction to ensure success. They proceeded through the material in small, quickly grasped steps and carefully asked questions that engendered short, correct answers. Azuma terms this approach, predominant in American education, the "quick and snappy" method of conducting lessons. He contrasts it with lessons in Japan, which he characterizes as "sticky and probing." Rather than moving briskly, Japanese teachers linger over topics, encouraging students to examine important concepts from a variety of perspectives (Azuma 1983).

Teacher effectiveness research continues to exert a powerful influence. In many states, teacher evaluations are based on criteria drawn from this research, and many teacher education programs have designed curriculums with its prescriptions in mind. These teaching practices appear to be helpful not only to low ability students, who presumably need more structure, but also to high ability students.

The change in researchers' minds about the validity of these prescriptions can be attributed to two factors:

• the growing influence in this country of cognitive psychologists who, building on Piaget's work, have begun to listen seriously to what young people say.

• the influence of educational anthropologists like Shirley Brice

Heath and cultural psychologists like Michael Cole, who have alerted us to the role of "context" or "community" in explaining what young people know.

Ideas developed from these two perspectives altered the landscape for educational research in the '80s and '90s.

Subject Matter Within Context

As cognitive psychologists have discovered, *all* children, when they enter school, bring a wealth of informal knowledge. They are not, as was believed, "sponges" soaking up knowledge according to their ability levels. They have definite views about what they are taught. Like adults, they develop theories about nearly everything, from the sublime — for example, God and death — to the ridiculous — for example, whether or not worms have bones. Children use these theories to frame their interpretation of new information. Because these theories help them make sense of their world, children often are hesitant to change them. In one study, following an eight-week science unit on photosynthesis, less than 10 percent of the 5th graders understood that plants get their food by making it themselves. Most held on to their original theory that plants, like people, ingest their food from outside (Roth and Anderson 1991).

Piaget alerted us that "real learning" is not simply the parroting back of information. Real learning involves personal *invention* or *construction*, and the teacher's role in this process is a difficult one. On the one hand, the teacher must honor students' "inventions," or they will not share them. On the other hand, the teacher needs to guide students toward a more mature understanding, which frequently means challenging student constructions. One way to reconcile these conflicting demands is to alter classroom norms, encouraging students to view errors as natural, even useful, aspects of learning. For classrooms to be centers of intellectual inquiry, students and teachers must feel free to pursue ideas and make mistakes.

In comparing the role of specific experience with that of more general characteristics such as age and IQ, cognitive psychologists have identified "the former experience" as the most important predictor of a child's conceptual understanding. Several studies validate this finding. One study contrasted the performance of 10-year-olds and adults on a short-term learning task: recalling the placement of pieces during various phases of a chess game. The younger subjects, who were chess players, outperformed the adults, who were novices, despite the fact that the children demonstrated *less* general memory ability on scales typically used to assess this variable (Chi 1978).

The recent focus on conceptual understanding also questions the use of achievement tests to assess student learning. Lorrie Shepard, a prominent measurement specialist, criticizes the current practice of testing isolated, discrete skills (1991). Shepard advocates the use of alternative assessment instruments that better reflect current thinking about the nature of teaching and learning.

Cognitive psychologists aren't the only ones to contribute to recent changes in our views about teaching and learning. Anthropologists and cultural psychologists remind us that context plays a key role in shaping and constraining individual learning. Some of the most interesting work contrasts learning in the classroom with learning in out-of-school contexts; these studies often highlight the shortcomings associated with our traditional, didactic approach to formal education.

The learning that people do outside of school frequently surpasses what they can do in the classroom. In one study performed in a commercial dairy, workers used error-free arithmetic typical of 8th or 9th graders to fill orders despite the fact that they only had a 6th grade education (Scribner and Fahrmeier 1982). Contrast that with what researchers find when they examine in-school performance. In one study, three-quarters of the 2nd graders inter-

viewed by a researcher "solved" the following problem by simply adding the numbers 26 and 10: There are 26 sheep and 10 goats on a ship. How old is the captain? (Schoenfeld in press). The suspension of sense-making seems to be less common in out-of-school settings. Why?

Meaningful activity is perhaps the most salient feature of out-of-school learning. Out-of-school learning focuses on overall goals and strategies, the "big picture," rather than on isolated details. In the classroom, students are expected to master the details and may never see the big picture. A study that ties children's ideas about reading to their reading group experience illustrates this. Children in the lower reading groups, where the focus was on isolated skills, defined reading as "using materials correctly and sounding out words," all discrete skills. Children in the higher reading groups, who were encouraged to read for meaning, stressed the importance of comprehension in their definitions of reading (Eisenhart and Cutts-Dougherty 1991).

Shared activity is another key feature of out-of-school learning. In apprenticeship situations, novices often learn as much from each other as they do from the master craftsman. Collaborative learning tends to be more the norm than the exception. In contrast, the focus in school is almost always on the individual. The most important activities — listening to the teacher, homework, in-class exercises — are carried out by individual students, operating in splendid isolation from each other.

Just as Piaget's research opened up the possibility of a learner who is continually developing and testing important theories about the world, so have anthropologists and cultural psychologists altered our views about the context of teaching. Not only do we more fully appreciate the importance of social environment in the learning process, we also appreciate that a school's learning environment — with its emphasis on individual learning and the mastery of isolated knowledge and skill — differs from

The learning that people do outside of school frequently surpasses what they can do in the classroom.

most other cultural learning arrangements. Clearly, we should no longer consider the classroom the prototype of effective learning. It is just one among many such arrangements. While it may be disconcerting to talk about the inadequacies of current classroom environments, the talk liberates us to search for alternative ways of structuring instruction. More important, it lessens the likelihood that school culture will be used as a benchmark for evaluating other learning environments. In the past, this practice led teachers and researchers alike to consider alternative environments as deficient compared to that norm.

By no longer viewing the school culture as an absolute standard for teaching and learning, we may value the contributions of other cultures. This puts behavior that used to be considered incompetent in a new light. Heath's classic study, *Ways with Words* (1983), illustrates how teachers can come to see differences in a child's language use — the child's use of stories to entertain and control, for example — as an asset rather than a liability during reading group. Thus, behaviors initially regarded as evidence of a deficiency in manners can be seen as an alternative form of self-expression upon which the teacher could build.

The Teacher as Community-Builder

This emerging picture of teaching and learning contrasts dramatically with that of the recent past. Our long fixation with individual differences appears to be waning. If learning is a social act, more akin to the process of socialization than instruction (Resnick 1990), the criteria for judging teacher effectiveness shifts from that of delivering good lessons to that of being able to build or create a classroom "learning community."

This, of course, raises a host of new questions for teachers and researchers to ponder: What is the nature of the classroom working environment? Does the work resemble authentic or realistic out-of-school activity or performance? Is there, for example, any relation between what students are asked to do in school mathematics or history and the kinds of activities engaged in by practitioners of those disciplines? Too often, school history involves the memorization of facts, and "problem solving" in school mathematics is little more than the search for syntactic cues in story problems — like the word "left" in "How many are left?"

Another vital question relates to the norms of interaction that govern how members of the community relate to one another: Do the ground rules for classroom discourse establish a context conducive to collaborative problem solving on the part of *all* students?

That many educators are grappling with these complex issues illustrates the role that educational research and theory typically play in education. They encourage us to look at the world through new conceptual lenses, thus creating new opportunities for development and change in classroom teaching. In addition to changing existing practices, educational research can bolster creative practitioners who decide to "teach against the grain" (Cochran-Smith 1991) based on their personal experiences with students. Susan Moran is one such teacher. She provides a moving example of the sort of practice current research supports. Her goal, she wrote, was to dispel the idea that English majors are the only people who know how to talk about books. She abandoned the practice of

having her 8th graders read one book together. Instead, students were invited to choose their own books, talk with one another about the books in class, and write to her about them in their journals:

> To get things under way, I asked students to bring in their favorite book from the summer. The next day, the first person to speak was Matthew, who had brought in *The Incredible Journey*. "It's the best book I've ever read," he announced. "Actually," he added quietly, "it's the only book I've ever read all the way through." I held my breath when the first hand shot up, afraid that someone might sneer at Matthew for having read such a "babyish" book. Instead, there was an outpouring of enthusiasm for this book and praise for Matthew for having discovered and read it. "Didn't you hate for it to be over?" Tali asked.
> We were off and running. The classroom became . . . like a dining-room table, where people could converse easily about books and poems and ideas. I would watch my students leave the classroom carrying on animated conversations about which book was truly Robert Cormier's best, why sequels are often disappointing, which books they planned to reread . . . (1991 pp. 437-439).

As this passage suggests, in classroom learning communities, individuals engage in animated conversations about important intellectual issues. Ideally, such conversations will occur at the school level as well, involving all teachers and focusing on concerns about curriculum, learning and teaching, alternative approaches to assessment, and the like.

Many reformers believe that the creation of schoolwide learning communities is a necessary if not sufficient condition for the creation of classroom learning communities. Figuring out how to accomplish these two goals is a task that could engage the productive energies of teachers and researchers well into the next century. If this comes to pass, current

educational theory and research will have pointed the way.

References

Azuma, H. (1983). "Two Models of Teachability: U.S. and Japan." Unpublished paper, Shirayuri College, Tokyo.

Chi, M. T. H. (1978). "Knowledge Structures and Memory Development." In *Children's Thinking: What Develops?*, edited by R. S. Siegler. Hillsdale, N.J.: Erlbaum.

Cochran-Smith, M. (1991). "Learning to Teach Against the Grain." *Harvard Educational Review* 61, 3: 279-310.

Eisenhardt, M. A., and K. Cutts-Dougherty. (1991). "Social and Cultural Constraints on Students' Access to School Knowledge." In *Literacy for a Diverse Society. Perspectives, Practices, and Policies*, edited by E. H. Hiebert. New York: Teachers College.

Engelmann, S. (1991). "Teachers, Schemata, and Instruction." In *Teaching Academic Content to Diverse Learners*, edited by M. Kennedy. New York: Teachers College.

Heath, S. B. (1983). *Ways with Words: Language, Life, and Work in Communities and Classrooms*. Cambridge, UK: Cambridge University Press.

Moran, S. (July/August 1991). "Creative Reading: Young Adults and Paperback Books." *The Horn Book Magazine*: 437-441.

Prawat, R. S. (In press). "Teachers' Beliefs About Teaching and Learning: A Constructivist Perspective." *American Journal of Education*.

Resnick, L. (1990). "Literacy in School and Out." *Daedalus* 119, 2: 169-185.

Roth, K., and C. W. Anderson. (1991). "Promoting Conceptual Change Learning from Science Textbooks." In *Improving Learning: New Perspectives*, edited by P. Ramsden. London: Kogen Page.

Schoenfeld, A. (In press). "On Mathematics as Sense-Making: An Informal Attack on the Unfortunate Divorce of Formal and Informal Mathematics." In *Informal Reasoning and Education*, edited by D. W. Perkins and G. J. Voss. Hillsdale, N.J.: Erlbaum.

Scribner, S., and E. Fahrmeier. (1982). "Practical and Theoretical Arithmetic: Some Preliminary Findings. Industrial-Literacy Project," Working Paper No. 3. Graduate Center, City University of New York.

Shepard, L. A. (1991). "Psychometricians' Beliefs About Learning." *Educational Researcher* 20, 7: 2-16.

Resolving Teacher-Student Conflict:

A Different Path

STANLEY C. DIAMOND

Stanley C. Diamond is the director of Mill Creek School, Institute of Pennsylvania Hospital, Philadelphia, and serves as a consulting editor for The Clearing House.

It is the last period of the day. Patience has worn thin for teachers and students alike. Jack enters the class after it has begun, nothing new for him. The door slams behind him, disrupting the class. Mr. Gross turns and indicates to Jack that he has come late to his class for the last time. He is to report to the office for the remainder of the period and is to serve a detention after school for the next three days. Jack mumbles some comment not designed to be heard, making Mr. Gross even angrier. He threatens suspension if Jack doesn't move along immediately. Jack makes some rebellious gesture but walks out of the class to report to the office. The class becomes quiet, and the lecture begins.

In most classrooms, conflict between the teacher and a student is a regular occurrence, part of the daily routine. When the contention is successfully resolved, the scenario is likely to involve the student's being reprimanded, punished, limited, excluded, or simply corrected. But what happens to the feelings that are generated by the conflict? More than likely, anger is experienced by both student and teacher. What passes for resolution of the conflict is often the same thing that occurs in the child's home. Order must be established; we all know that. The teacher (parent) is the authority; we know that also. The authority bears the responsibility for the program (family life) proceeding so that the tasks of the day and the goals of the setting can be successfully achieved. But, what happens to the feelings?

In most educational settings, they are simply stored. A student misbehaves. The teacher reacts. If the reaction achieves its purpose, the student's misbehavior ends and the future relationship between the teacher and that student includes the results of that transaction. If it is resolved effectively, the student learns that he cannot misbehave in that teacher's room without unpleasant consequences, and the class is a more orderly learning environment. Im-

agine a class where the teacher's interventions are unsuccessful. Not a very pleasant thought. We can all agree that little positive activity is likely to take place in a setting that is out of control. But, what happens to the feelings?

Almost invariably, whatever feelings arise in a teacher-student conflict are left for each party to deal with alone. More often than not, neither person is likely to share his or her personal experience with the incident with anyone at all, much less with each other. If the kind of interaction that gives rise to the teacher's interventions is repetitive or includes powerful negative reactions in the students, it is likely that angry feelings, or at least strong personal dislike, can develop between the two parties. The problem is that such feelings color the student's ability to respond to whatever that teacher has to offer to him or her in a way that makes learning less positive, less enriching, less effective. If the student is an angry person, his or her anger is augmented in a way that is likely to result in acting out in some other setting or in that classroom in a manner that can be self-destructive or, at the very least, unsatisfying.

What I have described is the usual process that takes place in most classrooms most of the time. The vast majority of students survive such situations and simply have an angry experience included in their life that is unresolved but quantitatively insignificant. Their otherwise sturdy egos and their many positive experiences that support a healthy self-image will balance things out. For them, life will go on. The feelings remain unexpressed. One small step for mild detachment, or pessimism, or self-deprecation on some future occasion. This is an unnecessary but uneventful development.

Yet there are students for whom such experiences are more wounding, whose lives are more fragile, whose sense of themselves is more brittle, whose anger defeats them from moment to moment. Can they afford to leave an interaction in which they have experienced humiliation, loss of status, loss of control, or any other reversal without an opportunity to process the interaction so that

From *The Clearing House*, Vol. 65, No. 3, January/February 1992, pp. 141-143. Reprinted with permission of the Helen Dwight Reid Educational Foundation. Published by Heldref Publications, 1319 Eighteenth St., NW, Washington, DC 20036-1802.

they understand it, integrate it into their psyche, and learn from it? Or are they doomed to repeat such defeats over and over?

The youngsters I am thinking of are those that we often call emotionally disturbed or behaviorally disordered or "high risk" for failure. Being sent from the room to the principal's office or being scolded in class or being given an extra assignment for talking with a neighbor increases the tension that exists between that student and the teacher. By no means am I criticizing a teacher's responding to undesirable behavior. That is clearly a necessity. Nor do I mean to be critical of a particular technique. Some are more desirable and more helpful than others, but those distinctions are not the purpose of this article. My concern is that customarily such interventions solve the problem of the behavior but do not deal in any useful way with the feelings that are generated.

I recently visited an alternative school for disturbed adolescents. I was asked to consult with the faculty and to lead a workshop on effective management of such students. To my surprise the teachers seemed to feel that they did not have real control over the students. They felt that the students seemed angry and uncooperative much of the time. Of course, some of this behavior was to be expected; their students had a lifetime of experience with that kind of response. Upon further discussion, I learned that there was a comprehensive behavioral system at work in the school that appeared to be well thought-out and quite effective at motivating the students to modify their responses. On the surface, it seemed that the teachers had a great deal of power in the classroom. As we talked, however, I realized that, although the teachers were able to take action with their students and had the support of both the administration and the system in which they worked, they felt that they never quite got things settled. The students left their classes angry and returned angrier. No matter what rewards the system included for encouraging compliance, doling out positive responses did not seem to take care of the residual bad feelings that were caused by previous negative interactions. As we talked, the teachers began to supply their own answers. They noted that they never got a chance to talk with the student about what happened between them. Without that opportunity, matters did not seem settled and they felt that they were beginning where they left off each time. That was indeed an accurate observation.

For such students, it seems necessary that two other ingredients must be introduced into that school setting. I would contend that these should be present in all schools, but are absolutely essential for a school that works with disturbed children. The first is a need for relationship-building experiences for the teachers and students. The second is a commitment on the part of all parties that feelings that arise between members of the school community are to be confronted, discussed, and resolved insofar as that is possible. Both of these are important and difficult ends to achieve.

Relationship-building experiences can take many shapes and forms. What characterizes them, however, is that they are opportunities for the individuals involved to touch each other in personal, human ways. That can include sharing of interests, experiences, feelings, skills, or values, or just relaxing or playing or laughing together, activities that are not bound by tasks and roles but depend on the voluntary association of the two people and the free sharing of themselves. A school can encourage such experiences by designing settings in which they are likely to occur. What is required are trips, games, informal times for students and teachers to associate at leisure, arrangements for mentoring or advising in manageable teacher-student ratios, joint activities wherein roles are not highly defined, joint learning experiences, and other nontypical arrangements that are rarely present in most schools. If one believes that effective growth requires processing of feelings and the development of interpersonal intimacy as a resource for individual growth, space and time must be found to make sure such events take place.

This is obviously no easy task. The fact that such opportunities are rarely present in school is an indication that either the notion of people getting to know one another in personal ways is deemed to be undesirable or it is too difficult to program into the school day. When working with disturbed adolescents, it is foolish to expect that long-term, positive changes in the ways students deal with tension and conflict can be truly altered without improving the nature of the relationships between them, their teachers, and their peers. To create an environment for resolving bad feelings between the members of the school community is no easy task, but a commitment to do so is essential. For disturbed students an open and interactive environment is a requirement; for less needy youngsters it is most desirable so that they may grow into powerful and confident adults.

The notion that there is a need to process and resolve feelings that arise in the conflicts that occur in the classroom is another matter altogether. The nature of the environment is of little consequence unless the people involved understand that a community that is dedicated to the growth of the students involves—indeed, requires—the risky, painful, arduous commitment of all the staff to confront their own as well as their students' feelings. Teachers need to be willing to hear criticism and tolerate hostility in order to provide a setting in which students feel comfortable being truthful and open, being close and real. This requires that the staff feel relaxed and secure about themselves. That surely rules out many of the teachers who are presently in our classrooms; unfortunately, there is much to be done before any staff would be amenable to putting themselves in such a vulnerable position. Those who can naturally function in this kind of setting are a minority. They should be treasured, rewarded, and given leadership opportunities so that others can learn from them. The students will gladly follow. They need only see that they are guaranteed respect and justice and that their feelings and opinions are valued in the school. However reserved and untrusting they may be initially, it will take little for most students to realize that an open and responsive school is to their advantage. Those who are too damaged in self-esteem or too hurt by their earlier life experiences may not any longer be able to act in their own best interest, but they will be the minority.

Certain facts follow from the notion that a school is a place where students, and especially those with emotional problems, can and should learn about the proper expression of feelings, about trust between individuals, about the value of being heard and of hearing others, about being in the other person's shoes and caring about what happens to all who exist in the community. No pipe dream this. Some of the most difficult tasks are the most urgent ones for us to strive toward. Every school for emotionally disturbed adolescents should provide its students the opportunity and lessons I describe. But no school of any kind should be unaware of the difference between control and resolution of conflict. If we wish our young people to grow into adults who can experience and share their joy as well as their pain, who care about themselves and others, who respect their society while guarding their own rights and powers within it, who seek intimacy and do not run from it, who are powerful enough personally to restructure their world, perhaps we shall have to go to extraordinary ends to reach that goal.

Teachers cannot change an institution single-handedly, but they can have impact upon it by dialogue and by example. More informal, relationship-building activities with the students are often possible:

• Leaving a few moments in a class for students to come to the desk with relevant questions or issues about the discussion can be structured into the day.

• Conversations that enable teachers and students to introduce to one another some personal aspects of their lives can be encouraged during or between classes.

• Discipline can be seen as a matter of concern by the teacher even after the external responses are achieved and the intervention has been made. For example, one can meet the student in the detention room to process the interaction that led up to the problem.

We can learn to listen as well as demand, to value the student as much as we do his or her performance. The change is not overwhelming, but the results can be most significant for the students involved.

It is the last period of the day. Patience has worn thin for teachers and students alike. Jack enters the class after it has begun, nothing new for him. Walking over to Jack's desk, Mr. Gross quietly indicates to him that he wishes him to remain at the end of the period and then he continues with the lesson. When the others leave, Mr. Gross tells Jack how disruptive it is for the class and how distracting it is for him when Jack comes in late. He cannot allow that and will insist that Jack get a detention each time it happens again.

Jack responds that the class comes right after gym and he has trouble getting himself together and stopping at the bathroom quickly enough to get to class on time. Besides, Mr. Gross is the only one who closes his door just as the bell rings. Jack does not want to be late, but it seems like the teacher wants him to be. Mr. Gross explains that it makes him angry when he finally gets things started and someone walks into the class. Getting underway is the hardest thing for him to do, and Jack is making it more difficult for him. Mr. Gross expects him to solve the problem of lateness but offers to help if Jack needs him to. Jack says he will try harder and will just accept the detention if he is late again. They won't need to talk about it; it will just be automatic. Mr. Gross expresses his appreciation of Jack's understanding and wishes him luck in handling the problem—no hard feelings, just one more challenge in the day for two well-meaning people in a high school that is a little too big for each of them. No egos bruised either.

It takes no more effort to enhance the dignity of each individual in the classroom than it does to diminish it.

Equality of Educational Opportunity

There are several serious debates in progress regarding how the schools should respond to the equity needs of students. The "equity agenda" for the schools deals with issues relating to fairness and justice for students from all cultural backgrounds. This has led to debate over how school curricula should or should not change to reflect the culturally pluralistic populations of students in the schools. The "Western canon" is being challenged by advocates of multicultural perspectives in school curriculum development. Multicultural educational programming, which will reflect the rapidly changing cultural demographics of North American schooling, is being fiercely advocated by some and strongly opposed by others. This controversy centers around several different issues regarding what it means to provide equality of opportunities for culturally diverse nations. This debate is reflected in the essays in this unit. The traditional Western cultural content of general and social studies and language arts curricula is being challenged as "Eurocentric."

Helping teachers to broaden their cultural perspectives and to take a more global view of curriculum content is something the advocates of culturally pluralistic approaches to curriculum development would like to see integrated into the entire elementary and secondary school curriculum structure. There are calls for teachers

to be more sensitive and responsive to the many cultural heritages represented in today's school populations. The debate over how to approximate equality of educational opportunity is turning more and more to questions as to how educational systems can integrate comparative and international cultural perspectives into the content of what students learn in school.

North America is as multicultural a region of the world as exists anywhere on Earth. Our enormous cultural diversity encompasses populations from many indigenous "First Americans" as well as peoples from every European culture, plus many peoples of Asian, African, and Latin American nations and the Central and South Pacific Island groups. There is spirited controversy as to how to help all Americans to better understand the multicultural heritage of America. There are spirited defenders and opponents to the traditional Eurocentric heritage of the established North American knowledge base. We must deal with this controversy as well as with many others having to do with issues regarding what constitutes equality of opportunity from different perspectives.

The problems of inequality of educational opportunity are still of great concern to American educators. One in four American children do not have all of their basic needs met and live under poverty conditions. Almost one in three live in single-parent homes, not that this is necessarily a disadvantage, but under conditions of poverty it often is. More and more concern is expressed over how to help children of poverty. The equity agenda of our time has to do with many issues related to gender, race, and ethnicity. All forms of social deprivation or discrimination are aggravated by great disparities in family income and accumulated wealth. How can students be helped to have an equal opportunity to succeed in school? We have wrestled with this great practical and moral dilemma in educational policy development for decades. How can we advance the just cause of the educational interests of our young people more effectively?

Discrimination on the basis of sex and race is still a great challenge to North American societies in spite of the great progress we have made. We must resolve never to stop the just and right struggle to secure equal rights for all our youth.

Some of us are still proud to say we are a nation of immigrants. There are powerful demographic and economic forces impacting on the makeup of the populations of Canada and the United States. In addition to the traditional minority-majority group relationships in the

United States, new waves of immigrants are making concerns for achieving equality of opportunity in education as important as ever. The new immigrations from Asia and Latin America reemphasize the already preexistent reality that we are a nation forged from many cultures. Both Canada and the United States are deeply committed to improving intercultural relations in education and society at large. The sociological and demographic changes in North American population development are very significant, and they represent trends that ensure that we will remain multicultural democracies.

The social psychology of prejudice is something North American psychiatrists, social psychologists, anthropologists, and sociologists have studied in great depth since the 1930s. Tolerance, acceptance, and a commitment to the unique worth of every person are teachable and learnable attitudes. The dream of the Founders and of the martyrs for human rights lives. It will never die.

The struggle for equality of opportunity is an endless challenge; poverty reduces windows of opportunity for those affected by it. A just society is constantly challenged to find meaningful ways to raise human aspirations, to heal human hurt, and to help in the task of optimizing every citizen's potential. Education is a vital component of all efforts to alleviate, or even eradicate, the causes of poverty. Yet poverty is not the only obstacle to equality of opportunity. Any form of discrimination against persons because of their identity or socioeconomic status is an impediment to democratic social aspirations. Educational systems and the teachers who labor within them can be a bulwark and a source of hope for those who struggle to fulfill the full promise of their humanity.

Teachers have enormous opportunities to reach out to their students as examples of justice and fairness in their day-to-day instructional activities. They can incorporate into their lessons an emphasis on acceptance of difference, toleration of and respect for the beliefs of others, and the skills of reasoned debate and dialogue.

We have witnessed a great struggle to secure our civil liberties in the schools. There is yet much to be done. There are many civil rights issues still affecting the lives of students in the schools. The courts have ruled on many of them. We still must be alert to keep our constitutional promises. It is not easy to maintain fair opportunity structures in a culturally pluralistic society in which about a fourth of the students in the schools cannot meet all of their basic needs. There are a plurality of cultural interests competing for inclusion in school curricula. What counts as fair treatment of students' cultural interests is a complex issue. The struggle for optimal, best possible representation of minority perspectives in the schools will be a matter of serious concern to educators for the foreseeable future. From the many court decisions upholding the rights of women and cultural minorities in the schools over the past 40 years has emerged a national consensus that we must strive for the greatest degree of equality in education as may be possible. The triumph of constitutional law over prejudice and bigotry must continue.

People honestly disagree on many questions relating to civil rights in the field of education. We still believe in the possibility of social justice under constitutional law. The struggle to enhance and expand the opportunity structures of our young people will continue. The mid-1990s find us facing serious challenges in our efforts to achieve both social justice and higher levels of achievement in the schools. Every citizen has benefited from the civil rights legislation and court cases of the past 40 years. The work, however, is far from finished. The social problems facing many American children and adolescents are critically severe and complex. We look with hope to our future, and we seek compassion for our respective visions of the world.

Looking Ahead: Challenge Questions

How do you respond to calls for the integration of more multicultural content into school studies?

What do you know about how it feels to be poor? How do you think it would feel in school? How would you respond?

If you are a female, have you ever felt that you were discriminated against, or at least ignored?

If you are a male, have you ever felt that you were being favored?

How can schools address more effectively the issue of gender bias?

How do children learn to be prejudiced? How can they learn tolerance?

What were the constitutional precedents for the school desegregation cases?

What academic freedoms should every teacher and student have?

What do you understand to be the interrelationship between the effects of poverty and racial or sexual discrimination?

How can a classroom teacher help his or her students adopt tolerant multicultural perspectives?

The Canon Debate, Knowledge Construction, and Multicultural Education

JAMES A. BANKS

JAMES A. BANKS *is professor and director, Center for Multicultural Education, University of Washington, Seattle, WA 98195. He specializes in social studies education and multicultural education.*

I review the debate over multicultural education in this article, state that all knowledge reflects the values and interests of its creators, and illustrate how the debate between the multiculturalists and the Western traditionalists is rooted in their conflicting conceptions about the nature of knowledge and their divergent political and social interests. I present a typology that describes five types of knowledge and contend that each type should be a part of the school, college, and university curriculum.

Educational Researcher, Vol. 22, No. 5, pp. 4–14.

A heated and divisive national debate is taking place about what knowledge related to ethnic and cultural diversity should be taught in the school and university curriculum (Asante, 1991a; Asante & Ravitch, 1991; D'Souza, 1991; Glazer, 1991; Schlesinger, 1991; Woodward, 1991). This debate has heightened ethnic tension and confused many educators about the meaning of multicultural education. At least three different groups of scholars are participating in the canon debate: the Western traditionalists, the multiculturalists, and the Afrocentrists. Although there are a range of perspectives and views within each of these groups, all groups share a number of important assumptions and beliefs about the nature of diversity in the United States and about the role of educational institutions in a pluralistic society.

The Western traditionalists have initiated a national effort to defend the dominance of Western civilization in the school and university curriculum (Gray, 1991; Howe, 1991; Woodward, 1991). These scholars believe that Western history, literature, and culture are endangered in the school and university curriculum because of the push by feminists, ethnic minority scholars, and other multiculturalists for curriculum reform and transformation. The Western traditionalists have formed an organization called the National Association of Scholars to defend the dominance of Western civilization in the curriculum.

The multiculturalists believe that the school, college, and university curriculum marginalizes the experiences of people of color and of women (Butler & Walter, 1991; Gates, 1992; Grant, 1992; Sleeter, personal communication, October 26, 1991). They contend that the curriculum should be reformed so that it will more accurately reflect the his-

tories and cultures of ethnic groups and women. Two organizations have been formed to promote issues related to ethnic and cultural diversity. Teachers for a Democratic Culture promotes ethnic studies and women studies at the university level. The National Association for Multicultural Education focuses on teacher education and multicultural education in the nation's schools.

The Afrocentrists maintain that African culture and history should be placed at the "center" of the curriculum in order to motivate African Americans students to learn and to help all students to understand the important role that Africa has played in the development of Western civilization (Asante, 1991a). Many mainstream multiculturalists are ambivalent about Afrocentrism, although few have publicly opposed it. This is in part because the Western traditionalists rarely distinguish the Afrocentrists from the multiculturalists and describe them as one group. Some multiculturalists may also perceive Afrocentric ideas as compatible with a broader concept of multicultural education.

The influence of the multiculturalists within schools and universities in the last 20 years has been substantial. Many school districts, state departments of education, local school districts, and private agencies have developed and implemented multicultural staff development programs, conferences, policies, and curricula (New York City Board of Education, 1990; New York State Department of Education, 1989, 1991; Sokol, 1990). Multicultural requirements, programs, and policies have also been implemented at many of the nation's leading research universities, including the University of California, Berkeley, Stanford University, The Pennsylvania State University, and the University of Wisconsin system. The success that the multiculturalists have had in implementing their ideas within schools and universities is probably a major reason that the Western traditionalists are trying to halt multicultural reforms in the nation's schools, colleges, and universities.

The debate between the Western traditionalists and the multiculturalists is consistent with the ideals of a democratic society. To date, however, it has resulted in little productive interaction between the Western traditionalists and the multiculturalists. Rather, each group has talked primarily to audiences it viewed as sympathetic to its ideologies and visions of the present and future (Franklin, 1991; Schlesinger, 1991). Because there has been little productive dialogue and exchange between the Western traditionalists and the multiculturalists, the debate has been polarized, and writers have frequently not conformed to the established rules of scholarship (D'Souza, 1991). A kind of forensic social science has developed (Rivlin, 1973), with each side stating briefs and then marshaling evidence to support its position. The debate has also taken place primarily in the popular press rather than in academic and scholarly journals.

Valuation and Knowledge Construction

I hope to make a positive contribution to the canon debate in this article by providing evidence for the claim that the positions of both the Western traditionalists and the multiculturalists reflect values, ideologies, political positions, and human interests. Each position also implies a kind of knowledge that should be taught in the school and university curriculum. I will present a typology of the kinds of knowledge that exist in society and in educational institutions. This typology is designed to help practicing educators and researchers to identify types of knowledge that reflect particular values, assumptions, perspectives, and ideological positions.

Teachers should help students to understand all types of knowledge. Students should be involved in the debates about knowledge construction and conflicting interpretations, such as the extent to which Egypt and Phoenicia influenced Greek civilization. Students should also be taught how to create their own interpretations of the past and present, as well as how to identify their own positions, interests, ideologies, and assumptions. Teachers should help students to become critical thinkers who have the knowledge, attitudes, skills, and commitments needed to participate in democratic action to help the nation close the gap between its ideals and its realities. Multicultural education is an education for functioning effectively in a pluralistic democratic society. Helping students to develop the knowledge, skills, and attitudes needed to participate in reflective civic action is one of its major goals (Banks, 1991).

I argue that students should study all five types of knowledge. However, my own work and philosophical position are within the transformative tradition in ethnic studies and multicultural education (Banks, 1988, 1991; Banks & Banks, 1989). This tradition links knowledge, social commitment, and action (Meier & Rudwick, 1986). A transformative, action-oriented curriculum, in my view, can best be implemented when students examine different types of knowledge in a democratic classroom where they can freely examine their perspectives and moral commitments.

The Nature of Knowledge

I am using knowledge in this article to mean the way a person explains or interprets reality. *The American Heritage Dictionary* (1983) defines knowledge as "familiarity, awareness, or understandings gained through experience or study. The sum or range of what has been perceived, discovered or inferred" (p. 384). My conceptualization of knowledge is broad and is used the way in which it is usually used in the sociology of knowledge literature to include ideas, values, and interpretations (Farganis, 1986). As postmodern theorists have pointed out, knowledge is socially constructed and reflects human interests, values, and action (Code, 1991; Foucault, 1972; S. Harding, 1991; Rorty, 1989). Although many complex factors influence the knowledge that is created by an individual or group, including the actuality of what occurred, the knowledge that people create is heavily influenced by their interpretations of their experiences and their positions within particular social, economic, and political systems and structures of a society.

In the Western empirical tradition, the ideal within each academic discipline is the formulation of knowledge without the influence of the researcher's personal or cultural characteristics (Greer, 1969; Kaplan, 1964). However, as critical and postmodern theorists have pointed out, personal, cultural, and social factors influence the formulation of knowledge even when objective knowledge is the ideal within a discipline (Cherryholmes, 1988; Foucault, 1972; Habermas, 1971; Rorty, 1989; Young, 1971). Often the researchers themselves are unaware of how their personal experiences and positions within society influence the knowledge they produce. Most mainstream historians were unaware of how their regional and cultural biases influenced their interpretation of the Reconstruction period until W. E. B. DuBois published a study that challenged the accepted and established interpretations of that historical period (DuBois, 1935/1962).

Positionality and Knowledge Construction

Positionality is an important concept that emerged out of feminist scholarship. Tetreault (1993) writes:

> Positionality means that important aspects of our identity, for example, our gender, our race, our class, our age ... are markers of relational positions rather than essential qualities. Their effects and implications change according to context. Recently, feminist thinkers have seen knowledge as valid when it comes from an acknowledgment of the knower's specific position in any context, one always defined by gender, race, class and other variables. (p. 139)

Positionality reveals the importance of identifying the positions and frames of reference from which scholars and writers present their data, interpretations, analyses, and instruction (Anzaldúa, 1990; Ellsworth, 1989). The need for researchers and scholars to identify their ideological positions and normative assumptions in their works—an inherent part of feminist and ethnic studies scholarship—contrasts with the empirical paradigm that has dominated science and research in the United States (Code, 1991; S. Harding, 1991).

The assumption within the Western empirical paradigm is that the knowledge produced within it is neutral and objective and that its principles are universal. The effects of values, frames of references, and the normative positions of researchers and scholars are infrequently discussed within the traditional empirical paradigm that has dominated scholarship and teaching in American colleges and universities since the turn of the century. However, scholars such as Mydral (1944) and Clark (1965), prior to the feminist and ethnic studies movements, wrote about the need for scholars to recognize and state their normative positions and valuations and to become, in the apt words of Kenneth B. Clark, "involved observers." Myrdal stated that valuations are not just attached to research but permeate it. He wrote, "*There is no device for excluding biases in social sciences than to face the valuations and to introduce them as explicitly stated, specific, and sufficiently concretized value premises*" (p. 1043).

Postmodern and critical theorists such as Habermas (1971) and Giroux (1983), and feminist postmodern theorists such as Farganis (1986), Code (1991), and S. Harding (1991), have developed important critiques of empirical knowledge. They argue that despite its claims, modern science is not value-free but contains important human interests and normative assumptions that should be identified, discussed, and examined. Code (1991), a feminist epistemologist, states that academic knowledge is both subjective and objective and that both aspects should be recognized and discussed. Code states that we need to ask these kinds of questions: ''Out of whose subjectivity has this ideal [of objectivity] grown? Whose standpoint, whose values does it represent?'' (p. 70). She writes:

> The point of the questions is to discover how subjective and objective conditions together produce knowledge, values, and epistemology. It is neither to reject objectivity nor to glorify subjectivity in its stead. Knowledge is neither value-free nor value-neutral; the processes that produce it are themselves value-laden; and these values are open to evaluation. (p. 70)

In her book, *What Can She Know? Feminist Theory and the Construction of Knowledge,* Code (1991) raises the question, ''Is the sex of the knower epistemologically significant?'' (p. 7). She answers this question in the affirmative because of the ways in which gender influences how knowledge is constructed, interpreted, and institutionalized within U.S. society. The ethnic and cultural experiences of the knower are also epistemologically significant because these factors also influence knowledge construction, use, and interpretation in U.S. society.

Empirical scholarship has been limited by the assumptions and biases that are implicit within it (Code, 1991; Gordon, 1985; S. Harding, 1991). However, these biases and assumptions have been infrequently recognized by the scholars and researchers themselves and by the consumers of their works, such as other scholars, professors, teachers, and the general reader. The lack of recognition and identification of these biases, assumptions, perspectives, and points of view have frequently victimized people of color such as African Americans and American Indians because of the stereotypes and misconceptions that have been perpetuated about them in the historical and social science literature (Ladner, 1973; Phillips, 1918).

Gordon, Miller, and Rollock (1990) call the bias that results in the negative depiction of minority groups by mainstream social scientists ''communicentric bias.'' They point out that mainstream social scientists have often viewed diversity as deviance and differences as deficits. An important outcome of the revisionist and transformative interpretations that have been produced by scholars working in feminist and ethnic studies is that many misconceptions and partial truths about women and ethnic groups have been viewed from different and more complete perspectives (Acuña, 1988; Blassingame, 1972; V. Harding, 1981; King & Mitchell, 1990; Merton, 1972).

More complete perspectives result in a closer approximation to the actuality of what occurred. In an important and influential essay, Merton (1972) notes that the perspectives of both ''insiders'' and ''outsiders'' are needed to enable social scientists to gain a complete view of social reality. Anna Julia Cooper, the African American educator, made a point similar to Merton's when she wrote about how the perspectives of women enlarged our vision (Cooper, 1892/1969, cited in Minnich, 1990, p. viii).

> The world has had to limp along with the wobbling gait and the one-sided hesitancy of a man with one eye. Suddenly the bandage is removed from the other eye and the whole body is filled with light. It sees a circle where before it saw a segment.

A Knowledge Typology

A description of the major types of knowledge can help teachers and curriculum specialists to identify perspectives and content needed to make the curriculum multicultural. Each of the types of knowledge described below reflects particular purposes, perspectives, experiences, goals, and human interests. Teaching students various types of knowledge can help them to better understand the perspectives of different racial, ethnic, and cultural groups as well as to develop their own versions and interpretations of issues and events.

I identify and describe five types of knowledge (see Table 1): (a) personal/cultural knowledge; (b) popular knowledge; (c) mainstream academic knowledge; (d) transformative academic knowledge; and (e) school knowledge. This is an ideal-type typology in the Weberian sense. The five categories approximate, but do not describe, reality in its total complexity. The categories are useful conceptual tools for thinking about knowledge and planning multicultural teaching. For example, although the categories can be conceptually distinguished, in reality they overlap and are interrelated in a dynamic way.

Since the 1960s, some of the findings and insights from transformative academic knowledge have been incorporated into mainstream academic knowledge and scholarship. Traditionally, students were taught in schools and universities that the land that became North America was a thinly populated wilderness when the Europeans arrived in the 16th century and that African Americans had made few contributions to the development of American civilization (mainstream academic knowledge). Some of the findings from transformative academic knowledge that challenged these conceptions have influenced mainstream academic scholarship and have been incorporated into mainstream college and school textbooks (Hoxie, no date; Thornton, 1987). Consequently, the relationship between the five categories of knowledge is dynamic and interactive rather than static (see Figure 1).

The Types of Knowledge

Personal and Cultural Knowledge

The concepts, explanations, and interpretations that students derive from personal experiences in their homes, families, and community cultures constitute personal and cultural

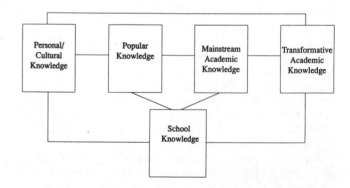

FIGURE 1. *The interrelationship of the types of knowledge. This figure illustrates that although the five types of knowledge discussed in this article are conceptually distinct, they are highly interrelated in a complex and dynamic way.*

Table 1

Types of Knowledge

Knowledge Type	Definition	Examples
Personal/cultural	The concepts, explanations, and interpretations that students derive from personal experiences in their homes, families, and community cultures.	Understandings by many African Americans and Hispanic students that highly individualistic behavior will be negatively sanctioned by many adults and peers in their cultural communities.
Popular	The facts, concepts, explanations, and interpretations that are institutionalized within the mass media and other institutions that are part of the popular culture.	Movies such as *Birth of a Nation, How the West Was Won,* and *Dances With Wolves.*
Mainstream academic	The concepts, paradigms, theories, and explanations that constitute traditional Western-centric knowledge in history and the behavioral and social sciences.	Ulrich B. Phillips, *American Negro Slavery;* Frederick Jackson Turner's frontier theory; Arthur R. Jensen's theory about Black and White intelligence.
Transformative academic	The facts, concepts, paradigms, themes, and explanations that challenge mainstream academic knowledge and expand and substantially revise established canons, paradigms, theories, explanations, and research methods. When transformative academic paradigms replace mainstream ones, a scientific revolution has occurred. What is more normal is that transformative academic paradigms coexist with established ones.	George Washington Williams, *History of the Negro Race in America;* W. E. B. DuBois, *Black Reconstruction;* Carter G. Woodson, *The Mis-education of the Negro;* Gerda Lerner, *The Majority Finds Its Past;* Rodolfo Acuña, *Occupied America: A History of Chicanos;* Herbert Gutman, *The Black Family in Slavery and Freedom 1750–1925.*
School	The facts, concepts, generalizations, and interpretations that are presented in textbooks, teacher's guides, other media forms, and lectures by teachers.	Lewis Paul Todd and Merle Curti, *Rise of the American Nation;* Richard C. Brown, Wilhelmena S. Robinson, & John Cunningham, *Let Freedom Ring: A United States History.*

knowledge. The assumptions, perspectives, and insights that students derive from their experiences in their homes and community cultures are used as screens to view and interpret the knowledge and experiences that they encounter in the school and in other institutions within the larger society.

Research and theory by Fordham and Ogbu (1986) indicate that low-income African American students often experience academic difficulties in the school because of the ways that cultural knowledge within their community conflicts with school knowledge, norms, and expectations. Fordham and Ogbu also state that the culture of many low-income African American students is oppositional to the school culture. These students believe that if they master the knowledge taught in the schools they will violate fictive kinship norms and run the risk of "acting White." Fordham (1988, 1991) has suggested that African American students who become high academic achievers resolve the conflict caused by the interaction of their personal cultural knowledge with the knowledge and norms within the schools by becoming "raceless" or by "ad hocing a culture."

Delpit (1988) has stated that African American students are often unfamiliar with school cultural knowledge regarding power relationships. They consequently experience academic and behavioral problems because of their failure to conform to established norms, rules, and expectations. She recommends that teachers help African American students learn the rules of power in the school culture by explicitly teaching them to the students. The cultural knowledge that many African American, Latino, and American Indian students bring to school conflict with school norms and values, with school knowledge, and with the ways that teachers interpret and mediate school knowledge. Student cultural knowledge and school knowledge often conflict on variables related to the ways that the individual should relate to and interact with the group (Hale-Benson, 1982; Ramírez & Castañeda, 1974; Shade, 1989), normative communication styles and interactions (Heath, 1983, Labov, 1975; Philips, 1983; Smitherman, 1977), and perspectives on the nature of U.S. history.

Personal and cultural knowledge is problematic when it conflicts with scientific ways of validating knowledge, is oppositional to the culture of the school, or challenges the main tenets and assumptions of mainstream academic knowledge. Much of the knowledge about out-groups that students learn from their home and community cultures consists of misconceptions, stereotypes, and partial truths (Milner, 1983). Most students in the United States are socialized within communities that are segregated along racial, ethnic, and social-class lines. Consequently, most American youths have few opportunities to learn firsthand about the cultures of people from different racial, ethnic, cultural, religious, and social-class groups.

The challenge that teachers face is how to make effective instructional use of the personal and cultural knowledge of students while at the same time helping them to reach beyond their own cultural boundaries. Although the school should recognize, validate, and make effective use of student personal and cultural knowledge in instruction, an important goal of education is to free students from their cultural and ethnic boundaries and enable them to cross cultural borders freely (Banks, 1988, 1991/1992).

In the past, the school has paid scant attention to the personal and cultural knowledge of students and has concentrated on teaching them school knowledge (Sleeter & Grant, 1991a). This practice has had different results for most White middle-class students, for most low-income students, and for most African American and Latino students. Because school knowledge is more consistent with the cultural experiences of most White middle-class students than for most other groups of students, these students have generally found the school a more comfortable place than have low-income students and most students of color—the majority of whom are also low income. A number of writers have described the ways in which many African American, American Indian, and Latino students find the school culture alienating and inconsistent with their cultural experiences, hopes, dreams, and struggles (Hale-Benson, 1982; Heath, 1983; Ramírez & Castañeda, 1974; Shade, 1989).

It is important for teachers to be aware of the personal and cultural knowledge of students when designing the curriculum for today's multicultural schools. Teachers can use student personal cultural knowledge as a vehicle to motivate students and as a foundation for teaching school knowledge. When teaching a unit on the Westward Movement to Lakota Sioux students, for example, the teacher can ask the students to make a list of their views about the Westward Movement, to relate family stories about the coming of the Whites to Lakota Sioux homelands, and to interview parents and grandparents about their perceptions of what happened when the Whites first occupied Indian lands. When teachers begin a unit on the Westward Movement with student personal cultural knowledge, they can increase student motivation as well as deepen their understanding of the schoolbook version (Wiggington, 1991/1992).

Popular Knowledge

Popular knowledge consists of the facts, interpretations, and beliefs that are institutionalized within television, movies, videos, records, and other forms of the mass media. Many of the tenets of popular knowledge are conveyed in subtle rather than obvious ways. Some examples of statements that constitute important themes in popular knowledge follow: (a) The United States is a powerful nation with unlimited opportunities for individuals who are willing to take advantage of them. (b) To succeed in the United States, an individual only has to work hard. You can realize your dreams in the United States if you are willing to work hard and pull yourself up by the bootstrap. (c) As a land of opportunity for all, the United States is a highly cohesive nation, whose ideals of equality and freedom are shared by all.

Most of the major tenets of American popular culture are widely shared and are deeply entrenched in U.S. society.

However, they are rarely explicitly articulated. Rather, they are presented in the media and in other sources in the forms of stories, anecdotes, news stories, and interpretations of current events (Cortés, 1991a, 1991b; Greenfield & Cortés, 1991).

Commercial entertainment films both reflect and perpetuate popular knowledge (Bogle, 1989; Cortés, 1991a, 1991b; Greenfield & Cortés, 1991). While preparing to write this article, I viewed an important and influential film that was directed by John Ford and released by MGM in 1962, *How the West Was Won*. I selected this film for review because the settlement of the West is a major theme in American culture and society about which there are many popular images, beliefs, myths, and misconceptions. In viewing the film, I was particularly interested in the images it depicted about the settlement of the West, about the people who were already in the West, and about those who went West looking for new opportunities.

Ford uses the Prescotts, a White family from Missouri bound for California, to tell his story. The film tells the story of three generations of this family. It focuses on the family's struggle to settle in the West. Indians, African Americans, and Mexicans are largely invisible in the film. Indians appear in the story when they attack the Prescott family during their long and perilous journey. The Mexicans appearing in the film are bandits who rob a train and are killed. The several African Americans in the film are in the background silently rowing a boat. At various points in the film, Indians are referred to as *hostile Indians* and as *squaws*.

How the West Was Won is a masterpiece in American popular culture. It not only depicts some of the major themes in American culture about the winning of the West; it reinforces and perpetuates dominant societal attitudes about ethnic groups and gives credence to the notion that the West was won by liberty-loving, hard-working people who pursued freedom for all. The film narrator states near its end, "[The movement West] produced a people free to dream, free to act, and free to mold their own destiny."

Mainstream Academic Knowledge

Mainstream academic knowledge consists of the concepts, paradigms, theories, and explanations that constitute traditional and established knowledge in the behavioral and social sciences. An important tenet within the mainstream academic paradigm is that there is a set of objective truths that can be verified through rigorous and objective research procedures that are uninfluenced by human interests, values, and perspectives (Greer, 1969; Kaplan, 1964; Sleeter, 1991). This empirical knowledge, uninfluenced by human values and interests, constitute a body of objective truths that should constitute the core of the school and university curriculum. Much of this objective knowledge originated in the West but is considered universal in nature and application.

Mainstream academic knowledge is the knowledge that multicultural critics such as Ravitch and Finn (1987), Hirsch (1987), and Bloom (1987) claim is threatened by the addition of content about women and ethnic minorities to the school and university curriculum. This knowledge reflects the established, Western-oriented canon that has historically dominated university research and teaching in the United States. Mainstream academic knowledge consists of the theories and interpretations that are internalized and accepted by most university researchers, academic societies, and organizations such as the American Historical Association, the American Sociological Association, the American Psychological Association, and the National Academy of Sciences.

It is important to point out, however, that an increasing number of university scholars are critical theorists and postmodernists who question the empirical paradigm that dominates Western science (Cherryholmes, 1988; Giroux, 1983; Rosenau, 1992). Many of these individuals are members of national academic organizations, such as the American Historical Association and the American Sociological Association. In most of these professional organizations, the postmodern scholars—made up of significant numbers of scholars of color and feminists—have formed caucuses and interest groups within the mainstream professional organizations.

No claim is made here that there is a uniformity of beliefs among mainstream academic scholars, but rather that there are dominant canons, paradigms, and theories that are accepted by the community of mainstream academic scholars and researchers. These established canons and paradigms are occasionally challenged within the mainstream academic community itself. However, they receive their most serious challenges from academics outside the mainstream, such as scholars within the transformative academic community whom I will describe later.

Mainstream academic knowledge, like the other forms of knowledge discussed in this article, is not static, but is dynamic, complex, and changing. Challenges to the dominant canons and paradigms within mainstream academic knowledge come from both within and without. These challenges lead to changes, reinterpretations, debates, disagreements and ultimately to paradigm shifts, new theories, and interpretations. Kuhn (1970) states that a scientific revolution takes place when a new paradigm emerges and replaces an existing one. What is more typical in education and the social sciences is that competing paradigms coexist, although particular ones might be more influential during certain times or periods.

We can examine the treatment of slavery within the mainstream academic community over time, or the treatment of the American Indian, to identify ways that mainstream academic knowledge has changed in important ways since the late 19th and early 20th centuries. Ulrich B. Phillips's highly influential book, *American Negro Slavery*, published in 1918, dominated the way Black slavery was interpreted until his views were challenged by researchers in the 1950s (Stampp, 1956). Phillips was a respected authority on the antebellum South and on slavery. His book, which became a historical classic, is essentially an apology for Southern slaveholders. A new paradigm about slavery was developed in the 1970s that drew heavily upon the slaves' view of their own experiences (Blassingame, 1972; Genovese, 1972; Gutman, 1976).

During the late 19th and early 20th centuries, the American Indian was portrayed in mainstream academic knowledge as either a noble or a hostile savage (Hoxie, 1988). Other notions that became institutionalized within mainstream academic knowledge include the idea that Columbus discovered America and that America was a thinly populated frontier when the Europeans arrived in the late 15th century. Frederick Jackson Turner (Turner, 1894/1989) argued that the frontier, which he regarded as a wilderness, was the main source of American democracy. Although Turner's thesis is now being highly criticized by revisionist historians, his essay established a conception of the West that has been highly influential in American mainstream scholarship, in the popular culture, and in schoolbooks. The conception of the West he depicted is still influential today in the school curriculum and in textbooks (Sleeter & Grant, 1991b).

These ideas also became institutionalized within mainstream academic knowledge: The slaves were happy and contented; most of the important ideas that became a part of American civilization came from Western Europe; and the history of the United States has been one of constantly expanding progress and increasing democracy. African slaves were needed to transform the United States from an empty wilderness into an industrial democratic civilization. The American Indians had to be Christianized and removed to reservations in order for this to occur.

Transformative Academic Knowledge

Transformative academic knowledge consists of concepts, paradigms, themes, and explanations that challenge mainstream academic knowledge and that expand the historical and literary canon. Transformative academic knowledge challenges some of the key assumptions that mainstream scholars make about the nature of knowledge. Transformative and mainstream academic knowledge is based on different epistemological assumptions about the nature of knowledge, about the influence of human interests and values on knowledge construction, and about the purpose of knowledge.

An important tenet of mainstream academic knowledge is that it is neutral, objective, and was uninfluenced by human interests and values. Transformative academic knowledge reflects postmodern assumptions and goals about the nature and goals of knowledge (Foucault, 1972; Rorty, 1989; Rosenau, 1992). Transformative academic scholars assume that knowledge is not neutral but is influenced by human interests, that all knowledge reflects the power and social relationships within society, and that an important purpose of knowledge construction is to help people improve society (Code, 1991, S. Harding, 1991; hooks & West, 1991; King & Mitchell, 1990; Minnich, 1990). Write King and Mitchell: "Like other praxis-oriented Critical approaches, the Afrocentric method seeks to enable people to understand social reality in order to change it. But its additional imperative is to transform the society's basic ethos" (p. 95).

These statements reflect some of the main ideas and concepts in transformative academic knowledge: Columbus did not discover America. The Indians had been living in this land for about 40,000 years when the Europeans arrived. Concepts such as "The European Discovery of America" and "The Westward Movement" need to be reconceptualized and viewed from the perspectives of different cultural and ethnic groups. The Lakota Sioux's homeland was not the West to them; it was the center of the universe. It was not the West for the Alaskans; it was South. It was East for the Japanese and North for the people who lived in Mexico. The history of the United States has not been one of continuous progress toward democratic ideals. Rather, the nation's history has been characterized by a cyclic quest for democracy and by conflict, struggle, violence, and exclusion (Acuña, 1988; Zinn, 1980). A major challenge that faces the nation is how to make its democratic ideals a reality for all.

Transformative academic knowledge has a long history in the United States. In 1882 and 1883, George Washington Williams (1849–1891) published, in two volumes, the first comprehensive history of African Americans in the United States, *A History of the Negro Race in America From 1619 to 1880* (Williams, 1982–1983/1968). Williams, like other African American scholars after him, decided to research and write about the Black experience because of the neglect of African Americans by mainstream historians and social scientists and because of the stereotypes and misconceptions about African Americans that appeared in mainstream scholarship.

W. E. B. DuBois (1868–1963) is probably the most prolific African American scholar in U.S. history. His published writings constitute 38 volumes (Aptheker, 1973). DuBois devoted his long and prolific career to the formulation of new data, concepts, and paradigms that could be used to reinterpret the Black experience and reveal the role that African Americans had played in the development of American society. His seminal works include *The Suppression of the African Slave Trade to the United States of America, 1638–1870*, the first volume of the Harvard Historical Studies (DuBois, 1896/1969). Perhaps his most discussed book is *Black Reconstruction in America: An Essay Toward a History of the Part Which Black Folk Played in the Attempt to Reconstruct Democracy in America, 1860–1880*, published in 1935 (1935/1962). In this book, DuBois challenged the accepted, institutionalized interpretations of Reconstruction and emphasized the accomplishments of the Reconstruction governments and legislatures, especially the establishment of free public schools.

Carter G. Woodson (1875–1950), the historian and educator who founded the Association for the Study of Negro Life and History and the *Journal of Negro History*, also challenged established paradigms about the treatment of African Americans in a series of important publications, including *The Mis-education of the Negro*, published in 1933. Woodson and Wesley (1922) published a highly successful college textbook that described the contributions that African Americans have made to American life, *The Negro in Our History*. This book was issued in 10 editions.

Transformative Scholarship Since the 1970s

Many scholars have produced significant research and theories since the early 1970s that have challenged and modified institutionalized stereotypes and misconceptions about ethnic minorities, formulated new concepts and paradigms, and forced mainstream scholars to rethink established interpretations. Much of the transformative academic knowledge that has been produced since the 1970s is becoming institutionalized within mainstream scholarship and within the school, college, and university curricula. In time, much of this scholarship will become mainstream, thus reflecting the highly interrelated nature of the types of knowledge conceptualized and described in this article.

Only a few examples of this new, transformative scholarship will be mentioned here because of the limited scope of this article. Howard Zinn's *A People's History of the United States* (1980): *Red, White and Black: The Peoples of Early America* by Gary B. Nash (1982): *The Signifying Monkey: A Theory of African-American Literacy Criticism* by Henry Louis Gates, Jr.

(1988); *Occupied America: A History of Chicanos* by Rodolfo Acuña (1988); *Iron Cages: Race and Culture in 19th-Century America* by Ronald T. Takaki (1979); and *The Sacred Hoop: Recovering the Feminine in American Indian Traditions* by Paul Gunn Allen (1986) are examples of important scholarship that has provided significant new perspectives on the experiences of ethnic groups in the United States and has helped us to transform our conceptions about the experiences of American ethnic groups. Readers acquainted with this scholarship will note that transformative scholarship has been produced by both European-American and ethnic minority scholars.

I will discuss two examples of how the new scholarship in ethnic studies has questioned traditional interpretations

---

Students should be given opportunities to investigate and determine how cultural assumptions, frames of references, perspectives, and the biases within a discipline influence the ways knowledge is constructed.

---

and stimulated a search for new explanations and paradigms since the 1950s. Since the pioneering work of E. Franklin Frazier (1939), social scientists had accepted the notion that the slave experience had destroyed the Black family and that the destruction of the African American family continued in the post–World War II period during Black migration to and settlement in northern cities. Moynihan (1965), in his controversial book, *The Negro Family in America: The Case for National Action*, used the broken Black family explanation in his analysis. Gutman (1976), in an important historical study of the African American family from 1750 to 1925, concluded that "despite a high rate of earlier involuntary marital breakup, large numbers of slave couples lived in long marriages, and most slaves lived in double-headed households" (p. xxii).

An important group of African and African American scholars have challenged established interpretations about the origin of Greek civilization and the extent to which Greek civilization was influenced by African cultures. These scholars include Diop (1974), Williams (1987), and Van Sertima (1988, 1989). Cheikh Anta Diop is one of the most influential African scholars who has challenged established interpretations about the origin of Greek civilization. In *Black Nations and Culture*, published in 1955 (summarized by Van Sertima, 1989), he sets forth an important thesis that states that Africa is an important root of Western civilization. Diop argues that Egypt "was the node and center of a vast web linking the strands of cultures and languages; that the light that crystallized at the center of this early world had been energized by the cultural electricity streaming from the heartland of Africa" (p. 8).

Since the work by Diop, Williams, and Van Sertima, traditional interpretations about the formation of Greek civilization has been challenged by Bernal (1987–1991), a professor of government at Cornell University. The earlier challenges to established interpretations by African and African Americans received little attention, except within the African American community. However, Bernal's work has received wide attention in the popular press and among classicists.

Bernal (1987–1991) argues that important aspects of Greek civilization originated in ancient Egypt and Phoenicia and that the ancient civilization of Egypt was essentially African. Bernal believes that the contributions of Egypt and Phoenicia to Greek civilization have been deliberately ignored by classical scholars because of their biased attitudes toward non-White peoples and Semites. Bernal has published two of four planned volumes of his study *Black Athena*. In Volume 2 he uses evidence from linguistics, archeology and ancient documents to substantiate his claim that "between 2100 and 1100 B.C., when Greek culture was born, the people of the Aegean borrowed, adapted or had thrust upon them deities and language, technologies and architectures, notions of justice and polis" from Egypt and Phoenicia (Begley, Chideya, & Wilson, 1991, p. 50). Because transformative academic knowledge, such as that constructed by Diop, Williams, Van Sertima, and Bernal, challenges the established paradigms as well as because of the tremendous gap between academic knowledge and school knowledge, it often has little influence on school knowledge.

School Knowledge
School knowledge consists of the facts, concepts, and generalizations presented in textbooks, teachers' guides, and the other forms of media designed for school use. School knowledge also consists of the teacher's mediation and interpretation of that knowledge. The textbook is the main source of school knowledge in the United States (Apple & Christian-Smith, 1991; Goodlad, 1984; Shaver, Davis, & Helburn, 1979). Studies of textbooks indicate that these are some of the major themes in school knowledge (Anyon, 1979, 1981; Sleeter & Grant, 1991b): (a) America's founding fathers, such as Washington and Jefferson, were highly moral, liberty-loving men who championed equality and justice for all Americans; (b) the United States is a nation with justice, liberty, and freedom for all; (c) social class divisions are not significant issues in the United States; (d) there are no significant gender, class, or racial divisions within U.S. society; and (e) ethnic groups of color and Whites interact largely in harmony in the United States.

Studies of textbooks that have been conducted by researchers such as Anyon (1979, 1981) and Sleeter and Grant (1991b) indicate that textbooks present a highly selective view of social reality, give students the idea that knowledge is static rather than dynamic, and encourage students to master isolated facts rather than to develop complex understandings of social reality. These studies also indicate that textbooks reinforce the dominant social, economic, and power arrangements within society. Students are encouraged to accept rather than to question these arrangements.

In their examination of the treatment of race, class, gender, and disability in textbooks, Sleeter and Grant (1991b) concluded that although textbooks had largely eliminated sexist language and had incorporated images of ethnic minorities into them, they failed to help students to develop an understanding of the complex cultures of ethnic groups, an understanding of racism, sexism and classism in American society, and described the United States as a nation that had largely overcome its problems. Sleeter & Grant write:

The vision of social relations that the textbooks we analyzed for the most part project is one of harmony and equal opportunity—anyone can do or become whatever he or she wants; problems among people are mainly individual in nature and in the end are resolved. (p. 99)

A number of powerful factors influence the development and production of school textbooks (Altbach, Kelly, Petrie, & Weis, 1991; FitzGerald, 1979). One of the most important is the publisher's perception of statements and images that might be controversial. When textbooks become controversial, school districts often refuse to adopt and to purchase them. When developing a textbook, the publisher and the authors must also consider the developmental and reading levels of the students, state and district guidelines about what subject matter textbooks should include, and recent trends and developments in a content field that teachers and administrators will expect the textbook to reflect and incorporate. Because of the number of constraints and influences on the development of textbooks, school knowledge often does not include in-depth discussions and analyses of some of the major problems in American society, such as racism, sexism, social-class stratification, and poverty (Anyon, 1979, 1981; Sleeter & Grant, 1991b). Consequently, school knowledge is influenced most heavily by mainstream academic knowledge and popular knowledge. Transformative academic knowledge usually has little direct influence on school knowledge. It usually affects school knowledge in a significant way only after it has become a part of mainstream and popular knowledge. Teachers must make special efforts to introduce transformative knowledge and perspectives to elementary and secondary school students.

Teaching Implications
Multicultural education involves changes in the total school environment in order to create equal educational opportunities for all students (Banks, 1991; Banks & Banks, 1989; Sleeter & Grant, 1987). However, in this article I have focused on only one of the important dimensions of multicultural education—the kinds of *knowledge* that should be taught in the multicultural curriculum. The five types of knowledge described above have important implications for planning and teaching a multicultural curriculum.

An important goal of multicultural teaching is to help students to understand how knowledge is constructed. Students should be given opportunities to investigate and determine how cultural assumptions, frames of references, perspectives, and the biases within a discipline influence the ways the knowledge is constructed. Students should also be given opportunities to create knowledge themselves and identify ways in which the knowledge they construct is influenced and limited by their personal assumptions, positions, and experiences.

I will use a unit on the Westward Movement to illustrate how teachers can use the knowledge categories described above to teach from a multicultural perspective. When beginning the unit, teachers can draw upon the students' personal and cultural knowledge about the Westward Movement. They can ask the students to make a list of ideas that come to mind when they think of "The West." To enable the students to determine how the popular culture depicts the West, teachers can ask the students to view and analyze the film discussed above, *How the West Was Won*. They can also ask them to view videos of more recently made films about the West and to make a list of its major themes and images. Teachers can summarize Turner's frontier theory to give students an idea of how an influential mainstream historian described and interpreted the West in the late 19th century and how this theory influenced generations of historians.

Teachers can present a transformative perspective on the West by showing the students the film *How the West Was Won and Honor Lost*, narrated by Marlon Brando. This film describes how the European Americans who went West, with the use of broken treaties and deceptions, invaded the land of the Indians and displaced them. Teachers may also ask the students to view segments of the popular film *Dances With Wolves* and to discuss how the depiction of Indians in this film reflects both mainstream and transformative perspectives on Indians in U.S. history and culture. Teachers can present the textbook account of the Westward Movement in the final part of the unit.

The main goals of presenting different kinds of knowledge are to help students understand how knowledge is constructed and how it reflects the social context in which it is created and to enable them to develop the understandings and skills needed to become knowledge builders themselves. An important goal of multicultural education is to transform the school curriculum so that students not only learn the knowledge that has been constructed by others, but learn how to critically analyze the knowledge they master and how to construct their own interpretations of the past, present, and future.

Several important factors related to teaching the types of knowledge have not been discussed in this article but need to be examined. One is the personal/cultural knowledge of the classroom teacher. The teachers, like the students, bring understandings, concepts, explanations, and interpretations to the classroom that result from their experiences in their homes, families, and community cultures. Most teachers in the United States are European American (87%) and female (72%) (Ordovensky, 1992). However, there is enormous diversity among European Americans that is mirrored in the backgrounds of the teacher population, including diversity related to religion, social class, region, and ethnic origin. The diversity within European Americans is rarely discussed in the social science literature (Alba, 1990) or within classrooms. However, the rich diversity among the cultures of teachers is an important factor that needs to be examined and discussed in the classroom. The 13% of U.S. teachers who are ethnic minorities can also enrich their classrooms by sharing their personal and cultural knowledge with their students and by helping them to understand how it mediates textbook knowledge. The multicultural classroom is a forum of multiple voices and perspectives. The voices of the teacher, of the textbook, of mainstream and transformative authors—and of the students—are important components of classroom discourse.

Teachers can share their cultural experiences and interpretations of events as a way to motivate students to share theirs. However, they should examine their racial and ethnic attitudes toward diverse groups before engaging in cultural sharing. A democratic classroom atmosphere must also be created. The students must view the classroom as a forum where multiple perspectives are valued. An open and democratic classroom will enable students to acquire the skills and abilities they need to examine conflicting knowledge claims and perspectives. Students must become critical consumers of knowledge as well as knowledge producers if they are to acquire the understandings and skills needed to function in the complex and diverse world of tomorrow. Only a broad and liberal multicultural education can prepare them for that world.

Notes

This article is adapted from a paper presented at the conference "Democracy and Education," sponsored by the Benton Center for Curriculum and Instruction, Department of Education, The University of Chicago, November 15–16, 1991, Chicago, Illinois. I am grateful to the following colleagues for helpful comments on an earlier draft of this article: Cherry A. McGee Banks, Carlos E. Cortés, Geneva Gay, Donna H. Kerr, Joyce E. King, Walter C. Parker, Pamela L. Grossman, and Christine E. Sleeter.

References

Acuña, R. (1988). *Occupied America: A history of Chicanos* (3rd ed.). New York: Harper & Row.

Alba, R. D. (1990). *Ethnic identity: The transformation of White America*. New Haven, CT: Yale University Press.

Allen, P. G. (1986). *The sacred hoop: Recovering the feminine in American Indian traditions*. Boston: Beacon Press.

Altbach, P. G., Kelly, G. P., Petrie, H. G., & Weis, L. (Eds.). (1991). *Textbooks in American Society*. Albany, NY: State University of New York Press.

The American heritage dictionary. (1983). New York: Dell.

Anyon, J. (1979). Ideology and United States history textbooks. *Harvard Educational Review, 49*, 361–386.

Anyon, J. (1981). Social class and school knowledge. *Curriculum Inquiry, 11*, 3–42.

Anzaldúa, G. (1990). Haciendo caras, una entrada: An introduction. in G. Anzaldúa (Ed.), *Making face, making soul: Haciendo caras* (pp. xv-xvii). San Francisco: Aunt Lute Foundation Books.

Apple, M. W., & Christian-Smith, L. K. (Eds.). (1991). *The politics of the textbook*. New York: Routledge.

Aptheker, H. (Ed.). (1973). *The collected published works of W. E. B. Dubois* (38 Vols.). Millwood, NY: Kraus.

Asante, M. K. (1991a). The Afrocentric idea in education. *The Journal of Negro Education, 60*, 170–180.

Asante, M. K. (1991b, September 23). Putting Africa at the center. *Newsweek, 118*, 46.

Asante, M. K., & Ravitch, D. (1991). Multiculturalism: An exchange. *The American Scholar, 60*, 267–275.

Banks, J. A. (1988). *Multiethnic education: Theory and practice* (2nd ed.). Boston: Allyn & Bacon.

Banks, J. A. (1991). *Teaching strategies for ethnic studies* (5th ed.). Boston: Allyn & Bacon.

Banks, J. A. (1991/1992). Multicultural education: For freedom's sake. *Educational Leadership, 49*, 32–36.

Banks, J. A., & Banks, C. A. M. (Eds.). (1989). *Multicultural education: Issues and perspectives*. Boston: Allyn & Bacon.

Begley, S., Chideya, F., & Wilson, L. (1991, September 23). Out of Egypt, Greece: Seeking the roots of Western civilization on the banks of the Nile. *Newsweek, 118*, 48–49.

Bernal, M. (1987–1991). *Black Athena: The Afroasiatic roots of classical civilization* (Vols. 1–2). London: Free Association Books.

Blassingame, J. W. (1972). *The slave community: Plantation life in the Antebellum South*. New York: Oxford University Press.

Bloom, A. (1987). *The closing of the American mind*. New York: Simon & Schuster.

Bogle, D. (1989). *Toms, coons, mulattoes, mammies & bucks: An interpretative history of Blacks in American films* (new expanded ed.). New York: Continuum.

Butler, J. E., & Walter, J. C. (1991). (Eds.). *Transforming the curriculum: Ethnic studies and women studies*. Albany, NY: State University of New York Press.

Cherryholmes, C. H. (1988). *Power and criticism: Poststructural investigations in education*. New York: Teachers College Press.

Clark, K. B. (1965). *Dark ghetto: Dilemmas of social power.* New York: Harper & Row.

Code, L. (1991). *What can she know? Feminist theory and the construction of knowledge.* Ithaca, NY: Cornell University Press.

Cooper, A. J. (1969). *A voice from the South.* New York: Negro Universities Press. (Original work published 1982)

Cortés, C. E. (1991a). Empowerment through media literacy. In C. E. Sleeter (Ed.), *Empowerment through multicultural education.* Albany: State University of New York Press.

Cortés, C. E. (1991b). Hollywood interracial love: Social taboo as screen titillation. In P. Loukides & L. K. Fuller (Eds.), *Beyond the stars II: Plot conventions in American popular film* (pp. 21–35). Bowling Green, OH: Bowling Green State University Press.

Delpit, L. D. (1988). The silenced dialogue: Power and pedagogy in educating other people's children. *Harvard Educational Review, 58,* 280–298.

Diop, C. A. (1974). *The African origin of civilization: Myth or reality?* New York: Lawrence Hill.

D'Souza, D. (1991). *Illiberal education: The politics of race and sex on campus.* New York: Free Press.

DuBois, W. E. B. (1962). *Black reconstruction in America 1860–1880: An essay toward a History of the part which Black folk played in the attempt to reconstruct democracy in America, 1860–1880.* New York: Atheneum. (Original work published 1935)

DuBois, W. E. B. (1969). *The suppression of the African slave trade to the United States of America, 1638–1870,* Baton Rouge, LA: Louisiana State University Press. (Original work published 1896)

Ellsworth, E. (1989). Why doesn't this feel empowering? Working through the repressive myths of critical pedagogy. *Harvard Educational Review, 59,* 297–324.

Farganis, S. (1986). *The social construction of the feminine character.* Totowa, NJ: Russell & Russell.

FitzGerald, F. (1979). *America revised: History schoolbooks in the twentieth century.* New York: Vintage.

Foucault, M. (1972). *The archaeology of knowledge and the discourse on language.* New York: Pantheon.

Fordham, S. (1988). Racelessness as a factor in Black students' school success: Pragmatic strategy or Pyrrhic victory? *Harvard Educational Review, 58,* 54–84.

Fordham, S. (1991). Racelessness in private schools: Should we deconstruct the racial and cultural identity of African-American adolescents? *Teachers College Record, 92,* 470–484.

Fordham, S., & Ogbu, J. (1986). Black students' school success: Coping with the burden of 'acting White.' *The Urban Review, 18,* 176–206.

Franklin, J. H. (1991, September 26). Illiberal education: An exchange. *New York Review of Books, 38,* 74–76.

Frazier, E. F. (1939). *The Negro family in the United States.* Chicago: University of Chicago Press.

Gates, H. L., Jr. (1988). *The signifying monkey: A theory of African-American literary criticism.* New York: Oxford University Press.

Gates, H. L., Jr. (1992). *Loose canons: Notes on the culture wars.* New York: Oxford University Press.

Genovese, E. D. (1972). *Roll Jordan roll: The world the slaves made.* New York: Pantheon.

Giroux, H. A. (1983). *Theory and resistance in education.* Boston: Bergin & Garvey.

Glazer, N. (1991, September 2). In defense of multiculturalism. *The New Republic,* 18–21.

Goodlad, J. I. (1984). *A place called school: Prospects for the future.* New York: McGraw-Hill.

Gordon, E. W. (1985). Social science knowledge production and minority experiences. *Journal of Negro Education, 54,* 117–132.

Gordon, E. W., Miller, F., & Rollock, D. (1990). Coping with communicentric bias in knowledge production in the social sciences. *Educational Researcher, 14*(3), 14–19.

Grant, C. A. (Ed.). (1992). *Research and multicultural education: From the margins to the mainstream.* Washington, DC: Falmer.

Gray, P. (1991, July 8). Whose America? *Time, 138,* 12–17.

Greenfield, G. M., & Cortés, C. E. (1991). Harmony and conflict of intercultural images: The treatment of Mexico in U.S. feature films and K–12 textbooks. *Mexican Studies/Estudios Mexicanos, 7,* 283–301.

Greer, S. (1969). *The logic of social inquiry.* Chicago: Aldine.

Gutman, H. G. (1976). *The Black family in slavery and freedom 1750–1925.* New York: Vintage.

Habermas, J. (1971). *Knowledge and human interests.* Boston: Beacon.

Hale-Benson, J. E. (1982). *Black children: Their roots, culture, and learning styles* (rev. ed.). Baltimore: John Hopkins University Press.

Harding, S. (1991). *Whose science? Whose knowledge? Thinking from women's lives.* Ithaca, NY: Cornell University Press.

Harding, V. (1981). *There is a river: The Black struggle for freedom in America.* New York: Vintage.

Heath, S. B. (1983). *Ways with words: Language, life and work in communities and classrooms.* New York: Cambridge University Press.

Hirsch, E. D., Jr. (1987). *Cultural literacy: What every American needs to know.* Boston: Houghton Mifflin.

hooks, b., & West, C. (1991). *Breaking bread: Insurgent Black intellectual life.* Boston: South End Press.

Howe, I. (1991, February 18). The value of the canon. *The New Republic,* 40–47.

Hoxie, F. E. (Ed.). (1988). *Indians in American history.* Arlington Heights, IL: Harlan Davidson.

Hoxie, F. E. (no date). *The Indians versus the textbooks: Is there any way out?* Chicago: The Newberry Library, Center for the History of the American Indian.

Kaplan, A. (1964). *The conduct of inquiry: Methodology for behavioral science.* San Francisco: Chandler.

King, J. E., & Mitchell, C. A. (1990). *Black mothers to sons: Juxtaposing African American literature with social practice.* New York: Lang.

Kuhn, T. S. (1970). *The structure of scientific revolutions* (2nd ed.). Chicago: University of Chicago Press.

Labov, W. (1975). *The study of nonstandard English.* Washington, DC: Center for Applied Linguistics.

Ladner, J. A. (Ed.). (1973). *The death of White sociology.* New York: Vintage.

Meier, A., & Rudwick, E. (1986). *Black history and the historical profession 1915–1980.* Urbana, IL: University of Illinois Press.

Merton, R. K. (1972). Insiders and outsiders: A chapter in the sociology of knowledge. *The American Journal of Sociology, 78,* 9–47.

Milner, D. (1983). *Children and race.* Beverly Hills, CA: Sage.

Minnich, E. K. (1990). *Transforming knowledge.* Philadelphia: Temple University Press.

Moynihan, D. P. (1965). *The Negro family in America: A case for national action.* Washington, DC: U.S. Department of Labor.

Myrdal, G. (with the assistance of R. Sterner & A. Rose). (1944). *An American dilemma: The Negro problem in modern democracy.* New York: Harper.

Nash, G. B. (1982). *Red, White and Black: The peoples of early America.* Englewood Cliffs, NJ: Prentice-Hall.

New York City Board of Education. (1990). *Grade 7, United States and New York state history: A multicultural perspective.* New York: Author.

New York State Department of Education. (1989, July). *A curriculum of inclusion* (Report of the Commissioner's Task Force on Minorities: Equity and excellence). Albany, NY: The State Education Department.

New York State Department of Education. (1991, June). *One nation, many peoples: A declaration of cultural interdependence.* Albany, NY: The State Education Department.

Ordovensky, P. (1992, July 7). Teachers: 87% White, 72% women. *USA Today,* p. 1A.

Philips, S. U. (1983). *The invisible culture: Communication in classroom and community on the Warm Springs Indian Reservation.* New York: Longman.

Phillips, U. B. (1918). *American Negro slavery.* New York: Appleton.

Ramírez, M., III, & Castañeda, A. (1974). *Cultural democracy, bicognitive development and education.* New York: Academic Press.

Ravitch, D., & Finn, C. E., Jr. (1987). *What do our 17-year-olds know? A report on the first national assessment of history and literature.* New York: Harper & Row.

Rivlin, A. M. (1973). Forensic social science. *Harvard Educational Review, 43,* 61–75.

Rorty, R. (1989). *Contingency, irony, and solidarity.* New York: Cambridge University Press.

Rosenau, P. M. (1992). *Post-modernism and the social sciences: Insights, inroads, and intrusions.* Princeton, NJ: Princeton University Press.

Schlesinger, A., Jr. (1991). *The disuniting of America: Reflections on a multicultural society.* Knoxville, TN: Whittle Direct Books.

Shade, B. J. R. (Ed.). (1989). *Culture, style and the educative process.* Springfield, IL: Thompson.

Shaver, J. P., Davis, O. L., Jr., & Helburn, S. W. (1979). The status of social studies education: Impressions from three NSF studies. *Social Education, 43,* 150–153.

6. EQUALITY OF EDUCATIONAL OPPORTUNITY

Sleeter, C. E. (1991). (Ed.). *Empowerment through multicultural education.* Albany: State University of New York Press.

Sleeter, C. E., & Grant, C. A. (1987). An analysis of multicultural education in the United States. *Harvard Educational Review, 57,* 421–444.

Sleeter, C. E., & Grant, C. A. (1991a). Mapping terrains of power: Student cultural knowledge versus classroom knowledge. In C. E. Sleeter (Ed.), *Empowerment through multicultural education* (pp. 49–67). Albany: State University of New York Press.

Sleeter, C. E., & Grant, C. A. (1991b). Race, class, gender and disability in current textbooks. In M. W. Apple & L. K. Christian-Smith (Eds.), *The politics of textbooks* (pp. 78–110). New York: Routledge.

Smitherman, G. (1977). *Talkin and testifyin: The language of Black America.* Boston: Houghton Mifflin.

Sokol, E. (Ed.). (1990). *A world of difference: St. Louis metropolitan region, preschool through grade 6, teacher/student resource guide.* St. Louis: Anti-Defamation League of B'nai B'rith.

Stampp, K. M. (1956). *The peculiar institution: Slavery in the ante-bellum South.* New York: Vintage.

Takaki, R. T. (1979). *Iron cages: Race and culture in 19th-century America.* Seattle, WA: University of Washington Press.

Tetreault, M. K. T. (1993). Classrooms for diversity: Rethinking curriculum and pedagogy. In J. A. Banks & C. A. M. Banks (Eds.), *Multicultural education: Issues and perspectives* (2nd ed.) (pp. 129–148). Boston: Allyn & Bacon.

Thornton, R. (1987). *American Indian holocaust and survival: A population history since 1492.* Norman: University of Oklahoma Press.

Turner, F. J. (1989). The significance of the frontier in American history. In C. A. Milner II (Ed.), *Major problems in the history of the American West* (pp. 2–21). Lexington, MA: Heath. (Original work published 1894)

Van Sertima, I. V. (Ed.). (1988). *Great Black leaders: Ancient and modern.* New Brunswick, NJ: Rutgers University, Africana Studies Department.

Van Sertima, I. V. (Ed.). (1989). *Great African thinkers: Vol. 1. Cheikh Anta Diop.* New Brunswick, NJ: Transaction Books.

Wiggington, E. (1991/1992). Culture begins at home. *Educational Leadership, 49,* 60–64.

Williams, G. W. (1968). *History of the Negro Race in America from 1619 to 1880: Negroes as slaves, as soldiers, and as citizens* (2 vols.). New York: Arno Press. (Original work published 1892 & 1893)

Williams, C. (1987). *The destruction of Black civilization: Great issues of a race from 4500 B.C. to 2000 A.D.* Chicago: Third World Press.

Woodson, C. G. (1933). *The Mis-education of the Negro.* Washington, DC: Associated Publishers.

Woodson, C. G., & Wesley, C. H. (1922). *The Negro in our history.* Washington, DC: Associated Publishers.

Woodward, C. V. (1991, July 18). Freedom and the universities. *The New York Review of Books, 38,* 32–37.

Young, M. F. D. (1971). An approach to curricula as socially organized knowledge. In M. F. D. Young (Ed.), *Knowledge and control* (pp. 19–46). London: Collier-Macmillan.

Zinn, H. (1980). *A people's history of the United States.* New York: Harper & Row.

Teachers and Cultural Styles in a Pluralist Society

Asa G. Hilliard III

Asa G. Hilliard, III, is Professor of Urban Education at Georgia State University. He recently co-authored Saving the African American Child.

I have been an educator for more than 30 years. During most of that time I have been a teacher educator. I have had the opportunity to observe thousands of teachers. I have had the opportunity to read extensively in the area of teaching strategies. I have been interested in locating teachers and schools where students who normally are expected to have low achievement are actually helped to have superior achievement. Many of the students who have been helped are the same students who, some argue, require a unique pedagogical style to match their cognitive or learning styles.

Since I have been interested in behavioral style and have conducted research on the topic, I have taken every opportunity to focus my observations and to query teachers—both successful and unsuccessful ones—in order to determine, if possible, the role that style considerations play in the work of teachers.

What I have learned is that the behavioral style is important and useful in some limited circumstances—I will address them later—but that it is very premature to draw conclusions for classroom strategy based on style; or to prescribe pedagogical practice in a general way.

I do believe that greater sensitivity to style issues will make meaningful contributions to pedagogy in the future. Yet I remain unconvinced that the explanation for the low performance of culturally different "minority" group students will be found by pursuing questions of behavioral style. Since students are adaptable, the stylistic difference explanation does not answer the question of why "minority groups" perform at a low level.

The most accurate description we can give of present circumstances is that teachers generally have the freedom to create their own unique, ad hoc approach to the design of instructional strategy.

In short, I believe that the children, no matter what their style, are failing primarily because of systematic inequities in the delivery of whatever pedagogical approach the teachers claim to master—not because students cannot learn from teachers whose styles do not match their own.

Low Expectations

In fact, there is a protocol of interactive behaviors of teachers who, for whatever reasons, have low expectations for students. Excellent evidence of this conclusion can be found in the research summarized by Jere Brophy and cited by Eva Chun in 1988. The research shows that teachers tend to:

• demand less from low-expectation students ("lows") than from high-expectation students ("highs").

• wait less time for lows to answer questions.

• give lows the answer or call on someone else rather than try to improve the lows' response through repeating the question, providing clues, or asking a new question.

• provide lows with inappropriate reinforcement by rewarding inappropriate behaviors or incorrect answers.

• criticize lows more often than highs for failure.

• fail to give feedback to lows' public responses.

• pay less attention to lows and interact with them less frequently.

• call on lows less often than highs to respond to questions.

• seat lows farther away from the teacher than highs.

• use more rapid pacing and less extended explanations or repetition of definitions and examples with highs than with lows.

• accept more low-quality or more incorrect responses from low-expectation students.

• interact with lows more privately than publicly.

• in administering or grading tests or assignments, give highs but not lows the benefit of the doubt in borderline cases.

• give briefer and less informative feedback to the questions of lows than to those of highs.

• use less intrusive instruction with highs than with lows, so that they have more opportunity to practice independently.

• when time is limited, use less effective and more time-consuming instructional methods with lows than with highs.

This range of teacher behavior toward low-performing students is only one aspect of an even larger reality. Another aspect has to do with the real world of pedagogy.

Reprinted from *Rethinking Schools*, December 1989/January 1990, p. 3. Reprinted by permission from The National Education Association.

6. EQUALITY OF EDUCATIONAL OPPORTUNITY

I believe most educators operate on the belief that our pedagogy is systematic, that there is a generally accepted professional practice. As mentioned above, we tend to believe that this practice can be differentiated. We imply exactly that when we group children in tracks or assign them to special education categories. But this assumption simply does not fit the empirical facts. The most accurate description we can give of present circumstances is that teachers generally have the freedom to create their own unique, ad hoc approach to the design of instructional strategy. Uniform strategies are generally not required. This fact alone would make it difficult to change in any consistent way the manner in which all teachers react to various styles, assuming that it were desirable to do so.

There may be very good reasons for using what we know about style in the design of teaching. This has less to do with matters of inequity, however, than with making pedagogy better for all. The traditional approaches to pedagogy have tended to be rigid and uncreative. They are far from exhausting the wonderful possibilities for teaching and learning.

The Uses of Style

Where, then, does this leave us? What can now be said about the utility of the style phenomenon for educators? I believe that the meaning of style for us at our present level of understanding can be found in four main areas.

First, the misunderstanding of behavioral style leads educators to make mistakes in estimating a student's or a cultural group's intellectual potential. The consequences of such errors are enormous, producing mislabeling, misplacement, and the ultimate mistreatment—inappropriate teaching—of children. If stylistic differences are interpreted as evidence of capacity rather than as an expression of preference, a long chain of abuses is set in motion.

Some children, for example, develop a habit of focusing on the global characteristics of a problem rather than on its particulars: Others do the reverse.

Ideally, a student would be flexible enough to do either. Since schools traditionally give more weight to analytical approaches than to holistic approaches, however, the student who does not manifest analytical habits is at a decided disadvantage.

There is often a gross mismatch between the storytelling styles of African American children and those of their teachers.

Second, the misunderstanding of behavioral styles leads educators to misread achievement in academic subjects such as creative expression. Orlando Taylor, a sociolinguist and dean of the School of Communications at Howard University, has shown, for example, that there is often a gross mismatch between the storytelling styles of African American children and those of their teachers.

Many teachers from Eurocentric cultures have a linear storytelling style. Many African American children, on the other hand, exhibit a spiraling storytelling style, with many departures from an initial point, but with a return to make a whole. Many teachers of these children are unable to follow the children's coherent stories. Some teachers even believe that the children's stories have no order at all. Some lose patience with the children and indicate that they're doing badly.

Third, the misunderstanding of behavioral style can lead educators to misjudge students' language abilities. When students and teachers differ in language, teachers sometimes use their own language as a normative reference. They are regarding common English as language, instead of a language. As a result, any child who speaks a different version of English is seen as having a "language deficiency" rather than a "common English deficiency." This judgement makes a big difference in how the problem is defined.

On the one hand, there is a deficiency in the student; on the other, there is an objective for instruction, with no suggestion that the student is somehow impaired.

Finally, the misunderstanding of behavioral style can make it difficult to establish rapport and to communicate. The literature on teachers' expectations of students is generally very clear. The images that teachers and others hold of children and their potential have a major influence on their decisions to use the full range of their professional skills.

If a teacher mistakes a child's differing style for lack of intellectual potential, the child will likely become educationally deprived as the teacher "teaches down" to the estimated level.

As I have mentioned, this involves simplifying, concretizing, fragmenting, and slowing the pace of instruction.

What We Know of Style

There is something we can call style—a central tendency that is a characteristic of both individuals and groups.

This style is cultural—learned.

It is meaningful in the teaching and learning interaction.

Students' style is not, however, to be used as an excuse for poor teaching or as an index of low capacity.

It is too early for us to say how or whether pedagogy (classroom teaching strategy) should be modified in response to learning styles.

A proper sensitivity to style can provide a perspective for the enrichment of instruction for all children and for the improvement both of teacher-student communications and of the systematic assessment of students.

Educators need not avoid addressing the question of style for fear they may be guilty of stereotyping students. Empirical observations are not the same as stereotyping. But the observations must be empirical, and must be interpreted properly for each student. We must become more sensitive to style out of a basic respect for our students, for their reality, and for their tremendous potential for learning.

Forging an Anti-racist Response
The Crisis in Education

The following is adapted from a speech presented this summer in Milwaukee at the annual conference of the National Coalition of Education Activists.

Enid Lee

Enid Lee is a consultant in anti-racist education and organizational change. She works with community groups and government institutions across Canada and the United States. She is also author of Letters to Marcia: a Teacher's Guide to Anti-Racist Education. *For the full text of Enid Lee's speech call her office at 416-869-1308.*

The National Coalition of Education Activists is a multiracial organization of parents, teachers, students, and union and community activists who are working for fundamental education reform. This speech was delivered at its fifth annual conference that was held in Milwaukee this past August. 200 people attended the conference from 30 states and Canada. Rethinking Schools co-sponsored the conference.

For more information on the NCEA write PO Box 405, Rosendale, NY 12472.

Some of the common descriptions of the crisis in education include words like, low self-esteem of students, lack of motivation, violent and disruptive behavior by students, and the problem of single-parent households. These are essentially victim-blaming terms. They locate the problem with the children and their parents. They pay no attention to the systems and the state that create the problem.

These explanations of the crisis are not a multicultural explanation. They

are monocultural, racist, white supremacist ways of talking about the problem. A multicultural or anti-racist perspective would cause us to see the crisis in other ways.

In case you're wondering why I use the term anti-racist, let me tell you. In Canada, the debate is between multiculturalism and anti-racism. Multiculturalism is described as the "soft" stuff and anti-racism as the "hard" stuff. In fact, when I do my workshops and people are trying to get me to do sessions, they say, "Enid, do you do the 'hard' stuff or the 'soft' stuff?" And I say I do the hard stuff. Because by the hard stuff, I'm talking about addressing the issue in terms of power, in terms of history, in terms of relationships, and definitely in terms of transformation.

The crisis, in my view, has to do with the systems and the practices in schools that contribute to low self-esteem. Low self-esteem is produced daily as the hand of the clock moves. And that is an image I want us to think about. We are working towards equality or inequality at every turn of the clock, at every time the hand moves to another number. It is not magical; it can be seen. It is taking place at 10 o'clock, at 10:15, at 10:30.

Possibilities of Transformation

When I think of it in that way, I know that I can do something. I know

that when we take an anti-racist perspective, we are challenging all of those practices and ideas and explanations that keep people in their place based on the color of their skin. We are challenging all of those practices that deny people the opportunity to become more than previous generations of their social group have been allowed to become; to know more about those forces which have directly contributed to their oppression and to have more of the resources and the rewards to which they are entitled.

Taking an anti-racist perspective allows possibilities for transformation. And I want to spend some minutes now on what I think can be done to begin to reduce the crisis.

We often ask ourselves what we can do with our colleagues who are resistant. One of the first things is to realize that you are not alone. You might say to yourself, "Enid doesn't know the kind of school that I work in." Believe me, I do know. But it is absolutely important not to see the rest of the staff as an unyielding block.

Usually, every staff can be divided into three groups, and I can figure them out within five minutes of coming into a workshop.

You have the people who change because they feel a moral imperative. They see themselves as upstanding citizens, as good people, and so they want to do the right thing. And those people can be appealed to on principle. Then there are those who are entirely prag-

The Backlash against Multiculturalism

Because some gains have been made in anti-racist education, there is a backlash from those who want to reclaim what they have lost in the struggles over the last two decades. The attack on multiculturalism is here; it's in Canada; it's in Britain. It manifests itself in all kinds of guises. And I thought I would just warn you of two of those.

Part of what happens is that people say, "Well, if multicultural is in, then everything that we do is multicultural." But even South Africa describes itself as a multicultural society. The language has been co-opted, and one of the key things is to look at what is being done under any given name.

It's a little bit like the label on food. You have to look at the fine print and see what exactly is in it. I always say I like to see the degree of BS that's in the particular food product that's being offered here, and I think you know what I mean. So when people say they're into the multicultural thing, I try to get the ingredients of what they're talking about. I look for things like outcomes, I look for who's benefiting.

The struggle has also been set back by the charge of reverse discrimination. People sometimes describe this charge in polite terms—as a need for balance, for example. Especially with old Columbus on the agenda, people are getting very concerned that we not name issues too closely, that we not attribute in very specific terms the kind of loss and damage and theft that has gone on in the name of European civilization and progress over the past 500 years. People want a rewriting of history in order to salve their consciences, in order to ease their discomfort. We cannot allow that to happen. We need to recall history with enormous accuracy and with great specificity.

—Enid Lee

matic, who will change out of enlightened self-interest. Things are not going well within the classes; they can't control the kids. So they want to do something to change this annoying situation. And then there are those who will change because it's legislated, because they are told they have to. So we have three motivations: it's right; it will help me; I must.

In my experience, those three groups can be found almost everywhere. And I think we attack accordingly. I do use the word "attack" advisedly, because we are engaged in a struggle. We are attempting to reorganize the state of the universe, certainly the state of the school, and definitely the state of the class.

I think we need to remember too that, when it comes to change, people go through stages of awareness, analysis, action, and eventually attitude change. Remember, we were not born activists.

One of the sure signs that you're making headway is resistance from the person you're speaking to. I get very disturbed when people say, "Yeah, yeah, yeah, yeah, that was great, that was great." They're trying to get rid of you. They're trying to get you to stop. A much more healthy response is, "Yes but, yes but." It means that it's taking. It's like a vaccination. So

don't think that you are not making headway because people are arguing with you. They're arguing with you because you're hitting home!

Above all, we must not assume a holier-than-thou attitude. I think that is one of the things that puts off many of our colleagues. We need to remember that we are not the first people to have thought about these things, and that can be very humbling.

Whatever we're doing in this strategy for change, we must have a healthy dose of self-interest in it. Because if we don't do that, we will become overly discouraged. We will feel that people are not appreciating us; we will forget the point of it. I hope that these changes that you are making in the school and in the society are for you, so that you can live in a society that is decent and fair. We also want to do it for the children, we want to do it for the generations to come, but you need to do it for yourself. So you do not have to wait for applause and approval. And it may never come!

A healthy dose of self-interest keeps you going. You're not doing anyone a favor, and even if you are on the privileged side of the line, remember it's a very narrow, thin, precarious line, because the day will come when those who have been disadvantaged will cross that line, and the privilege will

no longer be ours. And I say this because to me, it is one of the key things that trips us up, that prevents us from making the change.

Changing Curriculum

I want to spend a few minutes speaking very specifically about changing the curriculum. And there are two kinds of curriculum: the formal and the hidden curriculum that comes from the general climate and culture of schools.

We need to ensure that, first of all, we uncover the bias that's in the curriculum. We must get away from the notion that anything we're doing is neutral, because that's part of the problem. Everything we're doing currently is political. The question is, who is benefiting from that political thrust? We need to uncover the politics in all aspects of the curriculum, whether it's the yearbook and who's in it, whether it's the selection of texts, or whether it's how parents are allowed to get involved.

In almost all cases, that curriculum has to be named as Eurocentric—as having more than its share of that which has come from Western Europe in particular. And that piece of the curriculum has to be moved to the side so that other pieces may become part of what the picture is. It doesn't have to be moved out; it must be moved to its proper place. And its proper place is not the center; it is to the side so that all the other pieces of human experience can be placed along side it not in a spirit of negative comparison, but clearly as equally valid and valuable.

A true anti-racist curriculum requires that restructuring. It doesn't require sprinkling bits and pieces of other cultures on top. It means rearranging in order to make space for the histories, the experiences, the values of Native Americans, of African Americans, of Asian Americans, and of Latinos.

Let me give you a concrete example in math, which people tend not to think about too much in terms of an anti-racist curriculum. In grade 10 in some cities, the math curriculum has a lot of statistics in it. And the statistics in that curriculum frequently deal with weather and sports, you know, those interesting topics that everyone likes to talk about. A math coordinator in one city said to me, I want to do some anti-racist math curriculum. And I thought, bold fellow, let's get to it. So I offered him the statistics in terms of employment along lines of race in his school system. And he redesigned the math curriculum and took out the weather and sports and put those kinds of statistics in it.

And did he ever get discussion! We're not just turning out numbers; we are talking about the social content of math. The students wanted to know why there was such a discrepancy in the rates of employment among certain groups. So we had to do a social answer book for the math teachers. You know, so they would know what to say to a student when perceptive questions are asked about racism in employment.

Anyway, a lot of interest got generated in the math, among the math teachers, among the students. They saw that statistics had to do with real people. No major infusion of money happened, yet this teacher took a unit and changed not only what was there, but also changed his way of teaching.

Student Talk

I also remember a school in another city, where I heard two boys in grade 4 talking about some experiment that they were doing. It had to do with putting foil paper into an empty roll of toilet paper. I'm not sure of the scientific significance, but I know that they were trying to do it to prove something.

There were two kids who couldn't get the experiment and one boy said, "The paper won't cooperate." Another boy said, "I can't do it."

Selected Thoughts

What follows are excerpts from Enid Lee's speech on various aspects of the struggle against racism.

Discrimination is Not One-Sided

Oftentimes when we discuss the question of discrimination we forget to note what is on the other side of the balance sheet, because, you see, discrimination not only limits some people, it enhances other people's opportunities. It's not simply one-sided. As we try to bring about balance, one of the things we forget is that while discriminatory, racist practice is at work and some people are being disadvantaged, others are being enhanced. Their sense of who they are, their self-esteem is being elevated. Their experiences become what constitutes knowledge, their ways of learning become the ways that we teach. The kinds of outcomes that they have ensure them future employment. So that is the insidious nature of this thing that we call racism and the other forms of discrimi-

nation. It works against some, and it moves others forward.

Calling Individuals 'Racist'

I want to say something about using the word racist to describe individuals. In my work, I have not found it helpful to describe a person as a racist. I describe individual acts or words as racist behavior. I say, "You have engaged in racist behavior" or "that's racist language."

You might say that's just dancing around things diplomatically. But I think that some descriptions make it hard for people to change. And when I describe an act, or language as racist, they have a chance to change it. And this is what I'm interested in. What I want is for them to treat the children fairly, to treat the parents respectfully and to ensure equitable outcomes for people of color. That's the bottom line.

Racism and Power

I was talking to some people who wanted to know why something might be

called racism if it's against somebody of color, but not against people who are white. Let's say two children are playing and fall and hurt themselves. One child is a hemophiliac and the other child doesn't have anything the matter with her. Both kids are going to bleed, both kids are going to hurt. But you can't attend to the children in the same way. Because if you do the same thing for both kids, one of the children is going to die because they don't have the capacity to start the clotting.

It's the same thing about racism and other kinds of discrimination. If you have power, it's one kind of experience. It is entirely different if you are from a marginalized group. In the latter case, you have fewer options and less social power to back you up. It's the same with class, it's the same with gender. In social terms, the implications are significant. The individual experience with discrimination becomes part of a historic pattern and feeds into the larger picture of systemic oppression.

6. EQUALITY OF EDUCATIONAL OPPORTUNITY

I don't think I need to tell you the racial background of each of those children and the difference in who made which statement. I think you know who said, "I can't do it," and you know who said, "It's the paper's fault." I think those two statements capture how it is our children see school; how it is they experience success and how they understand their potential.

Now for those two students, different things have to be done in order to assist them. We have to respond individually and differently to different groups of students in order to respond fairly. The kid who said, "I can't do it," he needs to know that he can do it. He needs to be provided with enough support and opportunity that he can get it done. It definitely didn't need to be done for him. He needed to have a chance to do it himself. And he needs to know that if he can't get it, then it's nothing to do with him; he just hasn't quite got it and someone needs to help him. And it is at those moments that we are making a difference in terms of expectations, in terms of outcome.

Classroom Organization

I go into classrooms and I look at the way in which they're organized. I look at who is sitting where. And then when I'm asked, "How can you help us to improve the performance rate of the Black male students in the school?" I only have to take a look at where people are sitting. I will change it automatically, and overnight a different message could be got, and overnight a different result could be experienced.

So while we are waiting for a grand revolution, specific changes can be made that will make a major difference in what happens to students and in the messages that they get.

We need to look, as well, at the language that is part of the curriculum, how things are described. We need to challenge ourselves on such terms like ethnic literature. A person is teaching a course in ethnic literature, and then they are teaching regular literature.

Credit: Rick Reinhard

Each child deserves a chance at success.

Well, every literature is ethnic. It's just that some ethnicities are not named; they just are. We need to recognize that when we say we're teaching a course in music that's classical, that we're talking about Western classical music or European classical music, because every continent has had its classical period, and some of them we have missed because of our own limitations.

And you can go through your course description and your course outline. In fact, one day I was in a school and while I was there waiting to speak with the principal, I'm looking at this course description: "Eurasian Geography: Europe and Asia. For a Canadian student, the study of the geography of Eurasia offers an opportunity to investigate the fascinating variety of different people and places who make up the world's largest continent. The struggling and crowded masses of south Asia, the successful Japanese, and the highly advanced Western Europeans all provide a highly interesting example of people with a different approach to life from us Canadians."

I'm happy to say that this course description and the content have been altered. But I'm saying here that something as simple as a description is a beginning of looking at the bias of the curriculum. If we are to provide curriculum that reflects the human experience, it needs to be far more inclusive and it also needs to connect the relationships of various groups of people. Right now, what happens is that we have descriptions of isolated groups. We don't talk about how those groups impact and affect each other. Even in this course description, these struggling and crowded masses didn't just get to be struggling and crowded masses from the beginning of time and totally on their own. And these advanced people that we're describing didn't get to be advanced just through their entire genius and brilliance and everything else. Of course not. It needs to be talked about in context.

I want to say as I close that the unions need to attend to certain matters. Those of you in teachers' unions have a particular responsibility to make sure that anti-racist language is in the bargaining arrangement. Because it is from that source that many decisions can be made and we can begin to change things that are unacceptable in the schools. I would say that an anti-racist environment should be one of the conditions of employment—in the same way that you don't want to see people working with overcrowded classrooms or with low wages.

All of us, I think, have an opportunity to make some difference. We need to identify our points of power, to ask ourselves what is in my power to do, individually and collectively. And as we do that, remember to celebrate what has been accomplished. Because part of our despair is that we are constantly beginning from the beginning and starting as though this were the first time that anyone discussed the topic. It is absolutely important for us to celebrate every single step that we take forward, every time change has been made, every student that has been rescued, every colleague that has been influenced. Every time we have made a breakthrough in the system, we need to publicize it and to celebrate it.

Part of why we forget to celebrate is that we lose sight of the facts: there are people who have gone before us; our time is going to end but others will continue it. You are one in a long line of people struggling to make a difference in terms of the crisis in education.

Investing in Our
CHILDREN:
A Struggle for America's Conscience and Future

"Too many young people of all races and classes are growing up unable to handle life, without hope or steady compasses to navigate a world that is reinventing itself technologically and politically at a kaleidoscopic pace."

Marian Wright Edelman

Ms. Edelman is president of the Children's Defense Fund, Washington, D.C.

THE 1990S' STRUGGLE is about the U.S.'s conscience and future. Many of the battles will not be as dramatic as Gettysburg or Vietnam or Desert Storm, but they are going to shape this nation's place in the 21st century. Every American in this last decade of the last century of this millennium must struggle to redefine success in the U.S., asking not "How much can I get?," but "How much can I do without and share?"; not "How can I find myself?," but "How can I lose myself in service to others?"; not just how I can take care of me and mine, but how I can help as one American to strengthen family and community values and help this great nation regain her moral and economic bearings at home and abroad.

When I was growing up, service was as essential as eating and sleeping and going to church and school. Caring black adults were buffers against the segregated outside world which told me that, as a black girl, I wasn't worth anything and was not important. However, I didn't believe it because my parents, teachers, and preachers said it wasn't so. The childhood message I internalized, despite the outside segregation and poverty all around, was that, as God's child, no man or woman could look down on me, and I could look down on no man or woman.

I couldn't play in segregated playgrounds or sit at drugstore lunch counters, so my father, a Baptist minister, built a playground and canteen behind our church. Whenever he saw a need, he tried to respond. There were no black homes for the aged in South Carolina at that time, so my parents began one across the street, and our entire family had to help out. I didn't like it a whole lot of the time, but that is how I learned that it was my responsibility to take care of elderly family members and neighbors, and that everyone was my neighbor.

I went everywhere with my parents and the members of my church and community who were my watchful extended family. The entire black community took responsibility for protecting its children. They reported on me when I did wrong, applauded me when I did well, and were very clear as adults about what doing well meant. It meant being helpful to others, achieving in school, and reading. We all finally figured out that the only time our father wouldn't give us a chore was when we were reading, so we all read a lot.

Children were taught, by example, that nothing was too lowly to do and that the work of our heads and hands were both valuable. As a child, I went with an older brother—I was eight or nine or 10 and remember the debate between my parents as to whether I was too young to go help clean the bedsores of a poor, sick woman—but I went and learned just how much the smallest helping hands can mean to a lonely person in need.

Our families, churches, and community made kids feel useful and important. While life often was hard and resources scarce, we always knew who we were and that the measure of our worth was inside our heads and hearts, not outside in material possessions or personal ambition. We were taught that the world had a lot of problems; that black people had an *extra* lot of problems, but that we could struggle and change them; that extra intellectual and material gifts brought with them the privilege and responsibility of sharing with others less fortunate; and that service is the rent each of us pays for living—the very purpose of life and not something you do in your spare time or after you have reached your personal goals.

I am grateful for these childhood legacies of a living faith reflected in daily service, the discipline of hard work, and stick-to-itiveness—a capacity to struggle in the face of adversity. Giving up, despite how bad the world was outside, simply was not a part of my childhood lexicon. You got up every morning and did what you had to do, and you got up every time you fell down and tried as many times as you had to until you got it right. I was 14 the night my father died. He had holes in his shoes, but he had two children who graduated from college, one in college, another in divinity school, and a vision that he was able to convey to me even as he was dying in an ambulance—that I, a young black girl, could be and do anything, that race and gender are shadows, and that character, self-discipline, determination, attitude, and service are the substance of life.

What kind of vision are we conveying to our children today as parents, political and business leaders, and professionals? Our children are growing up in an ethically polluted nation where instant sex without responsibility, instant gratification without effort, instant solutions without sacrifice, getting rather than giving, and hoarding rather than sharing are the too frequent signals of our mass media, popular culture, and political life.

The standard of success for far too many Americans has become personal greed, rather than common good. The standard for striving and achievement has become getting, rather than making an extra effort or service to others. Truth-telling and moral example have become devalued commodities. Nowhere is the paralysis of public or private conscience more evident than in the neglect and abandonment of millions of our shrinking pool of youngsters, whose futures will determine our nation's ability to compete economically and lead morally as much as any child of privilege and as much as any other issue.

We need to understand that investing in our children is not investing in a special interest group or helping out somebody else—it is absolutely essential to every American's well-being and future. Only two out of every 10 new labor force entrants in this decade will be white males born in the U.S. As an aging population with a shrinking pool of kids, we don't have a child to waste—we need every one of them. We either can decide to invest in them up front and give them a sense of nurturing and caring adults that are part of a community and a society that guarantees them a future, or we can continue to fear them, build more and more prisons, and worry about them shooting at us. We don't have a choice about investing in our children, only when we are going to invest and whether it's going to be positive or negative investment.

Every 16 seconds of every school day, as we talk about a competitive workforce in the future, one of our children drops out of school. Every 26 seconds of every day, an American child runs away from home. These are not just poor or black children— they are all of our children. This is not something affecting just a few families— these are national problems. Every 47

seconds, a youngster is abused. Every 67 seconds, a teenager has a baby. We produce the equivalent of the city of Seattle each year with children having children. Every seven minutes, a child is arrested for a drug offense. Every 30 minutes, one of our children is charged with drunken driving. Every 53 minutes, in the richest land on Earth, an American child dies because of poverty.

It is disgraceful that children are the poorest Americans and that, in the last year alone, 840,000 youngsters fell into poverty and that there has been a 26% increase since 1979 in poverty among children. The majority of poor youngsters in America are not black and not in inner cities. They are in rural and suburban areas and in working and two-parent families. A lot of folk who were middle class last year around the country are now in poverty and on food stamps. It can happen to any of us.

We are in a sad state when the American Dream for many middle-class young people has become a choice between a house and a child. They are worrying about how their offspring are going to make it through college, pay off their higher education loans, and get off the ground and form families. We have to begin investing in all of our kids and all of our families. I believe we have lost our sense of what is important as a people. Too many children of all races and classes are growing up unable to handle life, without hope or steady compasses to navigate a world that is reinventing itself technologically and politically at a kaleidoscopic pace. Too many are growing up terribly uncertain and fearful about the future.

Despite the global realities the nation faces and a lot of the economic and moral uncertainty of the present, there are some enduring values we have lost sight of. I agree with poet Archibald MacLeish that there is only one thing more powerful than learning from experience and that is *not* learning from experience. It is the responsibility of every adult—parent, teacher, preacher, professional, and political leader—to make sure that youngsters hear what adults have learned from the lessons of life. Author James Baldwin wrote some years back that children really don't ever do what we tell them to do, but they almost always do what we do.

Americans have to move away from the idea of being entitled to something because they are men, or wealthy, or white, or black. It is time to come together to work quietly and systematically toward building a more just America and ensuring that no child is left behind. We should resist quick-fix, simplistic answers and easy gains that disappear as fast as they come. I am sick of people talking big and making great promises, then not following up and getting it done. Too often, we get bogged down

in our ego needs and lose sight of deeper community and national needs.

Family values vs. hypocrisy

As a nation, we mouth family values we do not practice. Seventy countries provide medical care and financial assistance to all pregnant women and to children—the U.S. is not one of them. Seventeen industrialized nations have paid maternity / paternity leave programs—the U.S. is not one of them. In 1992, Pres. George Bush vetoed an unpaid leave bill that would have allowed parents to stay at home when a child is sick or disabled. We need to stop the hypocrisy of talking about families when all our practices are the opposite. It is time for parents to have a real choice about whether to remain at home or work outside the home without worrying about the safety of their children.

Many families have had to put a second parent into the workforce in order to make ends meet. Even when both parents work, a vast number are not able to meet their basic housing and health care needs.

The new generation of young people must share and stress family rituals and values and be moral examples for their children, just as this generation must try even harder to be. If people cut corners, their children will too. If they are not honest, their children will not be either. If adults spend all of their money and tithe no portion of it for colleges, synagogues or churches, and civic causes, their children won't either. If they tolerate political leaders who don't tell the truth or do what they say, their children will lose faith as too many are doing in the political process.

If we snicker at racial and gender jokes, another generation will pass on the poison that our generation still has not had the will to snuff out. Each of us must counter the proliferating voices of racial, ethnic, and religious division that separates us as Americans. It's important for us to face up to, rather than ignore, our growing racial problems, which are America's historic and future Achilles' heel. Whites didn't create black or brown people; men didn't create women; Christians didn't create Jews—so what gives anybody the right to feel entitled to diminish another?

We need to ask ourselves as Americans—how many potential Martin Luther King, Jrs. or Colin Powells, Sally Rides or Barbara McClintocks our nation is going to waste before it wakes up and recognizes that its ability to compete in the new century is as inextricably intertwined with poor and non-white children as with its white and privileged ones, with girls as well as its boys? As Rabbi Abraham Heschel put it, ''We may not all be equally guilty for the problems that we face, but we are all equally responsible'' for building a decent and just

America and seeing that no child is left behind.

People who are unwilling or unable to share and make complicated and sometimes hard choices may be incapable or taking courageous action to rebuild our families and community and nation. Nevertheless, I have great hopes about America and believe we can rebuild community and begin to put our children first as a nation. It is going to require that each of us figure out what we're going to be willing to sacrifice and share.

Many whites favor racial justice as long as things remain the same. Many voters hate Congress, but love their own Congressman as long as he or she takes care of their special interests. Many husbands are happier to share their wives' added income than share the housework and child care. Many Americans deny the growing gap between the rich and the poor, and they are sympathetic and concerned about escalating child suffering as long as somebody else's program is cut.

Americans have to grow up beyond this national adolescence. Everybody wants to spend, but nobody wants to pay. Everybody wants to lower the deficit, but also to get everything that they can. We have to ask ourselves how we're going to come together as a people to begin to make sure that the necessities of the many are taken care of and that every child gets what he or she needs to achieve a healthy start in life. If we're not too poor to bail out the savings and loan institutions, if we're not too poor to build all those B-2 bombers, we're not too poor to rescue our suffering children and to ensure that all youngsters get what they need.

In a time of economic uncertainty and fear about the future, of rising crime, rising costs, and rising joblessness, we must never give in to the urge to give up, no matter how hard it gets. There's an old proverb that says, "When you get to your wits end, remember that God lives there." Harriet Beecher Stowe once said that, when you get into a "tight place and everything goes against you, till it seems as though you could not hang on for a minute longer, never give up then, for that is just the place and the time when the tide will turn."

We can not continue as a nation to make a distinction between our children and other people's kids. Every youngster is entitled to an equal share of the American Dream. Every poor child, every black child, every white child—every child living everywhere—should have an equal shot. We need every one of them to be productive and educated and healthy.

Let me end this article with a prayer, written by a schoolteacher in South Carolina. She urges us to pray and accept responsibility for children who sneak popsicles before supper, erase holes in math workbooks, and never can find their shoes, but let's also pray and accept responsibility for children who can't bound down the street in a new pair of sneakers, who don't have any rooms to clean up, whose pictures aren't on anybody's dresser, and whose monsters are real. Let each of us commit to praying and accepting responsibility for children who spend all their allowance before Tuesday, throw tantrums in the grocery store, pick at their food, shove dirty clothes under the bed, never rinse out the tub, squirm in church or temple, and scream in the phone, but let's also pray and accept responsibility for those children whose nightmares come in the daytime, who will eat anything, who have never seen a dentist, who aren't spoiled by anybody, who go to bed hungry and cry themselves to sleep all over this rich nation. Let's commit to praying and accepting responsibility for children who want to be carried and for those who must be carried. Let's commit to protecting those children whom we never give up on, but also those children who don't get a second chance. Let each of us commit to praying and voting and speaking and fighting for those children whom we smother, but also for those who will grab the hand of anybody kind enough to offer it.

Concerns About Teaching Culturally Diverse Students

Patricia L. Marshall

Patricia L. Marshall is Assistant Professor at North Carolina State University where she teaches courses in multicultural education and elementary school curriculum. Her current research interests involve cognitive developmental theory within multicultural education in teacher education programs. Dr. Marshall is a member of Omicron Rho Chapter.

The one word that best describes contemporary students, curricula, and school philosophies is *diverse*. A 1991 report conducted by the College Board and Western Interstate Commission for Higher Education report indicated that diverse student populations in the United States are expected to increase dramatically by the year 1994. Specifically, Asian and Pacific Islander student populations are predicted to increase by 70 percent, Hispanic by 54 percent, and African-American by 13 percent. While this diverse climate presents challenges, undoubtedly it also creates concerns among school personnel. Teachers may feel a definite need to develop a heightened sensitivity and cross-cultural awareness for teaching today's student populations.

The professional concerns that teachers hold about student diversity may potentially affect how teachers approach teaching tasks as well as how they interact with students. An examination of teachers' concerns about working with diverse students and ways they can address these concerns follows.

Identifying Concerns

Research (Fuller 1969; Gehrke 1987; Katz 1972; Marshall et al. 1990) suggests that teachers have varying levels of concern about working in classrooms. Heretofore, the research literature has not explicitly addressed the nature of teachers' concerns about working with diverse student populations. The phrase *multicultural teaching concern* refers to those concerns teachers have about working in contemporary culturally diverse school settings. Such teaching concerns are distinctive because they are held about students whose cultural backgrounds differ most from the teacher's background. Most multicultural teaching concerns are related to teacher and student racial or ethnic differences. Some concerns may reflect differences between individuals of the same racial or ethnic background but different socioeconomic backgrounds.

Surveying Concerns

Groups of teachers and university juniors and seniors were recently invited to respond to an open-ended questionnaire about multicultural education. They were asked to submit concerns they or their peers hold about teaching in diverse or "multicultural" school environments. More than 300 concerns were collected from this survey. Because the professional experiences with multicultural student populations varied among the groups, it was expected the concerns identified would also differ. However, the teachers and university students identified similar professional concerns about working—or the prospect of working—with culturally diverse students.

A group of multicultural education specialists analyzed the open-ended surveys and organized the original 300 concerns into a 64-item instrument called

Questions on the MTCS survey are presented in four categories. Within each category, samples are provided.

Multicultural Teaching Concerns Survey

Familial or Group Knowledge

Concerns about the completeness of teachers' knowledge about diverse students' familial/group culture and background.

Examples:

▼ How will I learn about the family culture of students and how it affects performance and attitudes toward school?

▼ How do I differentiate student values and behavior patterns that are culturally based?

▼ In what ways do parent expectations impact or dictate behaviors exhibited in my class?

Strategies and Techniques

Concerns about utilizing appropriate techniques and including the most appropriate and inclusive content in curriculum and general school program.

Examples:

▼ How should I vary my teaching techniques when teaching culturally diverse students?

▼ How should I go about selecting materials and resources to incorporate multicultural perspectives into the existing curricula?

Interpersonal Competence

Concerns about the impact of personal attitudes, actions, and/or beliefs on interactions with diverse student populations.

Examples:

▼ Will my students be prejudiced against me?

▼ Will students perceive me as biased simply because my background is different from theirs?

▼ Will I be able to be myself when working with culturally diverse students without appearing uncaring and aloof?

School Bureaucracy

Concerns about whether the structure of schools (e.g., grouping patterns) and the actions of other school personnel impact efforts to effectively address school issues related to student diversity.

Examples:

▼ How do I combat school district policies that are inequitable for diverse students?

▼ How do I deal with intolerance among my colleagues?

▼ What can I do when my classroom actually reflects the community in which I teach?

---

the *Multicultural Teaching Concerns Survey* (MTCS)[1]. Each item within the MTCS corresponds to one of four concern categories, which are outlined in the table above.

Ways to Address Concerns in the Classroom

Teachers who have concerns about teaching diverse student populations are often apprehensive about not being able to meet the needs of their students. Selecting the most appropriate teaching techniques and strategies involves constant vigilance on the part of every professional educator. Similar to other professionals, classroom teachers must constantly stay abreast of the latest interpretations of content and

[1]Pilot testing for Phase I of the MTCS included a survey of 300 teachers and university education majors. Analysis of the results revealed high construct validity and promising reliability coefficients. Currently in Phase II of its development, the MTCS is being refined using a larger, more diverse population of classroom teachers. For more information about the study, contact the author at North Carolina State University; Department of Curriculum and Instruction; 402 Poe Hall, Box 7801; Raleigh, NC 27695-7801.

teaching techniques. One of the greatest tragedies is that many teachers simply have not had a formal professional opportunity to explore techniques and strategies more appropriate for their work with diverse student populations. In addition, the basic content knowledge that many teachers may have studied while training to become teachers may not have been comprehensive to the extent that it included varying cultural perspectives. Consequently, these teachers should work to lessen or eliminate multicultural teaching concerns. When this is done, teachers can redirect their attention toward those aspects of classroom interaction that will allow them to meet the needs of all students. Below are ways multicultural teaching concerns can be addressed:

✔ Make a concerted effort to learn more about the family structure of your students.
✔ Personalize contacts with students' parents by visiting homes and neighborhoods.
✔ Enroll in classes or workshops devoted to the past and more recent history of the ethnic or racial groups of students in your classes.
✔ Visit community centers, places of worship, civic events, or cultural or religious celebrations of members of nonmajority cultures.

✔ Begin a self-study project to read contemporary literature written by authors from diverse backgrounds.

✔ Subscribe to or borrow from a library monthly magazines published for ethnic populations.

✔ Explore research on individual learning styles.

✔ Involve students in unit planning.

✔ Enroll in a race awareness or cross-cultural sensitivity workshop.

✔ Form professional collaborations with colleagues of a different race or ethnicity and with whom you can share concerns and questions about working with diverse students.

The MTCS offers opportunities to explore a new dimension of teachers' concerns about working in classrooms. It examines the nature of teachers' concerns as they relate to diversity in contemporary schools. Cultural diversity in schools will continue to increase, resulting in significant changes in the way schools operate. These changes need not cause major anxiety for teachers. Instead, diversity can be viewed as an opportunity for teachers to engage in analyzing their professional selves. These changes can also be perceived as opportunities for professional—and perhaps personal—growth.

Recommended Reading on Multicultural Education

Presently, multicultural education is the major schooling innovation that challenges teachers to explore their own attitudes and behaviors toward culturally diverse students. The following books are excellent sources of information on this growing field of study.

Banks, J. A., and C. McGee Banks, eds. 1993. *Multicultural education: Issues and perspectives.* Boston: Allyn and Bacon. Exploration of various dimensions of multicultural education including teaching about women, ethnic/racial minorities, and exceptionalities. Includes resources section and glossary list of culturally sensitive terminology.

Bennett, C. I. 1990. *Comprehensive multicultural education: Theory and practice.* Boston: Allyn and Bacon. Examines multicultural education as a "movement, curriculum approach, process and teacher commitment." Includes chapters on the role of individual learning styles on teaching and learning.

Grant, C. A. and C. E. Sleeter, 1989. *Turning on learning: Five approaches for multicultural teaching plans for races, class, gender, and disability.* Columbus: Merrill Publishing Company. Provides a collection of lesson plans for various subjects (including art and mathematics) and grade levels using five different approaches to multicultural education.

Gollnick, D. M., and P.C. Chinn, 1992. *Multicultural education in a pluralistic society.* Columbus: Merrill Publishing Company. Excellent introductory text on multicultural education. Includes one of the best all-around discussions on the basic tenets of multicultural education and the dominant culture in the United States.

Tiedt, P. L., and I. M. Tiedt, 1992. *Multicultural education teaching: A handbook of activities, information, and resources.* Boston: Allyn and Bacon. Collection of activities and ideas for incorporating multicultural education into existing curricula. Especially appropriate for elementary school teachers.

References

Fuller, F. F. 1969. Concerns of teachers: A developmental conceputalization. *American Educational Research Journal,* 6(2): 207-26.

Gehrke, N. 1987. *On Being A Teacher.* West Lafayette, Ind.: Kappa Delta Pi.

Katz, L. G. 1972. Developmental stages of preschool teachers. *Elementary School Journal,* 73(1): 50-54.

Marshall, P., S. Fittinghoff, and C. O. Cheney. 1990. Beginning teacher developmental stages: implications for creating collaborative internship programs. *Teacher Education Quarterly,* 17(3):25-35.

Serving Special Needs and Concerns

There are always many special issues of concern to educators everywhere. One major movement in curriculum and instruction in the United States is the move toward more "inclusive" scheduling of students in schools and away from ability grouping of students. This is really an offshoot of the "mainstreaming" movement of the 1970s and 1980s when all physically and cognitively handicapped students were required to be integrated into regular classes based on the criterion of "the least restrictive environment" possible for each child. This movement, in turn, has been a controversial issue in curriculum and instruction since the United States made its commitment to mass universal secondary education in the teens of this century; that issue is the controversy over "heterogeneous versus homogeneous" grouping (ability "tracking") of students. Advocates of inclusion today favor heterogeneously scheduling students in schools without regard to ability on the primary premise that all students will learn from one another. Academically, they will benefit from being in classes with fellow students representing a broad range of abilities and interests.

Each year we try to focus on a few special issues in this section of this volume. In addition to the topic of inclusion and the issue of ability grouping in schools, we look briefly at the issues of child care, what and how to teach about human sexuality in schools, and the role of vocational education in the preparation of students for both the world of work and postsecondary education.

Child care is a major concern for parents who choose to work outside the home. There is a major shortage of adequate child-care facilities in the United States. Frequently, it is also a major expense of working parents when they must rely on the services of private child care providers. Although there are some family income-based philanthropic child-care providers (sponsored by religious organizations, YWCAs, or other types of public outreach organizations), there is not nearly enough acceptable, safe child care available to working parents. It is also an issue that ties into the reasons why many low-income women cannot work, because minimum wage jobs cannot support both the costs of private child care and the mother and her children's needs.

Education in human sexuality for children and teenagers is a very important issue confronting American school systems. Because of the AIDS epidemic (still uncontrolled and spreading exponentially throughout the population each year), the high rate of teenage pregnancy in the United States (the highest in the industrialized world), the high rate of child abuse, as well as the fact that many young people are starting sexual activity at an earlier age than in previous decades, there is mounting pressure on the educational system to rethink the issue of education in human sexuality. This year we have included three articles on the issue of sex education that reflect concerns that we believe all teachers should understand.

Finally, we addressed the issue of vocational education (of some sort) for all students in addition to preparation for postsecondary educational opportunities. Several very original, creative proposals for helping young people to be better prepared to participate in the national work force while not necessarily foreclosing on their postsecondary educational opportunities are offered. The essays address how other nations have developed far more effective vocational educational goals and programs than we have in the United States.

Growing up has always involved a process of confronting change in one's self and others and of learning the folkways and mores of one's own culture. This enculturation process is experienced by every child and adolescent, and some children even learn the cultural values of other groups of persons with whom they interact in their neighborhood and school environments. The essays in this unit try to concentrate on some of the special emotional, psychological, and social concerns of importance to parents, teachers, and students.

Some issues that confront teachers and their students are unique to the teacher-student relationship. Other issues that affect teachers in their work with students have their origin in the problems of society at large. These problems impact on teachers because students bring these social problems to school with them. Since first issued in 1973, this anthology has sought to provide discussion of special social or curriculum issues affecting the teaching-learning conditions in schools. Fundamental forces at work in North American culture during the past several years have greatly affected millions of students. The social, cultural, and economic pressures on families have produced several special problems of great concern to teachers. There is demand for greater degrees of individualization of instruction and for greater development and maintenance of stronger self-concepts by students. The number of students who are either in single-parent situations or who have both parents working and maintaining careers has been growing. School systems and the teachers who work within them have been confronted with student populations that experience many problems that, traditionally at least, they were not expected to address. Teachers have an opportunity to shape the lives of young people by being good examples of stable personalities themselves and through individualizing interactions with their students. All children and adolescents do not have the same opportunity to be exposed to untroubled and stable men and women.

A teacher needs to see the work of the school as integrated with the activities of the general society that created and sustains it. There is too much superficial conceptualizing of schooling as not related to, or somehow separated from, the rest of the world. Teachers need to be good observers of the learning styles of their students. They need to modify instructional planning to provide learning experiences that are best for their students.

Teachers should become aware of the extraordinary circumstances under which many children and young adults strive to become educated. Teachers are interested in studying their options to respond constructively to the special needs of their students. They want to know how they can help build self-confidence and self-esteem in their students, and how they can help them to want to learn in spite of all of the distracting forces in their lives. There are even those who argue that all teachers can benefit from practicing certain parenting skills in their interactions with students. Development of constructive, positive student-teacher relationships to assist students in facing difficult life situations is a common theme in talk about curriculum and instruction.

The special needs and abilities that people possess are often called exceptionalities. Exceptionalities of certain kinds, whether they be physical or cognitive (mental), sometimes require special intervention or treatment skills. How can teachers address the unique needs, interests, abilities, and exceptionalities of students? How can teachers best serve their students' needs for attention and intellectual stimulation, demonstrate concern for the students, and also meet regular instructional responsibilities? Many children are not aware of their special needs and academic and social capabilities. School systems must find ways to help students discover these needs and

potentials, and they must create conditions for students to progress both academically and socially.

The issues discussed in this unit are ones that critically impact the working conditions of teachers. These issues have been produced either by social forces outside of the schools, or by the thought of improving how we serve students' needs as a profession.

Looking Ahead: Challenge Questions

What would be a philosophical justification for improving self-esteem as a general claim of education?

How do we teach children to be caring?

How should sex education be integrated into school curricula? What are the best sorts of educational curricula for teaching about human sexuality? What should be included in sex education?

What are the best methods for helping at-risk students to remain in school?

Can learning about one's own culture be integrated into the school curriculum?

How could more effective child care be made available to working parents?

What ought children and teenagers be taught about human sexual identity?

Why don't we have quality vocational education programming in the United States?

Should all students be fully prepared in at least one viable vocation in addition to their preparation for post-secondary education?

Blowing up the Tracks

Stop segregating schools by ability and watch kids grow

Patricia Kean

Patrician Kean is a writer in New York City.

It's morning in New York, and some seventh graders are more equal than others.

Class 7-16 files slowly into the room, prodded by hard-faced men whose walkie-talkies crackle with static. A pleasant looking woman shouts over the din, "What's rule number one?" No reply. She writes on the board. "Rule One: Sit down."

Rule number two seems to be an unwritten law: Speak slowly. Each of Mrs. H's syllables hangs in the air a second longer than necessary. In fact, the entire class seems to be conducted at 16 RPM. Books come out gradually. Kids wander about the room aimlessly. Twelve minutes into class, we settle down and begin to play "O. Henry Jeopardy," a game which requires students to supply one-word answers to questions like: "O. Henry moved from North Carolina to what state—Andy? Find the word on the page."

The class takes out a vocabulary sheet. Some of the words they are expected to find difficult include popular, ranch, suitcase, arrested, recipe, tricky, ordinary, humorous, and grand jury.

Thirty minutes pass. Bells ring, doors slam.

Class 7-1 marches in unescorted, mindful of rule number one. Paperbacks of Poe smack sharply on desks, notebooks rustle, and kids lean forward expectantly, waiting for Mrs. H. to fire the first question. What did we learn about the writer?

Hands shoot into the air. Though Edgar Allen Poe ends up sounding a lot like Jerry Lee Lewis—a booze-hound who married his 13-year-old cousin—these kids speak confidently, in paragraphs. Absolutely no looking at the book allowed.

We also have a vocabulary sheet, drawn from "The Tell-Tale Heart," containing words like audacity, dissimulation, sagacity, stealthy, anxiety, derision, agony, and supposition.

As I sit in the back of the classroom watching these two very different groups of seventh graders, my previous life as an English teacher allows me to make an educated guess and a chilling prediction. With the best of intentions, Mrs. H. is teaching the first group, otherwise known as the "slow kids," as though they are fourth graders, and the second, the

honors group, as though they are high school freshmen. Given the odds of finding a word like "ordinary" on the SAT's, the children of 7-16 have a better chance of standing before a "grand jury" than making it to college.

Tracking, the practice of placing students in "ability groups" based on a host of ill-defined criteria—everything from test scores to behavior to how much of a fuss a mother can be counted on to make—encourages even well-meaning teachers and administrators to turn out generation after generation of self-fulfilling prophecies. "These kids know they're no Einsteins," Mrs. H. said of her low-track class when we sat together in the teacher's lounge. "They know they don't read well. This way I can go really slowly with them."

With his grades, however, young Albert would probably be hanging right here with the rest of lunch table 7-16. That's where I discover that while their school may think they're dumb, these kids are anything but stupid. "That teacher," sniffs a pretty girl wearing lots of purple lipstick. "She talks so slow. She thinks we're babies. She takes a year to do anything." "What about that other one?" a girl named Ingrid asks, referring to their once-a-week student teacher. "He comes in and goes like this: Rail (pauses) road. Rail (pauses) road. Like we don't know what railroad means!" The table breaks up laughing.

Outside the walls of schools across the country, it's slowly become an open secret that enforced homogeneity benefits no one. The work of researchers like Jeannie Oakes of UCLA and Robert Slavin of Johns Hopkins has proven that tracking does not merely reflect differences—it causes them. Over time, slow kids get slower, while those in the middle and in the so-called "gifted and talented" top tracks fail to gain from isolation. Along the way, the practice resegregates the nation's schools, dividing the middle from the lower classes, white from black and brown. As the evidence piles up, everyone from the Carnegie Corporation to the National Governors Association has called for change.

Though some fashionably progressive schools have begun to reform, tracking persists. Parent groups, school boards, teachers, and administrators who hold the power within schools cling to the myths and wax apocalyptic about the horrors of heterogeneity. On their side is the most potent force known to man: bureaucratic inertia. Because tracking puts kids in boxes, keeps the lid on, and shifts responsibility for mediocrity and failure away from the schools themselves, there is little incentive to change a near-ly-century old tradition. "Research is research," the principal told me that day, "This is practice."

Back track

Tracking has been around since just after the turn of the century. It was then, as cities teemed with im-migrants and industry, that education reformers like John Franklin Bobbitt began to argue that the school and the factory shared a common mission, to "work up the raw material into that finished product for which it was best adapted." By the twenties, the sci-entific principles that ruled the factory floor had been applied to the classroom. They believed the IQ test—which had just become popular—allowed pure sci-ence, not the whims of birth or class, to determine whether a child received the type of education appro-priate for a future manager or a future laborer.

It hasn't quite worked out that way. Driven by standardized tests, the descendants of the old IQ tests, tracking has evolved into a kind of educational triage premised on the notion that only the least wounded can be saved. Yet when the classroom oper-ates like a battleground, society's casualties mount, and the results begin to seem absurd: Kids who enter school needing more get less, while the already en-riched get, well, enricher. Then, too, the low-track graduates of 70 years ago held a distinct advantage over their modern counterparts: If tracking prepared them for mindless jobs, at least those jobs existed.

The sifting and winnowing starts as early as pre-K. Three-year old Ebony and her classmates have won the highly prized "gifted and talented" label af-ter enduring a battery of IQ and psychological tests. There's nothing wrong with the "regular" class in this Harlem public school. But high expectations for Ebony and her new friends bring tangible rewards like a weekly field trip and music and computer lessons.

Meanwhile, regular kids move on to regular kindergartens where they too will be tested, and where it will be determined that some children need more help, perhaps a "pre-first grade" developmental year. So by the time they're ready for first grade reading groups, certain six-year-olds have already been marked as "sparrows"—the low performers in the class.

In the beginning, it doesn't seem to matter so much, because the other reading groups—the robins and the eagles—are just a few feet away and the class is together for most of the day. Trouble is, as they toil over basic drill sheets, the sparrows are slipping far-ther behind. The robins are gathering more challeng-ing vocabulary words, and the eagles soaring on to critical thinking skills.

Though policies vary, by fourth grade many of these groups have flown into completely separate class-rooms, turning an innocent three-tier reading system into three increasingly rigid academic tracks—honors, regular, and remedial—by middle school.

Unless middle school principals take heroic mea-sures like buying expensive software or crafting daily schedules by hand, it often becomes a lot easier to sort everybody by reading scores. So kids who do well on reading tests can land in the high track for math, science, social studies, even lunch, and move together as a self-contained unit all day. Friendships form, attitudes harden. Kids on top study together, kids in the middle console themselves by making fun of the "nerds" above and the "dummies" below, and kids on the bottom develop behavioral problems and get plenty of negative reinforcement.

> **It's easier for educators to tinker with programs and make cosmetic adjustments than it is to ask them to do what bureaucrats hate most: give up one method of doing things without having another to put in its place. Tracking is a system; untracking is a leap of faith.**

By high school, many low-track students are locked out of what Jeannie Oakes calls "gatekeeper courses," the science, math, and foreign language classes that hold the key to life after twelfth grade. Doors to college are slamming shut, though the kids themselves are often the last to know. When re-searcher Anne Wheelock interviewed students in Boston's public schools, they'd all insist they were going to become architects, teachers, and the like. What courses were they taking? "Oh, Keyboarding II, Earth Science, Consumer Math. This would be ju-nior year and I'd ask, 'Are you taking Algebra?' and they'd say no."

Black marks

A funny thing can happen to minority students on the way to being tracked. Even when minority chil-dren score high, they often find themselves placed in lower tracks where counselors and principals assume they belong.

In Paula Hart's travels for The Achievement Council, a Los Angeles-based educational advocacy group, she comes across district after district where black and Latino kids score in the 75th percentile for math, yet never quite make it into Algebra I, the classic gatekeeper course. A strange phenomenon occurs in inner city areas with large minority populations—high track classes shrink, and low track classes expand to fit humble expectations for the entire school population.

A few years ago, Dr. Norward Roussell's curiosity got the best of him. As Selma, Alabama's first black school superintendent, he couldn't help but notice that "gifted and talented" tracks were nearly lily white in a district that was 70 percent black. When he looked for answers in the files of high school students, he discovered that a surprising number of low track minority kids had actually scored higher than their white top track counterparts.

Parents of gifted and talented students staged a full-scale revolt against Roussell's subsequent efforts to establish logical standards for placement. In four days of public hearings, speaker after speaker said the same thing: We're going to lose a lot of our students to other schools. To Roussell, their meaning was clear: Put black kids in the high tracks and we pull white kids out of the system. More blacks and more low-income whites did make it to the top under the new criteria, but Roussell himself was left behind. The majority-white school board chose not to renew his contract, and he's now superintendent in Macon County, Alabama, a district that is overwhelmingly black.

Race and class divisions usually play themselves out in a more subtle fashion. Talk to teachers about how their high track kids differ from their low track kids and most speak not of intelligence, but of motivation and "family." It seems that being gifted and talented is hereditary after all, largely a matter of having parents who read to you, who take you to museums and concerts, and who know how to work the system. Placement is often a matter of who's connected. Jennifer P., a teacher in a Brooklyn elementary school saw a pattern in her class. "The principal put all the kids whose parents were in the PTA in the top tracks no matter what their scores were. He figures that if his PTA's happy, he's happy."

Once the offspring of the brightest and the best connected have been skimmed off in honors or regular tracks, low tracks begin to fill up with children whose parents are not likely to complain. These kids get less homework, spend less class time learning, and are often taught by the least experienced teachers, because avoiding them can become a reward for seniority in a profession where perks are few.

With the courts reluctant to get involved, even when tracking leads to racial segregation and at least the appearance of civil rights violations, changing the system becomes an arduous local battle fought school by school. Those who undertake the delicate process of untracking need nerves of steel and should be prepared to find resistance from every quarter, since, as Slavin notes, parents of high-achieving kids will fight this to the death. One-time guidance counselor Hart learned this lesson more than a decade ago when she and two colleagues struggled to introduce a now-thriving college curriculum program at Los Angeles' Banning High. Their efforts to open top-track classes to all students prompted death threats from an unlikely source—their fellow teachers.

Off track betting

Anne Wheelock's new book, *Crossing the Tracks*, tells the stories of schools that have successfully untracked or never tracked at all. Schools that make the transition often achieve dramatic results. True to its name, Pioneer Valley Regional school in Northfield, Massachusetts was one of the first in the nation to untrack. Since 1983, the number of Pioneer Valley seniors going on to higher education jumped from 37 to 80 percent. But, the author says, urban schools continue to lag behind. "We're talking about unequal distribution of reform," Wheelock declares. "Change is taking place in areas like Wellesley, Massachusetts and Jericho, Long Island. It's easier to untrack when kids are closer to one another to begin with."

It's also easier for educators to tinker with programs and make cosmetic adjustments than it is to ask them to do what bureaucrats hate most: give up one method of doing things without having another to put in its place. Tracking is a system; untracking is a leap of faith. When difficult kids can no longer be dumped in low tracks, new ways must be found to deal with disruptive behavior: early intervention, intensive work with families, and lots of tutoring. Untracking may also entail new instructional techniques like cooperative group learning and peer tutoring, but what it really demands is flexibility and improvisation.

It also demands that schools—and the rest of us—admit that some kids will be so disruptive or violent that a solution for dealing with them must be found *outside* of the regular public school system. New York City seems close to such a conclusion. Schools Chancellor Joseph Fernandez is moving forward with a voluntary "academy" program, planning separate schools designed to meet the needs of chronic troublemakers. One of them, the Wildcat Academy, run by a non-profit group of the same name, plans to enroll 150 students by the end of the year. Wildcat kids will attend classes from nine to five, wear uniforms, hold part-time jobs, and be matched with mentors from professional fields. Districts in Florida and California are conducting similar experiments.

Moving away from tracking is not about taking away from the gifted and talented and giving to the poor. That, as Wheelock notes, is "political suicide." It's not even about placing more black and Latino kids in their midst, a kind of pre-K affirmative action. Rather, it's about raising expectations for everyone. Or, as Slavin puts it: "You can maintain your tracking system. Just put everyone into the top track."

That's not as quixotic as it sounds. In fact, it's

long been standard practice in the nation's Catholic schools, a system so backward it's actually progressive. When I taught in an untracked parochial high school, one size fit all—with the exception of the few we expelled for poor grades or behavior. My students, who differed widely in ability, interest, and background, nevertheless got Shakespeare, Thoreau, and Langston Hughes at the same pace, at the same time—and lived to tell the tale. Their survival came, in part, because my colleagues and I could decide if the cost of keeping a certain student around was too high and we had the option of sending him or her elsewhere if expulsion was warranted.

The result was that my honor students wrote elegant essays and made it to Ivy League schools, right on schedule. And far from being held back by their "regular" and "irregular" counterparts, straight-A students were more likely to be challenged by questions they would never dream of asking. "Why are we studying this?" a big-haired girl snapping gum in the back of the room wondered aloud one day. Her question led to a discussion that turned into the best class I ever taught.

In four years, I never saw a single standardized test score. But time after time I watched my students climb out of whatever mental category I had put them in. Tracking sees to it that they never get that chance. Flying directly in the face of Yogi Berra's Rule Number One, it tells kids it's over before it's even begun. For ultimately, tracking stunts the opportunity for growth, the one area in which all children are naturally gifted.

CHILD CARE:
What Do Families Really Want?

Parents are hard-pressed to find facilities that are accessible, affordable, and reliable.

Photo courtesy of Kinder Care

Michael Schwartz

Mr. Schwartz is director, Center for Social Policy, Free Congress Research and Education Foundation, Washington, D.C.

WHEN PARENTS seek substitute care for their children, there are three fundamental considerations they weigh—accessibility, affordability, and reliability. The first two seem to be fairly obvious. A substitute caregiver must be accessible: near home and work. Any arrangement that entails substantial added commuting time is not practical. Similarly, the cost of child care must not take up such a large portion of a family's disposable income that it seriously would diminish the benefits of working.

These two factors so closely are related that they could be combined under affordability. If a family can afford to pay, accessible child care will be available. The market of providers is so flexible that it is potentially infinite. The Department of Labor concluded in 1988 that there is no lack of child care. There may be temporary, localized shortages, but the market has proved to be highly responsive to these situations. Where a need appears, someone inevitably and quickly moves to fill it.

The question of reliability is more problematic. When parents hire a babysitter for even one night, they want to be confident their offspring will be safe and secure. This concern is even greater when it is a matter of entering into an arrangement for substitute care on a regular basis over a long period of time.

What constitutes reliability is a highly individualized judgment. Most parents probably have experienced child care arrangements they found unsatisfactory for some reason, and have shopped around for a better one. The factors they weigh in making a judgment about the reliability of a substitute caregiver could be extremely varied.

Parents may be concerned about the meals their youngsters are served or the kind of entertainment offered to them, as well as the ages and behavior of the other children being cared for. The physical environment in which their kids are placed may be uppermost in their minds. In many cases, it may be a personal response to the substitute caregiver. If they find one they like, who inspires confidence and builds a positive relationship with their children, other, more easily measured factors may pale in significance.

Government is incapable of making these personal judgments. What it can do, and does, to address the reliability of child care is to establish certain minimum standards for commercial child care. This is reasonable because there are some objective, measurable conditions the state has a right to demand of those who offer a service on the market.

Yet, it must be admitted that a regulatory standard is a clumsy instrument for guaranteeing a satisfaction that depends so heavily on intangible factors. People will have various conceptions of what is acceptable, desirable, and ideal. Most of all, they will have different ideas about who is trustworthy. The main task of regulation is to protect children from foreseeable threats to their health and safety. As regulation goes beyond that point, it becomes a matter of replacing the personal judgment of parents with the abstract decisions of regulators not directly involved in the relationship.

Currently, Congress is considering legislation that would establish certain minimum regulatory standards for virtually all commercial child care providers. It is very important, in this connection, to bear in mind that the issue is not whether there should be regulatory standards, but whether they should be set at the state or Federal level. Each of the 50 states already has a set of regulatory standards they have determined are best suited to their particular circumstances and conditions.

Are Federal standards needed?

The question, then, is whether Federal law, in the interest of increasing the reliability of child care, should replace the standards set by the states with more stringent ones. This is ill-advised for several reasons.

In the first place, there is no evidence that the existing standards in any state are inadequate. Many of the tragedies that have occurred to youngsters while they were under the care of parental substitutes have resulted from unforeseeable accidents. Some have involved instances in which local regulatory standards were violated. Far more often, they have resulted from circumstances in which children were placed in situations beyond the reach of state regulation, frequently without adult supervision at all. In no instance has it been shown that a child has suffered harm because a state regulation was so lax that it placed his or her health and safety in danger.

The argument has been made that there are Federal standards for airline and consumer product safety and environmental pollution, so they should exist for child care as well. This analogy, however, fails in at least three ways:

● The safety of airplanes or the flammability of pajamas can be measured objectively, scientifically, and precisely. The reliability of child care is not amenable to this sort of laboratory analysis.

● It neither would be practical nor in the public interest to have 50 different sets of safety standards for products that are sold throughout the country. However, child care is not an interstate industry. It is a highly localized neighborhood business.

● There already are standards in all 50 states that—on the record, at least—are adequate to ensure the health and safety of all children covered by them. Thus, there is no reason to substitute the judgments of Federal regulators for those of the millions of consumers, providers, and state and local authorities who have established the existing standards.

A second significant consideration when weighing the advisability of Federal child care standards is that there is a trade-off between regulatory standards and the cost and availability of child care. The more stringent standards become, the more expensive it is for providers to meet them, and the more they must charge their clients. Those states with stricter regulatory standards tend to have a relatively smaller proportion of children cared for in a state-regulated setting, compared to the ones with more relaxed standards.

The states have had to strike a balance between maximizing standards at the cost of affordability and accessibility, or maximizing affordability and accessibility by placing fewer demands on child care providers. Connecticut, for example, has chosen to pursue the former course; Florida, the latter. Both of these decisions are honest attempts to serve the public good. It must be noted, however, that a far larger proportion of the children of Florida who are in substitute care are in regulated settings than in Connecticut.

Imposing stricter standards through Federal intervention will have at least two consequences. It will raise the cost of regulated child care in the affected states and prompt more providers and consumers to seek out arrangements that escape regulation, leaving a higher number of youngsters in unregulated care settings.

The industry trade journal, *Child Care Review,* conducted a study to assess the impact of Federal minimum standards on a single aspect of child care—staff-child ratios. It concluded that, if proposals pending before Congress become law, the cost of child care to consumers would increase by an average of $350 a year, and one-fifth of the licensed providers would go out of business, leaving more than 750,000 fewer places for children in licensed centers.

The impact of this single regulatory change would not fall evenly on the entire country. Some states would be unaffected, while others would suffer catastrophic dislocations in the child care market. In Arizona, for instance, parents would have to pay almost $750 a year more for licensed care. In South Carolina, the increase would be over $1,300. In Florida, more than 150,000 youngsters would be displaced from licensed care, while 250,000 places would disappear in Texas.

In those states that have chosen to emphasize accessibility and affordability by imposing lighter regulatory burdens on providers, licensed child care is plentiful and cheap. The system is working for families of modest means. Under Federal regulation, it would not, and they and their children would be hurt by strict standards.

Consumer choice is the key

In the final analysis, even the most stringent standards do not guarantee reliability because trust can not be imposed by regulation. What is far more effective than regulation is consumer choice. Where competition exists, consumers can ensure satisfaction by taking their business elsewhere if they lose confidence in a child care provider.

In order for the market to work this way, consumers must have the financial means to exercise choice. The family that can not afford more than $30 a week has very limited options. One that can spend $60 will have more choices open. Those who can pay $150 will have no problem finding care that meets their requirements. The problem is that there are a lot more families in the $30 than the $150 bracket.

Families of modest means have little choice except to take what is available at the price, and often that is not entirely to their liking. One mitigating circumstance is that churches—particularly in low-income neighborhoods which for-profit providers would not find attractive—have been generous in establishing child care programs at below-market cost. This has cushioned the hardship of meager resources for thousands of families in a way they find highly satisfactory. In addition, the natural solidarities of extended families and neighborhoods have enabled families of modest means to find reliable child care at low cost. Yet, despite these bright spots, the one element that assures parental choice and gives them real leverage over the reliability of child care is their ability to pay.

For this reason, it would make more sense to commit the resources of the Federal government toward strengthening the financial position of consumers instead of restructuring the child care industry. Putting money into the hands of parents obviously addresses the question of affordability, but also addresses the other two issues. When parents are able to pay for child care, providers emerge. Child care becomes accessible where it may not have

been before. When parents have the means to choose among providers, they are able to demand standards of reliability they find satisfactory.

The current dependent care credit in the tax code is a well-intentioned effort to attain this objective. However, for a number of reasons, it fails to aid most of those families who are most in need of help. The main weakness is that it is keyed to spending money for child care; in general, the more one can afford to spend, the larger the credit. Families of modest means would find it more in their interest to spend as little as possible for child care and forgo the benefits of the tax credit, rather than take fuller advantage of the credit by spending more.

The way out of this dilemma is to break the link between receiving the credit and spending money for substitute care. There are many parents who rely on non-monetary child care in exchange for some other service they can provide the substitute caregiver; who adjust their working hours—often sacrificing additional income and leisure time in the process—to ensure the presence of one parent at home all the time; or work at home and care for their offspring simultaneously.

Not everyone is in a position to do this, but those who do should not be penalized by the denial of a benefit they would qualify for if they hired someone else to watch their children. They often are people who place the welfare of their kids above short-term economic gain. In general, their children are better off because of the sacrifices their parents make. In effect, they are reducing the burden on the child care industry, thereby helping to keep accessibility up and costs down for those families who do patronize commercial providers.

The equitable approach to this is to issue an income supplement to families with young children in the form of a refundable tax credit. It should be scaled inversely to income, so that those with the greatest need would receive the most assistance. It need not be offered to families who earn significantly more than the median income, since that would amount to a transfer of income from the less to the more affluent. Clearly, budgetary considerations will determine the size of this credit and the number of families who will be eligible for it, but Federal resources should be stretched as far as possible to strengthen the economic position of families with children.

This solution goes directly to the heart of the child care dilemma—financial security. The only reason parents have to seek out substitute caregivers is so they can be free to earn enough money to support their kids. Enhancing the income of families with children will do more to help improve the quality of life for youngsters, and do so more effectively, than any other step that can be taken by government.

Helping Students Understand and Accept Sexual Diversity

To help all students realize their full potential, schools must acknowledge the special needs of homosexual students; but they must also enhance students' understanding of the sexual diversity within each person.

JAMES T. SEARS

James T. Sears is Senior Research Associate at the South Carolina Educational Policy Center and Associate Professor in the Department of Educational Leadership and Policies at the University of South Carolina, Columbia, SC 29208.

Back from summer vacation, Phillip ambled up the red brick steps of Strom Thurmond Junior High School. At the top of the steps stood Edith, a big-boned 9th grader. A group of "redneck brats" stood behind her. Phillip had feared something like this would happen. "The night before I started 7th grade, Edith called me up. She said, 'I hope you know I have a lot of friends. I told them *all* about you. We're going to make your junior high days pure hell.' "

Mary sat in study hall staring out into the unknown. "Are we deciding too fast? Maybe we should just not label ourselves and just experiment. But Connie says 'I don't think we should knock being with a boy until we've tried it.' I like boys—I just don't think about them so much sexually or emotionally. I like Connie. Am I the only one who feels this way?" Mary lays her head down on her unopened math book.

Though Phillip and Mary may feel alone, they are not. There are many Phillips and Marys who experience intimidation and suffer in fearful silence within our nation's schools. In response to their plight, the NEA, the AFT, and ASCD recently passed resolutions calling upon their members and school districts to acknowledge the special needs of students like Phillip and Mary, to provide supportive services to these students, and to adopt anti-harassment guidelines. The in-school counseling program for homosexual-identified youth established by the Los Angeles Unified School District, the Harvey Milk School supported by the New York public school system, and the anti-slur/anti-discrimination policies adopted by school districts in cities such as Cambridge, Des Moines, and Cincinnati exemplify such efforts (Grayson 1989, Rofes 1989, Sears 1987).

Educators, school board members, and parents who have spearheaded these efforts acknowledge the simple social fact that being sexually different in a society of sexual sameness exacts a heavy psychological toll. Struggling to cope with their sexual identity, gay and bisexual students are more likely than other youth to attempt suicide, to abuse drugs or alcohol, and to experience academic problems (Brown 1987, Gibson 1989, Martin and Hetrick 1988; Remafedi 1987, Sears 1989). Of course, gay and bisexual students do not always display these symptoms—in fact, they may excel in schoolwork, extracurricular activities, or sports as a means of hiding their sexual feelings from themselves or others (Sears 1991). When they hide their feelings, however, their emotional and sexual development languishes (Martin 1982).

The Diversity of Sexuality

Tagging these young people "at risk," providing supportive services, establishing policies and guidelines, and integrating homosexuality into sex education acknowledges sexual differences among people. Splitting the school and society into unequal heterosexual and homosexual categories, however, does not enhance an understanding of sexual diversity within each person.

Being gay or lesbian is a modern-day phenomenon. Just as "homosexual" is a 19th century, enlightened, medical construction, "gay" and "lesbian" are social artifacts popularized in contemporary America (Altman 1982, Greenberg 1988). However, the basic emotional and erotic attraction to members of one's own sex is not a social artifact. As Freud (1964), Bullough (1976), and Kinsey and Associates (1948, 1953) have shown, *human beings are diverse sexual creatures*: Our capacity to relate emotionally and physically to other human beings is not limited to the other gender.

More than 40 years ago, Alfred Kinsey and his associates found that nearly half of the adult population engaged in both heterosexual and homosexual activities—a finding that still troubles many Americans. Kinsey concluded that the world is not divided into sheep and goats; he contended that "patterns of heterosexuality and patterns of homosexuality represent learned behavior which depends, to a considerable degree, upon the mores of the particular culture in which the individual is raised" (Kinsey et al. 1948, p. 660). The construction of sexual identities does not take place within a social vacuum.

On the contrary, scholars such as Kenneth Plummer (1981), Carol Kitzinger (1987), and Michael Foucault (1978) have illustrated that *sexual biographies are integrally related to soci-*

By James T. Sears, "Helping Students Understand and Accept Sexual Diversity," *Educational Leadership*, Vol. 49, No. 1, September 1991, pp. 54-56. Reprinted with permission of the Association of Supervision and Curriculum Development.

> **From every vantage point, there are couples: couples holding hands as they enter school, couples dissolving into endless wet kisses between school bells.**

energy pulsating in even the most boring of classes.

At any given day in any particular school these feelings span the sexual continuum, yet only those at the heterosexual end are publicly acknowledged and peer approved. When sexuality is formally discussed in health or biology class, heterosexual mechanics are most often presented (leave it to schools to make even the most interesting subject emotionally dry, moralistically rigid, and intellectually sterile). Homosexuality, safer sex practices, abortion ethics, and sources of birth control are the topics least discussed by sex educators (Forrest and Silverman 1989, Sears in press).

In many school districts, developing critical thinking skills is a stated priority, yet few districts extend these skills across the curriculum. Sexuality education is a case in point: sexual values are taught, not explored; sexual danger is stressed while sexual pleasure is minimized; heterosexual intercourse is pre-

> **There is a great need for a healthy, frank, and honest depiction of the fluidity of sexual behavior and sexual identities.**

sented as the apex of the pyramid of sexual desire. Questions such as how being male or female defines one's sexual options, how sexual options and values vary across time and culture, why masturbation is considered less desirable than sexual intercourse, and how one distinguishs the "gays" from the "straights" are never asked, never encouraged, never addressed.

ety. Society provides the collective cultural history, social scripts, and language that form the foundation for these constructed identities. The personal meanings of our regional, social class, racial, gender, and sexual identities are inextricably woven into a culture in which being upper class or working class, black or white, male or female, homosexual or heterosexual, from the North or the South, have social significance. While the intersections of social class, race, gender, sexuality, and region vary for each person, their existence and importance within our culture are, for those who do not share membership in the dominant groups, social facts with social consequences.

Shaping Heterosexual Destinies

The culture of the school mirrors the larger society. Schools socialize boys and girls into their presumed heterosexual destiny. From every vantage point, there are couples: couples holding hands as they enter school; couples dissolving into endless wet kisses between school bells; couples exchanging rings with ephemeral vows of devotion and love. Sex, as many a high school student will freely admit, is an integral part of school life. And while educators may be reluctant to integrate this topic into the curriculum, covert sexual instruction comprises a large part of the hidden curriculum at any junior or senior high school: the exchange of lustful looks in the hallway or romantic notes in the classroom, the homoerotic comradery of sports teams, and the sexual

Resources for Teaching About Sexual Diversity

In Every Classroom: The Report of the President's Select Committee for Lesbian and Gay Concerns. A useful compilation of statistics, essays, and suggestions for teaching staff concerned about the quality of campus life for lesbian and gay students. Rutgers University, 301 Van Nest Hall, New Brunswick, NJ 98903.

Not All Parents Are Straight. A film that examines the various questions surrounding the issue of children raised by gay, lesbian, or bisexual parents. Cinema Guild, 1697 Broadway, New York, NY 10019.

Rappin', Teens, Sex, and AIDS. A comic book written in the language of adolescents in which African-American and Latino youth visit a health educator who speaks frankly to them about sexual issues. Multi-Cultural Training Resource Center, 1540 Markey St., Suite 320, San Francisco, CA 94102.

Sticks, Stones, and Stereotypes. This film gives viewers an appreciation of differences by examining the negative effects of name calling and the desire

for assimilation. Equity Institute, 48 N. Pleasant St., Amherst, MA 01002.

Dance On My Grave, by A. Chambers. The story of a first gay experience with an emphasis on friendship. New York: Harper and Row, 1982.

Annie on My Mind, by N. Garden. An account of a friendship between Liza Winthrop, an intelligent and successful high school senior from a wealthy section of Brooklyn who meets Annie Kenyon, a working class girl who attends public school in the city. The two quickly become friends, then slowly and sometimes painfully acknowledge that their relationship has both a romantic and a sexual component. New York: Farrar, Straus & Giroux, 1982.

National Gay and Lesbian Caucus of the American Federation of Teachers. P..O. Box 19856, Cincinnati, OH 45219.

Federation of Parents and Friends of Lesbian and Gay, P.O. Box 27605, Central Station, Washington, DC 20038.

Breaking Through the Conspiracy of Silence

There is a great need for a healthy, frank, and honest depiction of the fluidity of sexual behavior and sexual identities. Yet too many educators are partners in a conspiracy of silence in which sexual knowledge is what is salvaged after the scissors-and-paste philosophy of religious zealots or homosexual activists are applied.

The capacity of people to create and recreate their sexual identities is an integral component of the new holistic sexuality curriculum, which must redefine the meaning of "teaching for diversity." Then, we will not only recognize and support the development of the Phillips and Marys among us, but we will help all students realize their full human potential.

References

Altman, D. (1982). *The Homosexualization of America, The Americanization of the Homosexual*. New York: St. Martin's Press.

Brown, L. (1987). "Lesbians, Weight, and Eating: New Analyses and Perspectives." In *Lesbian Psychologies: Exploration and Challenges*, edited by the Boston Lesbian Psychologies Collective. Urbana: University of Illinois Press.

Bullough, V. (1976). *Sex, Society, and History*. New York: Science History.

Foucault, M. (1978). *The History of Sexuality*, Vol. 1. New York: Pantheon.

Freud, S. (1964). *Leonardo da Vinci and a Memory of Childhood*, translated by A. Tyson. New York: Norton.

Forrest, J., and J. Silverman. (1989). "What Public School Teachers Teach About Preventing Pregnancy, AIDS, and Sexually Transmitted Diseases." *Family Planning Perspectives* 21, 2:65–72.

Gibson, P. (1989). "Gay Male and Lesbian Youth Suicide." In *Report of the Secretary's Task Force on Youth Suicide, Vol. 3: Prevention and Interventions in Youth Suicide*. Washington, D.C.: U.S. Department of Health and Human Services.

Grayson, D. (1989). "Emerging Equity Issues Related to Homosexuality in Education." *Peabody Journal of Education* 64,4: 132-145.

Greenberg, D. (1988). *The Construction of Homosexuality*. Chicago: University of Chicago Press.

Kinsey, A., W. Pomeroy, and C. Martin. (1948). *Sexual Behavior in the Human Male*. Philadelphia: Saunders.

Kinsey, A., W. Pomeroy, C. Martin, and P. Gebhard. (1953). *Sexual Behavior in the Human Female*. Philadelphia: Saunders.

Kitzinger, C. (1987). *The Social Construction of Lesbianism*. London: Sage.

Martin, A. (1932). "Learning to Hide: The Socialization of the Gay Adolescent." In *Adolescent Psychiatry: Developmental and Clinical Studies,* edited by S. Feinstein and J. Looney, pp. 52–65. Chicago: University of Chicago Press.

Martin, A., and E. Hetrick. (1988). "The Stigmatization of Gay and Lesbian Adolescents." *Journal of Homosexuality* 15, 1-2: 163-185.

Plummer, K. (1981). *The Making of the Modern Homosexual*. London: Hutchinson.

Remafedi, G. (1987). "Adolescent Homosexuality: Psychosocial and Medical Implications." *Pediatrics* 79,3: 331-337.

Rofes, E. (1989). "Opening Up the Classroom Closet: Responding to the Educational Needs of Gay and Lesbian Youth." *Harvard Educational Review*, 59, 4: 444-453.

Sears, J. (1987). "Peering Into the Well of Loneliness: The Responsibility of Educators to Gay and Lesbian Youth." In *Social Issues and Education: Challenge and Responsibility*, edited by A. Molnar. Alexandria, Va.: Association for Supervision and Curriculum Development.

Sears, J. (1989). "The Impact of Gender and Race on Growing Up Lesbian and Gay in the South." *NWSA Journal* 1,3: 422-457.

Sears, J. (1991). *Growing Up Gay in the South: Race, Gender, and Journeys of the Spirit*. New York: Haworth Press.

Sears, J. (in press). "Reproducing the Body Politic: Dilemmas and Possibilities in Sexuality Education." In *Sexuality and the Curriculum*, edited by J. Sears. New York: Teachers College Press.

Teenage sex: Just say 'Wait'

The search is on for new and more effective ways to teach teens about the facts of life

JOSEPH P. SHAPIRO

Nine in 10 Americans agree: Schools should teach kids about sex. That, however, is the end of the consensus. Most adults fall into opposing camps on exactly *which* of the facts of life to teach. The "throw in the towel" crowd concedes, with value-free resignation, that having sex is normative teen behavior and the most that adults can do is teach young people how sperm meets egg, toss out loads of condoms and hope for the best. Meanwhile, the "stop it" forces call for scaring teens into premarital chastity with horror stories of shame and disease. Neither solution, however, works very well with today's sophisticated teenagers. That is clear from teen birthrates: After falling for more than a decade, they began climbing rapidly in the late 1980s and are now at their highest levels since the early 1970s—before the widespread availability of birth control and abortion.

Now, a third way of thinking has begun to emerge among sex educators and public-health workers that combines the abstemious and lenient approaches and stresses reaching younger children. The history of teen pregnancy prevention is littered with failure, and even this mixture of pragmatism and values-based teaching promises only modest results. But the results are positive enough to have drawn support from the woman who could be the nation's new sex-ed teacher, the blunt-spoken Joycelyn Elders, a sharecropper's daughter who became a pediatrician and who is now Bill Clinton's nominee to be surgeon general.

"Condom queen"? The debate over Elders makes clear that few subjects polarize the American public as easily as teen sex. As public-health chief of Arkansas, she started school-based health clinics, some of which distribute birth control devices, stirring opposition at home that is following her onto the national scene.

"Condom queen" is what Phyllis Schlafly calls Elders, echoing the many conservative groups opposing her nomination, for her support of abortion as well as of giving students birth control. Yet Elders's views on teen sex are mainstream enough to have garnered her endorsements from all the major medical and child health groups—from the American Medical Association to the Child Welfare League of America. Last week, however, questions over her personal finances forced a delay until this week of her confirmation hearings.

There is no denying that if she is confirmed, Surgeon General Elders will want a major change in federal policy. Since 1981, the federal response to teen pregnancy has been to teach students to remain chaste until marriage. Washington has spent some $31.7 million developing "abstinence only" curricula (or, as some of these programs put it, "secondary virginity" for those who have already lost theirs). Some of the programs have run into unexpected troubles. Earlier this year, the Department of Health and Human Services settled a suit that claimed these pro-chastity programs unconstitutionally promoted religion. In one classroom exercise, girls were told to imagine the ideal dating activities as things they would do if they were out with Jesus.

Beyond that, the main criticism is that such programs are unrealistic and ineffective because they never discuss birth control and simply expect teens to avoid sex, sometimes using almost comically out-of-touch techniques. "Pet your dog, not your date" is the slogan of the popular Sex Respect program, conducted in 1,100 school districts nationwide. While it is important to stress abstinence, notes Jerry Bennett, acting director of the HHS office that administers these programs, none of the "abstinence only" programs has a proven record of success.

Elders favors the middle road. She told *U.S. News* that she supports newer hybrid programs that "stress abstinence," particularly for the youngest teens, but believes it is unrealistic to demand abstinence only. She wants to "give kids the tools" to resist peer and societal pressures to have sex and aims to induce a new sense of social values in the young and teach children as early as kindergarten age that they have the right to decide who touches their bodies. "We need to have our kids understand that sex is good but it has to be appropriate," she says. Teens should be taught to make sound decisions about sex if they choose to have it, says Elders—including informed choices about birth control. But, says Family Research Council Director Gary Bauer, that approach sends a mixed message, akin to saying "it's illegal to shoplift, but if you do it, here are some tips on how to avoid getting caught."

Still, a decade of the abstinence-only approach has failed to end the long claim of the United States to the highest teenage pregnancy, abortion and childbirth rates in the West. Each year, 1 million girls under the age of 20—1 in 10—become pregnant; 43 percent of all adolescent girls will have been pregnant at least once by the time they turn 20. Black teens have the highest birthrates, but whites and Hispanics are closing the gap: In the last half of the 1980s, birthrates climbed by 25 percent for Hispanics, 19 percent for whites and 12 percent for blacks. It is clear that the problem cuts across racial, social and economic barriers. But for those who keep their babies, numerous studies have shown that parenthood is likely to lead to a trip down the economic scale into poverty.

The most troubling trend is that the largest jump in sexual activity is among teens under 16. It's not just that 72 percent of all students by their senior year of high school report having had sexual intercourse, but that 40 percent of 15-year-olds report the same, according to the Centers for Disease Control and Prevention—compared with just 10 percent of 15-year-olds in 1970. These and even younger children have the highest odds of contracting a sexually transmitted disease. Pregnant girls 16 and under are the most likely to drop out of school, then to deliver the sickest and smallest babies. And nearly 1 in 3 gives birth to a second child within two years.

Who is to blame? Social critics identify a welter of culprits, from media excesses and declining family values to—depending on which side is making the case—easy access to abortion (because it lets teens think sex can be risk-free) or the *decline* in abortion providers (because it leads to unwanted pregnancies). Even physiological reasons conspire: In the past 100 years, largely owing to improved nutrition, the average age of puberty for girls has dropped from 17 to 14.

There is no denying that the surge in teen pregnancies reflects larger developments in American society. Last year, according to a Census Bureau report released last week, 65 percent of teen births were to unmarried girls, up from 48 percent in 1980. That statistic mirrors America, as the same report showed. Nearly a quarter of unmarried women now become mothers, an increase of 57 percent in the past decade, and the rise has been sharpest among adults—particularly college-educated professionals.

Amid such statistics, America has been bombarded recently with harrowing scenes that confirm something is out of control when it comes to the way many teens think about sex. Most disturbing is the involvement of the youngest teens and even preteens. The molestation of a 10-year-old girl led to arrests in March of members of the Spur Posse, a group of middle-class boys in Lakewood, Calif., who proudly bragged of sex-for-points score keeping. In Yonkers, N.Y., last month, police charged nine elementary-school pupils, ages 9 to 13, with sexually abusing a 12-year-old girl. School officials had casually dismissed the incident as a "let's play rape" game. In most schools, sex education begins too late to instruct such young students—or even many older ones. One survey shows that among sexually active 15-year-olds, only 26 percent of boys and 48 percent of girls had had sex education by the time they first had intercourse.

Finding an answer. That it is the youngest who most need the abstinence message was clear to two Cincinnati doctors. For Dr. Reginald Tsang, the moment of recognition came as he watched a 13-year-old mother and father—who could have walked out of any junior-high school in America—peer over the rim of an incubator at their baby, no bigger than

Tsang's hand, and confide they had no idea what to do next. Tsang began to think about how "our societal chaos has overwhelmed our technological advances." After all, a computer-controlled neonatal unit like Tsang's at Cincinnati's Children's Hospital Medical Center now almost routinely saves 9 of every 10 babies born weighing as little as 2 pounds. At the same hospital, Dr. Joseph Rauh, an adolescent-medicine specialist, was similarly frustrated. He provided birth control to teens, but, he noted, 13- and 14-year-old girls were coming back pregnant, "bewildered and confused."

So, in 1991, Tsang (conservative and opposed to abortion) and Rauh (liberal and in favor of abortion rights) joined forces to find local funding for a new kind of sex-education program. The one they brought to Cincinnati grew out of a surprise discovery by Dr. Marion Howard in the late 1980s while she was surveying teens who received birth control information at her Atlanta clinic. Her clients wanted birth control, she says, but "84 percent wanted to know how to say no to someone pressuring them for sex—and to say no without hurting their feelings."

As a result, Howard developed a curriculum called Postponing Sexual Involvement. Discarding the old-fashioned approach—a gym teacher with a pointer and a reproductive-system poster giving rote lectures on sexual plumbing—Howard opted for a peer system that relies on teens as teachers. In PSI, older teens—especially school leaders and athletes—are chosen as believable messengers for the spiel: "I can postpone sex and still be cool." And teen leaders must also embrace abstinence themselves. "I'm happy because of my beliefs," says Monique Chattah, a Cincinnati peer leader. "I have a better self-image."

The heart of PSI is role-playing. In a recent PSI class in Cincinnati, seventh graders played out a classic confrontation: Boy takes girl on an expensive date and then insists on sex. The girls practiced handling the pressure, then the exercise was reversed, with the girl as the aggressor. This led to an open discussion of respect, values and even the way sex is glamorized in the media to sell products.

How to say no. The early signs are that PSI is filling an important need. National studies show that only 17 percent of girls say they planned their first sexual intercourse—meaning most apparently have sex because they don't know how to thwart advances, says Christopher Kraus, the coordinator of Cincinnati's PSI program. A 1991 survey of Atlanta students found that those who had gone through PSI training were five times less likely than other teens to have

started having sex by the end of eighth grade.

Still, the political divisiveness surrounding teen-sex programs—even those as neutral as PSI—threatens their effectiveness. Howard's curriculum omits specifics about how to use contraception, a concession to local authorities who typically want to decide on such teaching themselves. The result is a confusing muddle of programs. In Cincinnati itself, for instance, school officials opted for no birth control instruction. Meanwhile, across the Ohio River in suburban Newport, Ky., schools teach PSI to seventh graders—then give ninth graders a similar abstinence curriculum that, unlike PSI, provides birth control instruction. "It's being realistic," explains Maxine Jones of the Northern Kentucky District Health Department. And still another neighboring Kentucky county last week restricted the use of county taxes for any program that counsels any unmarried people about contraceptives.

In the end, the causes of teen pregnancy are so complex that even the most well-considered programs are limited in what they can accomplish. That is clear among some young Cincinnati women who meet at the Lower Price Community School in a neighborhood of brick tenements along the Ohio River. They are part of yet another teen-pregnancy program called the Birth Partner Project, which since last year has been helping young mothers try to avoid having a second child too soon, a development that often dooms their last chance to finish school or find jobs.

The women are at once realistic and naive. For example, Tina Daniels, 20, has enrolled in a local college this summer in hopes of becoming a social worker. Like most of her friends, Daniels planned her pregnancy—she knew that caring for a baby would give her the impetus she needed to leave a boyfriend she says was physically abusive—and her daughter is now 1½ years old. Although Daniels never took a PSI class, she still heard the abstinence message at the special school. She emerged as a leader among the mothers in the project and was the first to try Norplant, the surgically implanted birth control device that works up to five years.

Yet last month, Daniels had a doctor remove the Norplant. Her new boyfriend wanted a baby and then marriage next April. Now, the wedding is off but a second child is due in March. Daniels says the baby will not interfere with her dreams. Yet her pregnancy is a reminder that the causes of teen pregnancy are often ambiguous and trying to reduce teen birthrates is always formidable.

Everyone Is an Exception: Assumptions to Avoid in the Sex Education Classroom

More often than not, the teachers who are assigned to teach courses in sex education have little or no professional preparation to do so. Taking account of the difficulties inherent in the situation, Ms. Krueger provides helpful advice about how not *to proceed.*

MARY M. KRUEGER

MARY M. KRUEGER is the director of health education and an adjunct professor of public health at Emory University, Atlanta.

Illustration by Joe Lee

UNFORTUNATE though it may be, most public school teachers rarely have the opportunity (or luxury) to devote significant time to students as individuals. Such is the nature of our work — the classroom is made up of *groups* of people, and the moments in a school day when we can interact with our students one-to-one are infrequent at best. As a result, and in order to function with some degree of consistency, teachers usually develop and act on a set of generalizations and assumptions regarding students.

However, the unique nature of sex education — a field of growing importance as more and more states mandate its incorporation into the public school curriculum — necessitates a reexamination of some of these assumptions. To date 34 states have passed legislation requiring sex education in the schools, and additional state mandates are pending.[1] Nonetheless, there are no undergraduate degree-granting programs in the discipline, nor do any state boards of education certify teachers in sex education; most frequently, in fact, sex education courses are assigned to teachers with little or no professional training in the area.[2] Such teachers — who have been, in effect, *dumped* into the sex education classroom — are not only undertrained in method-

From *Phi Delta Kappan*, March 1993, pp. 569-572. Reprinted with permission of *Phi Delta Kappan* and the author.

165

ology and curriculum design but expected to facilitate activities and discussions in an exquisitely sensitive area. It is truly ironic that the sex education issues that are the most difficult for teachers (particularly undertrained teachers) to address are those in which teachers' assumptions have the potential to do the greatest disservice to students.

Regardless of their personal awkwardness or inexperience, sex education teachers have a special responsibility to avoid causing students embarrassment or pain. Above all, they have a duty to remember that their students are *individuals* with varying family backgrounds, experiences, and values.

During more than 12 years of experience in sex education, I have learned that sex education efforts are more effective when teachers respect students' individuality and interact with students in ways that make them feel unique and special. I have also become familiar with the most common (and dangerous) assumptions that teachers of sex education hold about students. I list them here, along with suggestions about how to avoid them. If teachers refrain from making these assumptions, their students will feel that their individuality is being honored and will thus be more willing to participate fully in and gain from lesson activities.

ASSUMPTIONS TO AVOID

1. *All students come from traditional nuclear families.* This misconception is especially relevant to the sex education classroom, with its (one hopes) frequent references to and encouragement of family communication about sexuality. Teachers who automatically refer to students' families with such phrases as "mom and dad" deny the experience of the majority of their students, as well as the realities of modern American culture.

In almost every region of the U.S., two-parent, traditionally structured families are now the exception.[3] Families no longer consist solely of nuclear groupings of heterosexual married couples and their biological children. Students' families may comprise such aggregations as single parents with children; married parents with children from the current and previous marriages; single or married parents with foster or adopted children; or cohabiting heterosexual or homosexual couples with biological, adopted, or foster children. If teachers are successfully to facilitate the full participation of

students in activities that involve parent/child communication and the clarification and validation of family values, we owe it to our students to remember that daily access to "mom and dad," in the traditional sense, is a fact of life for less than 20% of today's children.[4]

2. *All students are heterosexual.* Ten percent of students are *not* heterosexual, regardless of whether they have consciously internalized the fact yet.[5] It is common, yet potentially alienating to gay and lesbian students, to make unthinking references to male students' "girlfriends" or female students' "boyfriends." Such practices send a clear message to gay students that their sexual orientation is, at best, to be hidden and, at worst, abnormal and shameful.

In addition to promoting inclusive language with regard to sexual orientation, the field of sex education has an ethical obligation to condemn homophobic harassment and intimidation of gay, lesbian, and bisexual students. As one of society's most potent agents of socialization, schools are duty-bound to take a stand against hatred and ignorance and to allow all students to learn in a safe and nurturing environment. The denial of such an environment in the past has contributed to a suicide rate for gay and lesbian teenagers that is two to six times higher than that of heterosexual teens.[6] Gay and lesbian teens are also more likely than their heterosexual peers to drop out of school, become runaways, and abuse alcohol and other drugs.[7] Such self-destructive behavior is often the result of feeling overwhelmed by the challenge of learning to like oneself in a hostile world. Much of the self-doubt and inner turmoil that too often diminish the quality of life for these students can be averted by early and consistent messages of acceptance from adult authority figures. Sex education teachers are in a position to take significant steps toward that end.

3. *All students are sexually involved.* Many students are not sexually involved, and they need support for that decision. While we adults frequently wring our hands in concern over (and probably disapproval of) the percentage of "sexually active" teens, we must keep in mind that, in certain age groups and in many parts of the country, students who are not sexually involved are in the majority. However, they (like us) have been profoundly influenced by television, films, and the popular press, all of which send the

message that "everyone" is having sex. Because adolescence is a stage of life that so strongly emphasizes conformity, young people may respond to these societal pressures by feeling that virginity is something to be hidden — a source of embarrassment. In an environment that bombards teens at every turn with incentives to become involved with sex, the decision to resist — when one wants above all else to "fit in" — is difficult indeed.

In classroom presentations that address sexual behavior, teachers may unwittingly reflect this "of-course-all-teenagers-are-having-sex" mindset by, for example, phrasing references in the second person ("when you have sex, you need to be responsible"). Training oneself to speak almost exclusively in the third person when presenting lessons will allow students who choose abstinence to feel supported, normal, and comfortable with their decision (and respected for their courage in resisting peer pressure and acting in accordance with their own values).

4. *No students are sexually involved.* Despite all efforts to the contrary on the part of parents, teachers, and other concerned adults, students are becoming involved in sexual behavior with partners at increasingly younger ages. They need the skills to clarify their decisions and to protect their health. Surveys of American teenagers have found that the average age of first intercourse is 16. More than half of high school students have had intercourse at least once, and many participate in intercourse on a regular basis.[8]

With regard to these students, sex education teachers face another dilemma. While generally preferring that students avoid premature sexual involvement, with all its concomitant emotional and medical risks, savvy teachers realize that their preferences are irrelevant to the fact that significant numbers of young people are already involved in sexual behavior that was formerly considered the exclusive domain of adults. No truly caring teacher can choose to ignore the realities that accompany a young person's decision to be involved in sexual activity simply because the teacher is unwilling to face the fact that it is happening.

Teachers best serve the needs of sexually involved students by helping them to clarify their decisions and improve their decision-making skills, rather than making decisions for them; by educating them regarding the risks of early sexual activi-

> **M**ore than half of high school students have had intercourse at least once, and many participate in intercourse on a regular basis.

ty, without excluding the positive aspects of human sexual expression; and by expressing concern for their students' welfare, rather than standing in judgment of their behavior.

5. All students' sexual involvements are consensual. The faces we see in our classrooms every day include, by even the most rudimentary statistical calculations, more than one victim of sexual violence. It is estimated that 27% of girls and 16% of boys are sexually abused before they reach age 18.[9] Among adolescents, sexual abuse is the most common form of child abuse.[10] In addition, 50% of all rape victims are between the ages of 10 and 19, with half of that number under the age of 16.[11] Up to one-fourth of all college women report having experienced acquaintance rape.[12] (We must extrapolate from that figure to reflect the experience of junior high and high school girls, since the vast majority of research on acquaintance rape has focused on university populations.) Indeed, young people are being sexually exploited with frightening regularity.

Perhaps the best service a teacher can provide to students who have been sexually victimized is to be approachable, and certainly a sex education class offers a natural venue for students to approach a caring adult with questions and concerns. Among adolescents who have been sexually abused, 27% disclose the fact on their own initiative[13] — a figure that tells us that few adults are diligently looking for indicators of abuse or assertively seek-

ing information from survivors. By remembering that, for many students, sexual experience is, in fact, rape experience, sex education teachers can help students begin the necessary healing process, perhaps by putting students in touch with intervention services.

6. Students who are "sexually active" are having intercourse. A large number of young people are participating in sexual behaviors other than penis/vagina intercourse, thus rendering moot the overused and ill-defined catch phrase "sexually active." The most common expression of sexuality among teens is solo masturbation;[14] thus class discussions of sexual behavior that focus only on the risk of pregnancy or disease transmission exclude those students who are "sexually active" but not involved in behavior that puts them at medical risk.

Other nonintercourse behaviors, such as oral sex, partner masturbation, variations of "petting," and even such benign activities as kissing and hugging are part of the sexual repertoire of most adolescents. Ninety-seven percent of teenagers have kissed someone by the time they are 15; by age 13, 25% of girls have had their breasts touched by a partner. At least 40% of teens participate in partner masturbation.[15] By age 17, 41% of girls have performed fellatio on a partner, and 33% of boys have performed cunnilingus on a partner. Overall, 69% of young people who are sexually involved with a partner include oral sex in their behavior.[16]

When adults deny the full range of human sexual expression and regard only intercourse as "sex," students are denied an important educational opportunity. Many young people believe that there is no acceptable form of sexual behavior other than intercourse.[17] Operating under that assumption, students may put themselves at risk for unwanted pregnancy or sexually transmitted disease by engaging in intercourse when less risky sexual behavior would have been equally fulfilling. The myth that intercourse is the only way to act on one's sexual feelings has surely contributed significantly to such negative phenomena as premature pregnancy and the spread of sexually transmitted diseases (including AIDS). Clearly, ignorance is anything but bliss where sexual health is concerned. Teachers who help young people learn that intercourse is not required to enjoy one's sexuality not only broaden their students' horizons, but also impart knowledge that may help lower rates of adolescent preg-

nancy and sexually transmitted disease by lowering the rate of adolescent intercourse.

SCHOOLS ARE increasingly expected to address social problems that were formerly the province of the family, religious organizations, and social agencies. Understandably, teachers often feel overwhelmed by the prospect of dealing with sexuality, pregnancy, sexual abuse, and other complex issues facing young people. Complicating matters further are teachers' fears that sex education curricula are necessarily controversial, that they will incite negative community reaction, and that the majority of parents will disapprove. Indeed, both prospective and current sex education teachers are vociferous in expressing doubts about their ability to deal with potential objections to their curricula.[18]

Since the likelihood of avoiding all controversy when operating a school-based sex education program is slim, the best approach may be to expect and accept diversity of opinion among members of the community, to respect well-intentioned questioning of curricula and methodology, and to operate with unflagging vigor despite any limitations that may result from controversy.[19] Teachers' primary concern, however, *must* remain the well-being of the students, and the work of sex educators needs to be steeped in an awareness of the unique manner in which sexuality and well-being interact. If teachers know their material, believe in the importance of the program, and have clearly defined goals and objectives (one of which is the best possible quality of life for students), then they will be able to comfortably defend those curricular approaches that protect students' health, life, and individuality.

The sweeping alterations in American lifestyles, family structures, and interpersonal mores that have marked recent decades have been mind-boggling indeed. Precisely because modern society is so complicated, family organization so tenuous, and support systems so capricious, students need more than ever to be viewed as individuals. As teachers dealing with topics of an especially personal and sensitive nature, let us remember that, in one way or another, each of our students is an exception. Let us celebrate and respect the uniqueness of our students — because, when we do, we earn for ourselves the right to expect the same kind of treatment in return.

1. Debra Haffner, "1992 Report Card on the States: Sexual Rights in America," *SIECUS Report*, February/March 1992, pp. 1-7.

2. Mary M. Krueger, "Sex Education by State Mandate: Teachers' Perceptions of Its Impact" (Doctoral dissertation, University of Pennsylvania, 1990).

3. Steven Mintz and Susan Kellogg, *Domestic Revolutions: A Social History of American Family Life* (New York: Free Press, 1988); and Mary S. Calderone and Eric W. Johnson, *The Family Book About Sexuality* (New York: Harper & Row, 1985).

4. Calderone and Johnson, op. cit.

5. A. Damien Martin, "Learning to Hide: The Socialization of the Gay Adolescent," *Adolescent Psychiatry*, vol. 10, 1982, pp. 52-64.

6. "Suicide Major Cause of Death for Homosexual Youth," *Contemporary Sexuality*, September 1989, p. 3.

7. Laura Pender, "Growing Up Gay," *Cincinnati Magazine*, February 1990, pp. 26-29.

8. Mark O. Bigler, "Adolescent Sexual Behavior in the Eighties," *SIECUS Report*, October/November 1989, pp. 6-9.

9. Calderone and Johnson, op. cit.

10. Janet Eckenrode et al., "The Nature and Substantiation of Official Sexual Abuse Reports," *Child Abuse and Neglect*, vol. 13, 1988, pp. 311-19.

11. Donald E. Greydanus and Robert B. Shearin, *Adolescent Sexuality and Gynecology* (Philadelphia: Lea and Febiger, 1990).

12. Robin Warshaw, *I Never Called It Rape* (New York: Harper & Row, 1988); and Jean Hughes and Bernice Sandler, *Friends Raping Friends: Could It Happen to You?* (Washington, D.C.: Project on the Status and Education of Women, Association of American Colleges, 1987).

13. Warshaw, op. cit.

14. Kenneth R. Sladkin, "Counseling Adolescents About Sexuality," *Seminars in Adolescent Medicine*, vol. 1, 1985, pp. 223-30.

15. Robert Coles and Geoffrey Stokes, *Sex and the American Teenager* (New York: Harper & Row, 1985).

16. Susan F. Newcomer and J. Richard Udry, "Oral Sex in an Adolescent Population," *Archives of Sexual Behavior*, vol. 14, 1985, pp. 41-46.

17. Sladkin, op. cit.

18. Ione J. Ryan and Patricia C. Dunn, "Sex Education from Prospective Teachers' View Poses a Dilemma," *Journal of School Health*, vol. 49, 1979, pp. 573-75; and Krueger, op. cit.

19. Peter Scales, *The Front Lines of Sexuality Education* (Santa Cruz, Calif.: Network Publications, 1984).

Building a Smarter Work Force

Vocational education in the U.S. must be expanded and modernized, in the manner of other industrialized countries, to help build high-performance work organizations.

Ray Marshall and Marc Tucker

Ray Marshall, formerly secretary of labor under President Jimmy Carter, is a professor of economics and public affairs at the University of Texas at Austin. Marc Tucker is president of the National Center on Education and the Economy (based in Washington, D.C., and Rochester, N.Y.).

American enterprise has been organized on the principle that most workers do not need to know much, or be able to do much, beyond what's necessary to perform narrowly defined tasks. The high productivity growth that the United States enjoyed until recently was made possible by giving our workers the most advanced equipment on the market. Today, however, the same equipment is available to low-wage countries that can sell their products all over the world—including here in the United States—at prices way below ours. If we continue to compete with them on wages and hours, as we are now doing, real wages will continue the decline that began in the 1970s and hours will increase until they match the low-wage competition. In short, the U.S. standard of living will plummet.

The alternative is to join the ranks of countries such as Germany, Japan, Sweden, and Denmark that promote high-performance work organizations. In such businesses, highly skilled, well-paid front-line workers are given many of the responsibilities of managers—tasks such as scheduling production, ordering parts, and attending to quality control.

The advantages of this form of work organization are enormous. The ranks of middle management and many support functions are thinned out, creating a large productivity gain. Quality improves dramatically. There is better coordination of the myriad functions involved in manufacturing a product, and far fewer mistakes. Improvements in design and construction are made constantly, instead of waiting for new model introductions,

creating a strong market advantage. It becomes possible to go after small market segments, because success no longer depends on producing thousands or millions of identical products. Worker motivation and morale are greatly enhanced, because workers take real pride in their work. Taken together, these changes give firms a decisive edge over low-wage, low-skill competitors.

Unfortunately for the United States, high-performance work organizations hinge on a well-educated work force. The U.S. system of educating and training workers has been shaped around the meager demands of "scientific management," where employers design the jobs of their front-line workers so that they require little knowledge or ability. U.S. skill requirements look more like those of Third World countries than those of the leading industrial nations.

Third World skills are fine for companies that choose to compete with South Korea, Mexico, and the Philippines. But firms that want to take on Germany and Japan are finding themselves at a disadvantage. The scant minority—fewer than 5 percent—of American firms that are embracing high-performance forms of work organization report that they are experiencing or expect to face a shortage of skilled labor. If the vast majority of employers were to adopt high-performance organization, there would be a skilled-labor shortage of epic proportions.

The economic future of the United States depends mainly on the skills of the front-line work force, the people whose jobs will not require a baccalaureate degree. Success, then, depends on developing a program to prepare close to three-quarters of our work force to take on tasks in restructured workplaces that, up to now, have been assigned mainly to the college educated. The idea that Americans just turning 19 or 20 would come to the job equipped for such tasks might sound like the stuff of fantasy, but it is increasingly common in many European countries. If it does not happen here, the United States will simply be unable to attain the rates of productivity growth and deliver the quality that it must achieve.

7. SERVING SPECIAL NEEDS AND CONCERNS

So far, our record on educating workers has been grim. More than a quarter of American students—perhaps as much as half our future front-line workers—drop out of school. We do virtually nothing to recover them. We spend an average of about $4,300 a year on our high-school students, but only $235 a year trying to give those who drop out the education and job skills they will need to survive in our economy.

Half of our high-school students, and a much higher fraction of our future front-line workers, are in the "general" curriculum, enrolled neither in the academic track for the college-bound nor in the vocational track. Most of them emerge from school—with or without a diploma—with eighth-grade academic skills or worse. And they do no better with respect to vocational skills. Twenty-five percent of the vocational courses in the United States are taken by the general-curriculum students. The result is that most of our future front-line workers leave school with academic and vocational skills that fall below those of virtually all mature industrialized countries and many newly industrialized countries. In other words, they leave school with Third World skills.

U.S. employers spend about $30 billion a year to educate and train their workers. But two-thirds of that sum goes to college-educated employees, and 90 percent of it is paid out by only one-half of one percent of the nation's firms. Therefore the vast majority of American front-line workers get no further formal education or training after they leave school.

HOW OTHER COUNTRIES TRAIN STUDENTS

The extent of our failure can best be seen by comparing what we do with the job-training systems common in other countries. The methods by which Japan, Germany, Sweden, and Denmark arrange for a high level of vocational competence among their front-line workers differ greatly, but the result is the same: all four nations boast work forces that are among the most highly skilled in the world.

In Japan, the best vocational education occurs in companies. The country's well-known system of lifetime employment in the large firms, combined with the Japanese practice of shifting workers from one job to another, makes employers more than willing to pay for job training; they know that the investment will be recovered. By 1992, for example, Toyota plans to put all new high-school graduates it hires for the front line through a two-year full-time course in digital electronics and "mechatronics." The company's assembly-line workers will then have roughly the same qualifications as junior engineers in the United States.

Schools still play an important role. They are closely linked with employers and typically provide their graduates with a smooth transition to the workplace. Japanese firms look at the schools as they look at any other

supplier, cultivating close relations and demanding the highest possible quality.

The process by which young people enter the work force takes place in stages. First, firms send literature—and even videotapes—about themselves to schools at all levels. Recruiters stay in touch with high-school teachers, taking them to lunch, inquiring about the quality of their students, and urging them to encourage their best students to consider employment at their firm. Just before the students graduate, the big firms ask the principals of schools with which they have a special relationship to select the most qualified students for the available jobs on the basis of their academic performance as judged by the school staff.

The Japanese system provides a powerful motivation to all non-college-bound Japanese youth to do well in school, because the judgment of one's teachers is crucial. It also gives teachers far more authority than those of the non-college-bound in the United States have ever dreamed of having. Most important, it provides a swift, dependable entry for Japanese youth into real careers in the labor market.

In Germany, work is built on a centuries-old craft tradition, where workers tend to identify less with a particular company than with the trade or occupation in which they apprentice, become journeymen, and achieve—or hope to achieve—master status.

Germany's apprenticeship system provides the superb worker preparation that is a key factor in the country's economic success.

The German skills-development system begins early in school with the *Arbeitslehrer*, a formal program about industry that is compulsory for all grade-school students except those in a *Gymnasium*, a secondary school for college-bound students. Then, at age 15 or 16, most students not going on to college become apprentices with an employer in one of 480 trades and occupations.

Apprentices typically spend one day a week at a *Berufschule* (state vocational school) specializing in the student's trade and four days in a structured program of training at the employer's work site, guided by a master. In their two to three years of training, the apprentices receive a training wage, which gradually increases. At the end of the contract period, the apprentice faces a pencil-and-paper exam and a careful review of selected work samples. Apprentices who pass are awarded a certificate honored by employers all over Germany that attests to their having the skills required to assume journeyman status in their trade or occupation.

Given the costs that must be borne by the firms and the detailed regulations they must follow, one wonders why they don't just let the competition train future workers and then hire them away, much as U.S. firms would. But the companies view apprenticeship as a profitable investment. Since 90 percent of the apprentices remain employed by the firm that trains them, companies can tailor training to their specific needs. Many managers came up through the apprenticeship system and take great pride in continuing the tradition. And because all the large firms train, none are afraid that a nonparticipating firm will take unfair advantage.

These German apprenticeships constitute a national mentoring system, resulting in the superb preparation of the front-line worker that is a key factor in German economic success.

In Sweden, work experience begins at age seven, in first grade. Swedish students spend from one to several weeks a year in various kinds of workplaces, finding out what people do and how they do it. Representatives of employers visit schools as these kids are growing up, describing their industries and the careers within them.

When Swedish students are 16 and about to enter upper secondary school, they choose from among 27 courses of study within 6 divisions: arts and social sciences, care professions, economics and commerce, technology and science, technology and industry, and agriculture, horticulture, and forestry. All these programs include core courses in Swedish, English, and mathematics.

For the 75 percent of Swedish students who do not plan to go to college, 10 to 20 percent of their first and second years, and as much as 60 percent of their third year, are spent in the workplace. School vocational counselors, advised by industry committees, are responsible for organizing the "work-life" experiences of these students. Through the three years of upper secondary school, the student's field of vision narrows from familiarization with the occupational requirements of a broad industry group to the development of strong skills in a particular job. But the Swedish system, unlike the German, is designed *not* to commit youth to a narrow specialization for life. By exposing young people to a wide range of occupations, Swedish authorities hope to enable citizens to shift occupations with relative ease.

By guiding out-of-school youth into job-training programs, Sweden's Youth Centers put most dropouts back on track toward productive careers.

In stark contrast to the United States, Sweden also has a national dropout recovery program. In 1980, the Swedish Parliament enacted legislation holding every municipality responsible for locating disadvantaged and disaffected out-of-school youth between the ages of 16 and 18, recruiting them into a job-training program, and securing work opportunities for them. The result is the country's system of Youth Centers, which has been highly successful in putting the vast majority of dropouts back on track toward productive careers.

Denmark goes even further than Sweden in ensuring that its non-college-bound students will be able to apply their skills in a range of trades. As in Germany and Sweden, most Danish youth not going on to university participate in a three-year program of combined work and study after they complete the tenth grade. Periods of work alternate with time spent in study at a technical college. But the Danes also try to impart generic "work skills"—such as self-motivation, communication, organization, and creativity—that employers value in high-performance settings.

In a large company, the work-study program begins with a few days of orientation, followed by 6 to 12 months of training in teamwork and the functioning of self-governing groups. Then comes a brief period of formal individual training. The rest of the program, about two years long, consists of project-based, self-directed learning. Groups of trainees who intend to specialize in different but complementary areas are given complex long-term projects that require the skills of everyone in the group. The teams are expected to organize themselves and to reach their goal without supervision. They have access to any member of the firm and to any of its information sources, but they must locate the people and information on their own.

Team members keep diaries recording the problems they encounter, the approaches they are taking to address them, and the progress they make on acquiring the skills they need to meet the standards set by the employers. Each trainee meets regularly with his or her teachers to evaluate progress. The students are expected to constantly assess their learning; the teachers act like mentors and coaches but do not engage in direct instruction. This scheme has become a paradigm of the work environment in a high-performance organization.

Another appealing feature of the Danish vocational system is that it leaves the door open to higher education. As Danish youth progress through the job-training system, they are free to take courses that, if passed, qualify them for admission to university. In this way, the Danes have made explicit provisions for a no-dead-end system, one where people can always advance to the level of opportunity that more education affords.

REVAMPING VOCATIONAL EDUCATION

In describing what other countries do to ensure a successful transition from school to work, we do not mean to imply that nothing of value goes on in the United States. We know of secondary vocational schools, for-profit technical schools, and community colleges that prepare their students well for challenging and rewarding careers, that have strong ties to employers, that are responsive to shifting industry requirements, and that have the latest equipment on which their students can train. We know of good grade-school programs that acquaint students with a wide range of careers, dropout recovery programs that plainly do what they were intended to do, and curricula that are explicitly designed to help students develop generic work skills.

But these are all isolated occurrences, running against the grain of a system that produces, overall, dismal results. What the country sorely lacks is a system that embraces the great majority of our students and prepares them to become productive members of a highly capable front-line work force.

It is doubtful that we would serve this country well by replicating any of the systems of other industrialized nations. We can certainly learn from their successes, but we must keep in mind their different cultural contexts—and outright shortcomings. For example, the Germans are themselves concerned about the rigidity of their system of narrow lifelong specialization in trades and occupations. What's more, the strong pride in the ancient German craft system that motivates employers to invest large sums in vocational education voluntarily is wholly lacking in the American experience.

The Japanese system, where the schools are responsible for producing graduates with a high level of "general intelligence," would appear to be much better adapted to a world of changing job requirements. But this system, too, has liabilities. Although large employers make massive efforts to provide first-rate vocational skills to their new hires, these firms employ only about a third of Japanese workers, leaving the others to depend on a weak backup network of state-run vocational schools. The other drawback of the Japanese system is the lack of any formal national system for recognizing vocational qualifications. In a highly mobile country like the United States, such a system is essential if individuals are to invest in themselves and have the opportunity to realize that investment when they move.

The United States must construct its own system for developing strong technical and professional skills in high-school students not going directly to a four-year college—a system that builds on the best practices of the leading industrial nations. Specifically, that means:

Setting aside several weeks each year for grade-school students to visit work sites and learn about the range of career opportunities.

All students need this exposure, not just those headed for the workplace right out of school. Most of our children learn about what goes on at work from movies and television, which give a highly distorted picture. The problem is particularly severe for poor and minority children, but it applies in some measure to almost everyone. There is no substitute for visiting workplaces and talking to the people who work in them.

No nation in which a quarter of the students fail to complete secondary education can hope to have a world-class work force.

Many U.S. educators reject the idea that schools exist in part to prepare people for work. This view partly accounts for the primacy of college as the only goal worth working for in school—but this has to change. Teachers themselves will have to be persuaded that work not requiring a college degree can be challenging, rewarding, and the source of real status. That task should become easier as the number of high-performance work organizations grows.

Creating a system of youth centers through which municipalities recover dropouts.

No nation in which a quarter of the students fail to complete secondary education can hope to have a world-class work force. South Korea's dropout rate is only 10 percent, and Sweden's rate—thanks to its Youth Center program—is even less. Every state should require its municipalities to operate alternative education and work-experience programs based on the Swedish model. Whenever a student dropped out of school, the school district would have to notify the nearest youth center, which would then actively recruit that student.

Many existing programs—ranging from the Job Corps to programs run by churches and community organizations—already have the capacity to do some or all of the functions we would assign to youth centers. The youth centers would contract with such organizations and with school districts to get the job done. The point is not so much to create new institutions as to designate one local agency to take sole responsibility for recovering every dropout.

How to fund such a program? Every local, state, and federal dollar earmarked for a student's education in a regular high school should follow the dropout to the youth center. While this will not be an easy requirement to meet for states and localities experiencing hard fiscal times, there is overwhelming evidence that the nation would save far more in reduced welfare and prison costs.

Building the vocational education system on a base of real academic accomplishment.

Without exception, the countries with the most successful vocational education systems realize that job training must be complemented by solid academic skills. In most U.S. school districts, one can get a high-school diploma if one shows up most of the time and does not cause any trouble. The states that do impose some sort of performance requirement rarely set the standard above seventh-grade equivalency.

We urge adoption of "certificates of initial mastery," to be awarded to most students around age 16 when they pass an appropriate examination. The subject matter would encompass reading, writing, listening, and speaking, as well as mathematics, the sciences, history, and the social sciences, the arts, and work skills, but the examinations would place a premium on the capacity to integrate knowledge from many of these disciplines in solving problems. Students would be able to take the performance exams as often as they liked until they passed them.

By setting a single standard for everyone, we break ranks with the Europeans, who use their exams to sort students out, dividing those who will go to college from those who will not. Students who get their certificate would be able to choose whether to begin a technical and professional certificate program, enroll in a college preparatory program, or go directly into the work force.

Providing access for all students who want it to a high-quality on-the-job learning experience leading to a universally recognized qualification.

The United States ought to create a system of technical and professional certificates covering most trades and occupations not requiring a four-year college degree. The certificates would be awarded when students completed a three-year program of combined schooling and structured on-the-job training and passed a written and practical examination. Programs could be offered by many kinds of institutions—high schools, vocational schools, employers, community colleges, and for-profit technical schools among them—working singly or in combination, but always teamed with employers offering the job-site component. These institutions would compete for students' tuition.

Much of the money required to meet this commitment would come from a repackaging of government funds now spent on the last two years of secondary school and the first two years of college. But other funding could come from employers, especially if—as we recommend below—firms are required to contribute to the continued education and training of their employees.

Each state and industry should have a strong voice in constructing the system and an equally strong role in administering it, but it must be a national system, with national standards, nationally recognized certificates, and a system of occupational classifications that do not vary by jurisdiction. Anything less will lead to a system that will reduce the mobility of our work force or lower individuals' incentive to train, or both. The country will almost surely begin to create this system industry by industry and state by state, but the aim from the start must be to make it truly national.

Designing the work-based portion of the program so it develops the qualities needed for high-performance work organizations.

The United States faces something of a dilemma. On the one hand, a system of technical and professional

standards is urgently needed, and it is only common sense that these standards should be largely set by employers. On the other hand, most employers today would design standards around jobs that ask little of the people who have them.

Perhaps the United States should rely mainly on employers who are using advanced forms of work organization to formulate the new standards and then devise a curriculum, much like that of the Danes, explicitly to prepare our youth to function in the new work milieu. No doubt many young people will be employed at first by organizations that are not prepared to give them all the responsibility they have been trained to exercise or take advantage of all the skills they bring to the job. But these new employees can be powerful agents of change and can make it easier for forward-looking employers to restructure their workplaces.

Providing incentives to employers to invest in developing their employees.

Most advanced nations require companies to invest at least 1 percent of wages in continuing education and training. So should the U.S.

Most advanced nations and many newly industrialized countries require employers to invest a sum equal to at least 1 percent of salaries and wages for continuing education and training. The United States should require companies to do likewise—or, if they are unable or unwilling, to contribute to a government-operated Skills Development Fund, which would supply the education and training. Only expenditures on programs leading to state educational certificates, industry-wide training certificates, or recognized degrees would satisfy the requirement.

The situation is urgent. If we continue on our low-performance work track, real wages will fall much faster in the next 20 years than they have in the last 20. As that happens—and as the proportion of our population in the work force continues to drop—tax revenue will fall, and the investment capital required to educate and train our front-line workers will be increasingly hard to come by. Many states already find themselves in just such a bind. If we do not change course before 2010, when the baby boomers—77 million people—begin turning 65, and straining our pension and health resources, we could truly reach a point of no return.

If ever there was a time to make the choice for a high-skill work force, it is now.

What the 'V' Word Is Costing America's Economy

Ms. Aring outlines a new vocational system that she believes will shift the educational debate away from ensuring equal access to college and toward providing all students with a choice of the education and training system that best meets their own and the nation's needs.

MONIKA KOSMAHL ARING

MONIKA KOSMAHL ARING is director of the Institute for Education and Employment at the Education Development Center, Newton, Mass.

Illustration by Mario Noche

AT LEAST two other industrialized nations, Japan and Germany, have surpassed the U.S. in competitiveness in world markets and in growth of productivity. A report by the Commission on the Skills of the American Workforce and other studies conclude that the U.S. standard of living continues to drop as we teeter on the brink of an economic cliff.[1] The lack of a formal school-to-work transition system for both college-bound and non-college-bound youths is a major contributing factor. Even though the U.S. has the greatest number of employable youths, it is the only highly industrialized nation without a first-class system of vocational education. Perhaps that is so because in the U.S. *vocational* — the "V word" — is a dirty word, its negative connotations

From *Phi Delta Kappan*, January 1993, pp. 396-404. Reprinted with permission of *Phi Delta Kappan* and the author.

deeply embedded in language and culture.

Efforts are under way to change this situation. Within the past several years, a number of school-to-work demonstration projects have been started around the country, led in part by the U.S. Department of Labor, which in 1989 established an Office of Work-Based Learning.[2] In doing so, the department endorsed the concept that students in the K-12 system can more easily learn a number of valuable skills when classroom and workplace settings are connected. In 1990, acknowledging that future generations of workers were not acquiring valuable technical skills as students, Congress authorized the Department of Education to introduce a new, school-based track called "tech prep." The tech prep program would establish a formal technical track linking the last two years of high school with two years of community college.

Unfortunately, it is entirely possible that these and similar efforts will ultimately fail. The reason is this: if we think of the word *vocational* as a kind of "mental box," and if that box is considered "bad," then any new program we put into that box will become bad. Unlike Germans, who consider all education vocational because it leads to an occupation, Americans tend to associate "vocational education" with narrow training for marginal students and to think of it as preparation for manual, low-status work or, at best, work in the blue-collar trades. Economic data support our negative definition. The real income (adjusted for inflation) of Americans who have not attended college — 80% of the population — has consistently dropped during the past 20 years.[3] And as well-paying jobs for vocationally educated workers disappeared during the same time period, the negative view of things vocational was reinforced.

It must come as no surprise that today many middle-class parents insist that vocational education is definitely "not for my kid."[4] However, closer examination reveals that a number of different meanings for *vocational* coexist in the U.S. For example, consider the negative connotation of vocational tracks within comprehensive high schools, which are often dumping grounds for the worst students. Compare that with the positive perception of regional vocational centers, which offer better education and training and have students waiting in line for admission. To confuse matters even more, the term *vocational* has come to be identified in urban areas with inequities of race, gender, and language, as large concentrations of minorities, especially African-Americans and Hispanics, take part in vocational programs.[5]

> Americans tend to associate "vocational education" with narrow training for marginal students.

Given the high costs of defining vocational education in such a negative and charged way, what do we gain by doing so? Our negative definition gives us a way to sweep our marginal youths under the rug. But on a deeper level, our definition allows us to ignore the fact that our young people have different sets of skills and intelligences and that aptitudes for either practical or abstract skills are not dependent on racial origin or socioeconomic background.

HISTORICAL FACTORS AND VALUES

In general, the dominant values of the culture of American education grew out of the British system, which sent the sons of its aristocratic landowners to college to become managers who would not get their hands dirty in the production process. In Britain, only the lower classes were deemed fit to do the actual labor. Not surprisingly, Great Britain today faces economic problems similar to those of the U.S. It has been referred to as a "declining society," and its people now earn wages only one-half to two-thirds as high as those of their neighbors.[6]

We must also remember that the American colonies split from Britain during the height of that country's Industrial Revolution, at a time when even children were subjected to grueling working conditions for very low wages. Over the next two centuries, Britain would remain a society with a largely rigid class structure, a society whose educated elite went off to college and whose laboring classes left school early to go to work. Perhaps the fear of reproducing this sort of economic structure helped to make college such a desirable goal for everyone in the U.S., where the rhetoric of equal opportunity for all precluded a strictly class-based society.

HOW INDUSTRY DEVELOPED IN THE U.S.

The first 150 years of our nation's life were consumed with the acquisition and cultivation of large areas of land, as the nation grew westward. Cultivation of one's own land — as opposed to developing a craft — was the most widely followed avenue to a secure future. However, farming in the 18th and 19th centuries required enormous quantities of human labor, the demand for which was satisfied through the importation of slaves from Africa and the Caribbean.

The rapid westward expansion in turn created a need for a transportation infrastructure, which demanded an ever greater supply of new labor, drawn from endless streams of immigrants from Asia and Europe. The expansion of railroads and related industries led to the creation of a class of industrialists who became the American aristocracy. For the most part, such industrial leaders forgot as quickly as possible their own often humble beginnings and sent their sons to colleges, where they would receive the academic — not vocational — education they thought they would need to work in management. Despite a number of movements on behalf of vocational education, the push for academic or "abstract" education leading to college grew ever stronger.

EMPLOYMENT POLICY, LABOR UNIONS, AND MASS PRODUCTION

While American employers would continue to hire and fire as dictated by production cycles, employment laws in Europe made it virtually impossible to fire or lay off production workers. As a result, it was to the advantage of European employers to invest in the development of a broad base of skills, since a broadly skilled worker could more easily be moved to different tasks within the company as production needs changed. This strategy was supported by the labor unions, which argued for ever broader skills training and education.

In the U.S., mass production, which brought American productivity to its zenith in the 1940s and 1950s, did not require a broad base of skills. Labor unions bargained for their members' security and accepted fairly narrow job descriptions that were based on performing repetitive tasks on the mass production assembly line. Thus, instead of investing in developing the skills of production workers, U.S. industry focused almost all its resources on the further education and training of its college-educated managers — to the tune of $30 billion in 1989. This practice again reinforced the negative perception of the vocational track.

BEHAVIORIST THEORY IN THE U.S.

In the U.S. the strong push toward an academic education leading to college for all coincided with the birth of behaviorist theory in psychology during the 1930s. Behaviorism, which asserted that learning is a system of linear operations best accomplished by breaking a task into its minutest parts and then testing accordingly, appeared to provide U.S. educators with a pedagogy that could prepare anybody for college.[7] By building on the theory of behaviorism, U.S. educators differed from their colleagues in Europe, who followed the theories of Piaget and other developmental psychologists. Piaget argued that about half of any population does not develop the intellectual ability to handle "formal operations in an abstract context."[8] Only now are U.S. education theorists recognizing that many students may learn better in applied settings, something acknowledged all along in most European countries.[9] Ironically, the U.S. military, which successfully educates and prepares young men and women for skilled occupations in a variety of industrial sectors, consistently teaches its trainees in applied settings.

Within the U.S. public education system, incentives became increasingly structured so that teachers' and students' status rose in proportion to the level of abstraction being taught and learned. With notable individual exceptions, vocational teachers were relegated to the bottom of the heap, and "applied academics," as their courses came to be called, became so diluted that just about anyone could pass. Debates that could have focused more fruitfully on developing different educational opportunities for the needs of different students and different industries focused instead on how to guarantee all students equal access to the same goal: college.

THE INFLUENCE OF AN EXPORT-BASED ECONOMY

The 16th-century Protestant Reformation in Germany meant that, perhaps for

> Only now are U.S. theorists recognizing that many students may learn better in applied settings.

the first time in history, a man could be judged for his deeds, not his lands or inherited titles. This new emphasis on deeds as opposed to wealth and landholdings helped put a new value on production and quality. The development of powerful guilds further helped build a culture of excellence that focused on practical experience and know-how, as well as on the theoretical understanding required for the successful practice of a craft.

While Great Britain imported raw materials and exported technical assistance and goods within its empire, the Germanic countries depended more heavily on a strong and powerful export capacity. Only by exporting could they gain from other countries the raw materials they needed for their internal consumption and for the production of exportable goods. From the start this focus on exports required close collaboration between business, government, and education. This combination of circumstances led to the development of a middle-class population with a broad base of skills and knowledge. Status depended not on acreage owned, but on the ability to produce a high-quality product.

More recent developments in European history, such as the devastating inflation that hit in the first part of this century, led to a further emphasis on maintaining a close coordination between supply and demand in the labor market. Reasoning that an adequate pool of highly skilled workers is the best hedge against rising labor costs in their economy, the Germans — and now all other European countries — invest heavily in macro- and microeconomic policies that help ensure a continuous supply of the highly skilled labor necessary for the successful production of goods for the export market.

VOCATIONAL EDUCATION IN GERMANY

Since Germany is recognized as a world leader in vocational education, it is enlightening to compare vocational education in Germany and in the United States. Because all education is considered inherently vocational in Germany, the focus there is not on the quality of different types of education but on the setting in which the student learns and on the likelihood that he or she will enter an occupation on completion of a program of study. It is true that learning in an academic setting (that is, a university) is still considered more prestigious in a number of quarters in Germany, but approximately 70% of German youths between the ages of 16 and 19 elect to enter the dual system of youth apprenticeship, believing that they are more likely to get a good job by learning in an applied setting, even if they later go on to a university. Ray Marshall and Marc Tucker report that "fully one-third of German university-trained engineers came up through [that nation's] apprenticeship system and then attended university, a path that would be virtually unthinkable for most U.S. engineers."[10]

Since the German dual system is coming under increasing scrutiny in the U.S., a brief summary of its salient features may be useful.

1. The system is called *dual* because students learn in two interconnected settings — the workplace and the school — by means of an interrelated curriculum.

2. Students' education and training are provided in the context of a particular industrial sector.

3. Because students in the dual system have to meet very high standards of education and skills, educators and employers are willing to give them far more responsibility and at a much earlier age than their counterparts in the U.S.

4. Disadvantaged students are expected to meet the same requirements as

everyone else. However, they are provided with substantially more resources in the process.

5. Education and training are not test-oriented. Throughout their apprenticeship period, students are judged by how successfully they meet standards that are developed jointly by business, education, labor, and government. Students are seen as workers who are expected to acquire whatever competencies are necessary to do the job right.

6. The dual system of education requires that labor, business, education, and government collaborate closely. The relationships of these partners — unlike those of their counterparts in the U.S. — are supportive, not adversarial.

7. There appears to be no evidence of a "forgotten half," and there appears to be virtually no secondary labor market (for example, dead-end jobs in fast-food chains or mall stores) where young people spend significant amounts of time.

8. Education and training at the job site are not job-specific or entirely company-specific. Instead, the emphasis is on socialization and on broad, industry-wide training, so that the young person will have maximum job opportunities and mobility within the companies that make up the industry. It should be noted, however, that in Germany, as in the U.S., significant inequalities can be found with regard to gender within different occupational apprenticeships.

9. The career paths available in the dual system are not dead-end streets or one-way alleys. Instead, education and training paths are structured so that virtually all young people can pursue further education, enter an occupation with a good future, or change industries and retrain.

10. Students going through the dual system must meet stringent requirements set by industry/state examination boards. They must not only spend a certain amount of time in an apprenticeship but must demonstrate their knowledge and skills during a two- or three-day examination period. Performance standards for the final exam are determined by a consortium that represents the particular industrial sector along with the labor union and the ministry of education.

Young Germans completing an apprenticeship in metalworking, for example, must demonstrate through written, oral, and actual production work that they have mastered advanced algebra, calculus, probability, statistics, inorganic chemistry, metallurgy, written and spoken communications, business law and regulations governing the industry, and at least one foreign language. Students entering apprenticeships in banking are systematically rotated through all the departments of a bank, but only after having mastered curricular requirements for solving problems related to each department. Since many smaller banks cannot offer an apprentice training in such areas as export finance, small banks are required to send young apprentices to a regional training center, so that they can gain the knowledge and skills connected with financial transactions in the international market.

> Vocational education in the U.S. tends not to be seen as a viable preemployment training system.

Finally, it is important to note that student apprentices are taught in school and in the workplace by teachers who are respected and highly trained. The school and workplace teachers coordinate their teaching with assistance from *Ausbildungsberater*, industry experts whose function is to provide technical assistance to workplaces and educators. Curricula are determined by the requirements set by the consortium of representatives from the industrial sector, labor, and the ministry of education. Instruction is often project-centered, requiring students to work in teams to solve progressively more difficult problems.[11]

VOCATIONAL EDUCATION IN THE U.S.

The picture in the U.S. is quite different and for the most part reflects the pejorative use of the term *vocational*. In its 1989 report, *Made in America*, the MIT Commission on Industrial Productivity concluded that, "though high school vocational education in the U.S. has been supported by the federal government for over 70 years and enrolls about five million students annually, it has a very disappointing performance and is not generally viewed as a viable preemployment training system."[12] Co-op education fares little better. Perhaps because most current high school co-op programs are closely linked to vocational programs, co-op programs tend to suffer from similar problems facing students in vocational tracks.

In a recent study titled *Transition from School to Work*, the General Accounting Office cited the negative perception of co-op programs as a significant barrier to developing high-quality apprenticeship programs in the U.S.[13] Many comprehensive high schools offer co-op programs in the vocational trades. Ironically, while in the 1930s John Dewey strongly argued that comprehensive high schools were the means of avoiding the stigma and isolation of vocational education, 60 years later vocational students in comprehensive high schools tend to be the lowest academic achievers.[14] At best, these students get to work some time each day on real equipment (most of which is obsolete). Their teachers usually have little, if any, real experience in industry and are often considered the worst teachers in the system.[15] With few exceptions, most students never see the inside of a high-performance work environment, where statistical process control or other quality measures require sophisticated skills in problem "finding" and solving,[16] communication, and teamwork.

The curricula used to instruct such students generally do not reflect the needs of the future labor market, in which one worker will be required to do sophisticated tasks previously done by several workers. Academic courses for students in vocational tracks are usually out of date and watered down to the lowest possible level.[17] In most cases, "industry advisory panels" do little except rubber-stamp curricula developed by the schools. Teachers of college-prep math, science, or English would find little in common with teachers of vocational — or "applied" — math, science, or English. Finally, the method of instruction is almost always teacher-centered, and students gain little or no experience in teamwork, communication, and how to go about solving complex problems.

Generally speaking, employers do not

see vocational high school programs as a prime source of skilled or even trainable workers. Indeed, the mere fact of having participated in a vocational program often "stigmatizes workers in the eyes of employers."[18] U.S. industry does not recognize completion of a vocational program (with the possible exception of vocational training in the military) as a valid entry-level credential, since a formalized criterion of success — something like a vocational counterpart to the college boards — has never been established for such programs.[19]

WHAT OUR DEFINITION OF 'VOCATIONAL' COSTS US

Productivity. According to statistics from the U.S. Department of Labor, since 1969 the rate of increase in productivity has been lower in the U.S. than in Canada, France, West Germany, Italy, Japan, and the United Kingdom.[20] The MIT Commission on Industrial Productivity states that "the origins of the problem . . . lie in the institutions that educate Americans for work. We have concluded that, without major changes in the ways schools and firms train workers over the course of a lifetime, no amount of macroeconomic fine-tuning or technological innovation will be able to produce significantly improved economic performance and a rising standard of living."[21] The commission goes on to say that, although training that produces narrowly skilled workers has been part of the productivity problem, the same training methods were an integral part of a winning model for assembly line work in the heyday of the American economy.

Standard of living. A nation's standard of living largely depends on the rising productivity of its work force. A rising standard of living depends on the capacity of a nation's firms to achieve high levels of productivity and to increase productivity over time.[22] American productivity per worker has increased by very low percentages during the past 20 years. This has led to a decline in our standard of "material well-being," which is lower than that of many advanced, industrialized nations. From 1973 to the present, the income of the average Japanese and German went from 50% and 60% of U.S. average income to 120% and 130% of U.S. income respectively.[23]

Of the six major factors contributing to this decline,[24] three (outdated strategies, neglect of human resources, and failures of cooperation) directly relate to how we have devalued "vocational." An example of outdated strategies is our placing such a high premium on white-collar management jobs — not getting our hands dirty in the production process.

> To compete successfully, the U.S. must produce goods that cost less or display superior quality.

Compared to companies in other countries and to foreign companies producing in the U.S., American businesses are top-heavy.[25] Yet U.S. companies persist in spending virtually all of their training funds on management. Our neglect of human resources is reflected in our lack of investment in front-line workers in virtually every industrial sector. This neglect has been exacerbated by our economy's pronounced shift from manufacturing toward service industries — industries that generally suffer a low rate of productivity. Today, about 65% of all American employees work in some kind of service industry. No other industrialized nation has as high a percentage of workers in the service sector.[26] The third factor, failures of cooperation, shows up in the way our vocational education system is isolated from its academic cousin, college prep, and in the way individual companies fail to collaborate with one another in joint education and training strategies.

Ability to compete in the export market. During the past 20 years the balance of trade has shifted, so that the U.S. now imports more than it exports. American industries have consistently lost significant market shares in virtually every major industry. To compete successfully in the world market, the U.S. must produce goods that either cost less or display superior quality. Since labor costs in the U.S. are high compared to those in developing nations, U.S. firms must focus on superior quality, producing "differentiated products that command premium prices."[27] However, the production of such goods depends on a highly skilled, flexible work force. Creating such a work force, in turn, requires enormous investments in building the skills of front-line production workers, whose blue collars are turning white as they perform tasks that previously required several workers, including managers. Our current definition of "vocational" is too narrow and too pejorative to accommodate the complex academic, technical, and communication skills that such workers must possess.[28]

WHAT WE MUST DO

1. *Fully integrate minority groups into the economy.* By the year 2000, 85% of the incoming U.S. work force will be nonwhite and/or female. Only 15% of the new entrants into the work force will be white males, the population group that has traditionally held the best-paying jobs. As the pool of largely white, often immigrant craftsmen nears retirement, employers in a number of industrial sectors face an alarming shortage of new skilled workers. With the change in the makeup of the incoming work force, the major source of new, skilled workers will be the African-American, Hispanic, and female segments of the population — all groups that have, until now, filled the lower-skilled jobs.

In Chicago, the nation's metalworking center, several hundred jobs are opening up each year for a variety of metalworking crafts. A similar situation exists in Pennsylvania and in a number of states in the Great Lakes region, where the relatively low-skilled manufacturing jobs of the past have been replaced by jobs requiring sophisticated levels of numeracy, literacy, and communication. For example, as recently as 20 years ago, almost anyone with a little training in a high school shop could become a car mechanic. Today, automotive repair technicians must be able to read complex manuals, understand and use multisystem wiring charts, use a battery of sophisticated diagnostic instruments, cost out work, analyze their own performance with statistical process controls, and communicate with customers so that they feel their problems are understood. In Cleveland the number of new job openings in automotive repair is expected to top 20%, as aging skilled workers near retirement.[29] The starting salaries for many of these jobs are upward of $25,000 a year.

A similar situation exists in many other cities and in different manufacturing and service sectors, including health care, financial services, wholesale/retail, and hospitality. In many of these industries, the cost of finding new entry-level workers, particularly in the inner cities, is becoming prohibitive.[30] Furthermore, there is a rapidly growing demand for workers to fill a host of technical jobs, which call for fairly sophisticated mid- to upper-level skills that rely heavily on mathematics, the sciences, and communication. All of the jobs just mentioned require what Europeans would call "vocational education." But instead of preparing first-class vocational education systems for our young, Congress quietly lifts the immigration quotas to admit more skilled workers from abroad.[31]

2. *Recognize the importance of output measures: performance-based skill standards.* The concept of performance-based skill standards that allow students to demonstrate their mastery of high-level academic, technical, and communication skills lies at the heart of the first-class European vocational systems. In Germany, Austria, Switzerland, and Denmark, vocational students take three-day exams, which are every bit as respected as the exams that qualify students for entrance into a university.

Although in the U.S. the Secretary's Commission on Achieving Necessary Skills is developing basic skill standards for students within traditional school settings, many people — including parents and educators in the minority community — view any imposition of standards with skepticism, suspecting that it is another device to screen out certain youths. Ironically, performance-based skill standards would give minority parents a way to expose those institutions that do a poor job of preparing their children.

The exciting opportunity presented by performance-based skill standards is threefold. First, standards can serve as an externally accepted benchmark that can give students valuable feedback on what they still need to learn. Second, standards can provide a "floor of skills" on which students can build further learning or

training, depending on the career they choose. And third, they can be the impetus for devising a host of remedial strategies to help those who are not able to meet the standards. Unfortunately, many educators and parents viewed with alarm the less demanding version of academic performance standards set forth in America 2000, which leaves out the requirements of industry altogether. But performance-based skill standards that are accepted by an entire industry and that require students to demonstrate their skills for a group of experts are the one means by which students of any color or background could demonstrate that they are as skilled as anyone else.

TOWARD A NEW DEFINITION OF 'VOCATIONAL'

In many industrialized countries, front-line workers are already solving complex problems without the help of managers. The nature of front-line work has changed, while our language has not kept pace. We need a new word, a bigger word, one that recognizes that distinctions such as "vocational," "academic," and "technical" belong to the labor market of the last century and will not be valid in the high-performance workplaces of the future. In manufacturing and service industries, the advent of microelectronics has fundamentally reshaped the nature of work. If the incomes of our workers are to reverse direction and go back up, our new definition of *vocational* must include what Robert Reich has called the work of the "symbolic analyst, whose competitiveness depends not on the fortunes of any American corporation or industry, but on what function she or he serves in the global economy."[32]

Put simply, symbolic analysts manipulate information. On the shop floor, this function will require mastery of skills in mathematical areas such as probability, statistics, measurement, and calculus and in verbal areas such as reading, writing, and knowing how to use the many different kinds of documents encountered during the course of a week. Graduates of vocational programs under the new definition must also demonstrate that they can work effectively in teams, "find" and solve complex problems, and rapidly absorb new information. In addition, by the time students complete vocational programs they should have mastered whatever specific skills are required to meet

the technical demands associated with a particular industrial sector.

SELLING THE NEW DEFINITION TO PARENTS AND STUDENTS

If parents and students are to buy the idea of a newly redefined vocational education, they have to see that it does not condemn those who choose it to second-class status and dead-end jobs. They have to see that, by graduating from such a system, students would have at least as much upward mobility in their future jobs as they would have if they had participated in college-prep programs. The belief that college is the only path to a good job is very strong among most American parents. That perception could be changed if the new vocational programs were based on performance standards that were every bit as high as — or even higher than — those demanded of students in the college track. Such performance standards should qualify a graduate to enter any of a number of jobs within an entire industrial sector (rather than one specific job) or, if he or she chooses, to go on to college without penalty.

SELLING IT TO EMPLOYERS

Most American employers in the service and manufacturing industries do not put a premium on having their front-line workers develop broadly based skills.[33] But they quickly see the advantages of a system whose graduates have integrated technical, communication, and academic skills and are familiar with the basic requirements of the employer's industrial sector. Implementing such a system is an entirely different matter, however.

Several issues must be dealt with before American employers can function as an institutional partner in a first-class vocational system. First, can American employers agree to collaborate on the development of a work force for their industry? Second, can they muster the financial will to look beyond the next quarter's returns and join forces with educators to develop a viable system that won't reap rewards for a number of years? Third, given their dismal experience with non-college-prep students, are employers willing to believe that educators can deliver on their part of the bargain? Fourth, given the reluctance of most employers to seriously invest in and train their non-college-educated workers in a broad and systematic way, can educators believe that employers will deliver?

Let's examine the first issue, collaborating to prepare a future work force for an industrial sector. Currently, many U.S. employers see their in-house remedial education and training programs as a way to compete with other firms in their industry and within their region.[34] This situation is only exacerbated as labor shortages increase. Instead of collaborating to create a rising tide that lifts all boats, many American employers plug the holes in their own boat, hoping they can do so better and faster than their competitor down the street. This strategy reinforces the current practice of training workers for a narrow job category and makes it easy to lay workers off as capacity is exceeded. Not surprisingly, these practices reinforce Americans' belief that vocational education is undesirable. And, while this competitive strategy might help employers in the short run, in the long run it drives up wages as competitors try to lure workers away from one another with higher salaries.

The second issue — investing now in a system whose benefits will accrue only several years later — poses an equally formidable challenge. While employers in Europe and Asia implicitly assume that the future returns to their export-based economies are worth the present costs associated with the development of broad skills, American employers will have to be convinced with hard numbers that the returns on a superb vocational system are worth the considerable investment that will be required, especially during the time of transition.

The third issue, profound skepticism about our schools, is closely tied to the negative image of vocational education. In many urban centers, employers find that "vocational" or general track students — many of whom are nonwhite — are the schools' lowest achievers. This situation reinforces negative racial stereotypes and further solidifies the notion that vocational education is bad. Small wonder that a growing number of corporations are putting most of their education-related efforts into business/education partnerships that help guarantee students access to college and perhaps a job with the corporation. But many employers have become disillusioned even with the college-oriented programs. Clearly, employers would have to be convinced that what is pro-

> In many cities employers find that "vocational" or general track students are the lowest achievers.

posed is not another "business/education compact," but a radically different approach.

SELLING IT TO EDUCATORS

Ironically, the new definition for vocational education suggested in this article is likely to encounter vigorous resistance from several quarters in education and for several reasons, largely connected to survival. Vocational educators, faced with decreased federal funding and competition from a host of new school-to-work initiatives, are likely to protest that they are already doing what's suggested here. Teachers of high school college-prep courses who derive real status from teaching abstract academics are just as likely to resist an expanded definition of vocational education, claiming that a "liberal arts" education best prepares all students for a labor market that puts a premium on thinking and other advanced cognitive skills. Educators from four-year colleges, facing declines in enrollment, will see a first-class vocational system as a way of siphoning promising students away from their doors and coffers. They are likely to use the argument of 19th-century American liberals, claiming that the job of education is to prepare good citizens and that it is not the job of educators to prepare people for the labor market.[35] In their fight for survival, it is entirely possible that vocational educators on the one side and academic educators on the other will stifle any attempt to create a superb vocational system because it might draw on the best features of each side.

Perhaps even more threatening to survival is the notion of performance standards that hold schools and employers accountable. Teachers, whose job security depends on seniority, will not look kindly on a system that exposes them if they fail to prepare students to meet performance standards. Employers who have done a poor job of educating and training learners in the workplace will also be exposed as inadequate. If the new vocational system is to sell, the threatened parties will have to be convinced that they stand to gain from it.

Despite these challenges, there is a light at the end of the tunnel. One promising American-made model for a first-class vocational system is as close as the nearest professional school for law, medicine, dentistry, accounting, engineering, or the arts. There we can find the vocational education that is closest to the European understanding of the term. Interestingly, our professional schools are considered by most other nations to be the best in the world. It is virtually impossible to teach medicine, law, the arts, or architecture in a setting divorced from the practice of the profession.

Moreover, curricula in these disciplines are very demanding, and students in such schools have to take tough exams in order to qualify for a license to practice. Licensing boards are made up of practitioners, who periodically adjust the requirements reflected in the exams. The license to practice depends on more than time spent in school, as can be seen by the number of times many students take portions of their exams before being allowed to hang out a shingle. Licensing is strictly supervised by the state, which awards the professional credentials. Finally, the exit exam generally qualifies the graduate for jobs throughout the entire industry rather than for one specific task. Specialization does not occur until later.

How could we adapt the model of our "professional" education system so that American youths can match the skills of their European peers? Instead of waiting for the completion of high school or four years of college, students could enter our reinvented "vocational" system somewhat earlier — between grades 9 and 11 for many of our industrial sectors, such as health care, manufacturing, electronics, hospitality, wholesale/retail, and financial services. Students would enter the system having already studied a curriculum in the earlier grades that gradually acquainted them with economics and the labor market.

Once employers and educators have developed tough performance standards for each industrial sector, curricula could be designed around demanding team projects that require the integration of academic knowledge, technical knowledge, and interpersonal skills. Student teams would be coached by a teacher in the school and an industry mentor/supervisor in the workplace. Each satisfactorily completed stage of the project could be worth a credential, further building a student's confidence and credibility. Once performance standards are explicit and require demonstrated mastery, educators and workplace teachers will be freed up to invent a variety of strategies to help students reach those goals.

What about the students who discover that they would really rather go right on to college? Instead of being penalized for participating in this system, they could continue to finance some of their education by working in their field of interest, where they would already have gained valuable academic and work experience. Similarly, students who discover that they would prefer an entirely different industrial sector will have acquired valuable learning skills that they can readily transfer to another context.

A NEW DEFINITION REQUIRES A NEW STRUCTURE

A new, world-class vocational system will require a national commitment, starting with the President, the Departments of Labor and Education, national math organizations, the National Science Foundation, labor leaders, and our leading employers, who set quality standards for their suppliers. Regional boards made up of educators, employers, labor leaders, government representatives, and parents would monitor nationally developed skill standards that students would have to meet in order to qualify for entry into the various industrial sectors.[36] These standards would not be for today's jobs but would reflect the projected needs of the labor market five to 10 years in the future. Where appropriate, standards for each sector would be benchmarked to the best European and Japanese standards. Most important, such performance stan-

dards would provide educators and employers with a powerful incentive to pool their resources and to devise promising strategies to help students make the transition from school to work.

While the transition to such a system would be costly, the long-term returns would far exceed the initial expenses.[37] A new vocational system based on a powerful national and regional structure such as the one outlined above will shift the educational debate away from ensuring equal access to college and toward providing all students with a choice of the education and training system that will best meet their own and the nation's needs.

1. Commission on the Skills of the American Workforce, *America's Choice: High Skills or Low Wages?* (Rochester, N.Y.: National Center on Education and the Economy, 1990); Michael L. Dertouzos, Richard K. Lester, and Robert M. Solow, *Made in America: Regaining the Productive Edge* (Cambridge, Mass.: MIT Press, 1989); and William T. Grant Foundation Commission on Work, Family and Citizenship, *The Forgotten Half: Non-College-Bound Youth in America* (Washington, D.C.: William T. Grant Foundation, 1988).

2. For a complete listing of youth apprenticeship initiatives in the U.S., contact the William T. Grant Foundation Commission on Children and Youth, 1001 Connecticut Ave. N.W., Suite 301, Washington, DC 20036-5541.

3. Robert Reich, " 'As the World Turns': U.S. Income Inequality Keeps on Rising," *New Republic*, 1 May 1989, pp. 23-28.

4. *What Ohioans Say About Vocational Education* (Cincinnati: Institute for Policy Research, University of Cincinnati, 1988).

5. Alan Weisberg, "What Research Has to Say About Vocational Education and the High Schools," *Phi Delta Kappan*, January 1983, pp. 355-59.

6. Ira Magaziner and Mark Patinkin, *The Silent War* (New York: Random House, 1990), p. xi.

7. Therese H. Herman, *Creating Learning Environments: The Behavioral Approach to Education* (Boston: Allyn and Bacon, 1977).

8. Herbert P. Ginsburg and Sylvia Opper, *Piaget's Theory of Intellectual Development* (Englewood Cliffs, N.J.: Prentice-Hall, 1988).

9. Senta A. Raizen and Richard Lee Colvin, "On Apprenticeship: A Cognitive-Science View," *Education Week*, 11 December 1991, p. 26.

10. Ray Marshall and Marc Tucker, "The Best Imports from Japan and Germany," *Washington Post National Weekly Edition*, 9-15 November 1992, p. 24.

11. At the Vereins und Westbank of Hamburg, for instance, human resource managers assigned to supervise young apprentices recently developed a new curriculum for the workplace that is self-directed and requires the student to solve actual problems.

12. Dertouzos, Lester, and Solow, p. 85.

13. *Transition from School to Work: Linking Education and Worksite Training* (Washington, D.C.: General Accounting Office, August 1991).

14. Marvin Lazerson and W. Norton Grubb, eds., *American Education and Vocationalism: A Documentary History* (New York: Teachers College Press, 1974), p. 37.

15. Interestingly, England's Ministry of Education recommends that all secondary teachers spend a significant period of time in industry.

16. Sylvia Scribner and Patricia Sachs, *On the Job Training: A Case Study* (New York: Center on Education and Employment, Teachers College, Columbia University, Report No. 9, August 1990), p. 1.

17. Patricia Flynn Pannell, "Occupational Education and Training: Goals and Performance," in Peter B. Doeringer and Bruce Vermeulen, eds., *Jobs and Training in the 1980s: Vocational Policy and the Labor Market* (Boston: Martinus Nijhoff, 1982).

18. Dertouzos, Lester, and Solow, p. 85.

19. The American College Testing Service is in the process of developing a vocational equivalent of the college boards, called "Work Keys."

20. Dertouzos, Lester, and Solow, p. 29.

21. Ibid., p. 82.

22. Michael Porter, *The Competitive Advantage of Nations* (New York: Free Press, 1990).

23. Magaziner and Patinkin, p. 9.

24. The MIT Commission on Industrial Productivity lists six major reasons for the U.S. productivity crisis: outdated strategies and the mass production system, short time horizons, technological weaknesses in development and production, neglect of human resources, failures of cooperation, and government and industry at cross-purposes. See Dertouzos, Lester, and Solow, p.44.

25. Robert L. Heilbroner and Lester C. Thurow, *Economics Explained* (New York: Simon & Schuster, 1987).

26. Ibid., p. 147.

27. Porter, p. 10.

28. Reich, op. cit.

29. *The Great Lakes Economy and Technology Base: Charts and Tables* (Cleveland: Center for Regional Economic Initiatives, Case Western Reserve University, 31 January 1989).

30. Author's conversations with various chief executive officers.

31. Seth Mydans, "For Skilled Foreigners – Lower Hurdles to U.S.," *New York Times*, 5 November 1990, p. 8.

32. Reich, p. 26.

33. Commission on the Skills of the American Workforce, op. cit.

34. Author's interviews with employers in various cities, 1990-91.

35. In the City College of Chicago, for instance, teachers of "academic" subjects refuse to teach what they consider "applied" or "vocational" subjects, arguing just this point. Actual negotiated pay scales mirror this situation, as academic teachers earn considerably more than their "applied" colleagues.

36. In September 1992 the U.S. Departments of Labor and Education awarded a number of contracts to national consortia of employers, trade unions, associations, and educators to develop broadly based, industrywide standards for a number of industries.

37. I am working with Tom Kane and Jackie Kraemer of the Kennedy School of Government, Harvard University, to design a cost-benefit analysis of the dual system in Germany so as to identify the costs that U.S. employers would face in setting up such a system.

The Profession of Teaching Today

All of us who live the life of a teacher should reflect on those characterizing features of professional practice that we associate with the concept of a "good" teacher. In addition, we must remember that the teacher-student relationship is both a tacit and an explicit one—one in which teacher attitude and emotional outreach is as important as student response to instructional effort. The role of mutual teacher-student assent to the teaching-learning episode cannot be overemphasized. Teaching is a two-way street. Teachers must create an emotional set in the teacher-student relationship in which students will want to accept instruction if optimal student learning performance is to be achieved. What, then, constitute those most defensible standards to assess "good teaching"? This question will continue to be a matter of reflec-

tion within the teaching profession for the foreseeable future. Indeed, it has been a matter of thoughtful reflection among some of the world's greatest teachers since Socrates.

In-depth research on the various levels of expertise in the practice of teaching has occurred within the past decade. Much more is known now about specific teaching competencies and how they are acquired than was known in the 1970s. Expert teachers do differ from novices and advanced beginning teachers in terms of their capacity to exhibit accurate, integrated, and holistic perceptions and analyses of what goes on when students try to learn in classroom settings. There are qualitative differences in the levels of understanding students and their behavioral and learning patterns when "expert" teachers are compared with beginning teachers.

There has also been some interesting research comparing the performance of teachers who have graduated from different types of teacher education programs. Some research has suggested, for example, that novice (beginning) teachers who took subject matter majors for their undergraduate degrees are no better able to explain basic concepts in their fields of teaching than students who graduated from undergraduate teacher education programs. This flies in the face of the presuppositions of the Holmes Group and Carnegie reports on the preparation of teachers. Whether readers will consider such claims defensible or not is a matter they must assess for themselves. Mere structural (organizational) changes in teacher education programming will not, in and of themselves, produce that qualitative improvement in beginning teacher classroom performance that would come from a balance between increased subject matter knowledge and enhanced pedagogical classroom skill repertoires.

As the knowledge base on professional practice continues to expand, we will be able to certify with greater and greater precision what constitute acceptable ranges of teacher performance based on clearly defined standards of practice as in medicine and dentistry. Such standards are achievable. Medicine is a practical art as well as a science, as is teaching. The analogy in terms of professional practice is strong and can be made to hold logically. Yet the emotional pressure on teachers to face the idea that theirs is a performing art and that clear standards of practice can be applied to that performing art is a bitter pill to swallow for many of them. Hence, the intense reaction of many teachers against external competency testing and to being held to any rigorous classroom observation

standards. Yet the writing is on the wall. The profession cannot hide behind the tradition that teaching is a special art, unlike others, which cannot be subjected to objective observational standards, aesthetic critique, or to a standard knowledge base. Those years are behind us. The public demands the same levels of demonstrable professional standards of practice as are demanded of those in the medical arts.

Likewise, certain approaches to working with students in the classroom have been effective. Classroom practices such as cooperative learning strategies have won widespread support for inclusion in the knowledge base on teaching. The knowledge base of the social psychology of life in classrooms has been significantly expanded by collaborative research between classroom teachers and various specialists in psychology and teacher education. This has been accomplished by using anthropological field research techniques to ground theory of classroom practice in demonstrable phenomenological perspectives. So, there are many things to consider as the teaching professional rapidly moves to the dawn of a new century far better grounded in its knowledge base than at the beginning of this one.

Recent research by teachers and teacher educators on their professional practice in classrooms is greatly enriching our knowledge base on the teaching-learning process in schools. Many issues have been raised by basic ethnographic field observations, interviews, and anecdotal record-keeping techniques to understand more precisely how teachers and students interact in the classroom. There is a rich dialectic developing among teachers regarding the description of classroom teaching environments. The methodological issues raised by this research into the day-to-day realities of life in schools is transforming what we know about teaching as a professional activity. These developments are pertinent to the concerns of all teachers regarding how to best advance our knowledge of effective teaching strategies.

Creative, insightful persons who become teachers usually find ways to network their interests and concerns with other teachers. There are many opportunities for creative professional practice in teaching in spite of external assessment procedures. The science of teaching involves the observation and measurement of teaching behaviors. The art of teaching involves the humanistic dimensions of instructional activities. Interesting and original conceptions of teaching as a humanistic activity are still being developed. We continue to rediscover older methods of relating what is taught to the interests of students. The art of teaching involves not only alertness to the details of what is taught, but equal alertness to how students receive it. Teachers often guide class processes and formulate questions according to their perceptions of how students are responding to the material.

We are in the midst of a period in which fundamental revisions in the structure of the professional role and status of teachers are being considered and developed. Teachers want more input into how the profession is to be reformed. It will be interesting to see how many of the new proposals for career ladders for teachers will be implemented and how the teaching profession responds to the recommendations for licensure by the new national board for certification of teachers.

To build their hope as well as their self-confidence, teachers must be motivated to an even greater effort for professional growth. Teachers need support, appreciation, and respect. Simply criticizing them and refusing to alter those social and economic conditions that affect the quality of their work will not solve their problems, nor will it lead to excellence in education. Not only must teachers work to improve the public's image of and confidence in them, but the public must confront its own misunderstanding of the level of commitment required to achieve excellence. Teachers need to know that the public cares about and respects them enough to fund their professional improvement and to recognize them for the important force they are in the life of their nation. The articles in this unit consider the quality of education and the status of the teaching profession today.

Looking Ahead: Challenge Questions

What is "expertise" in teaching?

What are some ways in which teacher-student classroom interaction can be studied?

Why has the knowledge base on teaching expanded so dramatically in recent years?

List what you think are the five most important issues confronting the teaching profession today (with number one being the most important and number five the least important). What criteria did you use in ranking the issues? What is your position on each of them?

What does gaining a student's assent to your instructional effort mean?

What are the most defensible standards to assess the quality of a teaching performance?

What is the role of creativity in the classroom?

CREATING A COMPOSITE PICTURE

What Makes a Good Teacher?

Christopher M. Clark

Christopher Clark, a professor of educational psychology at Michigan State University, looks to researchers, teachers, and students—then creates a composite picture that "may inspire but not be imitated or mass produced."

We cannot hope for good education, from preschool to graduate school, in the absence of good teaching. For better and for worse, the quality of teaching defines the quality of education. And the quality of education, in turn, limits or enables the good that the next generation of teachers is able to do.

This portrayal of the good teacher draws on three sources: 1) empirical research on teaching, 2) the voices of teachers themselves, and 3) what children have to say about good teaching. I hope that this analysis will create a composite picture of the good teacher that may inspire but may not be imitated or mass produced—a heroic form on which we can project our best qualities and aspiration, through which we will come to a deeper appreciation of our own best moments.

Knowing something of the good teacher will not, by itself, solve the many problems of teacher education, certification, professional development, and life-long learning that we're all concerned about. But coming to a better vision of good teaching may serve to encourage each of us as we address specific local and national problems in our own creative and field-sensitive ways.

In the end, good teachers equip their students for confident, independent thought and action in an uncertain world. Good teachers prepare us for a world of difference. Good teachers know when to let us go. And this is almost always before we feel ready to be on our own.

The question "What makes a good teacher?" is fundamental to much of research in education. This is particularly true for three approaches to research on teaching conceived and led by educational psychologists: The Process-Product approach, the teacher thinking approach, and the teacher knowledge approach.

The Process-Product approach to research on teaching began in the early 1950s. The young educational psychologists of that time were fresh from designing emergency training programs for soldiers, sailors, and airmen in World War II. Naturally, they drew on their experiences and successes with task analysis, behavior reinforcement, and testing and measurement when they turned their attention to teachers and schooling. Their goals were to discover the most effective teachers' secrets and then to create teacher training programs that would transform all teachers into effective ones.

The reason this approach is called the Process-Product approach is that the researchers concerned themselves with two classes of variables. "Process" refers to the visible and audible behavior of teachers and students during classroom teaching. "Product" refers to the objectively measurable results of teaching, usually expressed as students' achievement test scores.

In this framework, the good teacher is one whose students, after receiving instruction, achieve the highest scores on tests of knowledge and skill. The research program is dedicated to describing the teaching skills and behaviors that reliably distinguish between the most effective teachers and less effective ones.

During 40 years of Process-Product research, many developments have taken place in the theoretical tools used to study teaching. Observation systems for describing teacher behavior and classroom interaction have become more sophisticated and complex.

Most importantly, thousands of researchers have spent tens of thousands of hours in school classrooms, carefully attending to teachers and teaching, students and learning. A scholarly community of research on teaching has developed internationally—a community of dedicated and intelligent professionals that has come to some consensus about what makes a good teacher.

What Teachers Do

What do these people say to us today about the good teacher?

To answer this question, I draw heavily on work by Jere Brophy and Thomas Good ("Teacher Behavior and Student Achievement," 1986). According to Brophy and Good, the most reliable findings about effective teaching depict a classroom teacher who is well organized, efficient, task oriented, and businesslike. They describe this form of active, direct instruction as follows:

Students achieve more in classes where they spend most of their time being taught or supervised by their teachers rather than working on their own (or not working at all). These classes include frequent lessons...in which the teacher presents information and develops concepts through lecture and demonstration, elaborates this information in the feedback given following responses to recitation or discussion questions, prepares the students for follow-up seatwork activities by giving instructions and going through practice examples, monitors progress on assignments after releasing the students to work independently, and follows up with appropriate feedback and reteaching when necessary.

So, the image of the good teacher offered by Process-Product researchers is of one who is an efficient director and manager of a three-part instructional process that involves lecture and demonstration, recitation with feedback, and supervised practice or seatwork. This body of research also offers detailed guidance about which behaviors constitute effective recitation or feedback, or appropriate seatwork.

For example, the researchers broke the recitation strategy of teaching into a pattern consisting of structuring information, asking questions, and responding to student answers. Breaking the strategy down even further, many studies have been done to discover which kinds of questions at what levels of difficulty are correlated with high student achievement.

The global image of the good teacher supported by this research is of a businesslike person who is clearly in control of the flow of work in an orderly, efficient classroom. Such a person is clear, well organized, enthusiastic, and direct.

The process of rapid and cumulative coverage of academic content, with clear feedback and remedial instruction

when necessary, leads to superior performance on tests of facts and skills. The culture of control, efficiency, and convergence of learning outcomes defines the world of the Process-Product teacher.

What Teachers Think

Partly as a reaction to the behavioral and managerial focus of Process-Product research on teaching, a new approach to the question "What makes a good teacher?" began in 1974. This approach has come to be called research on teacher thinking, and researchers in this field concern themselves with the mental lives of teachers—the planning, decision making, beliefs, and theories that invisibly guide and influence teacher action.

This field began with the image of a teacher as a diagnostician responsible for observing, categorizing, and acting in response to a complex array of cues and situations that describe self, students, and learning environment.

The metaphor of teacher as decision maker is central to this work, along with the assumption that teachers behave rationally almost all of the time. The challenge to researchers was to describe and understand the rationality underlying good teaching.

With my colleague Penelope Peterson, I conducted a review summarizing approximately 40 studies of teacher thinking. Our review concludes with this portrait of the good teacher:

The maturing professional teacher is one who has taken some steps toward making explicit his theories and beliefs about learners, curriculum, subject matter, and the teacher's role. This teacher has developed a style of planning for instruction that includes interrelated types of planning and that has become more streamlined and automatic with experience.

Much of this teacher's interactive teaching consists of routines familiar to the students, thus decreasing the collective information-processing load. During teaching, the teacher attends to

and intently processes academic and nonacademic . . . events and cues.

These experienced teachers have developed the confidence to depart from a planned course of action when they judge that to be appropriate. They reflect on and analyze the apparent effects of their own teaching and apply the results of these reflections to their future plans and actions. In short, they have become researchers on their own teaching effectiveness.

The good teacher knows when to let us go. And this is almost always before we feel ready to be on our own.

We leave research on teacher thinking with the impression that the good teacher's effective action depends as much on his or her thoughts, plans, and decisions as on efficient behavior and management ability. The mental lives of teachers are at least as important to understanding and supporting the profession as are their visible behaviors.

What Teachers Know

Let's now consider what the newest approach to research on teaching has to offer. This approach is called research on teacher knowledge and takes the position that what is most important and most neglected in teaching is the teacher's knowledge of subject matter.

Logic and common sense suggest that one cannot teach what one does not understand. But how many of us have had the experience of being taught by a teacher or professor who is clearly the master of a discipline, yet is unable to communicate that knowledge to struggling students?

This paradox has led Lee Shulman and his colleagues to do a series of case studies of the knowledge held by high school teachers and, most importantly, of the ways in which these teachers transform that knowledge for their students.

What these detailed case studies depict, in the teaching of history, literature, and mathematics is what anthropologists call a "conversation with the situation." This conversation takes place in the mind of the teacher as he or she reorganizes academic knowledge about Hamlet or photosynthesis or the Civil War to accommodate to local knowledge about the lives and minds of the children to be taught.

A delicate balance must be struck each day between appropriate transformation of knowledge and the danger of distorting what will be taught. In this framework, the teacher is both a knowledge representative of an academic discipline and also a translator who can faithfully express the big ideas of history or biology in the language of 16-year-olds.

This would be a difficult enough task if all 16-year-olds spoke the same language. But according to these researchers, the teacher is faced with many dialects and variations in students' ways of understanding.

One of the best known reports of this research effort is entitled "150 Different Ways of Knowing" (Wilson, Shulman & Richert, 1987). This title is intended to emphasize the claim that a high school teacher who teaches 150 students each day ought to aspire to a repertoire of 150 variations in ways to represent content.

In an article that describes the philosophy and assumptions of research on teacher knowledge, Shulman (1987) lists seven constituents of the knowledge that good teachers have. These are:

▶ content knowledge
▶ general pedagogical knowledge
▶ curriculum knowledge
▶ pedagogical content knowledge
▶ knowledge of learners and their characteristics
▶ knowledge of educational contexts
▶ knowledge of educational ends, purposes, and values.

In my opinion, the central contributions of this newest approach to research on teaching are the coining of the concept of pedagogical content knowledge and the descriptions of particular cases of teachers developing and acting on what Shulman calls the "special amalgam of content and pedagogy that is the unique province of teachers."

The good teacher, then, must not only know how to manage, give feedback, make practical plans and wise decisions. She must be more than a performer, more than a thinker. The good teacher must also be a practical scholar, a student of the academic disciplines, and a fluent translator. The good teacher becomes a life-long learner. The journey toward becoming a good teacher has barely begun on graduation day.

What Do Teachers Say?
So now we have a picture of the good teacher from the points of view of the educational research community. You probably know teachers who fit these descriptions. You or your children may have been taught by teachers who express these qualities. You may know yourself to be a good teacher in these ways.

But is it good enough to demonstrate comprehensive mastery of subject matter, exhibit skills in managing a classroom and explaining its complexities, and be an effective planner and decision maker? Is it good enough to score high on teacher evaluation checklists developed from research on teaching?

For some answers, let's turn to what teachers have said about what it takes to be a good teacher, to what good teachers have said about themselves, and to what ordinary teachers have said about times when their teaching was exceptionally good.

To teachers, the heart of good teaching is not in management or decision making or pedagogical content knowledge. No, the essence of good teaching, for teachers, is in the arena of human relationships.

Teaching is good when a class becomes a community of honest, nurturing, and mutually respectful people. Experienced teachers treasure the moments and memories of times when laughter, compassion, and surprise describe their day or year.

Cultivation of the self-esteem of young people is very high on the list of goals of the good teacher.

How many of us have been taught by a teacher who is clearly the master of a discipline, yet is unable to communicate that knowledge?

"Better to leave my class having learned a little math and love it than knowing a lot of math and hate it." Good humor was mentioned again and again as a quality of the best teachers.

Enthusiasm for teaching, fascination with content, and openness to admitting mistakes are important in good teachers. The good teacher is capable of expressing love, care, and respect in [150] different ways. The good teacher is an adult who takes children seriously. The good teacher, they say, "is the colleague who supports me and is open to my support."

When experienced educators speak of the good teacher, the word "good" takes on richer meaning. The good teacher is one who finds good in students, individually and collectively. The pedagogical challenge becomes celebrating and elaborating the noblest human qualities in the context of a school, for teaching is a social and a moral enterprise.

Teaching is more than the transmission of information. Intentionally or not, teachers shape the character of their students and influence the character of society for years after they retire. The good teacher attends to this human, social, moral dimension of life in schools as much as to the technical and academic. Good teaching is a vocation, a calling, as much as it is a profession.

The last voice to speak about the good teacher is, perhaps, the most important: the child's. What do the children say? I have listened to little children, to adolescents, and to adult students. I urge you to listen for the voice of your own children, to imagine or remember what they know to be true about their experiences of good teaching.

Almost invariably, their thoughts and stories about good teachers have to do with four fundamental human needs: to be known, to be encouraged, to be respected, and to be led. These four human needs are the positive side of the four primal fears that children and adults labor against throughout life: fear of abandonment, despair, ridicule, and fear of being lost.

What Do Children Say?

In the words of children, good teachers nurture students by treating them as intelligent people who can become even more intelligent, taking the time to learn who they are and what they love, treating them fairly by treating them differently. The good teacher explains why he teaches and acts as he does, tells stories of his own life outside school and listens to his students' stories, and lets his students have a bad day when they can't help it.

The good teacher is both funny and serious. Students say, "We can laugh together, and this makes me feel happy and close." "She surprises us in ways that we will never forget." "He draws pictures that show how ideas are connected." "We don't feel lost or afraid that we will be sent away or humiliated." "She loves what she's teaching but doesn't show off or put distance between us."

The good teacher sets things up so that children can learn how to learn from one another. The good teacher knows how to be a friend while still being a responsible adult.

Very often, the good teacher doesn't know of the good he has done at the time. A letter from a gifted, high achieving student written five years after college graduation closes with these words:

You were a good friend when I needed one. You listened to me ramble on. You said encouraging things at the right times. When I was a confused student, you made time for me. There were times when I was ready to burst that I came and took comfort from your confidence and your soothing voice.

The good teacher puts people first, say the children. The good teacher acts from love and caring and is loved and cared for in return.

Putting the Picture Together

Now we've heard from researchers, from teachers, and from children about the good teacher. The composite picture may seem overwhelming—too much for any human being to become, too much for any teacher preparation program, certification process, or national plan to guarantee.

Yet I'm optimistic. For these voices that speak of the good teacher describe real people, actual classrooms, true stories, powerful experiences. This is not wishful thinking, fantasy, or groundless idealization. These are the voices of inspiration and encouragement. One high school student I talked to estimated that 10 of the 30 teachers she had were good teachers in these ways.

Perhaps it's now time to change the question. Let's turn away from asking "What makes a good teacher?" Instead, let's ask "When is teaching good?"

How can we each do a better job of acknowledging the good teaching that's already happening every day in our schools? How can we improve policy, conditions, and support systems so that ordinary teachers can have good moments and good days more often?

We should begin to build an ethos of good teaching by learning to tell stories, even sagas, of heroic but invisible good teaching. We need help from minstrels, poets, biographers, historians, and film producers to create a vivid literature of good teaching.

We need help from clinical psychologists and from one another to heal our childhood wounds and to prevent us from unthinkingly passing on our wounds to the next generation. We, as teachers, need to learn to respect the children by learning to respect and love the wounded child within each of us. We must begin with ourselves.

Good teaching will never be easy. Nor will it ever be easy to be a good parent, a good nurse, a good scientist, or a good principal. The essence of these callings is a courageous willingness to form moral relationships, to embrace uncertainty, to do what seems right at the time, to lead but not to control. In these ways, good teaching happens every day in our schools and in our homes, in our workplaces and communities.

Perhaps the best preparation for the future of life-long learning is to cultivate and treasure a better appreciation of the present state of good teaching. We cannot change the past, but we can come to understand and cooperate with contemporary goodness more constructively.

References

▶ Brophy, J. J. & Good, T. (1986). "Teacher behavior and student achievement." In M.C. Wittrock (Ed.), *Handbook of research on teaching* (3rd ed., pp. 328-375). New York: MacMillan.

▶ Clark. C. M. & Peterson, P.L. (1986). "Teachers' thought processes." In M.C. Wittrock (Ed.), *Handbook of research on teaching* (3rd ed., pp. 255-296). New York: MacMillan.

▶ Shulman, L. S. (1987). "Knowledge and teaching: Foundations of the new reform." *Harvard Educational Review*, 57(1), 1-22.

▶ Wilson, S. M., Shulman, L. S. & Richert, A. (1987). "150 different ways of knowing: Representations of knowledge in teaching." In J. Calderhead (Ed.), *Exploring teacher thinking*. London: Cassell, pp. 104-124.

Probing the Subtleties of Subject-Matter Teaching

Building on the effective schools research of the 1970s, studies today focus on teaching for understanding and use of knowledge.

JERE BROPHY

Jere Brophy is University Distinguished Professor of Teacher Education and Co-director, Institute for Research on Teaching. He can be contacted at Michigan State University, Center for the Learning and Teaching of Elementary Subjects, College of Education, Erickson Hall, East Lansing, MI 48824-10341

Research on teaching, if interpreted appropriately, is a significant resource to teachers; it both validates good practice and suggests directions for improvement. All too often, however, reviews of the research assume an "out with the old, in with the new" stance, which fosters swings between extremes. Practitioners are left confused and prone to believe that research is not helpful. This summary of the research conducted during the last 25 years attempts not only to highlight the changing implications of research but also to emphasize how the research has built on what was learned before.

Process-Outcome Research

Especially relevant findings come from studies designed to identify relationships between classroom processes (what the teacher and students do in the classroom) and student outcomes (changes in students' knowledge, skills, values, or dispositions that represent progress toward instructional goals). Two forms of *process-outcome research* that became prominent in the 1970s were school effects research and teacher effects research.

School effects research (reviewed in Good and Brophy 1986) identified characteristics in schools that elicit good achievement gains from their students: (1) strong academic leadership that produces consensus on goal priorities and commitment to instructional excellence; (2) a safe, orderly school climate; (3) positive teacher attitudes toward students and expectations regarding their abilities to master the curriculum; (4) an emphasis on instruction in the curriculum (not just

on filling time or on nonacademic activities); (5) careful monitoring of progress toward goals through student testing and staff evaluation programs; (6) strong parent involvement programs; and (7) consistent emphasis on the importance of academic achievement, including praise and public recognition for students' accomplishments.

Teacher effects research (reviewed in Brophy and Good 1986) identified teacher behaviors and patterns of teacher-student interaction associated with student achievement gains. This research firmly established three major conclusions:

1. *Teachers make a difference.* Some teachers reliably elicit greater gains than others, because of differences in how they teach.

2. *Differences in achievement gains occur in part because of differences in exposure to academic content and opportunity to learn.* Teachers who elicit greater gains: (a) place more emphasis on developing mastery of

the curriculum, in establishing expectations for students, and defining their own roles; (b) allocate most of the available time for activities designed to foster such mastery; and (c) are effective organizers and managers who make their classrooms efficient learning environments, minimize the time spent getting organized or making transitions, and maximize student engagement in ongoing academic activities.

3. *Teachers who elicit greater achievement gains do not merely maximize "time on task"; in addition, they spend a great deal of time actively instructing their students.* Their classrooms feature more time spent in interactive lessons, featuring much teacher-student discourse and less time spent in independent seatwork. Rather than depend solely on curriculum materials as content sources, these teachers interpret and elaborate the content for students, stimulate them to react to it through questions, and circulate during seatwork times to monitor progress and provide assistance. They are active instructors, not just materials managers and evaluators, although most of their instruction occurs during interactive discourse with students rather than during extended lecture-presentations.

The process-outcome research of the 1970s was important, not only for contributing the findings summarized above but also for providing education with a knowledge base capable of moving the field beyond testimonials and unsupported claims toward scientific statements based on credible data. However, this research was limited in several respects. First, it focused on important but very basic aspects of teaching. These aspects differentiate the least effective teachers from other teachers, but they do not include the more subtle points that distinguish the most outstanding teachers.

Second, most of this research relied on standardized tests as the outcome measure, which meant that it focused on mastery of relatively isolated knowledge items and skill components without assessing the degree to which students had developed understanding of networks of subject-matter content or the ability to use this information in authentic application situations.

Research on Teaching for Understanding and Use of Knowledge

During the 1980s, research emerged that emphasized teaching subject matter for understanding and use of knowledge. This research focuses on particular curriculum units or even individual lessons, taking into account the teacher's instructional goals and assessing student learning accordingly. The researchers find out what the teacher is trying to accomplish, record detailed information about classroom processes as they unfold, and then assess learning using measures keyed to the instructional goals. Often these include detailed interviews or portfolio assessments, not just conventional short-answer tests.

Current research focuses on attempts to teach both the individual elements in a network of related content and the connections among them, to the point that students can explain the information in their own words and can use it appropriately in and out of school. Teachers accomplish this by explaining concepts and principles with clarity and precision and by modeling the strategic application of skills via "think aloud" demonstrations. These demonstrations make overt for students the usually covert strategic thinking that guides the use of the skills for problem solving.

Construction of Meaning

Current research, while building on findings indicating the vital role teachers play in stimulating student learning, also focuses on the role of the student. It recognizes that students do not merely passively receive or copy input from teachers, but instead actively mediate it by trying to make sense of it and to relate it to what they already know (or think they know) about the topic. Thus, students develop new knowledge through a process of *active construction*. In order to get beyond rote memorization to achieve true understanding, they need to develop and integrate a network of associations linking new input to preexisting knowledge and beliefs anchored in concrete experience. Thus, teaching involves inducing *conceptual change* in students, not infusing knowledge into a vacuum. Students' preexisting beliefs about a topic, when accurate, facilitate learning and provide a natural starting place for teaching. Students' misconceptions, however, must be corrected so that they do not distort the new learning.

To the extent that new learning is complex, the construction of meaning required to develop clear understanding of it will take time and will be facilitated by the interactive *discourse* that occurs during lessons and activities. Clear explanations and modeling from the teacher are important, but so are opportunities to answer questions about the content, discuss or debate its meanings and implications, or apply it in authentic problem-solving or decision-making contexts. These activities allow students to process the content actively and "make it their own" by paraphrasing it into their own words, exploring its relationships to other knowledge and to past experience, appreciating the insights it provides, or identifying its implications for personal decision making or action. Increasingly, research is pointing to thoughtful discussion, and not just teacher lecturing or student recitation, as characteristic of the discourse involved in teaching for understanding.

Researchers have also begun to stress the complementary changes in teacher and student roles that should occur as learning progresses. Early in the process, the teacher assumes most of the responsibility for structuring and managing learning activities and provides students with a great deal of information, explanation, modeling, and cueing. As students develop expertise, however, they can begin regulating their own learning by asking questions and by working on increasingly complex applications with increasing degrees of autonomy.

The teacher still provides task simplification, coaching, and other "scaffolding" needed to assist students with challenges that they are not yet ready to handle on their own. Gradually, this assistance is reduced in response to gradual increases in student readiness to engage in self-regulated learning.

Principles of Good Subject Matter Teaching

Although research on teaching school subjects for understanding and higher-order applications is still in its infancy, it already has produced successful experimental programs in most subjects. Even more encouraging, analyses of these programs have identified principles and practices that are common to most if not all of them (Anderson 1989, Brophy 1989, Prawat 1989). These common elements are:

1. The curriculum is designed to equip students with knowledge, skills, values, and dispositions useful both inside and outside of school.

2. Instructional goals underscore developing student expertise within an application context and with emphasis on conceptual understanding and self-regulated use of skills.

3. The curriculum balances breadth with depth by addressing limited content but developing this content sufficiently to foster understanding.

4. The content is organized around a limited set of powerful ideas (key understandings and principles).

5. The teacher's role is not just to present information but also to scaffold and respond to students' learning.

6. The students' role is not just to absorb or copy but to actively make sense and construct meaning.

7. Activities and assignments feature authentic tasks that call for problem solving or critical thinking, not just memory or reproduction.

8. Higher-order thinking skills are not taught as a separate skills curriculum. Instead, they are developed in the process of teaching subject-matter knowledge within application contexts that call for students to relate what they are learning to their lives outside of school by thinking critically or creatively about it or by using it to solve problems or make decisions.

9. The teacher creates a social environment in the classroom that could be described as a learning community where dialogue promotes understanding.

In-Depth Study of Fewer Topics

Embedded in this approach to teaching is the notion of "complete" lessons carried through to include higher-order applications of content. The breadth of content addressed, thus, is limited to allow for more in-depth teaching of the content. Unfortunately, typical state and district curriculum guidelines feature long lists of items and subskills to be "covered," and typical curriculum packages supplied by educational publishers respond to these guidelines by emphasizing breadth over depth of coverage. Teachers who want to teach for understanding and higher-order applications of subject-matter will have to both: (1) limit what they teach by focusing on the most important content and omitting or skimming over the rest, and (2) structure what they do teach around important ideas, elaborating it considerably beyond what is in the text.

Besides presenting information and modeling skill applications, such teachers will need to structure a great deal of thoughtful discourse by using questions to stimulate students to process and reflect on the content, recognize relationships among and implications of its key ideas, think critically about it, and use it in problem-solving or decision-making applications. Such discourse downplays rapid-fire questioning and short answers and instead features sustained examination of a small number of related topics. Students are invited to develop explanations, make predictions, debate alternative approaches to problems, or otherwise consider the content's implications or applications. Some of the questions admit to a range of possible correct answers, and some invite discussion or debate (for example, concerning the relative merits of alternative suggestions for

Clearly, the kind of instruction described here demands more from both teachers and students than traditional reading-recitation-seatwork teaching does.

solving problems). In addition to asking questions and providing feedback, the teacher encourages students to explain or elaborate on their answers or to comment on classmates' answers. The teacher also capitalizes on "teachable moments" offered by students' comments or questions (by elaborating on the original instruction, correcting misconceptions, or calling attention to implications that have not been appreciated yet).

Holistic Skills Instruction

Teaching for understanding and use of knowledge also involves holistic skills instruction, not the practice of skills in isolation. For example, most practice of writing skills is embedded within activities calling for authentic writing. Also, skills are taught as strategies adapted to particular purposes and situations, with emphasis on modeling the cognitive and metacognitive components involved and explaining the necessary conditional knowledge (of when and why the skills would be used). Thus, students receive instruction in when and how to apply skills, not just opportunities to use them.

Activities, assignments, and evaluation methods incorporate a much greater range of tasks than the familiar workbooks and curriculum-embedded tests that focus on recognition and recall of facts, definitions, and fragmented skills. Curriculum strands or units are planned to accomplish gradual transfer of responsibility for managing learning activities from the teacher to the students, in response to their growing expertise on the topic. Plans for lessons and activities are guided by overall curriculum goals (phrased in terms of student capabilities to be developed), and evaluation efforts concentrate on assessing the progress made.

Reading. Reading is taught as a sense-making process of extracting meaning from texts that are read for information or enjoyment, not just for practice. Important skills such as decoding, blending, and noting main ideas are taught and practiced, but primarily within the context of reading for meaning. Activities and assignments feature more reading of extended texts and less time spent with skills worksheets. Students often work cooperatively in pairs or small groups, reading to one another or discussing their answers to questions about the implications of the text. Rather than being restricted to the artificial stories written for basal readers, students often read literature written to provide information or pleasure (Anderson et al. 1985, Dole et al. 1991).

Writing. Writing is taught as a way for students to organize and communicate their thinking to particular audiences for particular purposes, using skills taught as strategies for accomplishing these goals. Most skills practice is embedded within writing activities that call for composition and communication of meaningful content. Composition activities emphasize authentic writing intended to be read for meaning and response. Thus, composition becomes an exercise in communication and personal craftsmanship. Students develop and revise outlines, develop successive drafts for meaning, and then polish their writing. The emphasis is on the cognitive and metacognitive aspects of composing, not just on mechanics and editing (Englert and Raphael 1989, Rosaen 1990, Scardamalia and Bereiter 1986).

Mathematics. Mathematics instruction focuses on developing students' abilities to explore, conjecture, reason logically, and use a variety of mathematical models to solve nonroutine problems. Instead of working through a postulated linear hierarchy from isolated and low-level skills to integrated and higher-level skills, and only then attempting application, students are taught within an application context right from the beginning through an emphasis on authentic problem solving. They spend less time working individually on computation skills sheets and more time participating in teacher-led discourse concerning the meanings of the mathematical concepts and operations under study (Carpenter et al. 1989; National Council of Teachers of Mathematics 1989, 1991; Steffe and Wood 1990).

Science. In science, students learn to understand, appreciate, and apply connected sets of powerful ideas that they can use to describe, explain, make predictions about, or gain control over real-world systems or events. Instruction connects with students' experience-based knowledge and beliefs, building on accurate current knowledge but also producing conceptual change by confronting and correcting misconceptions. The teacher models and coaches the students' scientific reasoning through scaffolded tasks and dialogues that engage them in thinking about scientific issues. The students are encouraged to make predictions or develop explanations, then subject them to empirical tests or argue the merits of proposed alternatives (Anderson and Roth 1989, Neale et al. 1990).

Social studies. In social studies, students are challenged to engage in higher-order thinking by interpreting, analyzing, or manipulating information in response to questions or problems that cannot be resolved through routine application of previously learned knowledge. Students focus on networks of connected content structured around powerful ideas rather than on long lists of disconnected facts, and they consider the implications of what they are learning for social and civic decision making. The teacher encourages students to formu-late and communicate ideas about the topic, but also presses them to clarify or justify their assertions rather than merely accepting and reinforcing them indiscriminately (Brophy 1990, Newmann 1990).

Greater Efforts, Greater Rewards

The type of teaching described here is not yet typical of what happens in most schools. For it to become more common, several things must occur. First, researchers need to articulate these principles more clearly. Second, states and districts must adjust their curriculum guidelines, and publishers must modify their textbooks and teachers' manuals. Finally, professional organizations of teachers and teacher educators must build on the beginnings that they have made in endorsing the goals of teaching subjects for understanding, appreciation, and life application by creating and disseminating position statements, instructional guidelines, videotaped examples, and other resources for preservice and inservice teachers. Clearly, the kind of instruction described here demands more from both teachers and students than traditional reading-recitation-seatwork teaching does. However, it also rewards their efforts with more satisfying and authentic accomplishments.

Author's note: This work is sponsored in part by the Center for the Learning and Teaching of Elementary Subjects, Institute for Research on Teaching, Michigan State University. The Center for Learning and Teaching of Elementary Subjects is funded primarily by the Office of Educational Research and Improvement, U.S. Department of Education. The opinions expressed here do not necessarily reflect the position, policy, or endorsement of the Office or Department (Cooperative Agreement No. G0087C0226).

References

Anderson, L. (1989). "Implementing Instructional Programs to Promote Meaningful, Self-Regulated Learning." In *Advances in Research on Teaching*, Vol. 1, edited by J. Brophy, pp. 311-343. Greenwich, Conn.: JAI.

Anderson, C., and K. Roth. (1989). "Teaching for Meaningful and Self-Regulated Learning of Science." In

Advances in Research on Teaching, Vol. 1, edited by J. Brophy, pp. 265-309. Greenwich, Conn.: JAI.

Anderson, R., E. Hiebert, J. Scott, and I. Wilkinson. (1985). *Becoming a Nation of Readers: A Report of the Commission on Reading*. Washington, D.C.: National Institute of Education.

Brophy, J., ed. (1989). *Advances in Research on Teaching*, Vol. 1. Greenwich, Conn.: JAI.

Brophy, J. (1990). "Teaching Social Studies for Understanding and Higher-Order Applications." *Elementary School Journal* 90: 351-417.

Brophy, J., and T. Good. (1986). "Teacher Behavior and Student Achievement." In *Handbook of Research on Teaching*, 3rd. ed., edited by M. Wittrock, pp. 328-375. New York: Macmillan.

Carpenter, T., E. Fennema, P. Peterson, C. Chiang, and M. Loef. (1989). "Using Knowledge of Children's Mathematics Thinking in Classroom Teaching: An Experimental Study." *American Educational Research Journal* 26: 499-532.

Dole, J., G. Duffy, L. Roehler, and P. D. Pearson. (1991). "Moving From the Old to the New: Research on Reading Comprehension Instruction." *Review of Educational Research* 61: 239-264.

Englert, C., and T. Raphael. (1989). "Developing Successful Writers Through Cognitive Strategy Instruction." In *Advances in Research on Teaching*, Vol. 1, edited by J. Brophy, pp. 105-151. Greenwich, Conn.: JAI.

Good, T., and J. Brophy. (1986). "School Effects." In *Handbook of Research on Teaching*, 3rd ed., edited by M. Wittrock, pp. 570-602. New York: Macmillan.

National Council of Teachers of Mathematics. (1989). *Curriculum and Evaluation Standards for School Mathematics*. Reston, Va.: NCTM.

National Council of Teachers of Mathematics. (1991). *Professional Standards for Teaching Mathematics*. Reston, Va.: NCTM.

Neale, D., D. Smith, and V. Johnson. (1990). "Implementing Conceptual Change Teaching in Primary Science." *Elementary School Journal* 91: 109-131.

Newmann, F. (1990). "Qualities of Thoughtful Social Studies Classes: An Empirical Profile." *Journal of Curriculum Studies* 22: 253-275.

Prawat, R. (1989). "Promoting Access to Knowledge, Strategy, and Disposition in Students: A Research Synthesis." *Review of Educational Research* 59: 1-41.

Rosaen, C. (1990). "Improving Writing Opportunities in Elementary Classrooms." *Elementary School Journal* 90: 419-434.

Scardamalia, M., and C. Bereiter. (1986). "Written Composition." In *Handbook of Research on Teaching*, 3rd ed., edited by M. Wittrock, pp. 778-803. New York: Macmillan.

Steffe, L., and T. Wood, eds. (1990). *Transforming Children's Mathematics Education: International Perspectives*. Hillsdale, N.J.: Erlbaum.

Exploring the Thinking of Thoughtful Teachers

JOSEPH J. ONOSKO

Joseph J. Onosko is Assistant Professor, University of New Hampshire, Department of Education, Morrill Hall, Durham, NH 03824-3595.

The development of higher-order thinking has been and will continue to be a fundamental goal in education, despite persistent reports that it is hard to find in classrooms (Cuban 1984, Goodlad 1984, Sirotnik 1983). To remedy this situation, concerned educators have enhanced our conceptual understanding of higher-order thinking, proposed instructional practices to promote it, designed curriculum and instructional materials that emphasize it, and developed assessment techniques that attempt to measure it.

Other researchers have begun to explore how teachers think about their work. Questions that drive this research include: How do teachers think about problems and issues related to promoting students' higher-order thinking? Do outstanding teachers conceptualize their work differently from their less-than-outstanding colleagues? Do their thoughts and beliefs reveal a consistent perspective on how to promote thinking? Here I report findings from a research project that attempted to answer these questions.

Teachers who reflect about their own practices, value thinking, and emphasize depth over breadth of coverage tend to have classrooms with a measurable climate of thoughtfulness.

Background to the Study

The 20 social studies teachers selected for this study were drawn from a pool of 48 teachers from 16 secondary schools as part of the Higher Order Thinking in the Humanities Project at the National Center on Effective Secondary Schools (for details, see Newmann 1991). We identified 10 teachers as outstanding and 10 as less than outstanding through classroom observations using the following six dimensions of instructional practice related to promoting students' thinking:

1. *There is sustained examination of a few topics rather than superficial coverage of many.* As Newmann (1988) has stated, there is little to probe or analyze in a curriculum that is "a mile wide and an inch deep."

2. *The lesson displays substantive coherence and continuity.* Lessons that contain factual and conceptual inaccuracies, gaps in logic, inappropriate transitions, and so on are detrimental to the development of higher-order thinking.

3. *Students are given an appropriate amount of time to prepare responses to questions.* Research has shown that increased "wait time" results in longer, more sophisticated student responses (Tobin 1987). Wait time also suggests to students that reflection is valued.

4. *The teacher asks challenging questions and/or structures challenging tasks.* By definition, thinking is unnecessary unless there is a problem, question, or task that challenges the mind (Schrag 1988).

5. *The teacher is a model of thoughtfulness.* Higher-order thinking involves a set of attitudes or dispositions as much as it does a set of skills or content understanding (Dewey 1933, Passmore 1967, Schrag 1988, Siegel 1988). Collectively, these dispositions might be called "thoughtfulness." Teachers model thoughtfulness by showing appreciation for students' ideas and for alternative approaches if based on sound reasoning, by acknowledging the difficulty of acquiring knowledge, and by explaining how they think through problems.

6. *Students offer explanations and*

reasons for their conclusions. During lessons students must talk if teachers are to determine whether higher-order thinking is being promoted. Students must share not only their answers, ideas, and opinions, but also the reasons that support them.

The 10 teachers whose classroom practice most consistently reflected the six dimensions will hereafter be called the "high scorers." The 10 whose practice least consistently reflected the dimensions will hereafter be called the "low scorers." The remaining group of 28 "middle scorers" were not included in the study.

Incidentally, the research team did not know which teachers from the pool of 48 would eventually compose the two groups of teachers; that is, the analysis of teachers' instructional practice to identify high and low scorers occurred months after the interview data were gathered.

We examined four areas of teachers' beliefs and theories: instructional goals, depth vs. breadth of content coverage, perceptions of students, and conceptions of thinking.

Instructional Goals

Teachers are asked to pursue a vast number of instructional goals. We were curious to see whether outstanding teachers of thinking place greater emphasis on the goal of thinking than their less successful colleagues. Here's what we found.

On a written questionnaire, high scorers unanimously mentioned the development of students' thinking as a fundamental goal of instruction, com-pared to only half of the low scorers. When we asked the two groups what gave them satisfaction as teachers, all of the high scorers, but only one low scorer, cited activities readily associated with thinking (for example, "students wrestling with values and making links," "seeing kids think and express their thoughts," "students citing reasons for their position"). Low scorers, on the other hand, referred to activities that may or may not involve thinking ("when students show interest," "when they feel

good about themselves," "helping them to understand the information being imparted.").

Equally dramatic differences showed up during our interviews with teachers. High scorers offered more elaborate responses when discussing their goals and placed greater emphasis on developing students' thinking. For example, Harold, a high scorer, wants to cultivate attitudes and skills related to thinking. Consider his comment:

> I want them to be able to study the material in my class and when they are finished with that course to be able to take the analytic skills and think through for themselves problems and situations that otherwise they would have ignored. To give them some confidence in their own mental abilities and what they can achieve; to examine, analyze, and decide. . . . Kids need to be "crap detectors," and they have to be able to think in order to put it into motion. . . . You've got to be able to think to filter out what's garbage and what's not; what's meaningful and what's not. The mind is a wonderful thing students can learn to use. It's not something that happens automatically. I really have a motivation to want them to think. It bothers me if they don't use their minds.

Except for two members, low scorers' responses to the question about instructional goals were generally much shorter and lacked the articulate, impassioned elaboration of high scorers — regardless of the goal cited. In addition, they emphasized teacher transmission rather than student exploration and critique of ideas. For example, unlike Harold, who has kids filtering, analyzing, and deciding, low scorer Laura wants her students to "know," "understand," and "pick up" knowledge:

> I want to relate my lesson to students' own lives. My goal is to have them know economic concepts that can help them become productive members of society. This can be as basic as staying in high school! In government the goal is to have them understand that these laws are for them, that this democracy is for them, to know their rights. This applies mostly to the hu-

manities students. The economics and government students are at a higher level, so I expect them to pick up more content in addition to relating it to their own lives.

Depth vs. Breadth

Clear, effective thinking about topics and issues requires a certain degree of immersion or depth of study. Immersion often comes in conflict with efforts to expose students to a breadth of content. We were curious to see how teachers think about the coverage dilemma.

Though both groups of teachers unanimously acknowledged their conflict over the issue, high scorers were more likely to believe content coverage impedes students' thinking and in turn were more willing to reduce coverage to pursue the goal of thinking. Further, high scorers identified their pressure to cover material as externally imposed (by the department chair, colleagues, state guidelines, and tests), whereas low scorers identified themselves as their primary source of coverage pressure.

Harold's statement is representative of many high scorers' disdain for extensive content coverage:

> I do not preoccupy myself with finishing the curriculum. Instead, I attempt to teach whatever I teach well and select classroom topics and materials very carefully. . . . It's ludicrous to attempt to cover 100 years of history in a month or two. I focus on concepts and ideas. The problem with most courses is that they are survey courses that are homogenized.

Conversely, Laura's statement highlights low scorers' self-imposed breadth orientation and awareness of its negative effect on promoting students' thinking:

> I'm more survey oriented. There's a conflict in my head, but I go for coverage. The kids like it, I like it, exposure is important. If they know a little, they can go on to further understanding themselves or in college. . . . Often times I feel like I squeeze information in and am not able to cover it all. It becomes a survey course. . . . Often times this reduces the ability to use critical

Using six dimensions of classroom practice that appear to promote thinking, we identified 10 teachers as outstanding and 10 as less than outstanding.

thinking skills because you want to try to cover the material more quickly.

Perceptions of Students

Research has documented the powerful impact teachers' perceptions of students have on their instructional practices and student achievement. Our analysis of teachers' perceptions of students revealed a defeatist orientation among half of all low scorers compared to none among the high scorers. While high scorers often acknowledged the difficulty of getting students to think (especially low achievers or early in the school year), their statements did not indicate frustration toward students or resignation about trying to promote their thinking. Instead, most high scorers expressed optimism about the prospects of engaging students' minds.

Group differences in the perception of students can be observed in the statements of low scorer Leonard and high scorer Howard. Leonard complains of student disinterest and low motivation, implicitly exonerating himself from responsibility for students' less-than-adequate performance:

What is most disappointing is that the students aren't interested in learning. . . . They are just not willing to put much effort into school. Their attention span is short, and they are apathetic. . . . High

achievers can be just as apathetic as low achievers.

Howard, on the other hand, believes that students of all achievement levels are capable of "responding favorably" to challenging tasks and that teachers must persist in challenging them. For Howard, factors that have created student resistance to thinking tasks can be overcome:

I believe many or even most students find a thinking task challenging and interesting. Some see it as too difficult and too much trouble. If the task is presented to them reasonably well, they respond favorably. . . . To think requires a lot more time and a lot more effort. But it is possible to change their attitudes. . . . There are a lot of teachers who could do more of it. . . . A lot of kids with limitations have been told, "You can't do this or that," so they aren't too motivated. Thinking can be fun. Low achievers can show good, solid thinking.

Conceptions of Thinking

Many staff development and reform efforts have assumed that developing teachers' conceptual understanding of thinking will help improve teachers' instruction in this area. We found that compared to low scorers, high scorers manifested lengthier, more elaborate, and more precise perspectives on what thinking entails. In part, this involves a greater ability to indicate the kinds of behaviors students and teachers should exhibit in a thoughtful classroom (for example, "critique but also defend a position," "understand the relevance of data to a central theme," "determine points of view and identify their effects," "formulate hypotheses and subject some to criticism").

In addition, high scorers identified a greater number of intellectual dispositions (curiosity, confidence, a thirst for reasons, willingness to take risk) and intellectual skills (interpret information, generalize from data, formulate conclusions) that cognitive scientists and other researchers typically associate with good thinkers.

Finally, high scorers include in their

statements points of clarification and subtle but important distinctions between their own views and possible alternative conceptions. For example, high scorer Hans challenges the notion that Benjamin Bloom's taxonomy of cognitive processes should be viewed hierarchically, observing that a Level Two "comprehension" question may be of greater difficulty to students than a Level Six "evaluation" question. In addition, he takes aim at skill approaches to thinking by calling "mindless" any activities that are not tied to the goal of understanding subject matter. Harriet, in her discussion of thinking, disagreed with the view that students need direct instruction in logical fallacies to become good thinkers. A third high scorer, Hilary, argued that "intellectual curiosity" can be cultivated and therefore should be distinguished from

Our conclusion is that thoughtful classroom practice requires thoughtful reflection on practice.

"cognitive capacity," which is physiologically determined. Distinctions of this kind were not found in the conceptions of thinking offered by low scorers.

Thoughtful Reflection on Practice

We began our study to compare outstanding teachers of thinking with their less successful colleagues. We looked at teachers' instructional goals, whether they emphasized depth or breadth of content coverage, their perceptions of students, and their understanding of thinking. What we found is that there is a correlation between teachers' goals and perspectives and the climate of thoughtfulness we perceived in their classrooms.

Reform efforts in the area of thinking that focus primarily on "how to" instructional techniques and that minimize opportunities for teachers to reflect upon and reconceptualize facets of their teaching are unlikely to produce significant, long-term change. Our conclusion is that thoughtful classroom practice requires thoughtful reflection on practice.

References

Cuban, L. (1984). *How Teachers Taught: Constancy and Change in American Classrooms: 1890-1980.* New York: Longman.

Dewey, J. (1933). *How We Think.* Boston: D.C. Heath.

Goodlad, J. (1984). *A Place Called School: Prospects for the Future.* New York: McGraw-Hill.

Newmann, F. M. (1988). "Can Depth Replace Coverage in the High School Curriculum?" *Phi Delta Kappan* 68, 5: 345-348.

Newmann, F. M. (1991). "Promoting Higher Order Thinking in Social Studies: Overview of a Study of Sixteen High School Departments." *Theory and Research in Social Education* 19, 4: 323-339.

Passmore, J. (1967). "On Teaching To Be Critical." In *The Concept of Education,* edited by R. S. Peters. London: Routledge and Kegan Paul.

Schrag, F. (1988). *Thinking in School and Society.* New York: Routledge and Kegan Paul.

Siegel, H. (1988). *Educating Reason.* New York: Routledge and Kegan Paul.

Sirotnik, K. (1983). "What You See Is What You Get — Constancy, Persistency, and Mediocrity in Classrooms." *Harvard Educational Review* 53, 1: 16-31.

Tobin, K. (1987). "The Role of Wait Time in Higher Cognitive Level Learning." *Review of Educational Research* 57, 1:69-95.

Author's note: This paper was supported by the National Center on Effective Secondary Schools; the U.S. Department of Education, Office of Educational Research and Improvement (Grant No. G-008690007); and the Wisconsin Center for Education Research, School of Education, University of Wisconsin-Madison. Contributions to this work have been made by Fred Newmann, Dae-Dong Hahn, Bruce King, Jim Ladwig, Robert Stevenson, Cameron McCarthy, Francis Schrag, and the cooperative staff in 16 high schools. The opinions expressed in this publication are mine and do not necessarily reflect the views of the supporting agencies or the contributors.

A BETTER WAY TO LEARN

Just 10% of classroom time can unlock children's creative thinking. A parent, physicist, and MacArthur 'genius' tells how.

Stephen H. Schneider

Stephen H. Schneider, winner of a Mac-Arthur "genius" award, is spending some of his MacArthur time working on science education and teaching at Stanford. He is senior scientist at the National Center for Atmospheric Research in Boulder, Colorado, and an international expert on global warming. He is also an advocate and practitioner of interdisciplinary teaching and learning at all levels—elementary to post-graduate. He frequently lectures on college campuses and says he "talks with elementary and secondary-school students, right on down to Congressional committees.

George Bush called himself the "education president." Bill Clinton has put "education for competitiveness" near the top of his priority list. The US Congress resonates whenever better schools are mentioned.

But the sad fact is that America has rededicated itself to improved education in every decade since World War II. And still the results don't measure up.

Can it be that American education is like the old line about the weather: Everybody talks about it, but nobody does anything about it?

In the interest of stimulating some doing, let me take you on a tour of some schools—and then put forward a modest but, I hope, extremely useful proposal, one involving only 10% of daily classroom time.

First the disclosure clause. I'm not an educator. (In fact, contrary to the old line, my career involves trying to do something about the weather and climate.) But I am a parent. I've served as chairman of a mid-American school-improvement team. And I'm using a Mac-Arthur Fellowship in part to study how science can be better taught. And that means going into school classrooms and finding what catches students' attention. Let me give you an example of what I mean. I have two kids, 11 and 13, and I have frequently visited their schools to talk with their classes. I went to their elementary school a few years ago, just after I'd been on a PBS program that discussed global warming. The ages of the kids I faced probably ranged from 8 to 12.

Now I should tell you that in a school situation I try to stuff my instinct to lecture like an expert. Instead, I like to conduct dialogues with the kids. Sure, they can give you a lot of "wrong" answers. But if you lead them through a dialogue, helping them to shape their own ideas and experiences—in other words, helping to empower them to think for themselves and have the courage to express it—they usually do amazingly well. I've learned what every good teacher already knows: Nine-year-olds really have no hesitation about telling you what they think if you free them of the stigma of having to be "right."

Anyway, we got a kind of Socratic dialogue going in that school that day. We started out talking about how climate works—why it is warmer in Kansas than in San Francisco in July, and just the opposite in January. They already knew the reason was being near or far from the ocean, and with a little help they even figured out why. Soon I asked them what was one of the biggest polluters of the atmosphere. "Coal," they replied, having seen the PBS program.

"OK," I said. "What should we do about that?"

"Well, I guess we better not use it," one kid replied. Fine. Nobody disagreed. So we went on to some other subjects.

But a few minutes later I came back to coal. "Where does coal come from?" I asked.

They started with dinosaurs, and, with a little shaping from me, worked their way back to prehistoric plants. But I told them I was not so much interested in where coal came from 100 million years ago. I wanted to know where it comes from today, and how we get it to power plants.

They knew—or easily guessed—that it is transported by trains and trucks, and gradually we got to the person who digs the coal out of the ground.

"Why does that person dig it up?" I asked. "Does that miner like going down in dark holes, or something?"

And the answer was, "No, of course not, but a miner needs money."

"Why?"

They laughed at my naiveté. "To eat, go to the movies, buy clothes and Nintendos for the kids."

So I said, "Well, what happens if we do what you guys said we ought to do? What happens if we stop using coal?"

All of a sudden the room was silent. For a long minute. They realized they had just unwittingly doomed some coal miner's kids to poverty.

"Maybe we can't ban coal," one kid said. "But what about the birds and fish if we don't?" another chimed in.

Finally one 11-year-old said, "Well, maybe we could find something else for miners to do."

"And maybe we could lower the age for serving in the US Senate," I joked, trying to conceal my goose-bumps. "Because they haven't figured that out yet!"

As we continued to talk about this issue, we explored the alternatives to coal—and to unemployment. But the best part of the discussion, to me, was that it took place in a realm that I like to think of as the realm of creative thinking—as opposed to rote, programmed learning.

I should add that I have tried this same exercise at the junior and senior high levels and at the university level, with freshmen and sophomores. And you know what happens there? Nothing. They look at one another or take notes. It is tough to get creative responses.

But creative responses are essential to teaching topics that are global, long-term, multidisciplinary, and cross-cutting. How do we teach about real problems—of peace, environment, productivity—when we tend to learn in boxes and organize ourselves in industry, government, and education into disciplinary niches—in departments of economics, chemistry, and biology? I think one answer can be found by changing the way we approach primary and secondary education in only 10% of daily classroom time.

Once I told some non-forthcoming college honors freshmen about what goes on in the elementary schools I visit, and I asked them, "What happens between the ages of 9 and 19 to kill your brains?"

"Junior high school," one nervous student mumbled out loud. The rest of the kids erupted like a geyser. And I heard virtually the same thing from all of them—that their classroom silence begins in junior high school.

Since then I've had other students confirm that they were afraid to speak up in junior high because their friends would think they were trying to show off. And there have been those who've said they were afraid of getting tagged as dumb.

College students also consistently tell me that their high school teachers rarely encouraged them to speak up creatively. They say teachers overwhelmingly wanted them to "learn" what was in the syllabus and the standardized tests, and not to question the curriculum or go off in directions that the teachers didn't know much about.

"Tell me about the good teachers you had in junior high and high school," I suggested. And then these same college students overflowed with enthusiasm.

I can remember the freshman who told me about a high school history teacher who'd set up the students to role-play different countries in famous conflict situations. And there was a math teacher who had asked the kids to invent examples from their lives to use in applying particular mathematical methods. Time after time, it seems that the teachers they truly learned from were the ones who

empowered students to have the courage to be creative and to express their opinions in class—right or wrong could be sorted out later.

HUMAN COGS

Creativity isn't simply learning the textbook. It is finding new ways to think or act. So, one problem that we have today in education, in my opinion, begins between the ages of 9 and 19. And the problem is the impression that "truth comes only from the front of the room," rather than from within individuals and by research, questioning, and group discussion.

Now, I know that every teacher has a curriculum and a syllabus to follow, and I know that time is limited, and that teachers sometimes have as many as 30 kids in a single classroom. And I don't oppose texts, tests, or achievement standards. And we all know that creativity is not measured by grades alone.

I think the problem is more gut level: that the US education system overall is set up to package information and to process people to be plastic cogs in the economic engine. And the vaunted Japanese system? It makes *titanium* parts for its economic juggernaut.

More than ever, what we need in the US is a system that encourages kids to ask questions.

I'm reminded of a trip I took to Tokyo several years ago for an international industrial congress. As it happened, I was the featured environment speaker, and my Japanese hosts very graciously invited me to dinner one evening. It was a spectacular sushi meal, and as we talked about the day's events and dined sumptuously, we began to relax and to genuinely feel like trusted friends.

I could tell that the environmental official who was sitting beside me had something on his mind. Finally he loosened his tie a bit, leaned over, and said, "I've got to ask you a question."

"Fine."

"I don't mean to be insulting," he began, "but everyone agrees that the

American public education system is poor, and that our workers are better trained in technical skills and better disciplined in their work habits than your workers. So why is it that we can *build* better products than you can, but we can't *invent* them?"

"Let me ask you a question," I replied. "Think back to your own school days. Can you remember a time when a teacher said something that you *knew*, from your own reading and study, was wrong? What did you do? Did you raise your hand, or ask for clarification?"

"Never!" he answered, visibly agitated. "That would have been inconceivable."

"Well," I said, "what you're asking me about goes to the heart of how you define creativity. What do you think it is? It's being different, isn't it? It has to do with not being afraid to ask questions, and not being afraid to take risks."

Very difficult," he said, glumly. "It would be very difficult in this culture to teach people to do such things, especially things that appear to insult seniority."

Remembering my Japanese friend's comments makes me realize more than ever that what we need in the United States is a system that encourages kids (and adults, too!) to ask questions—especially about whether they want to be turned into machine parts! Somehow we have to get kids participating creatively in the process of their education. Because if they continue to think that truth comes only from the front of the room, and that learning is a product that can be standardized, we are going to end up with sheeplike, uninformed citizens who are not capable of conducting public debate on difficult issues. And that will leave the "solutions" to the spin doctors, advertisers, elites, and lobbyists.

I can't help but remember a well-known British scientist-statesman who had the knack for getting right to the heart of an issue, and knowing exactly what questions to ask. I first met him when I was invited to a conference on nuclear winter in 1985 in Bellagio, Italy. The participants were divided between applied-physics types like me and theologians. There we were, in an incredibly beautiful, opulent setting, discussing gigadeaths and the fate of Earth.

One of the most remarkable panelists was Lord Zuckerman, a former chief scientific adviser to the British secretary of state for defense. He told a story about his early days in the Defense Ministry:

A TEACHER'S VIEW

Teacher Donna Luther says an education system that teaches children "the one right answer" turns out machines, not thinkers. She practices what Dr. Schneider is talking about every day. She has taught creativity to people of all ages (kindergartners to adults) for 19 years now—currently at Thayer Academy, a private school in Braintree, Massachusetts, and summers at the University of Buffalo's Creative Problem Solving Institute.

"On the first day of every year," Ms. Luther said in a recent interview with WM, "I read to all freshmen a story from 'A Whack on the Side of the Head,' a wonderful book by Roger von Oech. It's a wonderful story about a teacher in a sophomore English class who put a chalk dot on the board and asks, 'What is it?' And the class just sat there and looked and looked and looked, and finally somebody said, 'It's a chalk dot.' And he said, 'Isn't that interesting? I did this with a group of kindergartners yesterday, and they said it's an owl's eye, a cigar butt, a squashed egg, a pebble.'

"Those kindergartners just went on and on and on," Luther continued, "and how interesting that in all of those years [from kindergarten to sophomore year], we've beaten out all the questions and looked for the right answer, and in so many cases there are so many more than one right answer. I think that's very, very important to help kids understand—that I [the teacher] am not an expert and what's a right answer for me may be very different for them, and that's OK. As long as we learn to respect each other's right answer."

Luther said she's found it very effective to work with young children in dialogue, because they're so imaginative and natural about expressing their ideas.

One of the things they learn in that process is "to respect a lot of ideas along the way and understand that a lot of things are possible. It's not my idea, I'm saying to them. I'm not giving you the right answer," she said.

"Everything we teach has three parts to it," Luther said. "One is motivation: Let's figure out why we want to learn this, why it might be helpful to me. . . . Otherwise, you've got teachers saying, 'Today we're going to do Chapter 2, open to page 47.' That's not a motivator. That's 'we're all just going to plow through this stuff.'

"Then there's the exchange of information between teachers and students. But if you've opened up the doors of curiosity initially, then that stuff just pours in. . . .

"The last one is evaluation. And I think that's another place where our system falls apart.

"Because it's a test or a quiz, and what does that mean? Some kids are much better verbally than in writing, so a test is deadly for them. Why can't they just have a conversation and exchange information, or make a video, or do something that would help show what they know? Because that's an evaluation: What do we know here?"

Asked what she feels is the most important thing to make happen in a classroom, Luther said "mutual respect—not at the teacher-student level, but just for our fellow beings." That's one of the few rules she imposes on classes: "That we not criticize anyone—ever." With that established, people start to open up—even those sophomores in the "chalk-dot test."—WM

An admiral and a general came to him to discuss the details of three alternative designs for nuclear warheads. They had launched into an involved presentation when he brought them up short.

"Excuse me one moment, gentlemen," he said, "but what's it for? What's its strategic purpose? And how can we decide on the best design until we understand what it's for?"

I'm suggesting that we're never going to begin to solve any of the problems that I mentioned above—problems that are global, long-term, and multidisciplinary—until we ask the same question about our public education system: "What's it for?"

Should it be designed only to create tens of millions of stratified careerists for a system where only the elite are allowed to be creative? Or should it be designed to foster creativity wherever it's found?

10% = Q & A

Each of us has some component of creativity. I think that creativity is partly innate—and partly teachable. We may have different endowments as to how far we can go with our creative bents. But I'm quite certain that if those creative talents are beaten down for some individuals—as they may have been for my Japanese friend—such individuals will never have the same degree of inventiveness as those who are encouraged to challenge the system, and to do the hard, disciplined work of proving their challenges.

I'd therefore like to propose a "creativity tithe": that 10% of classroom time be devoted to encouraging individual initiative and creativity. Creative dialoguing is one way to get kids involved again in the education process. I'd like to propose that the education process be reinvigorated by rewarding teachers who aren't afraid to risk letting kids say what they think, and who aren't afraid to say that they don't have all the answers. I can't think of anything holding more promise for the future than a teacher who, in a dialogue with kids, is willing to say to a student, "I don't know the answer to your question, but how do you think we might find it together?"

I'm convinced that this kind of empowerment to ask questions and this process of learning how to learn will last a lifetime. Whereas the facts that are learned off a syllabus may not linger past the final exam.

EXTRA CREDIT

Now I'm not suggesting a return to something akin to the 1960s Berkeley free speech movement for fourth-graders. The idea isn't to go out and tear down the education system just because it's got problems. These are well-known to have multiple causes, including disparities in students' social and economic status.

What I *am* suggesting is that students of all status groups should be encouraged to challenge their teachers' premises—provided they take the next step, which is to back up their arguments with evidence, with logic, and with carefully reasoned suggestions even if these have to be labeled as speculative. And they should get extra credit, not censure, for such creative, thoughtful troublemaking.

WOULDN'T IT BE
NICE IF...?

Would there be a Nike shoe if inventor Bill Bowerman had not wondered what would happen if he poured rubber in his waffle iron?

Would there be a Sony Walkman if Masaru Ibuka hadn't wondered what it would be like to take the speaker and recorder out of a tape recorder and just make it a player with earphones?

Would there be a Federal Express if Fred Smith hadn't wondered why there couldn't be reliable overnight mail delivery service?

Such are the "questions of wonder" that Jim Collins of Stanford's School of Business has compiled, as noted in "The Creative Spirit," the book accompanying last year's PBS series by that name ("Notes From Practically Everywhere," WM, April 1992).

The trick is to ask the kind of questions children are not afraid to ask. The book suggests a simple exercise for anyone: "Each day, for a week, take a few minutes to ask yourself a question that begins: 'I wonder....' Ask this question about a particular area of your life, such as the workplace....It is essential not to censor yourself, no matter how impractical or outlandish the question sounds. After you have had some practice doing this, try going public with your questions by posing them to friends or colleagues....Listen carefully to their responses."

Another way to nudge the creative process is to begin "Wouldn't it be nice if...?" Once on vacation Edwin Land took some pictures of his daughter, and she asked why she couldn't see the results right away. He started thinking, and within an hour he had developed the concept of instant photography we know as Polaroid.

This episode is reported by management consultant William J. Altier in R&D Innovator, published by Winston J. Brill & Associates, Madison, Wisconsin. "Unfortunately," he writes, "a common barrier to creativity, the 'right answer' syndrome, is locked into people's brains shortly after they start school."

Author Stephen H. Schneider's dialogue approach is in keeping with the effort to "allow students and teachers to learn by discovery," as presented at this year's meeting of the American Association for the Advancement of Science (AAAS) in Boston in February. Some 60 participants' presentations had to do with educational reform—an indication of the impor-

tance given the subject by scientists.

The Computers for Classrooms Foundation asked the AAAS scientists for "an hour of your time every week" as school volunteers. In "SuperQuest" the Cornell Theory Center offered ways for students and their "teacher-coaches" to work together on projects using supercomputers to study everything from the environmental impact of high-rise buildings to the aerodynamics of bicycles to the patterns of a marching band. The Harvard-Smithsonian Center for Astrophysics announced its new Science Education Department, where teachers, scientists, and education specialists can work together to find new ways to make science education exciting. One program involves building portable robot observatories.

Seventh-grade teacher David J. Smith's "Making Maps from Memory" (WM, May 1989) describes a participatory way for teenagers to learn geography: drawing a map of the world from memory at the beginning of the school year—and again at the end of the year with all the accumulated learning represented.

Parents and teachers Jeannie Oakes and Martin Lipton tell how parents can continue a school dialogue—and communicate that ideas are important—by asking even small children what they think about issues of the day ("How Parents Can Help Children at School," WM, December 1989).

Biologist Joseph S. Levine explains how science teaching can be enhanced by involving students in participatory problem solving ("Your Child *Can* Learn Science," WM, February 1991).

C. Samuel Micklus, founder of Odyssey of the Mind, adds the element of international competition: Creative teams interact and cooperate to make a better rubber-band airplane (as the Chinese did), for example ("The World Finals of Creativity," WM, May 1991).—WM

I'd also like to propose that competition in the classroom or on the scholastic playing fields be mixed with some compassion. I'm not against competition, except that in many cases it insists on winner-take-all and loser-go-home. And somehow we have to teach kids (by example, perhaps?) that winning also has an obligation—to recognize how the loser feels. And to remember that winners are sometimes going to be losers.

Not everybody is going to like the idea of shifting 10% of class time from work on testable standard curriculum to more subjective "creativity training." I'm not remotely suggesting that I have worked out all the kinks. But let me offer replies to four of the concerns I have heard.

1. Some parents want every available second in class used to improve students' grades and test scores in order to get them early-decision admissions to elite colleges.

Such parents may be asking their children to carry out the parents' failed fantasies—a burden that some psychologists believe can reduce a child's ultimate adjustment to school and life. It has earned such guardians the unflattering label of "cannibal parents"—they devour their children's sense of self-determination. Psychological theory aside, the great achievements of creative people are not generally made by those who can best give back the canned curriculum, but rather by those free enough intellectually to find new ways to do things. Good grades or SAT scores are fine, but are just not enough to predict creativity.

2. If we encourage kids to question the curriculum or the purpose of school, they soon might doubt authority in general, for example, their parents, priests, or president.

In my value system it is the unthinking followers and the don't-make-waves types who keep some of our industrial and government agencies in neutral. The most successful, innovative companies (i.e., high-tech firms) reward creativity, helping to maintain America's competitive edge. Disciplined and rewarded iconoclasm is less likely to produce mediocrity or riot than suppression of open debate, of individuality, or of questioning standard practices.

3. Creative learning is hard to evaluate, and thus both student and teacher performance evaluations would become more subjective.

Several years ago I was chairman of my kids' elementary school's "School

Improvement Team"—a state-mandated committee of parents, teachers, community members, and the principal. The SIT's mission was to evaluate the school's performance in meeting educational goals set by the board and legislature. These included, rhetorically at least, both achievement and creativity. But virtually nothing existed to measure creativity. So, ignorant of any professional educational research that might have been under way, we met monthly for a year and a half to see what we could fathom for ourselves.

I can't think of anything more promising than a teacher willing to say 'I don't know the answer.'

First, with the active participation of Betsy Krill, the principal, we came up with a motto for the educational goal of the Mapleton Elementary School in Boulder, Colorado: "Shaping Education From Within." We felt that some of the best judges of what excites children are parents—if they'd watch and listen to their kids and report on their observations. So we designed a questionnaire asking parents to write down what aspects of school their kids talked about at home—negatively, neutrally, or enthusiastically. Most important, did the child on his/her own continue to read, draw, write, or sing about topics from school beyond assignments?

For teachers, we suggested devising a form—parallel to traditional report cards—on which observations about children's creative or self-motivated learning could be recorded.

Such observations would be subjective. But, by standardizing the format and tracking the responses over time, we felt we'd come up with consistent indicators of individual initiative and creative performance. (After all, even standardized tests have essay questions calling for subjective evaluation.)

Of course, for such parent/teacher measures to work, educational professionals need to take teaching and evaluating creativity seriously, devising many means to do so. This is an element of the "creativity tithe."

4. *Teachers have complained that some school boards and state legislatures are already threatening to tie teachers' pay to a "merit" system that objectively measures their performance based on how students do on standardized tests.*

If means like those above were available and maintained over time, they could be used along with other measures of creativity to help provide fairer evaluation of students' and teachers' overall performance. This delicate topic requires operating experience and constant renegotiations and reappraisals among teachers, administrators, parents, legislators, and students. But first it requires the will to experiment and take some risks in putting creativity higher on our education agenda.

NOT FLAKY

I realize what I am proposing isn't easy, given classroom sizes, school budgets, social problems, teachers' salaries, and the like. But I think that without this kind of fundamental change—from *product* and *facts* to a creative, questioning learning *process*—it will be very tough for schools to turn children into adults who can understand global, long-term problems, let alone feel competent to solve them creatively.

However, if we could give teachers a curriculum flexible enough to allow 10% of their classroom time each day—or even an hour or two a week at first—to encouraging, evaluating, and rewarding creative thinking, I think we could go a long way toward creating the citizenry that will be better able to diagnose and solve long-term, global problems.

Now when I say "creative," some people may think "flaky." And they may think that means we're not going to teach "hard facts," or that students won't be prepared to compete in the working world. But creativity means finding novel ways to solve problems—which means learning equally about products *and* process. If we can only get more teachers, parents, and administrators talking about this issue, it will become possible to take a small step or two, and over time a more comprehensive approach will evolve.

I'm not a flaming revolutionary. I don't argue that we have to can the traditional curriculum by next week. But I do think that we can't continue with "business as usual" in our schools—or political debates—for much longer. People have to feel competent to deal as citizens with perplexing, long-term, global, and multi-disciplinary problems. We have to make an effort to change our system, 10% by 10%. And before long, what might be thought radical today can become common sense tomorrow. And, like other "unthinkable" achievements, such as the crumbling of the Iron Curtain, it can happen within a single generation.

Exposing Our Students to Less Should Help Them Learn More

Mr. Dempster urges educators to take a close look at the composition of each instructional unit with an eye to separating the wheat from the chaff, so that they can get on with the serious business of effectively teaching the essentials.

Frank N. Dempster

FRANK N. DEMPSTER is a professor in the Department of Educational Psychology, University of Nevada, Las Vegas.

CURRICULAR change is hardly a newcomer to discussions of education reform in the U.S. However, only recently have concerns about the sheer size of the implemented curriculum threatened to move to center stage. Reform-minded scholars and educators have argued that decreasing the size of the curriculum will benefit students. Exposing students to less material but in more depth will, they contend, lead to greater learning than the current practice of exposing students to a large amount of often disconnected information.[1] So far, though, this claim has not received the rigorous scrutiny that an item on the national agenda with such far-reaching implications deserves. Teachers, administrators, policy makers, and others who seek to make such drastic changes in the curriculum will face difficult problems and will have to overcome many obstacles, including the nagging suspicion that students exposed to less will simply learn less, not more.

In this article I review relevant research on learning and discuss its implications for proposals to reduce the size of the curriculum. At the very least, these "lessons from learning research" illustrate the kinds of data on which curriculum decisions might be based. The results of this research arguably provide strong support for those who have adopted the old Bauhaus motto, "Less is more."[2] They lead to the conclusion that our students are exposed to too much material and that this practice is antithetical to what is known about effective learning.

The curriculum that now predominates in American schools seems to be based on three beliefs about human learning. First, curriculum decisions appear to be informed by the conviction that "more is better" and that just about anything that "enriches the meaning" of a lesson will assist learning. Second, there appears to be a pervasive belief among educators that exposing students to information contains little or no risk, that knowledge can't hurt. Third, the curriculum has been shaped according to the dual assumption that most students can learn most things quickly and that, once a student has satisfactorily demonstrated such learning, further practice is unnecessary. As the research presented below shows, each of these beliefs is false.

OVERSTUFFED AND UNDERNOURISHED

There is mounting evidence that students in a variety of curricular domains, including science, mathematics, and social studies, are receiving fleeting exposure to a vast amount of material.[3] The instructional medium most responsible for this state of affairs is the textbook. National surveys report that many classroom teachers look to textbooks for guidance in deciding what to teach, and the textbook to a great extent defines the content of what is taught in U.S. schools.[4] The textbook is both a subject-matter authority and a pedagogical guide. However, most textbooks present an abundance of material and encourage teachers to address a wide range of topics. According to one study, "The table of contents of most precollege texts reads like a course catalog for a four-year college. . . . The new vocabulary in a one-week science unit often exceeds that for a one-week unit in a foreign language."[5]

Cross-cultural comparisons, as well as historical studies, make a similar point, indicating that textbooks currently in use in the U.S. are unrivaled in size and amount of information covered.[6] U.S. science texts, for example, are considerably larger than their counterparts in Japan and Singapore, where students tend

 From *Phi Delta Kappan*, February 1993, pp. 433-437. Reprinted with permission of *Phi Delta Kappan* and the author.

to have higher achievement test scores than American students. The difference in the size of the texts seems to reflect the quantity of facts about each topic rather than the number of topics and key concepts covered. The texts used in Japan and Singapore are more concise and focus on a few examples, whereas the U.S. texts are laden with more information and detail.

As a result, U.S. textbooks and the tests designed to measure proficiency in a particular domain make so many, often conflicting, curricular demands that teachers cannot possibly cover all the material adequately. Thus teachers often make a practice of simply "mentioning" or "teaching for exposure," which means that students receive superficial exposure to a large amount of information.[7] That information includes the concepts, skills, and phenomena teachers are seeking to convey, as well as a variety of supporting material, such as details, embellishments, redundancies, illustrations, examples, facts, and names. Much of this information consists of what researchers refer to as "elaborations" — that is, material that is intended to enrich the meaning of the central information. Unfortunately, many texts are so packed with facts, names, and details that the real point of the lesson is often obscured.

In an effort to redress this imbalance, Project 2061 of the American Association for the Advancement of Science and the National Science Teachers Association have both initiated major reform efforts that seek to restructure science teaching in the U.S. While the two proposals recommend different approaches to the problem, both efforts share the same goals and are based on the explicit assumption that less content taught more effectively over successive years will lead to greater scientific literacy for the general public. Both efforts recommend that the number of topics taught and their accompanying baggage of facts and terminology be greatly reduced. According to the Project 2061 task force, the science and mathematics curricula are "overstuffed and undernourished." Consequently "the curricula must be changed to reduce the sheer amount of material covered."[8]

RESEARCH ON ELABORATIONS

From the early returns of research on elaborations, most researchers came

> Unfortunately, many texts are so packed with facts, names, and details that the real point of the lesson is obscured.

to believe that just about anything that would make information "more meaningful" would improve a student's ability to learn it. However, the early studies were conducted with traditional laboratory materials (e.g., lists of arbitrarily paired words) that have little or no meaning to begin with. More recent studies, using learning tasks that are less artificial, have not only dimmed this expectation but have shown that elaborations can be detrimental.[9] It appears that elaborations often divert attention away from the crucial point of a lesson.

In an especially informative series of studies of this sort, students learned better when they read text summaries that contained only main ideas (e.g., "Africa has had less rapid development in the 1960s than in the 1950s") than when they read the unabridged texts that contained both main ideas and the details, embellishments, and redundancies that typically accompany main ideas (e.g., "In the 1960s there was an unwise emphasis on manufacturing at the expense of agriculture").[10] This was the case even when total study time for main points was equated and subjects in the elaboration condition received additional time to study the elaborations. Not only did the elaborations hurt subjects' ability to retain the main points in the text, but they also hindered their subsequent ability to acquire new information that was related to the material presented in the summaries. Although it may be argued that the elaborations should have provided a richer knowledge base for acquiring new information, this is not what was found.

In these studies, the elaborations were

clearly relevant to the main ideas. But in many cases they are not. Consider, for example, the excerpt below, adapted from an elementary school text.

Aquaculture

One earth zone having to do with food production we have not yet investigated. It is the seas. Can they be farmed? The seas carry some of man's biggest manufactured items — his ships — and provide recreation for those who live along the shores. But the seas' greatest importance is the number of things found in their depths. Many of them are useful and necessary to man.

From his beginnings, man has probably hunted and caught fish. As he developed boats, he was able to get into deeper areas of water.

Recognizing the high nutritional value of fish, man has sought them more and more. He has been attracted to those fishing areas in which he could catch many fish of one kind. Tuna are caught with hooks and sardines with nets. Mackerel are packed in different size cans than sardines. And tuna and salmon in the same style of can are packed quite differently.

The authors were apparently trying to create a more meaningful, learner-friendly context for comprehension by elaborating on the main ideas. However, it is difficult to see what details about the size and style of cans for packing tuna and salmon have to do with farming the seas. Research suggests that the reader would be better off without these details. They are irrelevant and only serve to make it more difficult for the reader to extract the main ideas.

In another series of studies with a counterintuitive outcome, college students were given a lengthy list of unfamiliar vocabulary words to learn. One group received only the words and their definitions, while the other received the words, their definitions, and either one or three sentences in which the words were used in correct contexts. Although the group receiving the sentence-context elaboration was treated in a manner consistent with the popular "learning from context" approach to vocabulary learning, this group actually performed worse than the group receiving only the words and their definitions. Moreover, these same findings prevailed when the group receiving the sentences in context was given more total study time (to allow for processing the sentences) than the group receiving only words and definitions. The findings even held up when the measure of learning was the subjects' ability to use the vocabulary words correctly in sentences.[11] Clearly, these findings are contrary to the prevailing trends in such areas as language arts, which emphasize the importance of context.

In order to promote classroom learning, it appears that elaborations must meet at least four necessary, but not always sufficient, conditions. First, they must be personally meaningful.[12] If the student does not have sufficient domain-specific knowledge to comprehend an elaboration, he or she will not benefit from it; indeed, it may hinder learning. In one study, for instance, examples in text facilitated recall and comprehension — but only when the reader was very knowledgeable in the topic area. Otherwise, the elaborated text resulted in poorer performance than the unelaborated ones. Significantly, U.S. science texts tend to use examples that are remote from the experience of many children. Examples in foreign texts appear to provide a better connection to real life.

Second, the elaboration must be relevant and should not digress too far from the point that the teacher or textbook wishes to convey.[13] For example, illustrations that are not relevant but merely decorative, as they are in many texts, may actually impede learning.

Third, the elaboration must be precise. It should be logically or causally connected to the main point, so that the learner can either reconstruct or infer the main idea from the elaboration.[14]

Finally, elaborations are likely to be effective only to the extent that they encourage processing that is complementary to the processing invited by the material to be learned itself.[15] Research using material from textbooks has shown that elaborations do not facilitate learning if they help students focus on information that they would have processed easily in the first place.

RESEARCH ON INTERFERENCE

Interference is one of the most thoroughly investigated phenomena in the study of learning. Two kinds of interference — namely, *proactive* and *retroactive* interference — have received most of the attention. Proactive interference occurs when previously presented information hinders the learning of new material, while retroactive interference occurs when the retention of previously presented information is reduced by sub-

sequent learning. The risk of interference is highest when a lot of similar information is presented and the material is not well-learned. For example, a teacher who is introduced to an increasing number of students — but does not have an opportunity to learn their names very well — will probably find it increasingly difficult to learn the names of new students (proactive interference), as well as to remember the names of past students (retroactive interference).

Another form of interference is known as *coactive* interference. It arises when one information-processing activity impairs another that is occurring at essentially the same time. In the study that compared text summaries with unabridged texts, for example, the findings suggest that the embellishments to the text forced subjects into a "time-sharing" mode of information processing, which interfered with their ability to adequately focus attention on the main points. As with proactive and retroactive interference, coactive interference is also much influenced by the amount of material to which the learner is exposed and by the degree to which it has already been learned.

The early investigations gave little reason to believe that interference was of much practical significance, since interference seemed to be confined to artificial laboratory materials. However, more recent studies have shown that massive amounts of interference can occur in a variety of classroom activities.[16]

For example, research suggests that many, if not most, texts contain abundant sources of interference.[17] One section of a text can interfere with another section, particularly if the two sections are topically related. In one study, subjects who first read a passage about direct current and then read a passage about alternating current tended to perform worse on subsequent tests about electricity than did subjects who read only one of the sections and an unrelated passage. Reading about two related topics in succession, without having the opportunity to really understand the material, appears to result in a great deal of confusion and little learning. Given that instruction often occurs in blocks of time, with each block partitioned into related topics, this finding is of considerable practical significance.

RESEARCH ON PRACTICE

Research has shown that, under certain

conditions, practice may either reduce the effects of interference or result in proactive or retroactive facilitation of learning.[18] For example, the acquisition of skill in multiplication is normally hampered by brief exposures to problems with similar or identical digits and products, because problems encountered early in a sequence interfere with problems introduced later and vice versa. But with continuous practice on both old problems and new problems, these difficulties can be avoided. Likewise, several rereadings of the passage about direct current (cited above) completely eliminated the retroactive interference that normally comes about as a result of reading the passage about alternating current. The rereadings even resulted in some retroactive facilitation.

The conditions most favorable to such outcomes involve what learning researchers refer to as "distributed" or "spaced" practice — in the form of either multiple presentations of the information to be learned (e.g., reviews) or in the form of tests. The signature characteristic of distributed practice is that the practice sessions are distributed over a relatively lengthy period of time (e.g., three reviews in three months). Although "massed" practice, which occurs over a relatively brief period (e.g., three reviews in one week), may result in rapid acquisition of new material, the learning is not as durable or as resistant to interference as that acquired through frequent distributed practice.[19] Frequent distributed practice helps students maintain and develop concepts and skills introduced early in a sequence, and it gives them the time needed to find appropriate and meaningful ways of integrating information from a variety of sources. Research suggests that distributed practice does more than simply increase the amount learned; it frequently shifts the learner's attention away from the verbatim details of the material being studied to its deeper conceptual structure.[20]

Even insights seldom occur without repeated exposure to relevant material over a relatively lengthy period. Anyone who has arrived at a profound understanding of something will recognize the importance of distributed practice and the sense of accomplishment it affords. Sustained involvement in an area of inquiry — what Isaac Newton reportedly referred to as "patient thought" — is the key to success in a wide variety of endeavors.

IMPLICATIONS FOR THE CURRICULUM

In short, research on elaborations, interference, and practice has several implications for proposals to reduce the curriculum. First, it suggests that many of the elaborations found in textbooks and provided by teachers are of little value. Some probably hinder the realization of key educational objectives even as they consume limited instructional resources. Second, exposing students to information has a potential downside: it may actively interfere with the acquisition and retention of other information. Thus there is indeed some truth to the old adage "a little learning is a dangerous thing." Third, if there is one indispensable key to effective learning, it is distributed practice. But in an overstuffed curriculum there is little opportunity for distributed practice.

Together, these lessons from research on learning illustrate how research can be used to support efforts to streamline the curriculum. Of course, curriculum decisions are not based on research alone. As Theodore Sizer noted, "Coverage within subjects is a key priority."[21] What one sees and hears in the classroom is a torrent of disconnected facts, procedures, lists, and dates. When an imaginative teacher suggests the deletion of some material, the voices raised in protest have usually won out. Indeed, research suggests that teachers, curriculum planners, and administrators are much more eager to add topics and supporting material to the existing curriculum than they are to remove them.[22] On a different level, this practice parallels the phenomenon known as "course proliferation," which has been nicely chronicled in *The Shopping Mall High School*.[23]

For reform efforts to be successful, difficult choices will have to be made about what students ought to learn. Research provides guidelines for identifying elaborations and for distinguishing between effective and ineffective ones, but it says little about the range of topics or the specific concepts and skills within each topic that should remain. Supporting material must be distinguished from key educational objectives; only then can time-consuming elaborations that do not serve their purpose be weeded out.

I do not mean to suggest that textbooks and other sources of information in the classroom should be little more than glorified outlines. But with 20 or so states setting their own standards for what should go into textbooks, it's no wonder that the books often end up so crammed with definitions, facts, and embellishments that they read like a Sears catalogue. Textbook publishers are not likely to trim their texts unless it is worthwhile financially, and this is unlikely to happen unless states insist on cuts and coordinate their guidelines, as California and Texas have recently done on behalf of their science texts.

Educators will also need to be persuaded that poorly learned information can be harmful and that sound learning normally requires frequent practice, in the form of either reviews or tests. This will not be easy, since many educators have convinced themselves that "repetitive practice" stifles creativity, and they identify such practice with something called "rote learning." It is partly because of this belief that teachers avoid recycling curricular units throughout the term. Besides, recycling isn't tidy. It doesn't let teachers teach a unit and dust off their hands quickly with a nice sense of completion.

In short, truly effective learning requires frequent distributed practice, and this can only be achieved by reducing the size of the existing curriculum, which is dangerously overstuffed. But instead of focusing immediately on which topics to eliminate, educators should consider taking a close look at the composition of each instructional unit, with an eye to relieving the curriculum of elaborations that do not serve a purpose. In effect, such a reexamination would force educators to think about separating the wheat from the chaff, so that they can get on with the serious business of effectively teaching the essentials.

1. Bet-Sheva Eylon and Marcia C. Linn, "Learning and Instruction: An Examination of Four Research Perspectives in Science Education," *Review of Educational Research*, vol. 58, 1988, pp. 251-301; Donald J. Freeman et al., "Do Textbooks and Tests Define a National Curriculum in Elementary School Mathematics?," *Elementary School Journal*, vol. 83, 1983, pp. 501-13; Fred M. Newmann, "Can Depth Replace Coverage in the High School Curriculum?," *Phi Delta Kappan*, January 1988, pp. 345-48; and Andrew Porter, "A Curriculum out of Balance: The Case of Elementary School Mathematics," *Educational Researcher*, June/July 1989, pp. 9-15.

2. Theodore R. Sizer, *Horace's Compromise: The Dilemma of the American High School* (Boston: Houghton Mifflin, 1984.)

3. Eylon and Linn, op. cit.; Newmann, op. cit.; and Porter, op. cit.

4. Freeman et al., op. cit.

5. Eylon and Linn, op. cit.

6. Marilyn J. Chambliss and Robert C. Calfee, "Designing Science Textbooks to Enhance Student Understanding," *Educational Psychologist*, vol. 24, 1989, pp. 307-22; and Patricia Mulcahy and S. Jay Samuels, "Three Hundred Years of Illustrations in American Textbooks," in Harvey A. Houghton and Dale M. Willows, eds., *The Psychology of Illustration*, vol. 2 (New York: Springer-Verlag, 1987), pp. 1-52.

7. Porter, op. cit.

8. *Project 2061: Science for All Americans* (Washington, D.C.: American Association for the Advancement of Science, 1989).

9. John D. Bransford et al., "Differences in Approaches to Learning: An Overview," *Journal of Experimental Psychology: General*, vol. 3, 1982, pp. 390-98; Frank N. Dempster, "Informing Classroom Practice: What We Know About Several Task Characteristics and Their Effects on Learning," *Contemporary Educational Psychology*, vol. 13, 1988, pp. 254-64; idem, "Effects of Variable Encoding and Spaced Presentations on Vocabulary Learning," *Journal of Educational Psychology*, vol. 79, 1987, pp. 162-70; idem, "Retroactive Interference in the Retention of Prose: A Reconsideration and New Evidence," *Applied Cognitive Psychology*, vol. 2, 1988, pp. 97-112; and Lynne M. Reder, "Techniques Available to Author, Teacher, and Reader to Improve Retention of Main Ideas of a Chapter," in Susan F. Chipman, Judith W. Segal, and Robert Glaser, eds., *Thinking and Learning Skills*, vol. 2 (Hillsdale, N.J.: Erlbaum, 1985).

10. Reder, op. cit.

11. Dempster, "Effects of Variable Encoding."

12. Chambliss and Calfee, op. cit.

13. Reder, op. cit.; and Joel R. Levin, Gary J. Anglin, and Russell N. Carney, "On Empirically Validating Functions of Pictures in Prose," in Dale M. Willows and Harvey A. Houghton, eds., *The Psychology of Illustration*, vol. 1 (New York: Springer-Verlag, 1987), pp. 51-85.

14. Bransford et al., op. cit.

15. Mark A. McDaniel and Gilles O. Einstein, "Material-Appropriate Processing: A Contextualist Approach to Reading and Studying Strategies," *Educational Psychology Review*, vol. 1, 1989, pp. 113-45.

16. Gary B. Blumenthal and Donald Robbins, "Delayed Release from Proactive Interference with Meaningful Material: How Much Do We Remember After Reading Brief Prose Passages?," *Journal of Experimental Psychology: Human Learning and Memory*, vol. 3, 1977, pp. 754-61; Alan S. Brown, "Encountering Misspellings and Spelling Performance: Why Wrong Isn't Right," *Journal of Educational Psychology*, vol. 80, 1988, pp. 488-94; Jamie I. D. Campbell and Jeffrey D. Graham, "Mental Multiplication Skill: Structure, Process, and Acquisition," *Canadian Journal of Psychology*, vol. 39, 1985, pp. 338-66; and Dempster, "Retroactive Interference."

17. Dempster, "Retroactive Interference."

18. Campbell and Graham, op. cit.; Dempster, "Retroactive Interference"; and Perry W. Thorndyke and Barbara Hayes-Roth, "The Use of Schemata in the Acquisition and Transfer of Knowledge," *Cognitive Psychology*, vol. 2, 1979, pp. 82-106.

19. Frank N. Dempster, "Synthesis of Research on Reviews and Tests," *Educational Leadership*, April 1991, pp. 71-76.

20. Richard E. Mayer, "Can You Repeat That? Qualitative Effects of Repetition and Advance Organizers on Learning from Science Prose," *Journal of Educational Psychology*, vol. 75, 1983, pp. 40-49.

21. Sizer, p. 81.

22. Robert E. Floden et al., "Responses to Curriculum Pressures: A Policy-Capturing Study of Teacher Decisions About Context," *Journal of Educational Psychology*, vol. 73, 1981, pp. 129-41.

23. Arthur G. Powell, Eleanor Farrar, and David K. Cohen, *The Shopping Mall High School* (Boston: Houghton Mifflin, 1985).

Five Standards of Authentic Instruction

Fred M. Newmann and Gary G. Wehlage

Fred M. Newmann is Director of the Center on Organization and Restructuring of Schools and Professor of Curriculum and Instruction, University of Wisconsin-Madison, Wisconsin Center for Education Research, 1025 W. Johnson St., Madison, WI 53706. **Gary G. Wehlage** is Associate Director of the Center on Organization and Restructuring of Schools and Professor of Curriculum and Instruction, University of Wisconsin-Madison, same address.

What types of instruction engage students in using their minds well? A framework developed at Wisconsin's Center on Organization and Restructuring of Schools may be a valuable tool for teachers and researchers attempting to answer this complex question.

Why do many innovations fail to improve the quality of instruction or student achievement? In 1990, we began to explore this question by studying schools that have tried to restructure. Unfortunately, even the most innovative activities—from school councils and shared decision making to cooperative learning and assessment by portfolio—can be implemented in ways that undermine meaningful learning, unless they are guided by substantive, worthwhile educational ends. We contend that innovations should aim toward a vision of authentic student achievement, and we are examining the extent to which instruction in restructured schools is directed toward authentic forms of student achievement. We use the word *authentic* to distinguish between achievement that is significant and meaningful and that which is trivial and useless.

To define authentic achievement more precisely, we rely on three criteria that are consistent with major proposals in the restructuring movement:[1] (1) students construct meaning and produce knowledge, (2) students use disciplined inquiry to construct meaning, and (3) students aim their work toward production of discourse, products, and performances that have value or meaning beyond success in school.[2]

The Need for Standards for Instruction

While there has been much recent attention to standards for curriculum and for assessment,[3] public and professional discussion of standards for instruction tends to focus on procedural and technical aspects, with little attention to more fundamental standards of quality. Is achievement more likely to be authentic when the length of class periods varies, when teachers teach in teams, when students participate in hands-on activities, or when students spend time in cooperative groups, museums, or on-the-job apprenticeships?

We were cautious not to assume that technical processes or specific sites for learning, however innovative, necessarily produce experiences of high intellectual quality. Even activities that place students in the role of a more active, cooperative learner and that seem to respect student voices can be implemented in ways that do not produce authentic achievement. The challenge is not simply to adopt innovative teaching techniques or to find new locations for learning, but deliberately to counteract two persistent maladies that make conventional schooling inauthentic:

1. Often the work students do does not allow them to use their minds well.

2. The work has no intrinsic meaning or value to students beyond achieving success in school.

To face these problems head-on, we articulated standards for instruction that represented the quality of intellectual work but that were not tied to any specific learning activity (for example, lecture or small-group discussion). Indeed, the point was to assess the extent to which any given activity—traditional or innovative, in or out of school—engages students in using their minds well.

Instruction is complex, and quantification in education can often be as misleading as informative. To guard against oversimplification, we formulated several standards, rather than only one or two, and we conceptualized each standard as a continuous construct from "less" to "more" of a quality, rather than as a categorical (yes or no) variable. We expressed each standard as a dimensional construct on a five-point scale. Instructions for rating lessons include specific criteria for each score—1 to 5—on each standard. Space does not permit us to present criteria for every possible rating, but for each standard we first distinguish between high and low scoring lessons and then offer examples of criteria for some specific ratings. Raters consider both the number of students to which the criterion applies and the proportion of class time during which it applies.[4] The five standards are: higher-order thinking, depth of knowledge, connectedness to the world beyond the classroom, substantive conversation, and social support for student achievement (see fig. 1).

Higher-Order Thinking

The first scale measures the degree to which students use higher-order thinking.

Lower-order thinking (LOT) occurs when students are asked to receive or recite factual information or to employ rules and algorithms through repetitive routines. As information-receivers, students are given pre-specified knowledge ranging from simple facts and information to more complex concepts. Students are in this role when they recite previously acquired knowledge by responding to questions that require recall of pre-specified knowledge.

Higher-order thinking (HOT) requires students to manipulate information and ideas in ways that transform their meaning and implications, such as when students combine facts and ideas in order to synthesize, generalize, explain, hypothesize, or arrive at some conclusion or interpretation. Manipulating information and ideas through these processes allows students to solve problems and discover new (for them) meanings and understandings. When students engage in HOT, an element of uncertainty is introduced, and instructional outcomes are not always predictable.

Criteria for higher-order thinking:
3 = Students primarily engage in routine LOT operations a good share of the lesson. There is at least one significant question or activity in which some students perform some HOT operations.
4 = Students engage in an at least one major activity during the lesson in which they perform HOT operations. This activity occupies a substantial portion of the lesson, and many students perform HOT.

> We wanted to assess the extent to which any given activity— traditional or innovative, in or out of school— engages students in using their minds well.

Depth of Knowledge

From "knowledge is shallow" (1) to "knowledge is deep" (5), the next scale assesses students' depth of knowledge and understanding. This term refers to the substantive character of the ideas in a lesson and to the level of understanding that students demonstrate as they consider these ideas.

Knowledge is thin or superficial when it does not deal with significant concepts of a topic or discipline—for example, when students have a trivial understanding of important concepts or when they have only a surface acquaintance with their meaning. Superficiality can be due, in part, to instructional strategies that emphasize coverage of large quantities of fragmented information.

Knowledge is deep or thick when it concerns the central ideas of a topic or discipline. For students, knowledge is deep when they make clear distinctions, develop arguments, solve problems, construct explanations, and otherwise work with relatively complex understandings. Depth is produced, in part, by covering fewer topics in systematic and connected ways.

Criteria for depth of knowledge:
2 = Knowledge remains superficial and fragmented; while some key concepts and ideas are mentioned or covered, only a superficial acquaintance or trivialized understanding of these complex ideas is evident.
3 = Knowledge is treated unevenly during instruction; that is, deep understanding of something is countered by superficial understanding of other ideas. At least one significant idea may be presented in depth and its significance grasped, but in general the focus is not sustained.

Connectedness to the World

The third scale measures the extent to which the class has value and meaning beyond the instructional context. In a class with little or no value beyond, activities are deemed important for success only in school (now or later). Students' work has no impact on others and serves only to certify their level of compliance with the norms of formal schooling.

A lesson gains in authenticity the more there is a connection to the larger social context within which students live. Instruction can exhibit some degree of connectedness when (1) students address real-world public problems (for example, clarifying a contemporary issue by applying statistical analysis in a report to the city council on the homeless); or (2) students use personal experiences as a context for applying knowledge (such as using conflict resolution techniques in their own school).

Criteria for connectedness:
1 = Lesson topic and activities have no clear connection to issues or experience beyond the classroom. The teacher offers no justification for the work beyond the need to perform well in class.
5 = Students work on a problem or issue that the teacher and students see as connected to their personal experiences or contemporary public situations. They explore these connections in ways that create personal meaning. Students are involved in an effort to influence an audience beyond their classroom; for example, by communicating knowledge to others, advocating solutions to social problems, providing assistance to people, or creating performances or products with utilitarian or aesthetic value.

Substantive Conversation

From "no substantive conversation" (1) to "high-level substantive conversation" (5), the fourth scale assesses the extent of talking to learn and understand the substance of a subject. In classes with little or no substantive conversation, interaction typically consists of a lecture with recitation in which the teacher deviates very little from delivering a preplanned body of information and set of questions; students routinely give very short answers. Teachers' list of questions, facts, and concepts tend to make the discourse choppy, rather than coherent; there is often little or no follow-up of student responses. Such discourse is the oral equivalent of fill-in-the-blank or short-answer study questions.

High levels of substantive conversation are indicated by three features:

1. There is considerable interaction about the ideas of a topic (the talk is about disciplined subject matter and includes indicators of higher-order thinking such as making distinctions, applying ideas, forming generalizations, raising questions, and not just reporting experiences, facts, definitions, or procedures).

2. Sharing of ideas is evident in exchanges that are not completely scripted or controlled (as in a teacher-led recitation). Sharing is best illustrated when participants explain themselves or ask questions in complete sentences and when they respond directly to comments of previous speakers.

3. The dialogue builds coherently on participants' ideas to promote improved collective understanding of a theme or topic.

Criteria for substantive conversation:
To score 2 or above, conversation must focus on subject matter as in feature (1) above.
2 = Sharing (2) and/or coherent promotion of collective understanding (3) occurs briefly and involves at least one example of two consecutive interchanges.
4 = All three features of substantive conversation occur, with at least one example of sustained conversation

---

Figure 1

Five Standards of Authentic Instruction

1. Higher-Order Thinking
lower-order thinking only   1...2...3...4...5   higher-order thinking is central

2. Depth of Knowledge
knowledge is shallow   1...2...3...4...5   knowledge is deep

3. Connectedness to the World Beyond the Classroom
no connection   1...2...3...4...5   connected

4. Substantive Conversation
no substantive conversation   1...2...3...4...5   high-level substantive conversation

5. Social Support for Student Achievement
negative social support   1...2...3...4...5   positive social support

---

(that is, at least three consecutive interchanges), and many students participate.

Social Support for Student Achievement

The social support scale involves high expectations, respect, and inclusion of all students in the learning process. Social support is low when teacher or student behavior, comments, and actions tend to discourage effort, participation, or willingness to express one's views. Support can also be low if no overt acts like the above occur, but when the overall atmosphere of the class is negative as a result of previous behavior. Token acknowledgments, even praise, by the teacher of student actions or responses do not necessarily constitute evidence of social support.

Social support is high in classes when the teacher conveys high expectations for all students, including that it is necessary to take risks and try hard to master challenging academic work, that all members of the class can learn important knowledge and skills, and that a climate of mutual respect among all members of the class contributes to achievement by all. "Mutual respect" means that students with less skill or proficiency in a subject are treated in ways that encourage their efforts and value their contributions.

Criteria for social support:
2 = Social support is mixed. Both negative and positive behaviors or comments are observed.
5 = Social support is strong. The class is characterized by high expectations, challenging work, strong effort, mutual respect, and assistance in achievement for almost all students. Both teacher and students demonstrate a number of these attitudes by soliciting and welcoming contributions from all students. Broad student participation may indicate that low-achieving students receive social support for learning.

Using the Framework to Observe Instruction

We are now using the five standards to estimate levels of authentic instruction in social studies and mathematics in elementary, middle, and high schools that have restructured in various ways. Our purpose is not to evaluate schools or teachers, but to learn how authentic instruction and student achievement are facilitated or impeded by:

■ organizational features of schools (teacher workload, scheduling of instruction, governance structure);

■ the content of particular programs aimed at curriculum, assessment, or staff development;

■ the quality of school leadership;

■ school and community culture.

We are also examining how actions of districts, states, and regional or national reform projects influence instruction. The findings will describe the conditions under which "restructuring" improves instruction for students and suggest implications for policy and practice.

Apart from its value as a research tool, the framework should also help teachers reflect upon their teaching. The framework provides a set of standards through which to view assignments, instructional activities, and the dialogue between teacher and students and students with one another. Teachers, either alone or with peers, can use the framework to generate questions, clarify goals, and critique their teaching. For example, students may seem more engaged in activities such as cooperative learning or long-term projects, but heightened participation alone is not sufficient. The standards provide further criteria for examining the extent to which such activities actually put students' minds to work on authentic questions.

In using the framework, either for reflective critiques of teaching or for research, it is important to recognize its limitations. First, the framework does not try to capture in an exhaustive way all that teachers may be trying to accomplish with students. The standards attempt only to represent in a quantitative sense the degree of authentic instruction observed within discrete class periods. Numerical ratings alone cannot portray how lessons relate to one another or how multiple lessons might accumulate into experiences more complex than the sum of individual lessons. Second, the relative importance of the different standards remains open for discussion. Each suggests a distinct ideal, but it is probably not possible for most teachers to show high performance on all standards in most of their lessons. Instead, it may be important to ask, "Which standards should receive higher priority and under what circumstances?"[5]

Finally, although previous research indicates that teaching for thinking, problem solving, and understanding often has more positive effects on student achievement than traditional teaching, the effects of this specific framework for authentic instruction on student achievement have not been examined.[6] Many educators insist that there are appropriate times for traditional, less authentic instruction—emphasizing memorization, repetitive practice, silent study without conversation, and brief exposure—as well as teaching for in-depth understanding.

Rather than choosing rigidly and exclusively between traditional and authentic forms of instruction, it seems more reasonable to focus on how to move instruction toward more authentic accomplishments for students. Without promising to resolve all the dilemmas faced by thoughtful teachers, we hope the standards will offer some help in this venture.

---

[1] See Carnegie Corporation of New York (1989), Elmore and Associates (1990), and Murphy (1991).

[2] See Archbald and Newmann 1988, Newmann 1991, Newmann and Archbald 1992, Newmann et al. 1992, and Wehlage et al. 1989.

[3] For example, see the arguments for standards in National Council on Education Standards and Testing (1992), and Smith and O'Day (1991).

[4] In three semesters of data collection, correlations between raters were .7 or higher, and precise agreement between raters was about 60 percent or higher for each of the dimensions. A detailed scoring manual will be available to the public following completion of data collection in 1994.

[5] The standards may be conceptually distinct, but initial findings indicate that they cluster together statistically as a single construct. That is, lessons rated high or low on some dimensions tend to be rated in the same direction on others.

[6] Evidence for positive achievement effects of teaching for thinking is provided in diverse sources such as Brown and Palinscar (1989), Carpenter and Fennema (1992), Knapp et al. (1992), and Resnick (1987). However, no significant body of research to date has clarified key dimen-sions of instruction that produce *authentic* forms of student achievement as defined here.

References

Archbald, D., and F.M. Newmann. (1988). *Beyond Standardized Testing: Assessing Authentic Academic Achievement in the Secondary School*. Reston, Va.: National Association of Secondary School Principals.

Brown, A., and A. Palinscar. (March 1989). "Coherence and Causality in Science Readings." Paper presented at the annual meeting of the American Educational Research Association, San Francisco.

Carnegie Corporation of New York. (1989). *Turning Points: Preparing American Youth for the 21st Century*. Report on the Carnegie Task Force on the Education of Young Adolescents. New York: Carnegie Council on Adolescent Development.

Carpenter, T. P., and E. Fennema. (1992). "Cognitively Guided Instruction: Building on the Knowledge of Students and Teachers." In *Curriculum Reform: The Case of Mathematics in the United States*. Special issue of *International Journal of Educational Research*, edited by W. Secada, pp. 457-470. Elmsford, N.Y.: Pergamon Press, Inc.

Elmore, R. F., and Associates. (1990). *Restructuring Schools: The Next Generation of Educational Reform*. San Francisco: Jossey-Bass.

Knapp, M. S., P.M. Shields, and B.J. Turnbull. (1992). *Academic Challenge for the Children of Poverty: Summary Report*. Washington, D.C.: U.S. Department of Education, Office of Policy and Planning.

Murphy, J. (1991). *Restructuring Schools: Capturing and Assessing the Phenomenon*. Nashville, Tenn.: National Center for Educational Leadership, Vanderbilt University.

National Council on Education Standards and Testing. (1992). *Raising Standards for American Education*. A Report to Congress, the Secretary of Education, the National Education Goals Panel, and the American People. Washington, D.C.: U.S. Government Printing Office, Superintendent of Documents, Mail Stop SSOP.

Newmann, F. M. (1991). "Linking Restructuring to Authentic Student Achievement." *Phi Delta Kappan* 72, 6: 458-463.

Newmann, F.M., and D. Archbald. (1992). "The Nature of Authentic Academic Achievement." In *Toward a New Science of Educational Testing and Assessment*, edited by H. Berlak, F.M. Newmann, E. Adams, D.A. Archbald, T. Burgess, J. Raven, and T.A. Romberg, pp. 71-84. Albany, N.Y.: SUNY Press.

Newmann, F. M., G.G. Wehlage, and S.D. Lamborn. (1992). "The Significance and Sources of Student Engagement." In *Student Engagement and Achievement in American Secondary Schools*, edited by F.M. Newmann, pp. 11-30. New York: Teachers College Press.

Resnick, L. (1987). *Education and Learning to Think*. Washington, D.C.: National Academy Press.

Smith, M. S., and J. O'Day. (1991). "Systemic School Reform." In *The Politics of Curriculum and Testing: The 1990 Yearbook of the Politics of Education Association*, edited by S.H. Fuhrman and B. Malen, pp. 233-267. Philadelphia: Falmer Press.

Wehlage, G. G., R.A. Rutter, G.A. Smith, N. Lesko, and R.R. Fernandez. (1989). *Reducing the Risk: Schools as Communities of Support*. Philadelphia: Falmer Press.

Authors' note: This paper was prepared at the Center on Organization and Restructuring of Schools, supported by the U.S. Department of Education, Office of Educational Research and Improvement (Grant No. R117Q0005-92) and by the Wisconsin Center for Education Research, School of Education, University of Wisconsin-Madison. Major contributions to the development of these standards have been made by Center staff members. The opinions expressed here are those of the authors and do not necessarily reflect the views of the supporting agencies.

Why Teachers Must Become Change Agents

Teacher education programs must help teaching candidates to link the moral purpose that influences them with the tools that will prepare them to engage in productive change.

Michael G. Fullan

Michael G. Fullan is Dean of Education, University of Toronto, 371 Bloor St., West, Toronto, Ontario, Canada M5S 2R7.

Teaching at its core is a moral profession. Scratch a good teacher and you will find a moral purpose. At the Faculty of Education, University of Toronto, we recently examined why people enter the teaching profession (Stiegelbauer 1992). In a random sample of 20 percent of 1,100 student teachers, the most frequently mentioned theme was "to make a difference in the lives of students." Of course, such statements cannot be taken at face value because people have a variety of motives for becoming teachers. Nonetheless, there is a strong kernel of truth to this conclusion.

What happens in teacher preparation, the early years of teaching, and throughout the career, however, is another story. Those with a clear sense of moral purpose often become disheartened, and those with a limited sense of purpose are never called upon to demonstrate their commitment. In an extensive study of teacher burnout, Farber (1991) identifies the devastating effects of the growing "sense of inconsequentiality" that often accompanies the teacher's career. Many teachers, says Farber, begin their careers "with a sense that their work is socially meaningful and will yield great personal satisfactions." This sense dissipates, however, as "the inevitable difficulties of teaching . . . interact with personal issues and vulnerabilities, as well as social pressure and values, to engender a sense of frustration and force a reassessment of the possibilities of the job and the investment one wants to make in it" (1991, p. 36).

A Natural Alliance

Certainly calls for reestablishing the moral foundation of teaching are warranted, but increased commitment at the one-to-one and classroom levels alone is a recipe for moral martyrdom. To have any chance of making teaching a noble and effective profession—and this is my theme here— teachers must combine the mantle of moral purpose with the skills of change agency.

Moral purpose and change agency, at first glance, appear to be strange bedfellows. On closer examination they are natural allies (Fullan 1993). Stated more directly, moral purpose— or making a difference—concerns bringing about improvements. It is, in other words, a *change theme*. In addition to the need to make moral purpose more explicit, educators need the tools to engage in change productively. Moral purpose keeps teachers close to the needs of children and youth; change agentry causes them to develop better strategies for accomplishing their moral goals.

Those skilled in change appreciate its volatile character, and they explicitly seek ideas for coping with and influencing change toward some desired ends. I see four core capacities for building greater change capacity: personal vision-building, inquiry, mastery, and collaboration (see Senge 1990 and Fullan 1993). Each of these has its institutional counterpart: shared vision-building; organizational structures, norms, and practices of inquiry; the development of increased repertoires of skills and know-how among organizational members; and collaborative work cultures.

But we are facing a huge dilemma. On the one hand, schools are expected to engage in continuous renewal, and change expectations are constantly swirling around them. On the other hand, the way teachers are trained, the way schools are organized, the way the educational hierarchy operates, and the way political decision makers treat educators results in a system that is more likely to retain the status quo. One way out of this quandary is to make explicit the goals and skills of change agentry. To break the impasse, we need a new conception of teacher professionalism that integrates moral purpose and change agentry, one that works simultaneously on individual and institutional development. One cannot wait for the other.

Personal Vision-Building

Working on personal visions means examining and re-examining why we came into teaching. Asking "What difference am I trying to make personally?" is a good place to start.

For most of us, the reasons are there, but possibly buried. For the beginning teacher, they may be underdeveloped. It is time to make them front and center. Block emphasizes that "creating a vision forces us to take a stand for a preferred future"

(1987, p. 102). To articulate our vision of the future "is to come out of the closet with our doubts about the organization and the way it operates" (p. 105).

Personal vision comes from within. It gives meaning to work, and it exists independently of the organization or group we happen to be in. Once it gets going, it is not as private as it sounds. Especially in moral occupations like teaching, the more one takes the risk to express personal purpose, the more kindred spirits one will find. Paradoxically, personal purpose is the route to organizational change. When it is diminished, we see in its place groupthink and a continual stream of fragmented, surface changes acquired uncritically and easily discarded.

Inquiry

All four capacities of change are intimately interrelated and mutually reinforcing. The second one—inquiry—indicates that formation and enactment of personal purpose are not static matters but, rather, a perennial quest. Pascale (1990) captures this precisely: "The essential activity for keeping our paradigm current is persistent questioning. I will use the term *inquiry*. Inquiry is the engine of vitality and self-renewal" (p. 14, emphasis in original).

Inquiry is necessary for forming and reforming personal purpose. While the latter comes from within, it must be fueled by information and ideas in the environment. Inquiry means internalizing norms, habits, and techniques for continuous learning. For the beginner, learning is critical because of its formative timing. Lifelong learning is essential because in complex, ever-changing societies mental maps "cease to fit the territory" (Pascale 1990, p. 13). Teachers as change agents are career-long learners, without which they would not be able to stimulate students to be continuous learners.

Mastery

Mastery is a third crucial ingredient. People *behave* their way into new visions and ideas, not just think their

Who's Teaching America's Teachers?

Robert Ciscell

How much will a professor who taught for a few years in the late '50s know about the realities of elementary and secondary classrooms in the '90s?

Not much, you might answer, but one of the best-kept secrets in education is the fact that the typical education professor has fewer than five years of experience in the "real world" of K-12 education. For most, that experience occurred more than two decades ago. Even more frightening is the revelation that 30 percent of those who made up the education professoriat in the 1980s had no previous field experience (Ducharme and Agne 1983).

Would a medical school permit someone who hadn't worked in a medical facility for three decades to teach? Certainly not. Students in business or law wouldn't tolerate it either, yet generations of prospective teachers have been carried along in the deception.

It is a generally accepted premise in our society that anyone can teach, even without professional training. One recent study showed that as many as one-third of education majors believed they could begin teaching immediately without any coursework or experience in education (Book et al.

Education professors who haven't taught in a K-12 classroom in 20 years undermine preservice students' attitudes about teaching.

1985). Such assumptions have been bolstered by state legislatures scrambling to certify emergency teachers simply because they possess a degree in a "related" field.

Most children spend 180 days each year in the company of teachers—more than 14,000 hours between kindergarten and high school graduation. A few eventually choose a career in teaching, and as undergraduate education majors they look back upon their K-12 years as the true internship for prospective teachers. In fact, research suggests that most of them consider their public school years to be more important than preservice coursework as a source of knowledge about the professional realities of a career in teaching.

way into them. Mastery is obviously necessary for effectiveness, but it is also a means for achieving deeper understanding. New mind-sets arise from mastery as much as the reverse.

It has long been known that expertise is central to successful change, so it is surprising how little attention we pay to it beyond one-shot workshops and disconnected training. Mastery involves strong initial teacher education and career-long staff development, but when we place it in the

perspective of comprehensive change, it is much more than this. Beyond exposure to new ideas, we have to know where they fit, and we have to become skilled in them, not just like them.

To be effective at change, mastery is essential both in relation to specific innovations and as a personal habit.

Collaboration

There is a ceiling effect to how much we can learn if we keep to ourselves

Students consistently indicate that education professors offer limited information about teachers' professional problems. A survey of nearly 500 Michigan State University students enrolled in an introductory education course suggested that education coursework offered limited knowledge about the day-to-day life of a teacher (Book et al. 1983). Students looked forward to full-time teaching and predicted that educational foundations courses would contribute even less to their professional preparation than their own experiences as K-12 students.

In another study (Ciscell 1989), 227 junior-level education majors in three universities were asked to rank several possible sources of information about the realities of teaching. Respondents rated "student teaching/field experiences" as their most important source of preservice knowledge about the teaching profession. More importantly, these education majors ranked "first-hand observations of former K-12 teachers" as more important than preservice "methods courses." When asked if they felt ready to teach, nearly 70 percent of these junior-level respondents indicated that they were ready to start full-time teaching careers immediately.

Would a medical school permit someone who hadn't worked in a medical facility for three decades to teach? Certainly not.

The education reform movement has managed to focus some attention on the process of teacher preparation, but few concerns have been expressed about teacher educators themselves. Perhaps it's time to look more closely at who has been teaching America's teachers.

Clearly, restructuring teacher preparation to include a "cutting edge" professoriat—and move away from an emphasis on scholarly productivity—would be a formidable task. Yet the character of teacher education may be altered in this decade not by legislative mandates or creative preservice requirements but by the massive faculty retirements due before the end of the century. Intelligent recruitment of candidates with broad experience in contemporary elementary and secondary schools could be a logical response to the education reform movement and the basis for rebuilding trust among preservice teachers. ∎

References

Book, C., D. Freeman, and B. Brousseau. (1985). "Comparing Academic Backgrounds and Career Aspirations of Education and Non-Education Majors." *Journal of Teacher Education* 36: 27-30.

Book, C., J. Byers, and D. Freeman. (1983). "Student Expectations and Teacher Education Traditions with which We Can and Cannot Live." *Journal of Teacher Education* 34: 9-13.

Ciscell, R.E. (1989). "Ready or Not: The Career Perspectives of Preservice Teachers." *Issues in Education* 2, 1: 8-17.

Ducharme, E.R., and R.M. Agne. (1983). "The Education Professoriate and the Written Word: An Interim Statement." Paper presented at AERA Annual Meeting, Chicago, Ill.

Robert Ciscell is Senior Research Associate, Research and Training Associates, 10950 Grandview, Suite 300, 34 Corporate Woods, Overland Park, KS 66210. He is a former Indiana Teacher of the Year.

(Fullan and Hargreaves 1991). The ability to collaborate on both a small-and large-scale is becoming one of the core requisites of postmodern society. Personal strength, as long as it is open-minded (that is, inquiry-oriented), goes hand-in-hand with effective collaboration—in fact, without personal strength collaboration will be more form than content. Personal and group mastery thrive on each other in learning organizations.

In sum, the moral purpose of teaching must be reconceptualized as a change theme. Moral purpose without change agentry is martyrdom; change agentry without moral purpose is change for the sake of change. In combination, not only are they effective in getting things done, but they are good at getting the *right* things done. The implications for teacher education and for redesigning schools are profound.

Society's Missed Opportunity

Despite the rhetoric about teacher education today, there does not seem to be a real belief that investing in teacher education will yield results. With all the problems demanding immediate solution, it is easy to overlook a preventive strategy that would take several years to have an impact.

Currently, teacher education—from initial preparation throughout the career—is not geared toward continuous learning. Teacher education has the honor of being the worst problem and the best solution in education. The

Especially in moral occupations like teaching, the more one takes the risk to express personal purpose, the more kindred spirits one will find.

absence of a strong publicly stated knowledge base allows the misconception to continue that any smart person can teach. After visiting 14 colleges of education across the U.S., Kramer (1992) concludes:

> Everything [a person] needs to know about how to teach could be learned by intelligent people in a single summer of well-planned instruction (p. 24).

In a twisted way, there is some truth to this observation. It is true in the sense that many people did and still do take such minimal instruction and manage to have a career in teaching. It is true also that some people with a strong summer program would end up knowing as much or more as others who take a weak yearlong program. In her journey, Kramer found plenty of examples of moral purpose—caring people, committed to social equality. What she found wanting was an emphasis on knowledge and understanding. Caring and competence are of course not mutually exclusive (indeed this is the point), but they can seem that way when the knowledge base is so poorly formulated.

Teacher education institutions themselves must take responsibility for their current reputation as laggards rather than leaders of educational reform. I will not take up the critical area of recruitment and selection in the profession (for the best discussion, see Schlechty 1990, chapter 1). In many ways an "if you build it, they will come" strategy is called for. It is self-defeating to seek candidates who turn out to be better than the programs they enter. What is needed is a combination of selection criteria that focus on academics as well as experience (related, for example, to moral purpose), sponsorship for underrepresented groups, and a damn good program.

Teacher educators like other would-be change agents must take some initiative themselves. Examples are now happening on several fronts. At the University of Toronto, we embarked on a major reform effort in 1988. With a faculty of some 90 staff and 1,100 full-time students in a one-year post-baccalaureate teacher certification program, we piloted a number of field-based options in partnerships with school systems (see University of Toronto, *Making a Difference* Video, 1992a). In 1991 I prepared a paper for our strategic planning committee, taking as a starting point the following premise: *Faculties of Education should not advocate things for teachers or schools that they are not capable of practicing themselves.* Using a hypothetical "best faculty of education in the country" metaphor, I suggested that such a faculty would:

1. commit itself to producing teachers who are agents of educational and social improvement,

2. commit itself to continuous improvement through program innovation and evaluation,

3. value and practice exemplary teaching,

4. engage in constant inquiry,

5. model and develop lifelong learning among staff and students,

6. model and develop collaboration among staff and students,

7. be respected and engaged as a vital part of the university as a whole,

8. form partnerships with schools and other agencies,

9. be visible and valued internationally in a way that contributes locally and globally,

10. work collaboratively to build regional, national, and international networks (Fullan 1991).

To illustrate, consider items 3 and 6. It would seem self-evident that faculties of education would stand for exemplary teaching among their own staff. Faculties of education have some excellent (and poor) teachers, but I would venture to say that hardly any have effective *institutional* mechanisms for improving their own teaching. Regarding item 6, many faculties of education advocate collaborative work cultures for schools, and some participate in professional development schools. This leads to two embarrassing questions. First, to what extent are teacher preparation programs designed so that student teachers deliberately develop and practice the habits and skills of collaboration? Even more embarrassing, to what extent do university professors (arts and science, as well as education) value and practice collaboration in their own teaching and scholarship?

Key Images for Teacher Preparation

With such guiding principles, and some experience with them through our pilot projects, we at the University of Toronto have recently begun redesigning the entire teacher preparation program. Our Restructuring Committee has proposed that:

> Every teacher should be knowledgeable about, committed to, and skilled in:
>
> 1. working with *all* students in an equitable, effective, and caring manner by respecting diversity in relation to ethnicity, race, gender, and special needs of each learner;
>
> 2. being active learners who continuously seek, assess, apply, and communicate knowledge as reflective practitioners throughout their careers;
>
> 3. developing and applying knowledge of curriculum, instruction, principles of learning, and evaluation needed to implement and monitor effective and evolving programs for all learners;
>
> 4. initiating, valuing, and practicing

collaboration and partnerships with students, colleagues, parents, community, government, and social and business agencies;

5. appreciating and practicing the principles, ethics, and legal responsibilities of teaching as a profession;

6. developing a personal philosophy of teaching which is informed by and contributes to the organizational, community, societal, and global contexts of education (University of Toronto, B.Ed. Restructuring Committee, 1992b).

We are now developing the actual program, curriculum, and teaching designs. Everything we know about the complexities of change applies in spades to the reform of higher education institutions. Nonetheless, after four years, we have made good progress and look forward to the next four years as the ones when more comprehensive and systematic reform will be put into place (see also Goodlad 1991, Howey 1992, and the third report of the Holmes Group, forthcoming).

To summarize: Faculties of education must redesign their programs to focus directly on developing the beginner's knowledge base for effective teaching *and* the knowledge base for changing the conditions that affect teaching. Sarason puts it this way: "Is it asking too much of preparatory programs to prepare their students for a 'real world' which they must understand *and seek to change* if as persons and professionals they are to grow, not only to survive" (in press, p. 252, my emphasis). Goodlad (1991) asks a similar question: "Are a large percentage of these educators thoroughly grounded in the knowledge and skills required to bring about meaningful change?" (p. 4). The new standard for the future is that every teacher must strive to become effective at managing change.

Redesigning Schools
One of the main reasons that restructuring has failed so far is that there is no underlying conception that grounds what would happen within new structures. Restructuring has caused

changes in participation, in governance, and in other formal aspects of the organization, but in the majority of cases, it has not affected the teaching-learning core and professional culture (Berends 1992, Fullan 1993). *To restructure is not to reculture.*

The professional teacher, to be effective, must become a career-long learner of more sophisticated pedagogies and technologies and be able to form and reform productive collaborations with colleagues, parents, community agencies, businesses, and others. The teacher of the future, in other words, must be equally at home in the classroom and in working with others to bring about continuous improvements.

I do not have the space to elaborate—indeed many of the details have not been worked out. The general directions, however, are clear. In terms of pedagogy, the works of Gardner (1991) and Sizer (1992)—in developing approaches to teaching for understanding—exemplify the kinds of knowledge and skills that teachers must develop and enlarge upon throughout their careers.

Beyond better pedagogy, the teacher of the future must actively improve the conditions for learning in his or her immediate environments. Put one way, teachers will never improve learning in the classroom (or whatever the direct learning environment) unless they also help improve conditions that surround the classroom. Andy Hargreaves and I developed 12 guidelines for action consistent with this new conception of "interactive professionalism":

1. locate, listen to, and articulate your inner voice;

2. practice reflection in action, on action, and about action;

3. develop a risk-taking mentality;

4. trust processes as well as people;

5. appreciate the total person in working with others;

6. commit to working with colleagues;

7. seek variety and avoid balkanization;

8. redefine your role to extend beyond the classroom;

> The teacher of the future must be equally at home in the classroom and in working with others to bring about continuous improvements.

9. balance work and life;

10. push and support principals and other administrators to develop interactive professionalism;

11. commit to continuous improvement and perpetual learning;

12. monitor and strengthen the connection between your development and students' development (Fullan and Hargreaves 1991).

We also developed eight guidelines for principals that focus their energies on reculturing the school toward greater interactive professionalism to make a difference in the educational lives of students. However, as important as principals can be, they are a diversion (and perhaps a liability) as far as new conceptions of the professional teacher are concerned. In a real sense, what gives the contemporary principalship inflated importance is the absence of leadership opportunities on the part of teachers (Fullan 1993).

A New Professionalism
Teacher professionalism is at a threshold. Moral purpose and change agentry are implicit in what good teaching and effective change are about, but as yet they are society's (and teaching's) great untapped resources for radical and continuous improvement. We need to go public

with a new rationale for why teaching and teacher development are fundamental to the future of society.

Above all, we need action that links initial teacher preparation and continuous teacher development based on moral purpose and change agentry with the corresponding restructuring of universities and schools and their relationships. Systems don't change by themselves. Rather, the actions of individuals and small groups working on new conceptions intersect to produce breakthroughs (Fullan 1993). New conceptions, once mobilized, become new paradigms. The new paradigm for teacher professionalism synthesizes the forces of moral purpose and change agentry.

References

Berends, M. (1992). "A Description of Restructuring in Nationally Nominated Schools." Paper presented at the Annual Meeting of the American Educational Research Association, San Francisco.

Block, P. (1987). *The Empowered Manager*. San Francisco: Jossey-Bass.

Farber, B. (1991). *Crisis in Education*. San Francisco: Jossey-Bass.

Fullan, M. (1991). "The Best Faculty of Education in the Country: A Fable." Submitted to the Strategic Planning Committee. Faculty of Education, University of Toronto.

Fullan, M. (1993). *Change Forces: Probing the Depths of Educational Reform*. London: Falmer Press.

Fullan, M., and A. Hargreaves. (1991). *What's Worth Fighting for in Your School?* Toronto: Ontario Public School Teachers' Federation; Andover, Mass.: The Network; Buckingham, U.K.: Open University Press; Melbourne: Australian Council of Educational Administration.

Gardner, H. (1991). *The Unschooled Mind*. New York: Basic Books.

Goodlad, J. (1991). "Why We Need a Complete Redesign of Teacher Education." *Educational Leadership* 49, 3: 4-10.

Holmes Group. (In press). *Tomorrow's Colleges of Education*. East Lansing, Mich.: Holmes Group.

Howey, K. R. (1992). *The Network of Fifteen*. Columbus: Ohio State University.

Kramer, R. (1992). *Ed School Follies*. New York: Foss Press.

Pascale, P. (1990). *Managing on the Edge*. New York: Touchstone.

Sarason, S. (In press). *The Case for a Change: The Preparation of Educators*. San Francisco: Jossey-Bass.

Schlechty, P. (1990). *Reform in Teacher Education*. Washington, D.C.: American Association of Colleges of Education.

Senge, P. (1990). *The Fifth Discipline*. New York: Doubleday.

Sizer, T. (1992). *Horace's School: Redesigning the American High School*. Boston: Houghton Mifflin.

Stiegelbauer, S. (1992). "Why We Want to Be Teachers." Paper presented at the Annual Meeting of the American Educational Research Association, San Francisco.

University of Toronto, Faculty of Education. (1992a). *Making a Difference* Video, Toronto, Ontario.

University of Toronto, Faculty of Education. (1992b). "B.Ed. Restructuring Committee Report," Toronto, Ontario.

The Rewards of Learning

To teach without using extrinsic rewards is analogous to asking our students to learn to draw with their eyes closed, Mr. Chance maintains. Before we do that, we should open our own eyes.

PAUL CHANCE

Paul Chance (Eastern Shore Maryland Chapter) is a psychologist, writer, and teacher. He is the author of Thinking in the Classroom *(Teachers College Press, 1986) and teaches at James H. Groves Adult High School in Georgetown, Del.*

A man is seated at a desk. Before him lie a pencil and a large stack of blank paper. He picks up the pencil, closes his eyes, and attempts to draw a four-inch line. He makes a second attempt, a third, a fourth, and so on, until he has made well over a hundred attempts at drawing a four-inch line, all without ever opening his eyes. He repeats the exercise for several days, until he has drawn some 3,000 lines, all with his eyes closed. On the last day, he examines his work. The question is, How much improvement has there been in his ability to draw a four-inch line? How much has he learned from his effort?

E. L. Thorndike, the founder of educational psychology and a major figure in the scientific analysis of learning, performed this experiment years ago, using himself as subject.[1] He found no evidence of learning. His ability to draw a four-inch line was no better on the last day than it had been on the first.

The outcome of this experiment may seem obvious to us today, but it was an effective way of challenging a belief widely held earlier in this century, a belief that formed the very foundation of education at the time: the idea that "practice makes perfect."

It was this blind faith in practice that justified countless hours of rote drill as a standard teaching technique. Thorndike's experiment demonstrated that practice in and of itself is not sufficient for learning.

Based on this and other, more formal studies, Thorndike concluded that practice is important only insofar as it provides the opportunity for reinforcement.

To reinforce means to strengthen, and among learning researchers *reinforcement* refers to a procedure for strengthening behavior (that is, making it likely to be repeated) by providing certain kinds of consequences.[2] These consequences, called *reinforcers,* are usually events or things a person willingly seeks out. For instance, we might teach a person to draw a four-inch line with his eyes closed merely by saying "good" each time the effort is within half an inch of the goal. Most people like to succeed, so this positive feedback should be an effective way of reinforcing the appropriate behavior.

Hundreds of experimental studies have demonstrated that systematic use of reinforcement can improve both classroom conduct and the rate of learning. Yet the systematic use of reinforcement has never been widespread in American schools. In *A Place Called School,* John Goodlad reports that, in the elementary grades, an average of only 2% of class time is devoted to reinforcement; in the high schools, the figure falls to 1%.[3]

THE COSTS OF REWARD

There are probably many reasons for our failure to make the most of reinforcement. For one thing, few schools of education provide more than cursory instruction in its use. Given Thorndike's finding about the role of practice in learning, it is ironic that many teachers actually use the term *reinforcement* as a synonym for *practice.* ("We assign workbook exercises for reinforcement.") If schools of education do not teach future teachers the nature of reinforcement and how to use it effectively, teachers can hardly be blamed for not using it.

The unwanted effects of misused reinforcement have led some teachers to shy away from it. The teacher who sometimes lets a noisy class go to recess early will find the class getting noisier before recess. If high praise is reserved for long-winded essays, students will develop wordy and redundant writing styles. And it should surprise no one if students are seldom original in classrooms where only conventional work is admired or if they are uncooperative in classrooms where one can earn recognition only through competition. Reinforcement is powerful stuff, and its misuse can cause problems.

Another difficulty is that the optimal use of reinforcement would mean teaching in a new way. Some studies suggest that maximum learning in elementary and middle schools might require very high rates of reinforcement, perhaps with teachers praising someone in the class an average of once every 15 seconds.[4] Such a requirement is clearly incompatible with traditional teaching practices.

Systematic reinforcement can also mean more work for the teacher. Reinforcing behavior once every 15 seconds means 200 reinforcements in a 50-minute period — 1,000 reinforcements in a typical school day. It also implies that, in order to spot behavior to reinforce, the teacher must be moving about the room, not sitting at a desk marking papers. That may be too much to ask. Some studies have found that teachers who have been taught how to make good use of reinforcement often revert to their old style of teaching. This is so even though the teachers acknowledge that increased use of reinforcement means fewer discipline problems and a much faster rate of learning.[5]

Reinforcement also runs counter to our Puritan traditions. Most Americans have always assumed — occasional protestations to the contrary notwithstanding — that learning should be hard work and at least slightly unpleasant. Often the object of education seems to be not so much to teach academic and social skills as to "build character" through exposure to adversity. When teachers reinforce students at a high rate, the students experience a minimum of adversity and actually enjoy learning. Thus some people think that reinforcement is bad for character development.

All of these arguments against reinforcement can be countered effectively. Schools of education do not provide much instruction in the practical use of reinforcement, but there is no reason why they cannot do so. Reinforcement can be used incorrectly and with disastrous results, but the same might be said of other powerful tools. Systematic use of reinforcement means teaching in a new way, but teachers can learn to do so.[6] A great deal of reinforcement is needed for optimum learning, but not all of the reinforcement needs to come from the teacher. (Reinforcement can be provided by computers and other teaching devices, by teacher aides, by parents, and by students during peer teaching and cooperative learning.) No doubt people do sometimes benefit from adversity, but the case for the character-building properties of adversity is very weak.[7]

However, there is one argument against reinforcement that cannot be dismissed so readily. For some 20 years, the claim has been made that systematic reinforcement actually undermines student learning. Those few teachers who make extensive use of reinforcement, it is claimed, do their students a disservice because reinforcement reduces interest in the reinforced activity.

Not all forms of reinforcement are considered detrimental. A distinction is made between reinforcement involving intrinsic reinforcers — or rewards, as they are often called — and reinforcement involving extrinsic rewards.[8] Only extrinsic rewards are said to be harmful. An *intrinsic reward* is ordinarily the natural consequence of behavior, hence the name. We learn to throw darts by seeing how close the dart is to the target; learn to type by seeing the right letters appear on the computer screen; learn to cook from the pleasant sights, fragrances, and flavors that result from our culinary efforts; learn to read from the understanding we get from the printed word; and learn to solve puzzles by finding solutions. The Japanese say, "The bow teaches the archer." They are talking about intrinsic rewards, and they are right.

Extrinsic rewards come from an outside source, such as a teacher. Probably the most ubiquitous extrinsic reward (and one of the most effective) is praise. The teacher reinforces behavior by saying "good," "right," "correct," or "excellent" when the desired behavior occurs. Other extrinsic rewards involve nonverbal behavior such as smiles, winks, thumbs-up signs, hugs, congratulatory handshakes, pats on the back, or applause. Gold stars, certificates, candy, prizes, and even money have been used as rewards, but they are usually less important in teaching — and even in the maintenance of good discipline — than those mentioned earlier.

The distinction between intrinsic and extrinsic rewards is somewhat artificial. Consider the following example. You put money into a vending machine and retrieve a candy bar. The behavior of inserting money into a vending machine has been reinforced, as has the more general behavior of interacting with machines. But is the food you receive an intrinsic or an extrinsic reward? On the one hand, the food is the automatic consequence of inserting money and pressing buttons, so it would appear to be an intrinsic reward. On the other hand, the food is a consequence that was arranged by the designer of the machine, so it would seem to be an extrinsic reward.[9]

Though somewhat contrived, the distinction between intrinsic and extrinsic rewards has been maintained partly because extrinsic rewards are said to be damaging.[10] Are they? First, let us be clear about the charge. The idea is that — if teachers smile, praise, congratulate, say "thank you" or "right," shake hands, hug, give a pat on the back, applaud, provide a certificate of achievement or attendance, *or in any way provide a positive consequence (a reward) for student behavior* — the student will be less inclined to engage in that behavior when the reward is no longer available.

> # Extrinsic rewards are said to be damaging. Are they? First, let us be clear about the charge.

For example, teachers who offer prizes to students for reading books will, it is said, make the children less likely to read when prizes are no longer available. The teacher who reads a student's story aloud to the class as an example of excellent story writing actually makes the student less likely to write stories in the future, when such public approval is not forthcoming. When teachers (and students) applaud a youngster who has given an excellent talk, they make that student disinclined to give talks in the future. The teacher who comments favorably on the originality of a painting steers the young artist away from painting. And so on. This is the charge against extrinsic rewards.

No one disputes the effectiveness of extrinsic rewards in teaching or in maintaining good discipline. Some might therefore argue that extrinsic rewards should be used, even if they reduce interest in learning. Better to have students who read only when required to do so, some might say, than to have students who cannot read at all.

But if rewards do reduce interest, that fact is of tremendous importance. "The teacher may count himself successful," wrote B. F. Skinner, "when his students become engrossed in his field, study conscientiously, and do more than is required of them, but *the important thing is what they do when they are no longer being taught*" (emphasis added).[11] It is not enough for students to learn the three R's and a little science and geography; they must be prepared for a lifetime of learning. To reduce their interest in learning would be a terrible thing — even if it were done in the interest of teaching them effectively.

The question of whether rewards adversely affect motivation is not, then, of merely academic or theoretical importance. It is of great practical importance to the classroom teacher.

More than 100 studies have examined this question.[12] In a typical experiment, Mark Lepper and his colleagues observed 3- to 5-year-old nursery school children playing with various kinds of toys.[13] The toys available included felt tip pens of various colors and paper to draw on. The researchers noted the children's inclination to draw during this period. Next the researchers took the children aside and asked them to draw with the felt tip pens. The researchers promised some children a "Good Player Award" for drawing. Other children drew pictures without receiving an award.

Two weeks later, the researchers returned to the school, provided felt tip pens and paper, and observed the children's inclination to draw. They found that children who had been promised an award spent only half as much time drawing as they had originally. Those students who had received no award showed no such decline in interest.

Most studies in this area follow the same general outline: 1) students are given the opportunity to participate in an activity without rewards; 2) they are given extrinsic rewards for participating in the activity; and 3) they are again given the opportunity to participate in the activity without rewards.

The outcomes of the studies are also fairly consistent. Not surprisingly, there is usually a substantial increase in the activity during the second stage, when extrinsic rewards are available. And, as expected, participation in the activity declines sharply when rewards are no longer available. However, interest sometimes falls below the initial level, so that students are less interested in the activity than they had been before receiving rewards. It is this net loss of motivation that is of concern.

Researchers have studied this decline in motivation and found that it occurs only under certain circumstances. For example, the effect is most likely to occur when the initial interest in the activity is very high, when the rewards used are *not* reinforcers, and when the rewards are held out in advance as incentives.[14]

But perhaps the best predictor of negative effects is the nature of the "reward contingency" involved. (The term *reward contingency* has to do with the nature of the relationship between behavior and its reward.) Alyce Dickinson reviewed the research literature in this area and identified three kinds of reward contingency:[15]

Task-contingent rewards are available for merely participating in an activity, without regard to any standard of performance. Most studies that find a decline in interest in a rewarded activity involve task-contingent rewards. In the Lepper study described above, for instance, children received an award for drawing *regardless of how they drew*. The reward was task-contingent.

Performance-contingent rewards are available only when the student achieves a certain standard. Performance-contingent rewards sometimes produce negative results. For instance, Edward Deci offered college students money for solving puzzles, $1 for each puzzle solved. The rewarded students were later less inclined to work on the puzzles than were students who had not been paid. Unfortunately, these results are difficult to interpret because the students sometimes failed to meet the reward standard, and failure itself is known to reduce interest in an activity.[16]

Success-contingent rewards are given for good performance and might reflect either success or progress toward a goal. Success-contingent rewards do not have negative effects; in fact, they typically *increase* interest in the rewarded activity. For example, Ross Vasta and Louise Stirpe awarded gold stars to third- and fourth-graders each time they completed a kind of math exercise they enjoyed. After seven days of awards, the gold stars stopped. Not only was there no evidence of a loss in interest, but time spent on the math activity actually increased. Nor was there any decline in the quality of the work produced.[17]

Dickinson concludes that the danger of undermining student motivation stems not from extrinsic rewards, but from the use of inappropriate reward contingencies. Rewards reduce motivation when they are given without regard to performance or when the performance standard is so high that students frequently fail. When students have a high rate of success and when those successes are rewarded, the rewards *do not have negative effects*. Indeed, success-contingent

rewards tend to increase interest in the activity. This finding, writes Dickinson, "is robust and consistent." She adds that "even strong opponents of contingent rewards recognize that success-based rewards do not have harmful effects."[18]

The evidence, then, shows that extrinsic rewards can either enhance or reduce interest in an activity, depending on how they are used. Still, it might be argued that, because extrinsic rewards *sometimes* cause problems, we might be wise to avoid their use altogether. The decision not to use extrinsic rewards amounts to a decision to rely on alternatives. What are those alternatives? And are they better than extrinsic rewards?

ALTERNATIVES TO REWARDS

Punishment and the threat of punishment are — and probably always have been — the most popular alternatives to extrinsic rewards. Not so long ago, lessons were "taught to the tune of a hickory stick," but the tune was not merely tapped on a desk. Students who did not learn their lessons were not only beaten; they were also humiliated: they sat on a stool (up high, so everyone could see) and wore a silly hat.

Gradually, more subtle forms of punishment were used. "The child at his desk," wrote Skinner, "filling in his workbook, is behaving primarily to escape from the threat of a series of minor aversive events — the teacher's displeasure, the criticism or ridicule of his classmates, an ignominious showing in a competition, low marks, a trip to the office 'to be talked to' by the principal, or a word to the parent who may still resort to the birch rod."[19] Skinner spent a lifetime inveighing against the use of such "aversives," but his efforts were largely ineffective. While extrinsic rewards have been condemned, punishment and the threat of punishment are widely sanctioned.

Punishment is popular because, in the short run at least, it gets results. This is illustrated by an experiment in which Deci and Wayne Cascio told students that, if they did not solve problems correctly within a time limit, they would be exposed to a loud, unpleasant sound. The threat worked: all the students solved all the problems within the time limit, so the threat never had to be fulfilled. Students who were merely rewarded for correct solutions did not do nearly as well.[20]

But there are serious drawbacks to the

use of punishment. For one thing, although punishment motivates students to learn, it does not teach them. Or, rather, it teaches them only what *not* to do, not what *to* do. "We do not teach [a student] to learn quickly," Skinner observed, "by punishing him when he learns slowly, or to recall what he has learned by punishing him when he forgets, or to think logically by punishing him when he is illogical."[21]

Punishment also has certain undesirable side effects.[22] To the extent that punishment works, it works by making students anxious. Students get nervous before a test because they fear a poor grade, and they are relieved or anxious when they receive their report card depending on whether or not the grades received will result in punishment from their parents.[23] Students can and do avoid the anxiety caused by such punishment by cutting classes and dropping out of school. We do the same thing when we cancel or "forget" a dental appointment.

Another response to punishment is aggression. Students who do not learn easily — and who therefore cannot readily avoid punishment — are especially apt to become aggressive. Their aggression often takes the form of lying, cheating, stealing, and refusing to cooperate. Students also act out by cursing, by being rude and insulting, by destroying property, and by hitting people. Increasingly, teachers are the objects of these aggressive acts.

Finally, it should be noted that punishment has the same negative impact on intrinsic motivation as extrinsic rewards are alleged to have. In the Deci and Cascio study just described, for example, when students were given the chance to work on puzzles with the threat of punishment removed, they were less likely to do so than were students who had never worked under the threat of punishment.[24] Punishment in the form of criticism of performance also reduces interest in an activity.[25]

Punishment is not the only alternative to the use of extrinsic rewards. Teachers can also encourage students. Encouragement consists of various forms of behavior intended to induce students to perform. We encourage students when we urge them to try, express confidence in their ability to do assignments, and recite such platitudes as "A winner never quits and a quitter never wins."[26]

In encouraging students, we are not merely urging them to perform, however; we are implicitly suggesting a relationship between continued performance and certain consequences. "Come on, Billy — you can do it" means, "If you persist at this task, you will be rewarded with success." The power of encouragement is ultimately dependent on the occurrence of the implied consequences. If the teacher tells Billy he can do it and if he tries and fails, future urging by the teacher will be less effective.

Another problem with encouragement is that, like punishment, it motivates but does not teach. The student who is urged to perform a task is not thereby taught how to perform it. Encouragement is a safer procedure than punishment, since it is less likely to provoke anxiety or aggression. Students who are repeatedly urged to do things at which they ultimately fail do, however, come to distrust the judgment of the teacher. They also come to believe that they cannot live up to the expectations of teachers — and therefore must be hopelessly stupid.

Intrinsic rewards present the most promising alternative to extrinsic rewards. Experts on reinforcement, including defenders of extrinsic rewards, universally sing the praises of intrinsic rewards. Unlike punishment and encouragement, intrinsic rewards actually teach. Students who can see that they have solved a problem correctly know how to solve other problems of that sort. And, unlike extrinsic rewards, intrinsic rewards do not depend on the teacher or some other person.

But there are problems with intrinsic rewards, just as there are with extrinsic ones. Sometimes students lack the necessary skills to obtain intrinsic rewards. Knowledge, understanding, and the aesthetic pleasures of language are all intrinsic rewards for reading, but they are not available to those for whom reading is a difficult and painful activity.

Often, intrinsic rewards are too remote to be effective. If a student is asked to add 3 + 7, what is the intrinsic reward for answering correctly? The student who learns to add will one day experience the satisfaction of checking the accuracy of a restaurant bill, but this future reward is of no value to the youngster just learning to add. Though important in maintaining what has been learned, intrinsic rewards are often too remote to be effective reinforcers in the early stages of learning.

One problem that often goes unnoticed is that the intrinsic rewards for academic work are often weaker than the rewards available for other behavior. Students are rewarded for looking out the window, daydreaming, reading comic books, taking things from other students, passing notes, telling and listening to jokes, moving about the room, fighting, talking back to the teacher, and for all sorts of activities that are incompatible with academic learning. Getting the right answer to a grammar question might be intrinsically rewarding, but for many students it is considerably less rewarding than the laughter of one's peers in response to a witty remark.

While intrinsic rewards are important, then, they are insufficient for efficient learning.[27] Nor will encouragement and punishment fill the gap. The teacher must supplement intrinsic rewards with extrinsic rewards. This means not only telling the student when he or she has succeeded, but also praising, complimenting, applauding, and providing other forms of recognition for good work. Some students may need even stronger reinforcers, such as special privileges, certificates, and prizes.

REWARD GUIDELINES

Yet we cannot ignore the fact that extrinsic rewards can have adverse effects on student motivation. While there seems to be little chance of serious harm, it behooves us to use care. Various experts have suggested guidelines to follow in using extrinsic rewards.[28] Here is a digest of their recommendations:

1. Use the weakest reward required to strengthen a behavior. Don't use money if a piece of candy will do; don't use candy if praise will do. The good effects of reinforcement come not so much from the reward itself as from the reward contingency: the relationship between the reward and the behavior.

2. When possible, avoid using rewards as incentives. For example, don't say, "If you do X, I'll give you Y." Instead, ask the student to perform a task and then provide a reward for having completed it. In most cases, rewards work best if they are pleasant surprises.

3. Reward at a high rate in the early stages of learning, and reduce the frequency of rewards as learning progresses. Once students have the alphabet down pat, there is no need to compliment them each time they print a letter correctly. Nor is there much need to reward be-

havior that is already occurring at a high rate.

4. Reward only the behavior you want repeated. If students who whine and complain get their way, expect to see a lot of whining and complaining. Similarly, if you provide gold stars only for the three best papers in the class, you are rewarding competition and should not be surprised if students do not cooperate with one another. And if "spelling doesn't count," don't expect to see excellent spelling.

5. Remember that what is an effective reward for one student may not work well with another. Some students respond rapidly to teacher attention; others do not. Some work well for gold stars; others don't. Effective rewards are ordinarily things that students seek — positive feedback, praise, approval, recognition, toys — but ultimately a reward's value is to be judged by its effect on behavior.

6. Reward success, and set standards so that success is within the student's grasp. In today's heterogeneous classrooms, that means setting standards for each student. A good way to do this is to reward improvement or progress toward a goal. Avoid rewarding students merely for participating in an activity, without regard for the quality of their performance.

7. Bring attention to the rewards (both intrinsic and extrinsic) that are available for behavior from sources *other than the teacher*. Point out, for example, the fun to be had from the word play in poetry or from sharing a poem with another person. Show students who are learning computer programming the pleasure in "making the computer do things." Let students know that it's okay to applaud those who make good presentations so that they can enjoy the approval of their peers for a job well done. Ask parents to talk with their children about school and to praise them for learning. The goal is to shift the emphasis from rewards provided by the teacher to those that will occur even when the teacher is not present.[29]

Following these rules is harder in practice than it might seem, and most teachers will need training in their implementation. But reinforcement is probably the most powerful tool available to teachers, and extrinsic rewards are powerful reinforcers. To teach without using extrinsic rewards is analogous to asking our students to learn to draw with their eyes closed. Before we do that, we should open our own eyes.

1. The study is described in E. L. Thorndike, *Human Learning* (1931; reprint ed., Cambridge, Mass.: MIT Press, 1966).

2. There are various theories (cognitive, neurological, and psychosocial) about why certain consequences reinforce or strengthen behavior. The important thing for our purposes is that they do.

3. John I. Goodlad, *A Place Called School: Prospects for the Future* (New York: McGraw-Hill, 1984). Goodlad complains about the "paucity of praise" in schools. In doing so, he echoes B. F. Skinner, who wrote that "perhaps the most serious criticism of the current classroom is the relative infrequency of reinforcement." See B. F. Skinner, *The Technology of Teaching* (Englewood Cliffs, N.J.: Prentice-Hall, 1968), p. 17.

4. Bill L. Hopkins and R. J. Conard, "Putting It All Together: Superschool," in Norris G. Haring and Richard L. Schiefelbusch, eds., *Teaching Special Children* (New York: McGraw-Hill, 1975), pp. 342-85. Skinner suggests that mastering the first four years of arithmetic instruction efficiently would require something on the order of 25,000 reinforcements. See Skinner, op. cit.

5. See, for example, Bill L. Hopkins, "Comments on the Future of Applied Behavior Analysis," *Journal of Applied Behavior Analysis*, vol. 20, 1987, pp. 339-46. In some studies, students learned at double the normal rate, yet most teachers did not continue reinforcing behavior at high rates after the study ended.

6. See, for example, Hopkins and Conard, op. cit.

7. For example, Mihaly Csikszentmihalyi found that adults who are successful and happy tend to have had happy childhoods. See Tina Adler, "Support and Challenge: Both Key for Smart Kids," *APA Monitor*, September 1991, pp. 10-11.

8. The terms *reinforcer* and *reward* are often used interchangeably, but they are not really synonyms. A reinforcer is defined by its effects: an event that strengthens the behavior it follows is a reinforcer, regardless of what it was intended to do. A reward is defined by social convention as something desirable; it may or may not strengthen the behavior it follows. The distinction is important since some studies that show negative effects from extrinsic rewards use rewards that are *not* reinforcers. See Alyce M. Dickinson, "The Detrimental Effects of Extrinsic Reinforcement on 'Intrinsic Motivation,' " *The Behavior Analyst*, vol. 12, 1989, pp. 1-15.

9. John Dewey distrusted the distinction between extrinsic and intrinsic rewards. He wrote that "what others do to us when we act is as natural a consequence of our action as what the fire does to us when we plunge our hands in it." Quoted in Samuel M. Deitz, "What Is Unnatural About 'Extrinsic Reinforcement'?," *The Behavior Analyst*, vol. 12, 1989, p. 255.

10. Dickinson writes that "several individuals have demanded that schools abandon reinforcement procedures for fear that they may permanently destroy a child's 'love of learning.' " See Alyce M. Dickinson, "Exploring New Vistas," *Performance Management Magazine*, vol. 9, 1991, p. 28. It is interesting to note that no one worries that earning a school letter will destroy a student's interest in sports. Nor does there seem to be much fear that people who win teaching awards will suddenly become poor teachers. For the most part, only the academic work of students is said to be put at risk by extrinsic rewards.

11. Skinner, p. 162.

12. For reviews of this literature, see Edward L. Deci and Richard M. Ryan, *Intrinsic Motivation and Self-Determination in Human Behavior* (New York: Plenum, 1985); Dickinson, "The Detrimental Effects"; and Mark R. Lepper and David Greene, eds., *The Hidden Costs of Reward: New Perspectives on*

the Psychology of Human Motivation (Hillsdale, N.J.: Erlbaum, 1978).

13. Mark R. Lepper, David Greene, and Richard E. Nisbett, "Undermining Children's Intrinsic Interest with Extrinsic Rewards," *Journal of Personality and Social Psychology*, vol. 28, 1973, pp. 129-37.

14. See, for example, Dickinson, "The Detrimental Effects"; and Mark Morgan, "Reward-Induced Decrements and Increments in Intrinsic Motivation," *Review of Educational Research*, vol. 54, 1984, pp. 5-30. Dickinson notes that studies producing negative effects are often hard to interpret since other variables (failure, deadlines, competition, and so on) could account for the findings. By way of example, she cites a study in which researchers offered a $5 reward to top performers. The study was thus contaminated by the effects of competition, yet the negative results were attributed to extrinsic rewards.

15. Dickinson, "The Detrimental Effects."

16. Edward L. Deci, "Effects of Externally Mediated Rewards on Intrinsic Motivation," *Journal of Personality and Social Psychology*, vol. 18, 1971, pp. 105-15.

17. Ross Vasta and Louise A. Stirpe, "Reinforcement Effects on Three Measures of Children's Interest in Math," *Behavior Modification*, vol. 3, 1979, pp. 223-44.

18. Dickinson, "The Detrimental Effects," p. 9. See also Morgan, op. cit.

19. Skinner, p. 15.

20. Edward L. Deci and Wayne F. Cascio, "Changes in Intrinsic Motivation as a Function of Negative Feedback and Threats," paper presented at the annual meeting of the Eastern Psychological Association, Boston, May 1972. This paper is summarized in Edward L. Deci and Joseph Porac, "Cognitive Evaluation Theory and the Study of Human Motivation," in Lepper and Greene, pp. 149-76.

21. Skinner, p. 149.

22. For more on the problems associated with punishment, see Murray Sidman, *Coercion and Its Fallout* (Boston: Authors Cooperative, Inc., 1989).

23. Grades are often referred to as rewards, but they are more often punishments. Students study not so much to receive high grades as to avoid receiving low ones.

24. Deci and Cascio, op. cit.

25. See, for example, Edward L. Deci, Wayne F. Cascio, and Judy Krusell, "Sex Differences, Positive Feedback, and Intrinsic Motivation," paper presented at the annual meeting of the Eastern Psychological Association, Washington, D.C., May 1973. This paper is summarized in Deci and Porac, op. cit.

26. It should be noted that encouragement often closely resembles reinforcement in form. One teacher may say, "I know you can do it, Mary," as Mary struggles to answer a question; another teacher may say, "I knew you could do it, Mary!" when Mary answers the question correctly. The first teacher is encouraging; the second is reinforcing. The difference is subtle but important.

27. Intrinsic rewards are more important to the maintenance of skills once learned. An adult's skill at addition and subtraction is not ordinarily maintained by the approval of peers but by the satisfaction that comes from balancing a checkbook.

28. See, for example, Jere Brophy, "Teacher Praise: A Functional Analysis," *Review of Educational Research*, vol. 51, 1981, pp. 5-32; Hopkins and Conard, op. cit.; and Dickinson, "The Detrimental Effects."

29. "Instructional contingencies," writes Skinner, "are usually contrived and should always be temporary. If instruction is to have any point, the behavior it generates will be taken over and maintained by contingencies in the world at large." See Skinner, p. 144.

A Look to the Future

What are the realistic prospects for achieving specific benchmark standards for improving the instructional effort in the schools in the near future? The efforts to develop various choice proposals and privatized forms of schools will continue. Some important changes are at work in the formation of alternative ways to become an educated person. Several ambitious goals for American elementary and secondary school students were adopted by the states and the Bush administration. These goals were expected to be achieved by the year 2000. While it is not likely that all of the goals will be achieved in the few years remaining in this decade, they did serve the purpose of framing a set of student performance expectations.

We will see much more debate over equal achievement standards for students in the next few years. Calls for new forms of schooling that break away from traditional conceptions of American school schedules and that organize and group students for instruction differently than at present are being proposed. These proposals will be debated with fervor by their proponents and opponents in the remaining years to the turn of the century.

Some of the demographic changes involving young people in the United States are staggering. Ten percent of American teenage girls will become pregnant each year, the highest rate in the developed world. At least 100,000 American elementary school children get drunk once a week. Incidence of venereal disease has tripled among adolescents in the United States since 1965. The actual school dropout rate in the United States stands at 30 percent. A social crisis exists in the United States of America, and we will have to face it in the near-term future.

On other fronts, the student populations of North America reflect vital social and cultural forces at work. In the United States, a massive secondary school dropout problem has been developing steadily through the past decade. The 1990s will reveal how public school systems will address this and other unresolved problems brought about by dramatic upheavals in demographics. There is the issue, as well, of how great a shortfall in the supply of new teachers will be experienced in the 1990s. In the immediate future we will be able to see if a massive teacher shortage is beginning; if it is, how will emergency or alternative certification measures adopted by states affect achievement of the objectives of the reform agenda?

At any given moment in a people's history, several alternative future directions are open to them. Since 1970, North American educational systems have been subjected to one wave after another of recommendations for programmatic change. Is it any wonder that change is a sort of watchword for persons in teacher education on this continent? What specific directions it will take in the immediate future depend on which recommendations of the reform agenda are implemented. The direction of educational change depends on several other factors as well, not the least of which is the resolution of the issue of which agencies of government (local, state or provincial, and federal) will pay for the very high costs of reform.

The major demographic changes that have been occurring on this continent, particularly in the United States, will be critical in determining the needs of our educational systems in the coming years. Increased numbers of students in the schools from the faster-growing cultural groups will bring about shifts in perceived national educational priorities, and perhaps fundamental realignments of our educational goals. We shall see how state and provincial education agencies respond to these trends.

Basic changes in society's career patterns should also be considered. It is estimated that in the United States the average nonagricultural worker now makes a major job change about five times in his or her career. The schools will surely be affected, indirectly or directly, by such major social phenomena. Changes in the social structure due to divorce, unemployment, or job retraining efforts will also have an impact. Educational systems are integral parts of the broader social systems that created them. If the larger social system experiences fundamental change, this is reflected in the educational system.

In the area of information science and computer technologies applicable for use in educational systems, the development of new products is so rapid that we cannot predict what technological capacities may be available to schools 20 years from now. In addition, basic computer literacy is becoming more and more widespread in the population. We are entering—indeed we are in—a period of human history when knowledgeable people can control far greater information (and have immediate access to it) than at any previous time. As new information command systems evolve, this phenomenon will become more and more meaningful to all of us.

The future of education will be determined by the current debate concerning what constitutes a just, na-

tional response to human needs in a period of technological change. The history of technological change in all human societies since the beginning of industrial development clearly demonstrates that major advances in technology and breakthroughs in the basic sciences lead to more rapid rates of social change. Society is on the verge of discoveries that will lead to the creation of entirely new technologies in the dawning years of the twenty-first century. All of the social, economic, and educational institutions on Earth will be affected by these scientific breakthroughs. The basic issue is not whether the schools can remain aloof from the needs of industry or the economic demands of society, but how they can emphasize the noblest ideals of free persons in the face of inevitable technological and economic change. Another concern is how to let go of predetermined visions of the future that limit our possibilities as free people. The schools, of course, will be called upon to face these issues. We need the most enlightened, insightful, and compassionate teachers ever educated by North American universities to prepare the youth of the future in a manner that will humanize the high-tech world in which they live.

All of the articles included in this unit can be related to discussions on the goals of education, the future of education, or curriculum development. They also reflect highly divergent perspectives in the philosophy of education.

Looking Ahead: Challenge Questions

What might be the shape of school curricula by the year 2000?

What changes in society are most likely to affect educational change?

Based on all of the commission reports of recent years, is it possible to identify any clear directions in which teacher education in North America is headed? How can we build a better future for teachers?

How can information about population demographics, potential discoveries in the basic sciences, and the rate and direction of technological change in Canada and the United States assist in planning for our educational future?

How can schools prepare students to live and work in an uncertain future? What knowledge bases are most important? What skills are most important?

Will privatized schools represent an expansion of the educational opportunities for our children?

Should school "choice" proposals include the concept that tax dollars follow the student?

WHERE WE GO FROM HERE

At FORTUNE's Education Summit, executives, politicians, and educators agreed on how to fix America's schools. Now to do it.

NANCY J. PERRY

IT IS THE BEST of times and the worst of times for America's schools. Best, because after years of talking about it, the nation's political leaders finally seem dedicated to radical reform. In April, President Bush announced America 2000, a four-pronged assault on educational mediocrity intended to drive the U.S. toward the six ambitious national education goals that he and the governors of the 50 states adopted last year.

Worst, because the reasons reform is essential have never been more grimly apparent. In August the College Board announced that scores on the Scholastic Aptitude Test had declined four points from last year, to 896 out of a possible 1,600. The verbal score, which fell to 422, was the lowest on record. This is after a decade in which spending per student, after inflation, has risen roughly 33%, schools have stiffened graduation requirements, and practically every major U.S. corporation has increased its involvement in K–12 education.

The mood among the 300 executives, educators, and politicians who gathered in September in Washington, D.C., for FORTUNE's fourth annual education summit reflected a mix of anger and hope. Says Alcoa Chairman Paul O'Neill: "It makes me angry to go to business meetings and find that my colleagues don't know about the President's education goals. And it makes me very angry to find

REPORTER ASSOCIATE *Rosalind Klein Berlin*

that we're spending 95% of our time bashing each other about the things we disagree on and maybe 5% working on the things we agree on."

Tempering that frustration was the discovery that we now agree on quite a lot. We agree, for instance, on the need to educate *all* kids—not just those in the top half academically. We agree on the need for higher standards, more effective tests, a curriculum that teaches the skills industry needs, better teacher training, and more preschool education. As Secretary of Education Lamar Alexander observes: "There is an enormous amount of common ground about what to do. What's left is to figure out how to do it."

This report on our summit, which leads off a five-article special report on education, zeroes in on how business can make a difference. Robert Kennedy, CEO of Union Carbide, believes more executives should bang on their bully pulpits: "We can begin by communicating the urgency of the problem to our own employees and getting them involved."

Business must also be more vocal and articulate about what it needs from the schools. Says Ian Rolland, CEO of the Lincoln National insurance company in Fort Wayne: "We really have not done a very good job of telling the educational community what we expect—maybe because we're not sure." BellSouth Chairman John Clendenin knows what he'd like to see—more emphasis on student writing: "Demanding this of your local schools is a specific change that is achievable and will make a difference."

Above all, business can help raise expectations. Says RJR Nabisco Chairman Louis Gerstner Jr.: "We have reached this point of dismal academic performance because we as a country stopped demanding excellence. If we accept second rate, we will become second rate. We must demand the best, because you never get more than you demand."

NONE of the ideas proposed in President Bush's America 2000 program inspired more discussion at FORTUNE's summit than his call for setting national standards in math, science, English, history, and geography, and holding educators accountable for achieving them. The President wants the U.S. for the first time to develop voluntary national achievement tests for fourth-, eighth-, and 12th-graders, and to have the initial battery of those tests ready to go by September 1993.

In a country that has long cherished local control of education, just talking about national standards is revolutionary. Opponents complain that it isn't fair to judge schools on performance, since many are coping with forces like drugs and poverty that are beyond their control; that teachers will teach to the test; and that decentralized schools cannot be measured against a single national benchmark.

Rubbish. For starters, America's 110,000 schools are already being measured against a single benchmark—international competition—and are coming up disastrously short. As for teaching to the test, Keith Geiger, president of the National Education Association, the largest teachers' union, notes, "If our assessment instruments measure the learning goals we have for students, then it would be perfectly appropriate to teach to the test."

Another objection to standards is that poor performance on national tests might damage students' self-esteem. If you buy that, consider that on a 1988 international math test conducted by the Educational Testing Service, American students scored 12th out of 12 countries and provinces. Yet when asked how good they thought they were in math, 68% of the U.S. kids replied, "Very good." Says Lou Gerstner: "Clearly these kids do not have a self-esteem problem. They have a serious performance problem."

In a nation of diverse people and unequal schools, the challenge is to agree on exactly what those new standards should be and then how to test students against them. How to do both without imposing a standardized curriculum? Here business's help is critical. Says Labor Secretary Lynn Martin, whose Commission on Achieving Necessary Skills is trying to define the basic competencies needed for most entry-level jobs: "We have to have a better dialogue between business, schools, parents, and community leaders about what skills are needed and why."

SOME of that dialogue is taking place in a partnership led by the Learning Research and Development Center at the University of Pittsburgh and the National Center on Education and the Economy in Rochester, New York. Their New Standards Project aims to build a new generation of evaluation tools that replace multiple-choice tests with performance exams and project appraisals. Says Lauren Resnick, head of the Pittsburgh center: "Life doesn't come packaged in short answers and bubbles."

To design the exams, Resnick and Marc Tucker, her counterpart in Rochester, are working with teachers and corporations from 15 states and six major urban school districts. Collectively these account for 42% of U.S. school children. Allowing clusters of states to offer their own regional exams and grade them according to a national standard finesses the issue of state vs. federal control.

The key to turning out better students, of course, is better teaching. With support from AT&T, Chrysler, Du Pont, Ford Motor, and several other corporations, the National Board for Professional Teaching Standards, headed by former North Carolina governor Jim Hunt, is developing new ways to raise standards among teachers and to evaluate performance. Like board standards in the medical specialities, these evaluations will be voluntary. They will go beyond written tests and rely on in-class observation, classroom simulations, videotapes of teachers at work, and interviews.

Teachers who make the grade will receive an advanced certificate from the national board entitling them—in theory, at least—to more pay and other benefits. Says Hunt: "Assessment of teachers is essential for reform. We must learn what makes great teachers and encourage hundreds of thousands of them to achieve that status."

In America today two subjects that get little respect are math and science, a conclusion confirmed in the 22nd annual Gallup poll on education. Asked to rank the education goals set out in America 2000, Gallup's respondents deemed making U.S. students first in the world in math and science by the year 2000 the least important target. Not so, says Lamar Alexander, who thinks that America's failures in this area are so dismal that an alarm bell "ought to ring all night."

One man attempting to awaken U.S. kids to the excitement of science is Dr. Robert Ballard, discoverer of the Royal Mail Ship *Titanic* and director of the Center for Marine Exploration at the Woods Hole Oceanographic Institution. After a 1986 Turner Broadcasting System special showed him at work on the *Titanic* deep in the Atlantic, Ballard received more than 16,000 letters from youngsters asking how they could do what he does.

To capitalize on this enthusiasm, Ballard has persuaded several companies, among them Electronic Data Systems, Cray Research, TBS, and the National Geographic Society, to underwrite an educational innovation he calls the Jason Project. Jason is the name of the robot Ballard invented to explore and transmit images from hard-to-reach places like the mountains that lie beneath the sea.

Two years ago, Ballard began taking hundreds of thousands of high school students on annual two-week electronic field trips by hooking them up via satellite to his traveling laboratory. In 1989 the Jason team went to the Mediterranean Sea to the deepest known ancient shipwreck site. Last year they explored two sunken War of 1812 warships, complete with every kid's favorite: skeletons of sailors.

To participate, students go to one of several satellite receiving centers—there are now 20—where they view live, interactive broadcasts, ask questions of Ballard and his team, and even help control the robot. Beforehand the kids spend an average of 50 hours studying a special curriculum prepared by the National Science Teachers Association. The cost to the schools: just $3 or less per student.

In December some 600,000 students and 10,000 teachers will join the third Jason expedition—bound for the Galápagos Islands. Says Ballard: "Kids are born scientists. The first question out of their mouth is 'why?' "

Turned on as a student might be by skeletons and seaweed, he or she won't ever be a scientist without first learning math. In Fort Worth, under a program called C^3—community, corporation, and classroom—local businesses such as Tandy Corp., American Airlines, and Burlington Northern evaluated more than 1,000 jobs to determine what skills they needed and concluded that math was an area where the school system fell short. Students weren't required to take much, and the little they took was more theoretical than practical.

THE SOLUTION: Within three years the Fort Worth schools hope to require all students to take algebra in the eighth or ninth grade. To make sure the kids are ready, the College Board and several foundations brought a new program this year to Fort Worth called Equity 2000 to train teachers in innovative methods of math instruction, to counsel students and parents, and to motivate the youngsters to learn and to appreciate math.

In this area too, better performance hinges on improving both the quality and quantity of math and science teachers. The White House is aiming for a 50% increase by the year 2000 in the number of teachers with a substantial math or science background.

U.S. business can lend a hand by providing in-service training and teaching grants to those already in the classroom. Cray Research runs a staff development program each summer for some 900 math and science teachers in rural northwestern Wisconsin. GTE sponsors a program called GIFT—Growth Initiative for Teachers—that each year awards 50 teams of math and science teachers $12,000 grants, part of which must be spent on a classroom project they have designed. One GTE teacher-team built a space shuttle cockpit and took students to the Kennedy Space Center in Florida to observe a launch.

Also growing in popularity are programs that encourage corporate engineers to become math and science teachers. Polaroid, Hughes Aircraft, Rockwell International, and Digital Equipment are just a few of the companies that will pay for retirees, and in some cases active employees, to go back to school to get their teacher certification. This year Digital's Engineers in Education program will move another 60 to 70 people with bachelor of science degrees into education.

But will this kind of slow, incremental effort really change American education? No, says Chris Whittle, the chairman of Whittle Communications: "You can't make a light bulb out of a candle. Instead of trying to improve the current model, we need to take it completely apart and put it back together into a fundamentally different whole."

Lamar Alexander and his team agree. One way they hope to realize the goals of America 2000 is by challenging the country to build a "new generation of American schools." It's easier to say what these schools are not than what they are. Among other things, they will abandon the traditional assumption that schools close their doors at three; that subjects are taught in 50-minute classes; and that students must be grouped by age and grade.

The White House is fostering such new schools in two ways. First, Bush is asking Congress to provide grants of $1 million to each of at least 535 communities—one in each congressional district, plus two per state—so that they can create their own high-perfor-

mance New American Schools. At the same time he has asked U.S. business leaders to contribute $200 million to launch the New American Schools Development Corp., a private, nonprofit organization that will award contracts in 1992 to as many as seven design teams. These teams of companies, universities, and education consultants will fashion new kinds of learning environments for students and then help communities adapt them to their individual needs.

Meanwhile, a number of states and businesses are attempting to reinvent schools on their own. In 1990, RJR Nabisco launched its Next Century Schools project, which will invest $30 million over the next five years in 45 ideas to change the schools. For six years, Apple Computer's Apple Classrooms of Tomorrow project (ACOT) has been exploring how technology affects learning and teaching.

INSTEAD OF LISTENING to lectures all day, more than 3,000 ACOT students in 100 schools around the country work with Apple-donated technology, including personal computers, laser disk players, optic scanners, and video cameras. Using infrared satellite images called up over on-line databases, eighth-graders at the Booth Fickett Math Science Magnet School in Tucson, Arizona, were able to study Hurricane Bob as it ravaged the East Coast. Says student Casiano Armenta: "By doing this we learned that hurricanes are controlled by warm and cold fronts, high- and low-pressure areas, steering winds, and jet streams." ACOT research shows that students who use high technology to learn are more self-confident, more comfortable working in teams, and better able to solve problems.

So far the most radical scheme to restructure U.S. schools is the $2.5 billion project recently launched by Chris Whittle. Having learned the depth of public educators' resistance to change during his much-publicized battle to sell *Channel One*, an advertiser-supported news program, to high school students, Whittle now intends to end-run the whole system. His plan is to open 1,000 low-cost, state-of-the-art, for-profit school campuses around the country by 2010.

Whittle offers no apologies for the

fact that his schools will, if successful, make money. Says he: "We are all seriously kidding ourselves if we believe that business-led charity is the answer to the current crisis. It costs $250 million per hour to run American K–12 education. That means all the money business currently spends annually on philanthropy could run our schools for about 90 minutes."

Nonetheless, Whittle stresses that his will "not be BMW schools," designed for the top 1% of U.S. households. Rather, they will be "Beetle schools," open to all students, with an average annual tuition of $5,500— roughly what the public schools spend per student. If Whittle succeeds, he expects a pack of private competitors will follow—and hopes public schools might learn from and imitate his project as well.

Supporters of school choice see this kind of market-led competition for the hearts, minds, and dollars of K–12 students as the perfect tonic for what ails American education. And free-enterprise fans were surprised and cheered when the White House's America 2000 program broadened the debate by advocating that states and local districts give parents the right to use public money to send their kids to private and parochial schools. That turned an already heated controversy over public school choice into the rhetorical equivalent of a food fight, with both sides slinging barbs like broccoli.

Says Lewis Finch, superintendent of Jefferson County schools in Colorado: "Corporations want us to operate public schools like they operate their businesses. They can carefully select their raw materials to produce, say, the best Oreo cookies in the world. But out behind the plant is a pile of refuse made up of those that don't qualify. Is that the kind of school system we want for America? I think not."

Even some ardent backers of public school choice worry that a nationwide system of education vouchers might do more harm than good. Says Joe Nathan, director of the Center for School Change at the University of Minnesota: "Choice, like electricity, is a very powerful tool. If handled carefully, it can create enormous benefits for millions of youngsters. If not, it will create far more problems than it solves."

The consensus at FORTUNE's summit was that public school choice, which has proved its worth in a handful of school districts, such as Cambridge, Massachusetts, and East Harlem in New York City, should continue its slow expansion. But private schools, except in a few special situations—say, to help pregnant teenagers—won't be granted public dollars to join the party anytime soon.

THOUGH the first of America 2000's six education goals declares, "All children in America will start school ready to learn," there is no goal that says, "All children will graduate ready to work." The Administration's otherwise comprehensive program offers no specific plan to help the 40% of high school graduates who won't immediately go on to college and the roughly half of college-bound grads who later drop out.

Several governors are working to fill that gap. One is Arkansas Governor and likely Democratic presidential contender Bill Clinton. "We can no longer let kids get out of high school and wander around trying to figure out what to do," he says. "We've got to have a better school-to-work transition." Last spring, Clinton persuaded the Arkansas legislature to pass a bill that provides funding for at least five youth apprenticeship programs in areas critical to the state's future, among them health, machine tooling, and entrepreneurship.

Political leaders in Oregon are also aware that not everyone will grow up to be an astrophysicist or an investment banker. Earlier this year they passed a law that will eventually establish the nation's first statewide apprenticeship program for students who don't go on to college. Under the Oregon plan, all high school students would be required to demonstrate competence in math, science, reading, and other academic courses by the tenth grade. At that point, they would have to choose between a college prep or job-training curriculum.

Give Oregon's plan points for ambition. But its final realization may be years away. Several business leaders in the state note that at a time when manufacturing companies are reducing work forces, apprenticeships are an unwanted expense. Companies also complain about the safety rules, child labor laws, and liability issues they have to contend with. "We've got a long way to go," admits Gary Carlson, who serves as vice president of Associated Oregon Industries, a trade group that represents 15,000 companies in the state. "But companies can't just cheer on the sidelines. We have to get in and work with schools to provide workplace experiences, along with a structured curriculum."

One new industry-driven course of study that is beginning to catch on around the country goes by the name of Tech Prep, or 2+2. This curriculum aims to prepare high school kids for two years of community college. Tech Prep students take a full load of academic courses in addition to several technical courses, some of which count for community college credit.

In southern Maryland, high schools in three counties are working with Charles County Community College to offer Tech Prep programs in engineering technology, business and management, and health and human services. They provide a model for how to begin. First, the college invited ten electronics technicians to spend two days answering the question, What do I do as an electronics technician? Later it put a related question to the managers who hired the technicians. In phase three, the faculty of the college and participating high schools will work together to ensure that all these skills and tasks are incorporated into their Tech Prep program for engineering.

For all the public optimism and enthusiasm of FORTUNE's education summit, a number of executives privately expressed a deepening gloom over the willingness of the educational establishment to embrace new ideas. After several years of working to improve this sprawling bureaucratic system, they wonder if any significant progress is possible.

But RJR Nabisco's Lou Gerstner warns corporate America to hang in there. "We can't become complacent or lazy or tired just because things are taking longer than we want them to," he says. "Like the Soviet citizens who recently rejected the regime that would roll back their hard-won gains, we must be steadfast. For business, for all of us, this is not a matter of philanthropy. This is a matter of preserving our democracy and our standing in the world." Could any cause matter more?

EDUCATION 2000 A.D.

A Peek into the Future

Will the problems that plague education today continue in the 21st century?

Robert J. Simpson

Dr. Simpson is dean, School of Education, University of Miami, Coral Gables, Fla.

THIS article is one educator's attempt to predict what significant events will affect American schools and colleges by the year 2000. No logical sequence for the items exists because all have the common denominator of improving learning. School "merit," "accountability," "reform," and "restructuring" are popular terms. All recognize that reorganization and redirection are needed along with a meaningful system of rewards for achievement for both students and employees. The question is, how?

An inherent obstacle to reform exists. Schools in the U.S. are government operated. Even private ones are strongly controlled. The aim is to prepare students to succeed in a capitalistic society, and it often does so poorly.

Active criticism of education is not new. Parisian students rioted in the 18th century as their Ivy League counterparts did in the 19th. As Yogi Berra once said, "It's *deja vu* all over again!"

The faster things change, the more they stay the same. While criticisms are *deja vu* for school leaders, they tend to change focus according to the social ills that may be in vogue in the media.

School systems are established to perpetuate the government, democratic or totalitarian, and educate children so they will be good taxpayers, rather than tax receivers. Schools today are blamed for most of the nation's ills because so many responsibilities have been dumped upon them by other social agencies and parents. The old small-town triumvirate of home, school, and church guiding the young has vanished as a result of court orders and urbanization, among other factors. Thus, I predict, some school will establish effective partnerships with its families and social agencies and significantly increase student achievement and retention.

Using our educational institutions as a dumping-ground and scapegoat is a convenience for legislators who, historically, have been willing to accept credit, but not responsibility, as they present more demands and fewer resources to schools. I predict that some state legislature will realize that superior education is the key to economic growth and savings in criminal justice and social services costs. It will develop an incentive funding program for local schools that will save money for the state within 10 years and increase student learning.

In addition, Congress will recognize that economics will be the international battlefield during the next century and that the gap between literate and illiterate nations may continue to widen. Where reason fails, war will occur. The Federal government will establish an Education Corps to provide assistance in developing democratic schools systems in other countries as well as the U.S.

Legislators know education generally gets taxpayer backing. This is why some states were able to establish lotteries to increase the support of schools, then proceed to divert previous sources of school revenues to pet projects. For most politicians, education is like the weather—it always is discussed, but little is done about it. Although education is easier to change than climate, a look at the record of Congress and the state legislatures puts this in doubt even for the 1990s!

American governors want the dropout rate to be reduced to 10% and literacy to increase to 100% during the next decade. Like legislators, their public statements were not accompanied by any numbers indicating sources of funds. I predict that, during the 1990s, some governor will present a cogent and coherent education platform and will shepherd it through the state legislature.

Various studies and groups find that American students today are ignorant in many subject areas. Academic achievement in the basic skills—the original and basic purpose of the school—often is found in small-town and parochial schools and among Oriental families. The common denominator is parental involvement in their children's learning activities, rather than assuming teachers will do it all.

Objective measures of achievement other than standardized examinations will be necessary to avoid the problem of educators teaching for the test, rather than life. Graduation, retention, college entrance, and other measurements will be included. Percentages of students passing a state or national standardized test are convenient and economical quantitative cop-outs for qualitative planning and evaluation in education. I predict that some programs will measure students by success in life—including minimal problems with drugs and crime—instead of blind reliance upon national test norms.

Students increasingly are becoming aware of the importance of an education to the "good life." In the 1990s, those now called minorities will constitute a majority in our colleges and, after the year 2000, in our public schools. Many will need special assistance to succeed in high school and college and will not realize their potential unless educators become more aware of the unique needs of individual students.

Discipline problems and dropout rates will continue to increase. Assistance programs will become mandatory to some extent. Legislators must be made aware that individualized education can *not* occur when the economical approach of mass education is governmental policy. Any successful merit system that is legislated must include immediate rewards for student achievers, intrinsic and extrinsic.

Individual educational programs (IEPs) first were required by the Education for All Handicapped Children Act of 1975. IEPs are developed through careful diagnosis of the learner's needs and problems by a staff of specialists. These are reviewed regularly, and appropriate adjustments are made to keep each student in the mainstream of the academic program as much as possible. IEPs follow pupils through their school years, much like physicians use medical records.

I predict that IEPs will be developed for all students by the end of the century. Further, a clear plan, subscribed to by parents and educators, permits parent support and minimizes litigation. In effect, *all* students, elementary through higher education, will have individual education contracts (IECs). These now exist in some private schools and for some in-school disciplinary programs. While standardized instruments will be used in IECs to measure aptitude and achievement, over-reliance will cause claims of ethnic bias to be expanded. Constitutional liberty and property rights to an education will be raised.

Delivery of learning

Ninety percent of the research and technology concerning effective teaching and learning has been developed during the past 25 years. Most school programs continue along state guidelines that are oblivious to discoveries in either area. School boards point with pride at their "modern program" if teachers and students can use personal computers as type-writers and calculators.

School use. The typical multi-million-dollar school building is used less than 20% of the time when one considers a six-hour school day for 180 days per year. In the 21st century, the restructured meritorious school will remain open longer each day, week, and year. It will serve more learners of greater age differences literally from the womb to the tomb with pre-school day-care centers and adult education programs for the entire community. It also will provide an after-hours study center where students—who may attend another school—can do their homework and receive aid. Special assistance programs will include English as a second language and aid to those with other learning difficulties, as well as serving students who just want to progress faster.

Schools still might be able to be smaller if they can be open longer. This, of course, assumes that neighborhoods are safe and students have easy access to their schools.

Technology. While the minimal use of expensive facilities is ridiculous, schools may be able to become smaller for other

reasons. Gridlock, smog, increasing urban populations, and convenience in child supervision will cause greater reliance upon education technology that already has been developed for use over distances. A restructured merit school will provide the basic information in language arts, social studies, mathematics, and sciences on disks and tapes for delivery via satellites, modems, and/or library checkout systems. Distance education will work in sparsely settled areas as well as in urban communities where students' homes and schools are separated by long bus rides.

Master teachers. The best teachers in all fields should reach more students. There are many stories about exemplary educators who can teach the most difficult subjects to the most disadvantaged learners. National/international curriculum materials laboratories will make it possible for master teachers to reach all students at school or at home.

While a computer lacks a human touch, it often provides better delivery of content. Interesting materials on computers will compete favorably and positively with television. Parents will become more involved with homework and, subsequently, in improving their own knowledge and skills.

Some innovative district, probably with a grant from the Federal government or IBM, will develop a model for computer-assisted instruction (CAI) that will determine what is best taught by CAI and what isn't. Considerations include short-term halo effects, cost-effectiveness, inertia, variety of clientele, location of transmission facilities, and ease of obtaining replacement hardware.

While integration provided immediate positive help to minority students, it removed the family-support factor from many academic situations simply because of the distance between students' homes and schools. Many faculty wouldn't travel to inner-city homes, and parents couldn't arrange to visit schools after work—even if anyone was there. Three factors will help ethnic assimilation in the 1990s:

● CAI will close the gap between school and home. Personal computers will be inexpensive so that all students may purchase, lease, or borrow one or use hardware at neighborhood homework centers.
● Legislators and jurists finally will admit the real cause of segregated schools is segregated housing patterns encouraged by state and local laws. Stronger penalties on restrictive real estate covenants plus incentives for low-income housing will permit the return of integrated neighborhood schools, which will solve many of the dilemmas cited above.
● Magnet schools will continue to be established at the junior and senior high levels to attract a multi-ethnic student body based upon common career interests. While

this works when adequate transportation and academic quality are provided, some problems can occur. Magnet schools may have an elitism scale—*e.g.*, health professions might rate higher than the automotive trades.

Also, by virtue of vocational choice and history, magnet schools might perpetuate segregation if questionably legal quotas are used in lieu of affirmative advisement. More parents may opt for education at home or in other non-traditional settings, which will give rise to church and state issues.

A successful magnet school will incorporate CAI along with rewards for successful programs, teachers, and pupils, including, for students, early work experiences for pay. Partnerships with local businesses are essential.

Values. It's okay if you don't get caught. The end justifies the means. The insurance company will pay so no one gets hurt. These are common examples of eroding values. No common social conduct standards are being transmitted to the young or practiced by their elders.

Historically, American public schools taught Protestant values. Catholics and Jews who objected to the sectarian packaging started their own schools. Atheists still were in the legislative closet until three decades ago.

When courts voided racial segregation in public schools, advocacy of any one religion was also excommunicated from the classroom. At the same time, overreaction occurred. Any suggestion of advocating morality was considered sectarian and, therefore, illegal.

No court decision said public schools couldn't teach *about* religion. Indeed, religious pluralism is part of the historical and cultural fabric of our nation and must be taught. I predict that some state or private agency will fund the development of instructional materials on values and comparative religion for the public schools' curriculum.

Brain surgeons don't admit their patients to hospitals nor clean the operating rooms. Yet, teachers with a master's degree end up with duties of which 90% could be done by an intelligent high school graduate.

The million-dollar teacher

By the year 2000, I predict that a few lighthouse schools and colleges will be paying *teachers* $100,000 a year. These career professionals will earn more than $3,000,000 during their work life.

The "million-dollar teacher" will replace the principal. This principal/teacher will lead the planning, delivery, and evaluation of academic programs for a school or program unit (*e.g.*, Language Arts or Nursery-Primary).

9. A LOOK TO THE FUTURE

An educational career ladder will create a teaching team consisting of young volunteers, aides, interns, assistant and associate teachers, plus technological, social services, and clerical support personnel.

Institutions of higher education are not exercising the leadership role in meritorious reform of education. It is amazing how universities garner funds to support research and innovative practices, but few of these findings are institutionalized on campus.

Theoretically, colleges have a collegial form of governance in which professors make academic policy decisions. This may be a form of self-protection or sharing the blame because few college administrators have any formal training in management.

In the future, I predict that a few lighthouse colleges will form full-partnership teams with local districts and teachers' unions to restructure teacher education; recognize that teaching and service are as important as research for merit rewards for college faculty; and encourage and practice classroom research that gives trained teachers immediate feedback as to the success of different instructional styles and materials.

The crystal ball grows foggy, but other concerns loom in the mist:

● Administrators will be found civilly liable for hiring child-abusers. At the same time, employees must be protected against false claims of abuse by children and their parents.

● More personnel actions will occur on the grounds of incompetency when schools don't meet program goals and students fall short of individual education contract objectives.

● Measurable evaluative standards for instructors will become increasingly important as a forced retirement age vanishes and, thus, age discrimination suits inexorably proliferate.

● Strong debates will arise as to advertising in instructional materials, including not only student publications, but instructional television as well.

● Lighthouse schools and meritorious programs will remember that creativity comes from imagination, not intelligence, and that curiosity is the starting point.

How 'New' Will the 'New' Whittle American School Be?

A Case Study in Privatization

There have been signals that the Edison Project will go ahead regardless of who occupies the White House, Mr. Brodinsky says. And those who oppose the incursion of business and the profit motive into public education predict that Clinton's election may postpone movements toward privatization — but will not end them.

BEN BRODINSKY

BEN BRODINSKY, a former president of the Educational Press Association of America, is a consultant and education writer living in Bloomfield, Conn. © 1993, Ben Brodinsky.

AMERICAN public schools have been growing, changing, and serving the nation for more than 300 years. Today, a man in Tennessee says that these schools are outdated and inadequate and that he will build "a new American school" in about five or 10 or 15 or 20 years. His name is Christopher Whittle, and he calls his instrument for creating that new school the Edison Project. Critics call it an ominous step toward privatization of public schools.

During the past three centuries America's schools developed under the impact of philosophers, statesmen, and social reformers — from Horace Mann to John Dewey, from Thomas Jefferson to Lyndon Johnson (the latter now recognized as the quintessential Education President

because of his stewardship of the Elementary and Secondary Education Act of 1965).

But Whittle sets out to build the new American school with a core team of seven people. Four are specialists in management or mass media; one is a Chicago inner-city principal; one, a former Brookings Institution fellow; and one, a former professor. To preside over the core team, Whittle hired Benno Schmidt, former president of Yale University — a move that sent mild shock waves through some education circles (and which I take up below).

During the past three centuries, as Henry Steele Commager has said in a memorable essay, the schools have kept us free. They have helped to create an enlightened citizenry so that self-government might work; they have instilled a sense of national unity (common language, common history, common songs); they have Americanized millions of immigrants; and they have routed "the forces of special privilege and ruinous division."[1]

But the focus of the Edison Project, as critics see it, is none of the above. It is, rather, the creation of "efficient schools" driven by technology and the marketplace, whose students will generate high test scores and will become proficient workers so that this nation can challenge the productive capacity of Japan, Germany, and South Korea. Such objectives can best be achieved by a private, for-profit company "with a public agenda," says Whittle.

Quick to defend his views at every opportunity, Whittle met with a group of editors in Baltimore on 27 June 1992 and hammered at these points: "We are not

out to destroy or hurt the existing public school system. . . . Our efforts may eventually help traditional schools as they pick up our practices suitable to their purposes. . . . Our efforts are not about privatization. . . . not about vouchers. . . . not about profits. . . ."

When one participant in the Baltimore session asked, "In one word, then, what is the Edison Project about?" Whittle shot back, "Service."[2]

Christopher Whittle, age 45, has been called one of America's great salesmen (and also a man who is dangerous to public education because of his salesmanship skills). Whittle showed his salesmanship skills early in life when, as a student at the University of Tennessee in 1970, he launched a company that provided freshmen with condensations of textbooks. The success of this venture led Whittle to produce other school materials, including books, wall charts, and magazines, which today can be found on 300 college campuses and in thousands of elementary and secondary schools. His personal fortune is said to be around $40 million. Because of his wealth and showy lifestyle, he has been called the playboy of the education world. And there is no doubt that he is obsessed with a single idea — wherever there is an audience, captive or not, whether in doctors' and dentists' offices, hospitals, or schools, it should be exposed to Whittle salesmanship.

To take the true measure of Christopher Whittle, consider his most controversial venture so far, Channel One. Here is Whittle's own recounting of its history:

Three years ago we developed a national television show for America's

From *Phi Delta Kappan,* March 1993, pp. 540-543, 546-547. Copyright © 1993 by Ben Brodinsky. Reprinted with permission of *Phi Delta Kappan* and the author.

teenagers that we wanted to beam directly into high schools. What we discovered shocked us. America's schools couldn't receive Channel One. The typical American high school classroom did not have a television set, much less a satellite dish to receive the program. So, not only did we have to produce the news show, we had to build an electronic infrastructure. Which we did — in 24 months.

We laid 6,000 miles of cable down the hallways of America's schools; we installed 10,000 satellite dishes; we bought and installed over 300,000 television sets, quadrupling the number that were in use in our high schools. And so today, 40% of America's schools have an electronic infrastructure they did not have two years ago.[3]

Whittle says that this effort cost him over $200 million. To underwrite this expense, he decided to sell two minutes of commercials a day — and thereby started a firestorm in the education establishment.

I have before me, as I write, a stack nearly a foot high of legal documents, resolutions, newspaper columns, editorials, and texts of court documents — all opposing Channel One. The opposition comes from every major national education association — with the American Association of School Administrators, the National Parents and Teachers Association, and the National Education Association among the most vocal. The opposition includes state departments of education and groups representing consumers, Catholic activists, and children's interests.

The critics charge that the classroom is no place for commercials — that it is unethical to corral schoolchildren to watch sales pitches. They denounce Channel One on the ground that the showings take up class time that could be better used, say, for laboratory work in science or for examining controversial issues in social studies.

Critics warn that Channel One is a harsh intrusion into the classroom, a disturbance of the flow of the curriculum, and an infringement on the learning time of students. They warn that more such intrusions (and greater ones) will come if the menace is not stopped now.

Most troublesome to critics is the philosophical significance of Channel One. They declare that the venture spells triumph for the idea that education is no longer based on a set of democratic principles dedicated to the common good. In-

stead, education is now seen by entrepreneurs as a function of the marketplace — and schools, students, and curriculum are to be used for generating profit.

To this, Whittle and his cohort all but say, "Nonsense." Whittle points to the following "set of facts" generated by his company: 12,000 schools have contracted for Channel One. The offering has been cleared to air in the public schools of every state except New York. Some 65% of all Catholic high schools in the country are on-line. A challenge to bar Channel One from California public schools has been defeated. (In September 1992 the state supreme court denied the state's request for an injunction to stop the program. The judge was not impressed by the state's arguments that students are forced to watch Channel One and urged California schools to work out restrictions on watching, if they so desire. Both sides declared victory.)

In sum, Channel One is due for a phenomenal expansion — and private estimates are that during 1993 Whittle will earn up to three-quarters of a million dollars a day in advertising fees. In the flush of this success, Whittle turned full attention to his more ambitious venture, the Edison Project.

IT WAS A rare opportunity, and Chris Whittle made the most of it. In August 1992 he came to Princeton, New Jersey, to address the annual meeting of the National Governors' Association. His assignment was to explain how he would create the new American school, using the Edison Project as the take-off point. The governors' applause at the end of his talk had hardly died down when Tommy Thompson, the governor of Wisconsin, voiced the questions that were uppermost in the minds of the audience: "How do the states buy into this? How can I, as a governor, get your schools to come to Wisconsin?"

Whittle replied, "We'd like to work with each one of you on this question. Some of you may say, 'We want an Edison school in our inner cities.' Others are going to say, 'We want Edison schools in our rural areas.' We'll work with each state to determine that."

There was no question that the Whittle sales genius had worked. He began by telling the group the now-familiar parable that when Thomas Edison invented the light bulb he did not simply hot-wire a candle. "You can't make a light bulb out

of a candle," Whittle said. "And interestingly, a light bulb is now cheaper than a candle." He continued, "The Edison Project is of a similar mind about education. We want to start over. If there are three words to describe what we are doing, they are 'to start over': to redesign prekindergarten through 12th grade from scratch."

Speaking softly but with zeal, Whittle kept the governors' attention with such statements as:

> Edison Project could match Sputnik in its impact on public schools. . . . Our schools will be built to be copied. . . . We are the only business in America that is building in a desire for shoplifting of what we do. . . . I invite you to start with me on an educational odyssey. . . . We are not saying that all schools should be privatized. We are saying that radical change in education is more likely to come from a private effort, free of political boundaries and infused with a certain urgency.

Whittle then struck the economic notes: "Over the next four years we will be investing $2.5 billion in new educational infrastructure. That may be something you want to compete for. It includes over 20,000 construction jobs and more than 5,000 educational positions in the schools we will be developing."

As the governors leaned forward to take in these economic morsels, at least one had something else on her mind. Gov. Ann Richards of Texas rose to say:

> My immediate reaction is — fear. You are going to come in with your schools and strip off our African-American kids who are the smartest and the brightest. You're going to strip off the Mexican-American kids who are the role models in the public schools in South Texas, and whom we really need there. But you're not going to take our kids that are so disabled that they are literally diapered by the teachers, because by law that's whom we've got to teach. So how do I deal with my fear that the public school is going to be left with educating those you don't want, those who are hardest to educate, the most expensive to educate? As a consequence, my Texas public school system is not going to look very good when it's compared with the opportunities you're going to have to reject the kids we can't reject.

Whittle responded, "We are not designing another private school system that is elitist in nature. We plan to create a school that confronts as many of the problems [as] a typical public school confronts. . . ."[4] No sigh of relief swept through the chamber.

THROUGHOUT 1991 and the first part of 1992, Whittle and his doings were grist for news stories, editorials, articles in popular magazines, and radio and television reports. (In 18 months some 2,000 articles appeared on the subject, according to Whittle publicists.) Then came a Whittle *coup de maître*. In May 1992 Whittle announced that Benno Schmidt, who had just completed his fourth year as president of Yale University, would head the Edison Project. Inside and outside the world of education some were taken by surprise, and some were aghast,

---

Whittle's Plans And Projections

The goal for the Edison Project is to invent, develop, and operate a thousand new schools. The first new schools will open in 1995 on 200 campuses, enrolling 150,000 students between the ages of 1 and 6. These initial openings may cost $2.5 billion. In 1998 additional campuses will be opened, and by 2010 enrollment will have reached 2,000,000. Eventually, each campus will contain a day-care center and offer elementary, middle school, and high school courses.

Schools will be privately operated on a for-profit basis. The annual charge will be the equivalent of the annual cost per student in U.S. public schools, which was $5,500 in 1992. Twenty percent of the funds will go for scholarships. Schools will be built in all types of communities, "including the most desperate inner-city areas," Christopher Whittle told the nation's governors at the 1992 meeting of the National Governors' Association in Princeton, N.J.

The Edison Project now has $60 million in seed capital from Time Warner, Philips Electronics of Holland, Associated Newspapers (a British conglomerate), and Whittle Communications. The main job before Chris Whittle is raising the additional millions. — BB

---

but nearly all understood that it was a case of Whittle salesmanship in action. And the offer to Schmidt of a salary purported to be between $800,000 and $1 million a year was seen as more evidence that Whittle was unstoppable in his march toward his objectives.

As for Schmidt, he retreated to high ground. In an interview for this article, held in the New York City offices of the Whittle enterprises, Schmidt ignored the controversy swirling around the Edison Project and his appointment and instead expounded his philosophy about the venture.[5] Schmidt stressed that the Edison Project represents, in essence, a research and development effort of unprecedented size, devoted to the future of American education. He put it this way:

> The Edison Project is essentially a search for new ways to conduct education in the United States. The search may take up to 25 years. In our new schools we shall be free to ask questions and search for answers without the constraints that exist in public education. We shall look for new ways to teach and new ways to administer, new ways to involve parents and all sectors of the community, but we shall not ignore the good practices already in use. We shall borrow ideas and we shall share.

Well and good. But I came to the interview with a basic question: How new will the new American school be that Whittle has been propounding? I made clear to Schmidt that this question had dozens of subquestions and that getting the answers was the main objective of the interview.

No time for that, said Schmidt. But before parting, we agreed that I would submit my questions in writing. Fair enough. Subsequently, I drafted about 100 questions covering school aims, administration, instruction, students, and teachers. Too many — so I pruned the list to about 30 questions. Schmidt's response, which came from Knoxville, was prompt.

My first question was, What underlying principle will govern the new American school you seek to create? Schmidt's response (edited for brevity) was as follows:

> The system of schools we hope to create is committed to liberty and equality. First, the schools will be dedicated to helping every child to his or her full potential as a thoughtful human being. Our schools are determined to liberate students as individuals; to de-

velop in every child the confidence and capacity to think independently; to participate intelligently, work productively, and live happily in a free society. Second, by serving diverse student bodies, treating all students equally, and encouraging students to work cooperatively, each of our schools will aim to . . . maximize student appreciation for the interdependence of society and the responsibilities of individuals toward each other.

Less florid were Schmidt's answers to the following questions:

Q. Will teachers have a role in the administration of your schools?

A. Teachers must play a key role. But teachers will focus their energy and talent on teaching rather than on lunchroom duty.

Q. Will parents have a real, substantive role or only an advisory role?

A. Parents will have a real and substantive role. We don't know what form that will take, but it's clear to us that parental involvement is essential to our success.

Q. Where will you find the teachers?

A. We have been contacted by thousands of teachers eager to get involved. We shall draw from the pool of talented teachers already in the field, but we shall also look in nontraditional places for new teachers.

Q. Will teachers be free to join unions and other professional organizations?

A. Employees will be free to join — or not to join — any union or organization.

Q. How will you deal with teacher strikes or work stoppages?

A. We are creating a wonderful school system where we believe teachers will want to be in school, not out.

Q. How much emphasis will be given to individualized instruction? To independent study?

A. We shall emphasize both.

Q. What attention will you give to rural youths, economically poor students, students at risk, handicapped students, minority students, immigrant students?

A. We shall welcome all children into our schools.

We now come to a group of questions to which Schmidt responded, "We don't know," "We haven't come up with our design yet," or "We're working on it." These questions included: Will your schools have the equivalent of a board of education? How big a role will inservice education have? How will teacher salaries be determined? What will be the nature of discipline for students? Will corporal punishment have a place? Do you see a place for a dress code? Will reading instruction have a high place in the curriculum? Phonics — yes or no? Will vocational guidance have a place in your curriculum? Will your schools use such traditional methods as recitation and memory work? Any plans about teaching religious subjects? Where will the textbooks for the new school come from?

Finally, here are half a dozen questions that also brought the reply, "We don't know yet": What attention will be given to slow learners? Will you group students according to ability? How much emphasis will be given to homework? Will development of thinking skills have a place in your curriculum? How much emphasis will be given to testing — and will it be the alpha and omega of your instruction? Do you see a place in your curriculum for international education?

To the glittering generalities of purpose and to the avowals of "we don't know" can be added an array of putative characteristics for the Edison Project schools, drawn from the founder's statements. The new schools will be open 12 months of the year and 12 to 14 hours a day. They will operate with a pruned-down bureaucracy, variable class size, and flexible student grouping. Grade levels will be a thing of the past; students will move ahead as they complete the school's objectives, not as they put in their time. Parent participation will be heavily courted. And whereas, according to Schmidt, present-day schools "use mostly paper, pencils, blackboards, and books untouched by modern technology," the ideal for the new schools will be the electronic classroom and the electronic student workstation. The dream continues:

> Each student will have a computer, a monitor, a printer — in a sense, a personal office. The student workstation will be hooked up to electronic central libraries that will have every book that a student might need, every film, every speech, every image that can be accessed electronically. Students will be able to reach, electronically, any student, teacher, or resource specialist not only nearby but thousands of miles away.
>
> Student stations will be arranged in circles. For group work, people will be in motion. Teachers will visit students at their workstations and students will visit the teacher and other students at will. What used to be textbooks and reference works will be on discs.

There will probably be little homework in the new American school, because students will be at work from eight in the morning to six in the evening.[6]

The hardware of the new school may dazzle student, teacher, and parent. But what will be the content of the curriculum — how new, how old, how derived, how organized, with what objectives? I could find no answers to these questions; neither Whittle nor Schmidt nor the core team has answers at this time. Educators I talked with expressed the view that, for the next decade at least, the new schools will transmit old subject matter, even though they may use all but miraculous ways to do it.

The reaction of the education establishment, whether in Washington or in local communities, to the Edison Project is neither as volatile nor as shrill as the reaction to Channel One. "Hey, look, it's a free country. If Whittle wants to build private schools for profit — so be it. Some of us may not like it; some of us may. Some think Whittle will hurt the public schools; others of us will wait and see what happens."

One who is not waiting is Jonathan Kozol. The author of *Death at an Early Age* and the recent best seller, *Savage Inequalities*, has attacked Channel One and the Edison Project with equal vehemence. In speeches, articles, and private conversations, Kozol vents his contempt for Whittle and his doings. In a telephone conversation with me, Kozol said:

> Chris Whittle insists he wants to improve public education through competition. I don't believe it. You don't improve the public water supply by selling Coca-Cola.
>
> Whittle is dangerous — very dangerous — for American education. He's dangerous because he is selling the idea that the public schools can be used as a marketing place for commercial products. He's opening the doors for a massive new industry — the Educational Industrial Complex. This would replace the Military Industrial Complex of the Eisenhower years and would bring up for grabs 45 million captive customers in the schools. He's dangerous because he's a marketing genius and may succeed where others with ideas dangerous to public education have failed.

Taking a wide-angle view of Whittle and his ideas, Kozol sees him as the champion of eventual large-scale privatization of public schools and as the immediate proponent of vouchers — both charges that Whittle denies.

AT THIS POINT let's look at the two men who, next to Schmidt, are closest to Whittle and are at work in Knoxville shaping the future course of the Edison Project. Chester Finn, Jr., a product of private schools in Akron, Ohio, on leave from Vanderbilt University, became a founding partner of the Edison Project in July 1992. He assisted former Secretary of Education Lamar Alexander with planning the America 2000 strategy. His work at the Hudson Institute, a conservative think tank, and his authorship of *We Must Take Charge: Our Schools and Our Future* (Free Press, 1992) have securely established him as a leader of the push for privatization.

Like other critics of public schools, Finn can readily list the things that are wrong with them today. (The list is too familiar to repeat here.) He stresses, however, that the main reason for the inertia and complacency in public education is the captive audience that we guarantee every public school regardless of its quality. He complains that major barriers to better schooling are the district and municipal boundaries that function like Berlin Walls. "They've torn down the one in Germany. How about demolishing our own?" he asks. It is Finn's conviction that we need two things: choice and start-from-scratch schools. Privatization would take care of both. (And isn't the Edison Project an expression of both?)

John Chubb, now working full-time in Knoxville, has been a senior fellow at the Brookings Institution since 1984 and is the co-author, with Terry Moe, of *Politics, Markets, and America's Schools* (Brookings Institution, 1990). Chubb and Moe believe that a major evil of public education is state and local bureaucracy. Bureaucracy imposes goals, structure, and requirements — and, as a consequence, stifles teaching and learning. Chubb wants the state and its agents, the local school boards, to keep their hands off public education. Public schools should function according to market principles — meaning that there should be a system of parental choice, with schools competing for students.

Under the Chubb/Moe plan, a school

would have authority to decide how it is to be run — whether by teachers, parents, the union, the principal, or a committee. Each school would set its own criteria for curriculum, textbook selection, inservice programs, homework, or anything else. School districts would continue as local taxing jurisdictions, but a school would not be subject to control by a board of education, superintendent, central office, state department of education, or any other arm of government. (Deftly back-pedaling, the authors say that the state should exercise certain controls — over finance, graduation requirements, health and safety, and teacher eligibility, to name but a few areas.)

Chubb and Moe insist, just as Chris Whittle does about his Edison Project, that their plan has nothing to do with privatizing the nation's schools. Advocates of public education disagree.[7] Finn and Chubb represent a midpoint in the range of beliefs held by advocates of privatization. At one end we have such far-out views as those held by Myron Lieberman; at the other we have the views of David Bennett and his "public/private partnership." Lieberman's book, *Beyond Public Education* (Praeger, 1986), is one of the earlier treatises on the subject, as well as one of the more strident. He charges that nothing can save the public schools — nothing — and contends that the only solution is to create a nationwide network of profit-making entrepreneurial schools. The failure of the public schools, Lieberman argues, is due to the fact that no one is really in charge — not local governments, not the states, not the federal government. Each entity is, according to Lieberman, hopelessly involved in laws, regulations, and bureaucracies. Reluctantly, Lieberman suggests that vouchers and tuition tax credits might help. But the real cure is an end to public education and its replacement by the entrepreneurial school.

In contrast, David Bennett wants to "re-invent" school system governance through what he calls a public/private partnership. He is now testing his ideas in several pilot schools in Baltimore and at South Pointe Elementary School in Dade County, Florida. He also has plans for installing his mechanism in other school districts.

Under the Bennett plan, which he calls Education Alternatives, Inc., teachers, administrators, and other public school employees remain public but are subject to the private company's management. Bennett stresses that under his plan the board of education is relieved of operational details and sticks to policy — its real job — and the superintendent, remaining as the chief operating officer, has more time for carrying out board policy and evaluating the private company's practices.

A FEW DAYS after his appointment as Edison Project chieftain, Benno Schmidt received a dinnertime telephone call at his home. It came from Air Force One, and the caller was then-President George Bush. According to a reporter for the *New York Times*, Bush said, "Benno, I just want you to know that I think what you're doing is truly wonderful. We desperately need innovation in this country. We're very proud of what you've done at Yale, but this is more fundamental."

Some time later, a private meeting at the White House revealed the faint outlines of a Bush/Alexander/Schmidt/Whittle axis. Bush, a Yale graduate, and Schmidt, the former Yale president, also had in common the conviction that the public schools had failed and that new models for educating America's children had to be created. Lamar Alexander, as Bush's secretary of education, agreed with his President (at least publicly) that America's public schools constituted "failed experiments of the past." More-over, it was widely known that Alexander and Whittle had had common interests — financial as well as spiritual — in what Whittle was doing. And Whittle held for this group a new light to lead to new ways of educating America's children.

This incipient alliance went dead on November 3 with the election of Bill Clinton as President. Clinton has his own ideas about education, and they do not include any movement toward privatization. During the campaign, Hillary Clinton, who shares her husband's views on the matter, had several occasions to say, "If we let the public school system be turned over to market forces, we'd be signing the death warrant for most public schools." From Knoxville, after the elections, came signals that the Edison Project will go ahead regardless of who occupies the White House. And from those who oppose the incursion of business and the profit motive into public education came the prediction that the election of Clinton may postpone movements toward privatization — but will not end them.

---

1. Henry Steele Commager, a noted historian, published "Our Schools Have Kept Us Free" as an editorial in the special education issue of *Life*, 16 October 1950. It has since been widely reprinted.

2. Interview with Whittle by members of the Educational Press Association, 27 June 1992.

3. Speech by Whittle to the National Governors' Association, Princeton, N.J., 4 August 1992.

4. Ibid.

5. The interview took place on 21 September 1992, the same day that the liberal-tilting weekly *The Nation* carried a blistering attack on Whittle and Schmidt and their connection to Secretary of Education Lamar Alexander and the Bush White House. See especially pp. 272-75, *The Nation*, 21 September 1992.

6. Speech by Whittle before the annual meeting of the Ohio School Board Association, Columbus, 15 October 1990.

7. See, for example, a statement by the superintendent of schools in Fairborn, Ohio: Stephen P. Scovic, "Let's Stop Thinking Choice Is the Answer to Restructured Schools," *School Administrator*, January 1992, pp. 19-27.

American Schools: Good, Bad, or Indifferent?

As important as criticism is, it is only a call to arms, Mr. Doyle points out. It is necessary but not sufficient. Constructive critics know that the time has come for American education to move on — toward solutions.

DENIS P. DOYLE

DENIS P. DOYLE, a senior fellow with the Hudson Institute, Indianapolis, writes about education and human capital from his office in Washington, D.C.

ATTEMPTING to assess the temper of our times, historians of the next century will no doubt fall back on Dickens' memorable opening of *A Tale of Two Cities*: "It was the best of times, it was the worst of times." That at least captures the spirit of the fevered revisionism now unfolding. On the one hand, there are analysts such as *Kappan* contributor Gerald Bracey who argue that contemporary critics of education — myself included — are simply myopic naysayers who are attacking public schools for personal or ideological reasons. Luckily, there is nothing ideological about Bracey.

Then there is Jonathan Kozol. He believes that American education has gone to hell in a handcart (unlike Bracey, who appears to believe that reports of its decrepitude are greatly exaggerated). But Kozol's demonology turns out to be much the same as Bracey's: dread conservatives.

In Kozol's world, however, we are not just carping critics, misanthropes, and misguided methodologists; we are starving public schools into submission.

That the critics of the critics are themselves divided suggests the emergence of a modern scholasticism, in which fierce pleasure is taken in playing with the statement of the problem rather than with the problem itself. Numbers are marshaled to demonstrate that we critics have either over- or underreached: that is, things are not really as bad as they seem, or, as Kozol would have it, things are a lot worse. No matter, the critics are wrong. No doubt the next step will be to estimate the number of critics that can dance on the head of a pin. (In the case of angels, the scholastics contrived an appealing answer: an infinite number, because angels are immaterial. So too with critics?) One is reminded of Mark Twain's observation about Richard Wagner's music: "It is not as bad as it sounds."

Still, 10 years after the release of *A Nation at Risk*, it would be disingenuous not to admit that there is a powerful — and understandable — desire to assert that all is well. People do need a break. In particular, teachers and principals feel, with some justification, that they have been treated unkindly.

By and large, educators do not embrace the politicians' adage that the only thing worse than bad news is no news, and in fairness to educators it must be noted that the Eighties were not a pleasant decade in which to be an educator. But is it equally the case that educators have not, on balance, seized on the events of the Eighties as an opportunity to make things better? That, of course, was the reason for all the criticism to begin with.

As it happened, however, after the release of *A Nation at Risk* in 1983, most of the important books and reports of the Eighties did not dwell on a litany of complaint and criticism. We didn't need to. The projects with which I was associated — the Committee for Economic Development's 1985 report, *Investing in Our Children: Business and the Schools*; the book I co-authored with former Deputy Secretary of Education David Kearns, *Winning the Brain Race*; and the 175-page *Business Week* white paper, *Children of Promise* — deliberately steered away from the sorry state of public education, except for the briefest reprise to set the stage. My collaborators on these projects and I were convinced that a catalogue of horrors was not the way to stimulate change. Equally to the point, we believed that any description of how bad things are can only be justified if it is accompanied by constructive ideas about reform and renewal.

Not to put too fine a point on it, even in the best of times criticism serves only one legitimate function: to stimulate change. Without that objective it is both cynical and counterproductive. Yet the recent spate of revisionist arguments strikes me as equally cynical. Is it meant to suggest that we should leave well enough alone? Or that the only hope is a socialist workers' paradise? Attempting to unscramble the omelet is not only time-consuming, but it also diverts attention from real issues. We do have problems to solve.

And what might they be? The simple fact is that American education faces a productivity crisis. This assertion is neither name-calling nor carping criticism. It does not represent fantastical claims about either the problem or its solution. It is both an analytic perspective and a simple statement of fact with powerful policy implications. To date, its absence as an analytic perspective has been a source of disappointment and great mischief because that absence makes it almost impossible to answer such sensible questions as, "How well are American schools doing in light of their expenditures?" or "What is the value added by schooling?" or "How great are the returns on human capital investment?"

THIS VIEW OF education, of course, owes a debt to the dismal science, economics — particularly political economics — which is preoccupied with questions concerning the allocation of scarce resources. We never have as much of many things as we might like: education, fine wine, medical care, inexpensive transportation, leisure — select your own list. This proposition is self-evident. On occasion, however, the issue of relative scarcity becomes more important than at other times. In the Sixties, before Vietnam at least, we enjoyed both guns and butter. This is not to be in the Nineties.

President Clinton and the Congress face deficits — current accounts, trade, and budget — so large that there is little room to maneuver. Without reciting the numbers in detail, suffice it to say that there is not enough room in local, state, and federal budgets to buy our way out of the educational impasse. There may be some new money for education — but not much. Schools will simply have to work smarter.

Let us agree to the following propositions: budgets for American education are necessarily limited, and American education is not as efficient — or as humane — as it must be if we are to face the next century with confidence. Does anyone really doubt these statements? It should be clear that this is not solely an economic argument, though it includes an economic component.

By "productivity crisis" I mean that schools must learn to do more with less — or, better yet, much more with a little bit more. I do not mean that schools as they once were failed; indeed, historically they have met their purposes reasonably well. So, too, did Detroit, at least through the era of "muscle cars." Remember the movie *A Man and a Woman*? The story line's centerpiece was a Mustang, the American car that was to

> *There is not enough room in local, state, and federal budgets to buy our way out of the educational impasse.*

catapult Lee Iacocca to fame and fortune. Imagine the French glorifying an American car in the 1990s. How times have changed. The point is that Detroit's problem over the past few decades is not that it forgot how to make muscle cars or that someone else made them better or cheaper. Muscle cars are out. Period. Detroit didn't get it. Detroit couldn't figure out how to make the transition into the modern era. So too with schools.

But a problem remains. To most educators, no matter how the terms are defined or explained, such words as *efficiency* and *productivity* are verboten when talking about schools. They conjure up images of time-and-motion studies — of white-jacketed efficiency experts with stopwatches and clipboards, who understand the cost of everything and the value of nothing. But in the postindustrial world (or the postcapitalist world, as Peter Drucker now describes it), productivity has a very different meaning. It means the most efficient deployment of resources in the most effective work environment that can be designed.

Mine is not an argument for more or less spending on schools; it is an argument on behalf of better use of whatever we've got. The modern productivity model for schools is not Frederick Taylor's factory — but the symphony orchestra; Drucker's well-run, not-for-profit organization (e.g., the Red Cross or Girl Scouts); or the modern high-tech, high-performance firm. What do these modern organizational forms have in common with schools? In the days when the factory was king, when the gate clanged shut

at night, the capitalist's wealth was locked securely inside. At the end of the workday in these modern organizations, when the door swings closed behind the last worker, the organization's wealth, its capital (human in this case), has gone home for the evening.

Consider another analogy. Remember the days of the early mainframe computers? Not only did they produce great amounts of heat, but they were extremely sensitive to changes in temperature and humidity. As a consequence, the rooms that housed them were the first parts of an organization to be fully air-conditioned, 24 hours a day, 365 days a year. Workers should be so lucky. Yet in modern high-performance organizations, they are. Indeed, it is a matter not of luck but of good sense. Today's managers — at least those with their wits about them — recognize that their most valuable resource is their workers. And it is more often the case today that employees are not considered workers at all, but associates. The employer is the manager of production.

BEFORE I consider the implications of "productivity" as the central concern of the modern firm, however, let me turn briefly to the two questions that must be dealt with if we are to reform education rationally: What is good about American education? And what is bad about American education?

In important respects, the questions are not empirical but normative. True, test scores and other quantitative indicators can be marshaled in support of the schools' performance, but they are largely empty indicators, because they do not relate to an accepted metric. Such research can answer questions that ask, "How much?" But those that ask, "How much is enough?" can be answered only in the domains of philosophy and politics.

So how do I answer them? What is good about American education? What is bad? The two themes intertwine. American education is democratic, egalitarian, and meritocratic. It is robust, dynamic, and resilient. It is responsive — at least to fads of the moment — and it is well financed, by any measure. It is radically decentralized, at least by world standards, and each component of the education system, from humble rural school districts to great research universities, stands on its own bottom. Attempts to

> *American youngsters do not believe that their school performance will greatly affect their later life.*

centralize education have largely failed — save only the movement over the past 50 years to consolidate school districts. Yet even in this area the 15,700 that remain (of more than 100,000 before World War II) are largely "independent."

Indeed, the marked sameness that characterizes American education — the fact that most of our schools look alike and behave similarly — is a commentary on the power of the culture of education, rather than a reflection of statutes or administrative regulations. The similarity of statutes from state to state is as much a product as a cause of that uniformity.

The consequence of this decentralization (at least as it appears to foreigners) is a system that is a system in name only. In fact, American education is most accurately described as "measured anarchy." What does this mean to the participants? Enormous freedom, including the freedom to fail. As long as they observe the rituals of the school and respect the privacy of their office or classroom, teachers and principals are largely free to do as they like. So too are students. In fact, in no other aspect of American education is the anarchic tendency so strong as among students. As long as they observe the minimum conventions of civility and behavior, students may do pretty much what they like — to the chagrin of teachers, parents, administrators, and serious students alike, I might add. But this has always been so.

The upside of this set of arrangements is schooling without equal for those who are disciplined, energetic, motivated, and supported by family and friends. And in our anarchic system, these traits may surface at any time in a student's career, even though, as a practical matter, surfacing early is to be preferred to surfacing late. But surface late they do in the case of many students, in which event the American passion for "second chances" comes into full play. America, of course, is a nation of second chances; that is what we are all about. We are a nation of immigrants. As Octavio Paz notes in his marvelous account, *One Earth, Four or Five Worlds*, America is the quintessential second-chance society. A new people in a new world, freed of the baggage of hereditary class, Americans invent themselves anew with each generation.

Not surprisingly, these habits extend well beyond school. America is a global scandal in terms of the rate of small business failure; Europeans and Asians are simply aghast. But they are equally astonished and impressed by the rate of small business formation, which is the flip side of failure. It is not too much to assert that small business failure is the true school of hard knocks, in which entrepreneurs learn the ropes the hard way. So prevalent are such failures that, alone in the industrialized world, no stigma attaches to having failed in America — not as long as you get up and try again.

So too with school. The school dropout can, if sufficiently energetic, drop back in — if not to the school he left, then to another. Or he can earn an equivalency diploma or, on occasion, go straight to a community or four-year college. So "naturally" and so readily is this done that we take it for granted. Today, for example, the average age of postsecondary students hovers around 30, and it is the rare undergraduate who finishes a course of study in four consecutive years.

But if this fluid and dynamic system works well for some, it has a terrible downside for many. In particular, youngsters from disorganized backgrounds, broken homes, and poverty — and even more particularly, students who are members of microcultures that do not prize education — find themselves left out. Sadly, this lack of a support network too often characterizes poverty-stricken minority youths, students who need to capitalize on their first chance and who are unlikely to seek and find second chances.

As John Ogbu, a sociologist at the University of California, Berkeley, points out, profoundly disadvantaged Americans look like nothing so much as members of a lower caste: outcasts. This distinction helps explain why boat people — poor, dispossessed, speaking little or no English — can rise so rapidly and decisively in American public schools. They do not think of themselves as outcasts; they think of themselves as individuals who, through diligence and hard work, can significantly improve their life chances. And they are right. Ironically, it is they who best exemplify the American Dream.

This, then, is what is wrong with American education: it has no systematic and effective way to deal with youngsters who do not see themselves as part of the system — who, for whatever reason, are not *workers*. Neither American education nor the larger society motivates these youngsters. The enabling power that education confers is kept secret from them. Because they hate school, their lives become a cruel hoax. Unlike students in Japan and Europe — who know that their life chances will be decided by how well they do in school — American youngsters do not believe that their performance in school will have a great deal of impact on their later life. To many of these youngsters, education is not an opportunity but a burden, one to be tolerated at best or more frequently avoided altogether. When asked how he escaped Harlem's mean streets to become a Navy pilot, Drew Brown, son of boxing promoter Budini Brown, attributes his success to his devoted father's admonition: "College or death!"

HOWEVER, the views of American education I have set forth raise the risk of two unwelcome interpretations. First, it is possible to indulge in the popular sport of blaming the victim. As the late, unlamented Gov. Lester Maddox of Georgia observed, when asked about improving his state prison system, "It can't be done without a better class of prisoner."

The second possible unwelcome interpretation would lead us to ask the schools to bear more weight than they can carry. Because schools are first and foremost educational institutions, they are poorly suited to deliver noneducational services, popular impressions to the contrary notwithstanding.

The view that schools should somehow be social service providers has, of course, gained wide currency because of its superficial plausibility. Kids have problems; kids are in school; ergo, solve the problems in the school. There is a rough justice in this notion, and in theory it makes administrative sense. Inoculations, well-baby screening, feeding programs, Norplant implants, condom distribution, contacts with case workers, and similar activities can in fact take place in school buildings. And it is surely the case that schools are a convenient place to track down young people, at least as long as compulsory attendance is the law of the land. Moreover, hungry, sick, and disoriented children do not make good students, and ameliorating their problems is both a good thing to do in its own right and good for the schools.

But if the problems presented by youngsters from disorganized backgrounds make it difficult for schools to go about their business, it is not clear that schools should enter the business of providing social services. Put plainly, if schools can't teach a youngster to read, can they minister to his or her social needs? While the question is no doubt in part empirical, management theory provides some guidance. As Peter Drucker observes, effective organizations *optimize*; they do not maximize. They do what they are good at and let others do what they are good at.

What does this have to do with schools? They too should optimize. And what they are good at — one hopes — is educating youngsters. That some of their charges are poor and dispossessed does not lead ineluctably to the idea that schools should attempt to fill the social service breach. It is self-evidently true that a wealthy society that cares about its future must care for its children. But children's social needs are not necessarily best met in school.

I belabor this obvious point because so many defenders of the public schools have begun to assert that the problems of the public schools are the problems of their clients. Indeed, the assertion is so often made that schools cannot deal with "these" children that it is a commonplace. That it is usually offered as a rationale for school failure is too often overlooked. So close to "blaming the victim" is this assertion that one wonders if it is a distinction without a difference. Be that as it may, I am convinced that we must draw a distinction between the social and educational needs of children and not use the former as an excuse not to fulfill the latter.

To return to Drucker's distinction, the schools must optimize. They must ask

themselves what their mission is, who their clients are, how they are to deliver the service called education, how they measure its quality, and how they know when they've met their goals. If schools try to be all things to all students — if they try to maximize — they will serve no one well. If they decide that they are social service institutions first and educational institutions second, they are not likely to meet either objective successfully. But if they decide that they are first and foremost educational institutions, charged with the responsibility of educating children, there is at least a chance that they may succeed.

The sorry fact is that most schools are not doing what they should be doing. And what they are doing, they are not doing well. They remind me of the Woody Allen routine in which a little old lady complains to her companion about airplane food. "Isn't it awful?" she asks. "Yes," her companion responds, "it certainly is, and the portions are so small!"

The one thing schools can and should do about the issue of social services is best illustrated by a program unfolding in Charlotte, North Carolina. No stranger to disadvantaged children, the schools in Charlotte are undertaking a comprehensive inventory of the needs of children; creating a catalogue of community resources, public and private; identifying the gaps in services; and bringing these gaps — deliberately, even provocatively — to the attention of the community as a whole. The superintendent, John Murphy, meets each month with representatives of the Charlotte Interfaith Council to coordinate a response. The Interfaith Council plans to build a countywide preschool network — the first facility opened in February 1993 — and the Charlotte schools are creating a pre-K parent/teacher organization to orient new parents. As evidence of how seriously it takes the issue, the school system will soon provide a brochure for mothers in the maternity ward. The objective: to welcome the newborns, but also to let parents know what their responsibilities are in helping their children get ready for school.

The strategy behind these programs stems from Charlotte's refusal to let its education budget hemorrhage in a futile attempt to *improvise* children's services. The school can sound the alarm, act as an honest broker, and make its facilities available. But responsibility for providing children's services lies with the community as a whole.

WHAT, THEN, is my vision of the future for education? First, debating the question of the quality of American schools — Are they as bad as the critics say? Are they better? — is a sterile and counterproductive exercise. Truly, it is the intellectual equivalent of rearranging the deck chairs on the *Titanic*. No good purpose is served by the exercise. The only legitimate reason to raise the question of school quality is to improve the schools. The question we must ask is, Are schools good enough for the future? Does anyone truly believe that they are?

The list of what might be done to improve our schools is understandably long, and I propose to treat only two examples here. Earlier I suggested that we need a coordinated children's policy; schools cannot go it alone. But at the same time, American schools face a productivity crisis. That is, they expect too little of teachers and students, and expecting little gets little. Few penalties — other than the remote possibility of failure as an adult, an incomprehensible idea for most adolescents — attach to a failure to perform, and few rewards attach to academic success.

As to the first part of the problem, the details of a children's policy are simply beyond the scope of this essay. I note only that such a policy is desirable, probably necessary, and possible *only if* President Clinton, working with his domestic policy council and relevant Cabinet members, can actually bring about real — I emphasize *real* — collaboration among the federal Departments of Education, Health and Human Services, and Labor (he could even encourage Commerce, Defense, and Energy to play a role). As an opponent of the creation of the Department of Education, I am fascinated that the interest groups that insisted that President Carter create it now lament the lack of connection between education and children's services. Might they ask Mr. Clinton to put the "E" back into HEW?

Whatever the interest groups do or fail to do, Washington is a major part of the problem. Consider employment, welfare, and health policies for starters. Washington must become part of the solution, and that means employment, welfare, and health policy reform on a massive scale if any lasting improvements in the condition of children are to be made. And it should be clear to all that education reform will not reach the poorest of the

9. A LOOK TO THE FUTURE

poor unless their social conditions are ameliorated.

Let me close by returning to my initial assertion that the real problem of American schools is a productivity crisis. Yet this problem is also an opportunity. Ironically, inefficiency — slack in the system — provides opportunities to save and invest and to improve dramatically. As an analogy, consider Americans' profligate use of energy. Wasting as much as we do, it is relatively easy, through conservation, to save a great deal of energy. In this light, we can see that there is one thing that schools can do for themselves that would make a difference: they can "benchmark."

Benchmarking, originally a topographical and nautical practice of defining permanent reference points against which measurements are made, has been appropriated by U.S. business, first by the Xerox Corporation, now by most high-tech, high-performance organizations. Not widely understood among educators, it is worth describing briefly. First, it is a form of self-measurement; it cannot be imposed from the outside. It is not a club with which to beat an organization over the head; it is a tool to permit members of the organization to improve their own performance by better understanding how other successful organizations achieve their success.

By way of illustration, Xerox seeks and finds the best performers in industry — not just other copier manufacturers, though Xerox looks at them closely, but the best performers, period. For copiers and office equipment, Xerox looks first at its direct competitors. When Xerox discovered that the Japanese were designing, manufacturing, assembling, shipping, and retailing high-quality copiers for less

than it took Xerox to manufacture them, the company recognized a clear message: restructure or collapse. Xerox chose the first course and remains one of the few American corporations to recapture market share from the Japanese.

In looking at generic processes, however, such as inventory control and management, the best performer Xerox could find was not Toyota or Kodak but L. L. Bean, the clothing and outdoor-wear catalogue house in Freeport, Maine. That's the standard of quality to which Xerox compares itself today. For customer response, in terms of both timeliness and courtesy, Xerox compares itself to Florida Light and Power.

Benchmarking is a form of accountability with special significance for public sector organizations — insulated as they are from the play of market forces — because, if it is to work, benchmarking must be self-imposed. It cannot be ordered up by a remote bureaucracy. Benchmarking forces organizations to rethink everything they do, from recruiting to compensation, from objectives to measurement, from assessment to management.

What kinds of things should benchmarking make schools think about? Outputs rather than inputs. The role of effort rather than innate ability. The importance of "mastery" as the appropriate measure of success in education. Making students workers and teachers managers of instruction. Using administrators as facilitators and superintendents as choreographers rather than autocrats. Using technology to increase output and not simply as glitz. These are only a few of the ideas that benchmarking will force schools to deal with.

That is precisely the challenge — and

the opportunity — American schools face. If they begin to benchmark seriously, they will compare themselves to the best of the best, not just in public elementary and secondary schools, but also in high-performance organizations. The power of benchmarking is that it does internally what competition is supposed to do externally: it holds organizations to high standards of performance, measurement, and reporting. It accepts no excuses. It is continuous. There is no finish line.

What's right with American education? There's much that's right. It has a proud history and an honorable tradition, it is generously funded, it is staffed by men and women of good will, and it is resilient. What's wrong with American education? It misconceives its own best interests in the Nineties; it tries to maximize when it should optimize; it comes perilously close to playing Lester Maddox with its clients, hoping for a "better class of student" as its salvation; and it sees problems where it should see opportunities.

What are the prospects for the future of American education? They are good. Criticism — constructive criticism — is the lifeblood of healthy organizations, just as it is the keystone of democracy. With it, conditions may be improved; without it, progress never occurs. It is for that reason that closed societies will not tolerate criticism; they fear it because they know it is the engine of change and renewal. But as important as criticism is, it is only a call to arms. It begins, but does not end, the dialogue. It is necessary but not sufficient. Constructive critics know that the time has come for American education to move on — toward solutions.

Credits/ Acknowledgments

Cover design by Charles Vitelli

1. How Others See Us and How We See Ourselves
Facing overview—Dushkin Publishing Group photo.

2. Change and Rethinking of the Educative Effort
Facing overview—United Nations photo by Y. Nagata.

3. Striving for Excellence: The Drive for Quality
Facing overview—Apple Computers.

4. Morality and Values in Education
Facing overview—United Nations photo by Y. Nagata.

5. Managing Life in Classrooms
Facing overview—Dushkin Publishing Group photo.

6. Equality of Educational Opportunity
Facing overview—United Nations photo by Y. Nagata.

7. Serving Special Needs and Concerns
Facing overview—United Nations photo by W. A. Graham.

8. The Profession of Teaching Today
Facing overview—United Nations photo by Marta Pinter.

9. A Look to the Future
Facing overview—Woodfin Camp © J. Wilson.

ANNUAL EDITIONS ARTICLE REVIEW FORM

■ NAME: _____ DATE: _____

■ TITLE AND NUMBER OF ARTICLE: _____

■ BRIEFLY STATE THE MAIN IDEA OF THIS ARTICLE: _____

_____

_____

_____

_____

■ LIST THREE IMPORTANT FACTS THAT THE AUTHOR USES TO SUPPORT THE MAIN IDEA:

_____

_____

_____

_____

_____

■ WHAT INFORMATION OR IDEAS DISCUSSED IN THIS ARTICLE ARE ALSO DISCUSSED IN YOUR TEXTBOOK OR OTHER READING YOU HAVE DONE? LIST THE TEXTBOOK CHAPTERS AND PAGE NUMBERS:

_____

_____

_____

_____

_____

_____

■ LIST ANY EXAMPLES OF BIAS OR FAULTY REASONING THAT YOU FOUND IN THE ARTICLE:

_____

_____

_____

_____

■ LIST ANY NEW TERMS/CONCEPTS THAT WERE DISCUSSED IN THE ARTICLE AND WRITE A SHORT DEFINITION:

_____

_____

_____

_____

_____

ANNUAL EDITIONS: EDUCATION 94/95
Article Rating Form

Here is an opportunity for you to have direct input into the next revision of this volume. We would like you to rate each of the 46 articles listed below, using the following scale:

1. **Excellent: should definitely be retained**
2. **Above average: should probably be retained**
3. **Below average: should probably be deleted**
4. **Poor: should definitely be deleted**

Your ratings will play a vital part in the next revision. So please mail this prepaid form to us just as soon as you complete it.
Thanks for your help!

Annual Editions revisions depend on two major opinion sources: one is our Advisory Board, listed in the front of this volume, which works with us in scanning the thousands of articles published in the public press each year; the other is you—the person actually using the book. Please help us and the users of the next edition by completing the prepaid article rating form on this page and returning it to us. Thank you.

Rating	Article	Rating	Article
	1. Preserving the American Dream		25. The Crisis in Education
	2. Strengths and Weaknesses of American Education		26. Investing in Our Children: A Struggle for America's Conscience and Future
	3. American Education: The Good, the Bad, and the Task		27. Concerns About Teaching Culturally Diverse Students
	4. The Little Schools That Could		28. Blowing Up the Tracks
	5. The 25th Annual Phi Delta Kappa/Gallup Poll of the Public's Attitudes Toward the Public Schools		29. Child Care: What Do Families Really Want?
	6. U.S. Education: The Task Before Us		30. Helping Students Understand and Accept Sexual Diversity
	7. Changing Schools From Within		31. Teenage Sex: Just Say 'Wait'
	8. A World of Choice in Education		32. Everyone Is an Exception: Assumptions to Avoid in the Sex Education Classroom
	9. A Question of Choice		33. Building a Smarter Work Force
	10. Launching a Revolution in Standards and Assessments		34. What the 'V' Word Is Costing America's Economy
	11. How the National Board Builds Professionalism		35. What Makes a Good Teacher?
	12. Magnet Schools and Issues of Education Quality		36. Probing the Subtleties of Subject-Matter Teaching
	13. The Myth of Public School Failure		37. Exploring the Thinking of Thoughtful Teachers
	14. Should We Push the Button?		38. A Better Way to Learn
	15. Right and Wrong		39. Exposing Our Students to Less Should Help Them Learn More
	16. Why Johnny Can't Tell Right From Wrong		40. Five Standards of Authentic Instruction
	17. Ethical Communication in the Classroom		41. Why Teachers Must Become Change Agents
	18. Discipline With Dignity in the Classroom: Seven Principles		42. The Rewards of Learning
	19. A Constructivist Approach to Conflict Resolution		43. Where We Go From Here
	20. Practical Peacemaking Techniques for Educators		44. Education 2000 A.D.: A Peek Into the Future
	21. From Individual Differences to Learning Communities—Our Changing Focus		45. How 'New' Will the 'New' Whittle American School Be? A Case Study in Privatization
	22. Resolving Teacher-Student Conflict: A Different Path		46. American Schools: Good, Bad, or Indifferent?
	23. The Canon Debate, Knowledge Construction, and Multicultural Education		
	24. Teachers and Cultural Styles in a Pluralistic Society		

(Continued on next page)

ABOUT YOU

Name_____ Date_____
Are you a teacher? ☐   Or student? ☐
Your School Name _____
Department _____
Address _____
City _____ State _____ Zip _____
School Telephone #_____

YOUR COMMENTS ARE IMPORTANT TO US!

Please fill in the following information:

For which course did you use this book? _____
Did you use a text with this Annual Edition?   ☐ yes   ☐ no
The title of the text? _____
What are your general reactions to the Annual Editions concept?

Have you read any particular articles recently that you think should be included in the next edition?

Are there any articles you feel should be replaced in the next edition? Why?

Are there other areas that you feel would utilize an Annual Edition?

May we contact you for editorial input?

May we quote you from above?

ANNUAL EDITIONS: EDUCATION 94/95

BUSINESS REPLY MAIL

First Class   Permit No. 84   Guilford, CT

Postage will be paid by addressee

The Dushkin Publishing Group, Inc.
Sluice Dock
DPG **Guilford, Connecticut 06437**